# Students' English – Tibetan Colloquial Dictionary

(Text incorporating corrections listed in the Errata)

by

C.A. Bell

C.M.G., C.I.E.

D.K. Printworld (P) Ltd.

Publishers of Indian Traditions

**Cataloging in Publication Data — DK**
[Courtesy: D.K. Agencies (P) Ltd. <docinfo@dkagencies.com>]

Bell, Charles Alfred, *Sir*, 1870-1945.
Students' English-Tibetan colloquial dictionary.

ISBN 13: 9788124601594 (Hb)
ISBN 13: 9788124601600 (Pb)
1. English language — dictionaries — Tibetan.
I. Title.

*First published in India* 1905
*Second edition published in* 1920
*D.K. Printworld's Edition* 2000
*Second Impression* 2011
ISBN 13: 978-81-246-0159-4 (Hb) ISBN 10: 81-246-0159-3
ISBN 13: 978-81-246-0160-0 (Pb) ISBN 10: 81-246-0160-7

*Published and printed by*:
D.K. Printworld (P) Ltd.
*Regd. office* : *'Vedaśrī'*, F-395, Sudarshan Park
Ramesh Nagar Metro Station
New Delhi – 110 015
*Phones* : (011) 2545 3975; 2546 6019; *Fax* : (011) 2546 5926
*E-mail*: indology@dkprintworld.com
*Web*: www.dkprintworld.com

## PREFACE TO SECOND EDITION.

1. In the first edition this dictionary was published as the second part of a "Manual of Colloquial Tibetan," the first part consisting of a Grammar of Colloquial Tibetan. In this second edition both parts have not only been revised, but have also been considerably enlarged. The map accompanying this edition—the latest from the Indian Survey Department—is bulkier than the Royal Geographical Society's map of 1904, with which the first edition was furnished. It has therefore been found best to bring out the Grammar and Dictionary as separate books. The map accompanies the Grammar.

2. The Tibetan words are romanized, as in the first edition, for the convenience of those, who lack either the time or the inclination to master the Tibetan character. But the first Chapter of the Grammar, that on "The alphabet and its pronunciation," is reprinted at the commencement of this dictionary, in order that the student, who learns the Tibetan letters, may understand the structure and the pronunciation of the words more clearly than can be expressed by any system of romanization.

3. Some two thousand fresh words have been added in this edition, which now contains between eleven and twelve thousand words. As Political Officer in Sikkim,—a post to which I have recently been recalled, though I retired from the service of Government ten months ago,—I am in charge of the diplomatic relations of the British Government not only with Sikkim, but with Tibet and Bhutan also. Many therefore of these new words, as well as the revision of a few in the earlier edition, have been gained in conversation with my Tibetan friends of all classes, High Priests, Cabinet Ministers, civil and military officers, shopkeepers, mule-drivers, shepherds, peasants, etc., etc., during my fifteen years' service in Tibet and on the borderland. Among all

these my thanks are especially due to Rai Sahib Kusho Pahlese of the noble family of Pahla in Lhasa. And Mr. David Macdonald, British Trade Agent at Yatung, Tibet, has again rendered valuable assistance.

4. My acknowledgments are also due to the Government of Bengal, who have defrayed the cost of this edition also, in retnrn for its copyright.

5. This book has been adopted as one of the text-books in the High Proficiency examination in the Tibetan language, held under the auspices of the Government of India.

6. In conclusion I must express my pleasure at finding that a second edition was called for owing to the first edition being sold out,—a rare occurrence among books on Tibet,—for it may be hoped that some have found it useful.

GANGTOK, SIKKIM :
*January, 1920.*

C. A. BELL.

## PREFACE TO FIRST EDITION OF "MANUAL OF COLLOQUIAL TIBETAN."

1. The object of this little work is to provide a practical handbook for those who wish to acquire a speedy knowledge of Colloquial Tibetan. It, therefore, does not deal with the written language, which differs widely from the colloquial, and is useless for conversational purposes.

2. Notwithstanding the political and commercial importance of Tibet it is remarkable that so few Europeans are able to converse with the people in their own tongue. The language is undoubtedly a hard one to acquire on account of the complexity of the grammar, the intricacy of the spelling, the fine shades of pronunciation, the different terminology, known as the honorific, employed in addressing the higher classes, the variety of dialects, and the distinction, already noted, between the literary and spoken language. To minimise these difficulties and to make the approach to the colloquial as easy as possible, is the aim of this handbook. It seeks to do so by giving a minimum of grammatical notes, fully explained by examples, a clear statement of the rules of pronunciation, a simple system of phonetic spelling in the Roman character, a set of conversational exercises and a sufficiently full vocabulary of both common and honorific words to meet the ordinary requirements of conversation with all classes.

3. Tibet is essentially a country of dialects. A well-known proverb says—

། ལུང་པ་རེ་རེ་སྐད་ལུགས་རེ། །
། བླ་མ་རེ་རེ་ཆོས་ལུགས་རེ། ། 

"Every district its own dialect;
Every lama his own doctrine."

Under these circumstances it was necessary to select the dialect most widely spoken, and that of Lhasa has been chosen accordingly. It is not only the dialect of the Central Province, but may be said to be also the *lingua franca* of the whole of Tibet. It is more generally spoken than any other, and is recognized as the most correct form of speech by all.

4. The Vocabulary contains somewhat less than ten thousand Tibetan words, the number of separate English words being some seven thousand or about twice as many as those contained in any colloquial Tibetan vocabulary up to date. The remaining three thousand words are made up of about two thousand honorific words and one thousand extra Tibetan words. Where two or more Tibetan words are given for one English equivalent, all are in common colloquial use and the one placed first is the commonest. It is hoped that the honorific words given may be found useful. Existing vocabularies give but few. A knowledge of honorific words is essential for talking to or of Tibetans of good position. It is hoped also that the exercises in Tibetan handwriting given in Part I, Chapter XVII, may assist any student, who so desires, to learn how to write Tibetan letters and other documents in a clear and correct style.

5. It is recommended that the grammar be used as follows: The rules of each Chapter should be perused and their accompanying examples learnt by heart. The *Words* at the end of the Chapter should then be committed to memory as far as possible, and the exercise (for reading and copying) should be read aloud to the teacher to ensure correct pronunciation, and every word should be understood. After this the other Exercise (for translation) should be translated *vivâ voce* and then written down, care being taken, when writing, to verify the spelling, as very few Tibetan teachers can spell correctly. On the following day the Tibetan half of the reading exercise should be covered up, and the English half re-translated into Tibetan, first *vivâ voce* and then in writing. If the above plan is followed the student will gain the soundest possible knowledge of the language. But if the student has not time for the above thorough system, he should omit the writing of both exercises and limit himself to the *vivâ voce*.

6. As regards teachers it is best to obtain at first one who speaks English. If the teacher can speak the Lhasa language also, so much the better, but very few of the English-speaking Tibetans in the Darjeeling district or in Sikkim are really proficient in the latter. As soon as he can converse a little, the student should change to a Lhasa man that speaks Tibetan only, so as to be certain of always speaking in Tibetan. When the teacher knows English or Hindustani there is always a tendency for the conversation to drop into the latter languages. The Lhasa teacher should of course be as well educated a man as is procurable. The student should also, when he is able to understand and converse a little, call in Tibetans of the Lhasa province to talk to him, one at a time, changing them every two or three weeks. Tibetans are generally ready to talk; they have not the formal constraint of manner which characterizes so many of the Indian races. The more he calls in thus, the better will he be able to understand and reply to any chance Tibetan he meets.

7. A word as to the system of romanization. In this, which is believed to be as phonetic as possible, I had reluctantly to differ from the various systems of my predecessors, as none of them seemed to me to reproduce the sounds in the dialect of Lhasa, though some reproduced those in the Sikkimese and other dialects. The system followed in this book is nearly the same as that recommended to Government for official reports, etc., by Captain O'Connor, C.I.E., Trade Agent at Gyangtse, and the author, but distinguishes the different sounds with greater accuracy than was considered necessary in the Government system.

8. The Tibetan words and syllables in brackets are those used in the simple form of book-language. Where the pronunciation of the literary and spoken form of a word is the same, the literary form alone is given, since the sole object of entering the spoken form is to show the exact pronunciation of the word.

9. In conclusion, I must acknowledge my obligations to the Government of Bengal for their patronage, to the Grammars of the Rev. Graham Sandberg, the Rev. H. A. Jäschke and the Rev.

Father A. Desgodins, and especially to Mr. Henderson's Tibetan Manual, which marks a great advance in the Tibetan colloquial over any of its predecessors. And most of all are my thanks due to Mr. David Macdonald, who has revised this book throughout, and to whose unrivalled knowledge of both colloquial and literary Tibetan are largely due whatever merits the work may possess.

CHUMBI, TIBET: *March*, 1905. C. A. BELL.

# ABBREVIATIONS.

Adj. = adjective.
Adv. = adverb.
Art. = article.
Ch. = Chinese.
Conj. = conjunction.
C.T. = Central Tibet, *i.e.* the provinces of U and Tsang.
Def. = definite.
Do. = ditto.
E.G. = for instance.
F. = female, feminine.
Hin. = Hindi.
Hon. = honorific.
H. hon. = high honorific.
Imp. = imperative.
Inf. = inferior.
Interj. = interjection.
Interr. = interrogative.
Lit. = literally.
M. = male, masculine.
Mon. = Mongolian.
Neg. = negative.
Opp. = opposed.
Post. = postposition.
Pron. = pronoun.
Rel. = relative.
S. = substantive.
Sik. = Sikkimese.
Sup. = superior.
Ts. = Tsang province.
V.I. = verb intransitive.
V.T. = verb transitive.
W. = with.

**Attention Please !**

To facilitate our readers, all the corrections listed in the errata of the second edition have been carried out in the main text.

**D.K. Printworld (P) Ltd.**

NOTE.—Where the colloquial and the literary forms differ appreciably, the latter are given in brackets in the Tibetan character. In the romanized Tibetan the colloquial forms alone are given.

## THE ALPHABET AND ITS PRONUNCIATION.

1. The Tibetan Alphabet was originally taken from the Sanskrit Devanagari in the 7th century A.D., but many of the letters, especially in Central Tibet, now represent sounds different from their prototypes. Both the Sanskrit and the Tibetan pronunciations have changed considerably during this period.

2. The Tibetan letters are as follow :—

*Consonants and their romanized equivalents.*

| | Surds. | Aspirates. | Sonants. | Nasals. |
|---|---|---|---|---|
| Gutturals | ཀ་ *ka* | ཁ་ *kha* | ག་ *ḱa* | ང་ *nga* |
| Palatals | ཅ་ *cha* | ཆ་ *chha* | ཇ་ *ch́a* | ཉ་ *nya* |
| Dentals | ཏ་ *ta* | ཐ་ *tha* | ད་ *t́a* | ན་ *na* |
| Labials | པ་ *pa* | ཕ་ *pha* | བ་ *ṕa* | མ་ *ma* |
| Sibilants | ཙ་ *tsa* | ཚ་ *tsha* | ཛ་ *tśa* | |
| Semi-vowels | ཝ་ *wa* | ཞ་ *sh́a* | ཟ་ *śa* | འ་ (not romanized) |
| | ཡ་ *ya* | ར་ *ra* | ལ་ *la* | |
| | ཤ་ *sha* | ས་ *sa* | ཧ་ *ha* | ཨ་ *a* |

3. In this Chapter I endeavour to give as nearly as possible the sound represented by each Tibetan letter. The romanization throughout is intended only as a rough guide to the pronunciation for those who are unable to give the time for studying the exact pronunciation. The consonants when used as initials, *i.e.*, when immediately preceding the vowel of a syllable, are pronounced as below.

ཀ་ The *k* in the Hindustani word *kam*. To be pronounced with the tongue between the teeth and without breathing.

ཁ་ an aspirated *k*, e.g., *block-head*, pronounced in one breath. The same as the aspirated *k* in Hindustani words, *e.g.*, *khana*.

ག་ also a *k* but pronounced through the throat and in a lower tone than ཀ་

ང་ like the *ng* in *coming*. Say *coming in*, eliminating the first four letters *comi*.

ཅ་ *ch* in *chin*. To be pronounced with the tongue between the teeth and without breathing.

ཆ་ *ch* aspirated, e.g., *touch-hands* pronounced in one breath, *i.e.*, like the aspirated *ch* in Hindustani.

ཇ་ is also a *ch* pronounced through the throat and in a lower tone than ཅ་

ཉ་ as the initial sound in *nuisance*.

ཏ་ a Dental *t* to be pronounced with the tongue between the teeth and without breathing. This ཏ་ and ན་ differ from the English *t* and *n*, in that the English letters require the tongue to be placed against the roof of the mouth and so have a heavier sound.

ཐ་ aspirated *t*, e.g., *thora* in Hindustani; or—subject to the difference noted under ཏ་—*pat hard* pronounced in one breath. Not to be confused with the English *th* sound, in words like *the*.

ད་ is like ཏ་ but pronounced through the throat and in a lower tone than ཏ་

ན་ is like English *n*, e.g., in *nest* subject to the difference noted under ཏ་

པ་ like English *p* as in *pear*, to be pronounced with the tongue between the teeth and without breathing.

ཕ་ aspirated *p*, e.g., *stop here* pronounced as one word. Not to be confused with *ph* sound occurring in English words like *phantasy*, etc.

བ་ is also a *p* but pronounced through the throat and in a lower tone than པ་ If it forms the second syllable of a word whose first syllable ends with a vowel or with ང་འ་ར་ or ལ་ it is pronounced as *w*.

མ་ as English *m*, e.g., in *man*.

ཙ་ *ts* is pronounced like *weights* eliminating the letters *weigh*.

To be pronounced with the tongue between the teeth ,and without breathing.

ཚ་ as *ts* aspirated, *e g.*, in *pats hard* pronounced as one word.

ཛ་ is also a *ts*, but pronounced through the throat and in a lower tone than ཙ་

ཝ་ like *w* in English, *e.g.*, in *wing*.

ཞ་ Something like *sh* in English, but pronounced in a lower tone and more through the throat.

ཟ་ Something like *s* in English, but pronounced in a lower tone and more through the throat.

འ་ has no pronunciation of its own. When it precedes གཇདབ་ or ཛ་; these letters are pronounced respectively like *g* in *gun*, *j* in *jam*, *d* in *den*, *b* in *bend*, and *ds* in *pads*. See also para. 23

ཡ་ like *y* in English, *e.g.*, in *yacht*.

ར་ is short like *r* in English, *e.g.*, in *rat*. It is never rolled.

ལ་ like *l* in English, *e.g.*, in *linger*.

ཤ་ like *sh* in English, but pronounced sharply and through the teeth.

ས་ like *s* in English, but pronounced sharply and through the teeth.

ཧ་ like *h* aspirated in English, *e.g.*, in *hand.*

ཨ་ When a vowel is initial, either ཨ་ or འ་ is used as its base. The difference in pronunciation of these two is that the throat is opened for ཨ་ and kept closed for འ་ The result is that ཨ་ carries the ordinary vowel sound, whatever the vowel may be; while འ་ in the case of ུ or ོ gives a slight, but very slight sound of *w*; e.g., འུར་ *noise*=something between *ur* and *wur* though more like *ur.*

4. The five vowels are called དབྱངས་ལྔ་ *Yang-nga*: ཨ་ (a) ཨི་ (i) ཨུ་ (u) ཨེ་ (e) ཨོ། (o)

The four vowel-signs are ི *i* ུ *u* ེ *e* ོ *o*.

Every consonant implies a following *a*, unless another vowel is attached. This *a* is sounded like the English *u* in *rub.*

ི named གི་གུ་ *ki-ku,* like *i* in *in* or *tin,* e.g., མི་ man=*mi.*

ུ named ཞབས་ཀྱུ་ *skap-kyu,* like *oo* in *root* when initial or final. Like *u* in *pull,* when medial, *e.g.,* གྲུ་ boat=*tru;* ནུབ་ west=*nup.*

named འགྲེང་བུ་ *Deng-bu*, like *e* in *men*. But when final also often like *i* in *tin*, e.g., ལེན་པ་ to take=*lem-pa*; ལྡེ་མིག་ *key=di-mi.*

named ན་རོ་ *na-ro*, like *o* in hole; e.g., ལོག་པ་ to come back=*loḱ-pa*.

5. The Tibetan letters with the four vowel-signs are as follow:—

| | | | |
|---|---|---|---|
| ཀི་ *ki.* | ཁུ་ *khu.* | གེ་ *ḱe.* | ངོམས། *ngom.* |
| ཅི་ *chi.* | ཆུ་ *chhu.* | ཇེ་ *cḱe.* | ཉོན། *nyön.* |
| ཏི་ *ti.* | ཐུ་ *thu.* | དེ་ *ťe.* | ནོར། *nor.* |
| པི་ *pi.* | ཕུ་ *phu.* | བེ་ *ṕe.* | མོས། *mö.* |
| ཙི་ *tsi.* | ཚུ་ *tshu.* | ཛེ་ *tśe.* | ཝོལ། *wöl.* |
| ཞི་ *sḱi.* | ཟུ་ *śu.* | འེ་ *e.* | ཡོད། *yö.* |
| རི་ *ri.* | ལུ་ *lu.* | ཤེ་ *she.* | སོང་། *song.* |
| | ཧེ་ *he.* | ཨོཾ། *Om.* | |

(The *o* is named "*le-kor,*" and represents the letter མ་).

The above set of examples is that ordinarily used in Tibetan schools and monasteries.

6. **Final Consonants.**—The preceding paragraph shows the ordinary pronunciation of the vowels which is, however, further affected by some of the final consonants. Of final con-

sonants there are only ten; that is to say, though any consonant may begin a syllable only one of these ten consonants may end it. These ten final consonants are as follow:—

ག་ང་ད་ན་བ་མ་འ་ར་ལ་ས་ Let us briefly consider the pronunciation of each as a final, and its effect upon the pronunciation of the preceding vowel.

ག་ is pronounced so slightly as hardly to be heard and shortens the preceding vowel. When followed, however, by another consonant in a second syllable of the same word it is clearly pronounced, and does not affect the pronunciation of the preceding vowel, thus མིག་ eye =*mi*, but འཕོག་པ་ to hit=*phok-pa*.

ང་ is pronounced more sharply than when an initial. It does not affect the pronunciation of the preceding vowel, *e.g.*, མིང་ name=*ming*, but sounded sharply. The sound of final ག་ and ང་ can be obtained from the teacher with but little practice.

ད་ } These all modify the sounds of the preceding vowels *a*, *u*
ལ་ } and *o*; i.e., *a* into *e* (in French *les*); *u* into *ü* (in French
ས་ } *sur*); *o* into *ö* (*e.g.*, *hören* in German or *eu* in French *peu*). These modified sounds will, therefore, be romanized into *e*, *ö*, *ü*, respectively.

The final consonant itself is not pronounced; *e.g.*, ལུད་ manure=*lü*, བལ་ wool=*pē*, བྲོས་པ་ to flee=*trö-pa*.

ད་ makes the preceding vowel short; ལ་ and ས་

make it long, thus ལུད་ manure=*lü* (short *u*); but ལུས་ body=*lü* (long *u*).

ན་ modifies vowels as ད་ལ་ and ས་ modify them, but is itself pronounced, *e.g.*, ལན་ answer=*len*. When followed by པ་ཕ་བ་ or མ་ in the same word it is pronounced as *m*, e.g., རིན་པོ་ཆེ་ precious=*rim-po-chhe*.

བ་ མ་ ར་ } Do not affect the pronunciation of the vowel, and are themselves pronounced the same as when initial, *e.g.*, ཚབ་ delegate=*tshap̌*, ཟམ་པ་ bridge=*śam-pa*, ཟུར་ corner=*śur*. But ར་ like ག་ is sometimes pronounced so lightly as hardly to be heard.

འ་ is not itself pronounced but lengthens the sound of the vowel preceding it. No vowel except the indirect *a* precedes it, *e.g.*, ནམ་མཁའ་ sky=*nam-khā*.

7. **Affix.**—The letter ས་ also occurs as a second final consonant or affix after either of the four letters ག་ང་བ་མ་ It is not pronounced, but in the case of ག་ preceded by *a*, it has the effect of lengthening the *a*, e.g., ལགས་སི་ yes=*lā-si*. It is sometimes written in an incomplete form below the final consonant thus ལགྶི་

8. **Sanskrit Letters.**—The following six letters taken from the Sanskrit are occasionally used in the Colloquial language, namely :—

| ཊ་ | ཋ་ | ཌ་ | ཎ་ | ཥ་ | ཀྵ་ |
|---|---|---|---|---|---|
| *tra* | *thra* | *dra* | *na* | *kḣa* | *khya.* |

ཊ་ is known as *ta-lo-tra,* which means "*ta* reversed is *tra*";

ཎ་ as *na-lo-na,* "*na* reversed is *na*"; and so on.

9. **Examples.**

[The student is recommended to cover the romanized Tibetan letters with a piece of paper and thus to test his knowledge of the alphabet and its pronunciation.]

| | |
|---|---|
| ཀོ་བ་ leather = *ko-wa.* | ས་ earth = *sa.* |
| སྒར་ encampment = *gar.* | ཟ་བ་ to eat = *śa-wa.* |
| ཤིང་ tree = *shing.* | དད་པ་ faith = *ťe-pa.* |
| ཆུ་ water = *chhu.* | དང་ and = *ťang.* |
| ཨ་མ་ mother = *a-ma.* | ལས་ཀ་ work = *le-ka.* |
| འོད་ light, *s.* = *ö.* | ལུག་ sheep = *lŭ.* |
| ཕན་ profit = *phen.* | ལག་པ་ hand = *laḱ-pa.* |
| ཞོན་པ་ to ride = *sḱöm-pa.* | ཇོ་བོ་ lord = *cḱo-wo.* |

10. **Diphthongs.**—There are no real diphthongs, but under this head may be classed the combination *ai, oi, ui,* occurring when the one syllable of a word ends in *a, o,* or *u,*

and the next begins with *i*; e.g., རོ་ and འི་ of the corpse = *ro-i*, pronounced almost like *rö*, but with a slight sound of *i*; similarly ཁ and འི་ of the mouth = *kha-i* and almost = *khē*; བུ་ and འི་ of the son = *ṕu-ï* and almost = *ṕü*. In fact the འི་ modifies the preceding vowels in practically the same way as ས་ would do.

The other combinations of vowels are *ao, io, uo, eo, oo, au, iu, eu*; e.g., ཟའོ། ཤིའོ། དུའོ། ཚེའོ། ཇོའོ། གའུ། ཁྲིའུ། ལེའུ། They are not often used in the colloquial and are not really diphthongs, as each vowel is clearly though rapidly pronounced.

Note that འ་ and not ཨ་ is always used as the base of the second vowel; that is, the letter over which the second vowel must be written; *e.g.*, ཁ and འི་ and not ཁ་ and ཨི་

11. **Compound Consonants.**—These are of two kinds, namely Subjoined and Superadded. These subjoined consonants are:—

ཝ་ཡ་ར་ལ་ and ཧ་ They are known respectively as ཝ་ཟུར་ *wa-śur*, "*wa* on the edge"; ཡ་བཏགས་ *ya-ta*, "*ya* subjoined"; ར་བཏགས་ *ra-ta*, "*ra* subjoined"; ལ་བཏགས་ *la-ta*, "*la* subjoined"; and ཧ་བཏགས་ *ha-ta*, "*ha* subjoined."

12. **Wasurs.**—*Wasur* may be joined to sixteen consonants, *viz.* —

ཀྭ ཁྭ གྭ ཅྭ ཉྭ ཏྭ དྭ ཙྭ ཚྭ ཞྭ ཟྭ རྭ ལྭ ཤྭ སྭ ཧྭ

The effect on the pronunciation is to lengthen the sound of the vowel in the same way as final འ but not quite so much, *e.g.*, ཚྭ salt = *tshā*.

13. Of *yatas* there are seven, which are joined to the following letters, thus—

ཀྱ *kya*, ཁྱ *khya*, གྱ *ḱya*, པྱ *cha*, ཕྱ *chha*, བྱ *cḱa*, མྱ *nya*.

Note the pronunciation of the last four.

Thus གྱོང་པོ hard = *ḱyong-po*.

ཕྱིན་པ to go = *chhim-pa*.

བྱ bird = *cḱa*.

14. *Rata* is joined to thirteen consonants, namely :—

ཀྲ *tra*, ཁྲ *thra*, གྲ *ťra*.

ཏྲ *tra*, དྲ *ťra*.

པྲ pronounced *tra*, or *pa*, ཕྲ *thra*, བྲ pronounced *ťra*, *ṕa* or *ra*.

Note that gutturals and labials take the sound of dentals. *Rata* is also joined to ནྲ *na*, མྲ *ma*, ཤྲ *sha*, སྲ *sa* or

NOTE.—Several English grammars also give ཐྲ *thra*, but this is neither given in Tibetan primers nor used in the colloquial language.

*tra* or *hra*, ཧྲ་ *hra*, e.g., ཁྲག་ blood = *thra*, གྲུ་ boat = *t́ru*, དྲིལ་བུ་ bell = *t́ri-ṕu*, བྲིས་པ་ (འབྲི་བ་) to write = *t́ri-pa*, སྲས་ son = *se*, སྲབ་ bridle = *traṕ*.

Note that where any of the first nine *ratas* are followed by the vowels ི or ེ the *r* is pronounced less strongly than when followed by the other vowels. And in no case is the *r* pronounced as strongly as in English.

15. *Hata* in the colloquial language is not used except with ལ་, *e.g.*, ལྷ་ a god = *hla*, the *h* being pronounced before the *l*. It is also joined to ག་ད་བ་ཛ་ and ཌ་ and is then written གྷ་དྷ་བྷ་ཛྷ་ and ཌྷ་ respectively, but these last five cases only occur in transcribing Sanskrit words, and are of little use for colloquial purposes.

16. *La-ta* is joined to six consonants, thus—

ཀླ་གླ་བླ་ཟླ་རླ་སླ་ These are all sounded as *la* in a high tone, except ཟླ་ which is pronounced *da*, e.g., གླུ་ song = *lu*; ཟླ་བ་ month = *da-wa*.

17. **Examples.**

བྲག་ rock = *t́ra*.

སྨྱུ་གུ་ reed-pen = *nyu-gu*.

སླེ་ཀོག་ basket = *le-ko*.

ངའི་སྲབ་ my bridle = *nge-traṕ*.

ཁྱོད་ཀྱི་སྲོག་ your life = *khyö-kyi so.*

ཁོའི་གླུ་ his song = *khö lu.*

ཞབས་བྲོ་ dance = *sKap-ro.*

བྲང་ཁོག་ chest (of body) = *pang-kho.*

སྲང་འགག་ lane = *hrang-ga.*

18. **Superscribed Consonants.**—There are three of these, namely, ར་ལ་ and ས་ They are placed on the tops of other letters.

ར་ is placed on the top of twelve consonants, thus·

| | | | | | | | | | | | |
|---|---|---|---|---|---|---|---|---|---|---|---|
| རྐ་ | རྒ་ | རྔ་ | རྗ་ | རྙ་ | རྟ་ | རྡ་ | རྣ་ | རྦ་ | རྨ་ | རྩ་ | རྫ་ |
| *ka* | *ga* | *nga* | *ja* | *nya* | *ta* | *da* | *na* | *ba* | *ma* | *tsa* | *dza.* |

Note that the ར་ is written as ˉ ; except with ཉ་ when the full ར་ is written. Note also that རྒ་ is pronounced as *ga,* རྗ་ as *ja,* རྡ་ as *da,* རྦ་ as *ba* and རྫ་ as *dza.* The others differ from the ordinary ཀ་ང་ etc., in that they are pronounced in higher tone.

19. **Examples.**

རྐང་པ་ foot = *kang-pa,* རྒད་པོ་ old man = *ge-po,* རྒྱན་ ornament = *gyen,* རྡོ་ stone = *do,* རྣོ་པོ་ sharp = *no-po,* རྩ་བ་ root = *tsa-wa,* ལུག་རྫི་ shepherd = *luk-dzi.* The ར་ itself is not pronounced except sometimes when occurring in the second syllables of words; *e.g.*, རྡོ་རྗེ་ sacred thunder-bolt = *dor-je*. When ར་ surmounts a consonant as above, it is named ར་མགོ་ *rang-go,* i.e., ra-head, and the consonant is said to be "tied on" or "subjoined" as the *ya-tas, ratas,* etc., above. Thus རྐ་ is named *ra-ka-ta,* i.e., *ra* with *ka* subjoined, རྒ་ is named *ra-ga-ta,* and so on.

20. ལ་ similarly named ལ་མགོ་ *lang-go,* i.e., la-head, is superadded to ten consonants as follow:—

ལྐ་ ལྒ་ ལྔ་ ལྕ་ ལྗ་ ལྟ་ ལྡ་ ལྤ་ ལྦ་ ལྷ་

ལྷ་ is pronounced *hla.* The rest are pronounced in the same way as the corresponding consonants with superadded ར། ལྕ་ and ལྤ་ are pronounced in a high tone as *cha* and *pa* respectively.

21. ས་ similarly named ས་མགོ་ *sang-go,* i.e., sa-head, is superadded to eleven consonants as follow:—

སྐ་ སྒ་ སྔ་ སྙ་ སྟ་ སྡ་ སྣ་ སྤ་ སྦ་ སྨ་ སྩ་

These are pronounced in the same way as the corresponding consonants with superadded ར་ or ལ་ The consonants surmounted by ལ་ or ས་ are similarly said to be "tied on," e.g., ལྔ་ is named *la-nga-ta,* and སྡ་ is named *sa-da-ta.*

22. **Examples.**

ལྔ་ five = *nga.*

སྔ་དྲོ་ morning = *nga-t́ro.*

ལྕགས་ iron = *cha.*

ལྡིང་བ་ to soar (in the air) = *ding-wa.*

སྡིག་པ་ sin = *dik̄-pa.*

སྨན་ medicine = *men.*

23. **Prefixed Letters.**—The five letters ག་ད་བ་མ་འ་ are found in many words before the initial consonant. These prefixes are not themselves pronounced, but affect the pronunciation in the same way as superadded ར་ལ་ or ས་

ག་ occurs before ཅ་ཉ་ཏ་ད་ན་ཙ་ཞ་ཟ་ཡ་ཤ་ས་

ད་ before ཀ་ག་ང་པ་བ་མ་

བ་ before ཀ་ག་ཅ་ཛ་རྟ་ཏ་ད་ན་ཙ་ཛ་ཞ་ཟ་རྣ་ཤ་ས་

མ་ before ཁ་ག་ང་ཆ་ཇ་ཉ་ཐ་ད་ན་ཚ་ཛ་

འ་ before ཁ་ག་ཆ་ཇ་ཐ་ད་ཕ་བ་ཚ་ཛ་

**Examples.**

གཅིག་ one = *chi.*

གསར་པ་ new = *sa-pa.*

གདན་ bolster = *den.*

དངུལ་ silver = *ngü.*

བཏང་བ་ to send = *tang-wa.* བདུན་ seven = *dün.*

མཁས་པོ་ skilful = *khe-po.* འཛོམ་པ་ to assemble = *dzom-pa.*

24. Confusion might arise in the case of one of the prefixed letters making a word with one of the final consonants, the vowel being the inherent *a*, e.g., དག་ as to whether it represents *tă* or *gă*. The confusion is obviated as follows. If it is the initial ད་, the word is written དག་ *tă.* If it is the prefix, འ་ is added thus, དགའ་ = *gă.*

25. When བ་ as initial consonant follows ད་ as prefix, the combination is either sounded as *w* or not sounded at all. If accompanied by a *yata* or a vowel sign, it is not sounded at all; *e.g.,* དབུགས་ breath=*u,* དབྱངས་ tune, melody=*yang*; དབྱུག་པ་ to throw = *yuǩ-pa.* If accompanied by *rata,* it follows the ordinary rule of *ratas* (para. 14) and prefixed ད་ (para. 23) and is pronounced *dr.* In other cases it is pronounced as *w,* e.g., དབང་ power, authority = *wang.*

26. **Sentences for Pronunciation.**

Bring some hot water. ཆུ་ཚ་པོ་འཁྱེར་ཤོག་ *chhu tsha-po khe sho.*

This water is not hot. ཆུ་འདི་ཚ་པོ་མི་འདུག་ *chhu di tsha-po min-du.*

It is cold. གྲང་མོ་རེད་ *ťrang-mo re.*

You can go now. ད་འགྲོ་ཆོག་གི་རེད་ *ťa dro chhoǩ-ǩi-re.*

27. **Irregular Sounds.**—In the following cases the pronunciation is modified for the sake of euphony.

(*a*) *m* and *n* sounds.—When one syllable is followed by another beginning with a prefixed letter the sound of *m* or *n* is often introduced. This occurs especially when the first syllable ends in ག་ *e.g.*

ཕྱག་ལྡེ་ key, *hon.* = *chhan di.*

ཕྱག་འབྲུ་ grain, *hon.* = *chhan-dru.*

མི་འདུག་ is not = *min-du.*

ན་བཟའ་ clothes, *hon.* = *nam-śa.*

(*b*) *Reduplicated Sounds.*—When the following final consonants, or affixes, namely, ག་གས་ང་ངས་ར་ and ལ་, are followed by པ་ or བ་, the sound of the final consonant is reduplicated, *e.g.*, བཀག་ (འགོགས་) པ་གནང་བ་ to hinder, *hon.*=*kaḱ-ḱa nang-wa*; གསུངས་པ་རེད་ he said, *hon.*=*sung-nga-re.* ཉར་བ་ གནང་བ་ to take care of, *hon.* = *ngar-ra nang-wa*; ཚིལ་བུ་ fat = *tshil-lu*; དཔོན་པོས་གནང་བ་རེད། the official has given, *pöm-pö nang-nga-re.*

(*c*) བ་ following a vowel or ལ་. When བ་ follows a vowel its sound is sometimes omitted altogether, *e.g.*, ལྦ་བ་ goitre = *ba-a.*

ཀ་བ་ pillar = *ka-a.*

བ་ after ལ་ is often pronounced as *r*, e.g.,—

རྒྱལ་བ་གནང་བ་ to conquer, hon. = *gye-ra nang-wa.*

(*d*) Other changed sounds

བཞིས་ཐུར་ spoon = *sk̆ip̆-thu.*

རྒྱ་ར་ (རྒྱ་བྲ་) sweet buck-wheat = *gyap̆-ra.*

(*e*) There are also other irregular sounds, but it seems unnecessary to enumerate them all here. They will be picked up more easily in the course of conversation.

28. **The Tones.**—In Tibetan the tone, that is to say the pitch of the voice, varies, each word in this language having a tone in which it should be pronounced. It is very important for the student to render these tones with substantial accuracy; otherwise the pronunciation becomes uncertain and many of his words will assume meanings which he does not intend for them.

29. For practical purposes we must discriminate between three tones, *viz.* the high, the medium, and the low. The initial letter and the prefix govern the tone.

*High Tone.*—Use this in a word beginning with a prefix except when the initial letter is ཁ་ག་ཆ་ཇ་ཐ་ད་ཕ་བ་ཚ་ or ཛ་ Use it also with any of the following initials, *viz.* ཀ་ཅ་ཏ་པ་ ཙ་ཤ་ས་ཧ་

*Medium Tone.*—Use this in a word beginning with ཁ་ཆ་ཐ་ཕ་ཚ་ as initals whether with or without prefixes.

*Low Tone.*—Use this in a word beginning with any of the following letters as initials ག་ང་ཇ་ཉ་ད་ན་བ་མ་ཛ་ཝ་ཞ་ཟ་ཡ་ར་ལ་འ་ also in words in which a prefix precedes the initials ག་ཇ་ད་བ་ or ཛ་ Such initials are in this case, as previously noted in paragraph 23, pronounced as *g, j, d, b* and *dz,* respectively. For effect of ག་ང་ད་བ་ལ་ས་ in lengthening or shortening the preceding vowel see above paras. 6 and 7.

## Examples.

ཀོ་བ་ leather = *ko-wa,* high tone.

སྤོས་ incense = *pö,* high tone and lengthened.

ཕག་ brick = *pă,* high tone and shortened.

ཆམ་པ་ cold (in the head) = *chham-pa,* medium tone.

ཐབས་ opportunity = *thap̆,* medium tone.

ཐག་པ་ rope = *thak̆-pa,* medium tone and shortened.

ལ་ to (postposition) *la,* low tone.

ལགས་ yes (a polite affirmative) = *lā,* low tone and lengthened.

བོད་ Tibet = *p̆ö,* low tone and shortened.

Note the difference in above examples between སྤོས་ and བོད་ and between ལ་ and ལགས་

30. **Punctuation.**—It will have been noticed from the examples that at the end of each syllable a dot is placed at the top right-hand corner. This dot is named ཚེག *tshe.* A comma, semi-colon or colon is indicated by a vertical line (།) called *she,* a full-stop by a double line (།།) called *nyi-she,* and the end of a chapter by four lines (།། །།) called *sk̄i-she.* In hand-writing a mark ( ‘ ) is usually placed between each syllable instead of the *tshe,* but is sometimes incorporated with the last letter of the syllable.

31. **Spelling.**—The Tibetan method of spelling words should be acquired, as the teacher, in common with all Tibetans, will use it.

32. Pronounce the first consonant or compound consonant, add the vowel and pronounce the two together.

Thus, ཀོ་; *ka-na-ro, ko.* སྐི་; *sa-ka-ta, ka, ka k̄i-k̄u, ki.*

It is as if to say *sa* with *ka-ta* makes *ka, ka* with *k̄i-k̄u* makes *ki.*

33. If there is a final consonant, pronounce the whole word with it, then the consonant itself, and then the whole word again. Thus, ཀོང་; *ka-na-ro, ko, kong-nga-kong.* Again ཀྱོང་; *ka ya-ta, kya, kya-na-ro, kyo, kyong-nga, kyong.*

34. If the vowel is the inherent *a,* pronounce the first consonant, then the whole word, then the final consonant, and then the whole word again, *e.g.* ཁང་; *k̄a, k̄ang-nga, k̄ang.* སྒང་; *sa-ga-ta, ga, gang-nga, gang.* ལྟོགས་; *la-ta-ta, ta, ta-na-ro, to, tok̄-k̄a-sa, tok̄.*

35. When a prefixed letter begins the syllable, *e.g.* གད་ etc., it is pronounced as *ḱa-wo, t́a-wo*; *e.g.* གཉེན་; *ḱa-wo-nya-deng-bu, nye, nyen-na, nyen.* དགབ་; *t́a-wo-ga, gaṕ-ṕa gaṕ.* This *wo* is pronounced very shortly.

36. A syllable containing only a consonant and the inherent *a*, e.g., མ་, is called *ma-kyang, i e.* "only *ma*," to distinguish it from the consonant accompanied by one of the other vowels. Thus, to enquire whether a syllable is སོ་ or ས་, you may say, "Is it *sa-na-ro* or *sa-kyang*?"

36. **Examples.**

ལུང་ handle. *la sḱaṕ-kyu, lu, lung-nga, lung.*

རས་ cotton. *ra, re-sa, re.*

བཏང་བ་ to send. *ṕa-wo-ta-tang-nga, tang; wa: tang-wa.*

འཁྱུད་པ་ to embrace. *a-wo-kha-ya-ta khya, khya shaṕ-kyu, khyu, khyü-t́a, khyü; pa: khyü-pa.*

དགྲ་ enemy. *t́a-wo-ga-ra-ta, dra.*

ལྷ་ spirit. *la-ha-ta, hla.*

བསོད་ནམས་ good fortune. *ṕa-wo-sa-na-ro, so, sö-t́a, sö; na, nam-ma-sa, nam: sö-nam.*

ཞྭ་མོ་ hat. *sḱa-wa-sur, sḱa; ma na-ro, mo: sḱa-mo.*

དཔེ་ཆ་ book. *T́a-wo-pa-deng-bu, pe; chha: pe-chha.*

གློག་ lightning. *ḱa-la-ta, la, la-na-ro, lo, lo-ḱa, lo.*

རྒྱུག་པ་ to run. *ra-ga-ta, ga, ga ya-ta gya, gya sḱaṕ-kyu, gyu, gyuḱ-ḱa, gyuḱ; pa: gyuḱ-pa.*

རིགས་བརྒྱུད་ lineage. *ra-ḱi-ḱu, ri, ri-ḱa-sa, riḱ; ṕa-wo-ra-ga-ta, ga, ga ya-ta, gya, gya-sḱaṕ-kyu, gyu, gyü-t́a, gyü: riḱ-gyü.*

## 37. Sentences.

Where are you going to? ཁྱོད་ག་པ་འགྲོ་གི་ཡིན་པ་ *khyö ḱa-pa dro-ḱi yim-pa?*

I am going to Darjiling, Sir. ལགས་ང་རྡོ་རྗེ་གླིང་ལ་འགྲོ་གི་ཡིན་ *lā nga Dor-je-ling lă dro-ḱi yin.*

What have you got in the bundle? རྡོག་ཐྲེད་ནང་ལ་ག་རེ་ཡོད་པ་ *doḱ-thre nang-la ḱa-re yö-pa?*

Different kinds of things, Sir. ལགས་ཆ་ལག་སྣ་ཚོགས་ཡོད་ *lā cha-lă na-tsho yö.*

Have you a tea-pot among them? དེའི་ནང་ལ་ཁོ་ཏིང་ཡོད་པས་ *t́e-ï nang-la kho ting yö-pē?*

Yes, Sir, I have. ལགས་ཡོད་ *lā-yö.*

What is its price? གོང་ག་ཚོད་ཡིན་པ་ *ḱong ḱa-tshö yim-pa?*

Twenty rupees. ལགས་སྒོར་མོ་ཉི་ཤུ་ཐམ་པ་ཡིན་ *lā gor-mo nyi-shu tham-pa yin.*

Will you let me have it for fifteen rupees? སྒོར་མོ་བཅོ་ལྔ་ལ་གཏོང་གི་ཡིན་པས་ *gor-mo che-nga la tong-ḱi yim-pē?*

No, Sir. ལགས་མིན་ *la-men.*

Well, good-day! འོ་ན་ག་ལེ་རྒྱུག *o-na ḱa-le gyu.*

Good-day, Sir! ད་འོ་ན་ག་ལེ་འཆིབ་རྒྱུ་གནང་ *t́a o-na ḱa-le chhiṕ gyu-nang.*

# ENGLISH-TIBETAN COLLOQUIAL DICTIONARY.

## NOTE.

1. To understand fully the pronunciation of the Tibetan words, and the transliteration into the Roman character, reference should be made to the preliminary chapter on the "The Alphabet and its Pronunciation." It is not possible to represent all the Tibetan sounds by Roman letters with exactitude; hence the importance of mastering that chapter before using this dictionary.

2. Where the colloquial and the literary forms differ appreciably, the latter are given in brackets in the Tibetan character. In the romanized Tibetan the colloquial forms alone are given.

3. Where two or more Tibetan words are entered against the same English word, the first is the one most commonly used.

## A

| | | |
|---|---|---|
| **A, An,** ***art.*** | ཅིག་ | *chi.* |
| Do. (in the sense of full or complete) | ཁང་ | *kang.* |
| Aback | རྒྱབ་ལོགས་ལ་ | *gyap-lo-la.* |
| Abaft | གཞུག་ལ་ | *sKu-la.* |
| Abandon, to | བཞག་པ་ (འཇོག་པ།) སྤང་བ་ | *sKak-pa; pang-wa.* |
| Do. *hon.* | གཞོག་ག་ (འཇོག་པ་) གནང་བ་ | *sKok-ka nang-wa.* |
| | སྤོང་ང་ (བ་) གནང་བ་ | *pong-nga nang-wa.* |

| | | |
|---|---|---|
| Abate, to (in price) | བཅག་པ་ (གཅོག་པ་) | *chaḱ-pa.* |
| Do. *hon.* | གཅོག་ག་ (པ་། གནང་བ་ | *choḱ-ḱa nang-wa.* |
| Abbess | ཨ་ནི་དབུ་མཛད་ | *a-ni um-dze.* |
| Abbot | མཁན་པོ་ | *khem-po.* |
| Abbreviate, to | སྡུད་པ། དུམ་དུམ་བྱེད་པ་ | *dü-pa; dum dum cḱe-pa.* |
| Abdomen | གྲོ་ཁོག་ (གྲོད་ཁོག་) | *t́ro-kho.* |
| Do. *hon.* | གསོལ་གྲོད་ | *sö-t́rö.* |
| Abide, to | བསྡད་པ་ (སྡོད་པ་) | *de-pa.* |
| Do. *hon.* | བཞུགས་པ་ | *sḱu-pa* |
| Ability | དབང་ | *wang.* |
| Abject | སྡུག་པོ་ | *duḱ-po.* |
| Able, *adj.* | མཁས་པོ་ | *khe-po.* |
| Able, to be | ཐུབ་པ་ | *thuṕ-pa.* |
| Do. *hon.* | ཐུབ་པ་གནང་བ་ | *thuṕ-pa nang-wa.* |
| Able, to be (in the sense of knowing how) | ཤེས་པ་ | *she-pa.* |
| Do. *hon.* | མཁྱེན་པ་ | *khyem-pa.* |
| Able-bodied | སྟོབས་ཆེན་པོ་ | *toṕ chhem-po.* |
| Ablution | ཁྲུས་ | *thrü.* |
| Do. *hon.* | སྐུ་ཁྲུས་ | *ku-thrü.* |

| | | |
|---|---|---|
| **Abode** | ཁང་པ། ནང་ | *khang-pa ; nang.* |
| Do. *hon.* | གཟིམ་ཁང་ | *śim-khang.* |
| Do. *h. hon* | གཟིམ་ཤག་ | *śim-sho* |
| **Abolish, to** | མེད་པར་བཟོ་བ་ | *me-pa śo-wa.* |
| Do. *hon.* | མེད་པར་བཟོ་བ་གནང་བ་ | *me-pa śo-wa nang-wa.* |
| **Abominable** | སྐྱུག་བྲོ་པོ་ | *kyuḱ-t́ro-po.* |
| **Abortion** | བུ་གུ་ཤོར་བ་ | *pu-gu shor-wa.* |
| **About** (approximately) | ཙ་ (ཙམ་) | *tsa.* |
| **About** (concerning) | དོན་ལ། སྐོར་ལ་ | *t́ön-la ; kor-la.* |
| **Above** (on top of) | སྟེང་ལ། སྒང་ལ་ | *teng-la ; gang-la.* |
| **Above** (higher up a hill) | ཡར་ལ་ | *ya-la.* |
| **Abridge, to** | སྡུད་པ་ | *dü-pa.* |
| Do. *hon.* | སྡུད་པ་གནང་བ་ | *dü-pa nang-wa.* |
| **Abruptly** | ལམ་སང་ | *lam-sang.* |
| **Abscess** | ཤུ་བ་ | *shu-wa.* |
| Do. *hon.* | སྐུ་ཤུ་ | *ku-shu.* |
| **Abscond, to** | བྲོས་པ་ (འབྲོས་པ་) | *t́rö-pa.* |
| Do. *hon.* | བྲོས་ (འབྲོས་) ཕེབ་པ་ | *t́rö-phe-pa.* |
| **Absence** | མེད་དུས་ | *me-t́ü.* |
| **Absent, to be** | མེད་པ་ | *me-pa.* |

| | | |
|---|---|---|
| Absolutely (used negatively) | བད་དེ། ཁྱོན་ནས་ | *be te ; khyön-ne.* |
| Absolve, to | སེལ་བ་ | *sel-wa.* |
| Do. *hon.* | སེལ་ལ་ (བ་) གནང་བ་ | *sel-la nang-wa.* |
| Abstain from, to (certain kinds of food, &c.) | སྤང་བ་ | *pang-wa.* |
| | བཅད་པ་ (གཅོད་པ་) | *che-pa.* |
| Do. *hon.* | སྤོང་ང་ (བ་) གནང་བ་ | *pong-nga nang-wa.* |
| | བཅད་ (གཅོད་) པ་གནང་བ་ | *che-pa nang-wa.* |
| Absurd, to be | དོན་དག་མེད་པ་ | *ťön-ťa me-pa.* |
| Abundant | འབེལ་པོ། ཛག་ཏོ་ | *be-po ; dzaǩ-ťo.* |
| Abuse, *s.* | སྨད་ར་ | *me-ra.* |
| Abuse, to | སྨད་ར་བཏང་ (གཏོང་) བ་ | *me-ra tang-wa.* |
| Do. *hon.* | སྨད་ར་གཏོང་ང་ (བ་) གནང་བ་ | *me-ra tong-nga nang-wa.* |
| Do. *inf.* to *sup.* | སྨད་ར་ཞུ་བ་ | *me-ra sǩu-wa.* |
| Abyss | གཡང་གཟར་པོ་ | *yang-śar-po.* |
| Accede, to | ཁས་ལེན་པ་ | *khe-lem-pa.* |
| Do. *hon.* | ཞལ་བཞེས་གནང་བ། | *sǩe-sǩe nang-wa ;* |
| | ཞལ་གྱིས་བཞེས་པ་ | *sǩe-ǩyi sǩe-pa.* |
| Accept, to | ལེན་པ་ | *lem-pa.* |
| Do. *hon.* | བཞེས་པ་ | *sǩe-pa.* |
| Access, to have | འགྲོ་ཆོག་པ། ཕྱིན་ཆོག་པ་ | *dro-chhoǩ-pa ; chhin-chhoǩ-pa.* |

| | | |
|---|---|---|
| Access, *hon.* | ཕེབ་ཆོག་པ་ | *phe-chhoḱ-pa.* |
| Accident | བར་ཆད་ | *ṕar-chhe.* |
| Accommodation | ཤོང་ས་ | *shong-sa.* |
| Accompany, to | མཉམ་དུ་ཡོང་བ་ | *nyam-ťu yong-wa.* |
| Do. *hon.* | མཉམ་དུ་ཕེབ་པ་ | *nyam-ťu phe-pa.* |
| Do. *h. hon.* | ལྷན་རྒྱས་འཆིབ་རྒྱུ་གནང་བ་ | *hlen-gye chhiṕ-gyu nang-wa.* |
| Accomplice | རོགས་ | *ro.* |
| Accomplished, to be (completed) | འཚར་བ་ | *tshar-wa.* |
| Do. *hon.* | གྲུབ་པ་ | *ťruṕ-pa.* |
| According to | ནང་བཞིན་ | *nang-sḱin.* |
| Account | རྩིས་ | *tsi.* |
| Account Book | རྩིས་ཐོ་ | *tsi-tho.* |
| Do. *hon.* | ཕྱག་ཐོ་ | *chha-tho.* |
| Account of, on | རྐྱེན་གྱིས་ | *kyen-ḱyi.* |
| Accounts, to do | རྩིས་རྒྱབ་པ་ | *tsi-gyaṕ-pa.* |
| Do. *hon.* | ལྗགས་རྩིས་གནང་བ་ | *ja-tsi nang-wa.* |
| | ལྗགས་རྩིས་སྐྱོན་པ་ | *ja-tsi kyöm-pa.* |
| Accountant | རྩིས་པ་ | *tsi-pa.* |
| Do. Chief | རྩིས་དཔོན་ | *tsi-pön.* |

| | | |
|---|---|---|
| Accountant, Office of an | རྩིས་ཁང་ | *tsi-khang.* |
| Accumulate, to (money) | བསག་པ་ (གསོག་པ་) | *sak-pa.* |
| Do. *hon.* | བསག་ག་ (གསོག་ག་) གནང་བ་ | *sak-ka nang-wa.* |
| Accurate | ཏྲིག་ཏྲིག། ཏེན་ཏེན་ | *thrik-thrik ; ten-ten.* |
| Accusation | སྙད་ | *nye.* |
| Accuse, to | སྙད་བཙུགས་ (འཛུགས་) པ་ | *nye-tsuk-pa.* |
| Do. *hon.* | སྙད་བཙུགས་ག་ (འཛུགས་པ་) གནང་བ་ | *nye-tsuk-ka nang-wa.* |
| | སྙད་སྐོ་བ་གནང་བ་ | *nye-ko-wa nang-wa.* |
| Accustomed, to be | གོམས་པ་ | *kom-pa.* |
| Do. to become | གོམས་སོང་བ་ | *kom-song-wa.* |
| Ache, *s.* | གཟུག་ | *suk.* |
| Do. *hon.* | སྙུང་གཞི་ | *nyung-ski.* |
| Ache, to | ན་བ་ | *na-wa.* |
| Do. *hon.* | སྙུང་བ་ | *nyung-wa.* |
| Achieve, to | བྱེད་པ་ | *che-pa.* |
| Do. *hon.* | གནང་བ་ | *nang-wa.* |
| Acid | སྐྱུར་པོ་ | *kyur-po.* |
| Aconite | བཙན་དུག་ | *tsen-t'u.* |
| Acquaintance (friend) | ངོ་ཤེས་པའི་མི་ | *ngo-shem-pe-mi.* |

| | | |
|---|---|---|
| Acquainted, to be | ངོ་ཤེས་པ་ | *ngo-shem-pa.* |
| Do. *hon.* | ཐུགས་ངོ་མཁྱེན་པ་ | *thu-ngo-khyem-pa.* |
| Do. *inf.* to *sup.* | ཞལ་ཚོ་ (ཚོར་) བ་ | *sk̄e-tsho-wa.* |
| Acquainted, to get | ངོ་ཤེས་བཏང་ (གཏོང་) བ་ | *ngo she tang-wa.* |
| Do. *hon.* | ངོ་ཤེས་གཏོང་ང་ (བ་) གནང་བ་ | *ngo-she tong-nga nang-wa.* |
| Acquire, to | འབྱོར་བ། ཐོབ་པ་ | *jor-wa ; thop̄-pa.* |
| Do. *hon.* | ཕྱག་འབྱོར་བྱུང་བ་ | *chhan-jor ck̄ung-wa.* |
| Acquirement (skill) | ཡོན་ཏན་ | *yön-ten.* |
| Acquit, to | གློས་པ། བཏང་བ་ | *lö-pa ; tang-wa.* |
| Acquitted, to be (in a case) | བཏང་བཞག་པ་ | *tang-sk̄ak̄-pa.* |
| Do. *hon.* | བཏང་བཞག་ག་ (པ་) གནང་བ་ | *tang-sk̄ak̄-k̄a nang-wa.* |
| Across | ཕར་ | *pha.* |
| Act, to | བྱེད་པ་ | *ck̄e-pa.* |
| Do. *hon.* | གནང་བ་ | *nang-wa.* |
| Action (law suit) | ཁ་མཆུ་ | *kham-chhu.* |
| Do. (deed) | ལས་ཀ་ | *le-ka.* |
| Do. *hon.* | ཕྱག་ལས་ | *chha-le.* |
| Active | ཧུར་པོ་ | *hur-po.* |
| Actor | ཨ་ཆེ་ལྷ་མོ་ | *a-chhe-hla-mo.* |
| Actress | ཨ་ཆེ་ལྷ་མོ་ | *a-chhe-hla-mo.* |

| | | |
|---|---|---|
| Actual | ངོ་ཐོག་ | *ngo-tho.* |
| Acute (knife) | རྣོ་པོ་ | *no-po.* |
| Adage | གཏམ་དཔེ་ | *tam-pe.* |
| Adams-apple | ཨོག་ལྡོམ་ | *ok̄-dom.* |
| Add, to | སྣོན་འབེལ་སྤྲད་པ་ | *nöm-be tre-pa.* |
| Do. *hon.* | སྣོན་འབེལ་གནང་བ་ | *nöm-be nang-wa.* |
| Do. (figures) | སྡོམ་པ་ | *dom-pa.* |
| Additional | སྣོན་གས་ | *nön-k̄e.* |
| Adequate, to be | འགྲིག་པ་ | *drik̄-pa.* |
| Adhere, to, *v.i.* | འབྱར་བ་ | *jar-wa.* |
| Adieu (to a person departing) | ག་ལེ་ཕེབས་ | *k̄a-le phe.* |
| Do. (to a person remaining) | ག་ལེ་བཞུགས་ | *k̄a-le sK̄u.* |
| Adjourn, to | བཞག་པ་ ( འཛོག་པ་ ) | *sK̄ak̄-pa.* |
| Adjourn, to, *hon.* | གཞོག་ག་ ( འཛོག་པ་ ) གནང་བ་ | *sK̄ok̄-k̄a nang-wa.* |
| Adjust, to | སྒྲིག་པ་ | *drik̄-pa.* |
| Do. *hon.* | སྒྲིག་ག་ ( པ་ ) གནང་བ་ | *drik̄-k̄a nang-wa.* |
| Admiration | མོས་པ་ | *mö-pa.* |
| Admire, to | མོས་པ་བྱེད་པ་ | *mö-pa cK̄e-pa.* |

| | | |
|---|---|---|
| Admire, to (things) | སེམས་ཤོར་བ་ | *sem-shor-wa.* |
| Do. *hon.* | ཐུགས་སེམས་ཤོར་བ་ | *thu-sem shor-wa.* |
| Admittance, to grant | མཇལ་ཁ་གནང་བ་ | *je-kha nang-wa.* |
| Admonish, to | བསླབ་བྱ་བྱེད་པ་ | *lap-cKa cKe-pa.* |
| Do. *hon.* | བསླབ་བྱ་གནང་བ་ | *lap-cKa nang-wa.* |
| Admonition | བསླབ་བྱ་ | *lap-cKa.* |
| Adopted child | གསོས་ཕྲུག་ | *sö-thruk.* |
| Adore, to | མོས་གུས་བྱེད་པ་ | *mö-kü cKe-pa.* |
| Adorn, to | རྒྱན་ཆ་བཏགས་ (འདོགས་) པ་ | *gyen-chha tak-pa.* |
| Adornment | རྒྱན་ཆ་ | *gyen-chha.* |
| Do. *hon.* | སྐུ་རྒྱན་ | *ku-gyen.* |
| Adrift, to be | ཆུའི་སྒང་ལ་ལྡིང་བ་ | *chhü-gang-la ding-wa.* |
| Adroit | རྩལ་ཆེན་པོ་ | *tse-chhem-po.* |
| Adult | ལོ་དར་མ། གཞོན་པ་ | *lo-ťar-ma; shöm-pa.* |
| Adulterate, to | འདྲེས་བཏང་ (གཏོང་) བ་ | *dre-tang-wa.* |
| Do. *hon.* | འདྲེས་གཏོང་ང་ (བ་) གནང་བ་ | *dre-tong-nga nang-wa.* |
| Adulterer | ཆལ་པོ་ | *chhe po.* |
| Adulteress | ཆལ་མོ་ | *chhe-mo.* |
| Advance (of money) | སྔ་ཕྱི་ | *ngam-chhi.* |
| Advantage | ཕན། ཕན་ཐོགས་ | *phen; phen-tho.* |

| | | |
|---|---|---|
| Advantage, *hon.* | ཐུགས་ཕན་ | *thu-phen.* |
| Do. to be of | ཕན་ཐོགས་པ་ | *phen-thoḱ-pa.* |
| Do. *hon.* | ཐུགས་ཕན་གསོ་བ་ | *thu-phen so-wa.* |
| Adversary | དགྲ་ | *dra.* |
| Advice | གྲོས་ | *ťrö.* |
| Advice, to ask | གྲོས་དྲི་ (འདྲི་) བ་ | *ťrö-ťri-wa.* |
| Do. *hon.* | བཀའ་འདྲི་ཞུ་བ་ | *kan-dri sḱu-wa.* |
| Do. *h. hon.* | བཀའ་སློན་ (མོལ) ཞུ་བ་ | *ka-mön sḱu-wa.* |
| Advice, to give | གྲོས་བྱེད་པ་ | *ťrö-cḱe-pa.* |
| Do. *hon.* | བཀའ་གྲོས་གནང་བ་ | *ka-ťrö nang-wa.* |
| Aeroplane | གནམ་གྲུ་ | *nam-ťru.* |
| Afar, *adv.* | ཐག་རིང་པོ་ | *tha-ring-po.* |
| Affair (business) | ལས་ཀ། དོན་དག་ | *le-ka ; ťön-ťa.* |
| Do. *hon.* | ཕྱག་ལས། སྐུ་དོན་ | *chha-le ; ku-ťön.* |
| Affection | བྱམས་པོ་ | *cḱam-po.* |
| Affectionate, to be | བྱམས་པོ་བྱེད་པ་ | *cḱam-po cḱe-pa.* |
| Do. *hon.* | བྱམས་པོ་གནང་བ་ | *cḱam po nang-wa.* |
| Affirm, to | ལབ་པ་ | *laṕ-pa.* |
| Do. *hon.* | གསུང་བ་ | *sung wa.* |
| Affix, *s.* (grammatical) | རྗེས་འཇུག་ | *jen-ju.* |

| | | |
|---|---|---|
| Affix, to | སྦྲེལ་བ་ | *drel-wa.* |
| Do. *hon.* | སྦྲེལ་ལ་ (བ་) གནང་བ་ | *drel-la nang-wa.* |
| Afflicted, to be | དཀའ་ལས་བྱུང་བ་ | *ka-le cḱung-wa.* |
| Affliction | དཀའ་ལས་ | *ka-le.* |
| Afford, to | སྟེར་བ་ | *ter-wa.* |
| Do. *hon.* | གནང་བ་ | *nang-wa.* |
| Afloat, to be | ཆུའི་སྒང་ལ་གཡང་ (གཡེང་) བ་ | *chhü-gang-la yang-wa.* |
| Afoot (on foot) | རྐང་ཐང་ལ་ | *kang-thang-la.* |
| Do. *hon.* | ཞབས་ཐང་ལ་ | *sḱap̃-thang-la.* |
| Afraid, to be | ཞེད་པ་ | *sḱe-pa.* |
| Do. *hon.* | ཞེད་པ་གནང་བ་ | *sḱe-pa nang-wa.* |
| Affray, to commit an | ལག་འཛིང་བྱས་པ་ | *laḱ-dzing cḱe-pa.* |
| After | གཞུག་ལ། རྗེས་ལ་ | *sḱu-la ; je-la.* |
| Afternoon | དགོངས་དག་ | *gong-ťa.* |
| Afterwards | གཞུག་ལ། རྗེས་ལ་ | *sḱu-la ; je-la.* |
| Again | ཡང་སྐྱར་ | *yang-kyar.* |
| Against, over | ཁ་ཐུག་ལ་ | *kha-thu-la.* |
| Age (of a human being) . | ལོ་ | *lo.* |
| Do. *hon.* | དགོང་ལོ་ (དགུང་ལོ་) | *gong-lo.* |
| Age (of an animal) | ན་ | *na.* |

| | | |
|---|---|---|
| **Aged,** *m.* | རྒ་ཕུ་ (རྒན་པོ་) | *ga-p̄u.* |
| Do. *f.* | རྒ་སྨུ་ (རྒན་མོ་) | *ga-mu.* |
| Do. *hon.* | སྐུ་ནས་བགྲེས་པོ་ | *ku-ne dre-po.* |
| **Agent** | ལས་ཚབ་ | *le-tshap̄.* |
| Do. *hon.* | སྐུ་ཚབ་ | *ku-tshap̄.* |
| **Aggravated, to be (angry)** | ཚིག་པ་ཟ་བ་ | *tshik̄-pa śa-wa.* |
| Do. *hon.* | དགོངས་པ་ཚུང་པ་ | *gong-pa tshung-pa.* |
| **Agile** | ཧུར་པོ་ | *hur po.* |
| **Agitate, to (shake)** | དཀྲུག་པ་ | *truk̄-pa.* |
| Do. *hon.* | དཀྲུག་ག་ (པ་) གནང་བ་ | *truk̄-k̄a nang-wa.* |
| **Agitated, to be** | སེམས་འཚབས་པ་ | *sem tshap̄-pa.* |
| Do. *hon.* | ཐུགས་སེམས་འཚབས་པ་ གནང་བ་ | *thu-sem tshap̄-pa nang-wa.* |
| **Agony** | སྡུག་བསྔལ་ | *du-nge.* |
| Do. *hon.* | ཐུགས་འཁྲལ་ | *thu-thre.* |
| **Agree, to** | འགྲིག་པ། འཆམ་པ་ | *drik̄-pa ; chham-pa.* |
| **Agreeable** | མཐུན་པོ་ | *thüm-po.* |
| **Agreeable (in taste)** | ཞིམ་པོ་ | *sk̄im-po.* |
| Do. *hon.* | སྒྲོ་པོ་ | *tro-po.* |
| **Agreement (bond)** | གམ་རྒྱ་ (གན་རྒྱ་) | *k̄am-gya.* |

| | | |
|---|---|---|
| Agriculture | སོ་ནམས་ | *so-nam.* |
| Agriculturist | སོ་ནམས་བྱེད་མཁན | *so-nam cḱe-khen.* |
| Ague | ཚད་ནད་ | *tshe-ne.* |
| Ague, to have | འདར་རྒྱབ་པ་ | *dar-gyaṕ-p̣a* |
| Ahead (in front) | སྔན་ལ་ (སྔོན་ལ་) | *ngen-la.* |
| Aid | རོགས་ | *ro.* |
| Do. *hon.* | མགོ་འདྲེན་ | *gön-dren.* |
| Aid, to | རོགས་བྱེད་པ་ | *ro-cḱe-pa.* |
| Do. *hon.* | མགོ་འདྲེན་གནང་བ་ | *gön-dren nang-wa.* |
| Ail, to | ན་བ་ | *na-wa.* |
| Do. *hon.* | སྙུང་བ་ | *nyung-wa.* |
| Ailment | ན་ཚ་ | *na-tsha.* |
| Do. *hon.* | སྙུང་བ་ | *nyung-wa.* |
| Air (atmospheric wind) | ལྷགས་པ། རླུང་ | *hlaḱ-pa ; lung.* |
| Air (mien) | མདངས། གདོང་ | *dang ; dong.* |
| Alarm, to | ཞེད་སྐྲག་སླང་བ་ | *sḱe-tra lang-wa.* |
| Do. *hon.* | ཞེད་སྐྲག་སློང་ང་ (བ་) གནང་བ་ | *sḱe-tra long-nga nang-wa.* |
| Alas | ཨ་ཁ་ཁ་ (ཀྱི་མ་) | *a-kha-kha.* |
| Alert | གཅང་པོ་ | *chang-po.* |
| Do. *hon.* | ཐུགས་གཅང་པོ་ | *thu-chang-po.* |

| | | |
|---|---|---|
| Alien | ཕྱོགས་མི་ | *chho-mi.* |
| Alight, to (*e.g.*, from horse) | བབ་པ་ (འབབ་པ་) | *ṕaṕ-pa.* |
| Alight, to be (of fire) | འབར་བ་ | *bar-wa.* |
| Alike | གཅིག་པ་ | *chiḱ-pa.* |
| Alive, to be | གསོན་པོ་ཡོད་པ་ | *söm-po yö-pa.* |
| All | ཚང་མ། ཐམས་ཅད། སྒང་ཁ། རུ་ | *tshang-ma ; tham che ; gang-ḱha ; ru.* |
| All day | ཉིན་གང་ | *nyin-ḱang.* |
| All right (very well) | ལགས་སོ། ལགས་ལགས་སི་ | *la-so ; la-la-si.* |
| Allot, to | བགོད་པ་ | *gö-pa.* |
| Do. *hon.* | བགོད་པ་གནང་བ་ | *gö-pa nang-wa.* |
| Alliance (relation) | བརྒྱུད་རྩ་ | *gyü-tsa.* |
| Do. *hon.* | སྐུ་བརྒྱུད་ | *ku-gyü.* |
| Allied, to be | ཁ་མཐུན་པ་ | *kha-thüm-pa.* |
| Do. *hon.* | ཞལ་མཐུན་གནང་བ་ | *sḱe-thün-nang-wa.* |
| Allotment (share allotted) | སྐེ་ལ་ (སྐལ་བ་) | *ke-la.* |
| Do. *hon.* | སྐུ་སྐལ་ | *ku-ke.* |
| Allow, to | བཅུག་པ་ (འཇུག་པ་) | *chuḱ-pa.* |
| Do. *hon.* | བཅུག་ག་ (འཇུག་པ་) གནང་བ་ | *chuḱ-ka nang-wa.* |
| Allowed, to be | ཆོག་པ་ | *chhoḱ-pa.* |

| | | |
|---|---|---|
| Alloy | ལྷད་ | *hle.* |
| Allure, to | སླུ་བ་ | *lu-wa.* |
| All-wise | ཐམས་ཅད་མཁྱེན་པ་ | *tham-che khyem-pa.* |
| Almanack | ཟླ་ཐོ། ལེ་ཐོ་ (ལོ་ཐོ་) | *da-tho; le-tho.* |
| Do. *hon.* | གཟིགས་ཐོ་ | *śik̓-tho.* |
| Almighty | སྐུ་དབང་ཆེན་པོ་ | *ku-wang chhem-po.* |
| Almond | རྒྱ་དཀར་སྟར་ཀ་ | *gya-kar tar-ka.* |
| Almost | ཧ་ལམ་ | *ha-lam.* |
| Alms | སྦྱིན་པ་ | *jim-pa.* |
| Alms, to ask | སློང་བ་ | *long-wa.* |
| Alms, to give | སྦྱིན་པ་བཏང་ (གཏོང་) བ་ | *jim-pa tang-wa.* |
| Alone | གཅིག་པོ་ | *chik̓-po.* |
| Do. *hon.* | སྐུ་རྐྱང་ | *ku kyang.* |
| Along with | དང་མཉམ་དུ་ | *t̓ang-nyam-t̓u.* |
| Aloud | སྐད་ཆེན་པོ་བརྒྱབ་ནས་ | *ke-chhem-po gyap̓-ne.* |
| Do. *hon.* | གསུང་སྐད་ཆེན་པོ་སྐྱོན་ནས་ | *sung-ke chhem-po kyön-ne.* |
| Alphabet | ཀ་ཁ་ | *ka-kha.* |
| Already | ད་གི་ནས་ | *t̓a-ki-ne.* |
| Also | ཡང་ | *yang.* |
| Altar | མཆོད་བཤམས་ | *chhö-sham.* |

| | | |
|---|---|---|
| Alter, to, *v.t.* | རྗེ་བ། སྒྱུར་བ་ | *je-wa ; gyur-wa.* |
| Do. *hon.* | རྗེ་བ་གནང་བ། སྒྱུར་ར་ (བ་) གནང་བ་ | *je-wa nang-wa ; gyur-ra nang-wa.* |
| Alter, to (fit of clothes, etc.) | བཟོ་བཅོས་རྒྱབ་པ་ | *śop-chö gyap-pa.* |
| Do. *hon.* | བཟོ་བཅོས་སྐྱོན་པ་ | *śop-chö kyöm-pa.* |
| Alternately | རེ་མེད་ (མོས་) བྱས་ནས་ | *re-me cKe-ne.* |
| Although | ཀྱང་། རུང་། ན། ཡང་། | *kyang ; rung ; na ; yang.* |
| Altogether (in total) | ཐམས་ཅད་བསྡོམས་ནས་ | *tham-ehe dom-ne.* |
| Do. (quite) | བད་ | *be.* |
| Alum | སྐྱུར་མོ་ཚྭ་ | *kyu-mu-tsha.* |
| Always | རྣམ་རྒྱུན། དུས་རྒྱུན་ | *nam-gyün ; tü gyün.* |
| Am | ཡོད་ | *yö.* |
| Amass, to | སྡུད་པ་ | *dü-pa.* |
| Do. *hon.* | སྡུད་པ་གནང་བ་ | *dü-pa nang-wa.* |
| Amaze, to | ཡ་མཚན་བྱེད་པ་ | *yam-tshen cKe-pa.* |
| Do. *hon.* | ཡ་མཚན་གནང་བ་ | *yam-tshen nang-wa.* |
| Amazement | ཡ་མཚན་ | *yam-tshen.* |
| Amazing | ཡ་མཚན་པོ་ | *yam-tshem-po.* |
| Ambassador | སྐུ་ཚབ་ | *ku-tshap.* |

| | | |
|---|---|---|
| Amber | སྤོས་ཤེལ་ | *pö-she.* |
| Ambition | མཐོ་འདོད་ | *thon-dö.* |
| Ambitious | མཐོ་འདོད་ཆེན་པོ་ | *thon-dö chhem-po.* |
| Amble (of a horse) | འགྲོས་ | *drö.* |
| Amble, to (horse) | འགྲོས་རྒྱབ་པ་ | *drö-gyaṗ-pa.* |
| Do. *hon.* | ཆིབས་འགྲོས་རྒྱབ་པ་ | *chhim-drö gyaṗ-pa.* |
| Ambling pony | འགྲོས་མ་ | *drö-ma.* |
| Amend, to | བཟོ་སྐྱོར་བྱེད་པ་ | *ś́o-kyor cḰe-pa.* |
| Do. *hon.* | བཟོ་སྐྱོར་གནང་བ་ | *ś́o-kyor nang-wa.* |
| Amendment (correction) | ཞུ་དག་ | *sḰu-ṫa.* |
| Amicable | མཐུན་པོ་ | *thüm-po.* |
| Amicable relationship (state of) | མཐུན་ལམ་ | *thün-lam.* |
| Amidst | དཀྱིལ་ལ་ | *kyi-la.* |
| Ammunition | རྫས་རྡེ་ | *dzen-de.* |
| Among | དཀྱིལ་ལ་ | *kyi-la.* |
| Among ourselves (yourselves, themselves) | ནང་ཚག་ | *nang-tsa.* |
| Amount, total | ཁྱོན་བསྡོམས་ | *khyön-dom.* |
| Ample | མང་པོ་ | *mang-po.* |

| | | |
|---|---|---|
| Amusement | རྩེད་མོ་ | *tse-mo.* |
| Do. *hon.* | སྐུ་རྩེད་ | *ku-tse.* |
| Amusement, to have | ཐུགས་སྤྲོ་བཏང་ (གཏོང་) བ་ | *thu-tro tang-wa.* |
| Do. *hon.* | ཐུགས་སྤྲོ་གཏོང་ང་(བ་)གནང་བ་ | *thu-tro tong-nga nang-wa.* |
| Analogy | དཔེ་ | *pe.* |
| Ancestry | རིགས་བརྒྱུད། མི་བརྒྱུད་ | *ri-gyü ; mi-gyü.* |
| Do. *hon.* | སྐུ་བརྒྱུད་ | *ku-gyü.* |
| Ancestry of Lama | གདུང་བརྒྱུད་ | *dung-gyü.* |
| Anchor | གཏིང་རྡོ་ | *ťing-do.* |
| Ancient (of former time) | སྔོན་གྱི་ | *ngön-ḱyi.* |
| Do. (old) | རྙིང་པ་ | *nying-pa.* |
| Anciently | སྔོན་ལ། སྔོན་དུས་ | *ngön-la ; ngön-ťü.* |
| And | ཡང་། དང་ | *yang ; ťang.* |
| Anecdote | སྒྲུམ་ (སྒྲུངས་) | *drum.* |
| Anecdote, to relate | སྒྲུམ་ (སྒྲུངས་) བཤད་པ་ | *drum she-pa.* |
| Do. *hon.* | སྒྲུམ་ (སྒྲུངས་) གསུང་བ་ | *drum sung-wa.* |
| Angel | ཕོ་ཉ་ | *pho-nya.* |
| Anger | ཚིག་པ། ཁོང་ཁྲོ་ | *tshiḱ-pa ; khong-thro.* |
| Angle (corner) | ཟུར་ | *śur.* |
| Angry, to be | ཚིག་པ་ཟ་བ། ཁོང་ཁྲོ་ཟ་བ་ | *tshiḱ-pa śa-wa ; khong thro śa-wa.* |

| | | |
|---|---|---|
| **Angry, to be** *hon* | དགོངས་པ་ཚུང་བ་ རྣམ་མཁྱེན་འགལ་བ་ | *gong-pa tshung-pa ; nam-khyen gel-wa.* |
| **Angry and suspicious, to be** | བལྟ་ཕྱོགས་བྱེད་པ་ | *ta-chhok cke-pa.* |
| **Do.** *hon.* | གཟིགས་ཕྱོགས་གནང་བ་ | *śi-chhok nang-wa.* |
| **Angular** | ཟུར་མང་པོ་ཡོད་པ་ | *śur-mang-po yö-pa.* |
| **Animal** | སེམས་ཅན་ | *sem-chen.* |
| **Animal (wild)** | རི་དྭགས་ | *ri-ťa.* |
| **Animal (beast of prey)** | གཅན་གཟན་ | *chen-śen.* |
| **Ankle** | རྐང་པའི་ཚིགས་ཏོག་ | *kang-pe tshik-do.* |
| **Do.** *hon.* | ཞབས་ཀྱི་ཚིགས་ཏོག་ | *sKap-kyi tshik-do.* |
| **Annals** | ལོ་རྒྱུས་ | *lo-gyü.* |
| **Annals (of kings)** | རྒྱལ་རབས་ | *gye-rap.* |
| **Annihilate, to** | ཐམས་ཅད་མེད་པར་བཟོ་བ་ | *tham-che me-pa śo-wa.* |
| **Announce, to** | ལན་ (ལེན་) སྤྲོད་པ། ལན་ (ལེན་) སྐྱེལ་བ་ | *len-tre-pa ; len-kyel-wa.* |
| **Do.** *inf. to sup.* | ལྗགས་ལན་ཕུལ་ (འབུལ་) བ་ | *ja-len phü-wa.* |
| **Annoy, to** | ཁོང་ཁྲོ་སློང་བ | *khong-thro lang-wa.* |
| **Do.** *hon.* | དགོངས་པ་དཀྲུག་པ་ | *gong-pa truk-pa.* |
| **Annoyed, to be** | འཚེར་བ་ | *tsher-wa.* |
| **Do.** *hon.* | ཐུགས་འཚེར་གནང་བ་ | *thu-tsher nang-wa.* |

| | | |
|---|---|---|
| Annually | ལོ་རེ་རེ་ | *lo-re-re.* |
| Anoint, to | བྱུགས་པ་ (འབྱུག་པ།) སྐུ་བ་ | *cḱuḱ-pa ; ku-wa.* |
| Do. *hon.* | བྱུགས་ག་ (འབྱུག་པ་) གནང་བ། བསྐུས་པ་ (སྐུ་བ་) གནང་བ་ | *cḱuḱ-ḱa nang-wa ; kü-pa nang-wa.* |
| Another | གཞན་པ། ཡན་པ་ | *sḱem-pa ; yem-pa.* |
| Answer, *s.* | ལན་ | *len.* |
| Do. *hon.* | བཀའ་ལན་ | *ka-len.* |
| Answer, to | ལན་རྒྱབ་པ་ | *len-gyaṕ-pa.* |
| Do. *hon.* | ལྗགས་ལན་སྐྱོན་པ་ | *ja-len kyöm-pa.* |
| Answer, to (in anger) | ཁ་ལན་ལོག་པ་ | *kha-len loḱ-pa.* |
| Answer letter, to | ཡིག་ལན་ལོག་པ། ཡིག་ལན་བཏང་ (གཏོང་) བ་ | *yiḱ-len loḱ-pa ; yiḱ-len tang-wa.* |
| Do. *hon.* | ཕྱག་བྲིས་བཀའ་ལན་གནང་བ་ | *chha-ri ka-len nang-wa.* |
| Ant | གྲོག་མ་ | *t́ro-ma.* |
| Antagonist | དགྲ་ | *dra.* |
| Antelope | གཙོད་ | *tsö.* |
| Antique | རྙིང་པ་ | *nying-pa.* |
| Anus | ཀུབ་ | *kuṕ.* |
| Do. *hon.* | ཞབས་ཕོངས་ | *sḱam-phong.* |
| Anvil | འོག་ཙ་ | *oḱ-tsa.* |

| | | |
|---|---|---|
| **Anxiety** | སེམས་འཁྲལ་ | *sem-thre.* |
| Do. *hon.* | ཐུགས་འཁྲལ་ | *thu-thre.* |
| **Anxious, to be** | སེམས་འཁྲལ་བྱེད་པ་ | *sem-thre cḱe-pa.* |
| Do. *hon.* | ཐུགས་འཁྲལ་གནང་བ་ | *thuk-thre nang-wa.* |
| **Any** | གང་ཡང་ | *ḱang yang.* |
| **Anybody** (with negative) | སུ་གང་། སུ་ཡང་ | *su-ḱang; su-yang.* |
| **Anyhow** (in any case) | ག་རེ་ཡིན་ན་ཡང་ | *ḱa-re yin-ne yang.* |
| **Apartment** | ཁང་མིག་ | *khang-mik.* |
| Do. *hon.* | གཟིམ་ཆུང་ | *śim-chung.* |
| **Ape** | སྤེའུ་ (སྤྲེའུ་) | *pe-u.* |
| **Aperture** | སྒི་ཁུང་ | *gi-khung.* |
| **Apologize, to** | ཐུགས་དགོངས་དག་ཞུ་བ་ | *thu-gong-ťa sḱu-wa.* |
| **Apology** | ཐུགས་དགོངས་དག་ | *thu-gong-ťa.* |
| **Apoplexy** | གཟའ་རྒྱབ་པ་ | *sa gyaṕ-pa.* |
| **Apothecary's shop** | སྨན་ཁང་ | *men-khang.* |
| **Apparatus** | ལག་ཆ་ | *laḱ-chha.* |
| **Apparel** | ཆུ་པ་ | *chhu-pa.* |
| **Apparel,** *hon.* | ན་བཟའ་ | *nam-śa.* |
| **Appeal, to** | ཞུ་བ་ | *sḱu-wa.* |
| **Appear to be, to** | ཡིན་འགྲོ་ | *yin-dro.* |

| | | |
|---|---|---|
| Appear, to (to be seen) | མཐོང་བ་ | *thong-wa.* |
| Appear, to cause to (ghost, etc.) | སྤྱན་འདྲེན་ཞུ་བ་ | *chen-dren sḱu wa.* |
| Appearance | དབྱིབས། བཟོ་ལྟ་ | *y'p̓ ; sóp-ta.* |
| Appetite | དང་ག་ | *ťang-ḱa.* |
| Do. *hon.* | གསོལ་དང་ | *sö-ťang.* |
| Applaud, to | སྟོད་ར་བཏང་ (གཏོང་) བ་ | *tö-ra tang-wa.* |
| Do. *hon.* | སྟོད་ར་གཏོང་ང་ (བ་) གནང་བ་ | *tö-ra tong-nga nang-wa.* |
| Do. *inf.* to *sup.* | སྟོད་ར་ཞུ་བ་ | *tö-ra sḱu-wa.* |
| Applause | སྟོད་ར་ | *tö-ra.* |
| Apple | ཀུ་ཤུ་ | *ku-shu.* |
| Application (inferior to superior) | སྙན་ཞུ་ | *nye-sḱu.* |
| Application, written (by inferior to superior) | ཞུ་ཡིག་ | *sḱu-yi.* |
| Apply, to (by inferior to superior) | སྙན་ཞུ་ཕུལ་ (འབུལ་) བ་ | *nye-sḱu-phü-ua.* |
| Apply in writing, to (by inferior to superior) | ཞུ་ཡིག་ཕུལ་བ་ | *sḱu-yi phü-wa.* |
| Appoint, to (an officer) | སྐོ་བ་ | *ko-wa.* |
| Do. *hon.* | བསྐོས་བཞག་གནང་བ་ | *kö-sḱa nang-wa.* |
| Appoint, to (a menial servant) | བཞག་པ་ (འཛོག་པ་) | *sḱak-pa.* |

| | | |
|---|---|---|
| Appoint, to (a menial servant) *hon.* | གཞོག་ག་ (འཛོག་པ་) གནང་བ་ | *sḱok-ḱa nang-wa.* |
| Approach, to (an object) | འགྲམ་ལ་འགྲོ་བ། འགྲམ་ལ་ཡོང་བ་ | *dram-la dro-wa ; drum-la yong-wa.* |
| Do. *hon.* | འགྲམ་ལ་ཕེབ་པ་ | *dram-la phe-pa.* |
| Approve, to (sanction) | བཀའ་གནང་བ་ | *ka-nang-wa.* |
| Appurtenance | ཅ་ལག་ (ཆ་ལག་) | *cha-la.* |
| Do. *hon.* | སྐུ་ཅས་ (སྐུ་ཆས་) | *ku-che.* |
| Apricot | ཁམ་བུ་ | *kham-ṕu.* |
| Do. (a quick-growing, with good fruit) | ལོ་གསུམ་ཁམ་བུ་ | *lo-sum kham-ṕu.* |
| Do. (dried, from Balti) | མངའ་རིས་ཁམ་བུ་ | *nga-ri kham-ṕu.* |
| Apron | པང་གདན་ | *pang-den.* |
| Do. *hon.* | སྐུ་པང་ | *ku-pang.* |
| Aqueduct | ཡོ་པོ་ (ཡུར་པོ་) | *yo-po.* |
| Arbitrate, to | བར་མི་བྱེད་པ་ | *ṕar-mi cḱe-pa.* |
| Do. *hon.* | བར་མི་གནང་བ་ | *ṕar-mi nang-wa.* |
| Archer | མདའ་པ་ | *da-pa.* |
| Do. *hon.* | ཕྱག་མདའ་གནང་མཁན་ | *chhan-da nang-khen.* |
| Arduous | དཀའ་ལས་ཁག་པོ་ | *ka-le khaḱ-po.* |
| Do. *hon.* | སྐུ་མཉེལ་པོ་ | *ku-nye-po.* |

| | | |
|---|---|---|
| Are | ཡོད། འདུག། རེད་ | *yö ; du ; re.* |
| Area | རྒྱ་ | *gya.* |
| Argue, to | རྩེ་རྒྱབ་པ་ | *t e-gyap-pa.* |
| Do. *hon.* | ཞལ་རྩེ་སྐྱོན་པ་ | *sKe-tse kyöm-pa.* |
| Argument | རྩོད་པ་ | *tsö-pa.* |
| Arid | སྐམ་པོ་ | *kam po.* |
| Arise, to | ལང་བ་ | *lang-wa.* |
| Do. *hon.* | བཞང་བ་ (བཞེང་བ་) | *sKang-wa.* |
| Do. *h. hon.* | སྐུ་བཞང་ (བཞེང་) གནང་བ་ | *ku-sKang nang-wa.* |
| Arithmetic | རྩིས་ | *tsi.* |
| Do. *hon.* | ཕྱགས་རྩིས་ | *ja-tsi.* |
| Arm | ལག་པ་ | *laK-pa.* |
| Do. *hon.* | ཕྱག་ | *chha.* |
| Arm, upper | ལག་པའི་ཉ་ | *laK-pe-nya.* |
| Do. *hon.* | ཕྱག་གི་ཉ་ | *chha-Ki-nya.* |
| Armful | པང་ག་ (པ་) གང་ | *pang-Ka-Kang.* |
| Armlet | སྒྲོག་གདུང་ | *dro-dung.* |
| Do. *hon.* | ཕྱག་གདུང་ | *chha-dung.* |
| Armour | ཁྲབ་ | *thrap.* |
| Arm-pit | མཆན་ཁུང་ | *chhen-khung.* |

| | | |
|---|---|---|
| Arms (weapon) | མཚོན་ཆ་ | *tshön-chha.* |
| Army | དམག་དཔུང་ | *maḱ-pung.* |
| Do. (first militia, consisting of Tibetan laymen) | འདོན་དམག་ | *dön-ma.* |
| Do. (second militia consisting of Tibetan monks) | སེར་དམག་ | *ser-ma.* |
| Do. (last militia, consisting of all males between 18 and 60) | བཅོ་བརྒྱད་དྲུག་ཅུ་ | *choṕ-gye truḱ-chu.* |
| Around | འཁོར་ལ་ | *khor-la.* |
| Arouse, to (from sleep) | གཉིད་སད་པ་ | *nyi-se-pa.* |
| Do. *hon.* | གཉིད་སད་པ་གནང་བ་ | *nyi-se-pa nang-wa.* |
| Arrange, to | སྒྲིག་པ་ | *driḱ-pa.* |
| Do. *hon.* | སྒྲིག་ག་ (པ་) གནང་བ་ | *driḱ-ka nang-wa.* |
| Arrest, to | ཟིན་པ་ | *śim-pa.* |
| Do. *hon.* | ཟིན་པ་གནང་བ་ | *śim-pa nang-wa.* |
| Arrive, to | སླེབ་པ་ | *leṕ-pa.* |
| Do. *hon.* | ཕེབ་པ་ | *phe-pa.* |
| Do. *h. hon.* | འཆིབ་རྒྱུ་གནང་བ་ | *chhiṕ-gyu nang wa.* |
| Arrogant | ཉམས་ཆེན་པོ། ཛ་ཁོག་ཆེན་པོ་ | *nyam-chhem-po; dza-kho chhem-po.* |

| | | |
|---|---|---|
| Arrow | མདའ་ | *da.* |
| Do. *hon.* | ཕྱག་མདའ་ | *chhan-da.* |
| Art, *s.* | ཡོན་ཏན་ | *yön-ten.* |
| Artery | རྩ་ | *tsa.* |
| Artful | གཅང་པོ་ | *chang-po.* |
| Do. *hon.* | ཐུགས་གཅང་པོ་ | *thu-chang-po.* |
| Article | སྤྱད་ལག །དངོས་རིགས་ | *cha-la ; ngö ri.* |
| Artist (painter) | ལྷ་རི་ (འབྲི་) པ་ | *hla-ri-pa.* |
| As (like) | ནང་བཞིན། འདྲ་པོ་ | *nang-sḱin ; dra-po.* |
| As far as | བར་དུ ! ཐུག་ | *ṕar-ťu ; thu.* |
| Ascend, to | འཛག་པ་ (འཛེག་པ་) | *dzaḱ-pa.* |
| Do. *hon.* | འཛག་ག་ (འཛེག་པ་) གནང་བ་ | *dzaḱ-ḱa nang-wa.* |
| Ascent (uphill) | གྱེན་ | *ḱyen.* |
| Ascertain, to | ཧ་གོ་བ་བྱེད་པ་ | *ha-ḱo-wa cḱe-pa.* |
| Do. *hon.* | མཁྱེན་པ་གནང་བ་ | *khyem-pa nang-wa.* |
| Ascetic | སྒོམ་ཆེན་ | *gom-chhen.* |
| Ashamed | ངོ་ཚ་པོ་ | *ngo-tsha-po.* |
| Ashamed, to feel | ངོ་ཚ་བ་ | *ngo-tsha-wa.* |
| Do. *hon.* | ཐུགས་ངོ་ཚ་བ་ | *thu-ngo-tsha-wa.* |
| Ashes | གོག་ཐལ་ | *ḱo-the.* |

| | | |
|---|---|---|
| Aside | ཟུར་དུ་ | *śur-ťu.* |
| Ask, to | དྲི་བ་ (འདྲི་བ་) | *ťri-wa.* |
| Ask, to (inferior asking superior) | ཞུ་བ་ | *sḱu-wa.* |
| Asleep, to fall | གཉིད་ཁུག་པ་ | *nyi-khuḱ-pa.* |
| Do. *hon.* | མཉན་ (མཉལ་) གཟིམ་པ་ | *nye-śim-pa.* |
| Ass | བུང་གུ་ (བོང་བུ་) | *ṕung-ḱu.* |
| Do. (wild) | རྐྱང་ | *kyang.* |
| Assail, to | རུབ་རྒྱབ་པ་ | *ruṕ-gyaṕ-pa.* |
| Assassin | མི་གསོད་མཁན་ | *mi-sö-khen.* |
| Assassinate, to | བསད་པ་ (གསོད་པ་) | *se-pa.* |
| Assault, to | རྡུང་བ་ | *dung-wa.* |
| Do. *hon.* | ཕྱག་འཇུག་ (འཇུས་) གནང་བ་ | *chhan-juḱ nang-wa.* |
| Assemble, to | འཚོགས་པ་ | *tshoḱ-pa.* |
| Do. *hon.* | ཚོགས་འདུ་འཚོགས་ག་ (པ་) གནང་བ་ | *tshon-du-tshoḱ-ḱa nang-wa.* |
| Assembly-hall | ཚོམས་ཆེན་ | *tshom-chhen.* |
| Do. for monks | འདུ་ཁང་ | *du-khang.* |
| Assiduous | བརྩོན་འགྲུས་ཆེན་པོ་ | *tsön-drü chhem-po.* |
| Do. to be | སྙིང་རུས་བྱེད་པ་ | *nying-rü cḱe-pa* |

| | | |
|---|---|---|
| Assiduous, to be *hon.* | ཐུགས་རུས་གནང་བ་ | *thu-rü nang-wa.* |
| Assist, to | རོགས་བྱེད་པ་ | *ro-che-pa.* |
| Do. *hon.* | མགོ་འདྲེན་གནང་བ་ | *gön-dren nang-wa.* |
| Assistance | རོགས་ | *ro.* |
| Do. *hon.* | མགོ་འདྲེན་ | *gön-dren.* |
| Assistant | རོགས་བྱེད་མཁན་ | *ro-che-khen.* |
| Do. *hon.* | མགོ་འདྲེན་གནང་མཁན་ | *gön-dren nang-khen.* |
| Associate | དགའ་པོ་ཉེ་པོ་ | *ga-po nye-po.* |
| Do. *hon.* | ཐུགས་ཉེ་ཆག་པོ་ | *thuk-nye chhak-po.* |
| Associate with, to | དགའ་པོ་ཉེ་པོ་ཡོད་པ་ | *ga-po nye-po yö-pa.* |
| Aster | བསྐལ་བཟང་མེ་ཏོག་ | *ke-sang me-to.* |
| Astonish, to | ཡ་མཚན་བྱེད་པ་ | *yam-tshen che-pa.* |
| Do. *hon.* | ཡ་མཚན་གནང་བ་ | *yam-tshen nang-wa.* |
| Astonished | ཡ་མཚན་པ་ | *yam-tshem-pa.* |
| Astonishing | ཡ་མཚན་པོ་ | *yam-tshem po.* |
| Astonishment | ཡ་མཚན་ | *yam-tshen.* |
| Astride, to put | སྐྱོན་པ་ | *kyöm-pa.* |
| Astrologer | རྩིས་པ་ | *tsi-pa.* |
| Astrology | སྐར་རྩིས་ | *kar-tsi.* |
| Astronomer | རྩིས་པ་ | *tsi-pa.* |

| | | |
|---|---|---|
| Astronomy | སྐར་རྩིས་ | *kar-tsi.* |
| Asunder | སོ་སོ་ | *so-so.* |
| At | ལ་ | *la.* |
| At all (negatively) | ཙ་ནས་ | *tsa-ne.* |
| Athletic | རྩལ་ཆེན་པོ་ | *tse-chhem-po.* |
| Atlas | ས་ཁྲ་ | *saṕ-thra.* |
| At once | ལམ་སང་ | *lam-sang.* |
| Attach, to | རྒྱབ་པ་ | *gyaṕ-pa.* |
| Do. *hon.* | སྐྱོན་པ་ | *kyöm-pa.* |
| Attach, to (by sticking together) | སྦྱར་བ་ | *jar-wa.* |
| Do. *hon.* | སྦྱར་ར་ (བ་) གནང་བ་ | *ćar-ra nang-wa.* |
| Attached, to be (long for) | དྲན་པ་ | *t́rem-pa.* |
| Do. *hon.* | དྲན་པ་གནང་བ་ | *t́rem-pa nang-wa.* |
| Attached, to be (love) | སེམས་ཆགས་པ་ | *sem chhaḱ-pa.* |
| Do. *hon.* | ཐུགས་སེམས་ཆགས་པ་ | *thu-sem chhaḱ-pa.* |
| Attack, to | རུབ་རྒྱབ་པ་ | *ruṕ-gyaṕ-pa.* |
| Attain, to | འབྱོར་བ། ཐོབ་པ་ | *jor-wa ; thoṕ-pa.* |
| Do. *hon.* | འབྱོར་ར་ (བ་) གནང་བ། ཕྱག་སོན་བྱུང་བ་ | *jor-ra nang-wa ; chhaḱ-sön ćhung-wa.* |

| | | |
|---|---|---|
| Attempt | བརྩོན་འགྲུས་ | *tsön-drü.* |
| Attempt, to | བརྩོན་འགྲུས་བྱེད་པ་ | *tsön-drü cKe pa.* |
| Do. *hon.* | བརྩོན་འགྲུས་གནང་བ་ | *tsön-drü nang-wa.* |
| Attend, to (servant on master) | ཞབས་ཕྱི་ཞུ་བ་ | *sKap-chhi sKu-wa.* |
| Attend, to (before a superior) | སྐུ་མདུན་ལ་བཅར་བ་ | *kun-dün-la char-wa.* |
| | སྐུ་བཅར་ཞུ་བ་ | *ku-char sKu-wa.* |
| Attend, to (before Lama) | སྐུ་མདུན་ལ་མཇལ་བ་ | *kun-dün-la je-wa.* |
| Attend, to (heed) | ཉན་པ། ཨམ་ཅོག་ཉན་པ་ | *nyem-pa ; am-cho nyem pa.* |
| Do. *hon.* | གསན་པ། སྙན་ལ་གསན་པ་ | *sem pa ; nyen-la-sem-pa.* |
| Attendant | གཡོག་པོ་ | *yoK-po.* |
| Do. *hon.* | ཞབས་ཕྱི་ | *sKap-chhi.* |
| Attendant, female | གཡོག་མོ་ | *yo mo.* |
| Do. *hon.* | ཞལ་ཏ་མ་ | *sKe-ta-ma.* |
| Attentive, to be | ཧུར་ཐག་བྱེད་པ་ | *hur-tha cKe-pa.* |
| Do. *hon.* | ཧུར་ཐག་གནང་བ་ | *hur-tha nang-wa.* |
| Aunt (paternal) | ཨ་ནི་ (ཨ་ནེ་) | *a ni.* |
| Do. (maternal) | སྲུ་མོ་ | *su-mo.* |
| Auspices (omens) | རྟེན་འབྲེལ་ | *tem-dre.* |
| Authentic | དངོས་ནས། ངོ་ཐོག་ | *ngö-ne ; ngo-tho* |
| Author | རྩོམ་མཁན་ | *tsom-khen.* |

| | | |
|---|---|---|
| Author, *hon.* | རྩོམ་པ་གནང་མཁན་ | *tsom-pa nang-khen.* |
| Authority | དབང་ | *wang.* |
| Authorize | དབང་སྤྲད་བ་ | *wang-tre-pa.* |
| Do. *hon.* | དབང་གནང་བ་ | *wang-nang-wa.* |
| Autumn | སྟོན་ཀ་ | *tön-ka.* |
| Auxiliary troops | རྒྱབ་སྐྱོན་ | *gyam-nön.* |
| Avalanche | གངས་རུད་ | *ƙang-rü.* |
| Avarice | ཧམ་པ་ | *ham-pa.* |
| Avaricious | ཧམ་པ་ཆེན་པོ་ | *ham-pa chhem-po.* |
| Avenge, to | དགྲ་ལན་ལོག་པ་ | *dra-len loƙ-pa.* |
| Do. *hon.* | དགྲ་ལན་ལོག་ག་ (པ་) གནང་བ་ | *dra-len loƙ-ƙa nang-wa.* |
| Avoid, to (a person) | དབྱོལ་བ། ཟུར་ནས་འགྲོ་བ་ | *yö-wa; śur-ne dro-wa.* |
| Do. *hon.* | གཟུར་ནས་ཕེབ་པ་ | *śur-ne phe-pa.* |
| Awake, to | གཉིད་སད་པ་ | *nyi-se-pa.* |
| Do. *hon.* | མཉན་ (མཉལ་) སད་པ་ | *nyen-se-pa.* |
| Await, to | སྒུག་པ་ | *guƙ-pa.* |
| Do. *hon.* | སྒུག་པ་གནང་བ་ | *guƙ-pa nang-wa.* |
| Away | ཕར་ | *pha.* |
| Awkward | སྡུག་རུས་ | *duƙ-rü.* |
| Axe | སྟ་རི་ (སྟ་རེ་) | *ta-ri.* |

| | | |
|---|---|---|
| **Ay (yes)** | ལགས་སོ། ལགས་ལགས་སི། ལ་ཧྲོང་ | *la-so ; la-la-si ; la-ong.* |
| **Azure** | སྔོན་པོ་ | *ngöm-po.* |

# B

| | | |
|---|---|---|
| Baby (of few months) | མ་འབྲུར་ | *man-ja.* |
| Baby (older) | ཕྲུ་གུ་ཆུང་ཆུང་ | *pu-gu chhung-chhung.* |
| Do. *hon.* | ཨ་ཝ་ | *a-wa.* |
| Bachelor | ཕོ་ཧྲང་ང་ | *pho-hrang-nga.* |
| Back (of body) | རྒྱབ་ | *gyap̌.* |
| Do. *hon.* | སྐུ་རྒྱབ་ | *ku-gyap̌.* |
| Back (behind in place) | རྒྱབ་ལ་ | *gyap̌-la.* |
| Backbite | ཁ་བདང་ (གཏོང་) བ་ | *kha-tang-wa.* |
| Do. *hon.* | ཞལ་གཏོང་ང་ (བ) གནང་བ་ | *sǩe-tong-nga nang-wa.* |
| Backbone | སྒལ་ཚིགས་ | *ge-tshi.* |
| Do. *hon.* | སྐུ་སྟོད་ཚིགས་ | *ku-tö tshi.* |
| Backside | རྐུབ་ | *kup̌.* |
| Do. *hon.* | ཞབས་ཕོངས་ | *sǩam-phong.* |
| Backwards | རྒྱབ་ལོགས་ལ་ | *gyap̌-lo-la.* |
| Bad (wicked) | ངན་པ། སྐྱུག་བྲོ་པོ་ | *ngem-pa ; kyuǩ ťro-po.* |
| Do. (decomposed, *e.g.*, of meat) | རུལ་པ་ | *rü-pa.* |
| Do. (of things offensive in smell, &c.) | སྐྱུག་བྲོ་བོ། སྡུག་རུལ་ | *kyuǩ-ťro-po ; duǩ-rü.* |

| | | |
|---|---|---|
| Bad, to be (of things generally) | ཡག་པོ་མེད་པ་ | *yak-po me-pa.* |
| Bag (large) | སྒྲེ་མོ་ | *gye-mo.* |
| Do. (small) | ཕད་ཀོག་ | *phe-k̓o.* |
| Do. (made of leather) | རྐྱལ་པ་ | *kye-pa.* |
| Badge | རྟགས་ | *ta.* |
| Baggage | དོས་པོ་ | *t̓ö-po.* |
| Bail | ཁས་ཁྱགས་ | *khe-khya.* |
| Do. *hon.* | ཞལ་ཁྱགས་ | *sk̓e-khya* |
| Bail, to | ཁས་ཁྱགས་བྱེད་པ་ | *khe-khya ck̓e-pa.* |
| Do. *hon.* | ཞལ་ཁྱགས་གནང་བ་ | *sk̓e-khya nang-wa.* |
| Bake, to | བག་ལེབ་སྲེག་པ་ | *p̓a-le trak̓-pa.* |
| Bakshish | གསོལ་རས་ | *sö-re.* |
| Balance (what is wanting) | ལྷག་མ་ | *hla-ma.* |
| Do. (for small weights) | རྒྱ་འཐུར་ | *gya-thu.* |
| Do. (for larger weights) | ཉ་ག་ | *nya-k̓a.* |
| Do. (for very large weights) | རྒྱ་མ་ | *gya-ma.* |
| Balanced evenly, to be | ཡང་ལྗི་མེད་པ་ | *yang ji me-pa.* |
| Bald | ཟངས་ཁོགས་ | *śang-kho.* |
| Do. *hon.* | དབུ་རིལ་ | *u-ri.* |

| | | |
|---|---|---|
| Bale | དོས་པོ་ | *tö-po.* |
| Do. (of wool) | བལ་དོས་ | *ṕe-ťö.* |
| Ball | རྡིའུ་ (རྡེའུ་) | *di-u.* |
| Ball-cartridge | མདེ་རིལ་ | *diḱ-ri.* |
| Ball (of gun) | རྡིག་རིལ་ | *diḱ-ri.* |
| Balloon | རླུང་གྲུ་ | *lung-ťru.* |
| Bamboo | སྨྱུག་མ་ | *nyung-ma.* |
| Banana | སྐྱེ་སྡོང་ *Sik.* | *ḱye-dong.* |
| Band (gang of men) | ཚོགས་ | *tsho.* |
| Band (hoop) | ཤེན་ | *shen.* |
| Do. (of iron) | ལྕགས་ཤེན་ | *cha-shen.* |
| Do. (of silver) | དངུལ་ཤེན་ | *ngü-shen.* |
| Do. (of brass) | རག་ཤེན་ | *ra-shen.* |
| Do. (of gold) | གསེར་ཤེན་ | *se-shen.* |
| Bandit | ཇག་པ་ | *cḱaḱ-pa.* |
| Bandy-legged | རྐང་ཀྱོག་ | *kang-ḱyo.* |
| Do. *hon.* | ཞབས་ཀྱོག་ | *sḱaṕ-kyo.* |
| Banish, to | རྒྱང་ཕུད་ (འཕུད་) བཏང་ (གཏོང་) བ་ | *gyam-phü tang-wa.* |

| | | |
|---|---|---|
| Banish, to, *hon.* | རྒྱང་ཕུད་ (འབུད་) གཏོང་ང་ (བ་) གནང་བ་ | *gyam-phü tong-nga nang-wa.* |
| Bank (of river, &c.) | འགྲམ་ | *d̓ram.* |
| Banker | ཕུན་བདག་ | *p̓ün-da.* |
| Banner | དར་འཕྱར་ | *t̓ar-chhar.* |
| Do. (of victory) | རྒྱལ་མཚན་ | *gyen-tshen.* |
| Banquet | མགྲོན་པོ་ (མགྲོན་) | *dröm-po.* |
| Do. *hon.* | ཐུགས་སྤྲོ་ | *thuk̓-tro.* |
| Do. to give a | མགྲོན་པོ་ (མགྲོན་) བཏང་ (གཏོང་) བ་ | *dröm-po tang-wa.* |
| Do. *hon.* | ཐུགས་སྤྲོ་གཏོང་ང་(བ་)གནང་བ་ | *thuk̓-tro tong-nga nang-wa.* |
| Baptism | ཁྲུས་གསོལ་ | *thrü-sö.* |
| Baptize, to | ཁྲུས་གསོལ་གནང་བ་ | *thrü-sö nang-wa.* |
| Bar | དུམ་བུ་ | *t̓um-p̓u.* |
| Barbarian | མཐའ་འཁོབ་པ་ | *tha-khop̓-pa.* |
| Barber | སྐྲ་བཞར་ར་ (བ་) | *tra-sk̓ar-ra.* |
| Do. *hon.* | དབུ་སྐྲ་བཞར་མཁན་ | *u-tra sk̓ar-k̓ken.* |
| Bare (naked) | དམར་ཧྲང་ང་ | *ma-hrang-nga.* |
| Barefooted | རྐང་རྗེན་མ་ | *k̓ang-je-ma.* |
| Do. *hon.* | ཞབས་རྗེན་མ་ | *shap̓-je-ma.* |

| | | |
|---|---|---|
| Bargain, *s.* | ཚོང་ | *tshong.* |
| Do. to | ཚོང་རྒྱབ་པ་ | *tshong gyap-pa* |
| Do. *hon.* | རྒྱ་ཚོང་གནང་བ་ | *gya-tshong nang-wa.* |
| Bark | པགས་པ་ | *pak-pa.* |
| Bark, to (of dogs) | འཆང་བ་ | *chhang-wa.* |
| Barley | ནས་ | *ne.* |
| Do. *hon.* | ཕྱག་འབྲུ་ | *chhan-dru.* |
| Barley-flour | རྩམ་པ་ | *tsam-pa.* |
| Do. *hon.* | གསོལ་ཞིབ་ | *sö-skip.* |
| Barn | འབྲུ་ཁང་ | *dru-khang.* |
| Barrel (of gun) | ལྕགས་ཧྲང་ | *cha-hrang.* |
| Barren (of women) | རབས་ཆད་ | *rap-chhe.* |
| Do. (of cow) | བཞོས་སྐམ་ | *skö-kam.* |
| Barrier (fence) | ར་བ་ | *ra-wa.* |
| Barter | བརྗེ་བ་ | *je-wa.* |
| Bashful, to be | ངོ་ཚ་བ་ | *ngo-tsha-wa.* |
| Do. *hon.* | ཞལ་རས་ཚ་བ་ | *ske-re tsha-wa.* |
| Basin (for washing hands) | ཏུང་བན་ | *tung-pen.* |
| Do. (wooden) | གཞོང་པ་ | *skong-pa.* |
| Do. (round copper basin) | ཀ་ཏོ་ར་ | *ka-to-ra.* |

| | | |
|---|---|---|
| Basket | སླེ་ཀོག། སླེ་པོ་ | *le-ko̤; le-po.* |
| Bat | ཕྲམ་པོ་ (ཕྲ་ཝོང་) | *gam-po.* |
| Bath | ཆུ་གཞོང་ | *chhu-sk̄ong.* |
| Do. *hon.* | ཆབ་གཞོང་ | *chhap̄-sk̄ong.* |
| Bathe, to | འཁྲུད་པ་ | *thrü-pa.* |
| Do. *hon.* | འཁྲུད་པ་གནང་བ་ | *t̄hrü-pa nang-wa.* |
| Battle | དམག་ | *ma.* |
| Bay-coloured (horse) | སྐྱང་པོ་ | *kyang-po.* |
| Do. (light) | སྐྱང་དཀར་ | *kyang-ka.* |
| Do. (dark) | སྐྱང་ནག་ | *kyang-na.* |
| Bazaar | ཁྲོམ | *throm.* |
| Be, to | རེད་པ། ཡིན་པ། ཡོད་པ། འདུག་པ་ | *re-pa; yim-pa; yö-pa; duk̄-p̄a.* |
| Bead | འཕྲང་ང་ (འཕྲེང་བ་) | *thrang-nga.* |
| Do. *hon.* | ཕྱག་འཕྲེང་ | *chhan-threng.* |
| Beak | མཆོ་ལྟོ་ (མཆུ་ལྟོ་) | *chho-to.* |
| Beam, large | གདུང་མ་ | *dung-ma.* |
| Do. small | ལྕམ་ཤིང་ | *cham-shing.* |
| Bean | སྲན་མ་ | *tre-ma.* |
| Bear, to (bring forth). | སྐྱེད་པ་ | *kye-pa.* |

| | | |
|---|---|---|
| Bear, to (bring forth) *hon.* | འཁྲུང་བ་ | *thrung wa.* |
| Bear, to (carry) | འཁྱེར་བ་ | *khyer-wa.* |
| Bear, *s.* | དོམ་ | *tom.* |
| Beard | ཨོག་ཚོལ་ | *oḱ-sḱö.* |
| Do. (with whiskers) | རྒྱ་ | *gya.* |
| Beard, a person having a | རྒྱའུ་ (རྒྱ་བོ་) | *gya-u.* |
| Beast | དུད་འགྲོ། སེམས་ཅན་ | *ťün-dro ; sem-chen.* |
| Beast (of prey) | གཅན་ཟན་ | *chen-śen.* |
| Beat, to | རྡུང་བ་ | *dung-wa.* |
| Do. *hon.* | ཕྱག་འཇུག་གནང་བ་ | *chhan-ju nang-wa.* |
| Beaten, to be (in a contest) | འཕམ་པ་ | *pham-pa.* |
| Beautiful | མཛེས་པོ་ | *dze-po.* |
| Do. *hon.* | ཐུགས་ཚར་པོ་ | *thu tshar-po.* |
| Beaver | ཆུ་སྲམ་ | *chhu-tram.* |
| Because | རྐྱེན་གྱིས། དོན་ལ་ | *kyen-ḱyi ; tön-la.* |
| Beckon, to | གཡས་དབྱུག་རྒྱབ་པ་ | *ye-yu gyap̍-pa.* |
| Do. *hon.* | གཡས་དབྱུག་སྐྱོན་པ་ | *ye-yu kyöm-pa.* |
| Become, to | བྱུང་བ་ (འབྱུང་བ་) | *cḱung-wa.* |
| Becoming | འོས་པོ་ | *ö-po.* |

| | | |
|---|---|---|
| Bed | ཉལ་ཁྲི་ | *nye-thri.* |
| Do. *hon.* | གཟིམ་ཁྲི་ | *sim-thri.* |
| Bedaub, to | བྱུགས་པ་ (འབྱུག་པ།) སྐུ་བ་ | *chuk-pa; ku-wa.* |
| Do. *hon.* | བྱུགས་ག་ (འབྱུག་པ་) གནང་བ། སྐུ་བ་གནང་བ་ | *chuk-ka nang-wa; ku-wa nang-wa.* |
| Bedding | ཉལ་གཟན་ | *nye-śen.* |
| Do. *hon.* | གཟིམ་གཟན་ | *śim-śen.* |
| Bedroom | ཉལ་ས་ | *nye-sa.* |
| Do. *hon.* | གཟིམ་ཁང་ | *śim-khang.* |
| Bee | སྦྲང་མ་ | *drang-ma.* |
| Bee-hive | སྦྲང་ཚང་ | *drang-tshang.* |
| Beef | གླང་ཤ་ | *lang-sha.* |
| Beer | ཆང་ | *chhang.* |
| Do. *hon.* | མཆོད་ཆང་ | *chhö-chhang.* |
| Do. (spirit) | ཨ་རག་ | *a-ra.* |
| Do. *hon.* | བཞེས་རག་ | *ske-ra.* |
| Beer-shop | ཆང་ཁང་ | *chhang-khang.* |
| Beer-seller | ཆང་མ། འཕྲུང་མ་ | *chhang-ma; thrung-ma.* |
| Bees-wax | སྦྲ་ཚིལ་ | *trak tshi.* |
| Beetle | སྦྲང་བུ་ | *drang-pu.* |

| | | |
|---|---|---|
| Befitting, *adj*. | འོས་པོ་ | *ö-po.* |
| Befool, to | མགོ་སྐོར་བ་ | *go-kor-wa.* |
| Do. *hon.* | དབུ་སྐོར་ར་ (བ་) གནང་བ་ | *u-kor-ra nang-wa.* |
| Before (*adv.* & *prep.* of place) | མདུན་ལ་ | *dün-la.* |
| Do. *hon.* | སྐུ་མདུན་ལ་ | *kun-dün-la.* |
| Before (*adv.* & *prep.* of time) | སྔན་ལ་ (སྔོན་ལ) | *ngen-la.* |
| Do. (with verb) | མ་...གོང་ལ་ | *ma...ḱong-la.* |
| Beg, to (request) | ཞུ་བ་ | *sḱu-wa.* |
| Do. *hon.* | ཞུ་བ་གནང་བ་ | *sḱu-wa nang-wa.* |
| Do. to (alms) | སློང་བ་ | *long-wa.* |
| Do. *hon.* | བསོད་སྙོམས་ཞུ་བ་གནང་བ་ | *sö-nyom sḱu-wa nang-wa.* |
| Beget, to | སྐྱེད་པ་ | *kye-pa.* |
| Do. *hon.* | འཁྲུང་བ་ | *thrung-wa.* |
| Beggar | སྤྲང་གོ་ (སྤྲང་པོ་) | *pang-ḱo.* |
| Begin, to | མགོ་བཙུགས་ (འཛུགས་) པ་ | *go-tsuḱ-pa.* |
| Do. *hon.* | དབུ་བཙུགས་ཀ་ (འཛུགས་པ་) གནང་བ་ | *u-tsuḱ-ḱa nang-wa.* |
| Beginning | མགོ་ | *go.* |
| Do. in the | སྔོན་དང་པོ་ | *ngön-ťang-po.* |
| Beguile, to | མགོ་སྐོར་བ་ | *go-kor-wa.* |

| | | |
|---|---|---|
| Beguile, to, *hon.* | དབུ་སྐོར་ར་ (བ་) གནང་བ་ | *u-kor-ra nang-wa.* |
| Behalf of, on | དོན་ལ་ | *t́ön-la.* |
| Behaviour | བྱེད་སྟངས་ (སྤྱོད་པ་) | *cḱe-tang.* |
| Behead, to (common person) | སྐེ་བཅད་ (གཅོད་) པ་ | *ke-che-pa.* |
| Do. (superior person) | མགུལ་བཅད་ (གཅོད་) པ་ | *gül-che-pa.* |
| Behind (*adv.* & *prep.*) | རྒྱབ་ལ། གཤུག་ལ་ | *gyaṕ-la; sḱu-la.* |
| Behind hand, to be | ཕྱི་པོ་བྱེད་པ་ | *chhi-po cḱe-pa.* |
| Do. *hon.* | ཕྱི་པོ་གནང་བ་ | *chhi-po nang-wa.* |
| Behold, to | མཐོང་བ་ | *thong-wa.* |
| Do. *hon.* | གཟིགས་པ་ | *śi-pa.* |
| Belch, to | འགག་དྲི་རྒྱབ་པ་ | *gaḱ-t́ri gyaṕ-pa.* |
| Do. *hon.* | འགག་དྲི་སྐྱོན་པ་ | *gaḱ-t́ri kyöm-pa.* |
| Belief (religion) | དད་པ་ | *t́e-pa.* |
| Believe, to | ཡིད་ཆེས་པ་ | *yi-chhe-pa.* |
| Do. *hon.* | ཐུགས་ཡིད་ཆེས་པ་ | *thu-yi chhe-pa.* |
| Do. (in religious sense) | དད་པ་བྱེད་པ་ | *t́e-pa cḱe-pa.* |
| Do. *hon.* | དད་པ་གནང་བ་ | *t́e-pa nang-wa.* |
| Bell | དྲིལ་བུ་ | *t́ri-ṕu.* |
| Do. *hon.* | ཕྱག་དྲིལ་ | *chha-t́ri.* |
| Bell-metal | ལི་ | *li.* |

| | | |
|---|---|---|
| Bellows | སྦུད་པ་ | *bü-pa.* |
| Do. iron tube of | ཤན་མཆུ་ (སྦུད་མཆུ་) | *shen-chhu.* |
| Belly | གྲོ་ཁོག་ (གྲོད་ཁོག །) ཁོག་པ་ | *ťro-kho; khoḱ-pa.* |
| Do. *hon.* | གསོལ་གྲོད་ | *sö-ťrö.* |
| Belong, to (to me) | ཡིན་པ་ | *yim-pa.* |
| Do. (to you or to third person) | རེད་པ་ | *re-pa.* |
| Beloved | གཅེས་པོ་ | *che-po.* |
| Below (lower down) | མ་ | *ma.* |
| Do. *prep.* | འོག་ལ། གཤམ་ལ་ | *o-la; sham-la.* |
| Belt | སྐེ་རགས་ | *ke-ra.* |
| Do. *hon.* | སྐུ་རགས་ | *ku-ra.* |
| Bench | ཀུབ་ཀྱག། ཁྲིའུ་ཤིང་ | *kuṕ-kya; thri-u-shing.* |
| Do. *hon.* | ཞབས་ཀྱག་ | *sḱaṕ-kya.* |
| Bend, to, *v.t.* | བཀུག་པ་ (འགུག་པ་) | *kuḱ-pa.* |
| Do. *hon.* | བཀུག་ག་ (འགུག་པ་) གནང་བ་ | *kuḱ-ka nang-wa.* |
| Bend, to (stoop) | གུག་གུག་བྱེད་པ་ | *ḱu-ḱu cḱe-pa.* |
| Do. *hon.* | གུག་གུག་གནང་བ་ | *ḱu-ḱu nang-wa.* |
| Beneath | འོག་ལ་ | *o-la.* |
| Benediction | བྱིན་རླབས་ | *cḱin-laṕ.* |
| Benefaction | མགོ་འདྲེན་ | *gön-dren.* |

| | | |
|---|---|---|
| Benefactor | མགོན་འདྲེན་གནང་མཁན་ | gön-dren nang-khen. |
| Do. *hon.* | དབུ་འདྲེན་གནང་མཁན་ | *u-dren nang-khen.* |
| Benefit, to | ཕན་ཐོགས་པ་ | *phen-thoḱ-pa.* |
| Benefit of, for the | ཕན་པའི་དོན་ལ་ | *phen-pe-tön-la.* |
| Benevolence | དྲིན་ | *t́rin.* |
| Do. *hon.* | བཀའ་དྲིན་ | *ḱa-t́rin.* |
| Benevolent | དྲིན་ཆེན་པོ་ | *t́rin-chhem-po.* |
| Do. *hon.* | བཀའ་དྲིན་ཆེན་པོ་ | *ḱa-t́rin chhem-po.* |
| Benevolent, to be | དྲིན་བྱེད་པ་ | *t́rin-cḱe-pa.* |
| Do. *hon.* | བཀའ་དྲིན་གནང་བ་ | *ḱa-t́rin nang-wa.* |
| Bent, to be | གུག་གུག་བྱས་ནས་བསྐྱོད་ (སྐྱོད་) པ་ | *ḱu-ḱu cḱe-ne de-pa.* |
| Beseech, to | ཞུ་བ་ཕུལ་ (འབུལ་) བ་ | *sḱu-wa phü-wa.* |
| Beside | རྩ་ལ་ | *tsa-la.* |
| Besides, *prep.* | མ་གཏོགས། མིན་པ་ | *ma-to; mem-pa.* |
| Besmear, to | བྱུགས་པ་ (འབྱུག་པ་) | *cḱuk-pa.* |
| Do. *hon.* | བྱུགས་ཀ་ (འབྱུག་པ་) གནང་བ་ | *cḱuḱ-ka nang-wa.* |
| Besprinkle with water, to | ཆུ་ཆག་རྒྱབ་པ་ | *chhu-chha gyaṕ-pa.* |
| Best | ཡག་ཤོས། ཡག་ཐག་ཆོད་ | *yaḱ-shö; yaḱ-thaḱ-chhö.* |
| Bestow, to | སྟེར་བ་ | *ter-wa.* |

| | | |
|---|---|---|
| Bestow, to, *hon.* | གནང་བ་ | *nang-wa.* |
| Bet | རྒྱན་ | *gyen.* |
| Do. *hon.* | སྐུ་རྒྱན་ | *ku-gyen.* |
| Bet, to | རྒྱན་བཞག་ (འཛོག་) པ་ | *gyen-sKak-pa.* |
| Do. *hon.* | སྐུ་རྒྱན་གཞོག་ག་ (འཛོག་པ་) གནང་བ་ | *ku-gyen sKok-ka nang-wa.* |
| Betel-nut | གོ་ཡུ་ | *ko-yu.* |
| Betray, to | དགྲའི་དབང་ལ་བཏང་ (གཏོང་) བ་ | *dra-i wang-la tang-wa.* |
| Better | ཡག་ག་ | *yak-ka.* |
| Better, to get the (in a fight, &c.) | རྒྱལ་བ་ | *gye-wa.* |
| Between | བར་ལ་ | *ṕa-la.* |
| Beware, to | དོགས་ཟོན་བྱེད་པ་ | *tok-śön cKe-pa.* |
| Do. *hon.* | ཐུགས་ཟོན་གནང་བ་ | *thuk-śön nang-wa.* |
| Bewildered, to be | མགོ་འཁོར་བ་ | *go-khor-wa.* |
| Do. *hon.* | དབུ་འཁོར་ར་ (བ་) གནང་བ་ | *u-khor-ra nang-wa.* |
| Beyond | ཕར་ཕྱོགས་ལ་ | *pha-chho-la.* |
| Bhutan | འབྲུག་ཡུལ་ | *druk-yü.* |
| Bhutanese | འབྲུག་པ་ | *druk-pa.* |
| Bible | གསུང་རབ་ | *sung-rap.* |

| | | |
|---|---|---|
| Bicycle | རྐང་སྒ་རི་ | *kang-ga-ri.* |
| Bid, to | བཀའ་གནང་བ་ | *ka-nang-wa.* |
| Bier | ཤིང་ཁྲི་ | *ching-thri.* |
| Big | ཆེན་པོ་ | *chhem-po.* |
| Bile | མཁྲིས་པ་ | *thri-pa.* |
| Bill (amount) | རྩིས་ཐོ་ | *tsi-tho.* |
| Do. *hon.* | ཕྱག་ཐོ་ | *chha-tho.* |
| Bill (of bird) | མཆོ་ལྟོ་ (མཆུ་ལྟོ་) | *chho-to.* |
| Billow | བ་རླབས་ | *ba-lap.* |
| Bind, to | བསྡམས་པ་ (སྡོམ་པ་) | *dam-pa.* |
| Biography | རྣམ་ཐར་ | *nam-tha.* |
| Do. *hon.* | གསུང་ཐར་ | *sung-tha.* |
| Birch tree | སྟག་པ་ཤིང་ | *tak-pa-shing.* |
| Bird | བྱ་ | *cha.* |
| Bird-cage | རླུང་ཚེ་ | *lung-tse.* |
| Bird's-nest | བྱ་ཚང་ | *cha-tshang.* |
| Birthday | སྐྱེ་ཚེས་ | *kye-tshe.* |
| Do. *hon.* | འཁྲུང་ཚེས་ | *thrung-tshe.* |
| Birth, high | སྐྱེ་ས་མཐོ་པོ་ | *kye-sa tho-po.* |
| Birth, low | སྐྱེ་ས་དམའ་པོ་ | *kye-sa ma-po.* |

| | | |
|---|---|---|
| Birth-place | སྐྱེ་ས། སྐྱེ་སའི་ལུང་པ་ | *kye-sa; kye-se lung-pa.* |
| Do. *hon.* | འཁྲུངས་ས་ | *thrung-sa.* |
| Bishop | མཁན་པོ་ | *khem-po.* |
| Bit (of a bridle) | སྲབ་ལྕགས་ | *traṕ-cha.* |
| Bit (piece) | དུམ་བུ་ | *t́um-ṕu.* |
| Bitch | ཁྱི་མོ་ | *khyi-mo.* |
| Bite, to | སྨུག་པ། སོ་རྒྱབ་པ་ | *muḱ-pa; so-gyaṕ-pa.* |
| Bitter | ཁག་ཐིག་ | *khaḱ-thi.* |
| Black | ནག་པོ་ | *naḱ-po.* |
| Blacksmith | མགར་ར་ (བ་) | *gar-ra.* |
| Bladder | ལྒང་ཕུག་ | *gang-phu.* |
| Blade (of grass) | ལྗང་པ་ | *jang-pa.* |
| Blade (of sword) | དངོ་ | *ngo.* |
| Blame, to | སྐྱོན་བརྡོན་པ་ | *kyön töm-pa.* |
| Do. *hon.* | སྐྱོན་བརྡོན་པ་གནང་བ་ | *kyön töm-pa nang-wa.* |
| Blank | སྟོང་པ་ | *tong-pa.* |
| Blanket | ཉལ་གཟན་ | *nye-śen.* |
| Do. *hon.* | གཟིམ་གཟན་ | *śim-śen.* |
| Blaspheme, to | སྨད་ར་བཏང་ (གཏོང་) བ་ | *me-ra tang-wa.* |
| Do. *hon.* | སྨད་ར་གཏོང་ང་ (བ་) གནང་བ་ | *me-ra tong-nga nang-wa.* |

| | | |
|---|---|---|
| Blaze, *s.* | མེ་ | *me.* |
| Blaze, to (of fire) | འབར་བ་ | *bar-wa.* |
| Bleat, to | ལུག་སྐད་རྒྱབ་པ་ | *luḱ-ke gyaṕ-pa.* |
| Bleed, to, *v.i.* | ཁྲག་འཐོན་པ་ | *thra-thöm-pa.* |
| Do. (of doctor), *v.t.* | ཁྲག་རྒྱབ་པ་ | *thra-gyaṕ-pa.* |
| Blemish, *s.* | སྐྱོན་ | *kyön.* |
| Blend, to | འདྲེ་བ་ | *dre-wa.* |
| Do. *hon.* | འདྲེ་བ་གནང་བ་ | *dre-wa nang-wa* |
| Bless, to | བྱིན་རླབས་གནང་བ་ | *cḰin-laṕ nang-wa.* |
| Do. to (dead person) | སྔོ་བ་རྒྱབ་པ་ | *ngo-wa gyaṕ-pa.* |
| Blessing (by placing book on head) | བྱིན་རླབས་ | *cḰin-laṕ.* |
| Do. (by laying hand on head) | ཕྱག་དབང་ | *chha-wang.* |
| Blind | ལོང་ང་ (ལོང་བ་) | *long-nga.* |
| Do. *hon.* | སྤྱན་ལོང་ང་ (བ་) | *chen-long-nga.* |
| Blind of one eye | མིག་ཞར་ར་ (བ་) | *mik-sḰar-ra.* |
| Do. *hon.* | སྤྱན་ཞར་ར་ (བ་) | *chen-sḰar-ra.* |
| Blink, to | མིག་བརྩུམ་རྒྱབ་པ་ | *miḱ-tsum gyaṕ-pa.* |
| Do. *hon.* | སྤྱན་བརྩུམ་སྐྱོན་པ་ | *chen-tsum kyöm-pa.* |
| Blister, *s.* | ཆུ་གང་ | *chhu-Ḱang.* |

| | | |
|---|---|---|
| Blistered, to be | ཆུ་གང་འཐོན་པ་ | *chhu-k̄ang thöm-pa.* |
| Blithe | སྐྱིད་པོ་ | *kyi-po.* |
| Block, to | བཀག་པ་ (འགེགས་པ་) | *kak̄-pa.* |
| Blockhead | ལྐུགས་པ། གླེན་པ་ | *kuk̄-pa ; lem-pa.* |
| Blood | ཁྲག་ | *thra.* |
| Do. *hon.* | སྐུ་ཁྲག་ | *ku-thra.* |
| Blossom | མེ་ཏོག་ | *me-to.* |
| Blot, *s.* | ནག་ཐིག་ | *nak̄-thi.* |
| Blow (with fist) | ཛོག་རམ་ (ཛོག་རིལ་) | *dzo-ram.* |
| Do. (with open palm) | ཐལ་ལྕག་ | *the-cha.* |
| Blow, to, *v.t.* | ཕུ་རྒྱབ་པ་ | *phu-gyap̄-pa.* |
| Do. *hon.* | ལྗགས་ཕུ་གནང་བ་ | *ja-phu nang-wa.* |
| Do. (of wind), *v.i.* | རྒྱབ་པ་ | *gyap̄-pa.* |
| Blue | སྔོན་པོ་ | *ngöm-po.* |
| Blue, dark | སྔོ་ནག་ | *ngo-nak̄.* |
| Blue Book | དེབ་སྔོན་པོ་ | *t̄ep̄ ngöm-po.* |
| Blue, light | སྔོ་སྐྱ་ | *ngo-kya.* |
| Blunder, to | ཁ་ནོར་བ་ | *kha-nor-wa.* |
| Do. *hon.* | ཞལ་ནོར་ར་ (བ་) གནང་བ་ | *sk̄e-nor ra nang-wa.* |
| Blunt, to be | རྣོ་པོ་མེད་པ་ | *no-po me-pa.* |

| | | |
|---|---|---|
| Blush, to | ངོ་ཚ་བ་ | *ngo-tsha-wa.* |
| Do. *hon.* | ཞལ་རས་ཚ་བ་གནང་བ། ཐུགས་ངོ་ཚ་བ་གནང་བ་ | *sḱe-re tsha-wa nang-wa; thu-ngo tsha-wa nang-wa.* |
| Boar | ཕག་པ་ | *phaḱ-pa.* |
| Do. (wild) | རི་ཕག་ | *ri-pha.* |
| Board | སྤང་ལེབ་ | *pang-le.* |
| Boast, to | རང་སྟོད་བྱེད་པ་ | *rang-tö cḱe-pa.* |
| Boat (of wood) | གྲུ་ | *t́ru.* |
| Boatman (of wooden boat) | གྲུ་པ་ | *t́ru-pa.* |
| Do. *hon.* | གྲུ་དཔོན་ | *t́ru-pön.* |
| Boat (of hide) | ཀོ་བ་ | *ko-wa.* |
| Do. *hon.* | ཕེབ་ཀོ་ | *phe-ko.* |
| Boatman (of hide boat) | མཉན་པ་ | *nyem-pa.* |
| Do. *hon.* | མཉན་དཔོན་ | *nyem-pön.* |
| Body | གཟུགས་པོ། ལུས་ | *śuḱ-po; lü.* |
| Do. *hon.* | སྐུ་གཟུགས། སྐུ་ལུས་ | *ku-śuḱ; ku-lü.* |
| Body (corpse of human being) | རོ་ | *ro.* |
| Do. *hon.* | སྐུ་ཕུང་ | *ku-phung.* |
| Body (dead body of animal) | ཤི་རོ་ | *shi-ro.* |
| Boil | གཉན་བུར་ | *nyen-ṕur.* |

| | | |
|---|---|---|
| Boil (watery) | ཆུ་བུར་ | *chhu-p̄ur.* |
| Do. to, *v.i.* | འཁོལ་བ་ | *khöl-wa.* |
| Do. *v.t.* | བསྐོལ་བ་ (སྐོལ་བ་) | *kö-wa.* |
| Boiler (cauldron) | དཀྱིལ་ཁྲོ་ | *kyi-thro.* |
| Boiling, *adj.* | ཁོལ་མ་ | *khöl-ma.* |
| Bold | བློ་ཁོག་ཆེན་པོ་ | *lo-kho chhem-po.* |
| Do. *hon.* | ཐུགས་ཁོག་ཆེན་པོ་ | *thu-kho chhem-po.* |
| Bolt | སྒོ་ལྕགས་ | *gön-cha.* |
| Do. *hon.* | གཟིམ་ལྕགས། ཕྱག་ལྕགས་ | *śim-cha; chha-cha.* |
| Bolt, to (of horse), *v.i.* | ངར་ནས་ཕྱིན་པ་ | *ngar-ne chhim-pa.* |
| Bolt, to (door, &c.) | སྒོ་ལྕགས་རྒྱབ་པ་ | *gön-cha gyap-pa.* |
| Do. *hon.* | གཟིམ་ལྕགས་སྐྱོན་པ་ | *śim-cha kyöm-pa.* |
| Bolting, *adj.* (of horse) | འདྲོག་པ་ | *drok-pa.* |
| Bond (for large amount) | གམ་རྒྱ་ (གན་རྒྱ་) | *k̄am-gya.* |
| Do. *hon.* | ཕྱག་གན་ | *chha-gen.* |
| Do. (for small amount) | འཛིན་ | *dzin.* |
| Do. *hon.* | ཕྱག་འཛིན་ | *chhan-dzin.* |
| | བཀའ་འཛིན་ | *kan-dzin.* |
| Bone | རུས་ཁོག་ | *rü-kho.* |
| Do. *hon.* | སྐུ་རུས་ | *ku-rü.* |

| | | |
|---|---|---|
| Book | དཔེ་ཆ་ | *pe-chha.* |
| Do. *hon.* | ཕྱག་དཔེ་ | *chha-pe.* |
| Book-language | ཆོས་ཚིག་ | *chhö-tshi.* |
| Book, printed | པར་མ་ | *par-ma.* |
| Do. written | བྲིས་མ་ | *t́ri-ma.* |
| Boon | དྲིན་ | *t́rin.* |
| Do. *hon.* | བཀའ་དྲིན་ | *ka-t́rin.* |
| Boot | ལྷམ། ལྷམ་ཁོག་ | *hlam ; hlam-kho.* |
| Do. *hon.* | ཞབས་ཆགས་ | *sh́aṕ-chha.* |
| Boot (of European style) | འཇུ་ཏ་ | *ju-ta.* |
| Bootmaker | ངོ་བཟོ་ | *ngoṕ-śo.* |
| Do. *hon.* | དབུ་མཛད་ | *um-dze.* |
| Borax | ཚ་ལི་ | *tsha-li.* |
| Border | ཟུར་ | *sur.* |
| Do. (of land) | ས་མཚམས་ | *san-tsham.* |
| Bore a hole, to | ཨི་ཁུང་ཕིད་ (འབིག་) པ་ | *i-khung pi-pa.* |
| Born, to be | སྐྱེ་བ་ | *kye-wa.* |
| Do. *hon.* | འཁྲུང་བ་ | *thrung-wa.* |
| Borrow, to | གཡར་བ་ | *yar-wa.* |
| Do. to (ask a loan) | སྐྱི་བ་ | *kyi-wa.* |

| | | |
|---|---|---|
| Borrow, to, *hon.* | གཡར་པོ་ཞུ་བ་གནང་བ་ | *yar-po sḱu-wa nang-wa.* |
| Bosom | ཕང་ཁོག་ (བྲང་ཁོག་) | *ṕang-kho.* |
| Do. *hon.* | སྐུ་ཕང་ (སྐུ་བྲང་) | *ku-ṕang.* |
| Both, *pron.* | གཉིས་ཀ་ | *nyi-ka.* |
| Bothersome | ཅ་སྙུན་པོ་ | *cha-sim-po.* |
| Do. *hon.* | ཐུགས་ཅ་སྙུན་པོ་ | *thu-cha sim-po.* |
| Bottle | ཤེལ་དམ་ | *she-ťam.* |
| Bottom | གཏིང་ | *ting.* |
| Do. (anus) | ཀུབ་ | *kuṕ.* |
| Do. *hon.* | ཞབས་ཕོངས་ | *sḱam-phong* |
| Bough | ཡལ་ག་ | *ye-ḱa.* |
| Bound, to (jump) | མཆོངས་པ། མཆོངས་རྒྱག་རྒྱབ་པ་ | *chhong-pa ; chhong-gya gyaṕ-pa.* |
| Do. *hon.* | མཆོངས་རྒྱག་སྐྱོན་པ་ | *chhong-gya kyöm-pa.* |
| Boundary | ས་མཚམས་ | *san-tsham.* |
| Bountiful | ལག་པ་ཤོག་པོ་ | *laḱ-pa shoḱ-po.* |
| Do. *hon.* | ཕྱག་ཤོག་པོ་ | *chha-shoḱ-po.* |
| Bow (for shooting) | གཞུ་ | *sḱu.* |
| Do. *hon* | ཕྱག་གཞུ་ | *chha-sḱu.* |
| Bow, to (taking hat) | ཕྱག་འབུལ་ཞུ་པ | *chham-bü sḱu-wa.* |

| | | |
|---|---|---|
| Bow-legged | རྐང་ཀྱོག་ | *ḱang-kyo.* |
| Bowel | རྒྱུ་མ་ | *gyu-ma.* |
| Bowl (for drinking tea, &c.) | ཕོར་པ་ | *phor-pa.* |
| Do. *hon.* | མཆོད་ཞལ་ | *chhö-sḱe.* |
| Bowl (of tobacco pipe) | གང་མགོ་ | *ḱang-go.* |
| Box (chest) | སྒམ་ | *gam.* |
| Do. *hon.* | ཕྱག་སྒམ་ | *chha-gam.* |
| Boy | བུ་གུ་ | *pu-gu.* |
| Do. *hon.* | ཨ་ཝ་ | *a-wa.* |
| Bracelet | སྒྲོག་གདུང་ | *dro-dung.* |
| Do. *hon.* | ཕྱག་གདུང་ | *chha-dung.* |
| Brahma | ཚངས་པ་ | *tshang-pa.* |
| Brahman (caste) | བྲམ་ཟེ་ | *t́ram-śe.* |
| Brain | ཀླད་པ་ | *le-pa.* |
| Bramble | ཚེར་མ་ | *tsher-ma.* |
| Bran | ཕུང་མ་ | *phung-ma.* |
| Branch | ཡལ་ག་ | *ye-ḱa.* |
| Brandish, to | དབྱུག་དབྱུག་བྱེད་པ་ | *yu-yu cḱe-pa.* |
| Do. *hon.* | དབྱུག་དབྱུག་གནང་བ་ | *yu-yu nang-wa.* |
| Brandy | ཨ་རག་ | *a-ra.* |

| | | |
|---|---|---|
| Brandy, *hon.* | བཞེས་རག་ | *sḰe-ra.* |
| Brass | རག་ | *ra.* |
| Brave, *adj.* | སྙིང་ཆེན་པོ་ | *nying-chhem-po.* |
| Do. *hon.* | ཐུགས་སྙིང་ཆེན་པོ་ | *thu-nying. chhem po.* |
| Brawl | རྒྱབ་འདྲེ། འཁྲུག་པ་ | *gyam-dre ; thruḱ-pa.* |
| Bray | བོང་སྐད་རྒྱབ་པ་ | *ṕong-ke-gyaṕ-pa.* |
| Bread | བག་ལེབ་ | *ṕa-le.* |
| Do. *hon.* | བཞེས་བག་ | *sḰe-ṕa.* |
| Breadth | ཞང་ (ཞེང་) | *sḰang.* |
| Break, to, *v.t.* | བཅག་པ་ (གཅོག་པ་) | *chaḱ-pa.* |
| Do. *hon.* | གཅོག་ག་ (གཅོག་པ་) གནང་བ་ | *choḱ-ḱa nang-wa.* |
| Break, to, *v.i.* | འཆག་པ་ | *chhaḱ-pa.* |
| Breakfast (at 10 or 11 A.M.) | ཚ་གདིང་མའི་ཁ་ལག་ | *tsha-ting-me kha-la.* |
| Do. *hon.* | ཚ་གདིང་མའི་ཞལ་ལག་ | *tshu-ting-me sḰe-la.* |
| Breakfast (at 7 to 9 A.M.) | ཞོགས་གའི་ཁ་ལག་ | *sḰo-ke kha-la.* |
| Do. *hon.* | ཞོགས་གའི་ཞལ་ལག་ | *sḰo-ke sḰe-la.* |
| Breast | བང་ཁོག་ (བྲང་ཁོག་) | *ṕang-kho.* |
| Do. *hon.* | སྐུ་བང་ (སྐུ་བྲང་) | *ku-ṕang.* |
| Breath | དབུགས་ | *u.* |

| | | |
|---|---|---|
| Breath, *hon.* | ལྗགས་དབུགས་ | *ja-u.* |
| Breathe, to | དབུགས་བཏང་ (གཏོང་) བ་ | *u-tang-wa.* |
| Do. *hon.* | ལྗགས་དབུགས་གཏོང་ང་ (བ་) གནང་བ་ | *ja-u tong-nga nang-wa.* |
| Breathless, to be | དབུགས་བསག་ (གསོག་) པ་ | *u saǩ-pa.* |
| Do. *hon.* | ལྗགས་དབུགས་བསག་ག་ (གསོག་པ་) གནང་བ་ | *ja-u saǩ-ǩa nang-wa.* |
| Breed (of men) | བརྒྱུད་ | *gyü.* |
| Do. *hon.* | སྐུ་བརྒྱུད་ | *ku-gyü.* |
| Do. (of animals) | བརྒྱུད་དག་ | *gyü-ťa.* |
| Breeze | ལྷགས་པ། རླུང་ | *hlaǩ-pa ; lung.* |
| Bribe | ཙིག་ཐོ་ | *tsiǩ-tho.* |
| Do. *hon.* | སྐྱབས་འཇུག་ | *kyam-ju.* |
| Bribe, to give | ཙིག་ཐོ་རྒྱབ་པ་ | *tsiǩ-tho gyap̌-pa.* |
| Do. (*inf.* to *sup.*) | སྐྱབས་འཇུག་ཞུ་བ་ | *kyam-ju sǨu wa.* |
| Bribe, to take | རྒྱུ་ཟ་བ་ | *gyu-śa-wa.* |
| Do. *hon.* | རྒྱུ་བཞེས་པ་ | *gyu sǨe-pa.* |
| Brick | ས་པག་ | *sa-pa.* |
| Brick of tea | ཇ་བག་ | *cǨa-p̌a.* |
| Do. *hon.* | གསོལ་ཇ་བག་ | *so-cǨa p̌aǩ-ǩa.* |

| | | |
|---|---|---|
| Bride | མནའ་མ་ | *na-ma.* |
| Bridegroom | མག་པ་ | *maḱ-pa.* |
| Bridesmaid | བག་རོགས་ | *ṕa·ro.* |
| Bridge | ཟམ་པ་ | *śam-pa.* |
| Do. *hon.* | ཕེབས་ཟམ་ | *phe-śam.* |
| Bridge, iron | ལྕགས་ཟམ་ | *cha-śam.* |
| Do. *hon.* | ལྕགས་ཀྱི་ཕེབ་ཟམ་ | *chạ-kyi phe-śam.* |
| Bridle | སྲབ་ | *traṕ.* |
| Do. *hon.* | ཆིབས་སྲབ་ | *chhiṕ-traṕ.* |
| Brief | ཐུང་ཐུང་ | *thung-thung.* |
| Brier | ཚེར་མ་ | *tsher-ma.* |
| Brigand | ཇག་པ་ | *cḱaḱ-pa.* |
| Bright (clear) | གསལ་པོ་ | *se-po.* |
| Do. (dazzling) | འོད་ཆེན་པོ་ | *ö-chhem-po.* |
| Brightness | འོད་ | *ö.* |
| Brilliant | འོད་ཆེན་པོ་ | *ö-chhem-po.* |
| Brim, to fill to the | དག་དག་ལྡུག་པ་ | *t́aḱ-t́aḱ luḱ-pa.* |
| Do. *hon.* | དག་དག་ལྡུག་ག་ (པ་) གནང་བ་ | *t́aḱ-t́aḱ luḱ-ka nang-wa.* |
| Brimstone | མུ་ཟི་ | *mu-śi.* |
| Bring, to (by carrying) | འཁྱེར་ཡོང་བ་ | *khyer-yong-wa.* |

| | | |
|---|---|---|
| Bring, to, *hon.* | བསྣམས་ (སྣོམ་) ཕེབ་པ་ | *nam-phe-pa.* |
| Bring, to (by leading along, *e.g.*, horse) | འཁྲིད་ཡོང་བ་ | *thri-yong-wa.* |
| Do. *hon.* | འཁྲིད་ཕེབ་པ་ | *thri-phe-pa.* |
| Brink | འགྲམ་ | *dram.* |
| Brisk | ཧུར་པོ་ | *hur-po.* |
| Bristle | ཕག་ཟེ་ | *phaǩ-ṡe.* |
| British | དབྱིན་ཇི་ | *in-ji.* |
| Do. Government | དབྱིན་གཞུང་ | *in-sǩung.* |
| Broadcloth | འགོ་སྣམ་ | *go-nam.* |
| Broad | ཞང་ (ཞེང་) ཆེན་པོ་ | *sǩang-chhem-po.* |
| Broad (of land) | རྒྱ་ཆེན་པོ་ | *gya-chhem-po.* |
| Broil | རྒྱབ་འདྲེ་ | *gyam-dre* |
| Broken, to be | ཆག་པ་ | *chhaǩ-pa.* |
| Bronchitis | གློ་ཡུའི་ནད་ | *lo-yü-ne.* |
| Bronze | ཁྲོ་ | *thro.* |
| Brooch | སྐེ་འཁྲུག་ | *ke thru.* |
| Do. *hon.* | མགུལ་འཁྲུག་ | *gü-thru.* |
| Brood, to (of fowls) | སྒོ་ང་བསྙལ་བ་ | *go-nga nyal-wa.* |
| Brook, *s.* | རྒྱུག་ཆུ་ | *gyuǩ-chhu.* |

| | | |
|---|---|---|
| Broom | ཕྱག་མ་ | *chha-ma.* |
| Broth | ཁུ་བ་ | *khu-a.* |
| Do. *hon.* | སྐྲུང་ཁུ་ (སྐྲུམ་ཁུ་) | *trung-khu.* |
| Broth (made from meat) | ཤ་ཁུ་ | *sha-khu.* |
| Do. *hon.* | སྐྲུང་ཁུ་ (སྐྲུམ་ཁུ་) | *trung-khu.* |
| Brother | སྤུན་ཀྱག་ | *pün-kya.* |
| Do. *hon.* | སྐུ་མཆེད་ | *kum-chhe.* |
| Brother, mother's | ཨ་ཞང་ | *a-sKang.* |
| Do. *hon.* | ཞང་ཞང་ལགས་ | *sKang-sKang-la.* |
| Brother, elder | ཇོ་ཇོ་ | *cKo-cKo.* |
| Do. *hon.* | ཇོ་ལགས་ | *cKo-la.* |
| Brother, younger | སྤུན་ཆུང་ང་ (བ་) | *pün-chhung-nga.* |
| Do. *hon.* | སྐུ་མཆེད་ཆུང་ང་ (བ་) | *kum-chhe chhung-nga* |
| Brother-in-law (wife's brother) | སྐྱེ་དམན་གྱི་སྤུན་ཀྱག་ | *kyi-men Kyi pün-kya.* |
| Do. *hon* | སྐུ་ཟླའི་སྐུ་མཆེད་ | *kum-de kum-chhe.* |
| Do. (sister's husband) | སྤུན་ཀྱག་གི་ཁྱོ་ག་ | *pün-Kya Ki khyo-ga.* |
| Do. *hon.* | སྐུ་མཆེད་ཀྱི་སྐུ་ཟླ་ | *kum-chhe kyi kum-da.* |
| Brown | སྨུག་པོ་ | *muK-po.* |
| Bruised, to be | སྤྲག་པ་ | *traK-pa.* |

| | | |
|---|---|---|
| Bruised, *hon.* | ཕྲག་ག་ (པ་) གནང་བ་ | *traǩ-ǩa nang-wa.* |
| Bruised, to be | ཀི་ཤུས་ལོག་པ་ | *ki-shü loǩ-pa.* |
| Brush | ཕག་ཟེ་ | *pha-śe.* |
| Brute | ཀྱོལ་སོང་ | *cǩö-song.* |
| Bubble | ལྦུ་བ་ | *bu-wa.* |
| Buck | ཤ་ (ཤ་བ་) | *sha-a.* |
| Bucket | ཆུ་བཟོམ་ | *chhu-śom.* |
| Do. *hon.* | ཆབ་བཟོམ་ | *chhaṕ-śom.* |
| Buck wheat, bitter | བྲའུ་ (བྲ་བོ་) | *t́ra-u.* |
| Do. sweet | རྒྱ་བྲ་ | *gyaṕ-ra.* |
| Bud, *s.* | ཐེའུ་ | *theu.* |
| Bud, to | སྐྱེ་བ་ | *kye-wa.* |
| Buddha | སངས་རྒྱས་ | *sang-gye.* |
| Buddhist | ནང་པ་ | *nang-pa.* |
| Buffalo | མ་ཧེ་ | *ma-he.* |
| Buffoonery | སྤྲེ་རྩེད་ | *tre-tse.* |
| Bug | འདྲེ་ཤིག་ | *dre-shi.* |
| Bugle | དམག་དུང་ | *maǩ t́ung.* |
| Build, to | བཟོ་བ་ | *śo-wa.* |
| Do. *hon.* | བཟོ་བ་གནང་བ་ | *śo-wa nang-wa.* |

| | | |
|---|---|---|
| **Building** | ཁང་པ་ | ***khang-pa.*** |
| Do. ***hon.*** | གཟིམ་ཁང་ | ***śim-khang.*** |
| Do. ***h. hon.*** | གཟིམ་ཤག་ | ***śim-sha.*** |
| Bulk | ཆེ་ཆུང་ | *chhe-chhung.* |
| Bulky | སྦོམ་པོ་ | *bom-po.* |
| Bull | གླང་། གླང་གོག་ | *lang ; lang-ḱo.* |
| Bullet | རྡིག་རིལ་ (མདེའུ་) | *diḱ-ri.* |
| Bullock | གླང་། གླང་གོག་ | *lang ; lang-ḱo.* |
| Bunch | ཆག་པ་ | *chhaḱ-pa.* |
| Bundle of clothes | གོས་སྒྲིལ་ | *ḱö-dril.* |
| Do. of papers | ཤུག་གུའི་ (ཤོག་བུའི་) ཆག་པ་ | *shuḱ-ḱu-i chhaḱ-pa.* |
| Do. of sticks | ཤིང་འཁུར་ | *shing-khur.* |
| Burden (of animal) | ཁལ། དོས་པོ་ | *khe ; t́ö-po.* |
| Do. (of human being) | རྡོག་ཁྲེད་། རྒྱབ་འཁུར་ | *doḱ-thre ; gyaṕ-khur.* |
| Buriat | སྤྲོ་རས་ཐུ་ | *po-re-thu.* |
| Burn, to, *v.i.* | འཚིག་པ་ | *tshiḱ-pa.* |
| Do. *v.t.* | སྲེག་པ་ | *traḱ-pa.* |
| Burnt-offering | སྦྱིན་སྲེག་ | *jin-se.* |
| Burrhel (sheep) | གནའ་བ་ | *na-wa.* |
| Burst, to, *v.i* | གས་པ་ (འགས་པ་) | *ḱe-pa.* |

| | | |
|---|---|---|
| Burst, to, *v.t.* | བཅག་པ་ (གཅོག་པ་) | *chaḱ-pa.* |
| Do. *hon.* | གཅོག་ག་ (གཅོག་པ་) གནང་བ་ | *chok-ḱa nang-wa.* |
| Bury, to | ས་ལ་སྦེད་པ་ | *sa-la be-pa.* |
| Do. *hon.* | ས་སྦེད་གནང་བ་ | *sa-be nang-wa.* |
| Burying-place | དུར་ཁྲོད་ | *t́u-thrö.* |
| Bush | ཤིང་སྡོང་ཆུང་ཆུང་ | *shing-dong chhung-chhung.* |
| Business | ལས་ཀ། དོན་དག་ | *le-ka.; t́ön-t́a.* |
| Do. *hon.* | ཕྱག་ལས། སྐུ་དོན་ | *chha-le ; ku-t́ön.* |
| Busy, I am | ང་ཅོག་གི་མི་འདུག། ང་དལ་གྱི་མི་འདུག་ | *nga cho-ki min-duk ; nga t́e-ḱyi min-du.* |
| Busy, he is, *hon.* | ཁོང་ཐུགས་ཅོག་ག་ གནང་གི་མི་འདུག་ | *ḱhong thu-choḱ-ḱa nang-gi min-du.* |
| Do. *h. hon.* | སྐུ་གཞོགས་ཐུགས་ཅོག་ག་ (པ་) གནང་གི་མི་འདུག་ | *ku-sḱo thu-cho-ḱa nang-gi min-du.* |
| But | ཡིན་ཀྱང་། ཡིན་ན་ཡང་ | *yin-kyang ; yin-na-yang.* |
| Butcher | ཤན་པ། ཡར་པོ་ | *shem-pa ; ya-po.* |
| Butler | གཟིམ་དཔོན་ | *śim-pön.* |
| Butt (of gun) | སྒྲུམ་ཤིང་། ཉ་གཞུག་ | *gum-shing ; nya-sḱu.* |
| Butter | མར་ | *mar.* |
| Do. *hon.* | གསོལ་མར་ | *sö-ma.* |

| | | |
|---|---|---|
| Butterfly | ཕྱེ་འདྲེན་མ་ | *chhem-drem-ma.* |
| Butter-milk | དར་ར་ (བ་) | *ťar-ra.* |
| Do. *hon.* | བཞེས་དར་ | *sǩe-ťar.* |
| Buttock | རྐུབ་ | *kuṕ.* |
| Do. *hon.* | ཞབས་ཕོངས་ | *sǩam-phong.* |
| Button | ཐུབ་ཆི་ | *thuṕ-chhi.* |
| Do. *hon.* | མགུལ་ཐུབ་ | *gü-thuṕ.* |
| Button-hole | ཐོབ་ལུང་ | *thoṕ-lung.* |
| Do. *hon.* | མགུལ་ལུང་ | *yü-lung.* |
| Button (of rank) | ཏོག་ | *to.* |
| Do. *hon.* | དབུ་ཏོག་ | *u-to.* |
| Buy, to | ཉོ་བ་ | *nyo-wa.* |
| Do. *hon.* | གཟིགས་པ་ | *śi-pa.* |
| Do. *h. hon.* | ལྗགས་གཟིགས་གནང་བ་ | *ja-śi nang-wa.* |
| Buzz, to | སྦྲང་སྐད་རྒྱབ་པ་ | *drang-ke gyaṕ-pa.* |
| By (*post*) | གིས། ཀྱིས། གྱིས། | *ǩi ; kyi ; ǩyi.* |
| By reason of | རྐྱེན་གྱིས་ | *kyen-ǩyi.* |

# C

| | | |
|---|---|---|
| Cabbage | པེ་ཚས་ *ch.* | *pe-tshe.* |
| Cage | ལྕགས་ཁྲ་ | *cha-thra.* |
| Cairn | རྡོ་སྤུང་ | *do-pung.* |
| Cake | ཏེན་ཤིན་ *ch.* | *ten-shin.* |
| Do. (of tea) | བག་ག་ | *ṕa-ḱa.* |
| Calamity | བཀྲ་མི་ཤིས་ | *t́ra-mi shi.* |
| Calculate, to | རྩིས་རྒྱབ་པ་ | *tsi gyaṕ-pa.* |
| Do. *hon.* | ཕྱག་རྩིས་སྐྱོན་པ་ | *ja-tsi kyöm-pa.* |
| Calculation | རྩིས་ | *tsi.* |
| Do. *hon.* | ཕྱག་རྩིས | *ja-tsi.* |
| Caldron | དཀྱིལ་ཁྲོ་ | *kyi-thro.* |
| Calendar | ཟླ་ཐོ་ | *da-tho.* |
| Do. *hon.* | གཟིགས་ཐོ་ | *śi tho.* |
| Calf (of the cow) | བེ་བེ་ (བེའུ་) | *ṕe-ṕe.* |
| Do. (of the leg) | རྐང་པའི་ཉ་ | *ḱang-pe nya.* |
| Do. *hon.* | ཞབས་ཀྱི་ཉ་ | *sḱaṕ ḱyi-nya.* |
| Call, to | སྐད་བཏང་ (གཏོང་) བ་ | *ḱe-tang-wa.* |
| Do. *hon.* | གསུང་གནང་བ། སྐད་གཏོང་ང་ (བ་) གནང་བ་ | *sung-nang-wa ; ke-tong-nga nang-wa.* |

| | | |
|---|---|---|
| Call! (a person) | སྐད་གཏོང་ཤོག་ | *ke-tong-sho.* |
| Do. *hon.* | ཕེབས་ཞུས་ཤོག་ | *pke-skü-sho.* |
| Do. *h. hon.* | འཆིབ་རྒྱུ་གནང་ཞུས་ཤོག་ | *chhip-gyu-nang skü-sho.* |
| Call, to (on a person) | བཙར་བ་ | *char-wa.* |
| Call, to (on superior) | སྐུ་མདུན་ལ་བཙར་བ་ | *kun-dün-la char-wa.* |
| Call up, to (a ghost, etc.) | སྤྱན་འདྲེན་ཞུ་བ་ | *chen-dren sku-wa.* |
| Calm (condition of country) | གླིངས་ཆག་པོ། འཇམ་ཐིང་ཐྲིང་ | *hling-chak-po ; jam-thing-thing.* |
| Cambric | དར་རས་ | *tar-re.* |
| Camel (male or female) | ཨ་མོང་ (ཛ་མོང་) | *a-mong.* |
| Camel hair | ཨ་མོང་སྤུ་ (ཛ་མོང་སྤུ) | *a-mong-pu.* |
| Camp | སྒར་ | *gar.* |
| Camping ground | སྒར་ས་ | *ga-sa.* |
| Camphor | ག་བུར་ | *ka-pur.* |
| Canal | ཡོ་པོ་ (ཡུར་པོ་) | *yo-po.* |
| Cancel, to (blot out) | སུབ་པ་ | *sup-pa.* |
| Do. *hon.* | སུབ་པ་གནང་བ་ | *sup-pa nang-wa* |
| Cancel, to (set aside) | མེད་པར་བཟོ་བ་ | *me-pa so-wa.* |
| Do. *hon.* | མེད་པར་བཟོ་བ་གནང་བ་ | *me-pa so-wa nang-wa.* |
| Cancel, to (writing) | བྲིས་སུབ་བཏང་ (གཏོང་) བ་ | *tri-sup tang-wa.* |
| Do. *hon.* | བྲིས་སུབ་གནང་བ་ | *tri-sup nang-wa.* |

| | | |
|---|---|---|
| Candid | དྲང་པོ་ | *ťrang-po.* |
| Do. *hon.* | ཐུགས་རྒྱུ་དྲང་པོ་ | *thu-gyu ťrang-po.* |
| Candle (of Chinese make) | ལྰ་ | *la.* |
| Candle (of English make) | རྒྱ་གར་ལྰ་ | *gya-ǩar-la.* |
| Cane | སྤ་ | *pa.* |
| Cannibal | མིའི་ཤ་ཟ་མཁན་ | *mi-i sha-śa-khen.* |
| Cannon | མེ་སྒྲོགས་ | *me-gyo.* |
| Cannon-ball | མེ་སྒྲོགས་ཀྱི་མདེའུ་ | *me-gyoǩ-ǩi di-u.* |
| Canter, to | འཛོག་རྒྱབ་པ་ | *dzo-gyap̌-pa.* |
| Cap | ཞྭ་མོ་ | *sǨa-mo.* |
| Do. *hon.* | དབུ་ཞྭ་ | *u-sǨa.* |
| Capable | ནུས་པོ་ | *nü-po.* |
| Capable, to be | ཐུབ་པ་ | *thup̌-pa.* |
| Do. *hon.* | ཐུབ་པ་གནང་བ་ | *thup̌-pa nang-wa.* |
| Capital, *s.* (as opposed to interest) | ངོ་བོ་ (དངོས་པོ་) | *ngo-po.* |
| Capital (letters) | དབུ་ཅན་ | *u-chen.* |
| Capital, *s.* (chief city) | རྒྱལ་ཁབ། རྒྱལ་ས་ | *gye-khap̌, gye-sa* |
| Capital, *adj.* (excellent) | ཡག་ཐག་ཆོད། ཨང་གི་དང་པོ་ | *yaǩ-thaǩ-chhö ; ang-gi ťang-po.* |

| | | |
|---|---|---|
| Capitulate, to | མགོ་དགུར་བ་ | *go-gur-wa.* |
| Do. *hon.* | དབུ་དགུར་ར་ (བ་) གནང་བ་ | *u-gur-ra nang-wa.* |
| Capsize, to | མགོ་གཞུག་ལོག་པ་ | *go sKu lok-pa.* |
| Captain (officer in command of 100 men) | བརྒྱ་དཔོན་ | *gya-pön.* |
| Captive | བཙོན་པ་ | *tsöm-pa.* |
| Capture, to | ཟིན་པ་ (འཛིན་པ་) | *śim-pa.* |
| Do. *hon.* | ཟིན་པ་ (འཛིན་པ་) གནང་བ་ | *śim-pa nang-wa.* |
| Carcass | རོ་ | *ro.* |
| Do. (of animal killed for meat) | ཤི་རོ་ | *shi-ro.* |
| Card | ཡི་གེ་ | *yi-ge.* |
| Cards, playing | ཤོན་ | *shön.* |
| Do. *hon.* | ཕྱག་ཤོན་ | *chha-shön.* |
| Cardamums | སུག་སྨེལ་ | *su-me.* |
| Care (anxiety) | སེམས་འཁྲལ་ | *sem-thre.* |
| Do. *hon.* | ཐུགས་འཁྲལ་ | *thu-thre.* |
| Care, to take (be careful) | བརྟན་བརྟན་བྱེད་པ་ | *ten-ten cKe-pa.* |
| Care of, to take (keep carefully) | ཉར་བ། ཆག་ག་བྱེད་པ་ | *nyar-wa; chak ka cKe-pa.* |

| | | |
|---|---|---|
| Care of, to take *hon.* | ཉར་ར་ (བ་) གནང་བ་ | *nyar-ra nang-wa.* |
| Do. *h. hon.* | ཐུགས་ཅག་གནང་བ་ | *thu-cha nang-wa.* |
| Career (manner of life) | བྱེད་སྟངས་ | *cḱe-tang.* |
| Do. *hon.* | གནང་སྟངས་ | *nang-tang.* |
| Carefully | ཅག་ག་བྱས་ནས་ | *cha-ḱa cḱe-ne.* |
| Do. *hon.* | ཐུགས་ཅག་གནང་ནས་ | *thu-cha nang-ne.* |
| Caress, to | བྱམས་པོ་བྱེད་པ་ | *cḱam-po cḱe-pa.* |
| Do. *hon.* | བྱམས་པོ་གནང་བ་ | *cḱam-po nang-wa.* |
| Carpenter | ཤིང་བཟོ་བ་ | *shing-ŝo wa.* |
| Do. *hon.* | དབུ་མཛད་ལགས་ | *um-dze-la.* |
| Carpet | ས་གདན་ | *sa-den.* |
| Carriage | ཤིང་རྟ་འཁོར་ལོ་ | *shing-ta ḱhor-lo.* |
| Carrier | དོས་པོ་འཁྱེར་མཁན་ | *tö-po ḱhyer-khen.* |
| Carrot | གུང་ལ་ཕུག་ | *ḱung-la-phuḱ.* |
| Carry, to | འཁྱེར་བ། འཁུར་བ་ | *khyer-wa ; khur-wa.* |
| Do. *hon.* | སྣོམ་པ་ | *nom-pa.* |
| Cart, bullock | གླང་སྒ་རི་ | *lang-ga-ri.* |
| Cartridge | རྡིག་རིལ་ | *diḱ-ri.* |
| Carve to (on wood, iron, etc.) | སྤྲོས་རྒྱབ་པ་ | *trö-gyap-pa.* |
| Do. *hon.* | སྤྲོས་སྐྱོན་པ་ | *trö-kyöm-pa.* |

| | | |
|---|---|---|
| Cascade | བབ་ཆུ་ (འབབ་ཆུ་) | *ṕaṕ-chhu.* |
| Do. (over rocks) | བྲག་ཆུ་ | *traḱ-chhu.* |
| Case (law suit) | ཁ་མཆུ་ | *kham-chhu.* |
| Do. (box) | སྒམ་ | *gam.* |
| Do. *hon.* | ཕྱག་སྒམ་ | *chha-gam.* |
| Do. (covering) | ཤུབས་ | *shuṕ.* |
| Cash | དངུལ་ | *ngü.* |
| Do. *hon.* | ཕྱག་དངུལ་ | *chha-ngü.* |
| Cashier | ཕྱག་མཛོད་ | *chhan-dzö.* |
| Cashmere | ཁ་ཆེའི་ལུང་པ་ | *kha-chhe lung-pa.* |
| Cask | ཆུ་རུམ་མ། ཆུ་བཟོམ་ | *chhu-rum-ma ; chhu-śom.* |
| Cast away, to | དབྱུག་པ་ | *yuḱ-pa.* |
| Do. *hon.* | དབྱུག་ག་ (པ་) གནང་བ་ | *yuḱ ḱa nang-wa.* |
| Caste | རུས་ | *rü.* |
| Do. *hon.* | སྐུ་རུས་ | *ku-rü.* |
| Castle | རྫོང་ | *dzong.* |
| Castrate, to | ཤ་བཅད་ (གཅོད་) པ་ | *sha-che-pa.* |
| Cat | ཞི་མི་ | *sḱi-mi.* |
| Cataract | ཧ་རི་ལོང་ང་ | *ha-ri-long-nga.* |
| Catarrh | ཆམ་པ་ | *chham-pa.* |

| | | |
|---|---|---|
| Catarrh, *hon.* | མགུལ་ཆམ་ | *gün-chham.* |
| Catch, to | ཟིན་པ་ (འཛིན་པ་) | *śim-pa.* |
| Do. *hon.* | ཟིན་པ་ (འཛིན་པ་) གནང་བ་ | *śim-pa nang-wa.* |
| Catechu | དོས་ཛ་ | *tö-ja.* |
| Caterpillar | ས་འབུ་ | *sa-bu.* |
| Cattle | བ་གླང་ | *ṕa-lang.* |
| Cattle-disease | ཕྱུགས་ནད་ | *chhu ne.* |
| Cauliflower | ཀོ་ཕི་མེ་ཏོག་ | *ko-pi me-tok̄.* |
| Cause (reason) | རྐྱེན། རྒྱུ་རྐྱེན་ | *kyen ; gyu-kyen.* |
| Cautious, to be | རྟེན་ལྡན་བྱེད་པ་ | *ten-den cK̄e-pa.* |
| Do. *hon.* | རྟེན་ལྡན་གནང་བ་ | *ten-den nang-wa.* |
| Cavalry | རྟ་དམག་ | *ta-ma.* |
| Cave of earth | ས་ཕུག་ | *sa-phu.* |
| Cave of rock | བྲག་ཕུག་ | *t̄rak̄-phu.* |
| Cavity | ཨི་ཁུང་ | *i-khung.* |
| Cease, to | འཆད་པ་ | *chhe-pa.* |
| Ceaseless | རྒྱུན་མི་ཆད་པ་ | *gyün-mi-chhe-pa.* |
| Ceiling | ཐོག་ཁ་ | *tho-kha.* |
| Celebrated | སྙན་གྲགས་ཆེན་པོ་ | *nyen-t̄ra chhem-po.* |
| Do. *hon.* | མཚན་སྙན་གྲགས་ཆེན་པོ་ | *tshen nyen-t̄ra chhem-po.* |

| | | |
|---|---|---|
| Cell (of hermit) | རི་ཁྲོད་ | *ri-thrö.* |
| Do. (of monks) | གྲྭ་ཤག་ | *ťra-sha.* |
| Cemetery | དུར་ཁྲོད་ | *ťu-thrö.* |
| Censer | སྤོས་ཕོར་ | *pö-phor.* |
| Censure, to | གཤེ་གཤེ་བཏང་ (གཏོང་) བ་ | *she-she tang-wa.* |
| Do. *hon.* | བཀའ་བཀྱོན་གནང་བ་ | *kaṕ-kyön nang-wa.* |
| Centipede | རྐང་བརྒྱ་ལག་བརྒྱ་ | *ḱang-gya laḱ-gya.* |
| Centre | དཀྱིལ་ | *ḱyi.* |
| Centurion | བརྒྱ་དཔོན་ | *gya-pön.* |
| Ceremony | ལུགས་སྲོལ་ | *luḱ-sö.* |
| Ceremony (religious) | ཆོ་ག། སྐུ་རིམ་ | *chho-ga ; ku-rim.* |
| Certain | ངེས་པ་ | *nge-pa.* |
| Do. *hon.* | ཐུགས་ངེས་པ་ | *thu-nge-pa.* |
| Certainly | ཏེན་ལྡན། ངོ་ཐོག་ | *ten-den ; ngo-tho.* |
| Certainty | བརྟན་པོ། ངེས་པ། ཏེན་ལྡན་ | *tem-po ; nge-pa ; ten-den.* |
| Certificate | བཀའ་ཤོག་ | *ka-sho.* |
| Chaff (of grain) | སྦུང་མ་ | *phung-ma.* |
| Chain, iron | ལྕགས་ཐག་ | *chaḱ-tha.* |
| Do. brass | རག་ཐག་ | *raḱ-tha.* |
| Chair | རྐུབ་ཀྱག། ཁྲིའུ་ཤིང་ | *kuṕ-kya ; thri-u-shing.* |

| | | |
|---|---|---|
| Chair, *hon.* | ཞབས་ཀྱག་ | *sKap-kya.* |
| Do. (high chair used as throne) | བཞུགས་ཁྲི་ | *sKuk-thri.* |
| Chairman | འཁྲིད་པ་ | *thri-pa.* |
| Chalk | ས་དཀར། དཀར་རྩི་ | *sa-kar ; kar-tsi.* |
| Chamber | ཁང་མིག་ | *khang-mi.* |
| Do. *hon.* | གཟིམ་ཆུང་ | *śim-chhung.* |
| Chamber, sleeping | ཉལ་ས་ | *nye-sa.* |
| Do. *hon.* | གཟིམ་ཁང་ | *śim-khang.* |
| Chamberlain | གཟིམ་དཔོན་ཆེན་པོ་ | *śim-pön chhem-po.* |
| Chance (accident) | བར་ཆད་ | *par-chhe.* |
| Do. (luck) | བསོ་བདེ་ (བསོད་བདེ་) | *so-de.* |
| Do. *hon.* | སྐུ་བསོད་ | *ku-sö.* |
| Change, to, *v.t.* | སྒྱུར་བ་ | *gyur-wa.* |
| Do. *hon.* | སྒྱུར་ར་ (བ་) གནང་བ་ | *gyur-ra nang-wa.* |
| Change, to, *v.i.* | འགྱུར་བ་ | *gyur-wa.* |
| Change, to, (exchange) | རྗེ་པོ་རྒྱབ་པ་ | *je-po gyap-pa.* |
| Do. *hon.* | རྗེ་པོ་སྐྱོན་པ་ | *je-po kyöm-pa.* |
| Channel (for irrigation) | ཡོ་པོ་ (ཡུར་པོ་) | *yo-po.* |
| Chap, to (of skin) | གས་པ་ | *ke-pa.* |

| | | |
|---|---|---|
| Chapel | ཆོས་ཁང་ | *chhö-khang.* |
| Chapter | ལེའུ་ | *li-u.* |
| Character | བྱེད་སྟངས་ | *cḱe-tang.* |
| Do. *hon.* | གནང་སྟངས་ | *nang-tang.* |
| Charcoal | སོལ་ལ་ (སོལ་བ་) | *sö-la.* |
| Charge, to (price) | གོང་ལབ་པ་ | *ḱong laṕ-pa.* |
| Charge of, to give into | རྩིས་སྤྲད་པ་ | *tsi tre-pa.* |
| Charge of, to take | རྩིས་ལེན་པ་ | *tsi lem-pa.* |
| Charitable | དགེ་སེམས་ཆེན་པོ་ | *ge sem chhem-po.* |
| Charity (alms) | སྦྱིན་པ། བསོད་སྙོམས་ | *jim-pa ; sö-nyom.* |
| Charity of mind | སྙིང་རྗེ། དགེ་སེམས་ | *nying-je ; ge-sem.* |
| Charm (amulet) | རྟེན་ | *ten.* |
| Do. (worn on person) | སྲུང་ང་ (སྲུང་བ་) | *trung-nga.* |
| Do. *hon.* | མགུལ་སྲུང་ | *gü-sung.* |
| Charm-box | གའུ་ | *ḱa-u.* |
| Do. *hon.* | མགུལ་གའུ་ | *gü-ḱa-u.* |
| Chase, to | གཉུག་དེད་ཕྱིན་པ་ | *sḱuk-ṫe chhim-pa.* |
| Do. *hon.* | གཉུག་དེད་ཕེབ་པ་ | *sḱuk-ṫe phe-pa.* |
| Chasm | སེར་ཀ་ | *ser-ka.* |
| Chat, to | ཁ་ལས་བ་ཤད་ (ཤོད་) པ་ | *khaṕ-le she-pa.* |

| | | |
|---|---|---|
| Chat, to *hon.* | ཞལ་ལས་གསུང་བ་ | *ske-le sung-wa.* |
| Cheap | ཁེ་པོ་ | *khe-po.* |
| Cheat, to | མགོ་སྐོར་བཏང་ (གཏོང་) བ། | *go-kor tang-wa.* |
| | མགོ་སྐོར་བ་ | *go kor-wa.* |
| Do. *hon.* | མགོ་སྐོར་གཏོང་ང་ (བ་) གནང་བ་ | *go-kor tong-nga nang-wa.* |
| Do. *inf.* to *sup.* | དབུ་སྐོར་ཞུ་བ་ | *u-kor sku-wa.* |
| Check, to (stop) | བཀག་པ་ (འགེགས་པ) | *kak-pa.* |
| Do. *hon.* | བཀག་ག་ (བཀག་པ་) གནང་བ་ | *kak-ka nang-wa.* |
| Cheek | འདན་ཁོག། འགྲམ་པ་ | *den-kho ; dram-pa.* |
| Do. *hon.* | ཞལ་འགྲམ་ | *sken-dram.* |
| Cheeky | གྱོང་པོ་ | *kyong-po.* |
| Cheerful, to be | སེམས་དགའ་བ་ | *sem-ga-wa.* |
| Do. *hon.* | ཐུགས་མཉེས་པ་ | *thu-nye-pa.* |
| Cheese | ཆུར་ར་ | *chhu-ra.* |
| Do. *hon.* | བཞེས་ཆུར་ | *skip-chhur.* |
| Do. (mixed with butter) | ཐུད་ | *thü.* |
| Do. *hon.* | བཞེས་ཐུད་ | *skip-thü.* |
| Do. (another kind) | ཆུར་ཞིབ་ | *chhur-skip.* |

| | | |
|---|---|---|
| Chemist | སྨན་ཚོང་པ་ | *men tshong-pa.* |
| Chess | མིག་དམག་ (མིག་མངས་) | *mi-ma.* |
| Do. *hon.* | སྤྱན་དམག་ (སྤྱན་མངས་) | *chen-ma.* |
| Chest | སྒམ་ | *gam.* |
| Do. *hon.* | ཕྱག་སྒམ་ | *chha-gam.* |
| Do. (of body) | བྲང་ཁོག་ | *ṕang-k̇ho.* |
| Do. *hon.* | སྐུ་བྲང་ | *ku-ṕang.* |
| Chestnut (horse), *m.* | སྐྱང་པོ་ | *kyang-po.* |
| Do. *f.* | སྐྱང་མོ་ | *kyang-mo.* |
| Chicken | བྱ་ཕྲུག་ | *cǩaṕ-thru.* |
| Chide, to | གཤེ་གཤེ་བཏང་ (གཏོང་) བ་ | *she-she tang-wa.* |
| Do. *hon.* | བཀའ་བཀྱོན་གནང་བ་ | *kaṕ-kyön nang-wa.* |
| Chief (among officials, etc.) | གཙོ་བོ་ | *tso-o.* |
| Chief Minister | བློན་ཆེན་ | *lön-chhen.* |
| Chiefly | ཕལ་ཆེར་ | *phe-chher.* |
| Chilblains, to suffer from | འཁྱགས་འབོས་འཐེབ་པ་ | *khyak̆-bö theṕ-pa.* |
| Child | བུ་གུ་ | *pu-gu.* |
| Do. *m. hon.* | སྲས་ | *se.* |
| Do. *f. hon.* | སྲས་མོ་ | *tre-mo* or *se-mo.* |
| Children | བུ་བུ་མོ་ | *ṕu ṕu-mo.* |

| | | |
|---|---|---|
| Children, *hon.* | ཨ་ལྦྲ་སྲས་སྲོས་ | *a-wa se-sö.* |
| Chilli | སིལ་པན་ | *si-pen.* |
| Do. *hon.* | སྲུམ་སྨན་ | *trum-men.* |
| Chilly | གྲང་མོ། བསིལ་པོ་ | *ťrang-mo ; si-po.* |
| Do. *hon.* | སྐུ་བསིལ་པོ་ | *ku-si-po.* |
| Chimney | དུ་ཁུང་ (དུད་ཁུང་) | *ťu-khung.* |
| Chin | མས་ལེ་ | *me-le.* |
| Do. *hon.* | ཞལ་མལ་ (ཞལ་མས་) | *sḱe-mel.* |
| China (country) | རྒྱ་ནག་ | *gya-na.* |
| China, *adj.* (porcelain) | དཀར་ཡོལ་ | *ka-yö.* |
| Do. *hon.* | ཞལ་དཀར་ | *sḱe-ka.* |
| Chinaman | རྒྱ་མི་ | *gya-mi.* |
| Chinese, *adj.* and *s.* | རྒྱ་མི་ | *gya-mi.* |
| Chinese Emperor | རྒྱ་ནག་གོང་མ། གོང་མ་ཆེན་པོ་ | *gya-na ḱong-ma ; ḱong-ma chhem-po.* |
| Chinese language | རྒྱ་སྐད་ | *gya-ke.* |
| Chink (in wall, etc.) | སེར་ཀ་ | *se-ka.* |
| Chisel | ཟོང་ | *śong.* |
| Choke, to | གློ་སུབ་རྒྱབ་པ་ | *lo-suṕ gyaṕ-pa.* |
| Do. *hon.* | གློ་སུབ་སྐྱོན་པ་ | *lo-suṕ kyöm-pa.* |

| | | |
|---|---|---|
| Choked, to be | འགགས་པ་ | *gaḱ-pa.* |
| Cholera | སྐྱུག་བཤལ་ | *kyuḱ-she.* |
| Choose, to (appoint) | སྐོ་བ་ | *ko-wa.* |
| Do. *hon.* | སྐོ་བ་གནང་བ་ | *ko-wa nang-wa.* |
| Choose, to (select) | འདམས་པ་ | *dam-pa.* |
| Do. *hon.* | འདམས་པ་གནང་བ་ | *dam-pa nang-wa.* |
| Chop (mutton chop) | ལུག་ཤའི་རྩིབ་མ་ | *luḱ-she tsi-ma.* |
| Do. *hon.* | གསོལ་སྐྲུམ་ལུག་ཤའི་རྩིབ་མ་ | *sö-trum luḱ-she tsi-ma.* |
| Do. to (meat) | བཙབ་པ་ | *tsaṕ-pa.* |
| Do. *hon.* | བཙབ་པ་གནང་བ་ | *tsaṕ-pa nang-wa.* |
| Do. to (wood, metal, etc.) | བཅད་པ་ (གཅོད་པ་) | *che-pa.* |
| Do. *hon.* | བཅད་ (གཅོད་) པ་གནང་བ་ | *che-pa nang-wa.* |
| Chopper | ཚས་དོ་ | *tshe-t́o.* |
| Chopsticks | ཁོ་ཙེ་ *ch.* | *khö-t́se.* |
| Do. *hon.* | བཞེས་ཙེ་ | *sḱe-tse.* |
| Christ | མ་ཤི་ཀ་ | *ma-shi-ka.* |
| Chronicle | ལོ་རྒྱུས་ | *lo-gyü.* |
| Chum (in a monastery) | ཆོས་གྲོགས་ | *chhö-t́ro.* |
| Church | ཆོས་ཁང་ | *chhö-khang.* |
| Churn, *s.* | ལྡོང་མོ་ | *dong-mo.* |

| | | |
|---|---|---|
| Churn for milk | ཞོ་ལྡོང་ | *sko-dong.* |
| Do. for tea | ཇ་ལྡོང་ | *ckan-dong.* |
| Do. *hon.* | གསོལ་ལྡོང་ | *sön-dong.* |
| Do. to (tea) | སྲུས་པ་ (སྲུབ་པ་) | *sü-pa.* |
| Do. *hon.* | སྲུས་ (སྲུབ་) པ་གནང་བ་ | *sü-pa nang-wa.* |
| Churn, to (milk) | ཞོ་དཀྲོག་པ་ | *sko-trok-pa.* |
| Cicatrice | རྨ་ཤུལ་ | *ma-shü.* |
| Cinder (hot) | མེ་མདག | *men-da.* |
| Cipher (zero) | ཀླད་ཀོར་ | *le-kor.* |
| Circle | སྒོ་སྐོར་ (སྒོར་སྒོར་) | *go-kor.* |
| Circular | ཀོར་ཀོར་ | *kor-kor.* |
| Circumference | སྒོར་ཐིག་ | *gor thik.* |
| Circumstance | རྐྱེན་ | *kyen.* |
| Citadel | རྫོང་ | *dzong.* |
| City | གྲོང་ཁྱེར་ | *trong-khyer.* |
| Civil, (honorific, of conversation) | ཞེ་ས་ | *ske-sa.* |
| Claim | ཐོབ་སྐལ་ | *thop-ke.* |
| Clairvoyance | མངོན་ཤེས་ | *ngön she.* |
| Do. *hon.* | མངོན་མཁྱེན་ | *ngön-khyen.* |
| Clamour | ཨུར་སྒྲ་ | *u-dra.* |

| | | |
|---|---|---|
| **Clap, the hands, to** | ལག་པ་རྡབ་པ་ | *laḱ-pa daṕ-pa.* |
| Do. *hon.* | ཕྱག་རྡབ་པ་ | *chha-daṕ-pa.* |
| **Clarified butter** | མར་ཁུ་ | *mar-khu.* |
| **Clarify, to (butter)** | མར་བཞུ་བ་ | *mar sḱu-wa.* |
| **Clarionet** | རྒྱ་གླིང་ | *gya-ling.* |
| **Clasp, to** | འཁྱུད་པ་ | *khyü-pa.* |
| Do. *hon.* | འཁྱུད་པ་གནང་བ་ | *khyü-pa nang-wa.* |
| **Class (kind)** | རིམ་པ་ | *rim-pa.* |
| Do. (in school) | གྲལ་ | *t́re.* |
| Do. *hon.* | བཞུགས་གྲལ་ | *sḱu-t́re.* |
| **Claw** | སྡེར་མོ་ | *der-mo.* |
| **Clay** | འདག་པ་ | *daḱ-pa.* |
| **Clean** | གཙང་མ་ | *tsang-ma.* |
| Do. to | འཁྲུ་བ་ | *thru-wa.* |
| Do. *hon.* | འཁྲུད་པ་གནང་བ་ | *thrü-pa nang-wa.* |
| **Clean, to (by wiping)** | འཕྱིད་པ་ | *chhi-pa.* |
| Do. *hon.* | འཇག་ཕྱིད་གནང་བ་ | *ja-chhi nang-wa.* |
| **Clean, to (by rubbing and wiping)** | འཕྱིད་དར་གཏོང་བ་ | *chhi-t́ar tong-wa.* |
| Do. *hon.* | འཇག་འཕྱིད་གནང་བ་ | *ja-chhi nang-wa.* |
| **Clean, to (by sweeping)** | གེ་རྒྱབ་པ་ | *ke-gyaṕ-pa.* |

| | | |
|---|---|---|
| Clean, to (by sweeping) *hon.* | གེ་སྐྱོན་པ་ | *ḱe-kyöm-pa.* |
| Cleansed (purified) | དག་པོ་ | *ṫak-po.* |
| Clear (of glass) | གསལ་པོ་ | *se-po.* |
| Do. (of air) | དྭངས་པོ་ | *ṫang-po.* |
| Cleave, to (wood etc.) | གཤགས་པ་ (གཤོག་པ་) | *shaḱ-pa.* |
| Do. *hon.* | གཤགས་ག་ (གཤོག་པ་) གནང་བ་ | *shaḱ-ḱa nang-wa.* |
| Cleft | སེར་ཀ་ | *se-ka.* |
| Clergy | གྲྭ་པ་ | *ṫra-pa.* |
| Do. *hon.* | དགེ་འདུན་ | *gen-dün.* |
| Clerk | དྲུང་ཡིག་ | *ṫrung-yi.* |
| Do. *hon.* | དྲུང་ཡིག་ལགས་ | *ṫrung-yi-la.* |
| Clever | རིག་པ་ཆེན་པོ་ | *riḱ-pa chhem-po.* |
| Do. *hon.* | ཐུགས་རིག་ཆེན་པོ་ | *thu-riḱ chhem-po.* |
| Climate | བསིལ་དྲོས་ | *si-ṫrö.* |
| Climb, to | འཛེག་པ་ (འཛེག་པ་) | *dzaḱ-pa.* |
| Do. *hon.* | འཛེག་ག་ (འཛེག་པ་) གནང་བ་ | *dzaḱ-ḱa nang-wa.* |
| Cling, to | འཛུས་པ་ | *jü-pa.* |
| Do. *hon.* | འཛུས་པ་གནང་བ་ | *jü-pa nang-wa.* |
| Cloak | ཆུ་པ་ | *chhu-pa.* |

| | | |
|---|---|---|
| Cloak, *hon.* | ན་བཟའ་ | *nam-śa.* |
| Clock | ཆུ་ཚོད་འཁོར་ལོ་ | *chhu-t́shö khor-lo.* |
| Cloisonné | གྲུ་གྲུ་ཤ་ | *ḱu-ḱu-sha.* |
| Close to, *adv.* and *post.* | ཙཱ་ (རྩར།) ཐག་ཉེ་པོ་ | *tsa ; tha-nye-po.* |
| Do. to | བཀག་པ་ (འགེགས་པ་) | *kaḱ-pa.* |
| Do. *hon.* | བཀག་ག་ (འགེགས་པ་) གནང་བ་ | *kaḱ-ḱa nang-wa.* |
| Close up, *v.i.* (of flowers, etc.) | ཁ་ཟུམ་པ་ | *kha-śum-pa.* |
| Close fisted | ལག་པ་དམ་པོ་ | *laḱ-pa t́am-po.* |
| Do. *hon.* | ཕྱག་དམ་པོ་ | *chha-t́am-po.* |
| Cloth, cotton | རས་ | *re.* |
| Do. *hon.* | སྐུ་རས་ | *ku-re.* |
| Cloth, woollen (of European or Indian make) | འགོ་སྣམ་ | *go-nam.* |
| Do. (of Tibetan make) | སྣམ་བུ་ | *nam-ṕu.* |
| Do. *hon.* | ཕྱག་སྣམ་ | *chha-nam.* |
| Clothe, to | གོན་པ་ | *ḱöm-pa.* |
| Do. *hon.* | བཞེས་པ་ | *sḱe-pa.* |
| Clothes | དུག་ལོག་ | *t́u-lo.* |
| Do. *hon.* | ན་བཟའ་ | *nam-śa.* |

| | | |
|---|---|---|
| Clothes, to put on | དུག་ལོག་གོན་པ་ | *ťu-lo ḱöm-pa.* |
| Do. *hon.* | ན་བཟའ་བཞེས་པ་ | *nam-śa sḱe-pa.* |
| Do. to take off | དུག་ལོག་ཕིས་ (འབུད་) པ་ | *ţu-lo ṕi-pa.* |
| Do. *hon.* | ན་བཟའ་བསིལ་བ་ | *nam-śa si-wa.* |
| Cloud (in sky) | སྤྲིན་པ་ | *trim-pa.* |
| Do. (fog) | རྨུགས་པ་ | *muḱ-pa.* |
| Cloudy, to become | འཐིབ་པ་ | *thiṕ-pa.* |
| Clove | ལི་ཤི་ | *li-shi.* |
| Clown | དབུ་འཁོར་ཞུ་མཁན་ | *wu-khor sḱu-khen.* |
| Clumsy | ལྡུག་རུལ་ | *duḱ-ru.* |
| Coagulate, to (of blood, etc.) | འཁྱག་པ་ | *khyaḱ-pa.* |
| Coal | རྡོ་སོལ་ | *do-sö.* |
| Coarse | རྩུབ་པོ་ | *tsuṕ-po.* |
| Coast | ཆུ་འགྲམ་ | *chhu-dram.* |
| Coat | ཆུ་པ་ | *chhu-pa.* |
| Do. *hon.* | ན་བཟའ་ | *nam-śa.* |
| Do. of mail | ཁྲབ་ | *thraṕ.* |
| Coax, to (for good object) | བསླབ་བྱ་རྒྱབ་པ་ | *laṕ cḱa gyaṕ-pa.* |
| Do. *hon.* | བཀའ་སློབ་གནང་བ་ | *ka-loṕ nang-wa.* |
| Coax, to (for bad object) | སླུ་བ་ | *lu-wa.* |

| | | |
|---|---|---|
| Coax, to (for bad object) *hon.* | སླུ་བ་གནང་བ་ | *lu-wa nang-wa* |
| Cobbler | ངོ་བཟོ་ | *ngop-so.* |
| Comforter. *hon.* | སེམས་གསོ་གཏོང་ང་ (བ) གནང་མཁན་ | *sem-so tong-nga nang-khen.* |
| Do. *hon.* (*inf.* to *sup.*) | ཐུགས་གསོ་ཕུལ་མཁན་ | *thuk so phü-khen.* |
| Confidential | གསང་བ་ | *sang-wa.* |
| Cobweb | སྡོམ་ཐག་ | *dom-tha.* |
| Cock | བྱ་ཕོ་ | *cka-pho.* |
| Code of law | ཁྲིམས་ཡིག་ | *thrim-yi.* |
| Coffer | སྒམ་ | *gam.* |
| Do. *hon.* | ཕྱག་སྒམ་ | *chha-gam.* |
| Coffin | རོ་སྒམ་ | *ro-gam.* |
| Do. *hon.* | སྤུར་སྒམ་ | *pur-gam.* |
| Cohere, to, *v.i.* (stick together) | འབྱར་བ་ | *jar-wa.* |
| Coil, to (of snake) | སྒོ་འཁོར་བྱེད་པ་ | *go-khor cke pa.* |
| Coin (silver, value four annas) | ཏཾ་ཀ་ | *tang-ka.* |
| Do. (silver, value two and half annas) | ཞོ་སྒང་ | *sko-kang.* |
| Do. (silver, value two annas) | ཕྱེད་གས་ | *chhi-ke.* |

| | | |
|---|---|---|
| Coin (silver, value one anna and one pice) | སྐར་མ་ལྔ་ | *ka-ma-nga.* |
| Do. (silver, value three pice) | ཁ་གང་ | *kha-ḱang.* |
| Do. (silver, value four pies) | ཁ་ཕྱེད་ | *khaṕ-chhe.* |
| Do. (Chinese pice) | ཏོང་ཙེ་ | *t́ong-tse.* |
| Cold, *adj.* (of body, meat, etc.) | གྲང་མོ། བསིལ་པོ་ | *t́rang-mo ; si-po.* |
| Do. *hon.* | སྐུ་བསིལ་པོ་ | *ku si-po.* |
| Do. (to feel) | འཁྱགས་པ་ | *khyaḱ-pa.* |
| Do. *hon.* | སྐུ་བསིལ་བ་ | *ku-si-wa.* |
| Cold, *s.* | འཁྱགས་པ་ | *khyaḱ-pa.* |
| Do. (catarrh) | ཆམ་པ་ | *chham-pa.* |
| Do. *hon.* | མགུལ་ཆམ་ | *gü-chham.* |
| Do. to have (in the head) | ཆམ་པ་ན་བ་ | *chham-pa na-wa.* |
| Do. *hon.* | མགུལ་ཆམ་སྙུང་བ་ | *gü-chham nyung-wa.* |
| Colic | རྒྱུ་གཟེར་ | *gyu-śer.* |
| Collar | གོང་ང་ (གོང་བ་) | *ḱong-nga.* |
| Do. (after Chinese fashion) | ལིང་ཙེ་ | *ling-tse.* |

| | | |
|---|---|---|
| Collar (after Chinese fashion) *hon.* | མགུལ་གླིང་ | *gü-ling.* |
| Colleague | རོགས་བྱེད་མཁན་ | *ro-cḱe-khen.* |
| Collect, to | སྡུད་པ་ | *dü-pa.* |
| Do. *hon.* | སྡུད་པ་གནང་བ་ | *dü-pa nang-wa.* |
| Collect, to (wood, etc.) | སྒྲུག་པ་ | *druḱ-pa.* |
| Do. *hon.* | སྒྲུག་ག་ (པ་) གནང་བ་ | *druḱ-ḱa nang wa.* |
| College (of monks) | གྲྭ་ཚང་ | *t́ra-tshang.* |
| Colloquial (language) | ཕལ་སྐད་ | *phe-ke.* |
| Colonel (officer in command of 500 men to 1,000 men) | མདའ་དཔོན་ | *de-pön.* |
| Colour (dye) | ཚོས་ | *tshö.* |
| Do. natural | མདོག་ | *do.* |
| Do. to lose | ཚོས་ཡལ་བ་ | *tshö-ye-wa.* |
| Colt | ཏི་གི་ (ཏི་ཙུ་) | *ti-ḱi.* |
| Do. of an ass | ཨུ་ཏྲི་ | *u-ti.* |
| Column | ཀ་ (ཀ་བ་) | *ka.* |
| Comb | སྐྲ་གཤད་ | *tra-she.* |
| Do. *hon.* | དབུ་བཤད་ | *u-she.* |
| Do. to | སྐྲ་གཤད་པ་ | *tra-she-pa.* |
| Do. *hon.* | དབུ་གཤད་སྐྱོན་པ་ | *u-she kyöm-pa* |

| | | |
|---|---|---|
| Combat | རྒྱབ་འདྲེ་ | *gyam-dre.* |
| Come, *imp.* | ཤོག་ | *sho.* |
| Do. to | ཡོང་བ་ | *yong-wa.* |
| Do. *hon.* | ཕེབ་པ་ | *phe-pa.* |
| Do. *h. hon.* | འཆིབ་རྒྱུ་གནང་བ་ | *chhiṕ-gyu nang-wa.* |
| Come back, to | ལོག་ཡོང་བ་ | *lo-yong-wa.* |
| Do. *hon.* | ལོག་ཕེབ་པ་ | *lo-phe-pa.* |
| Do. *h. hon.* | འཆིབ་རྒྱུ་གནང་བ་ | *chhiṕ-gyu nang-wa.* |
| Come, to (before *sup.*) | མཇལ་བ་ | *je-wa.* |
| Do. *hon.* | མཇལ་ར་ (བ་) གནང་བ་ | *je-ra nang-wa.* |
| Come out, to | འཐོན་པ་ | *thöm-pa.* |
| Do. *hon.* | ཕྱི་ལོགས་ལ་ཕེབ་པ་ | *chhi-lo la pheṕ-pa.* |
| Come together (of persons) | འཛོམ་པ། འཚོགས་པ་ | *dzom-pa ; tshoḱ-pa.* |
| Do. *hon.* | ལྷན་རྒྱས་ཚོགས་པ་གནང་བ་ | *lhen-gye tshoḱ-pa nang-wa.* |
| Comet | དུ་བ་མཇུག་རིང་ | *t́u-wa juḱ-ring.* |
| Comfortable | སྐྱིད་པོ་ | *kyi-po.* |
| Do. *hon.* | སྤྲོ་པོ་ | *tro-po.* |
| Comic | བགད་མོ་བྲོ་པོ་ | *ge-mo t́ro-po.* |
| Do. *hon.* | ཞལ་མོ་བྲོ་པོ་ | *sḱe-mo t́ro-po.* |
| Command, commandment | བཀའ་ | *ka.* |

| | | |
|---|---|---|
| Command, to (give order) | བཀའ་གནང་བ་ | *ka-nang-wa.* |
| Do. to (be in command of) | འགོ་བྱེད་བྱེད་པ་ | *go-ch̓e ch̓e-pa.* |
| Do. *hon.* | འགོ་བྱེད་གནང་བ་ | *go-ch̓e nang-wa.* |
| Commander | དམག་དཔོན་ | *mak̓-pön.* |
| Commander-in-Chief | སྤྱི་མདའ་ | *chin-da.* |
| Commence, to | མགོ་བཙུགས་ (འཛུགས་) པ་ | *go-tsuk̓-pa.* |
| Do. *hon.* | དབུ་བཙུགས་ (འཛུགས་) པ་ | *u-tsuk̓-pa.* |
| Commencement | ཐོག་མ་ | *tho-ma.* |
| Commend, to | བསྟོད་ར་བཏང་ (གཏོང་) བ་ | *tö-ra tang-wa.* |
| Do. *hon.* | བསྟོད་ར་གཏོང་ང་ (བ་) གནང་བ་ | *tö-ra tong-nga nang-wa.* |
| Commendation | བསྟོད་ར་ | *tö-ra.* |
| Commerce | ཚོང་ | *tshong.* |
| Do. *hon.* | རྒྱ་ཚོང་ | *gya-tshong.* |
| Commissary (delegate) | ཚབ་ | *tshap̓.* |
| Do. *hon.* | སྐུ་ཚབ་ | *ku-tshap̓.* |
| Commit, to | བྱེད་པ་ | *ch̓e-pa.* |
| Do. *hon.* | གནང་བ་ | *nang-wa.* |
| Do. to (to one's care) | བཅོལ་བ་ (འཆོལ་བ་) | *chöl-wa.* |
| Do. *hon.* | བཅོལ་ར་ (བ་) གནང་བ་ | *chö-ra nang-wa.* |

| | | |
|---|---|---|
| Common, *adj.* (vulgar) | དཀྱུས་མ་ | *kyü-ma.* |
| Do. (plentiful) | འབེལ་པོ་ | *be-po.* |
| Do. (of language *opp.* to *hon.*) | ཞེ་ས་མེད་པ་ | *sKe-sa me-pa.* |
| Do. in (jointly) | མཉམ་འབྲེལ་ | *nyam-dre.* |
| Do. *hon.* | ཕྱག་འབྲེལ་ | *chha-dre.* |
| Companion | རོགས་ | *ro.* |
| Do. (in work) | ལས་རོགས་ | *le-ro.* |
| Do. *hon.* | ཕྱག་འབྲེལ་ | *chha-dre.* |
| Company (of persons) | མི་ཚོགས་ | *mi-tsho.* |
| Compare, to | སྡུར་བ་ | *dur-wa.* |
| Do. *hon.* | སྡུར་ར་ (བ་) གནང་བ་ | *dur ra nang-wa.* |
| Comparison | དཔེ་ | *pe.* |
| Compasses (a pair of) | སྐོར་ཐིག་ | *kor-thi.* |
| Compassion | སྙིང་རྗེ་ | *nying-je.* |
| Do. *hon.* | ཐུགས་རྗེ་ | *thu-je.* |
| Compel, to | ཨུ་ཚུགས་བྱེད་པ་ | *u-tshu cKe-pa.* |
| Do. *hon.* | ཨུ་ཚུགས་གནང་བ་ | *u-tshu nang-wa.* |
| Compelled, to be | དགོས་པ་ | *gö-pa.* |
| Compensate, to | འགྲོ་སོང་སྟེར་བ་ | *dro-song ter-wa.* |
| Compensation | འགྲོ་སོང་ | *dro-song.* |

| | | |
|---|---|---|
| Compete, to | སྡུར་བ་ | *dur-wa.* |
| Do. *hon.* | སྡུར་ར་ (བ་) གནང་བ་ | *dur-ra nang-wa.* |
| Competent | འོས་པོ་ | *ö-po.* |
| Competitor | སྡུར་མཁན་ | *dur-khen.* |
| Do. *hon.* | སྡུར་ར་ (བ་) གནང་མཁན་ | *dur-ra nang-khen.* |
| Compile, to | སྒྲིག་པ་ | *drik-pa.* |
| Complain, to (in writing) | སྙན་ཞུ་ཕུལ་ (འབུལ་) བ་ | *nye-sku phü wa.* |
| Do. to (verbally) | ཞུ་ཐུག་བྱེད་པ་ | *sku-thu che-pa.* |
| Do. *hon.* | ཞུ་ཐུག་གནང་བ་ | *sku-thu nang-wa.* |
| Complaint (petition) | སྙན་ཞུ་ | *nye-sku.* |
| Complete, to | ཚར་བ་ | *tshar-wa.* |
| Do. *hon.* | འགྲུབ་པ་ | *drup-pa.* |
| Completely | བྱད་དེ་ | *be-te.* |
| Complicated | མགོ་ཉོག་ཚ་པོ་ | *go-nyo tsha-po.* |
| Compliment | ཕྱག་འབུལ་ | *chham-bü.* |
| Compliment, to (a superior) | ཕྱག་འབུལ་ཞུ་བ་ | *chham-bü sku-wa.* |
| Do. to (equals) | འདྲིས་མི་བཏང་ (གཏོང་) བ་ | *dri-me tang-wa.* |
| Compose, to (writing, &c.) | རྩོམ་པ་ | *tsom-pa.* |
| Do. *hon.* | རྩོམ་པ་གནང་བ་ | *tsom-pa nang-wa.* |
| Do. *h. hon.* | བཀའ་རྩོམ་གནང་བ་ | *ka-tsom nang-wa.* |

| | | |
|---|---|---|
| Comprehend, to (understand) | ཧ་གོ་བ་ | *ha-ḱo-wa.* |
| Do. *hon.* | མཁྱེན་པ་ | *khyem-pa.* |
| Compress, to | བཙིར་བ་ | *tsir-wa.* |
| Do. *hon.* | བཙིར་ར་ (བ་) གནང་བ་ | *tsir-ra nang-wa.* |
| Comprise, to | སྡུད་པ་ | *dü-pa.* |
| Compromise, to (by mutual concession) | ནང་འགྲིག་བྱེད་པ། བར་འདུམ་བྱེད་པ་ | *nang-driḱ ḱe-pa, par-dum cḱe-pa.* |
| Do *hon.* | བཀའ་བསྡུམ་གནང་བ་ | *nan-dum nang-wa.* |
| Computation | རྩིས་ | *tsi.* |
| Do. *hon.* | ཕྱགས་རྩིས་ | *ja-tsi.* |
| Compute, to | རྩིས་རྒྱབ་པ་ | *tsi-gyaṕ-pa.* |
| Do. *hon.* | ཕྱགས་རྩིས་གནང་བ་ | *ja-tsi nang-wa.* |
| Comrade | རོགས་ | *ro.* |
| Do. *hon.* | ཕྱག་འབྲེལ་ | *chha-dre.* |
| Concave | ཀོང་ཀོང་ | *kong-kong.* |
| Conceal, to | སྦེད་པ་ | *be-pa.* |
| Do. *hon.* | སྦེད་པ་གནང་བ་ | *be-pa nang-wa.* |
| Concede, to | སྟེར་བ་ | *ter-wa.* |
| Do. *hon.* | གནང་བ་ | *nang-wa.* |
| Conceited | ལྟ་བ་མཐོ་པོ་ | *ta-wa tho-po.* |

| | | |
|---|---|---|
| Conceive, to (a child) | བུ་གུ་འཁོར་བ། བུ་ཚ་འཆགས་པ་ | *pu-gu khor-wa, pu-tsha chhaḱ-pa.* |
| Do. *hon.* | ཨ་ལྭ་འཁོར་བ་ | *a-wa ḱhor-wa.* |
| Concerning | དོན་ལ། སྐོར་ལ་ | *t́ön-la; kor-la.* |
| Conch-shell | དུང་ | *t́ung.* |
| Do. bracelet | དུང་སྐོར་ | *t́ung-ko.* |
| Do. *hon.* | ཕྱག་དུང་ | *chha-t́ung.* |
| Conclude, to | འཚར་བ་ | *tshar-wa.* |
| Do. *hon.* | འགྲུབ་པ་ | *druṕ-pa.* |
| Concur, to | མཐུན་པ་ | *thüm-pa.* |
| Do. *hon.* | མཐུན་པ་གནང་བ་ | *thüm-pa nang-wa.* |
| Condemn, to (as judge) | ཁྲིམས་བཏང་ (གཏོང་) བ་ | *thrim-tang-wa.* |
| Condemn, to, *hon.* | ཁྲིམས་གཏོང་ང་ (བ་) གནང་བ་ | *thrim tong-nga nang-wa.* |
| Do. *h. hon.* | བཀའ་ཁྲིམས་གནང་བ་ | *ka-thrim nang-wa.* |
| Condiment | ཤ་སྨན་ | *sha-men.* |
| Condition (state) | གནས་ཚུལ་ | *ne-tshü.* |
| Condole, to | སེམས་གསོ་བཏང་ (གཏོང་) བ་ | *sem-so tang-wa.* |
| Conduct, *s.* | བྱེད་སྟངས | *cḱe-tang.* |
| Do. *hon.* | གནང་སྟངས་ | *naṇg-tang.* |
| Do. to (towards) | འཁྲིད་ཡོང་བ་ | *thri-yong-wa.* |
| Do. *hon.* | འཁྲིད་ཕེབ་པ་ | *thri-phe-pa.* |

| | | |
|---|---|---|
| Conduct to (away) | འཁྲིད་འགྲོ་བ་ | *thri-dro-wa.* |
| Do. *hon.* | འཁྲིད་ཕེབ་པ་ | *thri-phe-pa.* |
| Conduit (drain) | ཡོ་པོ་ (ཡུར་པོ་) | *yo-po.* |
| Cone of clay (with figures of gods) | ཚ་ཚ་ | *tsha-tsha.* |
| Confer, to (converse) | གྲོས་བྱེད་པ་ | *t́rö- cḱe-pa.* |
| Do. *hon.* | བཀའ་གྲོས་གནང་བ་ | *ka-t́rö nang-wa.* |
| Confer, to (give) | སྟེར་བ་ | *ter-wa* |
| Do. *hon.* | གནང་བ་ | *nang-wa.* |
| Conference | གྲོས་ | *t́rö.* |
| Do. *hon.* | བཀའ་གྲོས་ | *ka-t́rö.* |
| Confess, to | བཤགས་པ་ | *shaḱ-pa.* |
| Do. *hon.* | མཐོལ་བཤགས་ཕུལ་ (འབུལ་) བ་ | *thö-sha phü-wa.* |
| Do. *h. hon.* | མཐོལ་བཤགས་འབུལ་ལ་ (བ་) གནང་བ་ | *thö-sha bül-la nang-wa.* |
| Confide, to | བློ་གཏད་བྱེད་པ་ | *lo-te cḱe-pa.* |
| Do. *hon.* | བློ་གཏད་གནང་བ་ | *lo-te nang-wa.* |
| Confidence | བློ་གཏད་ | *lo-te.* |
| Confine, to | བཅུག་པ་ (འཇུག་པ་) | *chuḱ-pa.* |
| Do. *hon.* | བཅུག་ག་ (འཇུག་པ་) གནང་བ་ | *chuḱ-ḱa nang-wa.* |

| | | |
|---|---|---|
| Confirm, to (statement etc.) | གཏན་ལྡན་བྱེད་པ་ | *ten-den cḱe-pa.* |
| Do. *hon.* | གཏན་ལྡན་གནང་བ་ | *ten-den nang-wa.* |
| Confiscate, to | གཞུང་བཞེས་བཏང་ (གཏོང་) བ་ | *sḱung-sḱe tang-wa.* |
| Do. *hon.* | གཞུང་བཞེས་གནང་བ་ | *sḱung-sḱe nang-wa.* |
| Confiscation | གཞུང་བཞེས་ | *sḱung-sḱe.* |
| Conflict | རྒྱབ་འདྲེ་ | *gyam-dre.* |
| Confounded, to be | མགོ་འཁོར་བ། མགོ་འཐོམས་པ་ | *go-ḱhor-wa ; go-thom-pa.* |
| Do. *hon.* | དབུ་འཁོར་བ། དབུ་འཐོམས་པ་ | *u-khor-wa ; u-thom-pa.* |
| Confront, to | ར་འཕྲོད་བཏང་ (གཏོང་) བ་ | *raṕ-thrö tang-wa.* |
| Do. *hon.* | ར་འཕྲོད་གཏོང་ང་ (བ་) གནང་བ་ | *raṕ-thrö tong-nga nang-wa.* |
| Confused, to be | མགོ་འཁོར་བ་ | *go-khor-wa.* |
| Do. *hon.* | དབུ་འཁོར་བ་ | *u-khor-wa.* |
| Confusing (intricate) | མགོ་རྙོག་ཚ་པོ། མགོ་རྙོག་ཆེན་པོ་ | *go-nyo tsha-po ; go-nyo chem-po.* |
| Do. *hon.* | དབུ་རྙོག་ཚ་པོ་ | *u-nyo tsha-po.* |
| Confusion (of speech) | ཁ་རྗོད་ | *khan-jö.* |
| Confusion | མགོ་དཀྲོག་ | *go-tro.* |
| Congeal, to | འཁྱགས་པ་ | *khyaḱ-pa.* |
| Congregate, to | འཛོམས་པ་ | *dzom-pa.* |
| Do. *hon.* | ལྷན་རྒྱས་ཚོགས་པ་ | *hlen-gye tshoḱ-pa.* |

| | | |
|---|---|---|
| **Congregation** | ཚོགས་ | *tsho.* |
| **Conjure, to (do conjuring tricks)** | མིག་འཕྲུལ་རྩེད་པ་ | *mik-thrü tse-pa.* |
| Do. *hon.* | མིག་འཕྲུལ་རྩེད་པ་གནང་བ་ | *mik-thrü tse-pa nang-wa.* |
| **Conjure, to (implore)** | ནན་ཏན་ཞུ་བ་ | *nen-ten sḱu-wa.* |
| Do. *hon.* | ནན་ཏན་ཞུ་བ་གནང་བ་ | *nen-ten sḱu-wa nang-wa.* |
| **Conjure up, to (ghost, etc.)** | སྤྱན་འདྲེན་ཞུ་བ་ | *chen-dren sḱu-wa.* |
| Do. *hon.* | སྤྱན་འདྲེན་ཞུ་བ་གནང་བ་ | *chen-dren sḱu-wa nang-wa.* |
| **Conjuring tricks** | མིག་འཕྲུལ་ | *mik-thrü.* |
| Do. *hon.* | སྤྱན་འཕྲུལ་ | *chen-thrü.* |
| **Conjurer** | མིག་འཕྲུལ་རྩེད་མཁན་ | *mik-thrü tse-ḱhen.* |
| Do. *hon.* | མིག་འཕྲུལ་གནང་མཁན་ | *mik thrü nang-khen.* |
| **Connect, to (join together)** | འཐུད་པ་ | *thü-pa.* |
| Do. *hon.* | འཐུད་པ་གནང་བ་ | *thü-pa nang-wa.* |
| **Conquer, to** | རྒྱལ་བ་ | *gye-wa.* |
| Do. *hon.* | རྒྱལ་ར་ (བ་) གནང་བ་ | *gye-ra nang-wa.* |
| **Conquered, to be** | འཕམ་པ་ | *ṕham-pa.* |
| Do. *hon.* | ཐུགས་འཕམ་པ་གནང་བ་ | *thu pham-pa nang-wa.* |
| **Conscience, to have a** | བཟང་ངན་ཤེས་པ་ | *sang-ngen she-pa.* |
| Do. *hon.* | བཟང་ངན་མཁྱེན་པ་ | *śang-ngen khyem-pa.* |
| **Conscious, to be** | དྲན་པ་ | *ṫrem-pa.* |

| | | |
|---|---|---|
| Conscious, to be *hon.* | ཐུགས་དྲན་གསོ་བ་ | *thu-t́ren so-wa.* |
| Consecrate, to | རབ་གནས་བྱེད་པ་ | *raṕ-ne cḱe-pa.* |
| Do. *hon.* | རབ་གནས་གནང་བ་ | *raṕ ne nang wa.* |
| Consecration | རབ་གནས་ | *raṕ-ne.* |
| Consent, to | ཉན་པ་ | *nyem-pa.* |
| Do. *hon.* | གསན་པ་ | *sem pa.* |
| Consequence of, in | རྐྱེན་གྱིས་ | *kyen-ḱyi.* |
| Consequently | དེའི་རྐྱེན་བྱས་ནས་ | *t́ei-kyen cḱe-ne.* |
| Consider, to | བསམ་བློ་བཏང་ (གཏོང་) བ་ | *sam lo tang-wa.* |
| Do. *hon.* | ཐུགས་བསམ་བཞེས་པ་ | *thu-sam sḱe-pa.* |
| Considerable number of, a | མང་ཉུང་སྙོམ་པོ་གཅིག་ | *mang-nyung nyom-po-chi.* |
| Console, to | སེམས་གསོ་བཏང་ (གཏོང་) བ་ | *sem-so tang-wa.* |
| Do. *inf.* to *sup.* | སེམས་གསོ་ཞུ་བ་ | *sem so sḱu-wa.* |
| Consonant, *s.* | གསལ་བྱེད་ | *se-cḱe.* |
| Conspicuous | མངོན་གསལ་ཆེན་པོ་ | *ngön-se chhem-po.* |
| Constable | སྐོར་ཅག་པ་ | *ko-chaḱ-pa.* |
| Constant | བརྟན་པོ་ | *tem-po.* |
| Constantly | རྟག་པ་རེ་བཞིན་ | *taḱ-pa re-sḱi.* |
| Constellation | གཟའ་སྐར་ | *za-ka.* |
| Constipation | རྩ་འགག་པ་ | *tsa-gak pa.* |

| | | |
|---|---|---|
| Construct, to | བཟོ་བ་ | śo-wa. |
| Do. *hon.* | བཟོ་བ་གནང་བ་ | śo-wa nang-wa. |
| Consult, to | གྲོས་དྲི་ (འདྲི་) བ་ | t́rö-t́ri-wa. |
| Do. *hon.* | བཀའ་གྲོས་གནང་བ་ | ka t́rö nang-wa. |
| Consumed, to be | རྫོགས་པ་ | dzoḱ-pa. |
| Do. *hon.* | རྫོགས་ག་ (པ་) གནང་བ་ | dzoḱ-ḱa nang-wa. |
| Consumption (pulmonary) | གཅོང་ནད་ | chong-ne. |
| Contamination | གྲིབ་ | t́riṕ. |
| Do. *hon.* | སྐུ་གྲིབ་ | ku-t́riṕ. |
| Contemplate, to (consider) | བསམ་བློ་བཏང་ (གཏོང་) བ་ | sam-lo tang-wa. |
| Do. *hon.* | ཐུགས་བསམ་བཞེས་པ་ | thu-sam sḱe-pa. |
| Do. to (meditate on religious things) | སྒོམ་རྒྱབ་པ་ | gom-gyaṕ-pa. |
| Do. *hon.* | སྒོམ་སྐྱོན་པ་ | gom-kyöm-pa. |
| Contemporary | ལོ་ཟླ་ | lon-da. |
| Do. *hon.* | དགོང་ཟླ་ (དགུང་ཟླ་) | gong-da. |
| Contend, to (in war) | དམག་རྒྱབ་པ་ | ma-gyaṕ-pa. |
| Do. *hon.* | དམག་སྐྱོན་པ་ | ma-kyöm pa. |
| Contented, to be | འདོད་པ་གང་བ་ | dö-pa ḱang-wa. |
| Do. *hon.* | ཐུགས་འདོད་གང་བ་ | thung-dö ḱang-wa |

| | | |
|---|---|---|
| Continent, *s.* | གླིང་ | *ling.* |
| Continually | ནམ་རྒྱུན། དུས་རྒྱུན་ | *nam-gyün.; ṫü-gyün.* |
| Contract, a large written | གན་རྒྱ་ | *ḱam-gya.* |
| Do. a small written | འཛིན་ | *dzin.* |
| Do. *hon.* | བཀའ་འཛིན། ཕྱག་འཛིན་ | *kan-dzin; chha-dzin.* |
| Do. to let out on | ཕོགས་མ་ལ་བཏང་ (གཏོང་) བ་ | *ṕok-ma-la tang-wa.* |
| Do. *hon.* | ཕོགས་གཏོང་གནང་བ་ | *ṕok-tong nang-wa.* |
| Contractor | ཕོགས་འཛིན་པ་ | *ṕok-dzin-pa.* |
| Contradict, to | རྒྱབ་འགལ་བྱེད་པ་ | *gyam-ge cḱe-pa.* |
| Do. *hon.* | ཐུགས་འགལ་གནང་བ་ | *thuk-ge nang-wa.* |
| Contradictory | རྒྱབ་འགལ་ | *gyam-ge.* |
| Contrite, to be | འགྱོད་པ་སྐྱེད་པ་ | *gyö-pa kye-pa.* |
| Do. *hon.* | ཐུགས་འགྱོད་གནང་བ་ | *thung-gyö nang-wa.* |
| Contrition | འགྱོད་པ་ | *gyö-pa.* |
| Do. *kon.* | ཐུགས་འགྱོད་ | *thung-gyö.* |
| Control | དབང་ | *wang.* |
| Do. *hon.* | སྐུ་དབང་ | *ku-wang.* |
| Control, to | དབང་བྱེད་པ་ | *wang-cḱe-pa.* |
| Do. *hon.* | སྐུ་དབང་གནང་བ་ | *ku-wang nang-wa.* |
| Controversy | རྩོད་པ་ | *tsö-pa.* |

| | | |
|---|---|---|
| Convent | ཨ་ནིའི་དགོན་པ་ | *a-ni-i göm-pa.* |
| Conversation | སྐད་ཆ་ | *ke-chha.* |
| Do. *hon.* | གསུང་གྲོས་ | *sung-ťrö.* |
| Converse, to | སྐད་ཆ་བྱེད་པ་ | *ke-chha cȟe-pa.* |
| Do. *hon.* | གསུང་གྲོས་གནང་བ་ | *sung-ťrö nang-wa.* |
| Do. *inf.* to *sup.* | གསུང་གྲོས་ཞུ་བ་ | *sung-ťrö sȟu-wa.* |
| Convex | འབུར་འབུར་ | *bur-bur.* |
| Convey, to | སྐྱེལ་བ་ | *kye-wa.* |
| Do. *hon.* | སྐྱེལ་ར་ (ཟ་) གནང་བ་ | *kye-ra nang-wa.* |
| Convulsions (of baby, etc.) | རྒྱལ་གཟེར་རྒྱབ་པ་ | *ge-śer gyaṕ-pa.* |
| Cook | མ་ཆེན་ | *ma-chhen.* |
| Do. to | བཙོས་པ་ (འཚོད་པ་) | *tsö-pa.* |
| Cookroom | ཐབ་ཚང་ | *thaṕ-tshang.* |
| Do. *hon.* | གསོལ་ཐབ་ | *sö-thaṕ.* |
| Cool | གྲང་མོ། བསིལ་པོ་ | *ťrang-mo ; si-po.* |
| Do. *hon.* | སྐུ་བསིལ་པོ་ | *ku-si-po.* |
| Cooly (labourer) | ཨར་པོ་བ་ | *ar-po.* |
| Cooly (carrier of load) | དོས་པོ་འཁྱེར་མཁན། མི་ཧྲང་ | *ťö-po khyer-khen ; mi-hrang.* |
| Copious | མང་པོ། འབེལ་པོ་ | *mang-po ; be-po.* |
| Copper | ཟངས་ | *śang.* |

| | | |
|---|---|---|
| Coppersmith | ཟངས་བཟོ་བ་ | *śang-śo-wa.* |
| Do. *hon.* | དབུ་མཛེད་ | *um-dze.* |
| Copulate, to | སྦྱོ་བ་ | *gyo-wa.* |
| Copy | དཔེ་ | *pe.* |
| Do. to | དཔེ་ཤུ་བ་ | *pe-shu-wa.* |
| Do. *hon.* | དཔེ་ཤུ་བ་གནང་བ་ | *pe-shu-wa nang-wa.* |
| Copy, true | ངོ་ཤུས་ | *ngo-shü.* |
| Coral | བྱི་རུ་ | *cḱi-ru.* |
| Do. *hon.* | མགུལ་བྱི་ | *gü-cḱi.* |
| Cord | ཐག་པ་ | *thaḱ-pa.* |
| Cork (lid) | ཁ་གཅོད་ | *khaṗ-chö.* |
| Do. *hon.* | ཞལ་གཅོད་ | *śhe-chö.* |
| Corn (grain) | འབྲུ་ | *dru.* |
| Do. *hon.* | ཕྱག་འབྲུ་ | *chhan-dru.* |
| Do. parched | ཡོས་ | *yö.* |
| Do. *hon.* | བཞེས་ཡོས་ | *sḱe-yö.* |
| Corner | ཟུར་ | *śur.* |
| Corporal (in command of 10 men) | བཅུ་དཔོན་ | *chu-pön.* |
| Corpse | རོ་ | *ro.* |
| Do. *hon.* | སྐུ་ཕུང་ (སྐུ་སྤུར་) | *ku-phung.* |

| | | |
|---|---|---|
| Corpulent | རྒྱགས་པ་ | *gyak-pa.* |
| Do. *hon.* | སྐུ་ཤ་འབྱོར་པོ་ | *ku-sha jo-po.* |
| Correct (of words spoken) | སྒྲ་དག་པོ་ | *dra-ťak-po.* |
| Do. (of a thing done) | ཏེན་ལྡན་ | *ten-den.* |
| Do. to (any writing) | ཞུ་དག་བྱེད་པ་ | *sku-ťa cke-pa.* |
| Do. *hon.* | ཞུ་དག་གནང་བ་ | *sku--ťa nang-wa.* |
| Correction | ཞུ་དག་ | *sku-ťa.* |
| Correctly (of words spoken) | སྒྲ་དག་པོ་བྱས་ནས་ | *dra-ťak-po cke-ne.* |
| Do. (of a thing done) | ཏེན་ལྡན་བྱས་ནས་ | *ten-den cke-ne.* |
| Corrupt, to | མེད་པར་བཟོ་བ་ | *me-pa ŝo-wa.* |
| Do. *hon.* | མེད་པར་བཟོ་བ་གནང་བ་ | *me-pa ŝo-wa nang-wa.* |
| Cost | གོང་ | *kong.* |
| Do. *hon.* | ཕྱགས་གོང་ | *ja-kong.* |
| Costly | གོང་ཆེན་པོ་ | *kong-chhem-po.* |
| Do. *hon.* | ཕྱགས་གོང་ཆེན་པོ་ | *ja-kong chhem-po.* |
| Costume | ཆས་ | *chhe.* |
| Cotton | རས་ | *re.* |
| Cotton-cloth | རས་གོས། རས་ཆ་ | *re-kö ; re-chha.* |
| Cotton-thread | རས་སྐུད་ | *re-kü.* |
| Do. *hon.* | ཕྱག་སྐུད་ | *chha-kü.* |

| | | |
|---|---|---|
| Cotton-yarn | སྲིང་ | *sing.* |
| Cotton-wool | སྲིང་བལ་ | *trim-ṕe.* |
| Couch | ཀུབ་ཀྱག། ཁྲིའུ་ཤིང་ | *kuṕ-kya ; thri-u-shing.* |
| Do. *hon.* | ཞབས་ཀྱག་ | *sȟaṕ-kya.* |
| Cough, to | གློ་རྒྱབ་པ་ | *lo-gyaṕ-pa.* |
| Do. *hon.* | མགུལ་གློ་སྐྱོན་པ་ | *gü-lo kyöm-pa.* |
| Counsel | གྲོས་ | *t́rö.* |
| Do. *hon.* | བཀའ་གྲོས་ | *ka-t́rö.* |
| Do. to ask | གྲོས་དྲི་ (འདྲི་) བ་ | *t́rö-t́ri-wa.* |
| Do. *hon.* | བཀའ་གྲོས་གནང་བ་ | *ka-t́rö nang-wa.* |
| Council, Head | བཀའ་ག་ཤགས་ལྷན་རྒྱས་ | *ka-sha hlen-gye.* |
| Count, to | གྲངས་ཀ་རྒྱབ་པ་ | *t́rang-ka gyaṕ-pa.* |
| Do. *hon.* | ཕྱགས་གྲངས་སྐྱོན་པ་ | *ja-t́rang kyöm-pa.* |
| Countenance | གདོང་ | *dong.* |
| Do. *hon* | ཞལ་རས་ | *sȟe-re.* |
| Counterfeit, *adj.* (of coin) | མ་ཕིན་ | *ma-pin.* |
| Do. (of other things) | རྫུས་མ་ | *dzü-ma.* |
| Do. to (of coin) | མ་ཕིན་བཏང་ (གཏོང་) བ་ | *ma-pin tang-wa.* |
| Do. (of other things) | རྫུས་མ་བཏང་ (གཏོང་) བ་ | *dzü-ma tang-wa.* |
| Counting | གྲངས་ཀ་ | *t́rang-ka.* |

| | | |
|---|---|---|
| Counting, *hon.* | ལྗགས་གྲངས་ | *ja-ťrang.* |
| Country | ལུང་པ་ | *lung-pa.* |
| Do. (native land) | སྐྱེ་ས་ | *kye-sa.* |
| Do. *hon.* | འཁྲུང་ས་ | *thrung-sa.* |
| Country (as opposed to town) | གྲོང་སེབ་ | *ťrong-se.* |
| Country-house | གཞི་ཀ་ | *sǩi-ka.* |
| Couple, *s.* (a pair) | ཆ་ | *chha.* |
| Do. (two) | གཉིས། དོ་ | *nyi ; ťo.* |
| Do. a married | ནང་ཚང་གཉིས་ | *nang-tshang-nyi.* |
| Courageous | སྙིང་ཆེན་པོ། བློ་ཁོག་ཆེན་པོ་ | *nying-chhem po ; lo-kho chhem-po.* |
| Do. *hon.* | ཐུགས་སྙིང་ཆེན་པོ། ཐུགས་ཁོག་ཆེན་པོ་ | *thu-nying chhem-po ; thu-kho chhem-po.* |
| Courier | བང་ཆེན་ | *p̌ang-chhen.* |
| Do mounted | ཨ་དྲུང་རྟ་བཞོན་ | *a-trung tap̌-sǩön* |
| Court (of justice) | ཁྲིམས་ཁང་ | *thrim-khang.* |
| Court-yard | སྒོ་ར་ | *go-ra.* |
| Cousin | སྤུན་ཀྱག་ | *pün kya.* |
| Covenant | ཁ་རྟེན། ཁ་ཆད་ | *kha-ten ; kha-chhe.* |
| Do. *hon.* | ཞལ་རྟེན། ཞལ་ཆད་ | *sǩe-ten ; sǩe-chhe.* |
| Cover, *s.* (lid) | ཁ་གཅོད་ | *khap̌-chö.* |

| | | |
|---|---|---|
| Cover, to | བཀབ་པ་ (འགེབས་པ་) | *kaṕ-pa.* |
| Covering | ཁེབས་ | *kheṕ.* |
| Covet, to | ཧམ་པ་བྱེད་པ་ | *ham-pa cḱe-pa.* |
| Do. *hon.* | ཧམ་པ་གནང་བ་ | *ham-pa nang-wa.* |
| Covetous | ཧམ་པ་ཆེན་པོ་ | *ham-pa chhem-po.* |
| Covetousness | ཧམ་པ་ | *ham-pa.* |
| Cow | བ་ | *ṕa.* |
| Do. (of yak) | འབྲི་ | *dri.* |
| Coward | སེམས་ཆུང་ཆུང་ | *sem-chhung-chhung.* |
| Do. *hon.* | ཐུགས་སེམས་ཆུང་ཆུང་ | *thu-sem chhung-chhung.* |
| Cowherd | འབྲོག་པ་ | *drok-pa.* |
| Cowshed | བ་ར་ | *ṕa-ra.* |
| Cowry | འགྲོན་བུ་ | *dröm-ṕu.* |
| Crab | སྡིག་སྲིན་ | *diḱ-sing.* |
| Crack, to, *v.i.* | གས་པ་ (འགས་པ་) | *ḱe-pa.* |
| Do. *hon.* | གས་ (འགས་) པ་གནང་བ་ | *ḱe-pa nang-wa.* |
| Do. a | སེར་ཀ་ | *se-ka.* |
| Crafty | གཡོ་ཆེན་པོ་ | *yo-chhem-po.* |
| Cramp | རྩ་ཁུམ་པ་ | *tsa-khum-pa.* |

| | | |
|---|---|---|
| Crane (bird) | བྱ་ཁྲུང་ཁྲུང་ | *cḱa-thrung-thrung.* |
| Crawl, to | ཁ་བུབ་གོག་པ་ | *kha-ṕu ḱoḱ-pa.* |
| Crazy | སྨྱོན་པ་ | *nyöm-pa.* |
| Cream | སྤྲི་མ་ | *tri-ma.* |
| Do. *hon.* | བཞེས་སྤྲི་ | *sḱe-tri.* |
| Create, to | བཀོད་པ་ | *kö-pa.* |
| Do. *hon.* | བཀོད་པ་གནང་བ་ | *kö-pa nang-wa.* |
| Credible | འོས་པ་ | *ö-pa.* |
| Credit, to | ཡིད་ཆེས་པ་ | *yi-chhe-pa.* |
| Do. *hon.* | ཐུགས་ཡིད་ཆེས་པ་གནང་བ་ | *thu-yi chhe pa nang-wa.* |
| Creditor | བུན་བདག་ | *ṕün-da.* |
| Creed | དད་པ་ | *ťe-pa.* |
| Creek (in a lake) | མཚོ་ལག་ | *tsho-la.* |
| Do. (in a river) | ཆུ་ལག་ | *chhu-la.* |
| Creep, to | ཁ་བུབ་གོག་པ་ | *ḱa-ṕu ḱoḱ-pa.* |
| Crevice | སེར་ཀ་ | *se-ka.* |
| Crime, to commit | ཁྲིམས་འགལ་བ་ | *thrim gel-wa.* |
| Do. *hon.* | བཀའ་ཁྲིམས་འགལ་ར་ (བ་) གནང་བ་ | *ka-thrim ge-ra nang-wa.* |
| Criminal, *adj.* | འཛབ་ཆེན་ | *dzaṕ-chhen.* |

| | | |
|---|---|---|
| Crimson | དམར་པོ་ | *mar-po.* |
| Crippled | རྐང་ཀྱོག་ | *kang-kyo.* |
| Do. *hon.* | ཞབས་ཀྱོག་ | *sḱaṕ-kyo.* |
| Crocodile | ཆུ་སྲིན་ | *chhu-sin.* |
| Crooked (with one bend) | གུག་གུག་ | *ḱu-ḱu.* |
| Do. (with several bends) | ཀྱོག་ཀྱོག་ | *kyo-kyo.* |
| Crop (of corn, etc.) | སྟོན་ཐོག་ | *tön-tho.* |
| Cross, to | རྒལ་བ་ | *gel-wa.* |
| Do. *hon.* | བརྒལ་ནས་ཕེབ་པ་ | *ge-ne phe-pa.* |
| Do. *h. hon.* | བརྒལ་ནས་འཆིབ་རྒྱུ་གནང་བ་ | *ge-ne chhiṕ-gyu nang-wa.* |
| Cross, to be | ཚིག་པ་ཟ་བ་ | *tshiḱ-pa śa-wa.* |
| Do. *hon.* | དགོངས་པ་ཚུང་པ་ | *gong-pa tshung-wa.* |
| Cross of wood (on which criminals are bound) | རྒྱངས་ཤིང་ | *gyang-shing.* |
| Cross-legged | སྐྱིལ་ཀྲུམ་ (སྐྱིལ་ཀྲུང་) | *kyi-trum.* |
| Crow, *s.* | ཁྭ་ཏ་ | *kha-ta.* |
| Do. to (of cock) | བྱ་སྐད་རྒྱབ་པ་ | *cḱa-ke gyaṕ-pa.* |
| Crowd, *s.* | ཚོགས་ | *tshoḱ.* |
| Crown of the head | སྤྱི་གཙུག་ | *chi-tsu.* |
| Do. *hon.* | དབུ་གཙུག་ | *u-tsu.* |

| | | |
|---|---|---|
| Crucify, to | རྒྱངས་ཤིང་ལ་བརྒྱང་ (རྐྱོང་) བ་ | *gyang-shing-la. kyang-wa.* |
| Do. *hon.* | རྒྱངས་ཤིང་ལ་རྐྱོང་ང་ (བ་) གནང་བ་ | *gyang shing la kyong-nga nang-wa.* |
| Cruel, to be | སྙིང་རྗེ་མེད་པ་ | *nying-je me-pa.* |
| Crupper | རྨེད་ | *me.* |
| Crush, to | རྫི་བ་ | *dzi-wa.* |
| Do. *hon.* | རྫི་བ་གནང་བ་ | *dzi-wa nang-wa.* |
| Cry, to (weep) | ངུ་བ་ | *ngu-wa.* |
| Do. *hon.* | ཤུམ་པ་ | *shum-pa.* |
| Crystal | ཤེལ་ | *she.* |
| Cubit | ཁྲུ་ | *thru.* |
| Do. *hon.* | ཕྱག་ཁྲུ་ | *chha-thru.* |
| Cub of fox | ཝ་ཕྲུག་ | *wa-thru.* |
| Do. of bear | དོམ་ཕྲུག་ | *ťem-thru.* |
| Do. of leopard | གཟིག་ཕྲུག་ | *śiḱ-thru.* |
| Do. of tiger | སྟག་ཕྲུག་ | *ta-thru.* |
| Cuckoo | ཁུ་ཡུག་ | *khu-yu.* |
| Culprit | འཛབ་ཆེན་ | *dzaṕ-chhen.* |
| Cultivate, to | ཞིང་ལས་བྱེད་པ་ | *sḱing-le cḱe-pa.* |
| Cultivation | སོ་ནམས་ | *so-nam.* |

| | | |
|---|---|---|
| Cultivator | སོ་ནམས་བྱེད་མཁན་ | *so·nam ck̆e-khen.* |
| Cunning | གཅང་པོ་ | *chang-po.* |
| Do. *hon.* | ཐུགས་གཅང་པོ་ | *thu-chang-po.* |
| Cup (earthen-ware) | དཀར་ཡོལ་ | *ka-yö.* |
| Do. *hon.* | ཞལ་དཀར་ | *sk̆e-ka.* |
| Do. (wooden) | ཕོར་པ་ | *phor-pa.* |
| Do. *hon.* | མཆོད་ཞལ་ | *chhö-sk̆e.* |
| Curds | ཞོ་ | *sk̆o.* |
| Do. *hon.* | གསོལ་ཞོ་ | *sö-sk̆o.* |
| Cure, to | དྲག་པ་བཟོ་བ་ | *ṫrak̆-pa ṡo-wa.* |
| Do. *hon.* | དྲག་པ་བཟོ་བ་གནང་བ་ | *ṫrak̆-pa ṡo-wa nang·wa.* |
| Do. (patient, of good position) | སྐུ་དྭངས་ང་ (བ་) བཟོ་བ་ གནང་བ་ | *ku-ṫang·nga ṡo-wa nang wa.* |
| Cured, to be | དྲག་པ་ | *ṫrak̆-pa.* |
| Do. *hon.* | སྐུ་དྭངས་པ་ | *ku-ṫang·pa.* |
| Curious | ཁྱད་མཚར་པོ་ | *khye-tshar-po.* |
| Curly (of hair) | སུ་ལུ་ | *su-lu.* |
| Current | ཆུ་རྒྱུན་ | *chhu-gyün.* |
| Curse, to | དམོད་མོ་རྒྱབ་པ་ | *mö-mo gyap̆-pa.* |
| Do. *hon.* | དམོད་མོ་སྐྱོན་པ་ | *mö-mo kyöm-pa.* |

| | | |
|---|---|---|
| Curtail, to | ཉུང་རུ་(དུ་) བཏང་ (གཏོང་) བ་ | *nyung-ru tang-wa.* |
| Do. *hon.* | ཉུང་རུ་ (དུ་) གཏོང་ང་ (བ་) གནང་བ་ | *nyung-ru tong-nga nang-wa.* |
| Curtain | ཡོལ་ལ་ (ཡོལ་བ་) | *yö-la.* |
| Do. *hon.* | གཟིམ་ཡོལ་ | *śim-yö.* |
| Curve, to | ཀྱུག་ཀྱུག་བྱེད་པ་ | *ḱuk-ḱu cḱe-pa.* |
| Do. *hon.* | ཀྱུག་ཀྱུག་གནང་བ་ | *ḱuk-ḱu nang-wa.* |
| Curved | ཀྱུག་ཀྱུག་ | *ḱuk-ḱu.* |
| Cushion | གདན་ | *den.* |
| Do. *hon.* | བཞུགས་གདན་ | *sḱu-den.* |
| Cushion (small, placed on chair) | ཁ་གདན་ | *kha-den.* |
| Do. (large, placed on ground) | འབོལ་གདན་ | *bö-den.* |
| Custody (care) | རྩིས་ | *tsi.* |
| Custom (manner) | ལུགས་སྲོལ་ | *luḱ-sö.* |
| Customs (duty) | ཤོ་ཁྲལ་ | *sho-thre.* |
| Cut, *s.* (blow with whip, etc.) | ལྕག་ | *cha.* |
| Do. (wound) | རྨ་ | *ma.* |
| Cut, to | བཅད་པ་ (གཅོད་པ་) | *che-pa* |
| Do. *hon.* | བཅད་ (གཅོད་) པ་གནང་བ་ | *che-pa nang-wa.* |
| Cut, to (by chopping) | བཙབ་པ་ | *tsaṕ-pa.* |

| | | |
|---|---|---|
| Cut, to *hon.* (by chopping) | བཙབ་པ་གནང་བ་ | *tsap-pa nang wa.* |
| Cutch | སྟོད་ཛ་ | *tö-cKa.* |
| Cycle (of 12 years) | ལོ་འཁོར་ | *lo-khor.* |
| Do. (of 60 years) | རབ་བྱུང་ | *rab-cKung.* |
| Cyclone | རླུང་ཚུབ་ | *lung-tshup.* |
| Cylinder | འཁོར་ལོ་ | *khor-lo.* |
| Do. (praying) | མ་ཎི་ | *ma-ni.* |
| Cymbal | རོལ་མོ་ | *rö-mo.* |
| Cypress | ཤུག་པ་ | *shuk-pa.* |

# D

| | | |
|---|---|---|
| Dacoit | ཇག་པ་ | *cḱaḱ-pa.* |
| Dagger | ཨམ་གྲི། མགར་ཟོར་ | *am-t́ri ; ga-śo.* |
| Do. *hon.* | ཕྱག་ཤན་ | *chha-shen.* |
| Daily | ཉི་མ་རྟག་པ་རེ་བཞིན་ | *nyi-ma taḱ-pa ri-sḱi.* |
| Dainty | ཡག་པོ་ | *yaḱ-po.* |
| Dairy-farm | འབྲོག་ས་ | *droḱ sa.* |
| Dalai Lama | སྐྱབས་མགོན་རིན་པོ་ཆེ། རྒྱལ་བ་རིན་པོ་ཆེ་ | *kyam-gön rim-po-chhe.; gya-wa rim-po chhe.* |
| Dale | ཀླུངས་ | *lung.* |
| Dam, *s.* (for water) | ཆུ་རགས་ | *chhu-ra.* |
| Damage | སྐྱོན་ | *kyön.* |
| Do. to | སྐྱོན་བྱེད་པ་ | *kyön-cḱe-pa.* |
| Damp | རློན་པ་ | *löm-pa.* |
| Damsel | བུ་མོ་ | *ṕu-mo.* |
| Do. *hon.* | སྲས་མོ་ | *se-mo* or *tre-mo.* |
| Dance, ordinary | ཞབས་བྲོ་ | *sḱaṕ-ro.* |
| Do. with dramatic entertainment | འཁྲབ་པ་ | *thraṕ-pa.* |
| Do. religious, performed by monks | འཆམ་ | *chham.* |

| | | |
|---|---|---|
| Dance, to | ཞབས་བྲོ་རྒྱབ་པ་ | *skap-ro gyap-pa.* |
| Do. *hon.* | ཞབས་བཞེས་གནང་བ་ | *skap-ske nang-wa.* |
| Dandy (sedan-chair) | འཁྱོགས་དཔྱང་ | *gyo-chang.* |
| Do. *hon.* | ཕེབ་དཔྱང་ | *phe-chang.* |
| Danger | ཉེན་ | *nyen.* |
| Dangerous | ཉེན་ཀ་ཆེན་པོ་ | *nyen-ka chhem-po.* |
| Dare, to | ནུས་པ་ | *nü-pa.* |
| Do. *hon.* | ནུས་པ་གནང་བ་ | *nü-pa nang-wa.* |
| Daring | སྙིང་ཆེན་པོ་ | *nying-chhem-po.* |
| Do. *hon.* | ཐུགས་སྙིང་ཆེན་པོ་ | *thu nying chhem-po.* |
| Dark | ནག་པོ་ | *nak-po.* |
| Do. to become (from clouds) | འཐིབས་པ་ | *thip-pa.* |
| Darkness (of night) | མུན་ནག་ | *min-na.* |
| Darling (favourite) | སྙིང་སྡུག་ | *nying-du.* |
| Darn, to | གྲོག་ (སྒྲོག་) དུག་རྒྱབ་པ་ | *tro-tuk gyap-pa.* |
| Do. *hon.* | གྲོག་ (སྒྲོག་) དུག་སྐྱོར་པ་ | *tro-tuk kyöm-pa.* |
| Dart | མདའ་ | *da.* |
| Do. *hon.* | ཕྱག་མདའ་ | *chhan-da.* |
| Date | ཚེས་པ་ | *tshe-pa.* |
| Daub, to | སྐུ་བ་ | *ku-wa.* |

| | | |
|---|---|---|
| Daub, to *hon.* | སྐུ་བ་གནང་བ་ | *ku-wa nang-wa.* |
| Daughter | བུ་མོ་ | *ṕu-mo.* |
| Do. *hon.* | སྲས་མོ་ | *se-mo.* |
| Daughter-in-law | མནའ་མ་ | *na-ma.* |
| Dawn, *s.* | ནམ་ལངས་ | *nam-lang.* |
| Do. to | ཤར་མདའ་བཏང་ (གཏོང་) བ་ | *shan-da tang-wa.* |
| Day (as opposed to night) | ཉི་མ་ | *nyi-ma.* |
| Do. (of twenty-four hours) | ཞག་པོ་ | *sḱak-po.* |
| Do. *hon.* | བཞུགས་ཞག | *sḱu-sḱa.* |
| Do. (all the day long) | ཉིན་གང་ | *nyin-ḱang.* |
| Day, each | ཉི་མ་རེ་རེ་ | *nyi-ma re-re.* |
| Do. every | ཉི་མ་རྟག་པ་རེ་བཞིན་ | *nyi-ma taḱ-pa ri-sḱi.* |
| Day-break | ནམ་ལངས་ | *nam-lang.* |
| Day after to-morrow | ནངས་ | *nang.* |
| Day before yesterday | ཁའི་ཉི་མ་ | *khe-nyi-ma.* |
| Do. last of a month | གནམ་གང་ | *nam-ḱang.* |
| Dazzling | འོད་ཆེམ་ཆེམ་ | *ö-chhem-chhem.* |
| Dead man (corpse) | རོ་ | *ro.* |
| Do. *hon.* | སྐུ་ཕུང་ | *ku-phung.* |
| Dead, *adj.* (deceased) | ཤི་མཁན་ | *shi-ḱhen.* |

| | | |
|---|---|---|
| Dead, *adj.* (deceased) *hon.* | གྲོངས་མཁན་ | *t́rong-khen.* |
| Do. *h. hon.* | དམ་པ་ | *t́am-pa.* |
| Dead, is | ཤི་སོང་ | *shi-song.* |
| Do. *hon.* | གྲོངས་སོང་ | *t́rong-song.* |
| Do. *h. hon.* | གཤགས་སོང་ (གཤེགས་སོང་) | *sha-song.* |
| Deaf | འོན་པ་ | *öm-pa.* |
| Deal, a great (large quantity) | རྫག་ཏོ་ | *dzaḱ-t́o.* |
| Dealer | ཚོང་པ་ | *tshong-pa.* |
| Do. *hon.* | ཚོང་དཔོན་ལགས་ | *tshong-pön-la.* |
| Dear (expensive) | གོང་ཆེན་པོ། གུས་པོ་ | *ḱong-chhem-po ; ḱü-po.* |
| Do. *hon.* | ཕྱགས་གོང་ཆེན་པོ་ | *ja-ḱong chhem-po.* |
| Dear (beloved) | གཅེས་པོ་ | *che-po.* |
| Debar, to | བཀག་པ་ (འགོགས་པ་) | *kaḱ-pa.* |
| Do. *hon.* | བཀག་ག་ (འགོགས་པ་) གནང་བ་ | *kaḱ-ḱa nang-wa.* |
| Debate, to | རྩོད་པ་རྒྱབ་པ་ | *tsö-pa gyaṕ-pa.* |
| Do. *hon.* | ཐུགས་རྩོད་སྐྱོན་པ་ | *thuḱ-tsö kyöm-pa.* |
| Debt | བུ་ལོན་ | *ṕu-lön.* |
| Do. *hon.* | ཕྱག་བུན་ | *chha-ṕün.* |
| Debtor | བུ་ལོན་ལེན་མཁན་ | *ṕu-lön len-khen.* |

| | | |
|---|---|---|
| Debtor, *hon.* | ཕྱག་བུན་བཞེས་མཁན་ | *chha-ṕun sḱe-khen.* |
| Decapitate, to | སྐེ་བཅད་ (གཅོད་) པ་ | *ḱe-che-pa.* |
| Do. (person of high position) | མགུལ་བཅད་ (གཅོད་) པ་ | *gü-che-pa.* |
| Decay, to | རུལ་བ་ | *rül-wa.* |
| Deceased, the | ཤི་མཁན་ | *shi-khen.* |
| Do. *hon.* | གྲོངས་མཁན་ | *t́rong-khen.* |
| Do. *h. hon.* | དམ་པ་ | *t́am-pa.* |
| Deceit | མགོ་སྐོར་ | *go-kor.* |
| Do. *hon.* | དབུ་སྐོར་ | *u-kor.* |
| Deceitful | གཡོ་ཅན། བློ་སྐྱོགས་སྐྱོགས་ | *yo-chen; lo kyoḱ-kyoḱ.* |
| Do. *hon.* | ཐུགས་གཡོ་ཅན། ཐུགས་སྐྱོགས་སྐྱོགས་ | *thu yo-chen; thu kyoḱ-kyoḱ.* |
| Deceive, to | མགོ་སྐོར་བཏང་ (གཏོང་) བ་ | *go-kor tang-wa.* |
| Do. *hon.* | མགོ་སྐོར་གཏོང་ང་ (བ་) གནང་བ་ | *go-kor tong-nga nang-wa.* |
| Do. *inf.* to *sup.* | དབུ་སྐོར་ཞུ་བ་ | *u-kor sḱu-wa* |
| Deceiver | མགོ་སྐོར་གཏོང་མཁན་ | *go-kor tong-khen.* |
| Decent (becoming) | འོས་པོ་ | *ö-po.* |
| Deception | གཡོ་སྒྱུ་ | *yo-gyu.* |
| Decide, to (judge) | ཐག་བཅད་ (གཅོད་) པ་ | *tha-che-pa.* |

| | | |
|---|---|---|
| Decide, to (judge) *hon.* | ཐག་གཅོད་པ་གནང་བ་ | *tha-chö-pa nang-wa.* |
| Do. *h. hon.* | ཐུགས་ཐག་གཅོད་པ་གནང་བ་ | *thu-tha chö-pa nang-wa.* |
| Decidedly | ཐག་ཆོད་ | *thaḱ-chhö.* |
| Declare, to | བཤད་པ་ (འཆད་པ་) | *she-pa.* |
| Do. *hon.* | གསུང་བ་ | *sung-wa.* |
| Declivity | ཐུར་ | *thur.* |
| Decorate, to | རྒྱན་ཆ་བདགས་ (འདོགས་) པ་ | *gyen-chha taḱ-pa.* |
| Do. *hon.* | སྐུ་རྒྱན་བདགས་ག་ (འདོགས་པ་) གནང་བ་ | *ku-gyen taḱ-ḱa nang-wa.* |
| Decoration | རྒྱན་ཆ་ | *gyen-chha.* |
| Do. *hon.* | སྐུ་རྒྱན་ | *ku-gyen.* |
| Decrease, to (in numbers) | ཉུང་རུ་ (དུ་) ཕྱིན་པ་ | *nyung-ru chhim-pa.* |
| Do. to (in size) | ཆུང་རུ་ (དུ་) ཕྱིན་པ་ | *chhung-ru chhim-pa.* |
| Do. *hon.* | ཆུང་རུ་ (དུ་) ཕེབ་པ་ | *chhung-ru-phe-pa.* |
| Decree (of court of justice) | བཀའ་ཁྲིམས་ | *ka-thrim.* |
| Do. (of secular authority) | བཀའ་ཤོག་ | *ka-sho.* |
| Do. (religious) | ཆོས་ཁྲིམས་ | *chhö-thrim.* |
| Decrepit | འཁོགས་པ་ | *khoḱ-pa.* |
| Dedicate, to | རབ་གནས་བྱེད་པ་ | *ram-ne cḱe-pa.* |
| Do. *hon.* | རབ་གནས་གནང་བ་ | *ram-ne nang-wa.* |

| | | |
|---|---|---|
| Dedication | རབ་གནས་ | *ram-ne.* |
| Deduct, to | འཐྲེན་པ་ | *them-pa.* |
| Do. *hon.* | འཐྲེན་པ་གནང་བ་ | *them-pa nang-wa.* |
| Deed | ལས་ཀ་ | *le-ka.* |
| Do. *hon.* | ཕྱག་ལས་ | *chha-le.* |
| Deep | གཏིང་རིང་པོ་ | *ting-ring-po.* |
| Deer | ཤྭ་ (ཤྭ་བ་) | *sha.* |
| Do. male | ཤྭ་ཕོ་ | *sha-pho.* |
| Do. female | ཤྭ་མོ་ | *sha-mo.* |
| Do. young | ཤྭ་ཕྲུག་ | *sha-thru.* |
| Deface, to | སུབ་པ་ | *sup-pa.* |
| Do. *hon.* | སུབ་པ་གནང་བ་ | *sup-pa nang-wa.* |
| Defamation | སྨད་ར་ | *me-ra.* |
| Defame, to | སྨད་ར་བཏང་ (གཏོང་) བ་ | *me-ra tang-wa.* |
| Do. *hon.* | སྨད་ར་གཏོང་ང་ (བ་) གནང་བ་ | *me-ra tong-nga nang-wa.* |
| Defeat, to | རྒྱལ་བ་ | *gye-wa.* |
| Do. *hon.* | རྒྱལ་ར་ (བ་) གནང་བ | *gye-ra nang-wa.* |
| Defeated, to be | འཕམ་པ་ | *pham-pa.* |
| Do. *hon.* | འཕམ་པ་གནང་བ་ | *pham-pa nang-wa.* |
| Defect | སྐྱོན་ | *kyön.* |

| | | |
|---|---|---|
| **Defective** | སྐྱོན་ཆེན་པོ་ | *kyön-chhem-po.* |
| **Defend, to** | བསྐྱབས་པ་ (སྐྱོབ་པ།) སྐྱོང་བ་ | *kyaṕ-pa ; kyong-wa.* |
| **Do.** *hon.* | སྐྱབས་འཇུག་གནང་བ་ | *kyam-juḱ nang-wa.* |
| **Defendant** | སྐུ་གཏུག་བྱེད་པའི་ཁ་ཐེབ། | *sḱu-tuḱ cḱe-pe khaṕ-the.* |
| **Defer, to** | པ་རུ་བཞག་ (འཛོག་) པ་ | *pa-ru sḱaḱ-pa.* |
| **Do.** *hon.* | པ་རུ་གཞོག་ག་གནང་བ་ | *pa-ru sḱoḱ-ḱa nang-wa.* |
| **Deficient** | ཆད་པ་ | *chhe pa.* |
| **Defile, to** | བཙོག་པ་བཟོ་བ་ | *tsoḱ-pa śo-wa.* |
| **Do.** *hon.* | བཙོག་པ་བཟོ་བ་གནང་བ་ | *tsoḱ-pa śo-wa nang-wa.* |
| **Defilement** | གྲིབ་ | *t́riṕ.* |
| **Define, to** | དོན་དག་བཤད་ (འཆད་) པ་ | *t́ön-t́a she-pa.* |
| **Do.** *hon.* | སྐུ་དོན་གསུང་བ་ | *ku-t́ön sung-wa.* |
| **Definite (certain)** | ངེས་པ། ཏེན་ཏེན་ | *nge-pa ; ten-ten.* |
| **Do.** *hon.* | ཐུགས་ངེས་པ་ | *thu-nge-pa.* |
| **Definitely** | ཏེན་ཏེན་བྱས་ནས་ | *ten-ten cḱe-ne.* |
| **Deformed, to be** | དབང་པོ་མ་ཚང་བ་ | *wang-po ma-tshang-wa.* |
| **Defraud, to** | མགོ་སྐོར་བཏང་ (གཏོང་) བ་ | *go-kor tang-wa.* |
| **Do.** *hon.* | མགོ་སྐོར་གཏོང་ང་ (བ་) གནང་བ་ | *go-kor tong-nga nang-wa.* |
| **Degenerate, to** | ཉམས་པ་ | *nyam-pa.* |

| | | |
|---|---|---|
| Degenerate, to *hon.* | ཐུགས་ཉམས་པ་ | *thu-nyam-pa.* |
| Degrade, to | གོ་གནས་ཕབ་པ་ | *ḱo-ne ṕaṕ-pa.* |
| Degree (series) | རིམ་པ་ | *rim-pa.* |
| Do. (rank) | གོ་གནས་། གོ་ས་ | *ḱo-ne ; ḱo-sa.* |
| Degrees, by | རིམ་བཞིན་ | *rim-sḱin.* |
| Dejected, to be | མི་...དགའ་བ་ | *mi...ga-wa.* |
| Do. *hon.* | མཉེས་པོ་མི་...གནང་བ་ | *nye-po mi... nang-wa.* |
| Do. *h. hon.* | ཐུགས་དགྱེས་པོ་མི་...གནང་བ་ | *thu-gye-po mi ...nang-wa.* |
| Deity | ལྷ་ | *hla.* |
| Delay | འགོར་པོ་ | *gor-po.* |
| Delay, without | འགོར་པོ་མ་བྱེད་པར་ | *gor-po ma-cḱe-par.* |
| Do. *hon.* | ཐུགས་འགོར་མེད་པ་ | *thung-gor me-pa.* |
| Delay, to | འགོར་པོ་བྱེད་པ་ | *gor-po cḱe-pa.* |
| Do. *hon.* | ཐུགས་འགོར་གནང་བ་ | *thung-gor nang-wa.* |
| Delegate | ཚབ་ | *tshaṕ.* |
| Do. *hon.* | སྐུ་ཚབ་ | *ku-tshaṕ.* |
| Delegate, to | ངོ་ཚབ་བཏང་ (གཏོང་) བ་ | *ngo-tshaṕ tang-wa.* |
| Do. *hon.* | སྐུ་ཚབ་གཏོང་ང་ (བ་) གནང་བ་ | *ku-tshaṕ tong-nga nang-wa.* |
| Deliberate, to | གྲོས་བྱེད་པ་ | *ṫrö-cḱe-pa.* |
| Do. *hon.* | བཀའ་གྲོས་གནང་བ་ | *ka-ṫrö nang-wa.* |

| | | |
|---|---|---|
| **Delicate (weak), to be** | ཐང་པོ་མེད་པ་ | *thang-po me-pa.* |
| **Delicious** | ཞིམ་ཐག་ཆོད་ | *sk̄im-thak̄-chhö.* |
| Do. *hon.* | སྦྲོ་ཐག་ཆོད་ | *trö-thak̄-chhö.* |
| **Delight** | དགའ་ཚོར་ | *ga-tshor.* |
| Do. *hon.* | མཉེས་ཚོར་ | *nye-tshor.* |
| **Delight in, to take** | དགའ་བ་ | *ga-wa.* |
| Do. *hon.* | མཉེས་པོ་གནང་བ་ | *nye-po nang-wa.* |
| Do. *h. hon.* | ཐུགས་དགྱེས་པོ་གནང་བ་ | *thu-gye-po nang-wa.* |
| **Deliver, to (rescue)** | བསྐྱབས་པ་ (སྐྱོབ་པ།) སྐྱོང་བ་ | *kyap̄-pa; kyong-wa.* |
| Do. *hon.* | སྐྱབས་འཇུག་གནང་བ་ | *kyam-juk̄ nang wa.* |
| **Deliver, to (give)** | སྤྲད་པ་ | *tre-pa.* |
| Do. *hon.* | གནང་བ་ | *nang-wa.* |
| **Deliverance** | ཐར་པ་ | *thar pa.* |
| **Delude, to** | མགོ་སྐོར་བཏང་ (གཏོང་) བ་ | *go-kor tang-wa.* |
| Do. *hon.* | མགོ་སྐོར་གཏོང་ང་(བ་)གནང་བ་ | *go-kor tong-nga nang-wa.* |
| Do. *inf.* to *sup.* | དབུ་སྐོར་ཞུ་བ་ | *u-kor sk̄u-wa.* |
| **Deluge (flood)** | ཆུ་རུད་ | *chhu-rü.* |
| **Demand, to** | དགོ་ (དགོས་) ཟེར་བ་ | *go-śer-wa.* |
| Do. *hon.* | དགོ་ (དགོས) གསུང་བ་ | *go-sung-wa.* |

| | | |
|---|---|---|
| Demeanour | བྱེད་སྟངས་ | *cḱe-tang.* |
| Do. *hon.* | གནང་སྟངས་ | *nang-tang.* |
| Demented | སྨྱོན་པ་ | *nyöm-pa.* |
| Demi-god | ལྷ་མ་ཡིན་ | *lha-ma-yin.* |
| Demolish, to | བཤིག་པ་ (འཇིག་པ་) | *shiḱ-pa.* |
| Do. *hon.* | བཤིག་ག་ (འཇིག་པ་) གནང་བ་ | *shiḱ-ḱa nang-wa.* |
| Demon | གདོང་འདྲེ། བདུད་ | *dong-dre ; dü.* |
| Den | ཚང་ | *tshang.* |
| Denomination | ཆོས་ལུགས་ | *chhö-lu.* |
| Dense | འཐུག་པོ་ | *thuḱ-po.* |
| Deny, to | རྒྱབ་འགལ་བྱེད་པ་ | *gyam-ge cḱe-pa.* |
| Do. *hon.* | རྒྱབ་འགལ་གནང་བ་ | *gyam-ge nang-wa.* |
| Depart, to | འཐོན་པ་། ཕྱིན་པ་ | *thöm-pa; chhim-pa.* |
| Do. *hon.* | ཕེབ་པ་ | *phe-pa.* |
| Do. *h. hon.* | འཆིབ་རྒྱུ་གནང་བ་ | *chhiṕ-gyu nang-wa.* |
| Departed (deceased) | ཤི་མཁན་ | *shi-khen.* |
| Do. *hon.* | གྲོངས་མཁན་ | *ṫrong-khen.* |
| Do. *h. hon.* | དམ་པ་ | *ṫam-pa.* |
| Depend upon, to | བློས་ (བློ་) བཀལ་བ་ | *lö-kel-wa.* |

| | | |
|---|---|---|
| Depend upon, to *hon.* | ཐུགས་བློ་བཀལ་ར་ (བ་) གནང་བ་ | *thu-lo ke-ra nang-wa.* |
| **Deportment** | བྱེད་སྟངས་ | *cKe-tang.* |
| Do. *hon.* | གནང་སྟངས་ | *nang-tang.* |
| **Deposit, to** | བཞག་པ་ (འཇོག་པ་) | *sKak-pa.* |
| Do. *hon.* | གཞོག་ག་ (འཇོག་པ་) གནང་བ་ | *sKok-ka nang-wa.* |
| **Depositary** | མཛོད་ | *dzö.* |
| **Depraved,** *adj.* | སྡུག་རུལ་ | *duk-rü.* |
| **Deprive, to** | འཕྲོག་པ་ | *throk-pa.* |
| Do. *hon.* | འཕྲོག་ག་ (པ་) གནང་བ་ | *throk-ka nang wa.* |
| **Depth** | གཏིང་རིང་ཐུང་ | *ting-ring-thung.* |
| **Depute, to (send)** | ཚབ་བཏང་ (གཏོང་) བ་ | *tshap-tang-wa.* |
| Do. *hon.* | སྐུ་ཚབ་གཏོང་ང་ (བ་) གནང་བ་ | *ku-tshap tong-nga nang-wa.* |
| **Deputy** | ཚབ་ | *tshap.* |
| Do. *hon.* | སྐུ་ཚབ་ | *ku-tshap.* |
| **Derangement** | སྐྱོན་ | *kyön.* |
| **Descend, to** | བབ་ (འབབ་) ཡོང་བ་ (or འགྲོ་བ་) | *pap-yong-wa* (or *dro-wa*). |
| Do. *hon.* | བབ་ (འབབ་) ཕེབ་པ་ | *pap-phe-pa.* |

| | | |
|---|---|---|
| Descend, to *h. hon.* | བབ་ (འབབ་) འཆིབ་ཀྱུ་ གནང་བ་ | *pap-chhip-gyu nang-wa.* |
| Descendants | རིགས་བརྒྱུད། མི་བརྒྱུད་ | *ri-gyü ; mi-gyü.* |
| Do. *hon.* (of laymen) | སྐུ་བརྒྱུད་ | *ku-gyü.* |
| Do. *hon.* (of lamas) | གདུང་བརྒྱུད་ | *dung-gyü.* |
| Descent | ཐུར་ | *thur.* |
| Describe, to | བཤད་པ་ (འཆད་པ་) | *she-pa.* |
| Do. *hon.* | གསུང་བ་ | *sung-wa.* |
| Desert, *s.* | བྱེ་ཐང་ | *cKe-thang.* |
| Do. to | སྤང་བ་ | *pang-wa.* |
| Do. *hon.* | སྤོང་ང་ (བ) གནང་བ་ | *pong-nga nang-wa.* |
| Deserve, to | འོས་པ་ | *ö-pa.* |
| Design (sketch) | རི་མོ་ | *ri-mo.* |
| Do. (pattern) | དཔེ་ | *pe.* |
| Do. to (sketch, &c.) | རི་མོ་བྲིས་པ་ (འབྲི་བ་) | *ri-mo ťri-pa.* |
| Do. *hon.* | རི་མོ་བྲིས་པ་ (འབྲི་བ་) གནང་བ་ | *ri-mo ťri-pa nang-wa.* |
| Design, to (copy) | དཔེ་བྲིས་པ་ (འབྲི་བ་) | *pe ťri-pa.* |
| Do. *hon.* | དཔེ་བྲིས་པ་ (འབྲི་བ་) གནང་བ་ | *pe ťri-pa nang-wa.* |
| Desire, *s.* | འདོད་པ་ | *dö-pa.* |
| Do. *hon.* | ཐུགས་འདོད་ | *thung-dö.* |

| | | |
|---|---|---|
| Desire, to | འདོད་པ་བྱེད་པ་ | *dö-pa cḱe-pa.* |
| Do. *hon.* | ཐུགས་འདོད་གནང་བ་ | *thung-dö nang-wa.* |
| Desist, to | སྤང་བ་ | *pang-wa.* |
| Do. *hon.* | སྤོང་ང་ (བ) གནང་བ་ | *pong-nga nang-wa.* |
| Despair, to | ཡིད་མུག་པོ་བྱེད་པ་ | *yi-muḱ-po cḱe-pa.* |
| Despatch, to | བཏང་བ་ (གཏོང་བ་) | *tang-wa.* |
| Do. *hon.* | གཏོང་ང་ (བ་) གནང་བ་ | *tong-nga nang-wa.* |
| Desperate, to be (hopeless) | བློ་ (ཁོ་) ཐག་བཅད་ (གཅོད་) པ་ | *lo-tha che-pa.* |
| Despise, to | དམའ་འབེབས་བྱེད་པ་ | *ma-bep̍ cḱe-pa.* |
| Do. *hon.* | དམའ་འབེབས་གནང་བ་ | *ma-bep̍ nang-wa* |
| Do. *inf.* to *sup.* | དམའ་འབེབས་ཞུ་བ་ | *ma-bep̍ sḱu-wa.* |
| Despondent, to be | སེམས་སྐྱོ་བ་ | *sem-kyo-wa.* |
| Do. *hon.* | ཐུགས་སེམས་སྐྱོ་བ་གནང་བ་ | *thu-sem kyo-wa nang-wa.* |
| Destiny (fate) | བསོ་བདེ་ (བསོད་བདེ་) | *so-de.* |
| Do. *hon.* | སྐུ་བསོད་ | *ku-sö.* |
| Destitute | གང་ཡང་མེད་པ་ | *ḱang-yang me-pa.* |
| Destroy, to | མེད་པ་ (པར་) བཟོ་བ་ | *me-pa śo-wa.* |
| Do. *hon.* | མེད་པ་ (པར་) བཟོ་བ་གནང་བ་ | *me-pa śo-wa nang-wa.* |
| Detail, in | ཞིབ་པ་ | *sḱip̍-pa.* |

| | | |
|---|---|---|
| Detailed account | ཐོ་ | *tho.* |
| Do. *hon.* | ཕྱག་ཐོ་ | *chha-tho.* |
| Detain, to | བཀག་པ་ (འགེགས་པ་) | *kak-pa.* |
| Do. *hon.* | བཀག་ག་ (པ་) གནང་བ་ | *kak-ka nang-wa.* |
| Determine, to | ཐག་བཅད་ (གཅོད་) པ་ | *tha-che-pa.* |
| Do. *hon.* | ཐག་གཅོད་པ་གནང་བ་ | *tha-chö pa nang-wa.* |
| Do. *h. hon.* | ཐུགས་ཐག་གཅོད་པ་གནང་བ་ | *thu-tha chö-pa nang-wa.* |
| Detest, to | དགྲ་བྱེད་པ་ | *dra-cke-pa.* |
| Do. *hon.* | དགྲ་གནང་བ་ | *dra nang-wa.* |
| Device | ཇུས་ | *chü.* |
| Do. *hon.* | སྐུ་ཇུས་ | *ku-ckü.* |
| Devil | གདོང་འདྲེ། བདུད་ | *dong-dre ; dü.* |
| Devotee (hermit) | མཚམས་པ། སྒོམ་ཆེན་ | *tsham-pa ; gom-chhen.* |
| Devotion (faith) | དད་པ་ | *te-pa.* |
| Devour, to | ཧ་ཕེ་ཧོ་ཕེ་ (ཧབ་ཧོབ་) ཟ་བ་ | *ha-phe ho-phe sa-wa.* |
| Do. *hon.* | ཧ་ཕེ་ཧོ་ཕེ་ (ཧབ་ཧོབ་) བཞེས་པ་ | *ha-phe ho-phe ske-pa.* |
| Devout | ཆོས་སེམས་ཆེན་པོ་ | *chhö-sem chhem-po.* |
| Dew | ཟིལ་པ་ | *si-pa.* |
| Dexterous | གཅང་པོ་ | *chang-po.* |
| Do. *hon.* | ཐུགས་གཅང་པོ་ | *thu-chang-po.* |

| | | |
|---|---|---|
| Diadem | ཅོད་པན་ | *chö-pen.* |
| Dialect | སྐད་ལུགས་ | *ke-lu.* |
| Diamond | རྡོ་རྗེ་ཕ་ལམ་ | *do-je pha-lam.* |
| Diarrhœa | བཤལ་ནད་ | *she-ne.* |
| Do. to have | འགྲིམ་པ། བཤལ་བ་ | *drim-pa ; she-wa.* |
| Do. *hon.* | འགྲིམ་པ་གནང་བ། བཤལ་ར་ (བ་) གནང་བ་ | *drim-pa nang-wa ; she-ra nang wa.* |
| Dice, to play at | ཤོ་རྒྱབ་པ་ | *sho-gyaṕ-pa.* |
| Do. *hon.* | ཕྱག་ཤོ་སྐྱོན་པ་ | *chha-sho kyöm-pa.* |
| Dictionary | ཚིག་མཛོད་ | *tshiḱ-dzö.* |
| Die, Dice, *s.* | ཤོ་ | *sho.* |
| Do. *hon.* | ཕྱག་ཤོ་ | *chha-sho.* |
| Die, to | ཤི་བ་ | *shi-wa.* |
| Do. *hon.* | གྲོངས་པ་ (འགྲོང་བ་) | *t́rong-pa.* |
| Do. *h. hon.* | གཤགས་པ་ (གཤེགས་པ་) | *shaḱ-pa.* |
| Die, to (of great Lama) | སྐུ་ཞིང་ལ་ཕེབ་པ་ | *ku-sḱing-la phe-pa.* |
| Diet | ཁ་ལག། ལྟོ་ཆས་ | *kha-la ; toṕ-chhe.* |
| Do. *hon.* | ཞལ་ལག་ | *sḱe-la.* |
| Differ, to | ཁྱད་ཡོད་པ་ | *khye yö-pa.* |
| Do. *hon.* | ཐུགས་ཁྱད་ཡོད་པ་ | *thu-khye yö-pa.* |

| | | |
|---|---|---|
| Difference | ཁྱད། ཧེ་བག་ | *khye ; he-p̆a.* |
| Do. *hon.* | ཐུགས་ཁྱད་ | *thu-khye.* |
| Different | མི་གཅིག་པ་ | *mi-chik̆-pa.* |
| Difficult | དཀའ་ལས་ཁག་པོ་ | *ka-le khak̆-po.* |
| Do. *hon.* | སྐུ་མཉེལ་པོ་ | *ku-nye-po.* |
| Dig, to | རྐོ་བ་ | *ko-wa.* |
| Do. *hon.* | རྐོ་བ་གནང་བ་ | *ko-wa nang-wa.* |
| Digest, to | འཇུ་བ་ | *ju-wa.* |
| Do. *hon.* | འཇུ་བ་གནང་བ་ | *ju-wa nang-wa.* |
| Dignity | གོ་ས། གོ་གནས་ | *k̆o-sa ; k̆o-ne.* |
| Dilate, to | ཁ་ཕྱེ་བ་ | *kha-chhe wa.* |
| Dilatory | སྙ་སི་དགུ་སི་ | *nya-si gu-si.* |
| Diligence | སྙིང་རུས་ | *nying-rü.* |
| Do. *hon.* | ཐུགས་རུས་ | *thuk̆-rü.* |
| Diligence, to use | སྙིང་རུས་བྱེད་པ་ | *nying-rü ck̆e-pa.* |
| Do. *hon.* | ཐུགས་རུས་གནང་བ་ | *thuk̆-rü nang-wa.* |
| Diligent | སྙིང་རུས་ཆེན་པོ་ | *nying-rü chhem-po.* |
| Do. *hon.* | ཐུགས་རུས་ཆེན་པོ་ | *thuk̆-rü chhem-po.* |
| Diligently | སྙིང་རུས་བྱས་ནས་ | *nying-rü ck̆e-ne.* |
| Do. *hon.* | ཐུགས་རུས་གནང་ནས་ | *thuk̆-rü nang-ne.* |

| | | |
|---|---|---|
| Dim | སྲབ་སྲིབ་ | *hrap̍-hrip̍.* |
| Dimension | ཆེ་ཆུང་ | *chhe-chhung.* |
| Diminish, to (in number) | ཉུང་རུ་ (དུ་) འགྲོ་བ་ | *nyung-ru dro-wa.* |
| Do. to (in size) | ཆུང་རུ་ (དུ་) འགྲོ་བ་ | *chhung-ru dro-wa.* |
| Do. *hon.* | ཆུང་རུ་ (དུ་) ཕེབ་པ་ | *chhung-ru phe-pa.* |
| Dinner (in evening) | དགོང་མོའི་ཁ་ལག་ | *gong-mö kha-la.* |
| Do. *hon.* | དགོང་མོའི་ཞལ་ལག་ | *gong-mö sḱe-la.* |
| Dip, to (into water, &c.) | བཙུག་པ་ (འཛུག་པ་) | *chuḱ-pa.* |
| Do. *hon.* | བཙུག་ག་ (པ་) གནང་བ་ | *chuḱ-ḱa nang-wa.* |
| Diploma | བཀའ་ཤོག་ | *ka-sho.* |
| Direction | ཕྱོགས་ | *chho.* |
| Directly | ལམ་སང་ | *lam sang.* |
| Dirt | བཙོག་པ་ | *tsoḱ-pa.* |
| Do. *hon.* | སྐུ་བཙོག་ | *ku-tso.* |
| Dirt (mud) | རྫབ་ | *dzap̍.* |
| Dirty | བཙོག་པ་ | *tsoḱ-pa.* |
| Do. to make | བཙོག་པ་བྱེད་པ་ | *tsoḱ-pa cḱe-pa.* |
| Do. *hon.* | སྐུ་བཙོག་གནང་བ་ | *ku-tso nang-wa.* |
| Dirty, to become | བཙོག་པ་ཤོར་བ་ | *tsoḱ-pa shor-wa.* |
| Do. *hon.* | སྐུ་བཙོག་ཤོར་བ་ | *ku-tso shor-wa.* |

| | | |
|---|---|---|
| Disadvantageous, to be | ཕན་ཐོགས་མེད་པ་ | *phen-tho me-pa.* |
| Do. *hon.* | ཐུགས་ཕན་མི་གསོ་བ་ | *thu-phen mi so-wa.* |
| Disagree, to | མི་མཐུན་པ་ | *mi thüm-pa.* |
| Do. *hon.* | མཐུན་པ་མི་གནང་བ་ | *thüm-pa mı nang-wa.* |
| Disappear, to | ཡལ་བ་ | *ye-wa.* |
| Disbelieve, to | ཡིད་མི་ཆེས་པ་ | *yi mi chhe-pa.* |
| Do. *hon.* | ཐུགས་ཡིད་མི་ཆེས་པ་གནང་བ་ | *thu-yi mi chhe-pa nang-wa.* |
| Disc | འཁོར་ལོ་ | *khor-lo.* |
| Discharge, to (dismiss) | དགོངས་པ་སྟེར་བ་ | *gong-pa ter-wa.* |
| Do. *hon.* | དགོངས་པ་གནང་བ་ | *gong-pa nang-wa.* |
| Discharge, to (fire off) | རྒྱབ་པ་ | *gyap-pa.* |
| Do. *hon.* | སྐྱོན་པ་ | *kyöm-pa.* |
| Discharge to (free) | བཏང་བ་ (གཏོང་བ་) | *tang-wa.* |
| Do. *hon.* | གཏོང་ང་ (བ་) གནང་བ་ | *tong-nga nang-wa.* |
| Disciple | ཉེ་གནས་ | *nye-ne.* |
| Discipline | སྒྲིག་ལམ་ | *drik-lam.* |
| Discontented, to be | འདོད་པ་མི་ཁང་བ་ (འཁེངས་པ་) | *dö-pa mi khang wa.* |
| Do. *hon.* | ཐུགས་འདོད་མི་ཁང་བ་ (འཁེངས་པ་) | *thung-dö mi khang-wa.* |

| | | |
|---|---|---|
| Discourse | སྐད་ཆ་ | *ke-chha.* |
| Do. *hon.* | གསུང་གྲོས་ | *sung-ťrö.* |
| Discourse, to | སྐད་ཆ་བྱེད་པ་ | *ke-chha cḱe-pa.* |
| Do. *hon.* | གསུང་གྲོས་གནང་བ་ | *sung-ťrö nang-wa.* |
| Discover, to (see) | མཐོང་བ་ | *thong-wa.* |
| Do. *hon.* | གཟིགས་པ་ | *śi-pa.* |
| Discreet (in speech) | ཁ་བཙན་པོ་ | *kha tsem-po.* |
| Do. *hon.* | ཞལ་བཙན་པོ་ | *sḱe tsem-po.* |
| Discuss, to | རྩོད་པ་རྒྱབ་པ་ | *tsö-pa gyaṕ-pa.* |
| Do. *hon.* | རྩོད་པ་སྐྱོན་པ་ | *tsö-pa kyöm-pa.* |
| Disease | ན་ཚ་ | *na-tsha.* |
| Do. *hon.* | སྙུང་གཞི་ | *nyung-sḱi.* |
| Disgrace | ཞབས་འདྲེན་ | *sḱam-dren.* |
| Disgraced, to be | ཞབས་འདྲེན་ཞུ་བ་ | *sḱam-dren sḱu-wa.* |
| Do. *hon.* | ཞབས་འདྲེན་ཞུ་བ་གནང་བ་ | *sḱam-dren sḱu·wa nang-wa.* |
| Disguised, to be | ཆ་ལུགས་མི་གཅིག་པ་སྤྲད་པ་ | *chha-lu mi-chiḱ-pa tre-pa.* |
| Do. *hon.* | ཆ་ལུགས་མི་གཅིག་པ་བཞེས་པ་ | *chha-lu mi-chiḱ-pa sḱe-pa.* |
| Disgusting | སྐྱུག་བྲོ་པོ་ | *kyuḱ-ťro-po.* |
| Dish | སྡེར་མ་ | *der-ma.* |
| Do. *hon.* | གསོལ་སྡེར་ | *sö-der.* |

| | | |
|---|---|---|
| Disheartened | སེམས་སྐྱོ་པོ་ | *sem-kyo-po.* |
| Disk | འཁོར་ལོ་ | *khor-lo.* |
| Dislike, to | མི་དགའ་བ་ | *mi-ga-wa.* |
| Do. *hon.* | མི་མཉེས་པ་ | *mi-nye-pa.* |
| Dislocate, to (joint) | ཚིགས་སྒྲོག་པ་ | *tshiḱ-throḱ-pa.* |
| Dismantle, to | བཤིག་པ་ (འཇིག་པ་) | *shiḱ-pa.* |
| Do. *hon.* | བཤིག་ག་ (པ་) གནང་བ་ | *shiḱ-ḱa nang-wa.* |
| Dismiss, to (*e.g.*, servant) | དགོངས་འཕྱོག་བཏང་ (གཏོང་) བ། | *gong-pho tang-wa;* |
| | གནས་དབྱུང་བཏང་ (གཏོང་) བ་ | *ne-yung tang-wa.* |
| Do. *hon.* | གནས་དབྱུང་གཏོང་ང་ (བ་) གནང་བ། | *ne-yung tong-nga nang-wa,* |
| | དགོངས་འཕྱོག་གནང་བ་ | *gong-pho nang-wa.* |
| Dismount, to | བབ་པ་ (འབབ་པ་) | *ṕaṕ-pa.* |
| Do. *hon.* | ཆིབས་གཞོལ་གནང་བ་ | *chhiṕ-sḱö nang-wa.* |
| Disobey, to | ཁ་ལ་མི་ཉན་པ་ | *kha-la mi-nyen pa* |
| Do. *hon.* | ཞལ་ལ་མི་གསན་པ་ | *sḱe-la mi-sem-pa.* |
| Disorder | མགོ་དཀྲུག་ | *go-tro.* |
| Dispatch, to | བཏང་བ་ (གཏོང་བ་) | *tang-wa.* |
| Do. *hon.* | གཏོང་ང་ (བ་) གནང་བ་ | *tong-nga nang-wa.* |

| | | |
|---|---|---|
| Dispensary | སྨན་ཁང་ | *men-khang.* |
| Disperse, to, *v.i.* | གྲོལ་བ། གྱེས་པ་ | *t́röl-wa ; ḱye-pa.* |
| Do. *hon.* | ལྷན་རྒྱས་གྲོལ་ར་(བ་) གནང་བ་ | *lhen-gye t́rö-ra nang-wa.* |
| Disposition (temper) | སེམས་ | *sem.* |
| Do. *hon.* | ཐུགས་སེམས་ | *thu-sem.* |
| Disputation | རྩོད་པ་ | *tsö-pa.* |
| Dispute | ལབ་གཞི། རྩོད་པ་ | *laṕ-shi ; tsö-pa.* |
| Do. to | རྩོད་པ་རྒྱབ་བ་ | *tsö-pa gyaṕ-pa.* |
| Do. *hon.* | རྩོད་པ་སྐྱོན་པ་ | *tso-pa ḱyöm-pa.* |
| Disrobe, to | ཕྱིས་པ་ (འབུད་པ་) | *pi-pa.* |
| Do. *hon.* | ཕྱིས་ (འབུད་) པ་གནང་བ་ | *pi-pa nang-wa.* |
| Dissatisfied, to be | འདོད་པ་མི་ཁང་བ་(འཁེངས་པ) | *dö-pa mi-khang-wa.* |
| Do. *hon.* | ཐུགས་འདོད་མི་ཁང་བ་ (འཁེངས་པ་) | *thung-dö mi-khang-wa.* |
| Dissension | སྡེ་དཀྲུག་ | *de-tru.* |
| Dissimilar | མི་གཅིག་པ་ | *mi-chiḱ-pa.* |
| Dissimilarity | ཁྱད་པར་ | *khye-par.* |
| Do. *hon.* | ཐུགས་ཁྱད་ | *thu-khye.* |
| Dissolve, to | བཞུ་བ་ | *sḱu-wa.* |
| Do. *hon.* | བཞུ་བ་གནང་བ་ | *sḱu-wa nang-wa.* |

| | | |
|---|---|---|
| Dissuade, to | སེམས་སྒྱུར་བ་ | *sem-gyur-wa.* |
| Do. *hon.* | ཐུགས་སེམས་སྒྱུར་ར་ (བ་) གནང་བ་ | *thu-sem gyur-ra nang-wa.* |
| Distance | ཐག་རིང་ཐུང་ | *tha-ring-thung.* |
| Do. *hon.* | ཕེབ་ཐག་རིང་ཐུང་ | *pheṕ-tha-ring-thung.* |
| Distant | ཐག་རིང་པོ་ | *tha-ring-po.* |
| Do. *hon.* | ཕེབ་ཐག་རིང་པོ་ | *pheṕ-tha-ring-po.* |
| Distinct (clear) | གསལ་པོ་ | *se-po.* |
| Distinction, to make a | དབྱེན་ (དབྱེ་བ་) ཕྱེ་བ་ | *yen chhe-wa.* |
| Distinction (difference) | ཁྱད་ | *ḱhye.* |
| Do. *hon.* | ཐུགས་ཁྱད་ | *thu-ḱhye.* |
| Distinctly (intelligibly) | སྒྲ་དག་པོ་ | *dra-ťaḱ-po.* |
| Distinguish, to | དབྱེན་ (དབྱེ་བ་) ཕྱེ་བ་ | *yen-chhe-wa.* |
| Do. *hon.* | དབྱེན་ (དབྱེ་བ་) ཕྱེ་བ་གནང་བ་ | *yen-chhe-wa nang-wa.* |
| Distinguished (well-known) | སྐད་གྲགས་ཆེན་པོ་ | *ke-ťra chhem-po.* |
| Do. *hon.* | མཚན་སྙན་གྲགས་ཆེན་པོ་ | *tshen-nyen-ťra chhem-po.* |
| Distress | སྡུག་བསྔལ་ | *du-nge.* |
| Distressed, to be | སེམས་སྡུག་པ་ | *sem-duḱ-pa.* |
| Do. *hon.* | ཐུགས་སེམས་སྡུག་ག་ (པ་) གནང་བ་ | *thu-sem duḱ-ḱa nang-wa.* |

| | | |
|---|---|---|
| Distribute, to | བགོད་པ། བགོ་བཤའ་རྒྱབ་པ་ | *gö-pa ; goṕ-sha gyaṕ-pa.* |
| Do. *hon.* | བགོད་པ་གནང་བ། བགོ་བཤའ་སྐྱོན་པ་ | *gö-pa nang-wa ; goṕ-sha kyöm-pa.* |
| District (tract of country) | ལུང་པ། ཡུལ་ | *lung-pa ; yü.* |
| Do, (jurisdiction of a dzong pön) | རྫོང་ཁག་ | *dzong-kha.* |
| Distrust, to | བློས་མི་ཁེད་པ་ | *lö mi khe-pa.* |
| Do. *hon.* | ཐུགས་བློས་མི་ཁེད་པ་ | *thuk̓-lö mi khe-pa.* |
| Disturbance | རྒྱབ་འདྲེ་ | *gyam-dre.* |
| Do. *hon.* | གསུང་འཁྲུག་ | *sung-thru.* |
| Ditch | ཆུ་དོང་ | *chhu-t́ong.* |
| Dive, to | ཆུའི་གཏིང་ལ་འཛུལ་འགྲོ་བ་ | *chhu-i-ting-la dzü-dro-wa.* |
| Divers (various) | སོ་སོ་ | *so-so.* |
| Divest, to (of clothes) | ཕིས་པ་ (འབུད་པ་) | *pi-pa.* |
| Do. *hon.* | ཕིས་ (འབུད་) པ་གནང་བ་ | *pi-pa nang-wa.* |
| Divide, to | བགོད་པ། བགོ་བཤའ་རྒྱབ་པ་ | *gö-pa ; goṕ-sha gyaṕ-pa.* |
| Do. *hon.* | བགོད་པ་གནང་བ་ | *gö-pa nang-wa.* |
| Divorce, to | ཁ་བྲལ་ (འབྲལ་) བ་ | *kha-t́rel-wa.* |
| Do. *hon.* | ཁ་བྲལ་ར་ (འབྲལ་བ་) གནང་བ་ | *kha-t́re-ra nang-wa.* |
| Divorce money (paid to divorce) | དབྱུག་འཇལ་ | *yuk̓-je.* |
| Dizzy, to be | མགོ་ཡུ་འཁོར་བ་ | *go-yu khor-wa.* |

| | | |
|---|---|---|
| Dizzy, to be *hon.* | དབུ་ཡུ་འཁོར་བ་ | *u-yu khor-wa.* |
| Do, to | བྱེད་པ་ | *cḱe-pa.* |
| Do. *hon.* | གནང་བ་ | *nang-wa.* |
| Do, that will (that is enough) | ད་འགྲིག་ག་ | *t́a-driḱ-ḱa.* |
| Doctor | ཨམ་ཆི་ (ཨེམ་ཆི་) | *am-chhi.* |
| Do. *hon.* | ཨམ་ (ཨེམ་) ཆི་ལགས་ | *am-chhi-la.* |
| Doctrine | ཆོས་ལུགས་ | *chhö-lu.* |
| Document | འཛིན་ | *dzin.* |
| Do. *hon.* | ཕྱག་འཛིན་ | *chha-dzin.* |
| Dog | ཁྱི་ | *khyi.* |
| Do. *hon.* | གཟིམ་ཁྱི་ | *śim-khyi.* |
| Dog (for hunting) | ཤ་ཁྱི་ | *sha-khyi.* |
| Dominion | རྒྱལ་ཁག་ | *gye-kha.* |
| Dominoes, to play at | སྦག་རྒྱབ་པ་ | *ba gyaṕ-pa.* |
| Do. *hon.* | ཕྱག་སྦག་སྐྱོན་པ་ | *chha-ba kyöm-pa.* |
| Donkey | བུང་གུ་ (བོང་བུ་) | *ṕung-gu.* |
| Door | སྒོ་ | *go.* |
| Do. *hon.* | གཟིམ་སྒོ་ | *śim-go.* |
| Door (large outside) | རྒྱལ་སྒོ་ | *gye-go.* |
| Door-frame | སྒོའི་རི་བཞི་ | *gö-riṕ-sḱi.* |

| | | |
|---|---|---|
| Door-keeper | སྒོ་རག་པ་ (སྒོ་སྲུང་པ་) | *go-ra-pa.* |
| Dose (of medicine) | སྨན་ཐུན་ | *men-thün.* |
| Dot | ཚག་ (ཚེག) | *tsha.* |
| Double | གཉིས་ལྡབ་ | *nyi-daṕ.* |
| Doubt | ཐེ་ཚོམ་ | *the-tshom.* |
| Do. to | ཐེ་ཚོམ་ཟ་བ་ | *the-tshom śa-wa.* |
| Do. *hon.* | ཐེ་ཚོམ་གནང་བ་ | *the-tshom nang-wa.* |
| Doubtful | གཉིས་བཟོ་ | *nye-śo.* |
| Dough | སྤགས་ | *pa.* |
| Dove | ཏུད་ཏུད་ཀུ་ཀུ་ | *t́u-t́u ku-ku.* |
| Down | མར་ | *ma.* |
| Down hill | ཐུར་ | *thur.* |
| Down there | མ་གི་ | *ma-gi.* |
| Downwards | མར་ | *ma.* |
| Doze, to | གཉིད་ཙོག་རྒྱབ་པ་ | *nyi-tso gyaṕ-pa.* |
| Do. *hon.* | མཉན་ (མནལ་) ཙོག་སྐྱོན་པ་ | *nye-tso kyöm-pa.* |
| Drag, to | འཐེན་པ་ | *them-pa.* |
| Do. *hon.* | འཐེན་པ་གནང་བ་ | *them-pa nang-wa.* |
| Dragon | འབྲུག་ | *druḱ.* |
| Drain (on ground) | ཡོ་པོ་ (ཡུར་པོ་) | *yo-po.* |

| | | |
|---|---|---|
| Drain (on roof of house) | འོག་ཆུ་ | *o-chhu.* |
| Draw, to (pull) | འཐེན་པ་ | *them-pa.* |
| Do. *hon.* | འཐེན་པ་གནང་བ་ | *them-pa nang-wa.* |
| Draw lots, to | མོ་རྒྱབ་པ་ | *mo-gyaṕ-pa.* |
| Do. *hon.* | ཕྱག་མོ་སྐྱོན་པ་ | *chha-mo kyöm-pa.* |
| Draw up, to (documents &c.) | རྩོམ་པ་ | *tsom-pa.* |
| Do. *hon.* | རྩོམ་པ་གནང་བ་ | *tsom-pa nang-wa.* |
| Do. *h. hon.* | བཀའ་རྩོམ་གནང་བ | *ka-tsom nang-wa.* |
| Draw out, to (in length) | རིང་དུ་བཏང་ (གཏོང་) བ་ | *ring-t́u tang-wa.* |
| Do. *hon.* | རིང་དུ་གཏོང་ང་(བ་)གནང་བ་ | *ring-t́u tong-nga nang-wa.* |
| Draw pictures, to | རི་མོ་བྲིས་པ་ (འབྲི་བ་) | *ri-mo t́ri-pa.* |
| Do. *hon.* | རི་མོ་བྲིས་པ་ (འབྲི་བ་) གནང་བ་ | *ri-mo t́ri-pa nang-wa.* |
| Drawers (in table, &c.) | ཤུར་སྒམ་ (ཤུབས་སྒམ་) | *shur-gam.* |
| Drawers, chest of | སྒམ་ | *gam.* |
| Do. *hon.* | ཕྱག་སྒམ་ | *chha-gam.* |
| Drawers (garment) | གོ་ཐུང་ (གོས་ཐུང་།) དོར་མ་ | *ḱo-thung ; t́o-ma.* |
| Do. *hon.* | ཞབས་ཁྱེན། ཞབས་དོར་ | *sḱaṕ-khyen ; sḱaṕ-t́o.* |
| Dread, to | ཞེད་པ་ | *sḱe-pa.* |
| Do. *hon.* | ཞེད་པ་གནང་བ་ | *sḱe-pa nang-wa.* |

| | | |
|---|---|---|
| Dreadful | ཞེད་སྐྲག་ཚ་པོ་ | *ske-tra tsha-pa.* |
| Dream | གཉིད་ལམ་ | *nyi-lam.* |
| Do. *hon.* | མཉན་ལམ་ (མནལ་ལམ་) | *nye-lam.* |
| Dream, to | གཉིད་ལམ་བཏང་ (གཏོང་) བ་ | *nyi-lam tang-wa.* |
| Do. *hon.* | མཉན་ (མནལ་) ལམ་གཏོང་ང་ (བ་) གནང་བ་ | *nye-lam tong-nga nang-wa.* |
| Dress | དུག་ལོག་ | *tu-lo.* |
| Do. *hon.* | ན་བཟའ་ | *nam-sa.* |
| Dress, to (clothe) | གྱོན་པ་ | *kyöm-pa.* |
| Do. *hon.* | བཞེས་པ་ | *ske-pa.* |
| Dress ostentatiously, to | དང་འདོད་བྱེད་པ་ | *tang-dö chke-pa.* |
| Do. *hon.* | ཐུགས་དང་འདོད་གནང་བ་ | *thu tang-dö nang-wa.* |
| Dried | སྐམ་པོ་ | *kam-po.* |
| Drill, to (soldiers) | དམག་སྦྱོང་བྱེད་པ་ | *ma-jong chke-pa.* |
| Do. *hon.* | དམག་སྦྱོང་གནང་བ་ | *ma-jong nang-wa.* |
| Drink, to | འཐུང་བ་ | *thung-wa.* |
| Do. *hon.* | བཞེས་པ་ | *ske-pa.* |
| Drinking-water | འཐུང་ཡ་གི་ཆུ་ | *thung-ya-ki chhu.* |
| Do. *hon.* | བཞེས་ཡ་གི་ཆབ་ | *ske-ya-ki chhap.* |
| Drip, to (of water) | ཐིགས་པ་རྒྱབ་པ་ | *thik-pa gyap-pa.* |

| | | |
|---|---|---|
| Drive, to (pursue) | དེད་པ་ | *t́e-pa.* |
| Do. *hon.* | དེད་པ་གནང་བ་ | *t́e-pa nang-wa.* |
| Drop | ཐིགས་པ་ | *thiḱ-pa.* |
| Drop, to, *v.t.* | བཏང་བ་ (གཏོང་བ་) | *tang-wa.* |
| Do. *hon.* | གཏོང་ང་ (བ་) གནང་བ་ | *tong-nga nang-wa.* |
| Drop, to *v.i.* | གཟག་པ་ | *śaḱ-pa.* |
| Dropsy, to have | གཟུགས་པོ་ལ་ཆུ་བསགས་ (གསོག་) པ་ | *śuḱ-po-la chhu-saḱ-pa.* |
| Do. *hon.* | སྐུ་གཟུགས་ལ་ཆབ་བསགས་ (གསོག་) པ་ | *ku-śuḱ-la chhaṕ saḱ-pa.* |
| Dross (alloy) | ལྷད་ | *hle.* |
| Drowned, to be | ཆུ་ལ་ཤོར་བ་ | *chhu-la shor-wa.* |
| Do. *hon.* | ཆབ་ལ་ཤོར་ར་ (བ་) གནང་བ་ | *chhaṕ-la shor-ra nang-wa.* |
| Drug | སྨན་ | *men.* |
| Do. *hon.* | གསོལ་སྨན་ | *sö-men.* |
| Drum | རྔ་ | *nga.* |
| Do. *hon.* | ཕྱག་རྔ་ | *chha-nga.* |
| Drum-skin | རྔ་ལྤགས་ | *nga-pa.* |
| Drum-stick | རྔ་ཡོག་ (རྔ་དབྱུགས་) | *nga-yo.* |
| Drunk | ར་བཟི་ | *raṕ-śi.* |

| | | |
|---|---|---|
| Drunk, to be | ར་བཟི་བ་ | *ra-śi-wa.* |
| Do. *hon.* | སྐུ་ར་བྱེད་པ་ | *ku-ra be-pa.* |
| Drunken fit, to quarrel in a | ར་བཟི་བྱེད་པ། ཀྱོང་ཁོང་བྱེད་པ་ | *raṕ-śi cḱe-pa; kyong-khong cḱe-pa.* |
| Do. *hon.* | ར་བཟི་གནང་བ། ཀྱོང་ཁོང་གནང་བ་ | *raṕ-śi nang-wa; kyong-khong nang-wa.* |
| Dry | སྐམ་པོ་ | *kam-po.* |
| Dry to | བསྐམ་པ་ (སྐེམ་པ་) | *kam-pa.* |
| Duck | ཡ་ཚེ་ ch. | *ya-tse.* |
| Dull (stupid) | ལྐུགས་པ། གླེན་པ་ | *kuḱ-pa; lem pa.* |
| Dumb | ཁ་ལྐུགས་པ་ | *kha-kuḱ-pa.* |
| Do. *hon.* | ཞལ་ལྐུགས་པ་ | *sḱe-kuḱ-pa.* |
| Dung (of sheep, goats, mice, etc.) | རིལ་མ་ | *ri-ma.* |
| Do. of horse | རྟའི་སྦངས་ | *te-bang.* |
| Do. of cattle | ལྕུ་བ་ (ལྕི་བ་) | *chu-a.* |
| Do. of human beings. | སྐྱག་པ་ | *kyaḱ-pa.* |
| Dupe, to | མགོ་སྐོར་བཏང་ (གཏོང་) བ་ | *go-kor tang-wa.* |
| Do. *hon.* | མགོ་སྐོར་གཏོང་ང་ (བ་) གནང་བ་ | *go-kor tong-nga nang-wa.* |
| Durable | གྲོག་ཆེན་པོ་ | *tro-chhem-po.* |

| | | |
|---|---|---|
| During | དུས་ལ་ | ťü-la. |
| Dusk | ས་རིབ་ (སྲོད་རུབ་) | sa-riṕ. |
| Dust | ཐལ་ལ་ (ཐལ་བ་) | thel-la. |
| Dust-storm | ཐལ་རླུང་ | the-lung. |
| Duty (tax) | ཞོ་ཁྲལ་ | sho-thre. |
| Dwarf | མི་ཆུང་དེ་ལེབ་ | mi-chhung te-le. |
| Do. *hon.* | སྐུ་གཟུགས་ཆུང་ཆུང་ | ku-śuḱ chhung-chhung. |
| Dwell, to | བསྡད་པ་ (སྡོད་པ་) | de-pa. |
| Do. *hon.* | བཞུགས་པ་ | sḱu-pa. |
| Do. *h. hon.* | བཞུགས་གདན་འཇག་པ་ | sḱu-den jaḱ-pa. |
| Dweller | སྡོད་མཁན་ | dö-khen. |
| Do. *hon.* | བཞུགས་མཁན་ | sḱu-khen. |
| Do. *h. hon.* | བཞུགས་གདན་འཇག་མཁན་ | sḱu-den ja-khen. |
| Dwelling, *s.* | ཁང་པ། ནང་། སྡོད་ས་ | khang-pa ; nang ; dö-sa. |
| Do. *hon.* | གཟིམ་ཁང་། བཞུགས་ས་ | śim-khang ; sḱuḱ-sa. |
| Do. *h. hon.* | གཟིམ་ཤག། བཞུགས་གདན་འཇག་ས་ | śim-sha ; sḱu-den ja-sa. |
| Dwindle, to (in size) | ཆུང་རུ་ (དུ་) འགྲོ་བ་ | chhung-ru dro-wa. |
| Do. *hon.* | ཆུང་རུ་ (དུ་) ཕེབ་པ་ | chhung-ru phe-pa. |
| Dwindle, to (in numbers) | ཉུང་རུ་ (དུ་) འགྲོ་བ་ | nyung-ru dro-wa. |

| | | |
|---|---|---|
| **Dye** | ཚོས་ | *tshö.* |
| **Do. red lac** | རྒྱ་ཚོས་ | *gya-tshö.* |
| **Dye, to** | ཚོས་རྒྱབ་པ་ | *tshö-gyap-pa.* |
| **Do.** *hon.* | ཚོས་སྐྱོན་པ་ | *tshö-kyöm-pa.* |
| **Dynasty** | རྒྱལ་བརྒྱུད་ | *gye-gyü.* |
| **Dysentery** | འཁྲུ་ནད་ | *thru-ne.* |
| **Dyspepsia** | ལྟོ་མ་འཇུ་བའི་ནད་ | *to ma-ju-we ne.* |

# E

| | | |
|---|---|---|
| Each | རེ་རེ་ | *re-re.* |
| Eager | སྙིང་འདོད་པོ། སྙིང་སྤྲོ་པོ་ | *nying-dö-po ; nying-t́ro-po.* |
| Eager to do | བྱེད་སྙིང་འདོད་པོ་ | *cḱe nying dö-po.* |
| Eager to go | འགྲོ་སྙིང་འདོད་པོ་ | *dro-nying dö-po.* |
| Eagle | གོ་བོ་ | *ḱo-wo.* |
| Ear | ཨམ་མཆོག་ (རྣ་མཆོག་) | *am-chho.* |
| Do. *hon.* | སྙན་མཆོག་ | *nyen-chho.* |
| Ear-hole | ཨམ་མཆོག་ (རྣ་མཆོག་) གི་ཨི་ཁུང་ | *am-chho-ḱi i-khung.* |
| Do. *hon.* | སྙན་མཆོག་གི་ཨི་ཁུང་ | *nyen-chho-ḱi i-khung.* |
| Ear of corn | སྙེ་མ་ | *nye-ma.* |
| Early (in morning) | སྔ་པོ་ | *nga-po.* |
| Earnest, *adj.* | སྙིང་རུས་ཆེན་པོ་ | *nying-rü chhem-po.* |
| Do. *hon.* | ཐུགས་རུས་ཆེན་པོ་ | *thu-rü chhem-po.* |
| Earnestly | སྙིང་རུས་བྱས་ནས་ | *nying-rü cḱe-ne.* |
| Earring (man's) | སོ་བྱིས་ (སོ་གོང་) | *so-cḱi.* |
| Do. *hon.* | སྙན་བྱིས་ | *nyen-cḱi.* |
| Earring (woman's) | ཨལ་སྐོར་ | *e-kor.* |
| Do. *hon.* | སྙན་སྐོར་ | *nyen-kor.* |

| | | |
|---|---|---|
| Earring (of turquoises) | གཟི་གཡུ་ | *sí-yu.* |
| Do. *hon.* | སྙན་གཡུ་ | *nye-yu.* |
| Earth | ས་ | *sa.* |
| Earthen vessel | ཁོག་མ་ | *kho-ma.* |
| Do. *hon.* | བཞེས་ཁོག་ | *sḱe-kho.* |
| Earthenware | རྫ་སྣོད་ | *dza-nö.* |
| Earthquake | ས་གཡོས་ (ས་གཡོས།) ས་འགུལ་ | *sa-yom ; sa-gü.* |
| Earth-work | ས་ལས་ | *sap-le.* |
| Easily | ལས་སླ་པོ་ | *le·la-po.* |
| East | ཤར་ | *shar.* |
| Easy | ལས་སླ་པོ་ | *le-la-po.* |
| Eat, to | ཟ་བ་ | *śa-wa.* |
| Do. *hon.* | བཞེས་པ་ | *sḱe-pa.* |
| Eating-house | ཟ་ཁང་ | *śa-khang.* |
| Echo | བ་ཆ་ (བྲག་ཆ་) | *ṕa-chha.* |
| Do. to | བ་ཆ་ (བྲག་ཆ་) འཁོར་བ་ | *pa-chha khor-wa.* |
| Eclipse of the moon | ཟླ་འཛིན་ | *dan-dzin.* |
| Do. of the sun | ཉིན་འཛིན་ | *nyin-dzin.* |
| Edict | བཀའ་རྒྱ་ | *ka-gya.* |

| | | |
|---|---|---|
| Edge (of knife, etc.) | ངོ་ | *ngo.* |
| Do. (of land, water, etc.) | རྩར། འགྲམ་ | *tsa ; dram.* |
| Do. (of table, etc.) | ཟུར་ | *śur.* |
| Edged | རྣོ་པོ་ | *no-po.* |
| Edible, to be | ཟ་ཉན་པ་ | *śa-nyem-pa.* |
| Do. *hon.* | མཆོད་ཉན་པ་ | *chhö-nyem-pa.* |
| Editor | རྩོམ་པ་རྒྱབ་མཁན་ | *tsom-pa gyaṕ-khen.* |
| Educate, to | ཡི་གེ་བསླབས་ (སློབ་) པ། སྦྱོང་དར་སྤྲད་པ་ | *yi-ge laṕ-pa ; jong-ťar tre-pa.* |
| Do. *hon.* | ཕྱག་བྲིས་བསླབས་ (སློབ་) པ་གནང་བ་ | *chha-ri laṕ-pa nang-wa.* |
| Efface, to | སུབ་པ་ | *suṕ-pa.* |
| Do. *hon.* | སུབ་པ་གནང་བ་ | *suṕ-pa nang-wa.* |
| Effect, to (perform) | བྱེད་པ་ | *cḱe-pa.* |
| Do. *hon.* | གནང་བ་ | *nang-wa.* |
| Effects (goods) | ཅ་ལག་ (ཆ་ལག་) | *cha-la.* |
| Do. *hon.* | སྐུ་ཅས་ (སྐུ་ཆས་) | *ku-che.* |
| Effort | བརྩོན་འགྲུས་ | *tsön-drü.* |
| Effort, to make an | བརྩོན་འགྲུས་བྱེད་པ་ | *tsön-drü cḱe-pa.* |
| Do. *hon.* | ཐུགས་བརྩོན་གནང་བ་ | *thuḱ-tsön nang-wa.* |

| | | |
|---|---|---|
| Egg | སྒོ་ང་ | *go-nga.* |
| Do. *hon.* | བཞེས་སྒོང་ | *śe-gong.* |
| Egg, white of an | དཀར་སྤྲིན་ | *kar-trin.* |
| Eggs, to lay | སྒོ་ང་བཏང་ (གཏོང་) བ་ | *go-nga tang-wa.* |
| Eight | བརྒྱད་ | *gye.* |
| Eighteen | བཅོ་བརྒྱད་ | *choṕ-gye.* |
| Eighteenth | བཅོ་བརྒྱད་པ་ | *choṕ-gye-pa-* |
| Eighth | བརྒྱད་པ་ | *gye-pa.* |
| Eightieth | བརྒྱད་བཅུ་པ་ | *gye-chu-pa.* |
| Eighty | བརྒྱད་བཅུ་ | *gye-chu.* |
| Either, *conj.* | ཡང་མིན་ན། ཡང་ན་ | *yang-men-na ; yang-na.* |
| Eject to | བཏོན་པ་ (འདོན་པ་) | *töm-pa.* |
| Do. *hon.* | བཏོན་ (འདོན་) པ་གནང་བ་ | *töm-pa nang-wa.* |
| Elbow | གྲུ་མོ་ | *t́re-mo.* |
| Elder, *adj.* | རྒན་པ་ | *gem-pa.* |
| Elder brother | ཇོ་ཇོ་ | *ćo-ćo.* |
| Do. *hon.* | ཇོ་ལགས་ | *ćo-la.* |
| Eldest | རྒན་ཤོས་ | *gen-shö.* |
| Do. *hon.* | བགྲེས་ཤོས་ | *dre-shö.* |
| Elect, to (appoint) | སྐོ་བ་ | *ko-wa.* |

| | | |
|---|---|---|
| Elect, to (appoint) *hon.* | སྐོ་བ་གནང་བ་ | *ko-wa-nang-wa.* |
| Electric light | གློག་ཤུ་ | *loǩ-sǩu.* |
| Elegant | འདྲ་ཆགས་པོ་ | *dra-chhaǩ-po.* |
| Element (fire, earth, etc.) | འབྱུང་བ་ | *jung-wa.* |
| Elephant | གླང་པོ་ཆེ། གླང་ཆེན་ | *lang-po-chhe; lang-chhen.* |
| Elevation | མཐོ་དམན་ | *tho-men.* |
| Eleven | བཅུ་གཅིག་ | *chuǩ-chi.* |
| Eleventh | བཅུ་གཅིག་པ་ | *chuǩ-chi-pa.* |
| Else | དེ་མིན་ན་ | *ťe-min-na.* |
| Elsewhere | གཞན་པ་ | *sǩem-pa.* |
| Embarrassed, to be | མགོ་འཐོམས་པ་ | *go-thom-pa.* |
| Do. *hon.* | དབུ་འཐོམས་པ་ | *u-thom-pa.* |
| Ember | མེ་མདག་ | *men da.* |
| Emblem | རྟགས་ | *ta.* |
| Embrace, to | འཁྱུད་པ་ | *khyü-pa.* |
| Do. *hon.* | འཁྱུད་པ་གནང་བ་ | *khyü-pa nang wa.* |
| Embroidery | ཀྱིང་ཁབ་ (ཀྱིང་ཁེབས་) | *kying-khap̌.* |
| Do. gold | ཟར་བབས་ | *śur-p̌ap̌.* |
| Do. best quality | རྒྱ་གསེར་ | *gya-ser.* |
| Emerald | མ་རྐད་ | *ma-ge.* |

| | | |
|---|---|---|
| Emetic | སྐྱུག་སྨན་ | *kyuǩ-men.* |
| Eminence, *s.* | སྒང་། རྩེ་ | *gang ; tse.* |
| Eminent, *adj.* | སྐད་གྲགས་ཆེན་པོ་ | *ke-ťra chhem-po.* |
| Do. *hon.* | སྙན་གྲགས་ཆེན་པོ་ | *nyen-ťra Chhem-po.* |
| Emperor | རྒྱལ་པོ་ | *gye-po.* |
| Do. of China | རྒྱ་ནག་གོང་མ་ | *gya-na ǩong-ma.* |
| Emperor's administration | རྒྱལ་སྲིད་ | *gye-si.* |
| Empire | རྒྱལ་ཁམས་ | *gyeng-kham.* |
| Employ, to | སྐོ་བ་ | *ko-wa.* |
| Do. *hon.* | སྐོ་བ་གནང་བ་ | *ǩo-wa nang-wa.* |
| Employ, to (servant) | བཞག་པ་ (འཇོག་པ་) | *sǩaǩ-pa.* |
| Do. *hon.* | གཞོག་ག་ (པ་) གནང་བ་ | *sǩoǩ-ǩa nang-wa.* |
| Employment | ལས་ཀ་ | *le-ka.* |
| Do. *hon.* | ཕྱག་ལས་ | *chha-le.* |
| Empty, *adj.* | སྟོང་པ་ | *tong-pa.* |
| Do. to | སྟོང་པ་བཟོ་བ་ | *tong-pa śo-wa.* |
| Do. *hon.* | སྟོང་པ་བཟོ་བ་གནང་བ་ | *tong-pa śo-wa nang-wa.* |
| Enabled, to be | ཐུབ་པ་ | *thuṕ-pa.* |
| Do. *hon.* | ཐུབ་པ་གནང་བ་ | *thuṕ-pa nang-wa.* |
| Enamelware | གུ་གུ་ཤ་ | *ǩu-ǩu-sha.* |

| | | |
|---|---|---|
| Encamp, to | སྒར་རྒྱབ་པ་ | *gar-gyaṕ-pa.* |
| Do. *hon.* | སྒར་སྐྱོན་པ་ | *gar-kyöm-pa.* |
| Encampment | སྒར་ | *gar.* |
| Encircle, to | སྐོར་བ་ | *kor-wa.* |
| Do. *hon.* | སྐོར་ར་ (བ་) གནང་བ་ | *kor-ra nang-wa.* |
| Enclosure (fence) | ར་བ་ | *ra-wa.* |
| Encounter, to (meet) | ཐུག་པ་ | *thuḱ-pa.* |
| Do. *inf.* meeting *sup.* | མཇལ་བ་ | *jel-wa.* |
| Encourage, to | བློ་ཁོག་ཆེ་རུ་བཏང་ (གཏོང་) བ་ | *lo-kho chhe-ru tang-wa.* |
| Do. *hon.* | བློ་ཁོག་ཆེ་རུ་གཏོང་ང་ (བ་) གནང་བ་ | *lo-kho chhe-ru tong-nga nang-wa.* |
| End | མཐའ་ | *tha.* |
| Do. to be at an (consumed) | རྫོགས་པ་ | *dzoḱ-pa.* |
| Do. to be at an (accomplished) | འཚར་བ་ | *tshar-wa.* |
| Endeavour, to | བརྩོན་འགྲུས་བྱེད་པ་ | *tsön-drü cḱe-pa.* |
| Do. *hon.* | ཐུགས་བརྩོན་གནང་བ་ | *thu-tsön nang-wa.* |
| Endless | རྫོགས་རྒྱུ་མེད་པ་ | *dzo-gyu me-pa.* |
| Endure, to, *v.t.* | བཟོད་པ་སྒོམ་པ་ | *śö-pa gom-pa.* |
| Do. *hon.* | བཟོད་པ་སྒོམ་པ་གནང་བ་ | *śö-pa gom-pa nang-wa.* |
| Enemy. | དགྲ་ | *dra.* |

| | | |
|---|---|---|
| Energetic | བརྩོན་པོ། སྙིང་རུས་ཆེན་པོ་ | *tsöm-po ; nying-rü chhem-po.* |
| Do. *hon.* | ཐུགས་རུས་ཆེན་པོ་ | *thuḱ-rü chhem-po.* |
| Engage on hire, to | གླ་པ་ | *la-pa.* |
| Do. *hon.* | གླ་གནང་བ་ | *la nang-wa.* |
| Enhance, to | འཕར་བ་ | *phar-wa.* |
| Enjoin, to | བཀའ་གནང་བ་ | *ka-nang-wa.* |
| Enough, to be | འགྲིག་པ་ | *driḱ-pa.* |
| Enjoy, to | སྐྱིད་པོ་བྱེད་པ་ | *kyi-po cḱe-pa.* |
| Do. *hon.* | སྤྲོ་པོ་གནང་བ་ | *tro-po nang-wa.* |
| Enlarge, to | ཆེ་རུ་བཏང་ (གཏོང་) བ་ | *chhe-ru tang-wa.* |
| Do. *hon.* | ཆེ་རུ་གཏོང་ང་ (བ་) གནང་བ་ | *chhe-ru tong-nga-nang-wa.* |
| Enmity | གདིང་ནད་ | *ting-ne.* |
| Enormous | ཆེ་ཐག་ཆོད་ | *chhe-thaḱ-chhö.* |
| Enquire, to (ask) | དྲི་བ་ (འདྲི་བ་) | *ṫri-wa.* |
| Do. *hon.* | བཀའ་འདྲི་གནང་བ་ | *kan-dri nang-wa.* |
| Enquire, to (investigate) | ཞིབ་དཔྱོད་བྱེད་པ་ | *sḱip-chö cḱe-pa.* |
| Do. *hon.* | ཞིབ་དཔྱོད་གནང་བ་ | *sḱip-chö nang-wa.* |
| Do. *h. hon.* | བཀའ་ཞིབ་གནང་བ་ | *ka-sḱip nang-wa.* |
| Ensnare, to | རྙི་བཙུགས་ (འཛུགས་) པ་ | *nyi-tsuḱ-pa.* |

| | | |
|---|---|---|
| Ensnare, to *hon.* | རྙི་བཙུགས་ཀ་ (འཛུགས་པ་) གནང་བ་ | *nyi-tsuk-ka nang-wa.* |
| Enter, to | འཛུལ་བ་ | *dzü-wa.* |
| Do. *hon.* | ཕེབ་པ་ | *phe-pa.* |
| Do. *h. hon.* | འཆིབ་རྒྱུ་གནང་བ་ | *chhip-gyu nang-wa.* |
| Entertainment (feast) | མགྲོན་པོ་ | *dröm-po.* |
| Do. *hon.* | ཐུགས་སྤྲོ་ | *thu-tro.* |
| Entice, to | སླུ་བ་ | *lu-wa.* |
| Do. *hon.* | སླུ་བ་གནང་བ་ | *lu-wa nang-wa.* |
| Entire | ཚང་མ། ཐམས་ཅད། སྒང་ཁ་ | *tshang-ma ; tham che ; gang-kha.* |
| Entirely | ཐད་དེ་ | *be-te.* |
| Entomb, to | ས་སྦིད་བཏང་ (གཏོང་) བ་ | *sa-be tang-wa.* |
| Do. *hon.* | ས་སྦིད་གཏོང་ང་ (བ་) གནང་བ་ | *sa-be tong-nga nang-wa.* |
| Entrails | རྒྱུ་མ་ | *gyu-ma.* |
| Do. *hon.* | སྐུ་རྒྱུ་ | *ku gyu.* |
| Entreat, to | ཞུ་བ་ | *sku-wa.* |
| Entrust, to | བཅོལ་ (འཆོལ་) གཞོག་ (འཇོག་) པ་ | *chö-skok-pa.* |
| Do. *hon.* | བཅོལ་ (འཆོལ་) གཞོག་ཀ་ (འཇོག་པ་) གནང་བ་ | *chö-skok-ka nang-wa.* |

| | | |
|---|---|---|
| Envelope (Tibetan) | རྒྱ་མ་ | *gya-ma.* |
| Do. (English) | ཡིག་ཤུབས་ | *yiǩ-shuṕ.* |
| Envious | ཕྲ་དོག་ཚ་པོ་ | *thra-ťo tsha-po.* |
| Envoy | ཕོ་ཉ་ | *pho-nya.* |
| Envy, *s* | ཕྲ་དོག་ | *thra-ťo.* |
| Envy, to | ཕྲ་དོག་བྱེད་པ་ | *thra-ťo cǩe-pa.* |
| Do. *hon.* | ཕྲ་དོག་གནང་བ་ | *thra-ťo nang-wa.* |
| Epilepsy | གཟའ་ནད་ | *śa-ne.* |
| Epistle | ཡི་གེ་ | *yi-ge.* |
| Do. *hon.* | ཕྱག་བྲིས་ | *chha-ri.* |
| Equal | གཅིག་པ། འདྲ་འདྲ་ | *chiǩ-pa ; dran-dra.* |
| Equitable | འདྲ་དྲང་ | *dra-ťrang.* |
| Erase, to | སྤུབ་པ་ | *suṕ-pa.* |
| Do. *hon.* | སྤུབ་པ་གནང་བ་ | *suṕ-pa nang-wa.* |
| Erect | ཀྱེ་རེ་ | *kye-re.* |
| Do. to stand | ཀྱེ་རེ་ལང་བསྡད་ (སྡོད་) པ་ | *kye-re lang-de-pa.* |
| Do. *hon.* | ཀྱེ་རེ་བཞང་(བཞེང་)བཞུགས་པ་ | *kye-re sǩang-sǩu-pa.* |
| Erect, to (build) | རྩིག་པ་ | *tsiǩ-pa.* |
| Do. *hon.* | རྩིག་ག་ (པ་) གནང་བ་ | *tsiǩ-ǩa nang-wa.* |
| Err, to | ནོར་བ་ | *nor-wa.* |

| | | |
|---|---|---|
| Err, to *hon.* | ནོར་ར་ (བ་) གནང་བ་ | *nor-ra nang-wa.* |
| Error | ནོར་ | *nor.* |
| Eruption (on skin) | བྲ་ཚ་ (བྲ་པ་) | *ba-tsha.* |
| Escape, to | ཤོར་བ་ | *shor-wa.* |
| Escort, *s.* | སྐུ་སྲུང་། | *ku-sung.* |
| | དཔུང་རོགས་ | *pung-ro.* |
| Do. to | དཔུང་རོགས་འཁྲིད་པ་ | *pung-ro thri-pa.* |
| Do. *hon.* | དཔུང་རོགས་འཁྲིད་པ་གནང་བ་ | *pung-ro thri-pa nang-wa.* |
| Do. to (of person in superior position) | སྐུ་སྲུང་འཁྲིད་པ་གནང་བ་ | *ku-sung thri-pa nang-wa.* |
| Especially | ཁྱད་པར་དུ་ | *khye par-t́u.* |
| Eternal | རྫོགས་རྒྱུ་་་མེད་པ། མཐའ་མེད་པ་ | *dzo-gyu-me-pa; tha-me-pa.* |
| Europe | ཕྱི་གླིང་ | *chhi-ling.* |
| European, *adj.* | ཕྱི་གླིང་གི་ | *chhi ling-ḱi.* |
| Do. (a man) | ཕྱི་གླིང་གི་མི་ | *chhi-ling-ḱi-mi.* |
| Evaporate, to | ཡལ་བ་ | *ye-wa.* |
| Even, *adj.* (level) | སྙོམས་པོ་ | *nyom-po.* |
| Even, *adv.* | ཡང་ | *yang.* |
| Evening | དགོང་མོ་ | *gong-mo.* |
| Do. this | དེ་དགོང་ | *t́o-gong.* |

| | | |
|---|---|---|
| **Evenly balanced, to be** | ཡང་ལྗི་མེད་པ་ | *yang-ji me-pa.* |
| **Events, at all** | གང་ཨིན་ཀྱང་། ག་རེ་ཡིན་རུང་ | *ḱang-yin-kyang; ḱa-re yin-rung.* |
| **Ever** (always) | ནམ་རྒྱུན། དུས་རྒྱུན། རྟག་པ་རེ་བཞིན་ | *nam-gyün; ťü-gyün; taḱ-pa re-sḱi.* |
| **Everlasting** | ཛོགས་རྒྱུ་····མེད་པ། མཐའ་མེད་པ་ | *dzo-gyu me-pa; tha-me-pa.* |
| **Every** | རེ་རེ་ | *re-re.* |
| **Everybody** | མི་སྒང་ཁ་ | *mi gang-kha.* |
| **Every day** | ཞག་མ་རེ་རེ་ | *sḱa-ma re-re.* |
| **Every kind** | སྣ་ཚོགས་ | *na-tsho.* |
| **Everywhere** | ག་ས་ག་ལ་ | *ḱa sa ḱa-la.* |
| **Evidence** | རྒྱུ་མཚན་ | *gyum-tshen.* |
| **Evident** | ངེས་པ། དངོས་ནས་ | *nge-par; ngön-ne.* |
| **Evil** | ངན་པ་ | *ngen-pa.* |
| **Evil** spirit | འདྲེ་ | *dre.* |
| **Exact** | ཁྲིག་ཁྲིག་ | *thriḱ-thri.* |
| **Exactly** | རང་ | *rang.* |
| **Exactly** so | ད་ག་རེད་ | *ťa-ḱa-re.* |
| **Do.** *hon.* | ད་ག་རང་རེད་ | *ťa-ḱa rang-re.* |
| **Do.** *h. hon.* | བཀའ་གནང་རང་རེད་ | *ka-nang rang-re.* |

| | | |
|---|---|---|
| Exaggerate, to | སྐད་ཆ་སྒྲོ་འདོགས་པ་ | *ke-chha dro-doḱ-pa.* |
| Exalt, to | མཐོ་ས་སྐྱེལ་བ་ | *tho-sa kyel-wa.* |
| Do *hon.* | མཐོ་ས་སྐྱེལ་ར་ (བ་) གནང་བ་ | *tho-sa kye-ra nang-wa.* |
| Examination (of student) | རྒྱུགས་ | *gyuḱ.* |
| Do. (investigation) | ཞིབ་དཔྱོད་ | *sḱiṕ-chö.* |
| Do. *hon.* | བཀའ་ཞིབ་ | *ka-sḱiṕ.* |
| Examine, to (student) | རྒྱུགས་ལེན་པ་ | *gyuḱ-lem-pa.* |
| Do. *hon.* | རྒྱུགས་བཞེས་པ་ | *gyuḱ-sḱe pa.* |
| Examine, to (investigate) | ཞིབ་དཔྱོད་བྱེད་པ་ | *sḱiṕ-chö cḱe-pa.* |
| Do. *hon.* | ཞིབ་དཔྱོད་གནང་བ་ | *sḱiṕ-chö nang-wa.* |
| Do. *h. hon.* | བཀའ་ཞིབ་གནང་བ་ | *ka sḱiṕ nang-wa.* |
| Examined, to be (student) | རྒྱུགས་ཕུལ་ (འབུལ་) བ་ | *gyuḱ-phül-wa.* |
| Example | དཔེ་ | *pe.* |
| Example, for | དཔེ་ན་ཡིན་ན། དཔེ་ན་ (དཔེར་ན་) | *pe-na yin-na ; pe-na.* |
| Excavation | དོང་ | *ťong.* |
| Excavate, to | རྐོ་བ་ | *ko-wa.* |
| Do. *hon.* | རྐོ་བ་གནང་བ་ | *ko-wa nang-wa.* |
| Exceed, to | ལྷག་པ་ | *hlaḱ-pa.* |
| Exceedingly | ཐག་ཆོད་ | *thaḱ-chhö.* |

| | | |
|---|---|---|
| Exceedingly many | མང་ཐག་ཆོད་ | *mang-thak-chhö.* |
| Excellency, His | རིན་པོ་ཆེ་ | *rim-po-chhe.* |
| Excellent | ཡག་ཐག་ཆོད་ | *yak-thak-chhö.* |
| Except | མ་གཏོགས། མེན་པ་ (མིན་པ་) | *ma-to ; mem-pa.* |
| Exchange | རྗེ་པོ་རྒྱབ་པ་ | *je-po gyap-pa.* |
| Do. *hon.* | རྗེ་པོ་སྐྱོན་པ་ | *je-po kyöm-pa.* |
| Excessive | མང་ཐག་ཆོད། ཛག་དོ་ | *mang-thak-chhö ; dzak-to.* |
| Excessive appetite | གྲོད་ཁོག་ཆེན་པོ་ | *trö-kho chhem-po.* |
| Exclaim, to | སྐད་བཏང་ (གཏོང་) བ་ | *ke-tang-wa.* |
| Do. *hon.* | སྐད་གཏོང་ང་ (བ་) གནང་བ་ | *ke tong-nga nang-wa.* |
| Excluding (except) | མ་གཏོགས། མེན་པ་ (མིན་པ་) | *ma-to ; mem-pa.* |
| Excrement (human) | སྐྱག་པ་ | *kyak-pa.* |
| Excuse, *s.* | ཁ་འདྲི་ | *khan-dri.* |
| Do. *hon.* | ཞལ་འདྲི་ | *sken-dri.* |
| Excuses, to make | ཁ་འདྲི་བཤད་པ་ | *khan-dri she-pa.* |
| Do. *hon.* | ཞལ་འདྲི་གནང་བ་ | *sken-dri nang-wa.* |
| Do. *inf.* to *sup.* | ཁ་འདྲི་ཞུ་བ་ | *khan dri sku-wa.* |
| Exercise, literary | ཡིག་རྒྱུགས་ | *yik-gyu.* |
| Exert one's self, to | སྙིང་རུས་བྱེད་པ་ | *nying-rü che-pa.* |
| Do. *hon.* | ཐུགས་རུས་གནང་བ་ | *thuk-rü nang-wa.* |

| | | |
|---|---|---|
| Exhausted, to be (tired) | ཐང་ཆད་པ་ | *thang-chhe-pa.* |
| Do. *hon.* | སྐུ་ཐང་ཆད་པ་གནང་བ་ | *ku thang chhe-pa nang-wa.* |
| Exhaustion | ངལ་ | *ngel.* |
| Do. *hon.* | སྐུ་ངལ་ | *ku-ngel.* |
| Exhibit, to | བསྟན་པ་ (སྟོན་པ་) | *tem-pa.* |
| Exist, to | ཡོད་པ་ | *yö-pa.* |
| Exhort, to | བསླབ་བྱ་བྱེད་པ་ | *laṕ-cḱa cḱe-pa.* |
| Do. *hon.* | བསླབ་བྱ་གནང་བ་ | *laṕ-cḱa nang wa.* |
| Do. *h. hon.* | བཀའ་སློབ་གནང་བ་ | *ka-loṕ nang-wa.* |
| Exhortation | བསླབ་བྱ་ | *laṕ-cḱa.* |
| Do. *hon.* | བཀའ་སློབ་ | *ka loṕ.* |
| Exorcise, to | དམ་ལ་བཏགས་ (འདོགས་) པ་ | *ťam-la taḱ-pa.* |
| Do. *hon.* | དམ་འདོགས་གནང་བ་ | *ťam-doḱ nang-wa.* |
| Expanse | ཁ་ཞེང་ | *kha-sḱeng.* |
| Expect, to (wait for) | སྒུག་བསྡད་ (སྡོད་) པ་ | *gu-de pa.* |
| Do. *hon.* | སྒུག་བཞུགས་པ | *gu sḱu-pa.* |
| Expect, to (hope for) | རེ་བ་བྱེད་པ་ | *re-wa cḱe pa.* |
| Do. *hon.* | ཐུགས་རེ་གནང་བ་ | *thu-re nang-wa.* |
| Expectation | རེ་བ་ | *re-wa.* |
| Do. *hon.* | ཐུགས་རེ་ | *thu-re.* |

| | | |
|---|---|---|
| Expedite, to | བྲེལ་བ་བྱེད་པ་ | *ťre-wa cḱe-pa.* |
| Do. *hon.* | ཐུགས་བྲེལ་གནང་བ་ | *thuḱ-ťre nang-wa.* |
| Expel, to | བཏོན་པ་ (འདོན་པ་) | *töm-pa.* |
| Do. *hon.* | འདོན་པ་གནང་བ་ | *döm-pa nang-wa.* |
| Expense | འགྲོ་སོང་ | *dro-song.* |
| Do. *hon.* | ཐུགས་འགྲོན་ (ཐུགས་འགྲོ་) | *thung-drön.* |
| Expensive | གོང་ཆེན་པོ། གུས་པོ་ | *ḱong-chhem-po ; ḱü-po.* |
| Do. *hon.* | ལྗགས་གོང་ཆེན་པོ་ | *ja-ḱong chhem-po.* |
| Experienced (skilled) | མཁས་པོ་ | *khe-po.* |
| Explain, to | ངོ་སྤྲོད་སྤྲད་པ། དོན་དག་བཤད་པ་ | *ngo-trö tre-pa ; ton-ťa she-pa.* |
| Do. *hon.* | ངོ་སྤྲོད་གནང་བ། སྐུ་དོན་གསུང་བ་ | *ngo-trö nang-wa ; ku-ťön sung-wa.* |
| Explain, to (by sign) | ལག་བརྡ་བྱེད་པ་ | *laḱ-da cḱe-pa.* |
| Do. *hon.* | ཕྱག་བརྡ་གནང་བ་ | *chha-da nang-wa.* |
| Explanation (apology) | སེབ་བཀྲོལ་ | *seṕ-trö.* |
| Exports | འཐོན་ཁུངས་ | *thön-khung.* |
| Extensive | རྒྱ་ཆེན་པོ་ | *gya-chhem-po.* |
| External | ཕྱིའི་ | *chhi-i.* |
| Extinct, to become | ཆད་པ་ | *chhe-pa.* |

| | | |
|---|---|---|
| Extinguish, to | བསད་པ་ (གསོད་པ་) | *se-pa.* |
| Do. *hon.* | གསོད་པ་གནང་བ་ | *sö-pa nang-wa.* |
| Extort, to | དབང་ཡོད་བྱས་ནས་ལེན་པ་ | *wang-yö che-ne lem-pa.* |
| Extra | འཕྲིབ་པ་ | *thep-pa.* |
| Extract, to | བཏོན་པ་ (འདོན་པ་) | *töm pa.* |
| Do. *hon.* | འདོན་པ་གནང་བ་ | *döm-pa nang-wa.* |
| Extraction (descent) | རྒྱུད་ | *gyü.* |
| Extraordinary | ཡ་མཚན་པོ། ཁྱད་མཚར་པོ། | *yam-tshen po ; khye-tsha-po.* |
| Extremity | མཐའ་ | *tha.* |
| Exult, to (rejoice) | དགའ་བ་ | *ga-wa.* |
| Do. *hon.* | མཉེས་པོ་གནང་བ་ | *nye-po nang-wa.* |
| Do. *h. hon.* | ཐུགས་དགྱེས་པོ་གནང་བ་ | *thu-gye-po nang-wa.* |
| Exultation | དགའ་ཚོར་ | *ga-tshor.* |
| Eye | མིག་ | *mik.* |
| Do. *hon.* | སྤྱན་ | *chen.* |
| Eye-ball | མིག་རིལ་ | *mik-ri.* |
| Do. *hon.* | སྤྱན་རིལ་ | *chen-ri.* |
| Eye-brow | མིག་སྨི་ (མིག་ཛི་) | *mik-śi.* |
| Do. *hon.* | སྤྱན་ཟི་ (སྤྱན་ཛི་) | *chen-śi.* |
| Eye-glass | མིག་ཤེར་ (མིག་ཤེལ་) | *mik-sher.* |

| | | |
|---|---|---|
| Eye-glass, *hon.* | སྤྱན་ཤེར་ ( སྤྱན་ཤེལ་ ) | *chen-sher.* |
| Eye-lash | མིག་སྤུ་ | *mik-pu.* |
| Do. *hon.* | སྤྱན་སྤུ་ | *chem-pu.* |
| Eye-lid | མིག་ལྤགས་ | *mik-pa.* |
| Do. *hon.* | སྤྱན་ལྤགས་ | *chem-pa.* |
| Eye-lid, lower | མིག་ལྤགས་སྨད་ | *mik-pa me.* |
| Do. *hon.* | སྤྱན་ལྤགས་སྨད་ | *chem-pa me.* |
| Eye-lid, upper | མིག་ལྤགས་ཡས་ | *mik pa-ye.* |
| Do. *hon.* | སྤྱན་ལྤགས་ཡས་ | *chem-pa ye.* |
| Eye-shade (of hair) | མིག་ར་ | *mik-ra.* |
| Do. *hon.* | སྤྱན་ར་ | *chen-ra.* |

# F

| | | |
|---|---|---|
| Fable | སྒྲུམ་ (སྒྲུང་) | *drum.* |
| Do. *hon.* | ཞལ་སྒྲུམ་ (ཞལ་སྒྲུང་) | *sḱe-drum.* |
| Fabrication (lie) | ཧམ་པ། སྐྱག་རྫུན་ | *ham-pa ; kyaḱ-dzün.* |
| Do. *hon.* | ཞལ་རྫུན་ | *sḱe-dzün.* |
| Face | གདོང་ | *dong.* |
| Do. *hon.* | ཞལ་རས་ | *sḱe-re.* |
| Facsimile | འདྲ་ཤུས་ | *dra-shü.* |
| Fact | དོན་སྙིང་ | *ťön-nying.* |
| Factory | བཟོ་ཁང་ | *śo-khang.* |
| Fade, to (wither) | ཉིད་པ་ | *nyi-pa.* |
| Do. to (of colour) | གཞུད་པ་ | *sḱü pa.* |
| Fail, to (miss) | མི····ཐུབ་པ་ | *mi...thuṕ-pa.* |
| Do. *hon.* | མི····ཐུབ་པ་གནང་བ་ | *mi...thuṕ-pa nang-wa.* |
| Fail, without (in any event) | ཡིན་གཅིག་མིན་གཅིག། ཏེན་ལྡན་ | *yin-chi min-chi ; ten-den.* |
| Faint-hearted | སེམས་ཆུང་ཆུང་། སྙིང་ཆུང་ཆུང་ | *sem chhung-chhung ; nying-chhung-chhung.* |
| Do. *hon.* | ཐུགས་སེམས་ཆུང་ཆུང་ | *thu-sem chhung-chhung.* |

| | | |
|---|---|---|
| Faint, to | དྲན་མེད་བརྒྱལ་བ་ | *t́ren me gye-wa.* |
| Do. *hon.* | དྲན་མེད་བརྒྱལ་ར་ (བ་) གནང་བ་ | *t́ren me gye-ra nang-wa.* |
| Fair | མཛེས་པོ་ | *dze-po.* |
| Do. *hon.* | ཐུགས་ཚར་པོ་ | *thu tshar-po.* |
| Fair (just) | ཁྲིམས་དྲང་པོ་ | *thrim-t́rang-po.* |
| Do. *hon.* | བཀའ་ཁྲིམས་དྲང་པོ་ | *ka-thrim t́rang-po* |
| Fairy | ལྷ་མོ་ | *hla-mo.* |
| Faith | དད་པ་ | *t́e-pa.* |
| Faithful | དམ་ཚིག་ཡག་པོ་ | *t́am-tshi yaḱ-po.* |
| Fakir | གྲུབ་ཐོབ་ | *t́ruṕ-tho.* |
| Falcon | ཁྲ་ | *thra.* |
| Fall, to (on ground which one is already touching) | འགྱེལ་བ་ | *gye-wa.* |
| Do. *hon.* | འགྱེལ་ར་ (བ་) གནང་བ་ | *gye-ra nang-wa.* |
| Fall, to (from a height) | གཟགས་པ་ (འཛོག་པ་) | *śaḱ-pa.* |
| Do. *hon.* | གཟགས་ཀ་ (འཛོག་པ་) གནང་བ་ | *śaḱ-ḱa nang-wa.* |
| Fall, to (descend) | བབ་ (འབབ་) ཡོང་བ་ (or འགྲོ་བ་) | *ṕaṕ-yong-wa* (or *dro-wu*). |

| | | |
|---|---|---|
| Fall, to (descend) *hon.* | བབ་ (འབབ་) ཕེབ་པ་ | *ṕaṕ-phe-pa.* |
| Do. *h. hon.* | བབ་ (འབབ་) འཆིབ་རྒྱུ་ གནང་བ་ | *ṕaṕ-chhiṕ-gyu nang-wa.* |
| Fall head-over-heels, to | མགོ་གཞུག་ལོག་པ་ | *go-sḱu loḱ-pa.* |
| Do. to (in drops) | འཐིག་པ་རྒྱབ་པ་ | *thiḱ-pa gyaṕ-pa.* |
| Do. to (of flood, etc.) | ཆག་པ་ | *chhaḱ-pa.* |
| Fallow | ས་སྟོང་ | *sa-tong.* |
| False | ཧམ་བ། སྐྱག་རྫུན། | *ham-pa ; kyaḱ-dzün.* |
| Falsehood | ཧམ་པ། སྐྱག་རྫུན་ | *ham-pa ; ḱyaḱ-dzün.* |
| Do. *hon.* | ཞལ་རྫུན་ | *sḱe-dzün.* |
| Falter, to (waver) | ཐེ་ཚོམ་ཟ་བ་ | *the-tshom śa-wa.* |
| *Do. hon.* | ཐེ་ཚོམ་གནང་བ་ | *the-tshom nang-wa.* |
| Fame | སྐད་གྲགས་ | *ke-t́ra.* |
| Do. *hon.* | སྙན་གྲགས་ | *nyen-t́ra.* |
| Familiar | བློ་དཀར། ཉེ་པོ་ | *lo-ka ; nye-po.* |
| Family | མི་ཚང་ | *mi-tshang.* |
| Family (lineage) | རིགས་བརྒྱུད་ | *ri-gyü.* |
| Do. *hon.* | སྐུ་བརྒྱུད་ | *ku-gyü.* |
| Family, member of | ནང་མི་ | *nang-mi.* |
| Family priest | མཆོད་གནས་ | *chhö-ne.* |

| | | |
|---|---|---|
| amine | མུ་གེ་ | *mu-ke.* |
| amous (celebrated) | སྐད་གྲགས་ཆེན་པོ་ | *ke-tra chhem-po.* |
| Do. *hon.* | སྙན་གྲགས་ཆེན་པོ་ | *nyen-tra chhem-po.* |
| an | རླུང་ཡབ་ | *lung-yap.* |
| ancy (opinion) | བསམ་པ་ | *sam-pa.* |
| Do. *hon.* | ཐུགས་སེམས་ | *thu-sem.* |
| ancy (wish) | འདོད་པ་ | *dö-pa.* |
| Do. *hon.* | ཐུགས་འདོད་ | *thung-dö.* |
| ancy, to (like) | དགའ་བ་ | *ga-wa.* |
| Do. *hon.* | ཐུགས་མཉེས་པ་ | *thu-nye-pa.* |
| Do *h. hon.* | ཐུགས་དགྱེས་པ་ | *thu-gye-pa.* |
| ancy to, (suppose) | བསམ་པ་ | *sam-pa.* |
| Do. *hon.* | དགོངས་པ་ | *gong-pa.* |
| ang (of tiger, etc.) | མཆེ་བ་ | *chhe-wa.* |
| ar | ཐག་རིང་པོ་ | *tha-ring-po.* |
| Do. how | ཐག་རིང་ཐུང་ག་ཚོད་ | *tha-ring-thung ka-tshö.* |
| are (food) | ཁ་ལག། ལྟོ་ | *kha-la ; to.* |
| Do. *hon.* | ཞལ་ལག་ | *ske-la.* |
| rewell ! (to person going away) | འོ་ན་རྒྱུག་ཨ་ | *o-na gyu-a.* |
| Do. *hon.* | ག་ལེ་ཕེབས་ | *ka-le phe* |

| | | |
|---|---|---|
| **Farewell!** (to person going away) *h. hon.* | ག་ལེ་འཆིབ་རྒྱུ་གནང་ | *ka-le chhip-gyu nang.* |
| **Farewell!** (to person remaining) | འོ་ན་སྡོད་ཨ་ | *o-na dö-a.* |
| Do. *hon.* | ག་ལེ་བཞུགས་ | *ka-le sku.* |
| Do. *h. hon.* | ག་ལེ་བཞུགས་གདན་འཇག་ | *ka-le sku-den-ja* |
| **Farm** | ཕ་གཞིས་ | *pha-ski.* |
| **Farmer** | སོ་ནམས་བྱེད་མཁན་ | *so-nam cke-khen.* |
| **Farming,** *s.* (agriculture) | སོ་ནམས་ | *so-nam.* |
| **Farrier** | རྨིག་ལྕགས་རྒྱབ་མཁན་ | *mik-cha gyang-khen.* |
| **Farther** | ཕ་ཙ་ (ཕར་ཙམ་) | *pha-tsa.* |
| **Fascinate, to** | བློ་ལ་ཕྱིན་པ་ | *lo-la chhim-pa.* |
| Do. *hon.* | ཐུགས་ལ་ཕེབ་པ་ | *thu-la phe-pa.* |
| **Fashion** (custom) | ལུགས་སྲོལ་ | *luk-sö.* |
| Do. (form) | བཟོ་ལྟ་ | *sop-ta.* |
| Do. *hon.* | སྐུ་བཟོ་ | *ku-so.* |
| **Fast** (faithful) | དམ་ཚིག་ཡག་པོ་ | *tam-tshi yak-po* |
| Do. (firm) | བརྟན་པོ་ | *tem-po.* |
| Do. (quick) | མགྱོགས་པོ་ | *gyok-po.* |
| Do. *hon.* | རྩོལ་པོ་ | *tsö-po.* |
| **Fast, to** | སྨྱུང་གནས་སྲུང་བ་ | *nyung-ne sung-wa.* |

| | | |
|---|---|---|
| Fast, to, *hon.* | སྨྱུང་གནས་སྲུང་ང་ (བ་) གནང་བ་ | *nyung-ne sung-nga nang-wa.* |
| Fasten, to (with rope, etc.) | བསྡམས་པ་ (སྡོམ་པ་) | *dam-pa.* |
| Do. *hon.* | བསྡམས་ (སྡོམ་) པ་གནང་བ་ | *dam-pa nang-wa.* |
| Fasten, to (with glue, etc.) | སྦྱར་བ་ | *jar-wa.* |
| Do. *hon.* | སྦྱར་ར་ (བ་) གནང་བ་ | *jar-ra nang-wa.* |
| Fasten on, to (affix) | སྦྲེལ་བ་ | *drel-wa.* |
| Do. *hon.* | སྦྲེལ་ལ་ (བ་) གནང་བ་ | *drel-la nang-wa.* |
| Fasting, *s.* | སྨྱུང་གནས་ | *nyung-ne.* |
| Fat, *adj.* | ཤ་རྒྱགས་པ་ | *sha-gyak̄-pa.* |
| Do. *hon.* | སྐུ་ཤ་འབྱོར་པོ་ | *ku-sha jor-po.* |
| Fat, *s.* (suet, lard) | ཚིལ་ལུ་ (ཚིལ་བུ་) | *tshi-lu.* |
| Do. *hon.* | བཞེས་ཚིལ་ | *sk̄e-tshi.* |
| Fate | བསོ་བདེ་ (བསོད་བདེ་) | *so-de.* |
| Do. *hon.* | སྐུ་བསོད་ | *ku-sö.* |
| Father | ཨ་ཕ་ | *a-pha.* |
| Do. *hon.* | ཡབ་ | *yap̄.* |
| Fatherland | ལུང་པ་ | *lung-pa.* |
| Do. *hon.* | འཁྲུངས་ས་ | *thrung-sa.* |
| Father-in-law | ཕ་ལགས། གྱོས་པོ་ | *pa-la ; kyö-po.* |

| | | |
|---|---|---|
| Fatigue | ངལ་ | *ngel.* |
| Do. *hon.* | སྐུ་ངལ་ | *ku-ngel.* |
| Fatigued, to be | ཐང་ཆད་པ་ | *thang-chhe-pa.* |
| Do. *hon.* | སྐུ་ཐང་མཉེལ་བ་ | *ku-thang nye-wa.* |
| Fatiguing | དཀའ་ལས་ཁག་པོ་ | *ka-le khaḱ-po.* |
| Do. *hon.* | སྐུ་མཉེལ་པོ་ | *ku-nye-po.* |
| Fault | སྐྱོན་ | *kyön.* |
| Favonr | དྲིན་ | *t́rin.* |
| Do. *hon.* | བཀའ་དྲིན་ | *ka-t́rin.* |
| Favourite (official, etc.) | མིག་གསལ་ | *miḱ-se.* |
| Do. *hon.* | སྤྱན་གསལ་ | *chen-se.* |
| Fawn | ཤ་ཕྲུག་ | *sha-thru.* |
| Fear | ཞེད་སྐྲག་ | *sḱe-tra.* |
| Fear, to | ཞེད་པ་ | *sḱe-pa.* |
| Do. to *hon.* | ཞེད་པ་གནང་བ་ | *sḱe-pa nang-wa.* |
| Fearful | ཞེད་སྐྲག་ཚ་པོ་ | *sḱe-tra tsha-po.* |
| Fearless, to be | ཞེད་རྒྱུ་ཙ་ནས་མེད་པ་ | *sḱe-gyu tsa-ne me-pa.* |
| Feast | མགྲོན་པོ་ | *dröm-po.* |
| Do. *hon.* | ཐུགས་སྤྲོ་ | *thuḱ-tro.* |
| Feather (small) | སྤུ་ | *pu.* |

| | | |
|---|---|---|
| Feather (large) | སྒྲོ་ | *dro.* |
| Features | བཟོ་བལྟ་ | *sop-ta.* |
| Fee | རྔན་པ། བླ་ | *ngem-pa ; la.* |
| Feeble (infirm) | ཀྱ་རེ་ཀྱོ་རེ། ཉ་རེ་(ར)ཉོ་རེ་ | *kya-re kyo-re ; nya-re nyo-re.* |
| Do. *hon.* | སྐུ་ཀྱོར་ཀྱོར་ | *ku-kyor-kyor.* |
| Feed, to, *v.t.* | ལྟོ་སྟེར་བ་ | *to ter-wa.* |
| Do. *hon.* | ལྟོ་གསོལ་རས་གནང་བ་ | *to sö-re nang-wa.* |
| Do. *inf.* to *sup.* | ཞལ་ལག་ཕུལ་ (འབུལ་) བ་ | *sKe la phü-wa.* |
| Feed, to, *v.i.* | ཁ་ལག་ཟ་བ། ལྟོ་ཟ་བ་ | *kha-la sa-wa ; to śa-wa* |
| Do. *hon.* | ཞལ་ལག་བཞེས་པ་ | *sKe-la sKe-pa.* |
| Feel, to, (touch) | ཐུག་པ་ | *thuk-pa.* |
| Do. *hon.* | ཐུག་ག་ (པ་) གནང་བ་ | *thuk-ka nang-wa.* |
| Feel cold, to | འཁྱགས་པ་ | *khyak-pa.* |
| Do. *hon.* | སྐུ་བསིལ་ར་ (བ་) གནང་བ་ | *ku-si-ra nang-wa* |
| Feign, to | གྱོད་བཤད་པ་ | *Kyö-she-pa* |
| Do. *hon.* | གྱོད་གསུང་བ་ | *Kyö-sung-wa.* |
| Feign illness, to | ན་ཚུ་ (རྫུ) བདབ་ (འདེབས་) པ་ | *na-tshu tap-pa.* |
| Do. *hon.* | སྙུང་ཚུ་ (རྫུ) བདབ་ (འདེབས་) པ་ | *nyung-tshu tap-pa.* |
| Feign stupidity, to. | ལྐུགས་ཚུལ་བདབ་(འདེབས་)པ་ | *kuk-tshü tap-pa.* |

| | | |
|---|---|---|
| Feign stupidity, to, *hon.* | ལྐུགས་ཚུལ་གསུང་བ་ | *kuḱ-tshü sung-wa.* |
| Fellow-labourer | ལས་རོགས་ | *le-ro.* |
| Do. *hon.* | ཕྱག་སྒྲེལ་ | *chha-drel.* |
| Fellow-traveller | ལམ་རོགས་ | *lam-ro.* |
| Do. *hon.* | ཕེབ་རོགས་ | *pheṕ-ro.* |
| Felon | བཙོན་པ་ | *tsöm-pa.* |
| Felt | ཕྱིང་པ་ | *chhing-pa.* |
| Female | མོ་ | *mo.* |
| Fence | ར་བ་ | *ra-wa.* |
| Ferment, to (wine) | བསྙེལ་བ་ (སྙོལ་བ་) | *nyel-wa.* |
| Fern | སྐྱེ་མ་ | *kye-ma.* |
| Ferocious (of human beings) | ངན་པ་ | *ngem-pa.* |
| Do. (of animals) | ཚུབ་པོ་ | *tshuṕ-po.* |
| Ferry | གྲུ་ཁ་ | *t́ru-kha.* |
| Ferry-boat | གྲུ་ | *t́ru.* |
| Do. *hon.* | ཕེབ་གྲུ་ | *pheṕ t́ru.* |
| Ferry-man | གྲུ་པ་ | *t́ru-pa.* |
| Do. *hon.* | གྲུ་དཔོན་ | *t́ru-pön.* |
| Fertile | ལུད་ཆུ་འཛོམས་པོ་ | *lü-chhu dzom-po.* |
| Fervent | སྙིང་རུས་ཆེན་པོ་ | *nying-rü chhem-po.* |

| | | |
|---|---|---|
| Fervent, *hon.* | ཐུགས་རུས་ཆེན་པོ་ | *thu-rü chhem-po* |
| Festival | དུས་ཆེན་ | *tü-chhen.* |
| Fetch, to (by carrying) | འཁྱེར་བ་ | *khyer-wa.* |
| Do. *hon.* | སྣོམ་པ་ | *nom-pa.* |
| Fetch, to (by leading) | འཁྲིད་པ་ | *thri-pa.* |
| Do. *hon.* | འཁྲིད་པ་གནང་བ་ | *thri-pa nang-wa.* |
| Fetlock, fore (of horse) | ལག་གུག་ | *lak-ku.* |
| Do. hind | རྐང་གུག་ | *kang-ku.* |
| Fetters (for hands) | ལག་ལྕགས་ | *lak-cha.* |
| Do. (for feet) | རྐང་ལྕགས་ | *kang-cha.* |
| Fever | ཚད་པ་ | *tshe-pa.* |
| Do. *hon.* | སྐུ་ཚད་ | *ku-tshe.* |
| Fever, to have | ཚད་པ་ན་བ་ | *tshe-pa na-wa.* |
| Do. *hon.* | སྐུ་ཚད་སྙུང་བ་ | *ku-tshe nyung-wa.* |
| Few | ཏོག་ཙ་ (ཏོག་ཚོད་) | *tok-tsa.* |
| Do., only a | ཁ་ཤས་ཅིག་ | *kha-she-chi.* |
| Fibre | རྒྱུས་པ་ | *gyü-pa.* |
| Fickle, to be | བརྟན་པོ་……མེད་པ་ | *tem-po …… me-pa.* |
| Fiddle | པི་ཝང་ | *pi-wang.* |
| Field | ཞིང་ཁ་ | *sking-kha.* |

| | | |
|---|---|---|
| Fiend | བདུད་ | *dü.* |
| Fierce (of human beings) | ངན་པ་ | *ngem-pa.* |
| Do. (of animals) | ཚུབ་པོ་ | *tshuṕ-po.* |
| Fifteen | བཅོ་ལྔ་ | *chö-nga.* |
| Fifteenth | བཅོ་ལྔ་པ་ | *chö-nga-pa.* |
| Fifth | ལྔ་པ་ | *nga-pa.* |
| Fiftieth | ལྔ་བཅུ་པ་ | *ngaṕ-chu-pa.* |
| Fifty | ལྔ་བཅུ་ | *ngaṕ-chu.* |
| Fight | རྒྱབ་འདྲེ་ | *gyam-dre.* |
| Do. to (with words or blows) | རྒྱབ་འདྲེ་རྒྱབ་པ་ | *gyam-dre gyaṕ-pa.* |
| Do. *hon.* | གསུང་འཁྲུག་སྐྱོན་པ་ | *sung-thru kyöm-pa.* |
| Fight, to (make war) | དམག་རྒྱབ་པ་ | *ma-gyaṕ-pa.* |
| Do. *hon.* | དམག་སྐྱོན་པ་ | *ma-kyöm-pa.* |
| Fight, to (with blows) | འཛིང་བ་ | *dzing-wa.* |
| Do. *hon.* | འཛིང་རེས་གནང་བ་ | *dzing-re nang-wa.* |
| Figurative | སྙན་ངག་ | *nye-nga.* |
| Figure (painting) | རི་མོ་ | *ri-mo.* |
| Do. (number) | ཨང་གི་ | *ang-ki.* |
| Do. (shape) | བཟོ་བལྟ་ | *śoṕ-ta.* |
| Do. *hon.* | སྐུ་བཟོ་ | *ku-śo.* |

| | | |
|---|---|---|
| File | ལྕགས་སག་ | *chak-sa.* |
| Fill, to | གང་བླུག་པ་ | *kang-luk-pa.* |
| Do. *hon.* | གང་བླུག་ག་ (ཀ་) གནང་བ་ | *kang-luk-ka nang-wa.* |
| Do. *inf.* to *sup.* | གང་ཞུ་བ་ | *kang-sku-wa.* |
| Filter (for tea) | ཛ་ཚགས་ | *cka-tsha.* |
| Filthy | བཙོག་པ་ | *tsok-pa.* |
| Do. *hon.* | སྐུ་བཙོག་ | *ku-tso.* |
| Filthy, to be | བཙོག་པ་ཡོད་པ་ | *tsok-pa yö-pa.* |
| Do. to become | བཙོག་པ་ཤོར་བ་ | *tsok-pa shor-wa.* |
| Do. *hon* | སྐུ་བཙོག་ཤོར་བ་ | *ku-tso shor-wa.* |
| Fin | ཤོག་པ་ | *shok-pa.* |
| Final | གཞུག་ཤོས་ | *skuk-shö.* |
| Find, to | རྙེད་པ་ | *nye-pa.* |
| Do. *hon.* | རྙེད་པ་གནང་བ་ | *nye-pa nang-wa.* |
| Fine (beautiful) | མཛེས་པོ་ | *dze-po.* |
| Do. (minute) | ཞིབ་པོ་ | *skip-po.* |
| Do. (thin, of round objects) | ཕྲ་པོ་ | *thra-po.* |
| Do. (thin, of flat objects) | སྲབ་པོ་ | *trap-po.* |
| Fine, *s.* | དངོས་པོའི་ཉེས་པ་ | *ngö pö nye-pa.* |

| | | |
|---|---|---|
| Fine, *hon.* | དངོས་པོའི་བཀའ་ཉེས་ | *ngö-pö ka-nye.* |
| Fine, to | དངོས་པོའི་ཉེས་པ་བཏང་ (གཏོང་) བ་ | *ngö-pö nye-pa tang-wa.* |
| Do. *hon.* | དངོས་པོའི་བཀའ་ཉེས་གནང་བ་ | *ngö-pö ka-nye nang wa.* |
| Fine (for murder, paid as compensation to the relatives of the deceased) | སྟོང་ | *tong.* |
| Do. (for theft) | བཀུས་འཇལ་ (ཀུ་འཇལ་) | *kün-jel.* |
| Finger | མཛུག་གུ་ | *dzu-ku.* |
| Do. *hon.* | ཕྱག་མཛུག་ | *chhan-dzu.* |
| Finger (fore-finger) | མཛུག་གུ་ | *dzu-ku* |
| Do. (middle finger) | དཀྱིལ་མཛུག་ | *kyi-dzu.* |
| Do. (third finger) | སྲིན་མཛུག་ | *trin-dzu.* |
| Do. (little finger) | མཛུག་ཆུང་། ཨི་ཆུང་ང་ | *dzuk-chhung; i-chhung-nga.* |
| Finger-nail | སེན་མོ་ | *sen-mo.* |
| Do. *hon.* | ཕྱག་སེན་ | *chha-sen.* |
| Finish, to (complete) | འཚར་བ་ | *tshar wa* |
| Do. *hon.* | འགྲུབ་པ་ | *drup-pa.* |
| Fir-tree (Abies Webbiana) | གདུང་ཤིང་ | *dung-shing.* |

| | | |
|---|---|---|
| Fire | མེ་ | *me.* |
| Do. *hon.* | ཞུགས་མེ་ | *sḱu-me.* |
| Fire, to catch | མེ་ཤོར་བ་ | *me-shor-wa.* |
| Fire, to, *v.t.* | མེ་སྦར་བ་ | *me-bar-wa.* |
| Fire a gun, to | མེ་མདའ་རྒྱབ་པ་ | *men-da gyaṕ-pa.* |
| Do. to *hon.* | ཕྱག་མདའ་སྐྱོན་པ་ | *chhan-da-kyöm-pa.* |
| Fire-place | ཐབ་ | *thaṕ.* |
| Fire-works | ཤོག་པག་ | *sho-pa.* |
| Firm (not shaky) | བརྟན་པོ་ | *tem-po.* |
| Do. (tight) | དམ་པོ་ | *t́am-po.* |
| Firmament | གནམ། ནམ་མཁའ་ | *nam ; nam-kha.* |
| First | དང་པོ་ | *t́ang-po.* |
| Firstborn | རྒན་པ་ | *gem-pa.* |
| First class (excellent) | ཨང་གི་དང་པོ་ | *ang-ḱi t́ang-po.* |
| First-rate | ཨང་གི་དང་པོ་ | *ang-ḱi t́ang-po.* |
| Firstly | དང་པོ་ (དང་པོར་) | *t́ang-po.* |
| Fish | ཉ་ | *nya.* |
| Do. to | ཉ་ཟིན་པ་ | *nya śim-pa.* |
| Do. *hon.* | ཉ་ཟིན་པ་གནང་བ་ | *nya śim-pa nang-wa.* |
| Fish-bone | ཉ་རུས་ | *nya-rü.* |

| | | |
|---|---|---|
| Fisherman | ཉ་རྡུང་ང་། ཉ་ཟྲིན་མཁན་ | *nyap dung-nga; nya-sim khen.* |
| Fish-hook | ལྕགས་ཀྱུ། ཉ་ཀུག་ | *cha-kyu; nya-ku.* |
| Fishing-net | ཉ་དོལ་ | *nya-töl.* |
| Fish's fin | ཉའི་ཤོག་པ་ | *nya-i shoḱ-pa.* |
| Fissure | སེར་ཀ་ | *ser-ka.* |
| Fist | ཛོག་མགོ་ | *dzong-go.* |
| Fisted, close- | ལག་པ་དམ་པོ་ | *laḱ-pa t́am-po.* |
| Do. *hon.* | ཕྱག་དམ་པོ་ | *chha-t́am-po.* |
| Fit, to (of clothes, &c.) | འགྲིག་པ་ | *driḱ-pa.* |
| Do. *hon.* | འགྲིག་ག་ (པ་) གནང་བ་ | *driḱ-ḱa nang-wa.* |
| Fitful, to be | བརྟན་པོ་མེད་པ་ | *tem-po....me-pa.* |
| Fitting (proper) | འོས་པོ་ | *ö-po.* |
| Do. to be | འགྲིག་པ་ | *driḱ-pa.* |
| Five | ལྔ་ | *nga.* |
| Fix, to (place) | བཞག་པ་ (འཛོག་པ་) | *sḱaḱ-pa.* |
| Do. *hon.* | གཞོག་ག་ (པ་) གནང་བ་ | *sḱoḱ-ḱa nang-wa.* |
| Fix a time, to | དུས་ཚོད་བྱེད་པ་ | *tü-tshö cḱe-pa.* |
| Do. *hon.* | དུས་ཚོད་གནང་བ་ | *t́ü tshö nang-wa.* |
| Flag, large | དར་ཆེན་ | *t́ar-chhen.* |
| Do. small | དར་ལྕོག་ | *t́ar-cho.* |

| | | |
|---|---|---|
| lagstaff | དར་ཤིང་ | *ťar-shing.* |
| lame | མེ་ལྕེ་ | *me-che.* |
| lannel, thin | ཐེར་མ་ | *ther-ma.* |
| Do. thick | སྤུ་རུག་ | *pu-ru.* |
| lat | ལེབ་ལེབ་ | *leṕ-leṕ.* |
| latten, to | ལེབ་ལེབ་བཟོ་བ་ | *leṕ-leṕ śo-wa.* |
| Do. *hon.* | ལེབ་ལེབ་བཟོ་བ་གནང་བ་ | *leṕ-leṕ śo-wa nang-wa.* |
| latter, to | དཔལ་ལས་བཤད་པ་ | *pe-le she-pa.* |
| Do. *inf.* to *sup* | དཔལ་ལས་ཞུ་བ་ | *pe-le sḱu-wa.* |
| launt, to (boast) | རང་སྟོད་བྱེད་པ་ | *rang-tö cḱe-pa.* |
| lavour | བྲོ་བ་ | *ťro-wa.* |
| Do. *hon.* | ལྗགས་བྲོ་ | *ja-ťro.* |
| law | སྐྱོན་ | *kyön.* |
| ay, to | ཤུ་བ་ | *shu-wa.* |
| Do. *hon.* | ཤུ་བ་གནང་བ་ | *shu-wa nang-wa.* |
| ea | འཇོ་འོ་ (འཇུ་བ་) | *jo.* |
| ee, to | བྲོས་བྱིན་པ་ | *ṕö chhim-pa.* |
| Do. *hon.* | བྲོས་ཕེབ་པ་ | *ṕö-pheṕ-pa.* |
| Do. *h. hon.* | བྲོས་འཆིབ་རྒྱུ་གནང་བ་ | *ṕö chhiṕ-gyu nang-wa.* |

| | | |
|---|---|---|
| Fleet (quick) | མགྱོགས་པོ་ | *gyok-po.* |
| Do. *hon.* | རྩོལ་པོ་ | *tsö-po.* |
| Flesh | ཤ་ | *sha.* |
| Do. *hon.* | སྐུ་ཤ་ | *ku-sha.* |
| Flesh, for eating, *hon.* | གསོལ་སྤྲང་ (གསོལ་སྤྲམ་) | *sö-trung.* |
| Fleshy (fat) | ཤ་རྒྱགས་པ་ | *sha-gyak-pa.* |
| Do. *hon.* | སྐུ་ཤ་འབྱོར་པོ་ | *ku-sha jor-po.* |
| Flexible | མཉེན་པོ་ | *nyem-po.* |
| Fling, to | དབྱུག་པ་ | *yuk-pa.* |
| Do. *hon.* | དབྱུག་ག་ (པ་) གནང་བ་ | *yuk-ka nang-w* |
| Flint | མེ་རྡོ་ | *me do.* |
| Flip, to | ཨེ་ཀོག་གཞུ་བ་ | *e-ko sku-wa.* |
| Float, to | ལྡིང་བ་ | *ding-wa.* |
| Flock, *s.* | ཁྱུ་ | *khyu.* |
| Flog, to | གཞུ་བ་ | *sku-wa.* |
| Flood | ཆུ་རུད་ | *chhu rü.* |
| Do. to | ཆུ་ཡིས་གནོན་པ་ | *chhu-yi nem-p* |
| Floor, boarded | སྤང་ལེབ་ | *pang-lep.* |
| Do. of earth | ས་ | *sa.* |
| Do. plastered | ཞལ་ (ཞལ་ལ་ | *ska-la.* |

| | | |
|---|---|---|
| Flour, barley | ཙམ་པ་ | *tsam-pa.* |
| Do. *hon.* | གསོལ་ཞིབ་ | *sö-sḱiṕ.* |
| Flour, wheat | གྲོ་ཞིབ་ | *t́ro-sḱiṕ.* |
| Do. rice | འབྲས་ཙམ་ | *dre-tsam.* |
| Flourishing | གཡང་ཆེན་པ་ | *yang-chhem-po.* |
| Flout, to (scoff) | ཀྱག་ཀྱག་བྱས་ནས་ལབ་པ་ | *kya-kya cḱe-ne laṕ-pa.* |
| Do. *hon.* | ཀྱག་ཀྱག་གནང་ནས་གསུང་བ་ | *kya-kya nang-ne sung-wa.* |
| Flout, to (insult) | སྨད་ར་བཏང་ (གཏོང་) བ་ | *me-ra tang-wa.* |
| Do. *hon.* | སྨད་ར་གཏོང་ང་ (བ་) གནང་བ་ | *me-ra tong-nga nang-wa.* |
| Flow, to | རྒྱུག་པ་ | *gyuḱ-pa.* |
| Flow out, to | འཐོན་པ་ | *thöm-pa.* |
| Flower | མེ་ཏོག་ | *me-to.* |
| Do. garden. | མེ་ཏོག་ལྡུམ་ར་ | *me-to dum-ra.* |
| Fluently | ཆུ་རྒྱུག་རྒྱུག་ | *chhu-gyuḱ-gyu.* |
| Fluid (food) | ཁུ་བ་ | *khu-wa.* |
| Flute (small) | གླིང་བུ་ | *ling-ṕu.* |
| Flute (large, held across the body) | ཐྲེད་གླིང་ | *thre-ling.* |
| Do. *hon.* | ཞལ་གླིང་ | *sḱe-ling.* |
| Fly, *s.* | སྦྲང་མ་ | *drang-ma.* |
| Do. to (of bird) | འཕིར་བ་ (འཕུར་བ་) | *phir-wa.* |

| | | |
|---|---|---|
| Foal, *s.* | ཏི་ཀི་ (ཏེའུ་) | *ti-ki.* |
| Do. of an ass | ཨུ་ཏི་འི་ (ཨུ་ཏི་) | *u-ti-i.* |
| Foam | ལྦུ་བ་ | *bu-wa.* |
| Fodder (grass and grain) | རྩ་ཆག་ | *tsa-chha.* |
| Foe | དགྲ་ | *dra.* |
| Fog | རྨུགས་པ་ | *muk-pa.* |
| Fold, to | ལྟབ་རྩིས་ (རྩིགས་) རྒྱབ་པ་ | *tap-tsi gyap-pa.* |
| Do. *hon.* | ལྟབ་རྩིས་ (རྩིགས་) སྐྱོན་པ་ | *tap-tsi kyöm-pa.* |
| Foliage | ལོ་མ་ | *lo-ma.* |
| Folk | མི་ | *mi.* |
| Follow, to | གཞུག་ལ་ཕྱིན་པ་ | *sku-la chhim-pa.* |
| Do. *hon.* | གཞུག་ལ་ཕེབ་པ་ | *sku-la phe-pa.* |
| Do. *h. hon.* | གཞུག་ལ་འཆིབ་རྒྱུ་གནང་བ་ | *sku-la chhip-gyu nang-wa.* |
| Fond of, to be (of persons and things) | ཞེན་ཆགས་བྱེད་པ་ | *sken-chha cke-pa.* |
| Do. *hon.* | ཞེན་ཆགས་གནང་བ་ | *sken-chha nang-wa.* |
| Fondle, to | བྱམས་པོ་བྱེད་པ་ | *ckam po cke-pa.* |
| Do. *hon.* | བྱམས་པོ་གནང་བ་ | *ckam-po nang-wa.* |
| Fondness | བྱམས་པོ་ | *ckam-po.* |
| Food | ཁ་ལག། ལྟོ་ | *kha-la; to.* |
| Do. *hon.* | ཞལ་ལག་ | *ske-la.* |

| | | |
|---|---|---|
| **Fool** | གླེན་པ། ཀླུགས་པ་ | *lem-pa ; kuḱ-pa.* |
| **Foolhardy (rash)** | ཁ་མེད་མིག་མེད་ | *kha-me miḱ-me.* |
| **Foolish (weak in intellect)** | ཀླུགས་པ། གླེན་པ་ | *kuḱ-pa ; lem-pa.* |
| **Do. (senseless, of things)** | དོན་མེད་ | *tön-me.* |
| **Foot** | རྐང་པ་ | *kang-pa.* |
| Do. *hon.* | ཞབས་ | *sḱaṕ.* |
| **Foot, to go on** | རྐང་ཐང་ལ་འགྲོ་བ་ | *kang-thang-la dro-wa.* |
| Do. *hon.* | ཞབས་ཐང་ལ་ཕེབས་པ་ | *sḱaṕ-thang-la pheṕ-pa.* |
| Do. *h. hon.* | ཞབས་ཐང་ལ་འཆིབ་རྒྱུ་གནང་བ་ | *sḱaṕ-thang-la chhiṕ-gyu nang-wa.* |
| **Foot and mouth disease** | ཁ་ཚ་ | *kha-tsha.* |
| **Foot-bridge** | ཟམ་པ་ཆུང་ཆུང་ | *śam-pa chhung-chhung.* |
| Do. *hon.* | ཕེབ་ཟམ་ཆུང་ཆུང་ | *pheṕ-śam. chhung-chhung.* |
| **Foot-path** | རྐང་ཐང་ལ་འགྲོ་ས་ | *kang-thang-la dro-sa.* |
| Do. *hon.* | ཞབས་ཐང་ལ་ཕེབ་ས་ | *sḱaṕ-thang-la pheṕ-sa.* |
| **Foot-path (alongside of cliff)** | འཕྲང་ | *thrang.* |
| **Foot-print** | རྐང་རྗེས་ | *kang-je.* |
| Do. *hon.* | ཞབས་རྗེས་ | *sḱaṕ-je.* |
| **Foot-race** | མི་རྒྱུག | *mi-gyu.* |
| **Foot-soldier** | དམག་མི་ | *ma-mi.* |

| | | |
|---|---|---|
| Footstool | རྐང་སྟེགས་ | *kang-teḱ.* |
| Do. *hon.* | ཞབས་སྟེགས་ | *sḱap-teḱ.* |
| For (because) | ག་རེ་རེད་ཟེར་ན་ | *ḱa-re re śe-na.* |
| For instance | དཔེ་ན་ (དཔེར་ན་) | *pe-na.* |
| For the sake of | དོན་ལ་ | *ťön-la.* |
| Forage (grass) | རྩྭ་ | *tsa.* |
| Forbear, to | ཁོག་པ་བྱེད་པ་ | *khoḱ-pa cḱe-pa.* |
| Do. *hon.* | ཐུགས་ཁོག་གནང་བ་ | *thu-kho nang-wa.* |
| Forbear, to (of monks) | བཟོད་པ་སྒོམ་པ་ | *śö-pa gom-pa.* |
| Do. *hon.* | བཟོད་པ་བཞེས་པ་ | *śö-pa sḱe-pa.* |
| Forbid, to | བཀག་པ་ (འགེགས་པ་) | *kaḱ-pa.* |
| Do. *hon.* | བཀག་ག་ (འགེགས་པ་) གནང་བ་ | *kaḱ ḱa nang-wa.* |
| Forbidding (repulsive) | སྐྱུག་བྲོ་བོ་ | *kyuḱ-ťro-po.* |
| Force (strength) | ཤེད་ | *she.* |
| Do. *hon.* | སྐུ་ཤེད་ | *ku-she.* |
| Force (authority) | དབང་ | *wang.* |
| Do. *hon.* | སྐུ་དབང་ | *ku-wang.* |
| Force, to (compel) | ཨུ་ཚུགས་བྱེད་པ་ | *u-tshu cḱe-pa.* |
| Do. *hon.* | ཨུ་ཚུགས་གནང་བ་ | *u-tshu nang-wa.* |

| | | |
|---|---|---|
| Forcible | ཤུགས་ཆེན་པོ་ | *shuk-chhem-po.* |
| Ford, *s.* | རབ་ | *rap.* |
| Forearm | ལག་ངར་ | *la-ngar.* |
| Do. *hon.* | ཕྱག་ངར་ | *chha-ngar.* |
| Forecast | ལུང་བསྟན་ | *lung-ten.* |
| Do. *hon.* | བཀའ་ལུང་ | *ka-lung.* |
| Forego, to (renounce) | སྤང་བ་ | *pang-wa.* |
| Do. *hon.* | སྤོང་ང་ (བ་) གནང་བ་ | *pong-nga nang-wa.* |
| Foregoing | སྔོན་གྱི་ | *ngön-kyi.* |
| Forehead | དཔལ་ཁོག་ ( ཐོད་པ་ ) | *pe-kho.* |
| Do. *hon.* | དབུ་དཔལ་ | *u-pe.* |
| Foreign | ཕྱི་གླིང་ | *chhi-ling.* |
| Foreigner | ཕྱི་གླིང་ང་ (བ་) | *chhi-ling-nga.* |
| Foreign country | ཕི་ (ཕྱི་) གླིང་ལུང་པ་ | *phi-ling lung-pa.* |
| Foreign Secretary | ཕྱི་རྒྱའི་བློན་ཆེན་ | *chhi-gye lön-chhen.* |
| Foreknowledge | མངོན་ཤེས་ | *ngön-she.* |
| Do. *hon.* | མངོན་མཁྱེན་ | *ngön-khyen.* |
| Forenoon (8 a.m. to 10 a.m.) | ཚ་ཏིང་ | *tsha-ting.* |
| Forerunner | སྔན་ (སྔོན་) བགྲོད་པ་ | *ngen-drö-pa.* |
| Foretell, to | མངོན་ཤེས་ཤེས་པ་ | *ngön-she she-pa.* |

| | | |
|---|---|---|
| Foretell, to, *hon.* | མངོན་མཁྱེན་མཁྱེན་པ་ | *ngön-khyen khyem-pa.* |
| Foretell, to (in a trance) | ལུང་བསྟན་ (སྟོན་) པ་ | *lung-tem-pa.* |
| Do. *hon.* | ལུང་བསྟན་ ( སྟོན་ ) པ་གནང་བ་ | *lung-tem pa nang-wa.* |
| Forest | ཤིང་ནགས། ནགས་གསེབ་ | *shing-na ; naḱ-seṕ.* |
| Forever | ནམ་རྒྱུན། དུས་རྒྱུན་ | *nam-gyün ; ťü-gyün.* |
| Forge, *s.* | བཟོ་ཐབ་ | *śo-thaṕ.* |
| Forget, to. | རྗེད་པ། བརྗེད་ནས་མེད་པ་ | *je-pa ; je-ne-me-pa.* |
| Do. *hon.* | བསྙེལ་བ། ཐུགས་བསྙེལ་ཤོར་བ་ | *nyel-wa ; thu-nye shor-wa.* |
| Forgive, to | དགོངས་པ་བཏང་ (གཏོང་) པ། སྙིང་རྗེ་བལྟ་བ་ | *gong-pa tang-pa ; nying-je ta-wa.* |
| Do. *hon.* | དགོངས་པ་གཏོང་ང་ (བ་) གནང་བ། སྙིང་རྗེ་གཟིགས་པ་ | *gong-pa tong-nga nang-wa nying-je śik-pa.* |
| Fork | ཤ་འཛིན་ | *shan-dzin.* |
| Form, *s.* (shape) | བཟོ་བལྟ་ | *śoṕ-ta.* |
| Do. *hon.* | སྐུ་བཟོ་ | *ku-śo.* |
| Form, to (make) | བཟོ་བ་ | *śo-wa.* |
| Do. *hon.* | བཟོ་བ་གནང་བ་ | *śo-wa nang-wa.* |
| Formally | ལུགས་སྲོལ་ནང་བཞིན་ | *luḱ-sö nang sḱin.* |
| Former | སྔོན་གྱི། དང་པོ་ | *ngön-ḱyi ; ťang-po.* |

| | | |
|---|---|---|
| Formerly (a short time ago) | སྔན་ལ་ (སྔོན་ལ་) | *ngen-la.* |
| Do. (a long time ago) | སྔར་ | *ngar.* |
| Formidable | ཞེད་སྣག་ཚ་པོ་ | *sKe-tra tsha-po.* |
| Forsake, to | དབྱུག་བཞག་ (འཇོག་) པ་ | *yuk-sKak-pa.* |
| Do. *hon.* | དབྱུག་ག་ (པ་) གནང་བ་ | *yuk-ka nang-wa.* |
| Fort | རྫོང་ | *dzong.* |
| Forthwith | ལམ་སང་། ལམ་ཀྱང་ | *lam-sang ; lam-kyang.* |
| Fortieth | བཞི་བཅུ་པ་ | *sKip-chu-pa.* |
| Fortification | འཛིང་ར་ | *dzing-ra.* |
| Fortnight | བདུན་ཕྲག་གཉིས། བདུན་གཉིས་ | *dün-thra nyi ; dün-nyi.* |
| Fortress | རྫོང་ | *dzong.* |
| Fortunate | བསོ་ (བསོད་) བདེ་ཆེན་པོ། བསོད་ནམས་ཆེན་པོ་ | *so-de chhem-po ; sö-nam-chhem-po.* |
| Do. *hon.* | སྐུ་བསོད་ཆེན་པོ་ | *ku-sö chhem-po.* |
| Fortune, good | བསོ་བདེ་ (བསོད་བདེ་།) བསོད་ནམས་ | *so-de ; sö-nam.* |
| Do. *hon.* | སྐུ་བསོད་ | *ku-sö.* |
| Fortune, bad | བསོ་ (བསོད་) བདེ་སྐམ་པོ། བསོད་ནམས་ཆུང་ཆུང་ | *so-de kam-po ; sö-nam chhung-chhung.* |

| | | |
|---|---|---|
| Fortune, bad, *hon.* | སྐུ་བསོད་ཆུང་ཆུང་ | *ku-sö chhung-chhung.* |
| Forty | བཞི་བཅུ་ | *ship-chu.* |
| Foster, to | གསོ་བ་ | *so-wa.* |
| Do. *hon.* | གསོ་བ་གནང་བ་ | *so-wa nang-wa.* |
| Foul | བཙོག་པ་ | *tsok-pa.* |
| Do. *hon.* | སྐུ་བཙོག་ | *ku-tsho.* |
| Foul, to be | བཙོག་པ་ཡོད་པ་ | *tsok-pa yö-pa.* |
| Do. to become | བཙོག་པ་ཤོར་བ་ | *tsok-pa shor-wa.* |
| Do. *hon.* | སྐུ་བཙོག་ཤོར་བ་ | *ku-tso shor-wa.* |
| Found, to (institute) | བཙུགས་པ་ (འཛུགས་པ་) | *tsuk-pa.* |
| Do. *hon.* | བཙུགས་ག་ (འཛུགས་པ་) གནང་བ་ | *tsuk-ka nang-wa.* |
| Foundation of wall | རྩིག་རྟེན་ | *tsik-ten.* |
| Fountain | ཆུ་མིག | *chhu-mi.* |
| Four | བཞི་ | *ski.* |
| Fourth | བཞི་པ་ | *ski-pa.* |
| Fourteen | བཅུ་བཞི་ | *chup-ski.* |
| Fourteenth | བཅུ་བཞི་པ་ | *chup-ski-pa.* |
| Fowl | བྱ་ | *cka.* |
| Do. domestic | བྱ་དེ་ | *cka-te.* |

| | | |
|---|---|---|
| **Fox** | ཝ་མོ་ | *wa-mo.* |
| **Fractured, to be (of bones)** | རུས་ཁོག་ཆག་པ་ | *rü-kho chhak̄-pa.* |
| **Fragment** | ཆག་དུམ་ | *chhak̄-ťum.* |
| **Fragrance** | དྲི་མ་ | *ťri-ma.* |
| **Frail (infirm)** | ཀྱ་རེ་ཀྱོ་རེ། ཉ་རེ་ (ར་) ཉོ་རེ་ | *kya-re kyo-re ; nya-re nyo-re.* |
| Do. *hon.* | སྐུ་ཀྱོར་ཀྱོར་ | *ku-kyor-kyor.* |
| **Frame,** *s.* | ཁྲི་ | *thri.* |
| **Do. to (construct)** | བཟོ་བ་ | *śo-wa.* |
| Do. *hon.* | བཟོ་བ་གནང་བ་ | *śo-wa nang-wa.* |
| **Frank** | དྲང་པོ་ | *ťrang-po.* |
| Do. *hon.* | ཐུགས་རྒྱུ་དྲང་པོ་ | *thu-gyu ťrang-po.* |
| **Frankincense** | སྤོས་ | *pö.* |
| **Frankly** | མ་...གསང་བ་ | *ma...sang-wa.* |
| **Fraud, to commit** | མགོ་སྐོར་བ་ | *go-kor-wa.* |
| Do. *hon.* | མགོ་སྐོར་ར་ (བ་) གནང་བ་ | *go-kor-ra nang-wa.* |
| Do. *inf.* on *sup.* | དབུ་སྐོར་ཞུ་བ་ | *u-kor sK̄u-wa.* |
| **Free, to,** *v.t.* | ཐར་ར་ (བར་) བྱེད་པ། བཏང་ (གཏོང་) བ་ | *thar-ra cK̄e-pa ; tang-wa.* |
| Do. *hon.* | ཐར་ར་ (བར་) གནང་བ། གཏོང་ང་ (བ་) གནང་བ་ | *thar-ra nang-wa ; tong-nga nang-wa.* |

| | | |
|---|---|---|
| Free, to become | ཐར་བ་ | *thar-wa.* |
| Free, to (by ransom) | བླུ་བ་ | *lu-wa.* |
| Do. *hon.* | བླུ་བ་གནང་བ་ | *lu-wa nang-wa.* |
| Freedom | ཐར་པ་ | *thar-pa.* |
| Freeze, to | ཁྱགས་པ་ཆགས་པ་ | *khyaḱ-pa chhaḱ-pa.* |
| Frequently | ཚར་མང་པོ་ | *tshar mang-po.* |
| Fresco | རི་མོ་ | *ri-mo.* |
| Fresh | གསར་པ་ | *sa-pa.* |
| Fret, to | སེམས་འཁྲུལ་བྱེད་པ། སེམས་འཚབས་པ་ | *sem thre cḱe-pa ; sem-tshaṕ-pa.* |
| Do. *hon.* | ཐུགས་འཁྲུལ་གནང་བ། ཐུགས་སེམས་འཚབས་པ་གནང་བ་ | *thuḱ-thre nang-wa ; thu-sem tshaṕ-pa nang-wa.* |
| Friction (disagreement) | འཁྲུག་གཞི་ | *thruḱ-sḱi.* |
| Friday | གཟའ་སྤ་སངས་ | *śa-pa-sang.* |
| Friend, *m.* | གྲོགས་པོ་ | *ťroḱ-po.* |
| Friend, *f.* | གྲོགས་མོ་ | *ťro-mo.* |
| Friendly relationship (between governments, etc.) | མཐུན་ལམ་ | *thün-lam.* |
| Friends, to make | གྲོགས་པོ་རྒྱབ་པ་ | *ťroḱ-po gyaṕ-pa.* |

| | | |
|---|---|---|
| Friends, to make, *hon.* | གྲོགས་པོ་སྐྱོན་པ་ | *ťrok-po kyöm-pa.* |
| Fright (fear) | ཞེད་སྐྲག་ | *sḱe-tra.* |
| Frighten | ཞེད་སྐྲག་སླང་བ་ | *sḱe-tra lang-wa.* |
| Do. *hon.* | ཞེད་སྐྲག་སློང་ང་ (བ་) གནང་བ་ | *sḱe-tra long-nga nang-wa.* |
| Frightened, to be | ཞེད་པ་ | *sḱe-pa.* |
| Do. *hon.* | ཞེད་པ་གནང་བ་ | *sḱe-pa nang-wa.* |
| Frightful | ཞེད་སྐྲག་ཚ་པོ་ | *sḱe-tra tsha-po.* |
| Frigid | གྲང་མོ། བསིལ་པོ་ | *ťrang-mo ; si-po.* |
| Do. *hon.* | སྐུ་བསིལ་པོ་ | *ku-si-po.* |
| Fringe (of thread, etc.) | ཁ་ཚར། སྣེ་ཚར་ | *kha-tshar ; ne-tshar.* |
| Frivolous | དོན་གནད་ཆུང་ཆུང་ | *ťön-ne chhung-chhung.* |
| Do. *hon.* | ཐུགས་དོན་ཆུང་ཆུང་ | *thuḱ-ťön chhung-chhung.* |
| Frog | སྦལ་པ་ | *be-pa.* |
| From | ནས་ | *ne.* |
| From within | ནང་ནས་ | *nang-ne.* |
| Front of, in (ahead) | སྔན་ལ་ (སྔོན་ལ་) | *ngen-la.* |
| Do. (in presence of) | མདུན་ལ་ | *dün-la.* |
| Do. *hon.* | སྐུ་མདུན་ལ་ | *kun-dün-la.* |
| Front tooth | མདུན་སོ་ | *dün-so.* |
| Do. *hon.* | མདུན་གྱི་ཚེམས་ | *dün-ḱyi-tshem.* |

| | | |
|---|---|---|
| Frontier | ས་མཚམས | *san-tsham.* |
| Frost | ཁྱགས་པ | *khyak̄-pa.* |
| Frost-bitten, to be | གངས་ཀྱིས་འཚིག་པ | *k̄ang-k̄i tshik̄-pa.* |
| Froth | ལྦུ་བ | *bu-wa.* |
| Frown, to | ངོ་ནག་སྡུ་བ | *ngo-na du-wa.* |
| Frozen, to be | ཁྱགས་པ་ཆགས་པ | *khyak̄-pa chhak̄-pa.* |
| Fruit (of crops) | འབྲས་བུ | *dre-p̄u.* |
| Fruit of tree (as orange, etc.) | ཤིང་འབྲས | *shing-dre.* |
| Fruitful (fertile) | ལུད་ཆུ་འཛོམ་པོ | *lü--chhu dzom-po.* |
| Fruitless, to be (useless) | ཕན་མི་ཐོགས་པ | *phen mi thok̄-pa.* |
| Do. *hon.* | ཐུགས་ཕན་མི་གསོ་བ | *thu-phen mi so-wa.* |
| Fry, to | རྔོད་པ | *ngö-pa.* |
| Do. *hon.* | རྔོད་པ་གནང་བ | *ngö-pa nang-wa.* |
| Frying-pan | ཚལ་སླང | *tshe-lang* |
| Fuel | མེ་ཤིང | *me-shing.* |
| Fulfil, to | སྒྲུབ་པ | *drup̄-pa.* |
| Do. *hon.* | སྒྲུབ་པ་གནང་བ | *drup̄-p̄a nang-wa.* |
| Fulfilled, to be | ཚར་བ | *tshar-wa.* |
| Do. *hon.* | གྲུབ་པ | *t̄rup̄-pa.* |
| Full | གང | *k̄ang.* |

| | | |
|---|---|---|
| **Fun** | བལྟས་མོ་ | *te-mo.* |
| **Function** (work) | ལས་ཀ་ | *le-ka.* |
| Do. *hon.* | ཕྱག་ལས་ | *chha-le.* |
| **Functionary** | དཔོན་པོ་ | *pöm-po.* |
| **Fundament** | ཀུབ་ | *kuṕ.* |
| Do. *hon.* | ཞབས་ཕོངས་ | *sḰam-phong.* |
| **Fungus** | ཤ་མོ་ | *sha-mo.* |
| **Funny** | བགད་མོ་ བྲོ་པོ་ | *ge-mo t́ro-po.* |
| Do. *hon.* | ཞལ་མོ་བྲོ་པོ་ | *sḰe-mo t́ro-po.* |
| **Fur-coat** | པགས་ཚ་ | *paḱ-tsha.* |
| Do. *hon.* | སྐུ་ཚ་ | *ku-tsha.* |
| **Furnace** | ཐབ་ | *thaṕ.* |
| **Furnish, to** (supply) | སྒྲུབ་པ་ | *druṕ-pa.* |
| Do. *hon.* | སྒྲུབ་པ་གནང་བ་ | *druṕ-pa nang-wa.* |
| **Furniture** | ཅ་ལག་ (ཆ་ལག་) | *cha-la.* |
| Do. *hon.* | སྐུ་ཅས་ (སྐུ་ཆས་) | *ku-che.* |
| **Furrow** | རོལ་ | *rö.* |
| **Further** (in distance) | ཕ་ཙ་ (ཕར་ཙམ་) | *pha-tsa.* |
| Do. (again) | ད་རུང་ཡང་། ཡང་སྐྱར་ | *t́a-rung-yang; yang-kyar.* |
| **Fuse** (for gun) | སྦིད་དི་ (སྦིད་དེ) | *bi-di.* |

| | | |
|---|---|---|
| **Futile, to be (useless)** | ཕན་མི་ཐོགས་པ་ | *phen mi thok-pa.* |
| **Do.** *hon.* | ཐུགས་ཕན་མི་གསོ་བ་ | *thu-phen mi so-wa.* |
| **Future** | གཞུག་ལ་ | *sku-la.* |

# G

| | | |
|---|---|---|
| Gaiety | དགའ་ཚོར་ | *ga-tshor.* |
| Gain (profit) | ཁེ་བཟང་ | *kheṕ-śang.* |
| Do. *hon.* | སྐུ་ཁེ་ | *ku-khe.* |
| Gain a profit, to | ཁེ་བཟང་ཟ་བ་ | *kheṕ-śang śa-wa.* |
| Do. *hon.* | སྐུ་ཁེ་བཞེས་པ་ | *ku-khe sḱe-pa.* |
| Gain victory, to | རྒྱལ་བ་ | *gye-wa.* |
| Do. *hon.* | རྒྱལ་ར་ (བ་) གནང་བ་ | *gye-ra nang-wa.* |
| Gain, to (obtain) | འབྱོར་བ། ཐོབ་པ་ | *jor-wa ; thoṕ-pa.* |
| Do. *hon.* | ཕྱག་འབྱོར་ཡོང་བ་ | *chhan-jor yong-wa.* |
| Gainsay, to (deny) | རྒྱབ་འགལ་ལབ་པ་ | *gyam-ge laṕ-pa.* |
| Do. *hon.* | རྒྱབ་འགལ་གསུང་བ་ | *gyam-ge sung-wa.* |
| Gainsay, to (dispute) | རྩོད་པ་རྒྱབ་པ་ | *tsö-pa gyaṕ-pa.* |
| Do. *hon.* | རྩོད་པ་སྐྱོན་པ་ | *tsö-pa kyöm-pa.* |
| Gait | འགྲོ་སྟངས་ | *dro-tang.* |
| Do. *hon.* | ཕེབ་སྟངས་ | *pheṕ-tang.* |
| Gale | ལྷགས་པ་ཚ་པོ་ | *hlaḱ-pa tsha-po.* |
| Gall (malignant feeling) | གནོད་སེམས་ | *nö-sem.* |
| Gall-bladder | མཁྲིས་པ་ | *thri-pa.* |
| Gallant, *adj.* | སྙིང་ཆེན་པོ་ | *nying-chhem-po.* |

| | | |
|---|---|---|
| Gallant *hon.* | ཐུགས་སྙིང་ཆེན་པོ་ | *thu-nying chhem-po.* |
| Gallop, to | ཞམ་རིས་བཏང་ (གཏོང་) བ་ | *sKam-pe tang-wa.* |
| Do. *hon.* | ཆིབས་ཞམ་གནང་བ་ | *chhip-sKam nang-wa* |
| Gamble, to | ཤོ་རྒྱབ་པ་ | *sho-gyap-pa.* |
| Do. *hon.* | ཕྱག་ཤོ་སྐྱོན་པ་གནང་བ་ | *chha-sho kyöm-pa nang-wa.* |
| Gambler | ཤོ་པ་ | *sho-pa.* |
| Game (play) | རྩེད་མོ་ | *tse-mo.* |
| Do. *hon.* | སྐུ་རྩེད་ | *ku-tse.* |
| Game (wild animals) | རི་དྭགས་ | *ri-ṫa.* |
| Gander | འངང་པ་ (ངང་པ་) | *ang-pa.* |
| Gang | ཚོགས་ | *tsho.* |
| Gaol | བཙོན་ཁང་ | *tsön-khang.* |
| Gaoler | བཙོན་སྲུང་ང་ (པ་) | *tsön-sung-nga.* |
| Gap | སེར་ཀ་ | *se-ka.* |
| Gape, to (of wounds) | ཁ་བཞག་བསྟད་ (སྟོད་) པ་ | *kha-sKa de-pa.* |
| Do. (yawn) | ཨ་སྟོང་རྒྱབ་པ་ | *a-tong gyap-pa.* |
| Do. *hon.* | ཨ་སྟོང་སྐྱོན་པ་ | *a-tong kyöm-pa.* |
| Garb | དུག་ལོག་ | *ṫu-lo.* |
| Do. *hon.* | ན་བཟའ་ | *nam-śa.* |
| Garden | ལྡུམ་ར་ | *dum-ra.* |

| | | |
|---|---|---|
| Garden, flower | མེ་ཏོག་གི་ལྡུམ་ར་ | *me-tok-ki dum-ra.* |
| Do. vegetable | ཚས་གཡང་ཚེ་ *ch.* | *tshe-yang-tse.* |
| Do. public | གླིང་ག | *ling-ka.* |
| Gardener | གླིང་སྲུང་ང་ (པ) | *ling-sung-nga.* |
| Gargle, to | ཁ་བ་ཤལ་བ་ཤལ་བཏང་ (གཏོང་) བ་ | *kha-she-she tang wa.* |
| Do. *hon.* | ཞལ་བ་ཤལ་བ་ཤལ་གནང་བ་ | *ske she-she nang-wa.* |
| Garland | མེ་ཏོག་འཕྲང་ང་ (འཕྲེང་བ་) | *me-to thrang-nga.* |
| Garlic | སྒོག་པ་ | *gok-pa.* |
| Do. *hon.* | བཞེས་སྒོག | *ske-go.* |
| Garment | དུག་ལོག | *tu-lo.* |
| Do. *hon.* | ན་བཟའ་ | *nam-sa.* |
| Garnish, to (adorn) | རྒྱན་ཆ་བཏགས (འདོགས་) པ་ | *gyen-cha tak-pa.* |
| Garrison | དམག་སྒར་ | *ma-ga.* |
| Garter (for Tibetan boots) | ལྷམ་སྒྲོག | *hlam-dro.* |
| Do. *hon.* | ཞབས་སྒྲོག་ | *skap-dro.* |
| Gas | དུ་བའི་རླངས་པ་ | *tu-we lang-pa.* |
| Gas, poisonous | དུག་རླངས | *tuk-lang* |
| Gate (small) | ཕྱི་སྒོ | *chhi-go.* |

| | | |
|---|---|---|
| Gate (small), *hon.* | གཟིམ་སྒོ་ཕྱི་སྒོ་ | *śim-go chhi-go.* |
| Gate (large) | རྒྱལ་སྒོ་ | *gye-go.* |
| Do. *hon.* | གཟིམ་སྒོ་རྒྱལ་སྒོ་ | *śim-go gye-go.* |
| Gather, to (pick up) | སྒྲུག་པ་ | *druk-pa.* |
| Do. *hon.* | སྒྲུག་ག་ (པ་) གནང་བ་ | *druk-ka nang-wa.* |
| Gather, to (pluck off tree) | གཏོག་པ་ | *tok-pa.* |
| Do. *hon.* | གཏོག་ག་ (པ་) གནང་བ་ | *tok-ka nang-wa.* |
| Gather, to (collect) *v.t.* | སྡུད་པ་ | *dü-pa.* |
| Do. *hon.* | སྡུད་པ་གནང་བ་ | *dü-pa nang-wa.* |
| Gather, to (assemble) *v.i.* | འཚོགས་པ། འཛོམ་པ་ | *tsok-pa; dzom-pa.* |
| Do. *hon.* | ལྷན་རྒྱས་གནང་བ་ | *hlen-gye nang-wa.* |
| Gaunt | ཤ་སྐམ་པོ་ | *sha kam-po.* |
| Do. *hon.* | སྐུ་ཤ་སྐམ་པོ་ | *ku-sha kam-po.* |
| Gay, to be | དགའ་བ། སྐྱིད་པོ་བྱས་ནས་སྡོད་པ་ | *ga-wa; kyi-po che-ne dö-pa.* |
| Do. *hon.* | མཉེས་པོ་གནང་བ། སྤྲོ་པོ་གནང་ནས་བཞུགས་པ་ | *nye-po nang-wa; tro-po nang-ne shuk-pa.* |
| Do. *h. hon.* | ཐུགས་དགྱེས་པོ་གནང་བ་ | *thu-gye-po nang-wa.* |
| Gaze, to | ལྟ་བ་ | *ta-wa.* |
| Do. *hon.* | གཟིགས་པ་ | *śi-pa.* |

| | | |
|---|---|---|
| Gelding | ཕོ་རྟ་ | *pho-ta.* |
| Gem | ནོར་བུ་ | *nor-ṗu.* |
| Gender | ཕོ་མོ་ | *pho-mo.* |
| Genealogy (of laymen) | རིགས་བརྒྱུད། མི་བརྒྱུད་ | *ri-gyü ; mi-gyü.* |
| Do. *hon.* | སྐུ་བརྒྱུད་ | *ku-gyü.* |
| Do. *hon.* (of lamas) | གདུང་བརྒྱུད་ | *dung-gyü.* |
| Generally | ཕལ་ཆེར་ | *phe-chher.* |
| Generate, to | སྐྱེད་པ་ | *kye-pa.* |
| Generation | མི་བརྒྱུད་ | *mi-gyü.* |
| Generosity | དྲིན་ | *ťrin.* |
| Do. *hon* | བཀའ་དྲིན་ | *ka-ťrin.* |
| Generous | ལག་པ་ཤོག་པོ་ | *laǩ-pa shoǩ-po.* |
| Do. *hon.* | ཕྱག་ཤོག་པོ་ | *chha-shoǩ-po.* |
| Genius | རིག་པ་ | *riǩ-pa.* |
| Do. *hon.* | ཐུགས་རིག་ | *thu-ri.* |
| Gentian | ཏིག་ཏ་ | *tiǩ-ta.* |
| Gentile | ཕྱི་པ་ | *chhi-pa.* |
| Gentle | འཇམ་པོ་ | *jam-po.* |
| Do. in speech | ཁ་འཇམ་པོ་ | *kha jam-po.* |
| Do. *hon.* | ཞལ་འཇམ་པོ་ | *sǩe jam-po.* |

| | | |
|---|---|---|
| Gentle (tame, of animals) | མཉེན་པོ་ | *nyem-po.* |
| Gentleman | སྐུ་དྲག་ | *ku-ťra.* |
| Gently (slowly) | ག་ལེ་ | *ḱa-le.* |
| Do. (not roughly) | འཇམ་པོ་བྱས་ནས་ | *jam-po cḱe-ne.* |
| Do. *hon.* | འཇམ་པོ་གནང་ནས་ | *jam po nang-ne.* |
| Genuine | ངོ་ཐོག། དངོས་ནས་ | *ngo-tho ; ngö-ne.* |
| Geography | འཛམ་གླིང་རྒྱས་བཤད་ | *dzam-ling gye-she.* |
| Germinate, to | སྐྱེ་བ་ | *kye-wa.* |
| Do. to cause to | སྐྱེད་པ་ | *kye-pa.* |
| Gesture | བརྡབ་ (བརྡ་) | *daṕ.* |
| Gesture of hand | ལག་བརྡབ་ (ལག་བརྡ་) | *laḱ-daṕ.* |
| Do. *hon.* | ཕྱག་བརྡབ་ (ཕྱག་བརྡ་) | *chha-daṕ.* |
| Gesture of foot | རྐང་བརྡབ་ (རྐང་བརྡ་) | *kang daṕ.* |
| Do. *hon.* | ཞབས་བརྡབ་ (ཞབས་བརྡ་) | *sḱaṕ-daṕ.* |
| Get, to | འབྱོར་བ། ཐོབ་པ་ | *jor-wa ; thoṕ-pa.* |
| Do. *hon.* | ཕྱག་འབྱོར་ཡོང་བ་ | *chhan-jor yong-wa.* |
| Get by heart, to | བློ་ལ་ཟིན་པ་ | *lo-la śim-pa.* |
| Do. *hon.* | ཐུགས་བློ་ལ་ཟིན་པ་གནང་བ་ | *thu-lo-la śim-pa nang-wa.* |
| Get well, to | དྲག་པ་ | *ťraḱ-pa.* |
| Do. *hon.* | སྐུ་དང་བ་ | *ku-ťang-wa.* |

| | | |
|---|---|---|
| Get through, to | ཐར་བ་ | *thar-wa.* |
| Get up, to, *v.i.* | ལང་བ་ | *lang-wa.* |
| Do. *hon.* | བཞང་བ་ (བཞེངས་པ་) | *sKang-wa.* |
| Do. *h. hon.* | སྐུ་བཞང་ (བཞེངས་) གནང་བ་ | *ku-sKang nang-wa.* |
| Ghastly (horrible) | ཞེད་སྐྲག་ཚ་པོ་ | *sKe-tra tsha-po.* |
| Ghost | གདོང་འདྲེ། འདྲེ་ | *dong-dre ; dre.* |
| Giant | མི་ཆེན་པོ་ | *mi-chhem-po.* |
| Do. (mythological) | མི་རྒོད་ | *mi-gö.* |
| Gibberish | དོན་དག་མེད་པའི་སྐད་ཆ་ | *t́on-t́a me-pe ke-chha.* |
| Gibe, to | ཀྱག་ཀྱག་བྱས་ནས་ལབ་པ་ | *kya-kya cKe-ne lap̍-pa.* |
| Do. *hon.* | ཀྱག་ཀྱག་གནང་ནས་གསུང་བ་ | *kya-kya nang-ne sung-wa.* |
| Giddy, to be | མགོ་ཡུ་འཁོར་བ། བཟི་ཡོམ་ཡོམ་བྱེད་པ་ | *go-yu khor-wa ; śi-yom-yom cKe-pa.* |
| Do. *hon.* | དབུ་ཡུ་འཁོར་བ་ | *u-yu khor-wa.* |
| Gift (alms to poor) | སྦྱིན་པ་ | *jim-pa.* |
| Do. (to Lama) | འབུལ་བ་ | *bül-wa.* |
| Do. (tip) | ཆང་རིན་ | *chhang-rin.* |
| Do. *hon.* | གསོལ་རས། ཕྲུང་རིན་ | *sö-re ; thrung-rin.* |
| Gigantic | ཆེ་ཐག་ཆོད་ | *chhe-thak-chhö.* |
| Giggle, to | ཁ་ཚེ་ཚེ་བྱེད་པ་ | *kha tshe-tshe cKe-pa.* |

| | | |
|---|---|---|
| Giggle, to, *hon.* | ཞལ་ཚེ་ཚེ་གནང་བ་ | *sḱe tshe-tshe nang wa.* |
| Gild, to (images, etc.) | མཚར་གསེར་བཏང་ (གཏོང་) བ་ | *tsha-ser tang-wa.* |
| Do. *hon.* | མཚར་གསེར་གཏོང་ང་ (བ་) གནང་བ་ | *tsha-ser tong-nga nang wa.* |
| Gilding | མཚར་གསེར་ | *tsha-ser.* |
| Gilt, *s.* | མཚར་གསེར་ | *tsha-ser.* |
| Gilt, to | མཚར་གསེར་བཏང་ (གཏོང་) བ་ | *tsha-ser tang-wa.* |
| Gimlet | སོར་ | *sor.* |
| Ginger | སྒ་སྨུག་ | *ga-mu.* |
| Girdle | སྐེ་རགས་ | *ke-ra.* |
| Do. *hon.* | སྐུ་སྐེ། སྐུ་རགས་ | *ku-ke ; ku-ra.* |
| Girl | བུ་མོ་ | *ṕu-mo.* |
| Do. *hon.* | སྲས་མོ་ | *se-mo* or *tre-mo.* |
| Girth (of saddle) | གློ་ | *lo.* |
| Do. *hon.* | ཆིབས་གློ་ | *chhiṕ-lo.* |
| Gist (of letter, etc.) | དོན་སྙིང་ | *tön-nying.* |
| Give, to | སྟེར་བ་ | *ter-wa.* |
| Do. *hon.* | གནང་བ་ | *nang-wa.* |
| Give, to (to superior) | ཕུལ་བ་ (འབུལ་བ་) | *phü-wa.* |
| Do. *hon.* | འབུལ་ར་ (བ་) གནང་བ་ | *bü-ra nang-wa.* |

| | | |
|---|---|---|
| Give over, to (deliver) | སྤྲད་པ་ | *tre-pa.* |
| Do. *hon.* | གནང་བ་ | *nang-wa.* |
| Give up, to (sins, certain kinds of foods, etc.) | སྤང་བ་ | *pang-wa.* |
| Do. *hon.* | སྤོང་ང་ (བ་) གནང་བ་ | *pong-nga nang-wa.* |
| Glacier | འཁྱགས་རུམ་ | *khya-rum.* |
| Glad, to be | དགའ་བ་ | *ga-wa.* |
| Do. *hon.* | མཉེས་པོ་གནང་བ་ | *nye-po nang-wa.* |
| Do. *h. hon.* | ཐུགས་དགྱེས་པོ་གནང་བ་ | *thu-gye-po nang-wa.* |
| Gladness | དགའ་ཚོར་ | *ga-tshor.* |
| Do. *hon.* | མཉེས་ཚོར་ | *nye-tshor.* |
| Glaring | འོད་ཆེམ་ཆེམ་ | *ö-chhem-chhem.* |
| Glass | ཤེལ་ | *she.* |
| Do. (looking glass) | ཤེལ་སྒོ་ | *she-go.* |
| Do. *hon.* | སྤྱན་ཤེལ་ | *chen-she.* |
| Gleam, to | འོད་རྒྱབ་པ་ | *ö gyap-pa.* |
| Do. (of the sun) | ཤར་བ་ | *shar-wa.* |
| Do. (of the moon) | ཟླ་དཀར་ཤར་བ་ | *da-ka shar-wa.* |
| Glee | དགའ་ཚོར་ | *ga-tshor.* |
| Gleeful, to be | དགའ་བ་ | *ga-wa.* |

| | | |
|---|---|---|
| Gleeful, to be *hon.* | མཉེས་པོ་གནང་བ་ | *nye-po nang-wa.* |
| Do. *h. hon.* | ཐུགས་དགྱེས་པོ་གནང་བ་ | *thu-gye-po nang-wa.* |
| Glimmer, to | འོད་རྒྱབ་པ་ | *ö gyaṕ-pa.* |
| Do. (of the moon) | ཟླ་དཀར་ཤར་བ་ | *da-ka shar-wa.* |
| Glisten, to | འོད་རྒྱབ་པ་ | *ö gyaṕ-pa.* |
| Glistening, *adj.* | འོད་ཆེན་པོ་ | *ö chhem-po.* |
| Glitter, to | འོད་རྒྱབ་པ་ | *ö gyaṕ-pa.* |
| Globe | རིལ་རིལ་ | *ri-ri.* |
| Globular | རིལ་རིལ་ | *ri-ri.* |
| Gloom | མུན་ནག་ | *mi-na.* |
| Glomy, to be (low-spirited) | སེམས་སྐྱོ་སྣང་བྱེད་པ་ | *sem kyo-nang cḱe-pa* |
| Do. *hon.* | ཐུགས་སེམས་སྐྱོ་སྣང་གནང་བ་ | *thu-sem kyo-nang nang-wa.* |
| Glorious (in appearance) | གཟི་བརྗིད་ཆེན་པོ་ | *śi-ji chhem-po.* |
| Do. (celebrated) | སྐད་གྲགས་ཆེན་པོ་ | *ke-ťra chhem-po.* |
| Do. *hon.* | སྙན་གྲགས་ཆེན་པོ་ | *nyen-ťra chhem-po.* |
| Glory (splendour) | གཟི་བརྗིད་ | *śi-ji.* |
| Glossary | མིང་མཛོད་ | *ming-dzö.* |
| Glossy (of silk) | ཀོན་ཡག་པོ་ | *kön-yaḱ-po.* |
| Do. (of wool or cotton) | རྩིག་ག་ (པ་) ཡག་པོ་ | *tsiḱ-ḱa yaḱ-po.* |
| Glove | ལག་ཤུབས་ | *laḱ-shuṕ.* |

| | | |
|---|---|---|
| Glove, *hon.* | ཕྱག་ཤུབས་ | *chha-shuṕ.* |
| Glue | སྦྱིང་ (སྦྱིན་) | *ping.* |
| Gluttonous | གྲོད་ཆེན་པོ་ | *t́rö-chhem-po.* |
| Gnash teeth, to | སོ་བདར་བ་ | *so-dar-wa.* |
| Do. *hon.* | ཚེམས་བདར་ར་ (བ་) གནང་བ་ | *tshem dar-ra nang-wa.* |
| Gnat | སྦྲིན་སྦྲང་ | *sin-drang.* |
| Gnaw, to | སྨུར་བ་ | *mur-wa.* |
| Do. *hon.* | སྨུར་ར་ (བ་) གནང་བ་ | *mur-ra nang-wa.* |
| Go, to | འགྲོ་བ་ | *dro-wa.* |
| Do. *hon.* | ཕེབ་པ། ཐས་པ་ | *phe-pa ; the-pa.* |
| Do. *h. hon.* | འཆིབ་རྒྱུ་གནང་བ་ | *chhiṕ-gyu nang-wa* |
| Go after, to | གཞུག་ལ་ཕྱིན་པ་ | *sḱu-la chhim-pa.* |
| Do. *hon.* | གཞུག་ལ་ཕེབ་པ་ | *sḱu-la phe-pa.* |
| Do. *h. hon.* | གཞུག་ལ་འཆིབ་རྒྱུ་གནང་བ་ | *sḱu-la chhiṕ-gyu nang-wa.* |
| Go-between | བར་མི་ | *ṕar-mi.* |
| Godown | དོས་ཁང་ | *t́ö-khang.* |
| Go down, to (hill, etc.) | ཐུར་ལ་བབ་ (འབབ་) པ་ | *thur-la ṕaṕ-pa.* |
| Do. *hon.* | ཐུར་ལ་ཕེབ་པ་ | *thur-la phe-pa.* |
| Go down, to (diminish, of flood, etc.) | འཆག་པ་ | *chhaḱ-pa.* |
| Go out, to | འཐོན་པ་ | *thöm-pa.* |

| | | |
|---|---|---|
| Go out, to, *hon.* | འཐོན་པ་གནང་བ་ | *thöm-pa nang-wa.* |
| Go round, to | འཁོར་བ་ | *khor-wa.* |
| Do. *hon.* | འཁོར་ར་ (བ་) གནང་བ་ | *khor-ra nang-wa.* |
| Go up, to | འཛག་པ་ (འཛེག་པ་) | *dzak-pa.* |
| Do. *hon.* | འཛག་ག་ (འཛེག་པ་) གནང་བ་ | *dzak-ka nang-wa.* |
| Gaol | བཙོན་ཁང་ | *tsön-khang.* |
| Gaoler | བཙོན་སྲུང་ང་ (པ་) | *tsön-sung-nga.* |
| Goat | ར་ | *ra.* |
| Goat, he- | ར་ཕོ་ | *ra-pho.* |
| Goat, she- | ར་མོ་ | *ra-mo.* |
| Goblin | གདོང་འདྲེ། འདྲེ་ | *dong-dre ; dre.* |
| God | ཀུན་མཆོག་ (དཀོན་མཆོག་) | *kün-chho.* |
| God, a | ལྷ་ | *hla.* |
| Goddess, a | ལྷ་མོ་ | *hla-mo.* |
| Godless | ཆོས་སེམས་མེད་པ་ | *chho sem me-pa.* |
| Goggles | མིག་ཤེལ་ | *mik-she.* |
| Do. *hon.* | སྤྱན་ཤེལ་ | *chen-she.* |
| Goitre | ལྦ་བ་ | *ba-a.* |
| Do. *hon.* | མགྲུལ་ལྦ་ | *gü-ba.* |
| Gold | གསེར་ | *se.* |

| | | |
|---|---|---|
| Gold, *hon.* | ཕྱག་གསེར་ | *chha-se.* |
| Golden (made of gold) | གསེར་གྱི་ | *se ḱi.* |
| Do. (colour) | སེར་པོ་ | *se-po.* |
| Goldsmith | གསེར་བཟོ་བ་ | *ser-śo-wa.* |
| Gong | འཁར་རྔ་ | *kha-nga.* |
| Gonorrhoea | གྲང་གཞི་ | *ťrang-sḱi.* |
| Good, *adj.* | ཡག་པོ་ | *yaḱ-po.* |
| Do. (virtuous) | བཟང་པོ་ | *śang-po.* |
| Good, *s.* (advantage) | ཕན་ | *phen.* |
| Good for, to be | ཕན་ཐོགས་པ་ | *phen thoḱ-pa.* |
| Do. *hon.* | ཐུགས་ཕན་གསོ་བ་ | *thu-phen so-wa.* |
| Good-bye! (to person going) | འོ་ན་རྒྱུག་ཨ་ | *o-na gyu-a.* |
| Do. *hon.* | ག་ལེ་ཕེབས་ | *ḱa-le-phe.* |
| Do. *h. hon.* | ག་ལེ་འཆིབ་རྒྱུ་གནང་ | *ḱa-le chhiṕ-gyu-nang.* |
| Good-bye! (to person remaining) | འོ་ན་སྡོད་ཨ་ | *o-na dö-a.* |
| Do. *hon.* | ག་ལེ་བཞུགས་ | *ḱa-le sḱu* |
| Do. *h. hon.* | ག་ལེ་བཞུགས་གདན་འཇག་ | *ḱa-le sḱu-den ja.* |
| Goods | ཅ་ལག་ (ཆ་ལག་) | *cha-la.* |
| Do. *hon.* | སྐུ་ཅས་ (སྐུ་ཆས་) | *ku-che.* |
| Good-tempered | རྒྱུ་མ་རིང་པོ་ | *gyu-ma ring-po.* |

| | | |
|---|---|---|
| Good-tempered *hon.* | ཐུགས་རྒྱུ་རིང་པོ་ | *thuḱ-gyu ring-po.* |
| Goose | ངང་པ་ | *ngang-pa.* |
| Gorge | རོང་ | *rong.* |
| Gorgeous (of persons) | ངམ་ཟིག་ (བརྗིད་) ཆེན་པོ་ | *ngam-śi chhem-po.* |
| Gossamer | སྡོམ་ཐག་ | *dom-tha.* |
| Gossip, to | ལབ་ལབ་རྡུང་བ། ཁ་ལས་བཤད་པ་ | *laṕ-laṕ dung-wa; khaṕ-le she-pa.* |
| Do. *hon.* | ཞལ་ཞོག་གནང་བ། ཞལ་ལས་གསུང་བ་ | *sḱe-sḱo nang-wa; sḱel-le sung-wa.* |
| Gout | འབམ་ | *bam.* |
| Do. *hon.* | སྐུ་འབམ་ | *kun bam.* |
| Govern, to | དབང་བྱེད་པ་ | *wang-che-pa.* |
| Do. *hon.* | སྐུ་དབང་གནང་བ་ | *ku-wang nang-wa.* |
| Govern a country, to (secular government) | རྒྱལ་སྲིད་གནང་བ་ | *gye-si nang-wa.* |
| Do. (spiritual government) | ཆོས་སྲིད་གནང་བ་ | *chhö-si, nang-wa.* |
| Government | གཞུང་། གཞུང་ཐོག་ | *sḱung; sḱung tho.* |
| Do. Tibetan | སྡེ་པ་གཞུང་ | *de-pa sḱung.* |
| Government revenue | ཞུང་གི་འབབ་ | *sḱung gi baṕ.* |
| Governor | བཀའ་བློན་ | *ka-lön.* |
| Gown | ཆུ་པ་ | *chhu-pa.* |

| | | |
|---|---|---|
| Gown, *hon.* | ན་བཟའ་ | *nam-ṡa.* |
| Grace (favour) | བཀའ་དྲིན། ཐུགས་རྗེ་ | *ka-t́rin ; thuk-je.* |
| Graceful | མཛེས་པོ་ | *dze-po.* |
| Gracious | དྲིན་ཆེན་པོ་ | *t́rin-chhem-po* |
| Do. *hon.* | བཀའ་དྲིན་ཆེན་པོ་ | *ka-t́rin-chhem-po.* |
| Grade (rank) | གོ་ས། གོ་གནས། རིམ་པ་ | *ḱo-sa ; ḱo-ne ; rim-pa.* |
| Gradually | ག་ལེ་ག་ལེ་ | *ḱa-le ḱa-le.* |
| Grain (for human beings) | འབྲུ་ | *dru.* |
| Do. *hon.* | ཕྱག་འབྲུ་ | *chhan-dru.* |
| Grain (for animals) | ཆག་ | *chha.* |
| Grain, parched | ཡོས་ | *yö.* |
| Do. *hon.* | བཞེས་ཡོས་ | *sḱe-yö.* |
| Grammar (orthography) | དག་ཡིག་ | *t́ak-yi.* |
| Granary | འབྲུ་བཀང་འཇུག་<br>འབྲུ་ཁང་ | *dru-kang-juḱ ; dru-khang.* |
| Grand | ཆེན་པོ་ | *chhem-po.* |
| Grand-daughter | བུའི་བུ་མོ། བུ་མོའི་བུ་མོ་ | *ṕu-i ṕu-mo ; ṕu-mö ṕu-mo.* |
| Grandfather | པོ་འོ་ | *po-o.* |
| Do. *hon.* | པོ་འོ་ལགས་ | *po-o-la.* |
| Grandmother | རྨོ་འོ་ | *mo-o.* |

| | | |
|---|---|---|
| Grandmother, *hon.* | རྨོ་འོ་ལགས་ | *mo-o-la.* |
| Grandson (son's son) | བུའི་བུ་ | *ṕu-ï-ṕu.* |
| Do. (daughter's sou) | བུ་མོའི་བུ་ | *ṕu-mö-ṕu.* |
| Grant, to | སྟེར་བ་ | *ter-wa.* |
| Do. *hon.* | གནང་བ་ | *nang-wa.* |
| Grape (fruit) | རྒུན་འབྲུམ་ | *gün-drum.* |
| Grasp, to | ཟིན་པ་ (འཛིན་པ་) | *śim-pa.* |
| Do. *hon.* | ཟིན་ (འཛིན་) པ་གནང་བ་ | *śim-pa nang-wa.* |
| Grasp, to (understand) | ཧ་གོ་བ་ | *ha-ḱo-wa.* |
| Do. *hon.* | མཁྱེན་པ་ | *khyem-pa.* |
| Do. *h. hon.* | དགོངས་པ་རྟོགས་པ་ | *gong pa toḱ-pa.* |
| Grasping (avaricious) | ཧམ་པ་ཆེན་པོ་ | *ham-pa chhem-po.* |
| Grass | རྩྭ་ | *tsa.* |
| Grateful | བཀའ་དྲིན་ཆེན་པོ་ | *ka-t́rin chhem-po.* |
| Grateful, to be | དྲིན་དྲན་པ་ | *t́rin t́rem-pa.* |
| Do. *hon.* | དྲིན་དྲན་པ་གནང་བ་ | *t́rin t́rem-pa nang-wa.* |
| Do. *inf.* to *sup.* | བཀའ་དྲིན་དྲན་པ་ | *ka-t́rin t́rem-pa.* |
| Gratification (pleasure) | དགའ་ཚོར་ | *ga-tshor.* |
| Do. *hon.* | མཉེས་ཚོར་ | *nye-tshor.* |
| Gratified, to be | དགའ་བ་ | *ga-wa.* |

| | | |
|---|---|---|
| Gratified, to be, *hon.* | ཐུགས་མཉེས་པ་ | *thu-nye-pa.* |
| Do. *h. hon.* | ཐུགས་དགྱེས་པ་ | *thu-gye-pa.* |
| Grating (for windows) | ཁྲ་མ་ (དྲ་མ་) | *thra-ma.* |
| Do. iron | ལྕགས་ཁྲ་ (ལྕགས་དྲ་) | *chhak̄-thra.* |
| Gratitude | བཀའ་དྲིན་སྙིང་བཅང་ | *ka-t̄rin nying-chang.* |
| Gratuity (tip) | ཆང་རིན་ | *chhang-rin.* |
| Do. *hon.* | གསོལ་རས། ཁྲུང་རིན་ | *sö-re ; trung-rin.* |
| Grave, *s.* | དུར་ཁུང་ | *t̄ur-khung.* |
| Grave, *adj.* (important) | གནད་ཁག་ཆེན་པོ། གལ་ཆེན་པོ་ | *nen-kha chhem-po ; k̄e chhem-po.* |
| Gravity (importance) | གནད་ཁག་ | *nen-kha.* |
| Gravy | ཤ་ཁུ་ | *sha-khu.* |
| Do. *hon.* | སྐྱུང་ཁུ་ (སྐྱུམ་ཁུ་) | *trung-khu.* |
| Gray | སྔོ་སྐྱ་ | *ngop̄-kya.* |
| Graze, to (eat grass) | རྩ་ཟ་བ་ | *tsa śa-wa.* |
| Grease | ཚིལ་ལུ་ (ཚིལ་བུ་) | *tshi-lu.* |
| Do. liquid | སྣུམ་རྩི་ | *num-tsi.* |
| Greasy | ཞག་རྩི་ཆེན་པོ་ | *sk̄ak̄-tsi chhem-po.* |
| Great | ཆེན་པོ་ | *chhem-po.* |
| Greed | ཧམ་པ་ | *ham-pa.* |

| | | |
|---|---|---|
| Greedy (avaricious) | འདོད་པ་ཆེན་པོ་ | *dö-pa chhem-po.* |
| Do. (gluttonous) | གྲོད་ཆེན་པོ་ | *ťrö-chhem-po.* |
| Green | ལྗང་ཁུ་ | *jang-khu.* |
| Green (of grass) | སྔོན་པོ་ | *ngöm po.* |
| Greet, to (by raising the hands) | ཛབ་མཇལ་བྱེད་པ་ | *dam-jel cKe pa.* |
| Do. *hon.* | ཛབ་མཇལ་གནང་བ་ | *dam-jel nang-wa.* |
| Greet, to, *inf.* to *sup.* (by removing the hat) | ཕྱག་འབུལ་ཞུ་བ་ | *chham-bü sKu-wa.* |
| Do. (by kneeling) | ཕྱག་འཚལ་བ་ | *chha tshe-wa.* |
| Do. *hon.* | སྐུ་ཕྱག་འཚལ་ར་ (བ་) གནང་བ་ | *ku-chha tshe-ra nang-wa.* |
| Greet, to (by (postration) | བརྐྱང་ཕྱག་འཚལ་བ་ | *kyang-chha tshe-wa.* |
| Do. *hon.* | བརྐྱང་ཕྱག་འཚལ་ར་ (བ་) གནང་བ་ | *kyang-chha tshe-ra nang-wa.* |
| Grey | སྔོ་སྐྱ་ | *ngop-kya.* |
| Grief (in serious matters) | སྡུག་བསྔལ། སེམས་འཁྲལ་ | *du-nge ; sem-thre.* |
| Do. *hon.* | ཐུགས་འཁྲལ་ | *thuk-thre.* |
| Grieve, to, *v. i.* (in serious matters) | སྡུག་བསྔལ་བྱེད་པ། མྱ་ངན་བྱེད་པ་ | *du-nge cKe-pa ; nya-ngen cKe-pa.* |
| Do. *hon.* | ཐུགས་ངན་གནང་བ་ | *thu-ngen nang-wa.* |

| | | |
|---|---|---|
| Grieve, to, *v.i.* (in lesser matters) | སེམས་སྐྱོ་བ། སེམས་སྡུག་པ་ | *sem-kyo-wa* ; *sem-duk-pa.* |
| Do. *hon.* | ཐུགས་སེམས་སྡུག་ག་ (པ་) གནང་བ་ | *thu-sem duk-ka nang-wa.* |
| Grim | ཞེད་སྣྲག་ཚ་པོ་ | *sḱe-tra tsha-po.* |
| Grind, to (steel, the teeth) | བདར་བ་ | *dar-wa.* |
| Do. *hon.* | ཟདར་ར་ (བ་) གནང་བ་ | *dar-ra nang-wa.* |
| Grind, to (corn) | བཏགས་པ་ (འཐག་པ་) | *taḱ-pa.* |
| Grindstone (for knives, &c.) | རྡར་རྡོ་ | *dar-do.* |
| Do. (for corn) | རང་འཐག་ | *rang-tha.* |
| Grip, to | ཟིན་པ་ (འཛིན་པ་) | *śim-pa.* |
| Do. *hon.* | ཟིན་ (འཛིན་) པ་གནང་བ་ | *śim-pa nang-wa.* |
| Groan, to | སྐད་ཤོར་བ་ | *ke-shor-wa.* |
| Do. *hon.* | གསུང་སྐད་ཤོར་ར་ (བ་) གནང་བ་ | *sung-ke shor-ra nang-wa.* |
| Grog-shop | ཆང་ཁང་ | *chhang-khang.* |
| Grog-seller | ཆང་མ་ | *chhang-ma.* |
| Groom | ཆིབས་དཔོན་ | *chhiṕ-pön.* |
| Do. *hon.* | ཆིབས་དཔོན་ལགས་ | *chhiṕ-pön-la.* |
| Grotto | བྲག་ཕུག་ | *traḱ-phu.* |
| Ground | ས་ | *sa.* |

| | | |
|---|---|---|
| Ground-rent | ས་གླ་ | *sap-la.* |
| Group | ཚོགས་ | *tsho.* |
| Grouse, sand | གངས་ཀ་ལིང་ | *kang-ka-ling.* |
| Grove, pleasure | གླིང་ཀ་ | *ling-ka.* |
| Grow, to | ཆེ་རུ་ཆེ་རུ་འགྲོ་བ་ | *chhe-ru chhe-ru dro-wa.* |
| Do. *hon.* | ཆེ་རུ་ཆེ་རུ་ཕེབ་པ་ | *chhe-ru chhe-ru phe-pa.* |
| Grow dark, to | ས་རིབ་ (འཁྲིབས་) པ་ | *sa-rip-pa.* |
| Grow old, to | རྒད་རུ་རྒད་རུ་འགྲོ་བ་ | *ge-ru ge-ru dro-wa.* |
| Do. *hon.* | བགྲེས་རུ་བགྲེས་རུ་ཕེབ་པ་ | *dre-ru dre-ru phe-pa.* |
| Gruel | བག་ཐུག་ | *pa thu.* |
| Do. *hon.* | བཞེས་ཐུག་བག་ཐུག་ | *shé-thu pa-thu.* |
| Gruff (surly) | གྱོང་པོ་ | *kyong-po.* |
| Grunt, to | སྐད་རྒྱབ་པ་ | *ke-gyap-pa.* |
| Guarantee | ཁས་ཁྱགས་ | *khe-khya.* |
| Do. *hon.* | ཞལ་ཁྱགས་ | *ske-khya.* |
| Guarantee, to | ཁས་ཁྱགས་བྱེད་པ་ | *khe-khya cke-pa.* |
| Do. *hon.* | ཞལ་ཁྱགས་གནང་བ་ | *ske-khya nang-wa.* |
| Guarantor | ཁས་ཁྱགས་བྱེད་མཁན་ | *khe-khya cke-khen.* |
| Do. *hon.* | ཞལ་ཁྱགས་གནང་མཁན་ | *ske-khya nang-khen.* |
| Guard, *s.* | སྲུང་མཁན་ | *sung-khen.* |

| | | |
|---|---|---|
| **Guard,** to (a place, &c.) | སྲུང་བ་ | *sung-wa.* |
| Do. *hon.* | སྲུང་ང་ (བ་) གནང་བ་ | *sung-nga nang-wa.* |
| Guard, to (take care of goods, &c.) | ཉར་བ་ | *nyar-wa.* |
| Do. *hon.* | ཉར་ར་ (བ་) གནང་བ་ | *nyar-ra nang-wa.* |
| Do. *h. hon.* | ཐུགས་ཅག་གནང་བ་ | *thu-cha nang-wa.* |
| Guardian | མགོ་འདོན་བྱེད་མཁན་ | *gon-dön che-khen.* |
| Guess, *s.* | ཚོད་ | *tshö.* |
| Guest | མགྲོན་པོ་ | *dröm-po.* |
| Do. *hon.* | སྐུ་མགྲོན་ | *kun-drön.* |
| Guide, *s.* | ལམ་རྒྱུད་བྱེད་མཁན། ལམ་ཁ་བསྟན་ (སྟོན་) མཁན་ | *lam-gyü che-khen; lam-kha ten-khen.* |
| Do. *hon.* | ལམ་རྒྱུད་གནང་མཁན་ | *lam-gyü. nang-khen.* |
| Guide, to | ལམ་རྒྱུད་བྱེད་པ། ལམ་ཁ་བསྟན་ (སྟོན་) པ་ | *lam-gyü che-pa; lam-kha tem-pa.* |
| Do. *hon.* | ཕེབས་ལམ་རྒྱུད་གནང་བ་ | *phep-lam-gyü nang-wa.* |
| Guile | གཡོ་སྒྱུ་ | *yo-gyu.* |
| Guileful | གཡོ་སྒྱུ་ཚ་པོ་ | *yo-gyu tsha-po.* |
| Guilt | སྐྱོན། ཉེས་པ་ | *kyön; nye-pa.* |
| Guiltless | ཉེས་པ་མེད་པ་ | *nye-pa me-pa.* |

| | | |
|---|---|---|
| Guilty | སྐྱོན་ཆེན་པོ། ཉེས་པ་ཆེན་པོ་ | *kyön-chhem-po ; nye-pa chhem po* |
| Guinea-pig | ཨབ་ར་ | *ab-ra.* |
| Guitar | སྒྲ་སྙན་ | *dram-nyen.* |
| Do. *hon.* | ཕྱག་སྙན་ | *chha-nyen.* |
| Gull, to | མགོ་སྐོར་བཏང་ (གཏོང་) བ་ | *go-kor tang-wa.* |
| Do. *hon.* | མགོ་སྐོར་གཏོང་ང་ (བ་) གནང་བ་ | *go-kor tong-nga nang-wa.* |
| Do. *inf.* to *sup.* | དབུ་སྐོར་ཞུ་བ་ | *u-kor sKu-wa.* |
| Gullet | མིག་པ་ (མིད་པ་) | *mik-pa.* |
| Do. *hon.* | མགུལ་མིག་ | *gü-mi.* |
| Gully | ཤང་འགག་ | *hrang-ga.* |
| Gum | སྤྱིང་ (སྤྱིན་) | *ping.* |
| Do. for closing envelopes, etc. | ཁ་སྤྱིང་ (ཁ་སྤྱིན་) | *kha-ping.* |
| Do. *hon.* | ཞལ་སྤྱིང་ (ཞལ་སྤྱིན་) | *sKe-ping.* |
| Gum (of teeth) | སོ་རྙིང་ | *so-nying.* |
| Do. *hon.* | ཚེམས་རྙིང་ | *tshem-nying.* |
| Gun | མེ་མདར་ | *men-da.* |
| Do. *hon.* | ཕྱག་མདའ་ | *chhan-da.* |
| Gun-barrel | ལྕགས་ཧྲང་ | *cha-hrang.* |

| | | |
|---|---|---|
| Gun-fuse | སྦིད་རི་ (སྦིད་རེ་) | *bi-di.* |
| Gun, hammer of | སྐམ་པ་ | *kam-pa.* |
| Gun-powder | རྫས་ | *dze.* |
| Gun, ramrod of | སིན་འབིད་ | *sim-bi.* |
| Gun-rest (of Tibetan fashion) | མེ་མདའི་རུ་ | *men-de ru.* |
| Do. *hon.* | ཕྱག་མདའི་རུ་ | *chhan-de ru.* |
| Gun, stock of | སྒུམ་ཤིང་ | *gum-shing.* |
| Do. trigger of | སྐམ་པ་ | *kam-pa.* |
| Guts | རྒྱུ་མ་ | *gyu-ma.* |
| Do. *hon.* | སྐུ་རྒྱུ་ | *ku-gyu.* |
| Gutter (on ground) | ཡོ་པོ་ (ཡུར་པོ་) | *yo-po.* |
| Do. (on roof of house) | འོག་ཆུ་ | *o-chhu.* |

# H

| | | |
|---|---|---|
| Habit (custom) | ལུགས་སྲོལ་ | *luk̄-sö.* |
| Habitation | ཁང་པ། ནང་། སྡོད་ས་ | *khang-pa ; nang ; dö-sa.* |
| Do. *hon.* | གཟིམ་ཁང་། བཞུགས་ས་ | *śim-khang ; sk̄u-sa.* |
| Do. *h. hon* | གཟིམ་ཤག། བཞུགས་གདན་འཛགས་ས་ | *śim-sha ; sk̄u-den ja-sa.* |
| Habitually | རྟག་པར། རྣམ་རྒྱུན་ | *tak̄-pa ; nam-gyün.* |
| Haemorrhoids (piles) | གྲང་ཐོར་ | *ťrang-thor.* |
| Haft | ཡུ་བ་ | *yu-wa.* |
| Hag | མ་རྒན་ | *ma-gen.* |
| Hail, *s.* | སེར་ར་ (སེར་བ་) | *se-ra.* |
| Hail, to (hail-storm) | སེར་ར་ བཏང་ (གཏོང་) བ་ | *se-ra tang-wa.* |
| Do. to (call) | སྐད་བཏང་ (གཏོང་) བ་ | *ke-tang-wa.* |
| Do. *hon.* | གསུངས་སྐད་གནང་བ། སྐད་གཏོང་ང་ (བ་) གནང་བ་ | *sung-ke nang-wa ; ke tong-nga nang-wa.* |
| Hair (on human head) | སྐྲ་ | *tra.* |
| Do. *hon.* | དབུ་སྐྲ་ | *u-tra.* |
| Hair, to wash the | སྐྲ་འཁྲུད་པ་ | *tra thrü-pa.* |
| Do. *hon.* | དབུ་བསིལ་གནང་བ་ | *u-si nang-wa.* |
| Hair, a single | སྐྲ་ཀང་གཅིག་ | *tra-kang chi.* |

| | | |
|---|---|---|
| **Hairs**, two | སྐྲ་ཀང་གཉིས་ | *tra-kang-nyi.* |
| **Hair** (of animals, and human hair other than that on head) | སྤུ་ | *pu.* |
| Do. a single | སྤུ་ཀང་གཅིག་ | *pu-kang-chi.* |
| Do. two | སྤུ་ཀང་གཉིས་ | *pu-kang nyi.* |
| **Hair-brush** | ཕག་ཟེ་ | *phaḱ-śe.* |
| **Half** | ཕྱེད་ཀ་ | *chhe-ka.* |
| **Hall of assembly** | ཚོམས་ཆེན་ | *tshom-chhen.* |
| Do. for monks | འདུ་ཁང་ | *du-khang.* |
| **Halo** | འོད་སྐོར་ | *ö-kor.* |
| **Halt, to** | ཞག་ས་སྡོད་པ་ | *sḱak-sa dö-pa.* |
| Do. *hon.* | བཞུགས་ཞག་གནང་བ་ | *sḱuk-sḱa nang-wa.* |
| **Halter** | ཐོ་མགོ་ (ཐུར་མགོ་ | *thong-go.* |
| **Halting-place** (for the day) | ཞག་ས་ | *sḱak-sa.* |
| Do. *hon.* | བཞུགས་ཞག་ | *sḱu-sḱa.* |
| **Hammer** | ཐོ་བ་ | *tho-wa.* |
| Do. of gun | སྐམ་པ་ | *kam-pa.* |
| **Hamper**, *s.* | སླེ་ཀོག་ (སླེ་པོ་) | *le ko.* |
| Do. *hon.* | ཕྱག་སླེ་ | *chha-le.* |
| **Hamper, to** (hinder). | བཀག་པ་ (འགེགས་པ་) | *kaḱ-pa.* |

| | | |
|---|---|---|
| Hamper, to (hinder) *hon.* | བཀག་ག་ (འགེགས་པ་) གནང་བ་ | *kaḱ-ḱa nang-wa.* |
| Hand | ལག་པ་ | *laḱ-pa.* |
| Do. *hon.* | ཕྱག་ | *chha.* |
| Handcuff, to | ལག་ལྕགས་རྒྱབ་པ་ | *laḱ-cha gyaṕ-pa.* |
| Handcuffs | ལག་ལྕགས་ | *laḱ-cha.* |
| Handful, a | སྤར་ར་ (བ་) གང་ | *bar-ra ḱang.* |
| Do. *hon.* | ཕྱག་གང་ | *chha-ḱang.* |
| Handicraft | ལས་ཀ་ | *le-ka.* |
| Do. *hon.* | ཕྱག་ལས་ | *chha-le.* |
| Handkerchief | སྣ་འཕྱིད་ | *naṕ-chhi.* |
| Do. *hon.* | ཤངས་འཕྱིད་ | *shang-chhi.* |
| Handkerchief (compliment ary) | ཁ་བཏགས་ | *kha-ta.* |
| Do. *hon.* | མཇལ་དར་ | *je-t́ar.* |
| Handle, straight (of knife, &c.) | ཡུ་བ་ | *yu-wa.* |
| Do. *hon.* | ཕྱག་ཡུ་ | *chha-yu.* |
| Handle, curved (of kettle, &c.) | ལུང་ | *lung.* |
| Do. *hon.* | ཕྱག་ལུང་ | *chha-lung.* |
| Handle, to | འཆང་བ་ | *chhang-wa.* |
| Do. *hon.* | འཆང་ང་ (བ་) གནང་བ་ | *chhang-nga nang-wa.* |

| | | |
|---|---|---|
| Handmaid | གཡོག་མོ་ | *yo-mo.* |
| Do. *hon.* | ཞལ་ལྟ་མ་ | *sḱe-ta-ma.* |
| Handsome | ཚར་པོ། མཛེས་པོ་ | *tshar-po; dze-po.* |
| Do. *hon.* | ཐུགས་ཚར་པོ་ | *thu tshar po.* |
| Handwriting | ཡི་གེ་ | *yi-ge.* |
| Do. *hon.* | ཕྱག་བྲིས་ | *chha-ri.* |
| Hang, to, *v. t.* | བཀལ་བ་ (འགེལ་བ་) | *kel-wa.* |
| Do. *hon.* | བཀལ་ར་ (འགེལ་བ་) གནང་བ་ | *ke-ra nang-wa.* |
| Hang, to (a man) | སྐེ་ལ་ཐག་པ་བསྡམས་ནས་བསད་ (གསོད་) པ་ | *ke-la thaḱ-pa dam-ne se-pa.* |
| Hanker after, to | དྲན་པ་ | *t́rem-pa* |
| Do. *hon.* | ཐུགས་དྲན་པ་གནང་བ་ | *thu-t́rem-pa nang wa.* |
| Happen, to | བྱུང་བ་ (འབྱུང་བ་) | *cḱung-wa.* |
| Happiness | དགའ་ཚོར་ | *ga tshor.* |
| Do. *hon.* | མཉེས་ཚོར་ | *nye-tshor.* |
| Happy (comfortable) | སྐྱིད་པོ་ | *kyi-po.* |
| Do. *hon.* | སྤྲོ་པོ་ | *tro-po.* |
| Happy, to be | དགའ་བ་ | *ga-wa.* |
| Do. *hon.* | མཉེས་པོ་གནང་བ་ | *nye-po nang-wa.* |
| Do. *h. hon.* | ཐུགས་དགྱེས་པོ་གནང་བ་ | *thu-gye-po nang-wa.* |

| | | |
|---|---|---|
| Harass, to | སྡུག་པོ་བཏང་ (གཏོང་) བ་ | *duḱ-po tang-wa.* |
| Do. *hon.* | སྡུག་པོ་གཏོང་ང་ (བ་) གནང་བ་ | *duḱ-po tong-nga nang-wa.* |
| Hard (arduous) | དཀའ་ལས་ཁག་པོ་ | *ka-le khak-po.* |
| Do. *hon.* | སྐུ་མཉེལ་པོ། སྐུ་ལས་ཁག་པོ་ | *ku-nye-po ; ku-le khaḱ-po.* |
| Hard (of substance) | མཁྲགས་པོ་ (མཁྲེགས་པོ་) | *thraḱ-po.* |
| Hard-hearted, to be | སྙིང་རྗེ་མེད་པ་ | *nying-je me-pa.* |
| Do. *hon.* | ཐུགས་རྗེ་མེད་པ་ | *thuḱ-je me-pa.* |
| Hardship | དཀའ་ལས་ | *ka-le.* |
| Hardware (of iron things) | ལྕགས་ཅས་ (ལྕགས་ཆས་) | *cha-che.* |
| Do. (of copper things) | ཟངས་ཅས་ (ཟངས་ཆས་) | *śang-che.* |
| Hardy | གཟུགས་པོ་ཐང་པོ་ | *śuḱ-po thang-po.* |
| Do. *hon.* | སྐུ་གཟུགས་ཐང་པོ་ | *ku-śu thang-po.* |
| Hare | རི་གོང་ (རི་བོང་) | *re-ḱong.* |
| Hare-lip | ཞོ་རལ་ | *sho-re.* |
| Hare-year | ཡོས་ལོ་ | *yö-lo.* |
| Harlot | ཆལ་མོ། གཞང་ཚོང་མ། སྨད་ཚོང་མ་ | *chhe-mo ; sḱang-tshong-ma ; me-tshong-ma.* |
| Harm, *s.* | སྐྱོན་ | *kyön.* |
| Harm, to | སྐྱོན་བྱེད་པ་ | *kyön-cḱe-pa.* |
| Do. *hon.* | སྐྱོན་གནང་བ་ | *kyön-nang-wa.* |

| | | |
|---|---|---|
| Harm, to (by witchcraft, &c.) | གནོད་པ་ | *nö-pa.* |
| Do. *hon.* | གནོད་པ་གནང་བ་ | *nö-pa nang-wa.* |
| Harmony, to be in | མཐུན་པ་ | *thüm-pa.* |
| Harp | སྒྲ་སྙན་ | *dram-nyen.* |
| Do. *hon.* | ཕྱག་སྙན་ | *chha-nyen.* |
| Harsh | གྱོང་པོ་ | *ḱyong-po.* |
| Hart | ཤ་བ་ | *sha a.* |
| Harvest | སྟོན་ཐོག་ | *tön-tho.* |
| Haste | བྲེལ་བ་ | *t́re-wa.* |
| Do. *hon.* | ཐུགས་བྲེལ་ | *thu-t́re.* |
| Hasten, to | མགྱོགས་པོ་བྱེད་པ་ | *gyoḱ-po cḱe-pa.* |
| Do. *hon.* | ཚོལ་པོ་གནང་བ་ | *tsö-po nang-wa.* |
| Do. *h. hon.* | ཐུགས་ཚོལ་པོ་གནང་བ་ | *thu tsö-po nang-wa.* |
| Hastily | ལམ་སང་ | *lam-sang.* |
| Hasty (quick) | མགྱོགས་པོ་ | *gyoḱ-po* |
| Do. *hon.* | ཚོལ་པོ་ | *tsö-po.* |
| Hasty (rash) | ཁ་མེད་མིག་མེད་ | *kha-me miḱ-me.* |
| Hate, to | སྡང་པོ་བྱེད་པ་ | *dang po cḱe-pa.* |
| Do. *hon.* | སྡང་པོ་གནང་བ་ | *dang-po nang-wa.* |
| Hat | ཞྭ་མོ་ | *sḱa-mo.* |

| | | |
|---|---|---|
| Hat, *hon.* | དབུ་ཞྭ་ | *u-sḱa.* |
| Hatchet | སྟ་རི། སྟ་གྲི་ | *ta-ri ; ta-t́ri.* |
| Hateful | སྐྱུག་བྲོ་བོ་ | *kyuḱ-t́ro-po.* |
| Haughtiness | ཉམས། ཛ་ཁོག་ | *nyam ; dza-kho.* |
| Haughty | ཉམས་ཆེན་པོ། ཛ་ཁོག་ཆེན་པོ་ | *nyam-chhem-po; dza-kho chhem-po.* |
| Haul, to | འཐེན་པ་ | *them-pa* |
| Do. *hon.* | འཐེན་པ་གནང་བ་ | *them-pa nang-wa.* |
| Haunt, *s.* | ཚང་ | *tshang.* |
| Have, to | ཡོད་པ་ | *yö-pa.* |
| Have, I | ང་ལ་ཡོད་ | *nga-la yö.* |
| Haversack | རྟོ་ཕད་ | *to-phe.* |
| Hawk | ཁྲ་ | *thra.* |
| Hay | གཟན་པ། རྩྭ་སྐམ་པོ་ | *śem-pa ; tsa-kam-po.* |
| Do. *hon.* | ཆིབས་རྩྭ་ | *chhiṕ-tsa.* |
| Hay-fork | ཁེ་རག་ (ཁ་ཧྲག་) | *kheṕ-ra.* |
| Hay-sickle | ཟོར་ར་ (ཟོར་བ་) | *śor-ra.* |
| Hazard | ཉེན་ཁ་ | *nyen-kha.* |
| Hazardous | ཉེན་ཁ་ཆེན་པོ་ | *nyen-kha chhem-po.* |
| Haze | སྨུགས་པ་ | *muḱ-pa.* |
| He | ཁོ། ཁོ་རང་ | *kho ; kho-rang.* |

| | | |
|---|---|---|
| He, *hon.* | ཁོང་ | *khong.* |
| Head | མགོ་ | *go.* |
| Do. *hon.* | དབུ་ | *u.* |
| Head (leader) | མགོ་པ་ | *go-pa.* |
| Head, having a shaved (as a monk) | མགོ་རིལ་ | *go-ri.* |
| Do. *hon.* | དབུ་རིལ་ | *u-ri.* |
| Headache, to have | མགོ་ན་བ་ | *go-na-wa.* |
| Do. *hon.* | དབུ་སྙུང་བ་ | *u-nyung-wa.* |
| Headman | འགོ་བྱེད་ | *go-cḱe.* |
| Headstrong | གྱོང་པོ་ | *ḱyong-po.* |
| Heal, to | དྲག་ག་ (པ་) བཟོ་བ་ | *ťraḱ-ḱa śo-wa.* |
| Do. *hon.* | དྲག་ག་ (པ་) བཟོ་བ་གནང་བ་ | *ťraḱ-ḱa śo-wa nang-wa.* |
| Heal, to (patient of good position) | སྐུ་དངང་ (པ་) བཟོ་བ་གནང་བ་ | *ku-ťang-nga śo-wa nang-wa.* |
| Healed, to be | དྲག་པ་ | *ťraḱ-pa.* |
| Do. *hon.* | སྐུ་དང་བ་ | *ku-ťang-wa.* |
| Health | གཟུགས་པོ། ཁམས་ | *śuḱ-po ; kham.* |
| Do. *hon.* | སྐུ་གཟུགས། སྐུ་ཁམས་ | *ku-śuḱ ; kung-kham.* |
| Healthy | གཟུགས་པོ་བདེ་པོ་ | *śuḱ-po de-po.* |
| Do. *hon.* | སྐུ་གཟུགས་བཟང་པོ་ | *ku-śuḱ śang-po.* |

| | | |
|---|---|---|
| Heap, *s.* | སྤུང་ | *pung.* |
| Heap, to | སྤུང་བ་ | *pung-wa.* |
| Do. *hon.* | སྤུང་ང་ (བ་) གནང་བ་ | *pung-nga na wa.* |
| Hear, to | གོ་བ། ཨམ་མཆོག་གོ་བ་ | *ko-wa ; am-chho ko-wa* |
| Do. *hon.* | གསན་པ། སྙན་ལ་གསན་པ་ | *sem-pa ; nyen la sem-pa.* |
| Hearken, to | ཉར་བ་ | *nyem-pa.* |
| Do. *hon.* | གསན་པ་ | *sem-pa.* |
| Hearsay (report) | སྐད་ཆ། གཏམ་ | *ke-chha ; tam.* |
| Heart | སྙིང་ | *nying.* |
| Do. *hon.* | ཐུགས་སྙིང་། སྐུ་སྙིང་ | *thu-nying ; k… nying.* |
| Heart, to learn by | བློ་ལ་ཟིན་པ་ | *lo-la śim-pa.* |
| Do. *hon.* | ཐུགས་ལ་ཟིན་པ་གནང་བ་ | *thu-la śim-pa nang-wa.* |
| Hearth | ཐབ་ | *thaṕ.* |
| Do. *hon.* | གསོལ་ཐབ་ | *sö-thaṕ.* |
| Heartily | སྙིང་རུས་བྱས་ནས་ | *nying-rü cke-n…* |
| Do. *hon.* | ཐུགས་རུས་གནང་ནས་ | *thuk-rü nang-ne.* |
| Heat | ཚད་པ་ | *tshe-pa.* |
| Do. *hon.* | སྐུ་ཚད་ | *ku-tshe.* |
| Heathen | ཕྱི་པ་ | *chhi pa.* |
| Heaven (sky) | གནམ། ནམ་མཁའ་ | *nam ; nam-kh…* |

| | | |
|---|---|---|
| Heavy | ལྗི་པོ་ | *ji-po.* |
| Hedge | ར་བ་ | *ra-a.* |
| Hedgehog | གཟིག་མོ་ | *śik̄-mo.* |
| Heed, to | ཉན་པ་ | *nyem-pa.* |
| Do. *hon.* | གསན་པ་ | *sem-pa.* |
| Heel | རྟིང་པ་ | *ting-pa.* |
| Do. *hon.* | ཞབས་མཐིལ་ (ཞབས་རྟིང་) | *sk̄aṕ-thil.* |
| Heifer | པེ་བེ་ | *pe-ṕe.* |
| Height (of human being) | རིང་ཐུང་ | *ring-thung.* |
| Do. (of inanimate objects) | མཐོ་དམན་ | *tho-men.* |
| Heir | ནོར་གྱི་བདག་པོ་ | *nor-k̄yi dak-po.* |
| Heiress | ནོར་གྱི་བདག་པོ་ | *nor-k̄yi dak-po.* |
| Hell | དམྱལ་ལ་ (བ་) | *nyel-la.* |
| Helmet | རྨོག་ | *mo.* |
| Do. *hon.* | དབུ་རྨོག་ | *u-mo.* |
| Help | རོགས་ | *ro.* |
| Do. *hon.* | མགོན་འདྲེན་ | *gön-dren.* |
| Help, to | རོགས་བྱེད་པ་ | *ro ck̄e-pa.* |
| Do. *hon.* | མགོན་འདྲེན་གནང་བ་ | *gön-dren nang-wa.* |
| Helper | རོགས་བྱེད་མཁན་ | *ro-ck̄e-khen.* |

| | | |
|---|---|---|
| Helper, *hon.* | མགོན་འདྲེན་གནང་མཁན་ | *gön-dren nang-khen.* |
| Helpful, to be (useful) | ཕན་ཐོགས་པ་ | *phen-thoḱ-pa.* |
| Do. *hon.* | ཐུགས་ཕན་གསོ་བ་ | *thu-phen so-wa.* |
| Helpless | རོགས་ ·· མེད་པ་ | *ro .....me pa.* |
| Hem, *s.* | སྣེ། སྣེ་མོ་ | *ne ; ne-mo.* |
| Hem, to | སྣེ་ནས་འཚེམ་པ་ | *ne-ne tshem-pa.* |
| Do. *hon.* | སྣེ་ནས་འཚེམ་པ་གནང་བ་ | *ne-ne tshem-pa nang-wa.* |
| Hemp | སོ་མ་ར་ཙ་ | *so-ma ra-tsa.* |
| Hen | བྱ་མོ་ | *cḱa-mo.* |
| Hence (from this place) | འདི་ནས་ | *di-ne.* |
| Do. (therefore) | དེའི་རྐྱེན་བྱས་ནས། དེའི་རྐྱེན་གྱིས་ | *t́e-i-kyen cḱe-ne ; t́e-i kyen-ḱyi.* |
| Henceforth | ད་ནས་ཕྱིན་ཆད་ | *t́a-ne chhin-chhe.* |
| Her | མོའི་ | *mö.* |
| Herd | ཁྱུ་ | *khyu.* |
| Herdsman | རྫི་བོ་ | *dzi-o.* |
| Do. of cattle | བ་རྫི་ | *ṕa-dzi.* |
| Do. of goats | ར་རྫི་ | *ra-dzi.* |
| Do. of horses | རྟ་རྫི་ | *ta-dzi.* |
| Do. of hogs | ཕག་རྫི་ | *phaḱ-dzi.* |

| | | |
|---|---|---|
| Herdsman of sheep | ལུག་རྫི་ | *luḱ-dzi.* |
| Do. of yaks | གཡག་རྫི་ | *ya-dzi.* |
| Do. of donkeys | བོང་རྫི་ | *ṕong-dzi.* |
| Do. of fowls | བྱ་རྫི་ | *cḰa-dzi.* |
| Here | འདིར་ | *de.* |
| Hereafter | ད་ནས་ཕྱིན་ཆད་ | *t́a-ne chhin-chhe.* |
| Heresy | ཆོས་ལོག་ | *chhö lo.* |
| Heresy, to commit. | ཆོས་ལོག་བྱེད་པ་ | *chhö-lo cḰe-pa.* |
| Herewith | འདི་དང་མཉམ་དུ་ | *di-t́ang nyam-t́u.* |
| Heritage | ནོར་སྐལ་ | *nor-ke.* |
| Hermit | སྒོམ་ཆེན་ | *gom-chhen.* |
| Hermitage | དབེན་གནས་ | *en-ne.* |
| Hero | དཔའ་བོ་ | *pa-o.* |
| Heroine | དཔའ་མོ་ | *pa-mo.* |
| Hers | མོའི་ | *mö.* |
| Herself | མོ་རང་ | *mo-rang.* |
| Hesitate, to | ཐེ་ཚོམ་ཟ་བ་ | *the-tshom śa-wa.* |
| Do. *hon.* | ཐེ་ཚོམ་གནང་བ་ | *the-tshom nang-wa.* |
| Hesitation | ཐེ་ཚོམ་ | *the-tshom.* |
| Hew, to (length ways) | གཤག་པ་ | *shaḱ-pa.* |

| | | |
|---|---|---|
| Hew, to (breadthways) | བཙབ་པ་ | *tsap̃-pa.* |
| Hiccough, to | ཨི་ཀ་རྒྱབ་པ་ | *i-ka gyap̃-pa.* |
| Hidden (concealed) | སྦས་པ་ | *be-pa.* |
| Do. (secret) | གསང་བ་ | *sang-wa.* |
| Hide, *s.* (*e.g.* of yak, bullock, &c.) | ཀོ་བ་ | *ko-wa.* |
| Do. (*i.e.* skin of sheep, goat, &c.) | པགས་པ་ | *pak̃-pa.* |
| Hide, to, *v.t.* | སྦེད་པ་ | *be-pa.* |
| Do. *hon.* | སྦེད་པ་གནང་བ་ | *be-pa nang-wa.* |
| Hide, to, *v.i.* | ཡིབ་པ་ | *yip̃-pa.* |
| Do. *hon.* | ཡིབ་པ་གནང་བ་ | *yip̃-pa nang-wa.* |
| Hideous | ཞེད་སྐྲག་ཚ་པོ་ | *sk̃e-tra tsha-po.* |
| Hierarchy | ཆོས་སྲིད་ | *chhö-si.* |
| High (of things, rank of persons | མཐོ་པོ་ | *tho-po.* |
| Highway | རྒྱ་ལམ་ | *gya-lam.* |
| Hill | རི་ | *ri.* |
| Do. up | གྱེན་ | *kyen.* |
| Do. down | ཐུར་ | *thur.* |
| Hilt | ཡུ་བ་ | *yu-wa.* |
| Him | ཁོ་ལ་ | *kho-la.* |

| | | |
|---|---|---|
| Himself | ཁོ་རང་ | *kho-rang.* |
| Hinder, to | བཀག་པ་ (འཕེགས་པ) | *kaǩ-pa.* |
| Do. *hon.* | བཀག་ག་ (འགེགས་པ་) གནང་བ་ | *kaǩ-ǩa nang-wa.* |
| Hind-foot | རྐང་པ་ | *ǩang-pa.* |
| Hindrance | བཀག་ཆ་ | *kaǩ-chha.* |
| Hinge (of Tibetan make) | ཏིང་པ་ | *ting-pa.* |
| Hip (of body) | དཔྱི་མགོ་ | *ching-go.* |
| Hire (wages) | གླ། ཕོགས་ | *la ; pho.* |
| Hire, to | གླས་པ་ | *le-pa.* |
| Hired workman | མི་གླ། གླ་པ་ | *mi-la ; la-pa.* |
| His | ཁོའི་ | *khö.* |
| History | ལོ་རྒྱུས། རྣམ་ཐར་ | *lo-gyü ; nam-tha.* |
| Do. *hon.* | གསུང་ཐར་ | *sung-tha.* |
| Hit, to | ཁེས་པ། འཕོག་པ་ | *ǩhe-pa ; phoǩ-pa.* |
| Hit at to (with a stick, fists, &c.) | གཤུ་བ་ | *sǩu-wa.* |
| Hit, a | ལྕག་ | *cha.* |
| Hither | ཚུར། འདི་རུ་ | *tshur ; di-ru.* |
| Hitherto | ད་ཐུག་བར་དུ་ | *ta-thu ṕar-ťu.* |
| Hive (of bees) | སྦྲང་ཚང་ | *lrang-tshang.* |

| | | |
|---|---|---|
| Hoard | བཀང་འཇུག་ | *kang-juk.* |
| Hoar-frost | བ་མོ་ | *pa-mo.* |
| Hoarse, to be | སྐད་འཛེར་བ་ | *ke dzer-wa.* |
| Hobbling (lame) | རྐང་ཀྱོག་ | *kang-kyo.* |
| Do. *hon.* | ཞབས་ཀྱོག་ | *skap-kyo.* |
| Hobgoblin | གདོང་འདྲེ། འདྲེ་ | *dong-dre ; dre.* |
| Hoe | འཇོར་ (ཏོག་ཙེ་) | *jo.* |
| Hoe, to | རྐོ་བ་ | *ko-wa.* |
| Hog | ཕག་པ་ | *phak-pa.* |
| Hoist, to | ཡར་འཕྱར་བ་ | *yar-chhar-wa.* |
| Hold, to (catch hold of) | ཟིན་པ་ (འཛིན་པ་) | *sim-pa.* |
| Do. *hon.* | ཟིན་ (འཛིན་) པ་གནང་བ་ | *sim-pa nang-wa.* |
| Hold up, to | སྟེན་པ་ | *tem-pa.* |
| Hole (made by human being or animal) | ཁུང་ | *khung.* |
| Do. (formed by nature) | ཨི་ཁུང་ | *i-khung.* |
| Hole, peep- | སོ་ཁུང་ | *so-khung.* |
| Holiday | དགོངས་པ་ | *gong-pa.* |
| Hollo! *interj.* | ཝེ | *we.* |
| Hollow, *s.* (in the ground) | ཀོང་སྟོང་ | *kong-tong.* |

| | | |
|---|---|---|
| **Hollow**, *adj.* (of metals, manufactured articles, &c.) | ཁོག་སྟོང་ | *khoḱ-tong.* |
| **Hollyhock** | ཧ་ལོ་མེ་ཏོག་ | *ha-lo me-to.* |
| **Holy** | དམ་པ། ཆོས་ལྡན་ | *t́am-pa chhön-den.* |
| **Homage**, to do | ཕྱག་འཚལ་བ་ | *chha-tshe-wa.* |
| **Home** | ནང་། ཁང་པ་ | *nang ; khang-pa.* |
| Do. *hon.* | གཟིམ་ཁང་ | *śim-khang.* |
| Do. *h. hon.* | གཟིམ་ཤག་ | *śim-sha.* |
| **Home, at** | ནང་ལ་ | *nang-la.* |
| **Home-sick**, to be | ལུང་པ་དྲན་པ་ | *lung-pa t́rem-pa.* |
| **Honest** | དྲང་པོ་ | *t́rang-po.* |
| Do. *hon.* | ཐུགས་དྲང་པོ་ | *thu-t́rang-po.* |
| **Honey** | སྦྲང་རྩི་ | *drang-tsi.* |
| **Honour** (respect) | བསྙེན་བཀུར་ | *nyen-kur.* |
| **Honour**, to | བསྙེན་བཀུར་བྱེད་པ་ | *nyen-kur cḱe-pa.* |
| Do. *inf.* to *sup.* | བསྙེན་བཀུར་ཞུ་བ་ | *nyen-kur sḱu-wa.* |
| **Hood** (as scarf wound round the face to protect from cold, &c.) | ཁ་དཀྲིས་ | *kha-tri.* |
| Do. *hon.* | ཞལ་དཀྲིས་ | *sḱe-tri.* |
| **Hoof** | རྨིག་པ་ | *miḱ-pa.* |

| | | |
|---|---|---|
| Hook | ཀྱུག་ | *kuk.* |
| Hook, fish- | ཉ་ཀྱུག་ | *nya-kuk.* |
| Hook, iron- | ལྕགས་ཀྱུ་ | *cha-kyu.* |
| Hookah | ཧོར་ཁ་ *Hind.* | *hor-kha.* |
| Do. *hon.* | བཞེས་ཧོར་ | *ske-hor.* |
| Hookah, bowl of | ཅི་ལིམ་ *Hind.* | *chi-lim.* |
| Hoop | ཤན་ | *shen.* |
| Do. iron | ལྕགས་ཤན་ | *cha-shen.* |
| Hoopoe | པུ་པུ་ཁུ་ཤུད་ (ཕུ་ཤུད་) | *pu-pu khu-shü.* |
| Hope | རེ་བ་ | *re-wa.* |
| Do. *hon.* | ཐུགས་རེ་ | *thu-re.* |
| Hope, to | རེ་བ་བྱེད་པ་ | *re-wa che-pa.* |
| Do. *hon.* | ཐུགས་རེ་གནང་བ་ | *thu-re nang-wa.* |
| Hopeless, to be | རེ་བ་མེད་པ་ | *re-wa me-pa.* |
| Do. *hon.* | ཐུགས་རེ་མེད་པ་ | *thu re me pa.* |
| Horizon | མཐོང་བའི་འཁོར་ | *thong-we khor.* |
| Horn | རྭ་ཅོ་ | *ra-cho.* |
| Hornet | སྦྲང་མ་ | *drang-ma.* |
| Hornless | ཨ་ཡུ་ | *a-yu.* |
| Horoscope | སྐྱེ་སྐར་རྟགས་པ་ | *kye-ka tak-pa.* |

| | | |
|---|---|---|
| Horoscope, *hon.* | འཁྲུངས་སྐར་རྟགས་པ་ | *thrung-ka taḱ-pa.* |
| Horrible | ཞེད་སྐྲག་ཚ་པོ་ | *sḱe-tra tsha-po.* |
| Horrid | ཞེད་སྐྲག་ཚ་པོ་ | *sḱe-tra tsha-po.* |
| Horrifying | ཞེད་སྐྲག་ཚ་པོ་ | *sḱe-tra tsha-po.* |
| Horror | ཞེད་སྐྲག་ | *sḱe-tra.* |
| Horse | རྟ་ | *ta* |
| Do. *hon.* | ཆིག་པ་ ( ཆིབས་པ་ ) | *chhiḱ-pa.* |
| Horse, Chinese | སིང་རྟ་ | *sing-ta.* |
| Horse, Indian country-bred | རྟི་པི་ཙག་ | *ti pi-cha.* |
| Horse, saddle | ཞོན་རྟ་ | *sḱön-ta.* |
| Do. *hon.* | ཆིབས་པ་ | *chhiḱ-pa.* |
| Horse, pack | ཁལ་རྟ་ | *khe-ta.* |
| Horse, saddle (of very high official or lama) | ཆིབས་ཆེན་ | *chhiṕ-chhen.* |
| Horse-dung | རྟའི་སྦངས་ | *te-ƀang.* |
| Horse-hair (of the tail) | རྟ་རྔ་ | *ta-nga.* |
| Horse-whip | རྟ་ལྕག་ | *te-cha.* |
| Do. *hon.* | ཆིབས་ལྕག་ | *chhiṕ-cha.* |
| Horseman | རྟ་པ་ | *ta-pa.* |
| Horsemen, body of | རྟ་རག་ | *taṕ-ra.* |
| Do. *hon.* | ཆིབས་རག་ | *chhiṕ-ra.* |

| | | |
|---|---|---|
| Horse-shoe | རྨིག་ལྕགས་ | *mik-cha.* |
| Hospitable | ལག་པ་ཤོག་པོ་ | *lak-pa shok-po.* |
| Do. *hon.* | ཕྱག་ཤོག་པོ་ | *chha-shok-po.* |
| Hospital | སྨན་ཁང་ | *men-khang.* |
| Host (army) | དམག་ | *ma.* |
| Do. (crowd of persons) | མི་དཔུང་ | *mi-pung.* |
| Do. (owner of house, inn, &c.) | གནས་པོ་ | *ne-po.* |
| Hostess | གནས་མོ་ | *ne-mo.* |
| Hot | ཚ་པོ་ | *tsha-po.* |
| Hot-tempered | རླུང་ལང་པོ་ | *lung lang-po.* |
| Do. *hon.* | སྐུ་རླུང་བཞང་པོ་ | *ku lung skang-po.* |
| Hot (of weather) | ཚད་པ་ཚ་པོ་ | *tshe-pa tsha-po.* |
| Hot, to be (of body) | ཚད་པ་འཚིག་པ་ | *tshe-pa tshik-pa.* |
| Do. *hon.* | སྐུ་ཚད་ཚ་པོ་བྱུང་བ་ | *ku-tshe tsha-po ckung-wa.* |
| Hotel | གནས་ཚང་ | *ne-tshang.* |
| Hotel charges | གནས་གླ་ | *ne-la.* |
| Hotel-keeper | གནས་པོ་ | *ne-po.* |
| Do. *f.* | གནས་མོ་ | *ne-mo.* |
| Hound | ཁྱི་ | *khyi.* |
| Do. *hon.* | གཟིམ་ཁྱི་ | *sim-khyi.* |

| | | |
|---|---|---|
| Hour | ཆུ་ཚོད་ | *chhu-tshö.* |
| House | ནང་། ཁང་པ་ | *nang ; khang-pa.* |
| Do. *hon.* | གཟིམ་ཁང་ | *śim-khang.* |
| Do. *h. hon* | གཟིམ་ཤག་ | *śim-sha.* |
| House-owner | ཁང་བདག་ | *khang-dak̄.* |
| House agent | ཁང་གཉེར་ | *khang-nyer.* |
| House, care-taker of | ཁང་སྲུང་ང་ (བ་) | *khang-sung-nga.* |
| House-rent | ཁང་གླ་ | *khang-la.* |
| Household | ནང་མི་ | *nang-mi.* |
| Housewife | གནས་མོ་ | *ne-mo.* |
| Do. *hon.* | སྙི་སྙིང་ལགས་ | *nyi-nying-la.* |
| Hovel | ནང་ཆུང་། ཁང་ཆུང་ | *nang-chhung ; khang-chhung.* |
| How | ག་འདྲས་ | *k̄an-dre.* |
| How much | ག་ཚོད་ | *k̄a-tshö.* |
| Howbeit | ག་རེ་ཡིན་ནས་ | *ka-re yin-ne.* |
| However | ཡིན་ནས། ཡིན་ཀྱང་། ཡིན་ན་ཡང་ | *yin-ne ; yin-kyang ; yin-na-yang.* |
| Howl, to (of dogs) | སྦུག་སྐད་རྒྱབ་པ་ | *duk̄-k̄e gyap̄-pa.* |
| Do. (of children crying) | ངུ་བ་ | *ngu-wa.* |
| Hug, to | འཁྱུད་པ་ | *khyü-pa.* |

| | | |
|---|---|---|
| Huge | ཆེ་ཐག་ཆོད་ | *chhe-thaḱ-chhö.* |
| Hullo! (expression of surprise) | ཨ་ཙི་ | *a-tsi.* |
| Human | མིའི་ | *mi-i.* |
| Humble | སེམས་ཆུང་ཆུང་ | *sem-chhung-chhung.* |
| Do. *hon.* | ཐུགས་སེམས་ཆུང་ཆུང་ | *thuḱ sem chhung-chhung.* |
| Humid | རློན་པ་ | *löm-pa.* |
| Humorous | བགད་མོ་བྲོ་པོ་ | *ge-mo t́ro-po.* |
| Do. *hon.* | ཞལ་མོ་བྲོ་པོ་ | *sḱe-mo t́ro-po.* |
| Hunch-back | སྟོད་དགུར་ | *tö-gur.* |
| Hundred | བརྒྱ་ཐམ་པ་ | *gya-tham-pa.* |
| Hundredth | བརྒྱ་ཐམ་པ་ | *gya-tham-pa.* |
| Hunger | ལྟོགས་པ་ | *toḱ-pa.* |
| Do. *hon.* | བཀྲེས་པ་ | *tre pa.* |
| Hungry, to be | གྲོ་ (གྲོད་) ཁོག་ལྟོགས་པ་ | *t́ro kho toḱ-pa.* |
| Do. *hon.* | གསོལ་གྲོད་དཀྲེས་པ་ | *sö-t́rö tre-pa.* |
| Hunt, to | ཁྱི་ར་རྒྱབ་པ་ | *khyi-ra gyaṕ-pa.* |
| Hunter | ཁྱི་ར་བ་ | *khyi-ra-wa.* |
| Hurricane | ལྷགས་པ་ཚ་པོ་ | *hlaḱ-pa tsha-po.* |
| Do. (with rain) | ཆར་རླུང་ | *chhar-lung.* |
| Hurry, to | མགྱོགས་པོ་བྱེད་པ་ | *gyoḱ-po cḱe-pa.* |

| | | |
|---|---|---|
| Hurry, to, *hon.* | རྩོལ་པོ་གནང་བ་ | *tsö-po nang-wa.* |
| Do. *h. hon.* | ཐུགས་རྩོལ་པོ་གནང་བ་ | *thu tsö-po nang-wa.* |
| Hurry, in a great | བྲེལ་བ་ཚ་པོ་བྱས་ནས་ | *t́re-wa tsha-po cḱe-ne.* |
| Do. *hon.* | མཛད་བྲེལ་ཆེན་པོ་གནང་ནས་ | *dze-t́re chhem-po nang-ne.* |
| Hurt (physical) | རྨ་ | *ma.* |
| Do. (by witchcraft, etc.) | གནོད་པ་ | *nö-pa.* |
| Hurt, to (physically) | རྨ་བཟོ་བ་ | *ma-śo-wa.* |
| Do. (by witchcraft, etc.) | གནོད་པ་བྱེད་པ་ | *nö-pa cḱe-pa.* |
| Hurt, to (impair) | སྐྱོན་བྱེད་པ་ | *kyön-cḱe-pa.* |
| Do. *hon.* | སྐྱོན་གནང་བ་ | *kyön-nang-wa.* |
| Hurt, to be | སྐྱོན་བྱེད་པ་ | *kyön-cḱe-pa.* |
| Husband | ཁྱོ་ག་ | *khyo-ḱa.* |
| Husbandman | སོ་ནམས་བྱེད་མཁན་ | *sö-nam cḱe-khen.* |
| Husband and wife | བཟའ་ཚང་ | *śa-tshang.* |
| Husbandry (agriculture) | སོ་ནམས་ | *sö-nam.* |
| Husk (of grain) | པགས་པ་ | *paḱ-pa.* |
| Hut | ནང་ཆུང་། ཁང་ཆུང་ | *nang-chhung ; khang-chhung.* |
| Hydrophobia | ཁྱི་སྨྱོན་ | *khyim-nyön.* |
| Hymn | མགུར་མ་ | *gur-ma.* |

# I

| | | |
|---|---|---|
| **I** | ང་ | *nga.* |
| Do. myself | ང་རང་ | *nga-rang.* |
| **Ice** | ཁྱག་པ་ | *khyaḱ-pa.* |
| **Icicle** | ཁྱག་པ་ | *khyaḱ pa.* |
| **Icy, to be** | ཁྱག་པ་ཡོད་པ་ | *khyaḱ-pa yö-pa.* |
| **Idea (purport)** | དོན་ | *t́ön.* |
| Do. *hon.* | སྐུ་དོན་ | *ku-t́ön.* |
| **Idea (opinion)** | བསམ་པ་ | *sam pa.* |
| Do. *hon.* | ཐུགས་སེམས་ | *thu-sem.* |
| **Identical** | གཅིག་པ་ | *chiḱ-pa.* |
| **Identify, to** | ངོ་འཕྲོད་སྤྲད་པ་ | *ngo-thrö tre-pa.* |
| Do. *hon.* | ངོ་འཕྲོད་གནང་བ་ | *ngo-thrö nang-wa.* |
| **Idiom** | སྐད་ལུགས་ | *ke-lu.* |
| **Idiot** | རྐུགས་པ། གླེན་པ་ | *kuḱ-pa ; lem-pa.* |
| **Idiotic (stupid)** | རྐུགས་པ། གླེན་པ་ | *kuḱ-pa ; lem-pa.* |
| **Idle** | རྒྱུ་མ་རིང་པོ། ལེ་ལོ་ཆེན་པོ་ | *gyu-ma ring po; le-lo chhem-po.* |
| Do. *hon.* | ཐུགས་རྒྱུ་རིང་པོ་ | *thu-gyu ring-po.* |
| **Idol** | སྐུ་འདྲ་ | *kun-dra.* |
| **If** | གལ་སྲིད་....ན་ | *ḱe-si...na.* |

| | | |
|---|---|---|
| Ignite, to | འབར་བ་ | *bar-wa.* |
| Ignoble | སྐྱེ་ས་དམའ་པོ་ | *kye-sa ma-po.* |
| Ignominious | ངོ་ཚ་པོ་ | *ngo-tsha-po.* |
| Ignominy | ངོ་ཚ་ | *ngo-tsha.* |
| Ignoramus | ལྐུགས་པ་ | *kuḱ-pa.* |
| Ignorant | ཡོན་ཏན་མེད་པ་ | *yön-ten me-pa.* |
| Do. *hon.* | སྐུ་ཡོན་མེད་པ་ | *ku-yön me-pa.* |
| Ill, to be | ན་བ་ | *na-wa.* |
| Do. *hon.* | སྙུང་བ་ | *nyung-wa.* |
| Illegal | ཁྲིམས་མེད་ | *thrim-me.* |
| Ill-fated | བསོད་བདེ་མེད་པ། བསོད་བདེ་ཆུང་ཆུང་། | *so-de me-pa ; so-de chhung-chhung.* |
| Do. *hon.* | སྐུ་བསོད་མེད་པ། སྐུ་བསོད་ཆུང་ཆུང་ | *ku-sö me-pa ; ku-sö chhung-chhung.* |
| Ill-feeling, to cherish | སེམས་ལ་ངན་པ་བྱས་ནས་བཞག་ (འཇོག་) པ་ | *sem-la ngem-pa cḱe-ne sḱak-pa.* |
| Ill-luck | བསོད་བདེ་མེད་པ་ | *so-de me-pa.* |
| Do. *hon.* | སྐུ་བསོད་མེད་པ་ | *ku-sö me-pa.* |
| Ill-natured | སེམས་ངན་པ་ | *sem-ngem-pa.* |
| Do. *hon.* | ཐུགས་སེམས་ངན་པ་ | *thu-sem ngem-pa.* |

| | | |
|---|---|---|
| Ill-will | སྙིང་ནད་ | *nying-ne.* |
| Illegal | ཁྲིམས་མེད་ | *thrim-me.* |
| Illegitimate | ཁྲིམས་མེད་ | *thrim-me.* |
| Illicit | ཁྲིམས་མེད་ | *thrim-me.* |
| Illimitable | ཚོད་མེད་པ་ | *tshö-me-pa.* |
| Illiterate, to be | ཡོན་ཏན་མེད་པ་ | *yön-ten me-pa.* |
| Do. *hon.* | སྐུ་ཡོན་མེད་པ་ | *ku-yön me-pa.* |
| Illness | ན་ཚ་ | *na-tsha.* |
| Do. *hon.* | སྙུང་གཞི་ | *nyung-sḱi.* |
| Illuminate, to | འོད་རྒྱབ་པ་ | *ö-gyaṕ-pa.* |
| Illusion (optical) | མིག་འཁྲུལ་ | *miḱ-thrü.* |
| Illusive | མིག་འཁྲུལ་ཆེན་པོ་ | *miḱ-thrü chhem-po.* |
| Illustrate, to | དཔེ་སྦྱར་ནས་བཤད་པ་ | *pe-jar-ne she-pa.* |
| Do. *hon.* | དཔེ་སྦྱར་ནས་གསུང་བ་ | *pe-jar ne sung-wa.* |
| Illustration | དཔེ་ | *pe.* |
| Illustrious | སྐད་གྲགས་ཆེན་པོ་ | *ke-ťra chhem-po.* |
| Do. *hon.* | མཚན་སྙན་གྲགས་ཆེན་པོ་ | *tshen nyen-ťra chhem-po.* |
| Image (idol) | སྐུ་འདྲ་ | *kun-dra.* |
| Imagination | དམིགས་པ་ | *miḱ-pa.* |
| Imagine, to (think) | བསམ་པ་ | *sam-pa.* |

| | | |
|---|---|---|
| Imagine, to (think), *hon.* | ཐུགས་བསམ་བཞེས་པ་ | *thu-sam sKe-pa.* |
| Imbecile | ལྐུགས་པ། གླེན་པ་ | *kuk-pa ; lem-pa.* |
| Imbrue, to (soak) | སྦང་བ་ | *bang-wa.* |
| Do. *hon.* | སྦང་ང་ (བ་) གནང་བ་ | *bang-nga nang-wa.* |
| Imitate, to | མིག་འདྲེན་བྱེད་པ་ | *mik-dren cKe-pa.* |
| Immaculate, to be | སྐྱོན་མེད་པ་ | *kyön me pa.* |
| Immaterial (without substance) | གཟུགས་མེད་ | *śu-me.* |
| Immeasurable (very great) | ཆེ་ཐག་ཆོད་ | *chhe thaK chhö.* |
| Do. to be | ཚོད་མེད་པ་ | *tshö me pa* |
| Immediately | ལམ་སང་། ལམ་ཀྱང་ | *lam-sang ; lam-kyang.* |
| Immense | རྒྱ་ཆེན་པོ། ཆེ་ཐག་ཆོད་ | *gya-chhem-po ; chhe thaK-chhö.* |
| Immoderate, to be | ཚོད་མེད་པ་ | *tshö-me-pa.* |
| Do. *hon.* | ཐུགས་ཚོད་མེད་པ་ | *thuK-tshö me-pa.* |
| Immodest, to be | ངོ་ཚ་མེད་པ་ | *ngo-tsha me-pa.* |
| Immoral | བྱེད་སྟངས་ངན་པོ་ | *cKe-tang ngem-po.* |
| Do. *hon.* | གནང་སྟངས་ངན་པོ་ | *nang-tang ngem-po.* |
| Immortal, to be | ཤི་རྒྱུ་...མེད་པ་ | *shi-gyu...me-pa.* |
| Do *hon.* | བཞག (གཤེགས་) རྒྱུ་... མེད་པ་ | *sha-gyu...me-pa.* |
| Immovable | གཡོ་རྒྱུ་མེད་པ་ | *yo-gyu me-pa.* |

| | | |
|---|---|---|
| Impair, to | སྐྱོན་བྱེད་པ་ | *kyön-cḱe-pa.* |
| Do. *hon.* | སྐྱོན་གནང་བ་ | *kyön-nang-wa.* |
| Impale, to | ཤིང་ལ་བཀལ་ནས་བསད་ (གསོད་) པ་ | *shing-la ke-ne se-pa.* |
| Impart, to | སྟེར་བ་ | *ter-wa.* |
| Do. *hon.* | གནང་བ་ | *nang-wa.* |
| Impartial | ཉེ་རིང་མེད་པ་ | *nye-ring me-pa.* |
| Impartial (of judges) | ཁྲིམས་དྲང་པོ་ | *thrim t́rang-po.* |
| Do. *hon.* | བཀའ་ཁྲིམས་དྲང་པོ་ | *ka-thrim t́rang-po.* |
| Impassable, to be | མི་...ཐར་བ་ | *mi...thar-wa.* |
| Impassive | དྲན་པ་བརྒྱལ་བ་ | *t́rem-pa gyel-wa.* |
| Impede, to | བཀག་པ་ (འགེགས་པ་) | *kaḱ-pa.* |
| Do. *hon.* | བཀག་ག་ (འགེགས་པ་) གནང་བ་ | *kaḱ ḱa nang-wa.* |
| Impediment | བཀག་ཆ་ | *kaḱ-chha.* |
| Imperceptible, to be | མཐོང་རྒྱུ་....མེད་པ་ | *thong-gyu me-pa.* |
| Imperfect | མི་དག་པ་ | *mi t́ak-pa.* |
| Imperfection (defect) | སྐྱོན་ | *kyön.* |
| Imperial | རྒྱལ་པོའི་ | *gye-pö.* |
| Imperishable, to be | ཆག་རྒྱུ་མེད་པ་ | *chha-gyu me-pa.* |

| | | |
|---|---|---|
| Impertinent | འཛིང་པ་སྦོམ་པོ། གྱོང་པོ་ | *jing-pa bom-po ; kyong-po.* |
| Impetuous | རུ་ངར་པོ་ | *ru-ngar-po.* |
| Do. *hon.* | ཐུགས་རུ་ངར་པོ་ | *thuk-ru ngar-po.* |
| Impious | ཆོས་སེམས་མེད་པ་ | *chhö-sem me-pa.* |
| Implements | ལག་ཆ་ | *lak-chha.* |
| Implore, to | ཞུ་བ་ | *sku-wa.* |
| Do. *hon.* | ཞུ་བ་གནང་བ་ | *sku-wa nang-wa.* |
| Impolite | གྱོང་པོ་ | *kyong-po.* |
| Import (meaning) | དོན་དག་ | *tön-ta.* |
| Do. *hon.* | སྐུ་དོན་ | *ku-tön.* |
| Importance | གནད་ཁག་ | *nen kha.* |
| Important | གནད་ཁག་ཆེན་པོ། གལ་ཆེན་པོ་ | *nen-kha chhem-po ; ke-chhem-po.* |
| Impose, to (lay on) | སྐྱུལ་བ་ | *kü-wa.* |
| Impose on, to (deceive) | མགོ་སྐོར་བ་ | *go-kor-wa.* |
| Do. *hon.* | དབུ་སྐོར་ར་ (བ་) གནང་བ་ | *u-kor-ra nang-wa.* |
| Do. *inf.* to *sup.* | དབུ་སྐོར་ཞུ་བ་ | *u-kor sku-wa.* |
| Imposition (deceit) | མགོ་སྐོར་ | *go-kor.* |
| Do. *hon.* | དབུ་སྐོར་ | *u-kor.* |
| Impossible | མི་ཐུབ་པ་ | *mi-thup-pa.* |

| | | |
|---|---|---|
| Impost (general) | ཁྲལ། འབབ་ | *thre ; baṕ.* |
| Do. (customs-duty) | ཤོ་ཁྲལ་ | *sho-thre.* |
| Do. (on land) | ས་ཁྲལ་ | *sa-thre.* |
| Imposture | མགོ་སྐོར་ | *go-kor.* |
| Do. *hon.* | དབུ་སྐོར་ | *u-kor.* |
| Impotent, to be | སྟོབས་འཆག་པ་ | *toṕ-chhaḱ-pa.* |
| Do. *hon.* | སྐུ་སྟོབས་འཆག་པ་ | *ku-toṕ chhaḱ-pa.* |
| Impracticable, to be | བྱེད་...མི་ཐུབ་པ་ | *ćḱe...mi thuṕ-pa.* |
| Imprecate, to | དམོད་མོ་རྒྱབ་པ་ | *mö-mo gyaṕ-pa.* |
| Do. *hon.* | དམོད་མོ་སྐྱོན་པ་ | *mö-mo kyöm-pa.* |
| Impression, thumb | མཛུག་ཐེ་ | *dzuḱ-the.* |
| Imprison, to | བཙོན་ལ་བཅུག་ (འཇུག་) པ་ | *tsön-la chuḱ-pa.* |
| Improper | མི་ཆོག་པ་ | *mi-chhoḱ-pa.* |
| Improve, to | བཟོ་སྐྱོར་བྱེད་པ་ | *śo-kyor ćḱe-pa.* |
| Do. *hon.* | བཟོ་སྐྱོར་གནང་བ་ | *śo-kyor nang-wa.* |
| Impudent | འཛིང་པ་སྦོམ་པོ། གྱོང་པོ་ | *jing-pa bom-po ; ḱyong-po.* |
| Impure | སྐྱུག་བྲོ་པོ་ | *kyuḱ-t́ro-po.* |
| Impurity | གྲིབ་ | *t́riṕ.* |
| Impute wrongly, to | ཡ་ལ་བཞག་ (འཇོག་) པ་ | *ya-la sḱaḱ-pa.* |
| Do. *hon.* | ཡ་ལ་གཞོག་ག་ (པ་) གནང་བ་ | *ya-la-sḱoḱ-ḱa nang-wa.* |

| | | |
|---|---|---|
| In (inside) | ནང་ལ་ | *nang-la.* |
| Inaccessible | བཙན་པོ་ | *tsem-po.* |
| Inaccurate, to be | མི་ ··དག་པ་ | *mi...ťaḱ-pa.* |
| Inadequate, to be | མི་ ··འགྲིག་པ་ | *mi...driḱ-pa.* |
| Inattentive, to be | སེམས་གཡེང་ནས་བསྡད་ (སྡོད་) པ་ | *sem-yang-ne de-pa.* |
| Do. *hon.* | ཐུགས་སེམས་གཡེང་ནས་བཞུགས་པ་ | *thuḱ-sem yang-ne sḱuḱ-pa.* |
| Inauspicious day | གཡང་གཟའ་ | *yang-śa.* |
| Incalculable | གྲངས་མེད་ | *ťrang-me.* |
| Incantation | སྔགས་ | *nga.* |
| Incapable | མི་···ཐུབ་པ་ | *mi...thuṕ-pa.* |
| Incarcerate, to | བཙོན་ལ་བཅུག་ (འཇུག་) པ་ | *tsön-la chuḱ-pa* |
| Incarnate, to be | སྤྲུལ་བ་ | *trül-wa.* |
| Incarnation (of a deity) | སྤྲུལ་སྐུ་ | *trül-ku.* |
| Incautious | སྣང་དག་མེད་པ་ | *nang-ťa me-pa.* |
| Incense, *s.* | སྤོས་ | *pö.* |
| Incense, to | ཁོང་ཁྲོ་སློང་བ་ | *khong-thro lang-wa.* |
| Do. *hon.* | དགོངས་པ་དཀྲུག་པ་ | *gong-pa truḱ-pa.* |
| Incessant | རྒྱུན་ཆད་རྒྱུ་མེད་པ་ | *gyün-chhe-gyu me-pa.* |

| | | |
|---|---|---|
| Incessantly | ནམ་རྒྱུན། དུས་རྒྱུན་ | *nam-gyün ; ťü-gyün.* |
| Inch (breadth of a finger) | སོར་ | *sor.* |
| Inclination | འདོད་པ་ | *dö-pa.* |
| Do. *hon.* | ཐུགས་འདོད་ | *thung-dö.* |
| Incline, to (lean against) | སྦོ་སྙེ་རྒྱབ་པ་ | *bo-nye gyaṕ-pa.* |
| Do. *hon.* | སྦོ་སྙེ་སྐྱོན་པ་ | *bo-nye kyöm-pa.* |
| Inclined to be | འདོད་པ་ཡོད་པ་ | *dö-pa yö-pa.* |
| Do. *hon.* | ཐུགས་འདོད་ཡོད་པ་ | *thung-dö yö-pa.* |
| Inclosure | ར་བ་ | *ra-wa.* |
| Include, to | སྡོམ་པ་ | *dom-pa.* |
| Income | ཐོབ་ཐང་ | *thoṕ-thang.* |
| Incompetent, to be | འོས་པོ་མེད་པ་ | *ö-po me-pa.* |
| Do. *hon.* | ཐུགས་འོས་པོ་མེད་པ་ | *thuḱ-ö-po me-pa.* |
| Incomplete, to be | མི་ཚང་བ་ | *mi tshang-wa.* |
| Inconstant, to be | བརྟན་པོ་མེད་པ་ | *tem-po me-pa.* |
| Incorporeal | གཟུགས་པོ་མེད་པ་ | *śuḱ-po me-pa.* |
| Incorrect | མ་དག་པ་ | *ma-ťaḱ-pa.* |
| Increase, to (in numbers) | འཕེལ་བ་ | *phe-wa.* |
| Do. (in price) | འཕར་བ་ | *phar-wa.* |
| Do. (in size) | ཆེ་རུ་ཆེ་རུ་འགྲོ་བ་ | *chhe-ru chhe-ru dro-wa.* |

| | | |
|---|---|---|
| Increase, to (in size), *hon.* | ཆེ་རུ་ཆེ་རུ་ཕེབ་པ་ | *chhe-ru chhe-ru phe-pa.* |
| Indeed | ཏེན་ཏེན། ངོ་ཐོག་ | *ten-ten ; ngo-tho.* |
| Indefatigable | སྙིང་རུས་ཆེན་པོ་ | *nying-rü chhem-po.* |
| Do. *hon.* | ཐུགས་རུས་ཆེན་པོ་ | *thu-rü chhem-po.* |
| Indefinite | ཏན་པོ་མེད་པ་ | *tem-po me-pa.* |
| Indented | ཀྱོང་ཀྱོང་ | *kyong-kyong.* |
| Independent | རང་མགོ་འཐོན་པ་ | *rang-go thöm-pa.* |
| Indestructible | ཆག་རྒྱུ་མེད་པ་ | *chha-gyu me-pa.* |
| Index | ཐོ་ | *tho.* |
| India (plains of) | རྒྱ་ཐང་ | *gya-thang.* |
| India | རྒྱ་གར་ | *gya-ḱar.* |
| Indian | རྒྱ་གར་གྱི་ | *gya-ḱar-ḱyi.* |
| Indicate, to | མིག་སྟོན་པ་ | *mi-töm-pa.* |
| Do. *hon.* | མིག་སྟོན་པ་གནང་བ་ | *mi-töm-pa nang-wa.* |
| Do. *inf.* to *sup.* | སྤྱན་ཕེབ་ཞུ་བ་ | *chem-phe sḱu-wa.* |
| Indifferent, to be | སྣང་དག་མི་བྱེད་པ་ | *nang-ťa mi-cḱe-pa.* |
| Indigent | སྐྱོ་པོ་ | *kyo-po.* |
| Indigestion | ལྟོ་མ་འཇུ་བའི་ནད་ | *to ma ju-we ne.* |
| Indignant, to be | ཁོང་ཁྲོ་ཟ་བ། ཚིག་པ་ཟ་བ་ | *khong-thro śa-wa ; tshiḱ-pa śa-wa.* |

| | | |
|---|---|---|
| Indignant, to be, *hon.* | དགོངས་པ་ཚུང་པ། རྣམ་མཁྱེན་འགལ་བ་ | *gong-pa tshung-pa ; nam-khyen gel-wa.* |
| Indignation | ཚིག་པ། ཁོང་ཁྲོ་ | *tshik̇-pa ; khong-thro.* |
| Do. *hon.* | དགོངས་ཚུང་། རྣམ་མཁྱེན་ | *gong-tshung ; nam-khyen.* |
| Indigo | རམས་ | *ram.* |
| Indisposed, to be (unwell) | བདེ་པོ་མེད་པ། གཟུགས་པོ་ཐང་པོ་མེད་པ་ | *de-po me-pa ; śuk̇-po thang-po me-pa.* |
| Do. *hon.* | སྐུ་གཟུགས་ཐང་པོ་མེད་པ་ | *ku-śuk̇ thang-po me-pa.* |
| Indisposition (illness) | ན་ཚ་ | *na-tsha.* |
| Do. *hon.* | སྙུང་གཞི་ | *nyung-sk̇i.* |
| Indistinct | གསལ་པོ་མེད་པ་ | *se-po me-pa.* |
| Indolent | རྒྱུ་མ་རིང་པོ། ལེ་ལོ་ཆེན་པོ་ | *gyu-ma ring-po ; le-lo chhem-po.* |
| Do. *hon.* | ཐུགས་རྒྱུ་རིང་པོ་ | *thu-gyu ring-po.* |
| Indra | ལྷའི་དབང་པོ་རྒྱ་བྱིན་ | *hlaï-wang-po gya-jin.* |
| Induce, to | ཨུ་ཚུགས་བྱེད་པ་ | *u-tshu ck̇e-pa.* |
| Do. *hon.* | ཨུ་ཚུགས་གནང་བ་ | *u-tshu nang-wa.* |
| Industrious | སྙིང་རུས་ཆེན་པོ་ | *nying-rü chhem-po.* |
| Do. *hon.* | ཐུགས་རུས་ཆེན་པོ་ | *thu-rü chhem-po.* |
| Industry | སྙིང་རུས་ | *nying-rü.* |
| Do. *hon.* | ཐུགས་རུས་ | *thuk̇-rü.* |

| | | |
|---|---|---|
| Ineffaceable, to be | སྲུབ་...མི་ཐུབ་པ་ | *suṕ...mi thuṕ-pa.* |
| Inefficient, to be | འོས་པོ་...མེད་པ་ | *ö-po...me-pa.* |
| Inequitable, to be (unjust) | དྲང་པོ་...མེད་པ་ | *t́rang-po...me-pa* |
| Inert, to be | ཧུར་པོ་...མེད་པ་ | *hur-po . me-pa.* |
| Inexhaustible | རྫོགས་རྒྱུ་མེད་པ་ | *dzo-gyu me-pa.* |
| Inexorable | སྨྲ་བ་ལེན་གཅིག་ | *ma-wa len-chi.* |
| Inexpensive | ཁེ་པོ། གོང་ཆུང་ཆུང་ | *khe-po ; ḱong-chhung-chhung.* |
| Infallible, to be | མི་ནོར་བ་ | *mi-nor-wa.* |
| Infamy | མིང་ངན་ | *ming ngen.* |
| Infant | བྲུ་གུ་ཆུང་ཆུང་ | *ṕu-gu chhung-chhung.* |
| Do. *hon.* | ཨ་ལྷྭ་ཆུང་ཆུང་ | *a-wa chhung-chhung.* |
| Infant (of a few weeks only) | མ་འབྱར་ | *man-ja.* |
| Infantry | དམག་དཔུང་ | *maḱ-pung.* |
| Infelicitous (unfortunate) | བསོད་བདེ་མེད་པ། བསོད་བདེ་ཆུང་ཆུང་ | *so-de me-pa ; so-de chhung-chhung.* |
| Do. *hon.* | སྐུ་བསོད་མེད་པ། སྐུ་བསོད་ཆུང་ཆུང་ | *ku-sö me-pa ; ku-sö chhung-chhung.* |
| Inferior (of things) | སྡུག་པོ་ | *duḱ-po.* |
| Do. (in rank of persons) | དམའ་པོ་ | *ma-po.* |
| Infertile | རྩ་ཆུ་འཛོམ་པོ་...མེད་པ་ | *tsa-chhu dzom-po...me-pa.* |

| | | |
|---|---|---|
| Infidel | ཕྱི་པ་ | *chhi-pa.* |
| Infinite | ཚོད་མེད་པ་ | *tshö me-pa.* |
| Infirm | ཤེད་མེད་ང་ | *she me-pa.* |
| Do. *hon.* | སྐུ་ཤེད་ཆུང་ཆུང་ | *ku-she chhung-chhung.* |
| Inflame, to (with anger) | ཁོང་ཁྲོ་སློང་བ་ | *khong-thro lang-wa.* |
| Do. *hon.* | དགོངས་པ་དཀྲུག་པ་ | *gong-pa truk-pa.* |
| Inflammation | ཚ་བ་ | *tsha-wa.* |
| Do. of bone | རུ་གཟུག་རྒྱབ་པ་ | *ru-śuk gyap-pa.* |
| Do. of joint | ཚིགས་ཚ་བ་ | *tshi tsha-wa.* |
| Do. of muscle | རྩ་གཞི་འབར་བ་ | *tsap-ski bar-wa.* |
| Inflamed, to be (of hands, &c.) | འཚིག་པ་ | *tshik-pa.* |
| Inflate, to | གམ་ཕུ་རྒྱང་བ་ | *kam-phu gyang-wa.* |
| Inflexible (stubborn) | གྱོང་པོ་ | *kyong-po.* |
| Influence | དབང་ | *wang.* |
| Do. *hon.* | སྐུ་དབང་ | *ku-wang.* |
| Influential | དབང་ཆེན་པོ་ | *wang-chhem-po.* |
| Do. *hon.* | སྐུ་དབང་ཆེན་པོ་ | *ku-wang chhem-po.* |
| Inform, to | ལན་སྤྲོད་པ་ | *len-trö-pa.* |
| Do. *inf.* to *sup.* | ཞུགས་ལན་ཕུལ་ (འབུལ་) བ་ | *ja-len phü-wa.* |
| Do. *sup.* to *inf.* | བཀའ་ལན་གནང་བ་ | *ka-len nang-wa.* |

| | | |
|---|---|---|
| Information (news) | གནས་ཚུལ། གསར་འགྱུར་ | *ne-tshül ; sang gyu.* |
| Informer | ལན་སྤྲད་མཁན་ | *len-tre-khen.* |
| Ingenious | ཇུས་མཁས་པོ་ | *cK̇ü-khe-po.* |
| Do. *hon.* | སྐུ་ཇུས་མཁས་པོ་ | *ku-cK̇ü khe-po.* |
| Inhabit, to | བསྡད་པ་ (སྡོད་པ་) | *de-pa.* |
| Do. *hon.* | བཞུགས་པ་ | *sK̇u-pa.* |
| Inhale, to | དབུགས་འཐེན་པ་ | *u-them-pa.* |
| Do. *hon.* | ལྗགས་དབུགས་འཐེན་པ་ གནང་བ་ | *ja-u them-pa nang-wa.* |
| Inherit, to | སྐལ་ལ་ (བ་) ཐོབ་པ་ | *ke-la thop̊-pa.* |
| Do. *hon.* | སྐུ་སྐལ་ཐོབ་པ་ | *ku-ke thop̊-p̊a.* |
| Inheritance | ཐོབ་སྐལ་ | *thop̊-ke.* |
| Do. *hon.* | སྐུ་སྐལ་ | *ku-ke.* |
| Inhibit, to (forbid) | བཀག་པ་ (འགེགས་པ་) | *kaK̇-pa.* |
| Do. *hon.* | བཀག་ག་ (འགེགས་པ་) གནང་བ་ | *kaK̇-K̇a nang-wa.* |
| Inhuman, to be | སྙིང་རྗེ་མེད་པ་ | *nying-je me-pa.* |
| Do. *hon.* | ཐུགས་རྗེ་མེད་པ་ | *thuK̇-je me-pa.* |
| Inimical, to be | དགྲ་བྱེད་པ་ | *dra-cK̇e-pa.* |
| Do. *hon.* | དགྲ་གནང་བ་ | *dra-nang-wa.* |

| | | |
|---|---|---|
| Iniquitous | ངན་པོ་ | *ngem-po.* |
| Do. *hon.* | ཐུགས་ངན་པོ་ | *thu ngem-po.* |
| Iniquity | ཉེས་པ། སྡིག་པ་ | *nye-pa ; dik-pa.* |
| Do. *hon.* | སྐུ་སྡིག་ | *ku-di.* |
| Inject, to | བཙུག་པ་ (འཛུག་པ་) | *chuk-pa.* |
| Do. *hon.* | བཙུག་ག་ (འཛུག་པ་) གནང་བ་ | *chuk-ka nang-wa.* |
| Injunction | བཀའ་ | *ka.* |
| Injure, to (by witchcraft, etc.) | གནོད་པ་བྱེད་པ་ | *nö-pa che-pa.* |
| Do. (physically) | རྨ་བཟོ་བ་ | *ma-śo-wa.* |
| Do. (impair) | སྐྱོན་བྱེད་པ་ | *kyön-che-pa.* |
| Do. *hon.* | སྐྱོན་གནང་བ་ | *kyön-nang-wa.* |
| Injured, to be | སྐྱོན་བྱེད་པ་ | *kyön-che-pa.* |
| Injury | གནོད་པ་ | *nö-pa.* |
| Injustice, to do | ཁྲིམས་མེད་བྱེད་པ་ | *thrim-me che-pa.* |
| Do. *hon.* | ཁྲིམས་མེད་གནང་བ་ | *thrim-me nang-wa.* |
| Ink | སྣག་ཚ་ | *nak-tsha.* |
| Do. *hon.* | ཕྱག་སྣག་ | *chha-na.* |
| Ink-pot | སྣག་བུམ་ | *nak-pum.* |
| Do. *hon.* | ཕྱག་བུམ་ | *chha-pum.* |
| Ink, red | མཚལ་ | *tshe.* |

| | | |
|---|---|---|
| Inlet (bay) | ཆུ་ལྷག་ | *chhu-hla.* |
| Inmate (fellow-lodger) | ལྟོ་ཚང་། ཐབ་རོགས་ | *to-tshang ; thaṕ-ro.* |
| Inn | གནས་ཚང་ | *ne-tshang.* |
| Inn-keeper | གནས་པོ་ | *ne-po.* |
| Do. *f.* | གནས་མོ་ | *ne-mo.* |
| Inner | ནང་གི་ | *nang-ki.* |
| Innocent | ཉེས་པ་མེད་པ་ | *nye-pa me-pa.* |
| Innumerable | གྲངས་མེད་ | *t́rang me.* |
| Inoculate, to (for smallpox) | ལྷན་འབྲུམ་བཙུགས་ (འཛུག་) པ་ | *hlan-drum tsuḱ-pa.* |
| Do. *hon.* | ལྷན་འབྲུམ་བཙུགས་ག་ (འཛུགས་པ་) གནང་བ་ | *hlan-drum tsuḱ-ka nang-wa.* |
| Inordinate, to be. | ཚོད་མེད་པ་ | *tshö me-pa.* |
| Do. *hon.* | ཐུགས་ཚོད་མེད་པ་ | *thuḱ-tshö me-pa.* |
| Inquire, to (ask) | དྲི་བ་ (འདྲི་བ་) | *t́ri-wa.* |
| Do. *hon.* | བཀའ་འདྲི་གནང་བ་ | *kan-dri nang-wa.* |
| Do. *inf.* to *sup.* | ཞུ་བ་ | *sḱu-wa.* |
| Inquire, to (into a matter) | རྩད་གཅོད་པ་ | *tse chö-pa.* |
| Do. *hon.* | རྩད་གཅོད་གནང་བ་ | *tse-chö nang-wa.* |
| Inquire, to (investigate) | ཞིབ་དཔྱོད་བྱེད་པ་ | *sḱiṕ-chö cḱe-pa.* |
| Do. *hon.* | ཞིབ་དཔྱོད་གནང་བ་ | *sḱiṕ-chö nang-wa.* |

| | | |
|---|---|---|
| Inquire, to (investigate) *h. hon.* | བཀའ་ཞིབ་གནང་བ་ | *ka-sḱiṕ nang-wa.* |
| Inquiry (investigation) | ཞིབ་དཔྱོད་ | *sḱiṕ-chö.* |
| Do. *hon.* | བཀའ་ཞིབ་ | *ka-sḱiṕ.* |
| Insane | སྨྱོན་པ་ | *nyöm-pa.* |
| Insane, to be | སྨྱོ་བ་ | *nyo-wa.* |
| Inscription | རྡོ་བཀོད་ | *do-kö.* |
| Insect | འབུ་ | *bu.* |
| Insensible, to become | དྲན་པ་འཐོར་བ་ | *t́rem-pa thor-wa.* |
| Inseparable, to be | བྲལ་ (འབྲལ་) མི་ཐུབ་པ་ | *t́re...mi-thuṕ-pa.* |
| Insert, to | བཙུགས་པ་ (འཛུགས་པ་) | *tsuḱ-pa.* |
| Do. *hon.* | བཙུགས་ག་ (འཛུགས་པ་) གནང་བ་ | *tsuḱ-ḱa nang-wa.* |
| Inside, *prep.* | ནང་ལ་ | *nang-la.* |
| Insignificant (of matters) | དོན་དག་ཆུང་ཆུང་ | *t́ön-t́a chhung-chhung.* |
| Do. *hon.* | སྐུ་དོན་ཆུང་ཆུང་ | *ku-t́ön chhung-chhung.* |
| Insincere, to be | དྲང་པོ་...མེད་པ། དངོས་ནས་...མི་བྱེད་པ་ | *t́rang-po . me-pa; ngön-ne ...mi cḱe-pa.* |
| Insist, to | ཨུ་ཚུགས་བྱེད་པ་ | *u-tshu cḱe-pa.* |
| Do. *hon.* | ཨུ་ཚུགས་གནང་བ་ | *u tshu nang-wa.* |
| Insolent | འཇིང་པ་སྦོམ་པོ། རྒྱོང་པོ་ | *jing-pa bom-po; ḱyong-po.* |

| | | |
|---|---|---|
| Insoluble | ཞུ་...མི་ཐུབ་པ་ | *sKu...mi thup-pa.* |
| Inspect, to | ལྟ་བ་ | *ta-wa.* |
| Do. *hon.* | གཟིགས་པ་ | *śi pa.* |
| Installation (of a ruler) | ཁྲི་འདོན་ | *thrin-dön.* |
| Instance | དཔེ་ | *pe.* |
| Instance, for | དཔེ་ན་ (དཔེར་ན་) | *pe-na.* |
| Instant, in an (presently) | ཧྲིབ་ཙམ་ཅིག་ལ་ | *hrip-tsa-chi-la.* |
| Instantaneously | ལམ་སང་། ལམ་ཀྱང་ | *lam-sang ; lam-kyang.* |
| Instantly | ལམ་སང་། ལམ་ཀྱང་ | *lam-sang ; lam-kyang.* |
| Instead of | ཚབ་ལ་ | *tshap-la.* |
| Instigate, to | ངན་པ་བསླབས་ (སློབ་) པ་ | *ngen-pa lap-pa.* |
| Institute, to | བཙུགས་པ་ (འཛུགས་པ་) | *tsuk-pa.* |
| Instruct, to | བསླབས་པ་ (སློབ་པ་) | *lap-pa.* |
| Do. *hon.* | བསླབས་ (སློབ་) པ་གནང་བ་ | *lap-pa nang-wa.* |
| Instructor | དགེ་རྒན། སློབ་དཔོན་ | *ge-gen ; lo-pön.* |
| Do. (of Lama) | ཡོངས་འཛིན་ | *yong-dzin.* |
| Instrument | ལག་ཆ་ | *lak-chha.* |
| Insufficient | མི་...ལྡང་བ་ | *mi...dang wa.* |
| Insult, *s.* | སྨད་ར་ | *me-ra.* |
| Insult, to | སྨད་ར་བཏང་ (གཏོང་) བ་ | *me-ra tang-wa.* |

| | | |
|---|---|---|
| Insult, to, *hon.* | སྨད་ར་གཏོང་ང་ (བ་) གནང་བ་ | *me-ra tong-nga nang-wa.* |
| Insurrection | སྡེ་འཁྲུག་ | *de-thruḱ.* |
| Intellect | བློ་གྲོས་ | *lo-t́ro.* |
| Intellectual | བློ་གྲོས་ཆེན་པོ་ | *lo-t́ro chhem-po* |
| Do. *hon.* | དགོངས་པ་ཆེན་པོ་ | *gong-pa chhem-po.* |
| Intelligence (news) | གནས་ཚུལ། གསར་འགྱུར་ | *ne-tshül; sang-gyu.* |
| Do. (understanding) | རིག་པ་ | *riḱ-pa.* |
| Do. *hon.* | ཐུགས་རིག་ | *thu-ri.* |
| Intelligent | རིག་པ་ཡག་པོ་ | *riḱ-pa yaḱ-po.* |
| Do. *hon.* | ཐུགས་རིག་ཡག་པོ་ | *thu-ri yaḱ-po.* |
| Intemperate, to be | ཚོད་མེད་པ་ | *tshö-me-pa.* |
| Do. *hon.* | ཐུགས་ཚོད་མེད་པ་ | *thuḱ-tshö me-pa.* |
| Intend, to (purpose) | སེམས་ལ་བསམ་པ་ | *sem-la sam-pa.* |
| Do. *hon.* | ཐུགས་ལ་དགོངས་པ་ | *thuḱ-la gong-pa.* |
| Intent, *s.* | དོན་དག་ | *t́ön-t́a.* |
| Do. *hon.* | སྐུ་དོན་ | *ku-t́ön.* |
| Intention | དོན་དག་ | *t́ön-t́a.* |
| Do. *hon.* | སྐུ་དོན་ | *ku-t́ön.* |
| Inter, to (bury) | ས་ལ་སྦས་པ་ | *sa-la be-pa.* |
| Intercede, to | བར་མི་བྱེད་པ་ | *ṕar-mi cḱe-pa.* |

| | | |
|---|---|---|
| Intercede, to, *hon.* | བར་མི་གནང་བ་ | *par-mi nang-wa.* |
| Intercourse, to have (conversation) | སྐད་ཆ་བྱེད་པ་ | *ke-chha cḱe-pa.* |
| Do. *hon.* | གསུང་གྲོས་གནང་བ་ | *sung-t́rö nang-wa.* |
| Do. *inf. w. sup.* | གསུང་གྲོས་ཞུ་བ་ | *sung-t́rö sḱu-wa.* |
| Interdict, to (forbid) | བཀག་པ་ (འགེགས་པ) | *kaḱ-pa.* |
| Do. *hon.* | བཀག་ག་ (འགེགས་པ་) གནང་བ་ | *kaḱ-ka nang-wa.* |
| Interest (on loan) | སྐྱེད་ | *kye.* |
| Do. *hon.* | ལྷུགས་སྐྱེད་ | *ja-kye.* |
| Interior, *s.* (of a building) | ནང་ | *nang.* |
| Do. (of a country) | གྲོང་གསེབ་ | *t́rong-se.* |
| Internal | ནང་གི་ | *nang-ki.* |
| Interpose, to (intercede) | བར་མི་བྱེད་པ་ | *ṕar-mi cḱe-pa.* |
| Do. *hon.* | བར་མི་གནང་བ་ | *ṕar-mi nang-wa.* |
| Interpreter | ལོ་ཙ་བ་ | *lo-tsa-wa.* |
| Interrogate, to | དྲི་བ་ (འདྲི་བ་) | *t́ri-wa.* |
| Do. *hon.* | བཀའ་འདྲི་གནང་བ་ | *kan-dri nang-wa.* |
| Interrupt, to | བཀག་པ་ (འགེགས་པ་) | *kaḱ-pa.* |
| Do. *hon.* | བཀག་ག་ (འགེགས་པ་) གནང་བ་ | *kaḱ-ḱa nang-wa.* |

| | | |
|---|---|---|
| Interruption | བཀག་ཆ་ | *kak-chha.* |
| Interstice | སེར་ཀ་ | *ser-ka.* |
| Interview (with lama) | མཇལ་ཁ་ | *je-kha.* |
| Do. (with official) | སྐུ་མཇལ་ | *ku-ja* |
| Interview, to (lama) | མཇལ་ཁ་ཞུ་བ་ | *je-kha sku-wa.* |
| Do. (official) | སྐུ་བཅར་ཞུ་བ་ | *ku-cha sku-wa.* |
| Intestines | རྒྱུ་མ་ | *gyu-ma.* |
| Intimate, *adj.* | དགའ་པོ་ཉེ་པོ་ | *ga-po nye-po.* |
| Do. *hon.* | ཐུགས་ཉེ་ཆགས་པོ་ | *thuk-nye chhak-po.* |
| Intimidate, to | ཞེད་སྐྲག་སླང་བ་ | *ske-tra lang-wa.* |
| Do. *hon.* | ཞེད་སྐྲག་སློང་ང་ (བ་) གནང་བ་ | *ske-tra long-nga nang-wa.* |
| Into | ནང་ལ་ | *nang-la.* |
| Intolerable (pain) | སྒོང་ (སྒོམ་) མི་ཐུབ་པ་ | *gong mi thup-pa.* |
| Do. *hon.* | སྒོང་ང་ (སྒོམ་པ་) གནང་མི་ཐུབ་པ་ | *gong-nga nang mi thup-pa.* |
| Intonation | མདངས་ | *dang.* |
| Intoxicated | ར་བཟི་ | *ra-śi.* |
| Do. to be | ར་བཟི་བ་ | *ra-śi-wa.* |
| Do. *hon.* | སྐུ་ར་བྲད་པ་ | *ku-ra be-pa.* |

| | | |
|---|---|---|
| Intrepid. | སྙིང་ཆེན་པོ་ | *nying-chhem-po.* |
| Do. *hon.* | ཐུགས་སྙིང་ཆེན་པོ་ | *thu-nying chhem-po.* |
| Intricate | མགོ་ཉོག་ཚ་པོ་ | *go-nyo tsha-po.* |
| Do. *hon.* | དབུ་ཉོག་ཚ་པོ་ | *u-nyo tsha-po.* |
| Intrigue | གྲོས་ངན་ | *t'ö-ngen.* |
| Intrinsic (real) | ངོ་ཐོག། དངོས་ནས་ | *ngo tho ; ngö-ne.* |
| Inundate, to | ཆུ་ཡིས་གནན་ (གནོན་) པ་ | *chhu-yi nem-pa.* |
| Inundation | ཆུ་རུད་ | *chhu-rü.* |
| Invalid, *s.* | ནད་པ་ | *ne-pa.* |
| Do. *hon.* | སྙུང་མཁན་ | *nyung-khen.* |
| Invective | སྨད་ར་ | *me-ra.* |
| Inveigle, to | སླུ་བ་ | *lu-wa.* |
| Do. *hon.* | སླུ་བ་གནང་བ་ | *lu-wa nang-wa.* |
| Inventory | བརྗེད་ཐོ་ | *je-tho.* |
| Do. *hon.* | བསྙེལ་ཐོ་ | *nye-tho.* |
| Invert, to (upside down) | མགོ་གཞུག་ལོག་པ། ཨ་ལོག་རྒྱབ་པ་ | *go-sku lok pa ; a-lo gyap-pa.* |
| Do. *hon.* | མགོ་གཞུག་ལོག་ག་ (པ་) གནང་བ། ཨ་ལོག་རྒྱབ་པ་གནང་བ་ | *go-sku-lok-ka nang-wa ; a-lo gyap-pa nang wa.* |

| | | |
|---|---|---|
| Invert, to (back to front) | ཁ་ཕྱོགས་ལོག་པ་ | *kha-chho loḱ-pa.* |
| Do. *hon.* | ཞལ་ཕྱོགས་ལོག་ག་ (པ་) གནང་བ་ | *sḰe-chho loḱ-ḱa nang-wa.* |
| Investigate, to | ཞིབ་དཔྱོད་བྱེད་པ་ | *sḰiṕ-chö cḰe-pa.* |
| Do. *hon.* | ཞིབ་དཔྱོད་གནང་བ | *sḰiṕ-chö nang-wa.* |
| Do. *h. hon.* | བཀའ་ཞིབ་གནང་བ་ | *ka-sḰiṕ nang-wa.* |
| Investigation | ཞིབ་དཔྱོད་ | *sḰiṕ-chö.* |
| *Do.* *hon.* | བཀའ་ཞིབ་ | *ka-sḰiṕ.* |
| Invincible | གླགས་……མི་ཁ་བ་ | *la...mi kha-wa.* |
| Invisible | མི་……མཐོང་བ་ | *mi ..thong-wa.* |
| Invite, to (request) | ཞུ་བ་ | *sḰu-wa.* |
| Do. *hon.* | ཞུ་བ་གནང་བ་ | *sḰu-wa nang-wa.* |
| Invite, to (guest) | སྐད་བཏང་ (གཏོང་) བ་ | *ke-tang-wa.* |
| Do. *hon.* | གདན་འདྲེན་ཞུ་བ་ | *den-dren sḰu-wa.* |
| Involved (intricate) | མགོ་ཉོག་ཚ་པོ་ | *go-nyo tsha-po.* |
| Inward | ནང་གི་ | *nang-ḱi.* |
| Irascible | རུ་ངར་པོ་ | *ru-ngar-po.* |
| Do. *hon.* | ཐུགས་རུ་ངར་པོ་ | *thu-ru ngar-po.* |
| Ire | ཚིག་པ། ཁོང་ཁྲོ་ | *tshiḱ-pa ; khong-thro.* |
| Do. *hon.* | དགོངས་ཚུང་། རྣམ་མཁྱེན | *gong-tshung ; nam-khyen.* |

| | | |
|---|---|---|
| ris | སི་ལིང་ལྗང་པ་ | *si-ling jang-pa.* |
| rksome | དཀའ་ལས་ཁག་པོ་ | *ka-le khak-po.* |
| Do. *hon.* | སྐུ་མཉེལ་བོ་ | *ku-nye-po.* |
| ron, *s.* | ལྕགས་ | *cha.* |
| ron, *s.* (for clothes) | དབུར་དེ་ | *ur-te.* |
| ron, *adj.* | ལྕགས་ཀྱི་ | *cha-kyi.* |
| rrational | དོན་མེད་ | *tön-me.* |
| rreligious, to be | ཆོས་སེམས་མེད་པ་ | *chhö-sem me-pa.* |
| Do. *hon.* | ཆོས་སེམས་མི་གནང་བ་ | *chhö-sem mi-nang-wa.* |
| rreparable, to be | ཐབས་མེད་པ་ | *thap-me-pa.* |
| rresistible, to be | བཀག་……མི་ཐུབ་པ་ | *kak...mi thup-pa.* |
| rresolute, to be | བརྟན་བརྟན་……མེད་པ་ | *ten-ten...me-po.* |
| ritable | རུ་ངར་པོ་ | *ru-ngar-po.* |
| Do. *hon.* | ཐུགས་རུ་ངར་པོ་ | *thu-ru ngar-po.* |
| ritate, to | ཁོང་ཁྲོ་སློང་བ་ | *khong-thro lang-wa.* |
| Do. *hon.* | དགོངས་པ་དཀྲུག་པ་ | *gong-pa truk-pa.* |
| | རེད། འདུག་ | *re ; du.* |
| land | གླིང་ཕྲན་ | *ling-thren.* |
| olated place | དབེན་གནས་ | *en-ne.* |
| sue (result) | སྙིང་པོ་ | *nying-po.* |

| | | |
|---|---|---|
| Issue, to (come out) | འཐོན་པ་ | *thöm-pa.* |
| Do. *hon.* | ཕེབ་འཐོན་གནང་བ་ | *pheṕ-thön nang-wa.* |
| Do. *h. hon.* | ཕྱོགས་ཕེབས་གནང་བ་ | *chho-phe nang-wa.* |
| It | དེ། འདི་ | *t́e; di.* |
| Itch, *s.* | རྔོ་ | *ngo.* |
| Itch, to (of body) | ཟ་བ། གཡའ་བ་ | *śa-wa; ya-wa.* |
| Itching disease, to have | རྔོ་ཤོར་བ། རྔོ་རྒྱབ་པ་ | *ngo-shor-wa; ngo-gyaṕ-pa.* |
| Itself | འདི་རང་། དེ་རང་ | *di-rang; t́e-rang.* |
| Ivory | བ་སོ་ | *ṕa-so.* |
| Ivy | ཐག་འཁྱུད་མེ་ཏོག་ | *tha-khyü me-toḱ.* |

# J

| | | |
|---|---|---|
| **Jackal** | ཁྱི་སྤྱང་ | *khyiṕ-chang.* |
| **Jackass** | བུང་གུ་ (བོང་བུ་) | *ṕung-gu.* |
| **Jackdaw** | སྐྱུང་ཀ་ | *kyung-ka.* |
| **Jacket (without sleeves)** | སྦྱ་སྦྱར་ | *ja-ja.* |
| Do. *hon.* | ན་བཟའ་སྦྱ་སྦྱར་ | *nam-śa ja-ja.* |
| **Jacket (with sleeves)** | འགོག་རྩེ་ | *go-tse.* |
| Do. *hon.* | ན་བཟའ་འགོག་རྩེ་ | *nam-śa go-tse.* |
| **Jade (stone)** | གཡང་སྤྲི་ | *yang-tri.* |
| **Jail** | བཙོན་ཁང་ | *tsön-khang.* |
| **Jailor** | བཙོན་སྲུང་ང་ (བ་) | *tsön-sung-nga.* |
| **Jangle, to (wrangle)** | རྒྱབ་འདྲེ་རྒྱབ་པ་ | *gyam-dre gyaṕ-pa.* |
| Do. *hon.* | གསུང་འཁྲུག་སྐྱོན་པ་ | *sung-thru kyöm-pa.* |
| **Jar** | རྫ་བུམ་ | *dza-ṕum.* |
| **Jaundice** | སེར་ནད་ | *ser-ne.* |
| **Jaunt, to (ramble)** | ཆན་ཆམ་ (འཁྱམ་འཁྱམ་) བྱེད་པ་ | *chham-chham cḱe-pa.* |
| Do. *hon.* | སྐུ་ཆམ་ (འཁྱམ་) གནང་བ་ | *kün-chham nang-wa.* |
| **Javelin** | མདུང་ | *dung.* |

| | | |
|---|---|---|
| Javelin, *hon.* | ཕྱག་མདུང་ | *chhan-dung.* |
| Jaw | འགྲམ་པ་ | *dram-pa.* |
| Jealous | ཕྲག་དོག་ཚ་པོ་ | *thra-t́o tsha-po.* |
| Jealousy | ཕྲག་དོག་ | *thra-t́o.* |
| Jealousy (between husband and wife) | མིག་སེར་ | *miḱ-ser.* |
| Jeer, to | ཀྱག་ཀྱག་བྱས་ནས་ལབ་པ་ | *kya-kya ćhe-ne laṕ-pa.* |
| Do. *hon.* | ཀྱག་ཀྱག་གནང་ནས་གསུང་བ་ | *kya-kya nang-ne sung-wa.* |
| Jelly (meat) | ཕིག་ཕིག་ | *phiḱ-phi.* |
| Jest, to | ཁབ་ལས་བཤད་པ་ | *khaṕ-le she-pa.* |
| Do. *hon.* | ཞལ་ལས་གསུང་བ་ | *sḱe-le sung-wa.* |
| Do. *h. hon.* | ཞལ་ལས་གསུང་ང་ (བ་) གནང་བ་ | *sḱe-le sung-nga nang-wa.* |
| Jester | དབུ་འཁོར་ཞུ་མཁན་ | *u-khor sḱu-khen.* |
| Jesus | ཡེ་ཤུ་ | *ye-shu.* |
| Jew | ཡ་ཧུ་དཱ་པ་ | *ya-hu-da-pa.* |
| Jewel | ནོར་བུ་ | *nor-ṕu.* |
| Job (work) | ལས་ཀ་ | *le-ka.* |
| Jockey (for making horses) | རྟ་སྦྱོང་མཁན་ | *ta-jang-khen.* |
| Do. (for racing) | རྟ་རྒྱུག་བཏང་མཁན་ | *taṕ-gyu tang-khen.* |

| | | |
|---|---|---|
| Join, to | སྦྲེལ་བ། འཐུད་པ་ | *drel-wa ; thü-pa.* |
| Do. *hon.* | སྦྲེལ་ལ་ (བ་) གནང་བ། འཐུད་པ་གནང་བ་ | *drel-la nang-wa ; thü-pa nang-wa.* |
| Join, to (by glueing together, &c.) | སྦྱར་བ་ | *jar-wa.* |
| Do. *hon.* | སྦྱར་ར་ (བ་) གནང་བ་ | *jar-ra nang-wa.* |
| Joint, *s.* (of body) | ཚིགས་ | *tshiḱ.* |
| Jointlv | མཉམ་སྦྲེལ་ | *nyam-drel.* |
| Do. *hon.* | ཕྱག་སྦྲེལ་ | *chha-drel.* |
| Joke, to | ཁབ་ལས་བཤད་པ་ | *khaṕ-le she-pa.* |
| Do. *hon.* | ཞལ་ལས་གསུང་བ་ | *sḱe-le sung-wa.* |
| Do. *h. hon.* | ཞལ་ལས་གསུང་ང་ (བ་) གནང་བ་ | *sḱe-le sung-nga nang-wa.* |
| Jollity | དགའ་ཚོར་ | *ga-tshor.* |
| Do. *hon.* | མཉེས་ཚོར་ | *nye-tshor.* |
| Jolly | དགའ་པོ་ | *ga-po.* |
| Joss-stick | སྤོས་ | *pö.* |
| Do. *hon.* | གཟིམ་སྤོས་ | *śim-pö.* |
| Journey | ལམ་ཀ་ | *lang-ka.* |
| Do. *hon.* | ཕེབ་ལམ་ | *pheṕ-lam.* |
| Joviality | དགའ་ཚོར་ | *ga-tshor.* |

| | | |
|---|---|---|
| Joviality, *hon.* | མཉེས་ཚོར་ | *nye-tshor.* |
| Joy | དགའ་ཚོར་ | *ga-tshor.* |
| Do. *hon.* | མཉེས་ཚོར་ | *nye-tshor.* |
| Joyful, to be | དགའ་བ་ | *ga-wa.* |
| Do. *hon.* | མཉེས་པོ་གནང་བ་ | *nye-po nang-wa.* |
| Do. *h. hon.* | ཐུགས་དགྱེས་པོ་གནང་བ་ | *thu-gye-po nang-wa.* |
| Judge, *s.* (if a Chinaman) | ཁྲིམས་དཔོན་ | *thrim-pön.* |
| Do. (if a Tibetan) | མི་དཔོན་ | *mi-pön.* |
| Judge, to | ཁྲིམས་བཅད་ (གཅོད་) པ་ | *thrim-che-pa.* |
| Do. *hon.* | ཁྲིམས་གཅོད་པ་གནང་བ་ | *thrim-chö-pa nang-wa.* |
| Judgment (opinion) | བསམ་པ་ | *sam-pa.* |
| Do. *hon.* | ཐུགས་སེམས་ | *thu-sem.* |
| Judgment (legal) | བཅད་མཚམས། ཁྲ་མ་ | *che-tsham ; thra-ma.* |
| Do. to apply for | ཁྲ་མ་ཞུ་བ་ | *thra-ma sk̄u-wa.* |
| Do. to pass | ཁྲ་མ་གནང་བ་ | *thra-ma nang-wa.* |
| Judgment-hall | ལས་ཁུངས་ (ལས་ཁོངས་) | *le-khung.* |
| Jug | ཆུ་སྣོད་ | *chhu-nö.* |
| Do. *hon.* | ཆབ་སྣོད་ | *chhap̄-nö.* |
| Juggle, to (conjure) | མིག་འཕྲུལ་རྩེད་པ་ | *mik̄-thrü tse pa.* |
| Do. *hon.* | མིག་འཕྲུལ་རྩེད་པ་གནང་བ་ | *mik̄-thrü tse-pa nang-wa.* |

| | | |
|---|---|---|
| Juggler | མིག་འཕྲུལ་རྩེད་མཁན་ | *miḱ-thrü tse-khen.* |
| Do. *hon.* | མིག་འཕྲུལ་རྩེད་པ་གནང་མཁན་ | *miḱ-thrü tse-pa nang-khen.* |
| Jugglery | མིག་འཕྲུལ་ | *miḱ-thrü.* |
| Juice | ཁུ་བ་ | *khu-wa.* |
| Jump, to | མཆོངས་པ། མཆོངས་རྒྱག་རྒྱབ་པ་ | *chhong pa ; chhong-gya gyaṕ-pa.* |
| Do. *hon.* | མཆོངས་རྒྱག་སྐྱོན་པ་ | *chhong-gya kyöm-pa.* |
| Junction of roads | ལམ་འཛོམ་ | *lam-dzom.* |
| Do. of rivers | ཆུ་འཛོམ་ | *chhu-dzom.* |
| Jungle | ཤིང་ནགས་ | *shing-na.* |
| Juniper | ཤུག་པ་ | *shuḱ-pa.* |
| Do. (another kind) | སྤ་མ་ | *pa-ma.* |
| Jurisdiction | ས་གནས་ | *sa-ne.* |
| Just, *adj.* | ཁྲིམས་དྲང་པོ་ | *thrim-ťrang-po.* |
| Do. *hon.* | བཀའ་ཁྲིམས་དྲང་པོ་ | *ka-thrim ťrang-po* |
| Just, *adv.* | རང་ | *rang.* |
| Just by | རྩ་ལ་ (རྩར་) | *tsa-la.* |
| Just now | ད་ལྟ་རང་ | *ťan-da-rang.* |
| Just so! (like that) | ད་ག་རེད་ | *ťa-ḱa re.* |
| Do. *hon.* | ལགས་ད་ག་རང་རེད་ | *la-ťa-ḱa-rang re.* |

| | | |
|---|---|---|
| Just so ! (like that) *h. hon.* | ལགས་བཀའ་གནང་རང་རེད་ | *la ka nang-rang re.* |
| Justice | ཁྲིམས་དྲང་པོ་ | *thrim ťrang-po.* |
| Do. *hon.* | བཀའ་ཁྲིམས་དྲང་པོ་ | *ka-thrim ťrang-po.* |
| Justly | ཁྲིམས་ནང་བཞིན་ | *thrim nang-sǩin.* |
| Do. *hon.* | བཀའ་ཁྲིམས་ནང་བཞིན་ | *ka-thrim nang-sǩin.* |
| Jute | སོ་མ་ར་ཙ་ | *so-ma ra-tsa.* |
| Juvenile | གཞོན་པ། ལོ་གཞོན་གཞོན་ | *sǨöm pa ; lo sǨön-sǨön.* |

# K

| | | |
|---|---|---|
| Keen (not blunt) | རྣོ་པོ་ | *no-po.* |
| Keen (eager) | སྙིང་འདོད་པོ། སྙིང་བྲོ་པོ་ | *nying-dö-po ; nying tro-po.* |
| Keep, to (have the care of) | ཉར་བ། ཅག་ག་བྱེད་པ་ | *nyar-wa ; cha-ka che-pa.* |
| Do. *hon.* | ཉར་ར་ (བ་) གནང་བ། ཐུགས་ཅག་གནང་བ་ | *nyar-ra nang-wa ; thuk-cha nang-wa.* |
| Keep, to (retain) | བཞག་པ་ (འཛོག་པ་) | *skak-pa.* |
| Do. *hon.* | གཞོག་ག་ (འཛོག་པ་) གནང་བ་ | *skok-ka nang-wa.* |
| Keeper (guard) | སྲུང་མཁན་ | *sung-khen.* |
| Kennel | ཁྱི་ཚང་ | *khyi-tshang.* |
| Kerosene oil | ས་སྣུམ་ | *sa num.* |
| Kettle (for tea) | ཁོ་ཏི་ | *kho-ti.* |
| Do. *hon.* | གསོལ་ཏི་ | *sö-ti.* |
| Key | ལྡེ་མིག་ | *di-mi.* |
| Do. *hon.* | ཕྱག་ལྡེ་ | *chhan-di.* |
| Kham (province in Eastern Tibet) | ཁམས་ | *kham.* |
| Kham, inhabitant of | ཁམས་པ་ | *kham-pa.* |
| Kick | རྡོག་རྒྱག་ | *dong-gya.* |

| | | |
|---|---|---|
| Kick, to | རྡོག་རྒྱག་གཞུ་བ་ | *dong-gya sḱu-wa.* |
| Do. *hon.* | ཞབས་རྡོག་གཞུ་བ་གནང་བ་ | *shap-do sḱu-wa nang·wa.* |
| Kid, *s.* | རེ་ཀོག་ (ར་ཕྲུག་) | *re-ko.* |
| Kidney | ཨ་རི་མཁལ་རི་ | *a-ri khe-ri.* |
| Kill, to | བསད་པ་ (གསོད་པ་) | *se·pa.* |
| Do. *hon.* | བཀྲོངས་པ་ (འགྲོང་བ་) | *trong-pa.* |
| Do. *h. hon.* | བཀྲོངས་ང་ (འགྲོང་བ་) གནང་བ་ | *trong-nga nang wa.* |
| Kind, *s.* (sort) | རྒྱུ་ | *gyu.* |
| Kind, *adj.* | དྲིན་ཆེན་པོ་ | *t́rin chhem-po.* |
| Do. *hon.* | བཀའ་དྲིན་ཆེན་པོ་ | *ka-t́rin chhem-po.* |
| Kindle, to (fire) | བཏང་བ་ (གཏོང་བ་) | *tang-wa.* |
| Do. *hon.* | གཏོང་ང་ (བ་) གནང་བ་ | *tong-nga nang-wa.* |
| Kindly | དྲིན་ཆེན་པོ་ | *t́rin-chhem-po.* |
| Do. *hon.* | བཀའ་དྲིན་ཆེན་པོ་ | *ka-t́rin chhem-po.* |
| Kindness | དྲིན་ | *t́rin.* |
| Do. *hon.* | བཀའ་དྲིན་ | *ka-t́rin.* |
| Kindness, to do | དྲིན་བྱེད་པ་ | *t́rin cḱe-pa.* |
| Do. *hon.* | བཀའ་དྲིན་གནང་བ་ | *ka-t́rin nang-wa.* |
| Kindred (relatives) | ཉེ་བ་ | *nye-wa.* |

| | | |
|---|---|---|
| Kindred (relatives) *hon.* | སྐུ་གཉེན་ | *ku-nyen.* |
| Kinds, different | སྣ་ཚོགས་ | *na-tsho.* |
| King | རྒྱལ་པོ་ | *gye-po.* |
| King's business (administration) | རྒྱལ་སྲིད་ | *gye-si.* |
| Kingdom | རྒྱལ་ཁབ་ | *gye-khap̍.* |
| Kiss, to | ཁ་སྐྱེལ་བ་ | *kha-kyel-wa.* |
| Do. *hon.* | ཞལ་སྐྱེལ་ལ་ (བ་) གནང་བ་ | *sk̍e-kyel-la nang-wa.* |
| Kitchen | ཐབ་ཚང་ | *thap̍-tshang.* |
| Do. *hon.* | གསོལ་ཐབ་ | *sö-thap̍.* |
| Kitchen-garden | ཚལ་ཡང་ཙེ་ | *tshe-yang-tse.* |
| Kite (bird) | ཕིང་ཀྱུ་མ་ | *ping-kyu-ma.* |
| Kitten | ཞིམ་ཕྲུག་ | *sk̍im-thru.* |
| Knapsack | ལྟོ་ཕད་ | *to-phe.* |
| Knave | བསྟན་བཞིག། འཛབ་ཆེན་ | *ten-sk̍i; dzap̍-chhen.* |
| Knee | པུས་མོ་ | *pi mo.* |
| Do. *hon.* | ཞབས་པུས་ | *sk̍ap̍-pi.* |
| Knee-joint | པུས་མོའི་ཚིགས་ | *pi-mö-tshik̍.* |
| Do. *hon.* | ཞབས་པུའི་ཚིགས་ | *sk̍ap̍-pi-i tshik̍.* |
| Kneel, to | པུས་མོ་བཙུག་ (འཛུགས་) པ་ | *pi-mo tsuk̍-pa.* |

| | | |
|---|---|---|
| Kneel, to *hon.* | ཞབས་ཕྱིས་བཙུག་ག་ (འཛུགས་པ་) གནང་བ་ | *sḱaṕ-pi tsuk-ka nang-wa.* |
| Knife | གྲི་ | *t́ri.* |
| Do. *hon.* | ཕྱག་ཤན་ | *chha-shen.* |
| Knife, clasp | ལྟབ་གྲི་ | *taṕ-t́ri.* |
| Do. *hon.* | ཕྱག་ཤན་ལྟབ་གྲི་ | *chha-shen taṕ-t́ri.* |
| Knit, to | སླེ་བ་ | *le-wa.* |
| Do. *hon.* | སླེ་བ་གནང་བ་ | *le-wa nang wa.* |
| Knitting-needle | ལྕགས་མདའ་ | *chan-da.* |
| Knock, to | དག་དག་བཏང་ (གཏོང་) བ་ | *taḱ-ta tang-wa.* |
| Do. *hon* | དག་དག་གཏོང་ང་ (བ་) གནང་བ་ | *taḱ-ta tong-nga nang-wa.* |
| Knocking, *s.* (on door, &c.) | དག་དག་ | *taḱ-ta.* |
| Knot, *s.* | མདུད་པ་ | *dü-pa.* |
| Do. *hon.* | ཕྱག་མདུད་ | *chhan-dü.* |
| Knot, to | མདུད་པ་རྒྱབ་པ་ | *dü-pa gyaṕ-pa.* |
| Do. *hon.* | ཕྱག་མདུད་སྐྱོན་པ་ | *chhan-dü kyöm-pa.* |
| Knot, to untie a | མདུད་པ་བཤིག་པ་ | *dü-pa sḱiḱ-pa.* |
| Do. *hon.* | ཕྱག་མདུད་བཤིག་ག་ (པ་) གནང་བ་ | *chhan-dü sḱiḱ-ka nang-wa.* |

| | | |
|---|---|---|
| Know, to (things) | ཤེས་པ་ | *she-pa.* |
| Do. *hon.* | མཁྱེན་པ་ | *khyem-pa.* |
| Do. *h. hon.* | དགོངས་པ་རྟོགས་པ་ | *gong-pa tok-pa.* |
| Know, to (persons) | ངོ་ཤེས་པ་ | *ngo-shem-pa.* |
| Know, to (a person of good position) | ཞལ་ཚོ་ (ཚོར་) བ་ | *sKe-tsho-wa.* |
| Do. *hon.* | ཐུགས་ངོ་མཁྱེན་པ་ | *thu-ngo khyem-pa.* |
| Knowledge (in general) | ཤེས་བྱ། ཡོན་ཏན་ | *she-cKa ; yön-ten.* |
| Do. *hon.* | སྐུ་ཡོན་ | *ku-yön.* |
| Knowledge (as to a specific matter) | རྒྱུས་ | *gyü.* |
| Knuckle | ལག་པའི་ཚིགས་ | *lak-pe tshik.* |
| Do. *hon.* | ཕྱག་གི་ཚིགས་ | *chha-ki tshik.* |

## L

| | | |
|---|---|---|
| Laborious (difficult) | དཀའ་ལས་ཁག་པོ་ | *ka-le* ***khak-*** *po.* |
| Do. *hon.* | སྐུ་མཉེལ་པོ་ | *ku-nye-po.* |
| Labour (pangs of child-birth) | སྐྱེ་གཟུག་ | *kye-śu.* |
| Do. (work) | ལས་ཀ་ | *le-ka.* |
| Do. *hon.* | ཕྱག་ལས་ | *chha-le.* |
| Labour, forced | འུ་ལག་ | *u-la.* |
| Do. hired | མི་ལག་ | *mi-la.* |
| Labour, to | ལས་ཀ་བྱེད་པ་ | *le-ka cke-pa.* |
| Do. *hon.* | ཕྱག་ལས་གནང་བ་ | *chha-le nang-wa.* |
| Labourer | མི་གླ་ | *mi la.* |
| Labourer's hire, a | གླ་ | *la.* |
| Lac (dye) | རྒྱ་ཚོས་ | *gya-tshö.* |
| Lac (number) | འབུམ་ | *bum.* |
| Lacerate, to | གཤག་པ་ | *shak-pa.* |
| Do. *hon.* | གཤག་ག་ (པ་) གནང་བ་ | *shak-ka nang-wa.* |
| Lack, to | མི་··ཚང་བ་ | *mi. .tshang-wa.* |
| Lad | བུ་གུ་ | *pu-gu.* |
| Do. *hon.* | ཨ་ཝ་ | *a-wa.* |
| Ladak (name of province) | ལ་དྭགས་ | *la-dak.* |

| | | |
|---|---|---|
| Ladder | ཀན་རྩ་ (སྐས་འཛེག་) | *ken-tsa.* |
| Do. *hon.* | ཕེབ་སྐས་ | *phep̓-ke.* |
| Lade, to | ཁལ་བཀལ་ (འགེལ་) བ་ | *khe kel-wa.* |
| Do. *hon.* | ཁལ་བཀལ་ལ་ (བ་) གནང་བ་ | *khe kel-la nang-wa.* |
| Ladle, *s.* | སྐྱོགས་ | *kyo.* |
| Do. *hon.* | གསོལ་སྐྱོགས། ཕྱག་སྐྱོགས་ | *sö-kyo ; chha-kyo.* |
| Ladle, to | སྐྱོགས་ཀྱིས་བླུག་པ་ | *kyo-kyi luk̓-pa.* |
| Do. *hon.* | གསོལ་སྐྱོགས་ཀྱིས་བླུག་ག་ (པ་) གནང་བ་ | *sö-kyo-kyi luk̓-k̓a nang-wa.* |
| Ladle, to, *inf.* to *sup.* | གསོལ་སྐྱོགས་ཀྱིས་ཞུ་བ་ | *sö-kyo-kyi sk̓u-wa.* |
| Lady (wife of well-to-do villager) | སྙི་སྙིང་ལགས་ | *nyi- nying-la.* |
| Do. (wife of ordinary official) | ལྕམ་སྐུ་གཞོགས་ | *cham-ku-sk̓o.* |
| Do. (third grade and upwards) | ལྷ་ལྕམ་སྐུ་གཞོགས་ | *hla-cham ku-sk̓o.* |
| Lady, young | སྲས་མོ་ | *se-mo.* |
| Lag, to | འགོར་བ་ | *gor-wa.* |
| Do. *hon.* | ཕེབ་འགོར་གནང་བ་ | *phe-gor nang-wa.* |
| Lahoul (name of province) | གར་ཞ་ | *k̓ar-sk̓a.* |
| Laity | ཨའུ། འཇིག་རྟེན་པ་ | *a-u ; jik̓-tem-pa.* |

| | | |
|---|---|---|
| Lair | ཚང་ | *tshang.* |
| Lake | མཚོ་ | *tsho.* |
| Lakh (number) | འབུམ་ | *bum.* |
| Lama | བླ་མ་ | *la-ma.* |
| Lama, Grand (of Lhasa) | སྐྱབས་མགོན་རིན་པོ་ཆེ་ | *kyam-gön rim-po-chhe.* |
| Lama, Grand (of Tashi Hlüm-po) | པན་ཆེན་རིན་པོ་ཆེ་ | *pen-chhen rim-po-chhe.* |
| Lamb | ལུག་ཕྲུག། ལུ་གུ་ | *luḱ-thru ; lu-ḱu.* |
| Lame | ཀང་ཀྱོག་ | *kang-kyo.* |
| Do. *hon.* | ཞབས་ཀྱོག་ | *sḱaṕ-kyo.* |
| Lament, to | སྡུག་བསྔལ་བྱེད་པ། མྱ་ངན་བྱེད་པ་ | *du-nge cḱe pa ; nya-ngen cḱe-pa.* |
| Do. *hon.* | ཐུགས་ངན་གནང་བ་ | *thu-ngen nang-wa.* |
| Lamentation | མྱ་ངན་ | *nya-ngen.* |
| Lamp | ཞུ་མར་ | *sḱu-ma.* |
| Do. *hon.* | གཟིམ་ཞུ་ | *śim sḱu.* |
| Lamp (as offering to deity) | མཆོད་མེ་ | *chhö-me* |
| Lance, *s.* | མདུང་ | *dung.* |
| Do. *hon.* | ཕྱག་མདུང་ | *chhan-dung.* |
| Lancet | ཙའུ་ | *tsa-u.* |

| | | |
|---|---|---|
| Land (earth) | ས་ | *sa.* |
| Do. (landed property) | ས་ཆ་ | *sa-chha.* |
| Do. (country) | ལུང་པ། ཡུལ་ | *lung-pa ; yü.* |
| Landing-place | གྲུ་ཁ་ | *t́ru-kha.* |
| Landlady (of inn, etc.) | གནས་མོ་ | *ne-mo.* |
| Do. *hon.* | གནས་མོ་ལགས་ | *ne-mo-la.* |
| Landlord (of inn, etc.) | གནས་པོ་ | *ne-po.* |
| Do. *hon.* | གནས་པོ་ལགས་ | *ne-po-la.* |
| Landlord (of land) | སའི་བདག་པོ་ | *sa-i daḱ-po.* |
| Landslip | ས་རུད་ | *sa-rü.* |
| Land-tax | ས་ཁྲལ་ | *sa-thre.* |
| Lane | སྲང་འགག་ | *hrang-ga.* |
| Language | སྐད་ | *ke.* |
| Do. (honorific) | ཞེ་ས་ | *sḱe-sa.* |
| Language (common, *i.e.* non-honorific) | ཞེ་ས་མེད་པའི་སྐད་ཆ་ | *sḱe-sa me-pe ke-chha.* |
| Do. (colloquial) | ཕལ་སྐད། ཕལ་ཚིག་ | *phe-ke ; phe-tshi.* |
| Do. (literary) | ཆོས་སྐད། ཆོས་ཚིག་ | *chhö-ke ; chhö-tshi.* |
| Languid | ཉོབ་པོ་ | *nyoṕ-po.* |
| Lank (of persons and animals) | ཤ་སྐམ་པོ་ | *sha kam-po.* |
| Do. *hon.* (of persons) | སྐུ་ཤ་སྐམ་པོ་ | *ku-sha kam-po.* |

| | | |
|---|---|---|
| Lank (of animals) *hon.* | བཞེས་ཤ་སྐམ་པོ་ | *sḱe sha kam-po.* |
| Lantern | སྒང་ཀྲུ་ (སྒོང་ཀྲུ་) | *gang-sḱu.* |
| Do. *hon.* | ཕེབ་ཀྲུ་ | *pheṕ-sḱu.* |
| Lap, *s.* (of women) | པང་པ་ | *pang-pa.* |
| Do. *hon.* | སྐུ་པང་ | *ku-pang.* |
| Lap up, to (water, &c.) | ལྡག་པ་ | *daḱ-pa.* |
| Lapsus linguae, to make a | ཁ་ཤོར་བ་ | *kha-shor-wa.* |
| Do. *hon.* | ཞལ་བཞེས་གནང་བ་ | *sḱe-sḱe nang-wa.* |
| Larch | ཟྲ་ཤིང་ | *śa-shing.* |
| Lard | ཕག་ཚིལ་ | *phaḱ tshi.* |
| Large | ཆེན་པོ་ | *chhem-po.* |
| Large (of country, etc.) | གྱ་ཆེན་པོ་ | *gya-chhem-po.* |
| Larynx | སྐེ་ | *ke.* |
| Do. *hon.* | མགུལ་ | *gü.* |
| Lascivious | འདོད་ཆགས་ཆེན་པོ་ | *dö-chha chhem-po.* |
| Lasciviousness | འདོད་ཆགས་ | *dö-chha.* |
| Lash (of a whip) | རྟ་ལྕག་ | *ta-cha.* |
| Do. *hon.* | ཆིབས་ལྕག་ | *chhiṕ-cha.* |
| Lash, to | རྟ་ལྕག་གཞུ་བ་ | *ta-cha sḱu-wa.* |
| Do. *hon.* | ཆིབས་ལྕག་སྐྱོན་པ་ | *chhiṕ-cha kyöm-pa.* |

| | | |
|---|---|---|
| Lass | བུ་མོ་ | *ṕu-mo.* |
| Do. *hon.* | སྲས་མོ་ | *se-mo.* |
| Lassitude | ངལ་ | *ngel.* |
| Do. *hon.* | སྐུ་ངལ་ | *ku-ngel.* |
| Last, *adj.* | གཞུག་ཤོས་ | *sḱuḱ-shö.* |
| Do. *adv.* (at last) | གཞུག་ལ་ | *sḱuḱ-la.* |
| Last night | མདངས་དགོངས་ | *dang-yong.* |
| Last year | ཟླ་ཉིང་ (ན་ཉིང་) | *da-nying.* |
| Last, to | ཐུབ་པ་ | *thuṕ-pa.* |
| Lasting (durable) | ཀྲོག་ཆེན་པོ་ | *tro chhem-po.* |
| Latch | ཨ་ཤིང་ | *a-shing.* |
| Latchet | ལྷམ་སྒྲོགས་ | *hlam-dro.* |
| Do. *hon* | ཞབས་སྒྲོགས་ | *sḱaṕ-dro.* |
| Late | ཕྱི་པོ་ | *chhi-po.* |
| Late, to be | ཕྱི་པོ་བྱེད་པ་ | *chhi-po cḱe-pa.* |
| Late, the (the deceased) | ཤི་མཁན་ | *shi-khen.* |
| Do. *hon.* | གྲོང་མཁན་ | *t́rong-khen.* |
| Do. *h. hon.* | དམ་པ་ | *t́am-pa.* |
| Lately | ཁ་སང་ | *kha-sang.* |
| Latent | སྦེད་པ་ | *be-pa.* |

| | | |
|---|---|---|
| Later on (afterwards) | གཞུག་ལ་ | *sKu-la.* |
| Latest | གཞུག་ཤོས་ | *sKuk-shö.* |
| Latter | གཞུག་མ་ | *sKuk ma.* |
| Laud, to | སྟོད་ར་བཏང་ (གཏོང་) བ་ | *tö-ra tang-wa.* |
| Do. *hon.* | སྟོད་ར་གཏོང་ང་ (བ་) གནང་བ་ | *tö-ra tong-nga nang-wa.* |
| Do. *inf.* to *sup.* | སྟོད་ར་ཞུ་བ་ | *tö-ra sKu-wa.* |
| Laugh, *s.* | བགད་མོ་ | *ge-mo.* |
| Laugh, to | བགད་མོ་བགད་པ། བགད་མོ་ཤོར་བ་ | *ge-mo ge-pa ; ge mo shor-wa.* |
| Do. *hon.* | ཞལ་མོ་བཞེས་པ། ཞལ་མོ་ཤོར་བ་ | *sKe-mo sKe-pa ; sKe-mo shor-wa.* |
| Laughable | བགད་མོ་བྲོ་པོ་ | *ge mo t́ro-po.* |
| Do. *hon.* | ཞལ་མོ་བྲོ་པོ་ | *sKe-mo t́ro-po.* |
| Laughter | བགད་མོ་ | *ge-mo.* |
| Do. *hon.* | ཞལ་མོ་ | *sKe-mo.* |
| Lavish (profuse) | འབེལ་པོ། ཛག་ཏོ་ | *be po ; dzak-t́o.* |
| Law | ཁྲིམས་ | *thrim.* |
| Do. *hon.* | བཀའ་ཁྲིམས་ | *ka-thrim.* |
| Law (religious) | ཆོས་ཁྲིམས་ | *chhö-thrim.* |
| Law, to go to | རྒྱུ་རྐྱེན་ཞུ་བ། ཁྲིམས་ལ་ཞུ་བ་ | *gyu-kyen sKu-wa ; thrim-la sKu-wa.* |

| | | |
|---|---|---|
| **Laws, to obey** | ཁྲིམས་འཁྱེར་བ། ཁྲིམས་འཁུར་བ་ | *thrim khyer-wa ; thrim khur-wa.* |
| **Law-court** | ཁྲིམས་ས་ | *thrim-sa.* |
| Do. *hon.* | བཀའ་ཁྲིམས་ཀྱི་ས་ཆ་ | *ka-thrim-kyi sa-chha.* |
| **Lawful** | ཁྲིམས་མཐུན་ | *thrim-thün.* |
| **Lawfully** | ཁྲིམས་ནང་བཞིན་ | *thrim-nang-sk̄in.* |
| Do. *hon.* | བཀའ་ཁྲིམས་ནང་བཞིན་ | *ka-thrim nang-sk̄in.* |
| **Lawless** | ཁྲིམས་མེད་ | *thrim-me.* |
| **Lawn** | ཐང་ | *thang.* |
| **Law-suit** | ཁ་མཆུ་ | *kham-chhu.* |
| **Lay, to (place)** | བཞག་པ་ (འཛོག་པ་) | *sk̄ak-p̄a.* |
| Do. *hon.* | གཞོག་ག་ (འཛོག་པ་) གནང་བ་ | *sk̄ok-k̄a nang-wa.* |
| **Lay, to (spread)** | བཏིང་པ་ (འདིང་བ་) | *ting-pa.* |
| Do. *hon.* | བཏིང་ང་ (འདིང་བ་) གནང་བ་ | *ting-nga nang-wa.* |
| **Lay, to** | བཞག་པ་ (འཛོག་པ་) | *sk̄ak-pa.* |
| Do. *hon.* | གཞོག་ག་ (འཛོག་པ་) གནང་བ་ | *sk̄ok-k̄a nang-wa.* |
| **Lay, to (down)** | བསྙལ་བ་ (སྙོལ་བ་) | *nye-wa.* |
| Do. *hon.* | བསྙལ་ལ་ (སྙོལ་བ་) གནང་བ་ | *nye-la nang-wa.* |
| **Lay, to (eggs)** | བཏང་བ་ (གཏོང་བ་) | *tang-wa.* |
| **Lay the foundation of, to** | རྩིག་སྟན་བཏིང་ (འདིང་) བ་ | *tsik-ten ting-wa.* |

| | | |
|---|---|---|
| Lay the foundation of, to, *hon.* | རྩིག་སྟེན་བཏིང་ང་ (བ་) གནང་བ་ | *tsik-ten ting-nga nang-wa.* |
| Layman | ཨའུ། འཇིག་རྟེན་པ་ | *a-u ; jik-tem-pa.* |
| Lazy | རྒྱུ་མ་རིང་པོ། ལེ་ལོ་ཆེན་པོ་ | *gyu-ma ring-po ; le-lo chhem-po* |
| Do. *hon.* | ཐུགས་རྒྱུ་རིང་པོ་ | *thu-gyu ring-po.* |
| Lead, *s.* (metal) | ཞ་ནེ་ | *sKa-ni.* |
| Lead (red-lead) | སི་ནྡྷཱུ་ར་ | *sin-dhu-ra.* |
| Lead, to (towards) | འཁྲིད་ཡོང་བ་ | *thri-yong-wa.* |
| Do. *hon.* | འཁྲིད་ཕེབ་པ་ | *thri-phe-pa.* |
| Lead, to (away) | འཁྲིད་འགྲོ་བ་ | *thri-dro-wa.* |
| Do *hon.* | འཁྲིད་ཕེབ་པ་ | *thri-phe-pa.* |
| Leader | མགོ་པ་ | *go-pa.* |
| Leaf (of a tree) | ལོ་མ། འདབ་མ་ | *lo-ma ; da-ma.* |
| Do. (of a book) | ཤོག་ལེབ་ | *shoK-le.* |
| Leak, to (of water) | འཛག་པ་ | *dzaK-pa.* |
| Lean, *adj.* (of animals and persons) | ཤ་སྐམ་པོ་ | *sha-kam-po.* |
| Do. *hon.* (of persons) | སྐུ་ཤ་སྐམ་པོ་ | *ku-sha kam-po.* |
| Do. *hon.* (of meat) | བཞེས་ཤ་སྐམ་པོ་ | *sKe-sha kam-po.* |
| Lean, to (against) | སྙེ་བསྡད་ (སྡོད་) པ་ | *nye-de-pa.* |

| | | |
|---|---|---|
| Lean, to (against) *hon.* | སྐུ་སྙེ་གནང་ནས་བཞུགས་པ་ | *ku-nye nang-ne sKu-pa.* |
| Do. *h. hon.* | སྐུ་སྙེ་གནང་ནས་བཞུགས་གདན་འཇག་པ་ | *ku-nye nang-ne sKu-den ja-pa.* |
| Lean, to (back) | རྒྱབ་བསྙེས་བྱས་ནས་བསྡད་ (སྡོད་) པ་ | *gyap-nye cKe-ne de-pa.* |
| Do. *hon.* | སྐུ་བསྙེས་གནང་ནས་བཞུགས་པ་ | *ku-nye nang-ne sKu-pa.* |
| Leap, to | མཆོངས་པ། མཆོངས་རྒྱག་རྒྱབ་པ་ | *chhong-pa ; chhong-gya gyap-pa.* |
| Do. *hon.* | མཆོངས་རྒྱག་སྐྱོན་པ་ | *chhong-gya kyöm-pa.* |
| Learn, to | བསླབས་པ་ (སློབ་པ་) | *lap-pa.* |
| Do. *hon.* | བསླབས་ (སློབ་) པ་གནང་བ་ | *lap-pa nang-wa.* |
| Learn, to (by heart) | བློ་ལ་ཟིམ་པ་ (བཟུང་བ་) | *lo-la śim-pa.* |
| Do. *hon.* | ཐུགས་བློ་ལ་ཟིམ་པ་ (བཟུང་བ་) གནང་བ་ | *thuk-lo la śim-pa nang-wa.* |
| Learned | ཤེས་བྱ་ཆེན་པོ། ཡོན་དན་ཆེན་པོ་ | *she-cKa chhem-po ; yön-ten chhem po.* |
| Do. *hon.* | སྐུ་ཡོན་ཆེན་པོ་ | *ku-yön chhem-po.* |
| Learner (novice) | ཨེན་ཆུང་ | *en-chhung.* |
| Learning | ཤེས་བྱ། ཡོན་དན | *she-cKa ; yon-ten.* |

| | | |
|---|---|---|
| Learning, *hon.* | སྐུ་ཡོན་ | *ku-yön.* |
| Lease, *s.* | བཀའ་བརྟན་ | *ka-ten.* |
| Do. to (let out on) | བོགས་མ་ལ་བཏང་ (གཏོང་) བ་ | *p̓o-ma-la tang-wa.* |
| Do. *hon.* | བོགས་མ་ལ་གཏོང་ང་ (བ་) གནང་བ་ | *p̓o-ma-la tong-nga nang-wa.* |
| Least | ཆུང་ཤོས་ | *chhung-shö.* |
| Leather | ཀོ་བ་ | *ko-wa.* |
| Leave of absence | དགོངས་པ་ | *gong-pa.* |
| Leave, to (depart) | འཐོན་པ། ཕྱིན་པ་ | *thöm-pa ; chhim-pa.* |
| Do. *hon.* | ཕེབ་པ་ | *phep̓-pa.* |
| Do. *h. hon.* | འཆིབ་རྒྱུ་གནང་བ་ | *chhip̓-gyu nang-wa.* |
| Leave off, to (renounce) | སྤང་བ་ | *pang-wa.* |
| Do. *hon.* | སྤོང་ང་ (བ་) གནང་བ་ | *pong-nga nang-wa.* |
| Leave, to (a country, etc.) | བཞག་ནས་ཡོང་བ་ | *sḱa-ne yong-wa.* |
| Do. *hon.* | བཞག་ནས་ཕེབ་པ་ | *sḱa-ne phe-pa.* |
| Do. *h hon.* | བཞག་ནས་འཆིབས་རྒྱུ་གནང་བ་ | *sḱa-ne chhip̓ gyu nang-wa.* |
| Leave, to ask for | དགོངས་པ་ཞུ་བ་ | *gong-pa sḱu-wa.* |
| Do. *hon.* | དགོངས་ཞུ་གནང་བ་ | *gong-sḱu nang-wa.* |
| Leave, to grant | དགོངས་པ་སྟེར་བ་ | *gong-pa ter-wa.* |
| Do. *hon.* | དགོངས་པ་གནང་བ་ | *gong-pa nang-wa.* |

| | | |
|---|---|---|
| Leaven (for fermenting liquor) | ཆང་རྩི་ | *chhang-tsi.* |
| Do. (for fermenting dough for bread) | ཕྱེ་སྨན་ | *chhi-men.* |
| Leaves (in a book), number of | ཤོག་གྲངས་ | *shok-ťrang.* |
| Leavings (things left) | ལྷག་མ་ | *hla-ma.* |
| Lecherous | འདོད་ཆགས་ཆེན་པོ་ | *dö-chha chhem-po.* |
| Lechery | འདོད་ཆགས་ | *dö-chha.* |
| Leech | པད་པ་ | *pe-pa.* |
| Left, *adj.* (opp. to right) | གཡོན་ | *yön.* |
| Left, to be (not expended) | ལྷག་མ་ལུས་པ་ | *hla-ma lü-pa.* |
| Left, to be (behind) | ལས་ (ལུས་) ནས་མེད་པ་ | *le-ne me-pa.* |
| Do. *hon.* | ལས་ (ལུས་) པ་གནང་བ་ | *le-pa nang-wa.* |
| Left-handed | གཡོན་ལག་ | *yön-la.* |
| Do. *hon.* | ཕྱག་གཡོན་ལག་ | *chha-yön-la.* |
| Leg | རྐང་པ་ | *kang-pa.* |
| Do. *hon.* | ཞབས་ | *sKap.* |
| Leg (of mutton, etc.) | རྐང་ཤ་ | *kang-sha.* |
| Legal | ཁྲིམས་མཐུན་ | *thrim-thün.* |
| Legally | ཁྲིམས་ནང་བཞིན་ | *thrim-nang-sKin.* |

| | | |
|---|---|---|
| Legally, *hon.* | བཀའ་ཁྲིམས་ནང་བཞིན་ | *ka-thrim nang-sḱin.* |
| Legend | རྣམ་ཐར་ | *nam-thu.* |
| Legged, bandy | རྐང་ཀྱོག་ | *kang-kyo.* |
| Do. *hon.* | ཞབས་ཀྱོག་ | *sḱaṕ-kyo.* |
| Legible, to be | ཀློག་ཤེས་པ་ | *loḱ-she-pa.* |
| Do. *hon.* | ལྗགས་ཀློག་གནང་མཁྱེན་པ་ | *ja-lo nang khyem-pa.* |
| Legitimate (lawful) | ཁྲིམས་མཐུན་ | *ṫhrim-thün.* |
| Legitimately | ཁྲིམས་ནང་བཞིན་ | *thrim nang-sḱin.* |
| Do. *hon.* | བཀའ་ཁྲིམས་ནང་བཞིན་ | *ka-thrim nang-sḱin.* |
| Leisure | ལོང་ | *long.* |
| Leisure, to sit at | ལྷོད་ལྷོད་བསྡད་ (སྡོད་) པ་ | *hlö-hlö de-pa.* |
| Do. *hon.* | ཐུགས་ལྷོད་ལྷོད་བཞུགས་པ་ | *thu-hlö-hlö sḱu-pa.* |
| Lend, to | གཡར་བ་ | *yar-wa.* |
| Do. *hon.* | གཡར་པོ་གནང་བ་ | *yar-po nang wa.* |
| Length | རིང་ཐུང་ | *ring-thung.* |
| Length, at (afterwards) | གཞུག་ལ། རྗེས་ལ་ | *sḱu-la ; je-la.* |
| Lengthen, to | རིང་དུ་བཏང་ (གཏོང་) བ་ | *ring-t́u tang-wa.* |
| Do. *hon.* | རིང་དུ་གཏོང་ང་ (བ་) གནང་བ་ | *ring-t́u tong nga nang-wa.* |
| Lengthy | རིང་པོ་ | *ring-po.* |
| Lenient, to be | འཆྭ་ཡང་གནང་བ་ | *chha-yang nang-wa.* |

| | | |
|---|---|---|
| Leopard | གཟིག་ | *śiḱ.* |
| Leper (male) | མཛེ་པོ་ | *dze-po.* |
| Do. (female) | མཛེ་མོ་ | *dze-mo.* |
| Leprosy | མཛེ་ | *dze.* |
| Leprous, to be | མཛེ་རྒྱབ་པ་ | *dze-gyaṕ-pa.* |
| Do. *hon.* | མཛེ་སྐྱོན་པ་ | *dze kyön-pa.* |
| Less | ཉུང་བ་ | *nyung-wa.* |
| Lessen, to, *v.i.* | ཉུང་རུ་ཕྱིན་པ་ | *nyung-ru chhim pa.* |
| Do. to, *v.t.* | ཉུང་རུ་བཏང་ (གཏོང་) བ་ | *nyung-ru tang-wa.* |
| Do. *hon.* | ཉུང་རུ་གཏོང་ང་ (བ་) གནང་བ་ | *nyung ru tong-nga nang-wa.* |
| Lessen, to (price) | བཅག་པ་ (གཅོག་པ་) | *chaḱ-pa.* |
| Do. *hon.* | གཅོག་ག་ (པ་) གནང་བ་ | *choḱ-ḱa nang-wa.* |
| Lesson | ཡིག་རྒྱུགས་ | *yi-gyuḱ.* |
| Let, to (allow) | བཅུག་པ་ (འཇུག་བ་) | *chuḱ-pa.* |
| Do. *hon.* | བཅུག་ག་ (པ་) གནང་བ་ | *chuḱ-ḱa nang-wa.* |
| Let, to (down) | ཕབ་པ་ (འབེབས་པ་) | *phaṕ-pa.* |
| Let, to (let in, let loose, etc.) | བཏང་བ་ (གཏོང་བ་) | *tang-wa.* |
| Do. *hon.* | གཏོང་ང་ (བ་) གནང་བ་ | *tong-nga nang-wa.* |
| Let off, to | བཏང་བ་ (གཏོང་བ་) | *tang-wa.* |
| Do. *hon.* | གཏོང་ང་ (བ་) གནང་བ་ | *tong-nga nang-wa.* |

| | | |
|---|---|---|
| Letter (epistle) | ཡི་གེ་ | *yi-ge.* |
| Do. *hon.* | ཕྱག་བྲིས་ | *chha ri.* |
| Level, *adj.* | སྙོམས་པོ་ | *nyom-po.* |
| Lewd | འདོད་ཆགས་ཆེན་པོ་ | *dö chha chhem-po.* |
| Lewdness | འདོད་ཆགས་ | *dö-chha.* |
| Lhasa | ལྷ་ས་ | *hla-sa.* |
| Lhasa man, a | ལྷ་སཱ་ | *hla-sā.* |
| Liar | ཧམ་པ་ཤོད་མཁན་ | *ham-pa shö-khen.* |
| Libation | གསེར་སྐྱེམས་ | *ser-kyem.* |
| Libel, *s.* | སྨད་ར་ | *me-ra.* |
| Libel, to | སྨད་ར་བཏང་ (གཏོང་) བ་ | *me-ra tang-wa.* |
| Do. *hon.* | སྨད་ར་གཏོང་ང་ (བ་) གནང་བ་ | *me-ra tong-nga nang-wa.* |
| Do *inf.* to *sup.* | སྨད་ར་ཞུ་བ་ | *me-ra sk̄u wa.* |
| Liberal | ལག་པ་ཤོག་པོ་ | *lak̄-pa shok̄-po.* |
| Do. *hon.* | ཕྱག་ཤོག་པོ་ | *chha-shok̄-po.* |
| Liberate, to | བཏང་བ་ (གཏོང་བ་) | *tang-wa.* |
| Liberated, to be | ཐར་བ་ | *thar-wa.* |
| Liberty | ཚེ་ཐར་ | *tshe-thar.* |
| Do. to be at (to be allowed) | ཆོག་པ་ | *chhok̄-pa.* |

| | | |
|---|---|---|
| Liberty, to be set at | ཚེ་ཐར་བཏང་ (གཏོང་) བ་ | tshe-thar tang-wa. |
| Do. *hon.* | ཚེ་ཐར་གཏོང་ང་ (བ་) གནང་བ་ | *tshe-thar tong-nga nang-wa.* |
| Libidinous | འདོད་ཆགས་ཆེན་པོ་ | *dö-chha chhem-po.* |
| Library | དཔེ་ཆ་ཁང་ | *pe-chha-khang.* |
| Do. *hon.* | ཕྱག་དཔེ་ཁང་ | *chha-pe-khang.* |
| License | བཀའ་ཤོག་ | *ka-sho.* |
| Licentious | འདོད་ཆགས་ཆེན་པོ་ | *dö-chha chhem-po.* |
| Licentiousness | འདོད་ཆགས་ | *dö-chha.* |
| Lick, to (of animals) | ལྡག་པ་ | *daḱ-pa.* |
| Do. (of persons) | ལྕེ་ལྡ་ (ལྡག་) རྒྱབ་པ་ | *che-la gyaṕ-pa.* |
| Do. *hon.* | ལྕེ་ལྡ་ (ལྡག་) སྐྱོན་པ་ | *che-la kyöm-pa.* |
| Lid | ཁ་གཅོད། ཁ་ | *khaṕ-chö ; kha.* |
| Lid (of the eye) | མིག་པགས་ | *miḱ-pa.* |
| Lie, *s.* | ཧམ་པ། ཀྱག་རྫུན་ | *ham-pa ; kyaḱ-dzün.* |
| Do. *hon.* | ཞལ་རྫུན་ | *sḱe-dzün.* |
| Lie, to (tell untruth) | ཧམ་པ་བཤད་ (ཤོད་) པ། ཀྱག་རྫུན་བཤད་ (ཤོད་) པ་ | *ham-pa she-pa ; kyaḱ-dzün she-pa.* |
| Do. *hon.* | ཞལ་རྫུན་གནང་བ་ | *sḱe-dzün nang-wa.* |
| Lie, to (down) | ཉལ་བསྡད་ (སྡོད་) པ་ | *nye-de-pa.* |
| Do. *hon.* | གཟིམས་བཞུགས་པ་ | *śim-sḱu-pa.* |

| | | |
|---|---|---|
| Lieu of, in (instead of) | ཚབ་ | *tshap.* |
| Do. *hon.* | སྐུ་ཚབ་ | *ku-tshap.* |
| Life | སྲོག། ཚེ་ | *so* or *hro ; tshe.* |
| Do. *hon.* | སྐུ་སྲོག། སྐུ་ཚེ་ | *ku-so ; ku-tshe.* |
| Life-time | ཚེ་གང་ | *tshe-kang.* |
| Do. *hon.* | སྐུ་ཚེ་གང་ | *ku-tshe-kang.* |
| Lift, to | ཡར་ཀྱག་ (འཁྱོག་) པ། ཡར་ལེན་པ་ | *yar-kyak-pa ; yar-lem-pa.* |
| Do. *hon.* | ཡར་ཀྱག་ག་ (འཁྱོག་པ་) གནང་བ་ | *yar-kyak-ka nang-wa.* |
| Light, *s.* (lamp) | ཞུ་མར་ | *sku-ma.* |
| Do. *hon.* | གཟིམ་ཞུ་ | *sim-sku.* |
| Light, *s.* (brightness) | འོད་ | *ö.* |
| Light, *adj.* (bright) | འོད་ཆེན་པོ་ | *ö chhem-po.* |
| Light, *adj.* (not heavy) | ཡང་པོ་ | *yang-po.* |
| Light, to (fire) | བདང་བ་ (གདོང་བ་) | *tang-wa.* |
| Do. *hon.* | གདོང་ང་ (བ་) གནང་བ་ | *tong-nga nang-wa.* |
| Light, to (lamp) | སྦར་བ་ | *par-wa.* |
| Do. *hon.* | སྦར་ར་ (བ་) གནང་བ་ | *par-ra nang-wa.* |
| Lightning, *s.* | གློག་ | *lo.* |

| | | |
|---|---|---|
| Lightning (forked) | འཁྱུག་ | *khyu.* |
| Lightning (sheet), to flash | གློག་རྒྱབ་པ་ | *lo gyap̓-pa.* |
| Do. (forked), to flash | འཁྱུག་རྒྱབ་པ་ | *khyu gyap̓-pa.* |
| Like (similar) | ནང་བཞིན། འདྲ་པོ་ | *nang-sk̓in ; dra-po.* |
| Like, to | དགའ་བ་ | *ga-wa.* |
| Do. *hon.* | ཐུགས་མཉེས་པོ་གནང་བ་ | *thu-nye-po nang-wa.* |
| Do. *h. hon.* | ཐུགས་དགྱེས་པོ་གནང་བ་ | *thu-gye-po nang-wa.* |
| Like this | འདི་འདྲ་ | *din-dra.* |
| Like that | དེ་འདྲ་ | *t̓en-dra.* |
| Likely, it is | ཡིན་འགྲོ། ཡིན་པ་འདྲ་ | *yin-dro ; yim-pa-dra.* |
| Likeness (form) | བཟོ་བསྟ་ | *śop̓-ta.* |
| Do. *hon.* | སྐུ་བཟོ་ | *ku-śo.* |
| Likewise | ཡང་ | *yang.* |
| Limb (of human beings) | འཟུགས་ཀྱི་ཡན་ལག་ | *śuk̓-kyi yen-la.* |
| Do. *hon.* | སྐུ་གཟུགས་ཀྱི་ཡན་ལག་ | *ku-śuk-kyi yen-la.* |
| Limb (of animals) | སྲུག་ལག་ | *suk̓-la.* |
| Lime | ས་དཀར། དཀར་རྩི་ | *sa-kar ; kar-tsi.* |
| Limit | མཐའ་ | *tha.* |
| Limitation | ཚོད་ | *tshö.* |
| Do. *hon.* | ཐུགས་ཚོད་ | *thu-tshö.* |

| | | |
|---|---|---|
| Limp, to | རྐང་པ་འཁྱོག་འཁྱོག་བྱེད་པ་ | *kang-pa khyo-khyo cḱe-pa.* |
| Do. *hon.* | ཞབས་འཁྱོག་འཁྱོག་གནང་བ་ | *sḱaṕ khyo-khyo nang-wa.* |
| Limpid (clear) | དྭངས་པོ་ | *t́ang-po.* |
| Line | ཐིག་ | *thi.* |
| Line (in a book) | ཡིག་ཕྲེང་ | *yiḱ-threng.* |
| Lineage (of laymen) | རིགས་བརྒྱུད། མི་བརྒྱུད་ | *ri-gyü ; mi-gyü.* |
| Do. *hon.* | སྐུ་བརྒྱུད་ | *ku-gyü.* |
| Do. *hon.* (of lamas) | གདུང་བརྒྱུད་ | *dung-gyü.* |
| Linen | རས་ | *re.* |
| Do. *hon.* | སྐུ་རས་ | *ku-re.* |
| Linger, to | འགོར་བ་ | *gor-wa.* |
| Do. *hon.* | ཕེབ་འགོར་གནང་བ་ | *phe-gor nang-wa.* |
| Lining | ནང་ཤ་ | *nang-sha.* |
| Link, to | འཐུད་རྒྱབ་པ་ | *thü-gyaṕ-pa.* |
| Do. *hon.* | འཐུད་སྐྱོན་པ་ | *thü-kyöm-pa.* |
| Lion | སེང་གེ་ | *seng-ge.* |
| Lioness | སེང་གེ་མོ་ | *seng-ge-mo.* |
| Lip | མཆུ་ཏོ་ | *chho-to.* |
| Do. *hon.* | ཞལ་མཆུ་ | *sḱe-chhu.* |
| Lip, upper | ཡ་མཆུ་ | *yen-chhu.* |

| | | |
|---|---|---|
| Lip, lower | མ་མཆུ་ | *men-chhu.* |
| Liquefy, to | ཞུ་བ་ | *sKu-wa.* |
| Liquid | ཁུ་བ་ | *khu-wa.* |
| Liquid medicine | འཐུང་སྨན་ | *thung-men.* |
| Liquor, distilled | ཨ་རག་ | *a-ra.* |
| Do. *hon.* | བཞེས་རག་ | *sKe-ra.* |
| List | ཐོ་ | *tho* |
| Do. *hon.* | ཕྱག་ཐོ་ | *chha-tho.* |
| Listen, to | ཉན་པ། ཨམ་ཆོག་ཉན་པ་ | *nyem-pa ; am-chho nyem-pa.* |
| Do. *hon.* | གསན་པ། སྙན་ལ་གསན་པ་ | *sem-pa ; nyen-la sem-pa.* |
| Literary language | ཆོས་སྐད་ | *chhö-ke.* |
| Literature | ཆོས་ | *chhö.* |
| Little | ཆུང་ཆུང་ | *chhung-chhung.* |
| Little, a (few) | ཏོག་ཙ། ཉུང་ཉུང་ | *toK-tsa ; nyung-nyung.* |
| Little time, a | ཧྲིབ་ཙ་ (ཙམ་) ཅིག | *hrip-tsa-chi.* |
| Live, *adj.* | གསོན་པོ་ | *söm-po.* |
| Live, to (dwell) | བསྡད་པ་ (སྡོད་པ་) | *de-pa.* |
| Do. *hon.* | བཞུགས་པ་ | *sKu-pa.* |
| Do. *h. hon.* | བཞུགས་གདན་འཇག་པ་ | *sKu-den jaK-pa.* |
| Lively | ཧུར་པོ། གཅང་པོ་ | *hur-po ; chang-po* |

| | | |
|---|---|---|
| Liver | མཆིན་པ་ | *chhim-pa.* |
| Do. *hon.* | སྐུ་མཆིན་ | *ku-chhin.* |
| Living, *adj.* | གསོན་པོ་ | *söm-po.* |
| Lizard, sand (small) | བྱེ་མ་ཉུ་གུ་ | *cḱe-ma nyu-gu.* |
| Lizard, rock (large) | ཙམ་པ་ཁ་རེལ་ | *tsam-pa kha-re.* |
| Lo ! | ལྟོས་ཤིག་ | *tö-shi* |
| Load (of an animal) | ཁལ། ཏོ་པོ་ | *khe ; ťo-po.* |
| Do. (of human being) | རྡོག་ཁྲེད། རྒྱབ་འཁུར་ | *doḱ-thre ; gyaṕ-khur.* |
| Load, to (animal) | ཁལ་བཀལ་ (འགེལ་) བ་ | *khe-ke-wa.* |
| Do. to (of human being) | རྡོག་ཁྲེད་སྐུར་བ་ | *doḱ-thre kur-wa.* |
| Load, to (a gun) | རྫས་རྫོང་རྒྱབ་པ་ | *dze-dzong gyaṕ-pa.* |
| Do. *hon.* | རྫས་རྫོང་སྐྱོན་པ་ | *dze-dzong kyöm-pa.* |
| Loadstone | རྡོ་ཁབ་ལེན་ | *do-khaṕ-len.* |
| Loaf | བག་ལེབ་ | *ṕa-le.* |
| Loafer (tramp) | རྒྱལ་ཁམས་སྐོར་མཁན་ | *gyeng-kham kor-khen.* |
| Loan | བུ་ལོན་ | *ṕu-lön.* |
| Loathe, to | སྡང་པོ་བྱེད་པ་ | *dang-po cḱe-pa.* |
| Do. *hon.* | སྡང་པོ་གནང་བ་ | *dang-po nang-wa.* |
| Locality | ས་ཆ་ | *sa-chha.* |
| Lock, *s.* | སྒོ་ལྕགས་ | *gön-cha.* |

| | | |
|---|---|---|
| Lock, *hon.* | གཟིམ་ལྕུགས། ཕྱག་ལྕུགས་ | *śim-cha ; chha-cha.* |
| Lock, to | སྒོ་ལྕུགས་རྒྱབ་པ་ | *gön-cha gyaṕ-pa.* |
| Do. *hon.* | གཟིམ་ལྕུགས་སྐྱོན་པ་ | *śim-cha kyöm-pa.* |
| Locust | ཨ་ཚ་ཚག་པ་ | *a-tsha tshaḱ-pa.* |
| Lodging-house | གནས་ཚང་ | *ne-tshang.* |
| Lodging-house, landlady of | གནས་མོ་ | *ne-mo.* |
| Do. *hon.* | གནས་མོ་ལགས་ | *ne-mo-la.* |
| Lodging-house, landlord of | གནས་པོ་ | *ne-po.* |
| Do. *hon.* | གནས་པོ་ལགས་ | *ne-po-la.* |
| Lofty | མཐོ་པོ་ | *tho-po.* |
| Log (piece of wood) | ཤིང་དུམ་ | *shing-t́um.* |
| Loins | རྐེད་པ་ | *ke-pa.* |
| Do. *hon.* | སྐུ་རྐེད་ | *ku-ke.* |
| Loiter, to | འགོར་བ་ | *gor-wa.* |
| Do. *hon.* | ཕེབ་འགོར་གནང་བ་ | *phe-gor nang-wa.* |
| Lonely | གཅིག་པོ་ | *chiḱ-po.* |
| Do. *hon.* | སྐུ་རྐྱང་ | *ku-kyang.* |
| Lonely place | དབེན་གནས་ | *en-ne.* |
| Long | རིང་པོ་ | *ring-po.* |
| Long for, to | དྲན་པ་ | *t́rem-pa.* |

| | | |
|---|---|---|
| Long for, to, *hon.* | ཐུགས་དྲན་པ་གནང་བ་ | *thu-ťrem-pa nang-wa.* |
| Long life, to have | ཚེ་རིང་བ་ | *tshe-ring-wa.* |
| Do. *hon.* | སྐུ་ཚེ་རིང་བ་ | *ku-tshe ring-wa.* |
| Long-lived | ཚེ་རིང་པོ་ | *tshe-ring-po.* |
| Do. *hon.* | སྐུ་ཚེ་རིང་པོ་ | *ku-tshe ring-po.* |
| Look, to | ལྟ་བ་ | *ta-wa.* |
| Do. *hon.* | གཟིགས་པ་ | *śi-pa.* |
| Look for, to (search) | འཚོལ་བ་ | *ťshö-wa.* |
| Do. *hon.* | འཚོལ་ལ་ (བ་) གནང་བ་ | *tshö-la nang-wa.* |
| Looking-glass | ཤེལ་སྒོ་ | *she-go.* |
| Loom | འཐག་ཁྲི་ | *thak-thri* |
| Loop | ལུང་ | *lung.* |
| Loop-button | ཐུབ་ལུང་ | *thup-lung.* |
| Do. *hon.* | མགུལ་ལུང་ | *gü-lung.* |
| Loose (not tight) | ལྷུག་ལྷུག་ | *lhu-lhu.* |
| Do. (lascivious) | འདོད་ཆགས་ཆེན་པོ་ | *dö-chha chhem-po.* |
| Loose, to (liberate) | བཏང་བ་ (གཏོང་བ་) | *tang-wa.* |
| Do. *hon.* | གཏོང་ང་ (བ་) གནང་བ་ | *tong-nga nang-wa.* |
| Loose, to (slacken) | ལྷོད་ལྷོད་བཏང་ (གཏོང་) བ་ | *hlö-hlö tang-wa.* |

| | | |
|---|---|---|
| Loose, to (slacken), *hon.* | ལྷོད་ལྷོད་གཏོང་ང་ (བ་) གནང་བ་ | *hlö-hlö tong-nga nang-wa.* |
| Loosen, to | ལྷུག་ལྷུག་བྱེད་པ་ | *lhu-lhu cḱe-pa.* |
| Do. *hon.* | ལྷུག་ལྷུག་གནང་བ་ | *lhu-lhu nang-wa.* |
| Lord | དཔོན་པོ་ | *pöm-po.* |
| Lose, to | བརླགས་པ་ | *la-pa.* |
| Lose, to (in business transaction) | གྱོང་འཕོག་པ་ | *ḱyong phoḱ-pa.* |
| Do. *hon.* | སྐུ་གྱོང་འཕོག་ག་ (པ་) གནང་བ་ | *ku-ḱyong phoḱ-ḱa nang-wa.* |
| Lose, to (battle, law-suit, etc.) | ཤོར་བ | *shor-wa.* |
| Do. *hon.* | ཤོར་ར་ (བ་) གནང་བ་ | *shor-ra nang-wa.* |
| Loss | གྱོང་ | *ḱyong.* |
| Loss of appetite | དང་ཁ་མེད་པ་ | *ťang-kha me-pa.* |
| Do. *hon.* | གསོལ་དང་མེད་པ་ | *sö-ťang-me-pa.* |
| Lost, it is | བརླགས་ནས་མི་འདུག་ | *la-ne min-du.* |
| Do. *hon.* | བརླགས་ག་ (པ་) གནང་ནས་མི་འདུག་ | *laḱ-ḱa nang-ne min-du.* |
| Lot (many) | མང་པོ་ | *mang-po.* |
| Do. (very many) | གཡོ་མ་སུ་ | *yo-ma-su.* |
| Do. (chance) | མོ་ | *mo.* |
| Do. *hon.* | ཕྱག་མོ་ | *chha-mo* |

| | | |
|---|---|---|
| Lot (fortune) | བསོ་བདེ་ (བསོད་བདེ་) | *so-de.* |
| Do. *hon.* | སྐུ་བསོད་ | *ku-sö.* |
| Lot (share) | སྐལ་ལ་ (སྐལ་བ་) | *ke-la* |
| Do. *hon.* | སྐུ་སྐལ་ | *ku-ke.* |
| Lots, to draw | མོ་རྒྱབ་པ་ | *mo-gyaṕ-pa.* |
| Do. *hon.* | ཕྱག་མོ་སྐྱོན་པ་ | *chha-mo kyöm-pa.* |
| Lotus | པད་པ་ | *pe-ma.* |
| Loud (noisy) | སྐད་ཆེན་པོ་ | *ke chhem-po.* |
| Do. *hon.* | གསུང་སྐད་ཆེན་པོ་ | *sung-ke chhem-po.* |
| Louse | ཤིག་ | *shi.* |
| Do. *hon.* | སྐུ་ཤིག་ | *ku-shi.* |
| Love | བྱམས་པོ་ | *cḱam-po.* |
| Love, to | བྱམས་པོ་བྱེད་པ་ | *cḱam-po cḱe-pa.* |
| Do. *hon.* | བྱམས་པོ་གནང་བ་ | *cḱam-po nang-wa.* |
| Lovely | ཚར་པོ། མཛེས་པོ་ | *tshar-po ; dze-po.* |
| Do. *hon.* | ཐུགས་ཚར་པོ་ | *thu-tshar-po.* |
| Lover | སྙིང་སྡུག་ | *nying-du.* |
| Low | དམའ་པོ་ | *ma-po.* |
| Low (cheap) | ཁེ་པོ་ | *khe-po.* |
| Low, to be (shallow) | གཏིང་རིང་པོ་མེད་པ་ | *ting-ring-po me-pa.* |

| | | |
|---|---|---|
| Lower part of a thing | སྨད་ | *me.* |
| Lower tooth | སྨད་སོ་ | *me-so.* |
| Do. *hon.* | སྨད་ཀྱི་ཚེམས་ | *me-kyi tshem.* |
| Lowland | སྨད་ | *me.* |
| Lowly | སེམས་ཆུང་ཆུང་ | *sem-chhung-chhung.* |
| Do. *hon.* | ཐུགས་སེམས་ཆུང་ཆུང་ | *thuḱ-sem chhung-chhung.* |
| Low-spirited, to be | སེམས་སྐྱོ་སྣང་བྱེད་པ་ | *sem-kyo-nang cḱe-pa* |
| Do. *hon.* | ཐུགས་སེམས་སྐྱོ་སྣང་གནང་བ་ | *thu-sem kyo-nang nang-wa.* |
| Loyal, to be | བཀའ་མཐུན་ཞུ་བ་ | *ka-thün sḱu-wa.* |
| Lucid | སྒྲ་དག་པོ་ | *dra-ťaḱ-po.* |
| Luck (good) | བསོད་བདེ། བསོད་ནམས་ | *so-de ; sö-nam.* |
| Do. *hon.* | སྐུ་བསོད་ | *ku-sö.* |
| Luck (bad) | བསོད་བདེ་སྐམ་པོ། བསོད་ནམས་ཆུང་ཆུང་ | *so-de kam-po ; sö-nam chhung-chhung.* |
| Do. *hon.* | སྐུ་བསོད་ཆུང་ཆུང་ | *ku-sö chhung-chhung.* |
| Lucky | བསོད་བདེ་ཆེན་པོ། བསོད་ནམས་ཆེན་པོ་ | *so-de chhem-po ; sö-nam chhem-po.* |
| Do. *hon.* | སྐུ་བསོད་ཆེན་པོ་ | *ku-sö chhem-po.* |
| Ludicrous | དགོད་མོ་བྲོ་པོ་ | *ge-mo ťro-po.* |

| | | |
|---|---|---|
| Ludicrous, *hon.* | ཞལ་མོ་བྲོ་པོ་ | *sk̄e-mo t̄ro-po.* |
| Luggage | ཅ་ལག་ (ཆ་ལག་) | *cha-la.* |
| Do. *hon.* | སྐུ་ཅས་ (སྐུ་ཆས་) | *ku-che.* |
| Lugubrious, to be | སེམས་སྐྱོ་བ། སེམས་སྡུག་པ་ | *sem-kyo-wa : sem-duk̄-pa.* |
| Do. *hon.* | ཐུགས་སེམས་སྐྱོ་བ་གནང་བ། ཐུགས་སེམས་སྡུག་ག་ (པ་) གནང་བ་ | *thu-sem kyo-wa nang-wa. thu-sem duk̄-k̄a nang-wa.* |
| Lukewarm | དྲོས་འཇམས་ | *t̄rön-jam.* |
| Lumbago, to have | སྐེད་པ་ན་བ་ | *ke-pa na-wa.* |
| Do. *hon.* | སྐུ་སྐེད་སྙུང་བ་ | *ku-ke nyung-wa.* |
| Luminous | འོད་ཆེན་པོ་ | *ö chhem-po.* |
| Lump | རྡོག་རྡོག་ | *dok̄-do.* |
| Lunatic | སྨྱོན་པ་ | *nyöm-pa.* |
| Lunch | ཉིན་གུང་ཁ་ལག་ | *nyin-k̄ung kha-la.* |
| Do. *hon.* | ཉིན་གུང་ཞལ་ལག་ | *nyin-k̄ung sk̄e-la.* |
| Lungs | གློ་ (གློ་བ་) | *lo.* |
| Do. *hon.* | སྐུ་གློ་ | *ku-lo.* |
| Lurk, to | ཡིབ་ནས་བསྡད་ (སྡོད་) པ་ | *yip̄-ne de-pa.* |
| Do. *hon.* | ཡིབ་ནས་བཞུགས་པ་ | *yip̄-ne sk̄u-pa.* |
| Lust | འདོད་ཆགས་ | *dö-chha.* |

| | | |
|---|---|---|
| Lustful | འདོད་ཆགས་ཆེན་པོ་ | *dö-chha chhem-po.* |
| Lustre | གཟི་བརྗིད། འོད་ | *śi-ji ; ö.* |
| Lustrous | གཟི་བརྗིད་ཆེན་པོ། འོད་ཆེན་པོ་ | *śi-ji chhem-po ; ö chhem-po.* |
| Lusty | ཤེད་ཆེན་པོ་ | *she chhem-po.* |
| Do. *hon.* | སྐུ་ཤེད་ཆེན་པོ་ | *ku-she chhem-po.* |
| Luxuriant | འབེལ་པོ་ | *be-po.* |
| Lynx | དབྱི་ | *i.* |

# M

| | | |
|---|---|---|
| Machine, sewing | ཚེམ་བུའི་འཁོར་ལོ་ | tshem-bü khor-lo. |
| Mad | སྨྱོན་པ་ | nyöm-pa. |
| Mad, to be | སྨྱོ་བ་ | nyo-wa. |
| Madam | ལྕམ་སྐུ་གཞོགས་ | cham-ku-sḱo. |
| Magazine | མཛོད་ | dzö. |
| Magic | མིག་འཕྲུལ་ | miḱ-thrü. |
| Magician | མིག་འཕྲུལ་སྟོན་མཁན་ | miḱ-thrü tön-khen. |
| Magistrate, city (Chinaman) | ཁྲིམས་དཔོན་ | thrim-pön. |
| Do. (Tibetan) | མི་དཔོན་ | mi-pön. |
| Do. in charge of district | རྫོང་དཔོན་ | dzong-pön. |
| Magnanimity | དྲིན་ | t́rin. |
| Do. *hon.* | བཀའ་དྲིན་ | ka-t́rin. |
| Magnanimous | དྲིན་ཆེན་པོ་ | t́rin chhem-po. |
| Do. *hon.* | བཀའ་དྲིན་ཆེན་པོ་ | ka-t́rin chhem-po. |
| Magnet | རྡོ་ཁབ་ལེན་ | do-khaṕ-len. |
| Magnificent | གཡང་མཛེས་ | yang-dze. |
| Magnitude | ཆེ་ཆུང་ | chhe-chhung. |
| Magnolia | ཙམ་པ་ཀ་ *Hin.* | tsam-pa-ḱa. |
| Magpie | ཀྲ་ཀ་ (སྐྱ་ཀ་) | tra-ḱa. |

| | | |
|---|---|---|
| Mahommedan | ཁ་ཆེ་ | *kha-chhe.* |
| Maid, maiden | བུ་མོ་ | *ṕu-mo.* |
| Do. *hon.* | སྲས་མོ་ | *se-mo* or *tre-mo.* |
| Maid-servant | གཡོག་མོ་ | *yo-mo.* |
| Do. of person of high rank | ཞལ་ཏ་མ་ | *sKe-ta-ma.* |
| Main point | དོན་སྙིང་ | *t́ön-nying.* |
| Mainly | ཕལ་ཆེར་ | *phe-chher.* |
| Maintain, to (affirm) | ལབ་པ་ | *laṕ-pa.* |
| Do. *hon.* | གསུང་བ་ | *sung-wa.* |
| Maintain, to (nourish) | གསོ་བ་ | *so-wa.* |
| Do. *hon.* | གསོ་བ་གནང་བ་ | *so-wa nang-wa.* |
| Maize | ཀན་ཛོམ་ | *ken-dzom.* |
| Majestic | གཟི་བརྗིད་ཆེན་པོ་ | *śi-ji chhem-po.* |
| Majesty, His | རིན་པོ་ཆེ་ | *rim-po-chhe.* |
| Major (officer in command of 250 to 500 men) | རུ་དཔོན་ | *ru-pön.* |
| Majority, the | མང་ང་ (མང་བ་) | *mang-nga.* |
| Make, to | བྱེད་པ་ | *cKe-pa.* |
| Do. *hon.* | གནང་བ་ | *nang-wa.* |
| Make, to (construct) | བཟོ་བ་ | *śo-wa.* |

| | | |
|---|---|---|
| Make, to (construct), *hon.* | བཟོ་བ་གནང་བ་ | *śo-wa nang-wa.* |
| Maker | བཟོ་མཁན་ | *śo-khen.* |
| Do. *hon.* | བཟོ་བ་གནང་མཁན་ | *śo-wa nang-khen.* |
| Malady | ན་ཚ་ | *na-tsha.* |
| Do. *hon.* | སྙུང་གཞི་ | *nyung-sKi.* |
| Male | ཕོ་ | *pho.* |
| Malediction, to pronounce | དམོད་མོ་རྒྱབ་པ་ | *mö-mo gyap̃-pa.* |
| Do. *hon.* | དམོད་མོ་སྐྱོན་པ་ | *mö-mo kyöm-pa.* |
| Malefactor | འཛབ་ཆེན་ | *dzap̃-chhen.* |
| Malice | གནོད་སེམས་ | *nö-sem.* |
| Malicious | སེམས་ངན་པོ་ | *sem ngem-po.* |
| Do. *hon.* | ཐུགས་སེམས་ངན་པོ་ | *thu-sem ngem-po.* |
| Malign, to | སྨད་ར་བཏང་ (གཏོང་) བ་ | *me-ra tang-wa.* |
| Do. *hon.* | སྨད་ར་གཏོང་ང་ (བ་) གནང་བ་ | *me-ra tong-nga nang-wa.* |
| Do. *inf.* to *sup.* | སྨད་ར་ཞུ་བ་ | *me-ra sKu-wa.* |
| Malignant | སེམས་ངན་པོ་ | *sem ngem-po.* |
| Do. *hon.* | ཐུགས་སེམས་ངན་པོ་ | *thu-sem ngem-po.* |
| Malignity | གནོད་སེམས་ | *nö-sem.* |
| Mallet | ཤིང་གི་ཐོ་བ་ | *shing-Ki tho-a.* |
| Maltreat, to | སྡུག་པོ་བཏང་ (གཏོང་) བ་ | *duk̃-po tang-wa.* |

| | | |
|---|---|---|
| Maltreat, to, *hon.* | སྡུག་པོ་གཏོང་ང་(བ་) གནང་བ་ | *duk-po tong-nga nang-wa.* |
| Mamma | ཨ་མ་ | *a-ma.* |
| Do. *hon.* | ཡུམ་ | *yum.* |
| Mammon | ནོར་ལྷ་ | *nor-hla.* |
| Man | མི་ | *mi.* |
| Do. a short | ཏེ་པོ་ | *te-po.* |
| Man-servant | གཡོག་པོ་ | *yok-po.* |
| Do. of person in good position | ཞབས་ཕྱི་ | *shap-chhi.* |
| Manacles | ལག་ལྕགས་ | *lak-cha.* |
| Manage, to (supervise) | དོ་དམ་བྱེད་པ་ | *t́o-t́am che-pa.* |
| Do. *hon.* | དོ་དམ་གནང་བ་ | *t́o-t́am nang-wa* |
| Manager | དོ་དམ་པ་ | *t́o-t́am-pa.* |
| Do. *hon.* | དོ་དམ་གནང་མཁན་ | *t́o-t́am nang-khen.* |
| Mandate | བཀའ་ | *ka.* |
| Do. written (of Government) | བཀའ་རྒྱ་ | *ka-gya.* |
| Mane (of horse, etc.) | ཟེ་ | *śe.* |
| Do. (of lion) | རལ་པ་ | *re-pa.* |
| Mange | རྔོ་ | *ngo.* |
| Do. to have | རྔོ་ཤོར་བ་ | *ngo-shor-wa.* |

| | | |
|---|---|---|
| Manger | བྲེས་ར་ (བྲེས་) | *t́re-ra.* |
| Mangle, to (tear) | བཀོག་པ་ (འགོག་པ་) | *kok̇-pa.* |
| Do. *hon.* | བཀོག་ག་ (འགོག་པ་) གནང་བ་ | *kok̇-k̇a nang-wa.* |
| Maniac | སྨྱོན་པ་ | *nyöm-pa.* |
| Manifest, *adj.* | མངོན་ནས། ངོ་ཐོག་ | *ngön-ne ; ngo-tho.* |
| Manifold | སྣ་ཚོགས་ | *na-tsho.* |
| Mankind | མི་རིགས་ | *mi-ri.* |
| Manly (brave) | སྙིང་ཆེན་པོ། བློ་ཁོག་ཆེན་པོ་ | *nying-chhem-po ; lo-kho chhem-po.* |
| Do. *hon.* | ཐུགས་སྙིང་ཆེན་པོ། ཐུགས་ཁོག་ཆེན་པོ་ | *thu-nying chhem-po ; thu-kho chhem po.* |
| Manner (custom) | ལུགས་སྲོལ་ | *luk̇-sö.* |
| Do. (behaviour) | བྱེད་སྟངས་ | *ck̇e-tang.* |
| Do. *hon.* | གནང་སྟངས་ | *nang-tang.* |
| Manœuvre, to (troops) | དམག་སྦྱོང་བྱེད་པ་ | *ma-jong ck̇e-pa.* |
| Do. *hon.* | དམག་སྦྱོང་གནང་བ་ | *ma-jong nang-wa.* |
| Mansion | གཟིམས་ཤག། ཕོ་བྲང་ | *śim-sha ; pho-t́rang.* |
| Mantle | ཆུ་པ་ | *chhu-pa.* |
| Do. *hon.* | ན་བཟའ་ | *nam-śa.* |

| | | |
|---|---|---|
| Manufacture, to | བཟོ་བ་ | *ṡo-wa.* |
| Do. *hon.* | བཟོ་པ་གནང་བ་ | *ṡo-wa nang-wa.* |
| Manure | ལུད་ | *lü.* |
| Manuscript | བྲིས་མ་ | *t́ri-ma.* |
| Many | མང་པོ་ | *mang-po.* |
| Many, very | ཧ་ཅང་མང་པོ། གཡོ་མ་སུ་ | *ha chang mang-po ; yo-ma-su.* |
| Many, too | ལྷག་པོ་ | *hlaḱ-po.* |
| Many, how | ག་ཚོད་ | *ḱa-tshö.* |
| Map | ས་ཁྲ་ | *saṕ-thra.* |
| Mar, to | སྐྱོན་བྱེད་པ་ | *kyön-cḱe-pa.* |
| Do. *hon.* | སྐྱོན་གནང་བ་ | *kyön-nang-wa.* |
| March, to | འགྲོ་བ་ | *dro wa.* |
| Do. *hon.* | ཕེབ་པ་ | *phe-pa.* |
| Do. *h. hon.* | འཆིབ་ཀྱུ་གནང་བ་ | *chhiṕ-gyu nang-wa.* |
| Mare | རྒོད་མ་ | *gö-ma.* |
| Margin | མཐའ་ | *tha.* |
| Marigold | གུར་གུམ་མེ་ཏོག་ | *ḱur-ḱum me-to.* |
| Mark | རྟགས་ | *ta.* |
| Mark, to (observe) | མིག་ལྟ་བ་ | *miḱ-ta-wa.* |
| Do. *hon.* | གཟིགས་པ་ | *ṡi-pa.* |

| | | |
|---|---|---|
| **Marked (famous)** | སྐད་གྲགས་ཆེན་པོ་ | *ke-ťra chhem-po.* |
| Do. *hon.* | སྙན་གྲགས་ཆེན་པོ་ | *nyen-ťra chhem-po.* |
| **Market-place** | ཁྲོམ་ | *throm.* |
| **Marriage.** | ཆང་ས་ | *chhang-sa.* |
| Do. *hon.* | འཁྲུང་ས་ | *thrung-sa.* |
| **Marry, to (take a wife)** | མནའ་མ་ལེན་པ་ | *na-ma lem-pa.* |
| Do. *hon.* | མནའ་མ་བཞེས་པ་ | *na-ma sḱe-pa.* |
| **Marry, to (take a husband)** | མག་པ་བསླང་ (སློང་) བ་ | *mak-pa lang-wa.* |
| Do. *hon.* | སྐུ་བག་བཞེས་པ་ | *ku ṕa sḱe-pa.* |
| **Marvel,** *s.* | ཡ་མཚན་ | *yam tshen.* |
| **Marvel, to** | ཁྱད་མཚར་པོ་བྱེད་པ་ | *khye-tsha-po cḱe-pa.* |
| **Marvellous** | ཡ་མཚན་པོ། ཁྱད་མཚར་པོ་ | *yam-tshem-po ; khye-tsha-po.* |
| **Mask** | འབག་ | *ba.* |
| Do. *hon.* | ཞལ་འབག་ | *sḱem-ba.* |
| **Mason** | རྡོ་བཟོ་བ་ | *doṕ-ṡo-wa.* |
| **Masquerade** | འཆམ་ | *chham.* |
| Do. *hon.* | སྐུ་འཆམ་ | *kun-chham.* |
| **Massage, to** | འཕུར་འཕུར་བྱེད་པ་ | *phu-phu cḱe-pa.* |
| **Massive (bulky)** | སྦོམ་པོ་ | *bom-po.* |
| Do. (heavy) | ལྗི་པོ་ | *ji-po.* |

| | | |
|---|---|---|
| **Mast** (flag-staff) | དར་པོ་ཆེ་ | *tar-po-chhe.* |
| **Master** | སྦྱིན་བདག། བདག་པོ་ | *jin-da ; dak-po.* |
| Do. *hon.* | དཔོན་པོ་ | *pöm-po.* |
| **Mastery** (power) | དབང་ | *wang.* |
| Do. *hon.* | སྐུ་དབང་ | *ku-wang.* |
| **Mastiff** | འབྲོག་ཁྱི་ | *drok-khyi.* |
| **Mart** | ཁྲོམ་ | *throm.* |
| **Mat** | གདན་ | *den.* |
| **Match** (lucifer) | མུ་ཟི་ | *mu-śi.* |
| **Match-box** | མུ་ཟིའི་སྒམ་ཆུང་ | *mu-śi gam-chhung.* |
| **Mate** | རོགས་ | *ro.* |
| **Material**, *s.* | རྒྱུ་ | *gyu.* |
| **Material**, *adj.* (important) | གནད་ཁག་ཆེན་པོ། གལ་ཆེན་པོ་ | *nen-kha chhem-po ; ke chhem-po.* |
| **Maternal aunt** | སྲུ་མོ་ | *su-mo.* |
| **Matter** (substance) | རྒྱུ་ | *gyu.* |
| Do. (pus) | རྣག་ | *na.* |
| **Mattress** | འབོལ་གདན་ | *bö-den.* |
| Do. *hon.* | བཞུགས་འབོལ་ | *sKum-böl.* |
| **Mature, to be** | ཚོས་པ་ | *tshö-pa.* |

| | | |
|---|---|---|
| Maxim | གཏམ་དཔེ་ | *tam-pe.* |
| Me | ང་ལ་ | *nga-la.* |
| Meadow | སྤང་ | *pang.* |
| Meagre (lean) | ཤ་སྐམ་པོ་ | *sha-kam-po.* |
| Do. *hon.* | སྐུ་ཤ་སྐམ་པོ་ | *ku-sha kam-po.* |
| Meagre (scanty) | ཉུང་ཉུང་ | *nyung-nyung.* |
| Meal (food taken at one time) | ཁ་ལག། ལྟོ། ལྟོ་ཚས་ | *kha-la ; to ; top-chhe.* |
| Do. *hon.* | ཞལ་ལག་ | *sḱe-la.* |
| Mean (vulgar) | དཀྱུས་མ་ | *kyü-ma.* |
| Mean (stingy) | ལག་པ་དམ་པོ་ | *laḱ-pa ťam-po.* |
| Do. *hon.* | ཕྱག་དམ་པོ་ | *chha ťam-po.* |
| Mean, to (purpose) | སེམས་ལ་བསམ་པ་ | *sem-la sam-pa.* |
| Do. *hon.* | ཐུགས་ལ་དགོངས་པ་ | *thuḱ-la gong-pa.* |
| Meaning | དོན་དག་ | *ťön-ťa.* |
| Do. *hon.* | སྐུ་དོན་ | *ku-ťön.* |
| Means, *s.* | ཐབས་ | *thaṕ.* |
| Means, by all | ངེས་པར་ | *nge-par.* |
| Means, by what | ག་འདྲས་ | *ḱan-dre.* |
| Meantime, in the | ཁབ་སུ་ | *khaṕ-su.* |

| | | |
|---|---|---|
| Meanwhile, in the | ཁབ་སུ་ | *khaṕ-su.* |
| Measles | གསིལ་པ་ | *si-pa.* |
| Measure, *s.* | ཚད་ | *tshe.* |
| Measure, to | འཇལ་བ་ | *je-wa.* |
| Do. *hon.* | འཇལ་ར་ (བ་) གནང་བ་ | *je ra nang-wa.* |
| Meat | ཤ་ | *sha.* |
| Do. *hon.* | བཞེས་ཤ་ | *sKe-sha.* |
| Mechanic | བཟོ་མཁན་ | *śo-khen.* |
| Mediate, to | བར་མི་བྱེད་པ་ | *ṕar-mi cKe-pa.* |
| Do. *hon.* | བར་མི་གནང་བ་ | *ṕar-mi nang-wa.* |
| Mediator | བར་མི་བྱེད་མཁན་ | *ṕar-mi cKe-khen.* |
| Medicine | སྨན་ | *men.* |
| Medicine for internal use | ཁོང་སྨན་ | *khong-men.* |
| Medicine, mineral | ས་སྨན་ | *sa-men.* |
| Meditate, to | བསམ་པ་ | *sam-pa.* |
| Do. *hon.* | དགོངས་པ་ | *gong-pa.* |
| Meditate, to (on religious affairs) | སྒོམ་རྒྱབ་པ་ | *gom-gyaṕ-pa.* |
| Do. *hon.* | སྒོམ་སྐྱོན་པ་ | *gom-kyöm-pa.* |
| Meditation, religious | ཏིང་ངེ་འཛིན་ | *ting-nge dzin.* |

| | | |
|---|---|---|
| Medium (of quality) | འབྲིང་ཅིག། ཁྲིག་ཁྲིག་ཅིག་ | *dring-chi ; thriḱ-thri-chi.* |
| Meek | སེམས་ཆུང་ཆུང་ | *sem-chhung-chhung.* |
| Do. *hon.* | ཐུགས་སེམས་ཆུང་ཆུང་ | *thuḱ-sem-chhung-chhung.* |
| Meek in speech | ཁ་འཇམ་པོ་ | *kha jam-po.* |
| Do. *hon.* | ཞལ་འཇམ་པོ་ | *sḱe jam-po.* |
| Meet, to | ཐུག་པ་ | *thuḱ-pa.* |
| Do. (a superior) | མཇལ་བ་ | *je-wa.* |
| Do. (between two of high position) | མཇལ་ར་ (བ་) གནང་བ་ | *je-ra nang-wa.* |
| Meeting | ཐུག་ཕྲད་ | *thuḱ-thre.* |
| Do. *hon.* | མཇལ་ཕྲད་ | *je-thre.* |
| Melancholy, to be | སེམས་སྐྱོ་སྣང་བྱེད་པ་ | *sem-kyo-nang cḱe-pa.* |
| Do. *hon.* | ཐུགས་སེམས་སྐྱོ་སྣང་གནང་བ་ | *thu-sem kyo-nang nang-wa.* |
| Melt, to | ཞུ་བ་ | *sḱu-wa.* |
| Memoir (story) | རྣམ་ཐར་ | *nam-tha.* |
| Memory | དྲན་པ་ | *t́rem-pa.* |
| Do. *hon.* | ཐུགས་དྲན་ | *thu-t́ren.* |
| Menace, to | འཛིག་འཛིག་ (འཇིག་འཇིག་) བཏང་ (གཏོང་) བ་ | *dziḱ-dziḱ tang-wa.* |
| Mend, to | སྒྲོག་པ་ | *droḱ-pa.* |

| | | |
|---|---|---|
| Mend, to, *hon.* | སྒྲོག་ག་ (པ་) གནང་བ་ | *droḱ-ḱa nang-wa.* |
| Mend, to (by patching) | ལྷན་པ་རྒྱབ་པ་ | *hlem-pa gyaṕ-pa.* |
| Do. *hon.* | ལྷན་པ་སྐྱོན་པ་ | *hlem-pa kyöm-pa.* |
| Mendacious, to be | ཧམ་པ་ཤོད་པ། ཀྱག་རྫུན་ཤོད་པ་ | *ham-pa shö-pa ; kyaḱ-dzün shö-pa.* |
| Do. *hon.* | ཞལ་རྫུན་གསུང་བ་ | *sḱe-dzün sung-wa.* |
| Mendicant | སྤྲང་ཀོ་ (སྤྲང་པོ་) | *pang-ko.* |
| Menses | ཟླ་མཚན་ | *da-tshen.* |
| Menstruate, to | ཟླ་ཁྲག་རྒྱབ་པ་ | *da-thra, gyaṕ-pa.* |
| Mention, to | ལབ་པ་ | *laṕ-pa.* |
| Do. *hon.* | གསུང་བ་ | *sung-wa.* |
| Merchandise | ཚོང་ཟོག་ | *tshong-śo.* |
| Merchant | ཚོང་པ་ | *tshong-pa.* |
| Do. *hon.* | ཚོང་དཔོན་ | *tshong-pön.* |
| Merciful | སྙིང་རྗེ་ཆེན་པོ་ | *nying-je chhem-po.* |
| Do. *hon.* | ཐུགས་རྗེ་ཆེན་པོ་ | *thuḱ-je chhem-po.* |
| Merciless, to be | སྙིང་རྗེ་མེད་པ་ | *nying-je me-pa.* |
| Do. *hon.* | ཐུགས་རྗེ་མེད་པ་ | *thuḱ-je me-pa.* |
| Mercury | དངུལ་ཆུ་ | *ngü-chhu.* |
| Mercy | སྙིང་རྗེ་ | *nying-je.* |

| | | |
|---|---|---|
| Mercy, *hon.* | ཐུགས་རྗེ་ | *thuk-je.* |
| Merely | ཤ་སྟག་ | *sha-ta.* |
| Merit | དགེ་བ། ཚོགས་ | *ge-wa ; tsho.* |
| Do. to accumulate | ཚོགས་བསག་ (གསོག་) པ་ | *tsho sak-pa.* |
| Do. *hon.* | ཚོགས་གསོག་ག་ (པ་) གནང་བ་ | *tsho sok-ka nang-wa.* |
| Merit, to | འོས་པ་ | *ö-pa.* |
| Merriment | དགའ་ཚོར་ | *ga-tshor.* |
| Do. *hon.* | མཉེས་ཚོར་ | *nye-tshor.* |
| Merry, to be | དགའ་བ། སྐྱིད་པོ་བྱས་ནས་སྡོད་པ་ | *ga-wa ; kyi-po che-ne dö-pa.* |
| Do. *hon.* | མཉེས་པོ་གནང་བ། སྤྲོ་པོ་གནང་ནས་བཞུགས་པ་ | *nye-po nang-wa ; tro-po nang-ne shuk-pa.* |
| Do. *h. hon.* | ཐུགས་དགྱེས་པོ་གནང་བ་ | *thu-gye-po nang-wa.* |
| Message | ལན་ | *len.* |
| Do. *hon.* | བཀའ་ལན་ | *ka-len.* |
| Messenger | བང་ཆེན་ | *pang-chhen.* |
| Method (means) | ཐབས་ | *thap.* |
| Do. (custom) | ལུགས་སྲོལ་ | *luk-sö.* |
| Mewing, *s.* (of cat) | སྨྱེའོ་ | *me-o.* |

| | | |
|---|---|---|
| Mid-day | ཉིན་གུང་ | *nyin-k̄ung.* |
| Middle, *s.* | དཀྱིལ་ | *kyi.* |
| Do. (waist) | སྐེད་པ་ | *ke-pa.* |
| Do. *hon.* | སྐུ་སྐེད་ | *ku-ke.* |
| Middle, *adj.* | འབྲིང་ཅིག། ཁྲིག་ཁྲིག་ཅིག་ | *dring-chi ; thrik̄-thri-chi.* |
| Middle of, in the | དཀྱིལ་ལ་ | *kyi-la.* |
| Midnight | ནམ་ཕྱེད་ | *nam-chhe.* |
| Midst, in the | དཀྱིལ་ལ་ | *kyi-la.* |
| Mien | བཟོ་ལྟ་ | *śop̄-ta.* |
| Do. *hon.* | སྐུ་བཟོ་ | *ku-śo.* |
| Might (official authority) | དབང་ | *wang.* |
| Do. *hon.* | སྐུ་དབང་ | *ku-wang.* |
| Might (physical) | ཤེད་ | *she.* |
| Do. *hon.* | སྐུ་ཤེད་ | *ku-she.* |
| Mighty (officially) | དབང་ཆེན་པོ་ | *wang chhem-po.* |
| Do. *hon.* | སྐུ་དབང་ཆེན་པོ་ | *ku-wang chhem-po.* |
| Mighty (physically) | ཤེད་ཆེན་པོ་ | *she chhem-po.* |
| Do. *hon.* | སྐུ་ཤེད་ཆེན་པོ་ | *ku-she chhem-po.* |
| Milch cow | བཞོན་མ་ | *sk̄ö-ma.* |
| Mild in speech | ཁ་འཇམ་པོ་ | *kha jam-po.* |

| | | |
|---|---|---|
| Mild in speech, *hon.* | ཞལ་འཇམ་པོ་ | *sḱe jam-po.* |
| Mild (of climate) | བསིལ་དྲོས་སྙོམ་པོ་ | *si-ťrö nyom-po.* |
| Militia (first) see "army" | འདོན་དམག་ | *döm-ma.* |
| Do. (second) | སེར་དམག་ | *ser-ma.* |
| Do. (final) | བཅོ་བརྒྱད་དྲུག་ཅུ་ | *chop̔-gye truḱ-chu.* |
| Milk | འོ་མ་ | *o-ma.* |
| Do. *hon.* | བཞེས་འོ་ | *sḱe-o.* |
| Milk, to | བཞོ་བ་ | *sḱo-wa.* |
| Do. *hon.* | བཞོ་བ་གནང་བ་ | *sḱo-wa nang-wa.* |
| Milk-jug | འོ་སྣོད་ | *o-nö.* |
| Million | ས་ཡ་ | *sa-ya.* |
| Mimic, to | ལན་ཟློས་བྱེད་པ་ | *len-tö cḱe-pa* |
| Do. *hon.* | ལན་ཟློས་གནང་བ་ | *len-tö nang-wa.* |
| Mimicry | ལན་ཟློས་ | *len-tö* |
| Mina (bird) | མི་ན་ *Hin.* | *me-na.* |
| Mince, to | བཙབ་པ་ | *tsap̔-pa.* |
| Do. *hon.* | བཙབ་པ་གནང་བ་ | *tsap̔-pa nang-wa.* |
| Mind | བློ། སེམས་ | *lo ; sem.* |
| Do. *hon.* | ཐུགས་ | *thu.* |
| Mind, to (take care of) | ཉར་བ་ | *nyar-wa.* |

| | | |
|---|---|---|
| Mind, to (take care of), *hon.* | ཉར་ར་ (བ་) གནང་བ་ | *nyar-ra nang-wa.* |
| Mind! never | ཨའུ་ཙེ་ | *a-u-tse.* |
| Mine, *pron.* | ངའི་ | *nge.* |
| Mingle, to, *v.i.* | འདྲེ་བ་ | *dre-wa.* |
| Mingle, to, *v.t.* | བསྲེ་བ་ | *tre-wa.* |
| Do. *hon.* | བསྲེ་བ་གནང་བ་ | *tre-a nang-wa.* |
| Minister of the Grand Council at Lhasa | ས་དབང་ཆེན་པོ། ཞབས་པད། བཀའ་བློན་ | *sa-wang chhem-po ; sḱaṕ-pe ; ka-lön.* |
| Minister, Chief | བློན་ཆེན་ | *lön-chhen.* |
| Mint | དངུལ་པར་ཁང་ | *ngü-par-khang.* |
| Minute, *adj.* | ཞིབ་ཞིབ་ | *sḱiṕ-sḱiṕ.* |
| Miracle | ཡ་མཚན་ | *yam-tshen.* |
| Miraculous | ཡ་མཚན་པོ། ཁྱད་མཚར་པོ་ | *yam-tshem po ; khye-tsha-po.* |
| Mire | འདམ། རྫབ་ | *dam ; dzaṕ.* |
| Mirror | ཤེལ་སྒོ་ | *she-go.* |
| Mirth | དགའ་ཚོར་ | *ga-tshor.* |
| Do. *hon.* | མཉེས་ཚོར་ | *nye-tshor.* |
| Mirthful, to be | དགའ་བ་ | *ga-wa.* |
| Do. *hon.* | མཉེས་པོ་གནང་བ་ | *nye-po nang-wa.* |
| Do. *h. hon.* | ཐུགས་དགྱེས་པོ་གནང་བ་ | *thu-gye-po nang-wa.* |

| | | |
|---|---|---|
| Mischief | སྐྱོན་ | *kyön.* |
| Miscreant | འཛབ་ཆེན་ | *d̄zap̄-chhen.* |
| Miserable (unhappy) | སྡུག་བསྔལ་ཆེན་པོ་ | *dung-nge chhem-po.* |
| Do. *hon.* | ཐུགས་བསྔལ་ཆེན་པོ་ | *thuk̄-nge chhem-po.* |
| Miserliness | སེར་སྣ་ | *ser-na.* |
| Miserly | སེར་སྣ་ཆེན་པོ་ | *ser-na chhem-po* |
| Misery | སྡུག་བསྔལ་ | *dung-nge.* |
| Do. *hon.* | ཐུགས་བསྔལ་ | *thuk̄-nge.* |
| Misfortune | བསོད་བདེ་སྐམ་པོ་ | *so-de kam-po.* |
| Do. *hon.* | སྐུ་བསོད་ཆུང་ཆུང་ | *ku-sö chhung-chhung.* |
| Mist | རྨུགས་པ་ | *muk̄-pa.* |
| Mistake, to | ནོར་བ་ | *nor-wa.* |
| Do. *hon.* | ནོར་ར་ (བ་) གནང་བ་ | *nor-ra nang-wa.* |
| Mistake in speech, to make a | ཁ་ནོར་བ་ | *kha-nor-wa.* |
| Do. *hon.* | ཞལ་ནོར་བ་ | *s̄ke nor-wa.* |
| Mistress (wife of well-to-do villager) | སྙི་སྙིང་ལགས་ | *nyi-nying-la.* |
| Mistress (wife of ordinary official) | ལྕམ་སྐུ་གཞོགས་ | *cham-ku-s̄ko.* |
| Do. (third grade and upwards) | ལྷ་ལྕམ་སྐུ་གཞོགས་ | *hla-cham ku-s̄ko* |

| | | |
|---|---|---|
| Misunderstood, to be | གོ་ལོག་བྱུང་བ་ | *ḱo-loḱ cḱung-wa.* |
| Do. *hon.* | གསན་འཛོལ་བྱུང་བ་ | *sen-dzöl cḱung-wa.* |
| Mix, to, *v.t.* | བསྲེ་བ་ | *tre-wa.* |
| Do. *hon.* | བསྲེ་བ་གནང་བ་ | *tre-a nang-wa.* |
| Mix, to, *v.i.* | འདྲེ་བ་ | *dre-wa.* |
| Mock, to | ཀྱག་ཀྱག་བྱས་ནས་ལབ་པ་ | *kya-kya cḱe-ne laṕ-pa.* |
| Do. *hon.* | ཀྱག་ཀྱག་གནང་ནས་གསུང་བ་ | *kya kya nang-ne sung-wa.* |
| Mode (custom) | ལུགས་སྲོལ་ | *luḱ-sö.* |
| Do. (method) | ཐབས་ | *thaṕ.* |
| Model | དཔེ་ | *pe.* |
| Modelled well- (of metal-work, wood-work, etc.) | བཀོད་པ་དོད་པོ་ | *kö-pa t́ö-po.* |
| Moderate, to be | ཚོད་ཟིན་པ་ | *tshö-śim-pa.* |
| Modern | དེ་རིང་སང་གི་ | *t́e-ring sang-ḱi.* |
| Modest, to be | དམའ་ས་ཟིན་པ་ | *ma-sa śim-pa.* |
| Do. *hon.* | དམའ་ས་ཟིན་པ་གནང་བ་ | *ma-sa śim-pa nang-wa.* |
| Mohammadan | ཁ་ཆེ་ | *kha-chhe* |
| Moist | རློན་པ་ | *löm-pa.* |
| Moisten, to | སྦང་བ་ | *bang-wa.* |
| Do. *hon.* | སྦང་ང་ (བ་) གནང་བ་ | *bang-nga nang-wa.* |

| | | |
|---|---|---|
| Moisture (of ground) | བཞའ་ཚན་ | *sḱa-tshen.* |
| Molar tooth | འགྲམ་སོ་ | *dram-so.* |
| Do. *hon.* | ཞལ་འགྲམ་གྱི་ཚེམས་ | *sḱe-dram-ḱyi tshem.* |
| Mole | སྨེན་ (སྨེ་བ་) | *men.* |
| Molest, to | སྡུག་པོ་བཏང་ (གཏོང་) བ་ | *duḱ-po tang-wa.* |
| Do. *hon.* | སྡུག་པོ་གཏོང་ང་(བ་)གནང་བ་ | *duḱ-po tong-nga nang-wa.* |
| Moment (importance) | གནད་ཁག་ | *nen-kha.* |
| Moment, in a | ཧྲིབ་ཙ་ (ཙམ་) ཅིག་ | *hriṕ-tsa-chi.* |
| Momentous | གནད་ཁག་ཆེན་པོ། གལ་ཆེན་པོ་ | *nen-kha chhem-po ; ḱe chhem-po.* |
| Monarch | རྒྱལ་པོ་ | *gye-po.* |
| Monarch's administration | རྒྱལ་སྲིད་ | *gye-si.* |
| Monastery | དགོན་པ་ | *göm-pa.* |
| Monday | གཟའ་ཟླ་བ་ | *śa-da-wa.* |
| Money | དངུལ་ | *ngü.* |
| Mongol, Mongolian | སོག་པོ་ | *soḱ-po.* |
| Monk | གྲྭ་པ་ | *t́ra-pa.* |
| Do. *hon.* | དགེ་འདུན་ | *gen-dün.* |
| Monkey | སྤྲེའུ་ (སྤྲེའུ་) | *pe-u.* |
| Monstrous (huge) | ཆེ་ཐག་ཆོད་ | *chhe-thaḱ-chhö.* |

| | | |
|---|---|---|
| Monstrous (horrible) | ཞེད་སྐྲག་ཚ་པོ་ | *sKe-tra tsha-po.* |
| Month | ཟླ་བ་ | *da-wa.* |
| Month, 1st half of | ཟླ་སྟོད། ཚེས་ཤར་ | *da-tö ; tshe-shar.* |
| Do. middle of | ཟླ་དཀྱིལ། ཚེས་དཀྱིལ་ | *da-kyi ; tshe-kyi.* |
| Do. last half of | ཟླ་སྨད། ཟླ་མཇུག། ཚེས་གཞུག་ | *da-me ; dan-juk ; tshe-sKu.* |
| Do. last day of | ནམ་གང་ | *nam-Kang.* |
| Moon | ཟླ་བ་ | *da-wa.* |
| Moonlight | ཟླ་དཀར་ | *da-ka.* |
| Moonlight, to be | ཟླ་དཀར་ཤར་བ་ | *da-ka shar-wa.* |
| Moral, *adj.* (of persons) | ཚུལ་ལྡན་ | *tshün-den.* |
| Morality | ཚུལ་ཁྲིམས་ | *tshü-thrim.* |
| More | མང་ང་ (མང་བ།) ལྷག་ག་ (ལྷག་པ་) | *mang-nga ; hlak-ka.* |
| Moreover | ད་འདོ་ (ད་གདོས་) | *tan-do.* |
| Morning | ཞོགས་གས། སྔ་དྲོ་ | *sKok-Ke ; nga-tro.* |
| Do. (before dawn) | ཐོ་རངས་ | *tho-rang.* |
| Do. forenoon (eight to ten o'clock) | ཚ་དིང་ | *tsha-ting.* |
| Morrow | སང་ཉིན་ | *sang-nyi.* |

| | | |
|---|---|---|
| Morsel, a | དག་ག་ཅིག་ | *ťak-ǩa-chi.* |
| Mortal, *s.* | མི་ | *mi.* |
| Mortar (for pounding) | སྒོག་དིང་ | *goǩ-ting.* |
| Do. (cannon) | མེ་སྒྱོགས་ | *me-gyoǩ.* |
| Mortification (shame) | ངོ་ཚ་ | *ngo-tsha.* |
| Mortified, to feel | ངོ་ཚ་བ་ | *ngo-tsha-wa.* |
| Do. *hon.* | ཐུགས་ངོ་ཚ་བ་ | *thu-ngo tsha-wa.* |
| Mosquito | དུག་སྦྲང་ | *ťuǩ-drang.* |
| Most | མང་ཤོས་ | *mang-shö.* |
| Most part, for the | ཕལ་ཆེར་ | *phe-chher.* |
| Moth | ཕྱེ་འདྲེན་མ་ | *chhem-drem-ma.* |
| Mother | ཨ་མ་ | *a-ma.* |
| Do. *hon.* | ཡུམ་སྐུ་གཞོགས་ | *yum-ku-sǩo.* |
| Do. *h. hon.* | ལྷ་ཡུམ་སྐུ་གཞོགས་ | *hla-yum ku-sǩo* |
| Do. (of Dalai and Tashi Lamas) | རྒྱལ་ཡུམ་སྐུ་གཞོགས་ | *gye-yum ku-sǩo* |
| Mother of pearl | ཉ་ཕྱིས་ | *nyaṗ-chhi.* |
| Motive | དོན་དག་ | *ťön-ťa.* |
| Do. *hon.* | སྐུ་དོན་ | *ku-ťön.* |
| Mould (for shaping) | པར་ | *par.* |

| | | |
|---|---|---|
| Mouldy, to be | ཧམ་པ་རྒྱབ་པ་ | *ham-pa gyaṕ-pa.* |
| Mound | ས་ཕུང་ | *sa-phung.* |
| Mount for photograph | པར་གྱི་རྒྱབ་ཤ་ཤོག་བུ་ | *par-ḱyi gyaṕ-sha shoḱ-ḱu.* |
| Mount, to (a horse, &c.) | ཞོན་པ་ | *sḱöm-pa.* |
| Do. *hon.* | འཆིབ་པ་ | *chhiṕ-pa.* |
| Mount, to (rise) | ལང་བ་ | *lang-wa.* |
| Do. *hon.* | བཞང་བ་ (བཞེང་བ་) | *sḱang-wa.* |
| Do. *h. hon.* | སྐུ་བཞང་ (བཞེང་) གནང་བ་ | *ku-sḱang nang-wa.* |
| Mount, to (climb) | འཛག་པ་ (འཛེག་པ་) | *dzaḱ-pa.* |
| Do. *hon.* | འཛག་ག་ (འཛེག་པ་) གནང་བ་ | *dzaḱ-ḱa nang-wa.* |
| Mountain | རི་ | *ri.* |
| Do. snowy | གངས་རི་ | *ḱang-ri.* |
| Mountain-pass | ལ་ | *la.* |
| Mourn, to | སྡུག་བསྔལ་བྱེད་པ། མྱ་ངན་བྱེད་པ་ | *du-nge cḱe-pa; nya-ngen. cḱe-pa.* |
| Do. *hon.* | ཐུགས་ངན་གནང་བ་ | *thu-ngen nang-wa.* |
| Mouse | ཙི་ཙི་ | *tsi-tsi.* |
| Moustache | ཨ་ར་ | *a-ra.* |
| Do. *hon.* | ཞལ་ར་ | *sḱe-ra.* |

| | | |
|---|---|---|
| **Mouth** | ཁ་ | *kha.* |
| Do. *hon.* | ཞལ་ | *sḱe.* |
| **Mouthful** | ཁམ་རྡོག་ཅིག་ | *kham-do-chi.* |
| **Move, to** (go) | འགྲོ་བ་ | *dro-wa.* |
| Do. *hon.* | ཕེབ་པ། ཐེམས་པ་ | *phe-pa ; the-pa.* |
| Do. *h. hon.* | འཆིབ་སྒྱུ་གནང་བ་ | *chhiṕ-gyu nang-wa* |
| **Move, to** (persuade) | བསླབ་བྱ་བྱེད་པ་ | *laṕ-cḱa cḱe-pa.* |
| Do. *hon.* | བཀའ་སློབ་གནང་བ་ | *ka-loṕ nang-wa.* |
| **Mow, to** | རྔ་བ་ | *nga-wa.* |
| Do. *hon.* | རྔ་བ་གནང་བ་ | *nga-wa nang-wa.* |
| **Much** (many) | མང་པོ་ | *mang-po.* |
| Do. (very many) | གཡོ་མ་སུ་ | *yo-ma-su.* |
| **Much, too** | ལྷག་པ། ལྷག་མ་ | *hlaḱ-pa ; hla-ma.* |
| **Much, very** | ཧ་ཅང་མང་པོ་ | *ha-chang mang-po.* |
| **Mud** | འདམ། རྫབ་ | *dam ; dzaṕ.* |
| **Muddy** (of water) | རྙོག་པོ་ | *nyoḱ-po.* |
| **Muhammadan** | ཁ་ཆེ་ | *kha-chhe.* |
| **Mule** | དྲེ་ | *t́re.* |
| **Mule, baggage** | ཁལ་དྲེ་ | *khe-t́re.* |
| **Mule, riding** | ཞོན་དྲེ་ | *sḱön-t́re.* |

| | | |
|---|---|---|
| **Mule, riding, *hon.*** | ཆིབས་དྲེ་ | *chhiṕ-ťre.* |
| **Muleteer** | དྲེལ་པ་ | *ťre-pa.* |
| **Multitude** (of men) | མི་ཚོགས་ | *mi-tsho.* |
| **Mumps** | འགྲམ་པ་སྐྲང་བ་ | *dram-pa trang-wa.* |
| **Murder, to** | བསད་པ་ (གསོད་པ་) | *se-pa.* |
| Do. *hon.* (*inf.* to *sup.*) | བཀྲོངས་པ་ | *trong-pa.* |
| Do. *hon.* (between two of high position) | བཀྲོངས་ང་ (པ་) གནང་བ་ | *trong-nga nang-wa.* |
| **Murderer** | མི་བསད་མཁན་ | *mi-se-khen.* |
| **Murky, to become** (from clouds) | འཐིབས་པ་ | *thiṕ-pa.* |
| **Muscle** | རྩ་ | *tsa.* |
| **Muse, to** (meditate) | བསམ་པ་ | *sam-pa.* |
| Do. *hon.* | དགོངས་པ་ | *gong-pa.* |
| **Mushroom** (two kinds) | དཀར་ཤ། སེར་ཤ་ | *ka-sha ; se-sha.* |
| **Musk** | གླ་རྩི་ | *la-tsi.* |
| **Musk-deer** | གླ་བ་ | *la-wa.* |
| Do. the young one of a | གླ་ཕྲུག་ | *la-thru.* |
| **Musket** | མེ་མདའ་ | *men-da.* |
| **Musket ball** | རྡེའུ་ | *di-u.* |

| | | |
|---|---|---|
| Mussalman | ཁ་ཆེ་ | *kha-chhe.* |
| Must, *v.i.* | དགོ་བ་ (དགོས་པ་) | *go-wa.* |
| Mustard | ཡེ་གང་ | *pe-kang.* |
| Muster, to, *v.i.* | འཚོགས་པ། འཛོམ་པ་ | *tshok-pa ; dzom-pa.* |
| Do. *hon.* | ལྷན་རྒྱས་གནང་བ་ | *hlen-gye nang-wa.* |
| Musty, to be | ཧམ་པ་རྒྱབ་པ་ | *ham-pa gyap-pa.* |
| Mute, *s.* (dumb person) | ལྐུགས་པ་ | *kuk-pa.* |
| Mute, to be (silent) | ཁ་ཁ་བསྡད་ (སྡོད་) པ་ | *kha-kha de-pa.* |
| Do. *hon.* | ཞལ་རགས་བཞུགས་པ་ | *ske-ra sku-pa.* |
| Mutton | ལུག་ཤ་ | *luk-sha.* |
| My | ངའི་ | *nge.* |
| Myrabolam | ཨ་རུ་ | *a-ru.* |
| Myrrh | ཨ་ཀ་རུ་ | *a-ka-ru.* |
| Myself | ང་རང་ | *nga-rang.* |
| Mystified, to be | མགོ་འཐོམས་པ་ | *go-thom-pa.* |
| Do. *hon.* | དབུ་འཐོམས་པ་གནང་བ་ | *u-thom-pa nang-wa.* |
| Myth | སྒྲུང་ | *drum.* |

## N

| | | |
|---|---|---|
| Nail | གཟེར་ | *śer.* |
| Do. finger | ལག་པའི་སེན་མོ་ | *laḱ-p̣e se-mo.* |
| Do. *hon.* | ཕྱག་སེན་ | *chhaḱ-se.* |
| Nail, toe | རྐང་པའི་སེན་མོ་ | *kang-pe se-mo.* |
| Do. *hon.* | ཞབས་སེན་ | *sḱaṕ-se.* |
| Nail, iron | ལྕགས་གཟེར་ | *chaḱ-śer.* |
| Do. wooden | ཕུར་པ་ | *phur-pa.* |
| Nail, to | ལྕགས་གཟེར་རྒྱབ་པ་ | *chaḱ-śer gyaṕ-pa.* |
| Do. *hon.* | ལྕགས་གཟེར་སྐྱོན་པ་ | *chaḱ-śer kyöm-pa.* |
| Naked | དམར་ཧྲང་ང་ | *mar-hrang-nga.* |
| Name | མིང་ | *ming.* |
| Do. *hon.* | མཚན་ | *tshen.* |
| Name, to | མིང་འདོགས་པ་ | *ming doḱ-pa.* |
| Do. *hon.* | མཚན་འདོགས་པ་ | *tshen doḱ-pa.* |
| Nap (sleep) | གཉིད་ | *nyi.* |
| Do. *hon.* | མཉལ་ (མནལ་) | *nye.* |
| Napkin | པང་ཁེབས་ | *pang-kheṕ.* |
| Do. *hon.* | སྐུ་ཁེབས་ | *ku-kheṕ.* |
| Narrate, to | བཤད་པ་ | *she-pa.* |

| | | |
|---|---|---|
| Narrate, to, *hon.* | གསུང་བ་ | *sung-wa.* |
| Narrative | རྒྱུ་རྐྱེན། ལོ་རྒྱུས་ | *gyu-kyen; lo-gyü.* |
| Narrow | དོག་པོ། སྦུགས་སྦུབ་དོག་པོ་ | *ťoǩ-po; bu-su ťoǩ-po.* |
| Nasty | སྐྱུག་བྲོ་པོ་ | *kyuǩ-ťro-po.* |
| Nation | མི་བརྒྱུད། རིགས་བརྒྱུད་ | *mi-gyü; ri-gyü.* |
| Native land | སྐྱེ་ས་ | *kye-sa.* |
| Do. *hon.* | འཁྲུང་ས་ | *thrung-sa.* |
| Nature (species) | བརྒྱུད་ | *gyü.* |
| Do. of different | སྣ་ཚོགས་ | *na-tsho.* |
| Naught (cipher) | ཀླད་སྐོར་ | *le-kor.* |
| Naughty | ངན་པ་ | *ngem-pa.* |
| Nauseating | སྐྱུག་བྲོ་པོ་ | *kyuǩ-ťro-po.* |
| Navel | ལྟེ་ (ལྟེ་བ་) | *te.* |
| Near, *adj.* | ཉེ་པོ། ཐག་ཉེ་པོ། ཚར། འགྲམ་ལ་ | *nye-po; tha-nye-po; tsa; dram-la.* |
| Nearly (almost) | ཧ་ལམ། ག་ཆེན་ | *ha-lam; ǩa-chhen.* |
| Neat | འདྲ་ཆགས་པོ་ | *dra-chhaǩ-po.* |
| Necessary | དགོས་པ་ | *gö-pa.* |
| Necessity | དགོས་པ། མཁོ་ཆེ་ | *gö-pa; kho-chhe* |
| Neck | སྐེ་ | *ke.* |

| | | |
|---|---|---|
| Neck, *hon.* | མགུལ་ | *gü.* |
| Neck, back of | མཇིང་པ་ | *jing-pa.* |
| Do. *hon.* | མགུལ་མཇིང་ | *gü-jing.* |
| Necklace | སྐེ་རྒྱན་ | *ke-gyen.* |
| Do. *hon.* | མགུལ་རྒྱན་ | *gü-gyen.* |
| Nectar | བདུད་རྩི་ | *dü-tsi.* |
| Need, to (require) | དགོས་པ་ | *gö-pa.* |
| Do. *hon.* | ཐུགས་དགོས་པ་ | *thu-gö-pa.* |
| Need, *s.* (necessity) | དགོས་པ། མཁོ་ཆེ་ | *gö-pa; kho-chhe.* |
| Needful | དགོས་པ་ | *gö-pa.* |
| Needfulness | དགོས་པ། མཁོ་ཆེ་ | *gö-pa; kho-chhe.* |
| Needle | ཁབ་ | *khaṕ.* |
| Do. *hon.* | མགུལ་ཁབ་ | *gü-khaṕ.* |
| Needle, eye of | ཁབ་མིག་ | *khaṕ-mi.* |
| Do. *hon.* | མགུལ་ཁབ་མིག་ | *gü-khaṕ-mi.* |
| Needle, point of | ཁབ་རྩེ་ | *khaṕ-tse.* |
| Do. *hon.* | མགུལ་ཁབ་རྩེ་ | *gü-khaṕ-tse.* |
| Needy (poor) | སྐྱོ་པོ། སྙེམས་ཆུང་ (ཉམས་ཆུང་) | *kyo-po; nyem-chhung.* |
| Nefarious | ངན་པོ་ | *ngem-po* |

| | | |
|---|---|---|
| Nefarious, *hon.* | ཐུགས་ངན་པོ་ | *thu ngem-po.* |
| Negotiate, to | འགྲིག་ཆགས་བྱེད་པ་ | *driḱ-chha cḱe-pa.* |
| Do. *hon.* | འགྲིག་ཆགས་གནང་བ་ | *driḱ-chha nang-wa.* |
| Negotiation | བཀའ་མོལ། འགྲིག་ཆགས་ | *ka-mön ; driḱ-chha.* |
| Neigh, to | རྟ་སྐད་རྒྱབ་པ་ | *ta-ke gyaṕ-pa.* |
| Neighbour | ཁྱིམ་མཚེས་ | *khyim-tshe.* |
| Neighbourhood | ཉེ་འཁོར་ | *nye-khor.* |
| Nepal | བལ་ཡུལ་ | *ṕe-yü.* |
| Nepalese | བལ་པོ་ | *ṕe-po.* |
| Nephew | ཚ་བོ་ | *tsha-wo.* |
| Nerve | ཆུ་རྒྱུས་ | *chhu-gyü.* |
| Nest | ཚང་ | *tshang.* |
| Net | རྒྱ། དྲ་བ་ | *gya ; t́ra-a.* |
| Do. fish | ཉ་དོལ། ཉ་རྒྱ་ | *nya-t́ö ; nya-gya.* |
| Nettle, *s.* | ཟ་པོ་ | *śa-po.* |
| Nettle, to (irritate) | ཁོང་ཁྲོ་སློང་བ་ | *khong-thro lang-wa.* |
| Do. *hon.* | དགོངས་པ་དཀྲུག་པ་ | *gong-pa truḱ-pa.* |
| Neuralgia | ཡ་མ་ | *ya-ma.* |
| Never | ཙ་ནས་...མ། མ་ནས་...མ་ | *tsa-ne...ma ; ma-ne...ma.* |
| Never mind ! | ཨའུ་ཙེ་ | *a-u-tse.* |

| | | |
|---|---|---|
| Nevertheless | ཡིན་ནས། ཡིན་ཀྱང་། ཡིན་ན་ཡང་ | *yin-ne ; yin-kyang ; yin-na-yang.* |
| New | གསར་པ་ | *sa-pa.* |
| New year | ལོ་གསར་ | *lo-sa.* |
| News | གནས་ཚུལ། གསར་འགྱུར་ | *ne-tshü ; sang-gyu.* |
| Newspaper | གསར་འགྱུར་ཤོག་གུ | *sang-gyu shoḱ-ḱu.* |
| Next (at the side of) | ཙར། འགྲམ་ལ་ | *tsa ; dram-la.* |
| Next (afterwards) | གཤུག་ལ། རྗེས་ལ་ | *sḱu-la ; je-la.* |
| Nice (accurate) | ཁྲིག་ཁྲིག། ཏེན་ཏེན་ | *thriḱ-thriḱ ; ten-ten.* |
| Nice (in flavour) | ཞིམ་པོ་ | *sḱim-po.* |
| Do. *hon.* | སྤྲོ་པོ་ | *tro-po.* |
| Nice (pleasant) | དར་པོ། ཡག་པོ་ | *t́ar-po ; yaḱ-po.* |
| Nickname | མིང་འདོགས། མིང་ངན་ | *ming-do ; ming-ngen.* |
| Niece | ཚ་མོ་ | *tsha-mo.* |
| Niggardly | ལག་པ་དམ་པོ་ | *laḱ-pa t́am-po.* |
| Do. *hon.* | ཕྱག་དམ་པོ་ | *chha t́am-po.* |
| Nigh | ཉེ་པོ། ཐག་ཉེ་པོ། ཙར། འགྲམ་ལ་ | *nye-po ; tha-nye-po ; tsa ; dram-la.* |
| Night | མཚན། དགོངས་མོ་ | *tshen ; gong-mo.* |
| Night, last | མདང་དགོངས་ | *dang-gong.* |

| | | |
|---|---|---|
| Night, in the middle of the | ནམ་ནག་གུང་། མཚན་ནག་གུང་ | *nam-na ḱung ; tshen-na-ḱung.* |
| Night-attack, to make | མཚན་ཐིག་ (མཚན་ཐིབ་) རྒྱབ་པ་ | *tshen-thi gyaṕ-pa.* |
| Nimble | ཧུར་པོ། མགྱོགས་པོ་ | *hur-po ; gyoḱ-po.* |
| Do. *hon.* | རྩོལ་པོ་ | *tsö po.* |
| Nine | དགུ་ | *gu.* |
| Nineteen | བཅུ་དགུ་ | *chu-gu.* |
| Nineteenth | བཅུ་དགུ་པ་ | *chu-gu-pa.* |
| Ninetieth | དགུ་བཅུ་པ་ | *guṕ-chu-pa.* |
| Ninety | དགུ་བཅུ་ཐམ་པ་ | *guṕ-chu ťham-pa.* |
| Ninny | ལྐུགས་པ། གླེན་པ། | *kuḱ-pa ; lem-pa.* |
| Ninth | དགུ་པ་ | *gu-pa.* |
| Nipple (of breast) | འོ་མའི་རྩེ། ནུ་སོར་ | *o-me-tse ; nu-sor.* |
| Do. *hon.* | ཆབ་ཞོའི་རྩེ་ | *chhaṕ-sḱö-tse.* |
| Noble, *s.* | སྐུ་དྲག་ | *ku-ťra.* |
| Do. *adj.* (illustrious) | སྐད་གྲགས་ཆེན་པོ་ | *ke-ťra chhem-po.* |
| Do. *hon.* | མཚན་སྙན་གྲགས་ཆེན་པོ་ | *tshen-nyen-ťro chhem-po.* |
| Nobleman | སྐུ་དྲག་ | *ku-ťra.* |
| Nobody | སུ་ཡང་ w. neg. | *su-yang* (w. neg.) |
| Nod, to | མགོ་འཇོག་འཇོག་བྱེད་པ་ | *go joḱ-joḱ cḱe-pa.* |

| | | |
|---|---|---|
| **Nod, to,** ***hon.*** | དབུ་འཇོག་འཇོག་གནང་བ་ | *u jok-jok nang-wa.* |
| **Noise** | ཅུར་སྒྲ་ | *u-dra.* |
| **Noise, to make a** | ཅུར་སྒྲ་རྒྱབ་པ་ | *u-dra gyap-pa.* |
| **Do.** ***hon.*** | ཅུར་སྒྲ་སྐྱོན་པ་ | *u-dra kyöm-pa.* |
| **Noisome** | སྐྱུག་བྲོ་པོ་ | *kyuk-tro-po.* |
| **Nomad** | འབྲོག་པ་ | *drok-pa.* |
| **Nominate, to** | སྐོ་བ་ | *ko-wa.* |
| **Do.** ***hon.*** | སྐོ་བ་གནང་བ་ | *ko-wa nang-wa.* |
| **None (nobody)** | སུ་ཡང་ w. neg. | *su-yang* (w. neg.) |
| **Do. (nothing)** | ག་གས་ (གང་ཡང་) w. neg. | *ka-ke* (w. neg.) |
| **Nonsensical** | དོན་མེད་ | *tön-me.* |
| **Nook** | ཟུར་ | *sur.* |
| **Noon** | ཉིན་གུང་ | *nyin-kung.* |
| **Noose** | ཞགས་པ་ | *skak-pa.* |
| **North** | བྱང་ | *chang.* |
| **Northward** | བྱང་ངོས། བྱང་ཕྱོགས་ | *chang-ngö; chang-chho.* |
| **Nose** | སྣ་ཁུག་ (སྣ་) | *na-khu.* |
| **Do.** ***hon.*** | ཤངས་ | *shang.* |
| **Nostril** | སྣ་ཁུག་གི་ཨི་ཁང་ (སྣ་ཁུང་) | *na-khu-ki i-khang.* |

| | | |
|---|---|---|
| Nostril, *hon.* | ཤངས་ཀྱི་ཨི་ཁང་ (ཤངས་ཁུང་) | *shang-kyi i-khang.* |
| Not | མ། མི་ | *ma ; mi.* |
| Not at all | ཙ་ནས་ w. neg. | *tsa-ne* (w. neg.) |
| Notable (celebrated) | སྙན་གྲགས་ཆེན་པོ་ | *nyen-ťra chhem-po.* |
| Do. *hon.* | མཚན་སྙན་གྲགས་ཆེན་པོ་ | *tshen nyen-ťra chhem-po.* |
| Note, *s.* (letter) | ཡི་གེ་ | *yi-ge.* |
| Do. *hon.* | ཕྱག་བྲིས་ | *chha-ri.* |
| Note, *s.* (reputation) | སྐད་གྲགས་ | *ke-ťra.* |
| Do. *hon.* | སྙན་གྲགས་ | *nyen-ťra.* |
| Note, to (observe) | མིག་ལྟ་བ་ | *miǩ-ta-wa* |
| Do. *hon.* | གཟིགས་པ་ | *śi-pa.* |
| Noted | སྐད་གྲགས་ཆེན་པོ་ | *ke-ťra chhem-po.* |
| Do. *hon.* | མཚན་སྙན་གྲགས་ཆེན་པོ་ | *tshen-nyen-ťra chhem-po.* |
| Nothing | ག་གས་ (གང་ཡང་) w. neg. | *ǩa-ǩe* (w. neg.) |
| Notice | ལན་ (ལོན་) | *len.* |
| Notice, to (mention) | ལབ་པ་ | *lap̌-pa.* |
| Do. *hon.* | གསུང་བ་ | *sung-wa.* |
| Notice, to (see) | མིག་ལྟ་བ་ | *miǩ-ta-wa.* |
| Do. *hon.* | གཟིགས་པ་ | *śi-pa.* |

| | | |
|---|---|---|
| Notification (of Government) | བཀའ་རྒྱ་ | *ka-gya.* |
| Do. (of official) | བསྐུལ་གཏམ་ | *kü-tam.* |
| Notion (opinion) | བསམ་པ་ | *sam-pa.* |
| Do. *hon.* | ཐུགས་སེམས་ | *thu-sem.* |
| Notorious | སྐད་གྲགས་ཆེན་པོ་ | *ke-t́ra chhem-po.* |
| Notwithstanding | ཡིན་ནས། ཡིན་ཀྱང་། ཡིན་ན་ཡང་ | *yin-ne ; yin-kyang ; yin-na-yang.* |
| Noun | མིང་སྒྲ་ | *ming-dra.* |
| Nourish, to | གསོ་བ་ | *so-wa.* |
| Do. *hon.* | གསོ་བ་གནང་བ་ | *so-wa nang-wa.* |
| Novel (new) | གསར་པ་ | *sa-pa.* |
| Novice, religious | དགེ་ཚུལ་ | *ge-tshü.* |
| Now (at this time) | ད་ལྟ་ | *t́an-da.* |
| Now (well, yes) | འོ་ན་ | *o-na.* |
| Now-a-days | དེ་རིང་སང་། དེང་སང་ | *t́e-ring-sang ; t́eng-sang.* |
| Now and then | མཚམས་མཚམས་ | *tsham-tsham.* |
| Nowhere | ག་པ་...མ། ག་རེ་...མ་ | *ḱa-pa...ma ; ḱa-re...ma.* |
| Noxious | སྐྱུག་བྲོ་པོ་ | *kyuḱ-t́ro-po.* |
| Nude | དམར་ཧྲང་ང་ | *mar-hrang-nga.* |
| Nullify, to | མེད་པར་བཟོ་བ་ | *me-pa śo-wa.* |

| | | |
|---|---|---|
| Nullify, to, *hon.* | མེད་པར་བཟོ་བ་གནང་བ་ | *me-pa ŝo-wa nang-wa.* |
| Number (numeral) | གྲངས་ཀ། ཨང་གི་ | *t́rang-ka; ang-ki.* |
| Do. amount | མང་ཉུང་ | *mang-nyung.* |
| Number, to | གྲངས་ཀ་རྒྱབ་པ་ | *t́rang-ka gyaṕ-pa.* |
| Do. *hon.* | ཕྱགས་གྲངས་སྐྱོན་པ་ | *ja-t́rang kyöm-pa.* |
| Numberless | གྲངས་མེད་ | *t́rang-me.* |
| Numerous | མང་པོ་ | *mang-po.* |
| Numerous, very | གཡོ་མ་སྲུ་ | *yo-ma-su.* |
| Nun | ཨ་ནི་ | *a-ni.* |
| Do. *hon.* | རྗེ་བཙུན་ | *je-tsün.* |
| Nuptials | ཆང་ས་ | *chhang-sa.* |
| Do. *hon.* | འཁྲུང་ས་ | *thrung-sa.* |
| Nurse (of children) | དབུ་རྫི། ཕྲུ་རྫི་ | *u-dzi; ṕu-dzi.* |
| Do. *hon.* | ཞལ་ལྟ་མ་ | *sKe-ta-ma.* |
| Nurture, to | གསོ་བ་ | *so-wa.* |
| Do. *hon.* | གསོ་བ་གནང་བ་ | *so-wa nang-wa.* |
| Nutmeg | རྫ་ཏི་ | *dza-ti.* |
| Nutrition | ཁ་ལག། ལྟོ་ | *kha-la; to.* |
| Do. *hon.* | ཞལ་ལག་ | *sKe-la.* |

# O

| | | |
|---|---|---|
| Oar | གྲུ་སྐྱ་ | *ťru-kya.* |
| Oath | མནའ་ | *na.* |
| Do. *hon.* | དབུ་མནའ་ | *u-na.* |
| Oath, to take an | མནའ་སྐྱེལ་བ་ | *na kyel-wa.* |
| Do. *hon.* | དབུ་མནའ་བཞེས་པ་ | *u-na sḱe-pa.* |
| Obdurate, to be (hard-hearted) | སྙིང་རྗེ་མེད་པ་ | *nying-je me-pa.* |
| Do. *hon.* | ཐུགས་རྗེ་མེད་པ་ | *thuḱ-je me-pa.* |
| Obdurate, to be (obstinate) | གྱོང་པོ་ | *ḱyong-po.* |
| Obedient | ཁ་ལ་ཉན་པོ་ | *kha-la nyem-po.* |
| Do. *hon.* | ཞལ་ལ་གསན་པོ་ | *sḱe-la sem-po.* |
| Obeisance, to make (by kneeling) | ཕྱག་འཚལ་བ་ | *chha-tshe-wa.* |
| Do. *hon.* | སྐུ་ཕྱག་འཚལ་ལ་(བ་)གནང་བ་ | *ku-chha tshe-la nang-wa.* |
| Obeisance, to make (by removing hat) | རྡབ་མཇལ་བྱེད་པ་ | *ilam-jel cḱe-pa.* |
| Do. *hon.* | རྡབ་མཇལ་གནང་བ་ | *dam-jel nang-wa.* |
| Obeisance, to make (by raising hand) | ཕྱག་འབུལ་ཞུ་བ་ | *chham-bü sḱu-wa.* |
| Do. *hon.* | ཕྱག་འབུལ་ཞུ་བ་གནང་བ་ | *chham-bü sḱu-a nang-wa.* |
| Obeisance, to make (by prostration) | ཕྱག་འཚལ་བ་ | *chha-tshe-wa.* |

| | | |
|---|---|---|
| Obeisance, to make (by prostration), *hon.* | སྐུ་ཕྱག་འཚལ་བ་ | *ku-chha tshe-wa.* |
| Obese | ཤ་རྒྱགས་པ་ | *sha-gyaḱ-pa.* |
| Do. *hon.* | སྐུ་ཤ་འབྱོར་པོ་ | *ku-sha jor-po.* |
| Obey, to | ཁ་ལ་ཉན་པ་ | *kha-la nyem-pa.* |
| Do. *hon.* | ཞལ་ལ་གསན་པ་ | *sḱe-la sem-pa.* |
| Obey laws, to | ཁྲིམས་འཁྱེར་བ། ཁྲིམས་འཁུར་བ་ | *thrim khyer-wa; thrim khur-wa.* |
| Object (intention) | དོན་དག་ | *t́ön-t́a.* |
| Do. *hon.* | སྐུ་དོན་ | *ku-t́ön.* |
| Object, to | བཀག་པ་ (འགོགས་པ་) | *kaḱ-pa.* |
| Do. *hon.* | བཀག་ག་ (འགོགས་པ་) གནང་བ་ | *kaḱ-ḱa nang-wa.* |
| Obliged, to be (thankful) | དྲིན་དྲན་པ་ | *t́rin t́rem-pa.* |
| Do. *hon.* | དྲིན་དྲན་པ་གནང་བ་ | *t́rin t́rem-pa nang-wa.* |
| Do. *inf.* to *sup.* | བཀའ་དྲིན་དྲན་པ་ | *ka-trin t́rem-pa.* |
| Obliging | དྲིན་ཆེན་པོ་ | *t́rin chhem-po.* |
| Do. *hon.* | བཀའ་དྲིན་ཆེན་པོ་ | *ka-t́rin chhem-po.* |
| Oblique | ཀྱོག་ཀྱོག་ | *kyoḱ-kyo.* |
| Obliterate, to | སུབ་པ་ | *suṕ-pa.* |

| | | |
|---|---|---|
| Obliterate, to, *hon.* | སྲུབ་པ་གནང་བ་ | *sup̃-pa nang-wa.* |
| Obscure (dark) | ནག་པོ་ | *nak̃-po.* |
| Do. (undefined) | ཧྟན་པོ་མེད་པ་ | *tem-po me-pa.* |
| Obscurity (darkness) | སྨུན་ནག་ | *min-na.* |
| Observe, to | མིག་ལྟ་བ་ | *mik̃-ta-wa.* |
| Do. *hon.* | གཟིགས་པ་ | *śi-pa.* |
| Obstacle | བཀག་ཆ་ | *kak̃-chha.* |
| Obstinate | གྱོང་པྲོ་ | *k̃yong-po.* |
| Obstruct, to | བཀག་པ་ (འགེགས་པ་) | *kak̃ pa.* |
| Do. *hon.* | བཀག་ག་ (འགེགས་པ་) གནང་བ་ | *kak̃-k̃a nang-wa.* |
| Obtain, to | འབྱོར་བ། ཐོབ་པ་ | *jor wa ; thop̃-pa.* |
| Do. *hon.* | ཕྱག་འབྱོར་ཡོང་བ་ | *chhan-jor yong-wa.* |
| Obtuse (dull) | ལྐུགས་པ། གླེན་པ་ | *kuk̃-pa ; lem-pa.* |
| Occasion (cause) | རྐྱེན། རྒྱུ་རྐྱེན་ | *kyen ; gyu-kyen.* |
| Do. (opportunity) | ཐབས་ | *thap̃.* |
| Do. (time) | དུས། དུས་ཚོད་ | *t̃ü ; t̃ü-tshö.* |
| Occasionally | མཚམས་མཚམས་ | *tsham-tsham.* |
| Do. *hon.* | ཐུགས་སངས་ཐུགས་སངས་ལ་ | *thuk̃-sang thuk̃-sang la.* |
| Occupation | ལས་ཀ་ | *le-ka.* |

| | | |
|---|---|---|
| Occupation, *hon.* | ཕྱག་ལས་ | *chha-le.* |
| Occupied with work, to be | བྲེལ་བ་ཡོད་པ་ | *ťre-wa yö-pa.* |
| Do. *hon.* | ཐུགས་བྲེལ་ཡོད་པ་ | *thu-ťre yö-pa.* |
| Occur, to | ཡོང་བ་ | *yong-wa.* |
| Ocean | རྒྱ་མཚོ་ | *gyam-tsho.* |
| O'clock | ཆུ་ཚོད་ | *chhu-tshö.* |
| Odd (not a pair) | ཡ་གཅིག་ | *ya-chi.* |
| Odious | སྐྱུག་བྲོ་པོ་ | *kyuǩ-ťro-po.* |
| Odour | དྲི་མ་ | *ťri-ma.* |
| Odour, to have | དྲི་མ་ཁ་བ་ | *ťri-ma kha-wa.* |
| Of, *post.* | གི། ཀྱི། གྱི་ | *ǩi ; kyi ; ǩyi.* |
| Off, *adv.* | ནས་ | *ne.* |
| Offal | བཙོག་པ་ | *tsoǩ-pa.* |
| Offence (anger) | ཚིག་པ། ཁོང་ཁྲོ་ | *tshiǩ-pa ; khong thro.* |
| Do. (insult) | སྨད་ར་ | *me-ra.* |
| Do. (moral fault) | ཉེས་པ་ | *nye-pa.* |
| Offence, to commit | ཉེས་པ་བསག་ (གསོག་) པ་ | *nye-pa saǩ-pa.* |
| Do. *hon.* | སྐུ་སྡིག་བསག་ག་ (གསོག་པ་) གནང་བ་ | *ku-di saǩ-ǩa-nang-wa.* |
| Offence, to give | ཁོང་ཁྲོ་སློང་བ་ | *khong-thro lang-wa.* |

| | | |
|---|---|---|
| Offence, to give, *hon.* | དགོངས་པ་དཀྲུག་པ་ | *gong-pa truḱ-pa.* |
| Offence, to take | འཚེར་བ་ | *tsher-wa.* |
| Do. *hon.* | ཐུགས་འཚེར་གནང་བ་ | *thu-tsher nang-wa.* |
| Offend, to | དམའ་འབེབས་བྱེད་པ་ | *mam-be cḰe-pa.* |
| Do. *hon.* | དམའ་འབེབས་གནང་བ་ | *mam-be nang-wa.* |
| Offensive (disgusting) | སྐྱུག་བྲོ་པོ་ | *kyuḱ-t́ro-po.* |
| Do. (insolent) | འཛིང་པ་སྦོམ་པོ། གྱོང་པོ་ | *jing-pa bom-po ; Ḱyong-po.* |
| Offer, to | སྟེར་བ་ | *ter-wa.* |
| Do. *hon.* | གནང་བ་ | *nang-wa.* |
| Do. *inf.* to *sup.* | ཕུལ་བ་ (འབུལ་བ་) | *phü-wa.* |
| Offering (presents) | འབུལ་བ་ | *bül-wa.* |
| Do. (sacrifice) | མཆོད་པ་ | *chhö-pa.* |
| Office (employment) | ལས་ཀ་ | *le-ka.* |
| Do. *hon.* | ཕྱག་ལས་ | *chha-le.* |
| Office-room | ཡིག་ཚང་ | *yiḱ-tshang.* |
| Officer | དཔོན་པོ་ | *pöm-po.* |
| Official | དཔོན་པོ་ | *pöm-po.* |
| Officiate, to | ལས་ཚབ་བྱེད་པ་ | *le-tshaṕ cḰe-pa.* |
| Do. *hon.* | སྐུ་ཚབ་གནང་བ་ | *ku-tshaṕ nang-wa.* |
| Offspring | ཕྲུ་གུ་ | *pu-gu.* |

| | | |
|---|---|---|
| Often | ཚར་མང་པོ་ | *tshar mang-po.* |
| Oh ! | ཨ་ཁ་ཁ་ | *a-kha-kha.* |
| Oil | སྣུམ་ | *num.* |
| Do. (kerosene) | ས་སྣུམ་ | *sa-num.* |
| Ointment | བྱུགས་པ་ | *cḱuḱ-pa.* |
| Old (of persons and animals) | རྒ་པུ་ (རྒད་པོ་) | *ga-pu.* |
| Old man | རྒ་པུ་ (རྒད་པོ་) | *ga-pu.* |
| Do. *hon.* | བགྲེས་པོ་ | *dre-po.* |
| Old woman | རྒ་མུ་ (རྒད་མོ་) | *ga-mu.* |
| Do. *hon.* | བགྲེས་མོ་ | *dre-mo.* |
| Old (of things) | རྙིང་པ་ | *nying-pa.* |
| Old, to grow | རྒས་པ་ | *ge-pa.* |
| Do. *hon.* | བགྲེས་པ་ | *dre-pa.* |
| Omen | རྟེན་འབྲེལ་ | *tem-dre.* |
| Omit, to | སུབ་པ་ | *suṕ-pa.* |
| Do. *hon.* | སུབ་པ་གནང་བ་ | *suṕ-pa nang-wa.* |
| On | སྒང་ལ། སྟེང་ལ་ | *gang-la ; teng-la.* |
| Once | ཚར་གཅིག། ཐེངས་གཅིག་ | *tshar-chi ; theng-chi.* |
| Once, at (immediately) | ལམ་སང་ | *lam-sang.* |

| | | |
|---|---|---|
| Once more | ད་འདོ་ (ད་འདོས་) ཚར་གཅིག། ད་རུང་ཚར་གཅིག་ | *ťan-ťo tshar-chi ; ťa-rung tshar-chi.* |
| One | གཅིག་ | *chi.* |
| One (in the sense of one full or complete) | གང་ | *ǩang.* |
| One-eyed | ཞར་ར་ (ཞར་བ།) མིག་ཞར་ | *sǩar-ra ; miǩ-sǩar.* |
| Onion | བཙོང་ | *tsong.* |
| Only, *adj.* (alone) | གཅིག་པོ་ | *chiǩ-po.* |
| Do. *adv.* (entirely) | ཤ་སྟག་ | *sha-ta.* |
| Onward (forward) | སྔན་ལ་ (སྔོན་ལ་) | *ngen-la.* |
| Open, to | ཁ་ཕྱེས་ (འབྱེད་) པ་ | *kha-chhe-pa.* |
| Do. *hon.* | ཁ་ཕྱེས་ (འབྱེད་) པ་གནང་བ་ | *kha-chhe-pa nang wa.* |
| Open (frank) | དྲང་པོ་ | *ťrang-po.* |
| Do. *hon.* | ཐུགས་རྒྱུ་དྲང་པོ་ | *thu-gyu ťrang-po.* |
| Opening | ཨི་ཁུང་ | *i-khung.* |
| Openly (frankly) | མ་⋯⋯གསང་བ་ | *ma...sang-ẉa.* |
| Operation | གྲིས་བཤག་པ་ | *ťri-shaǩ-pa.* |
| Opinion | བསམ་པ་ | *sam-pa.* |
| Do. *hon.* | ཐུགས་སེམས་ | *thu-sem.* |
| Opium | གཡའ་ཕིན། *Ch.* ཉལ་ཐ་ཁ་ | *ya-phin ; nye-tha-ǩha.* |

| | | |
|---|---|---|
| Opponent | དགྲ་ | *dra.* |
| Opportunity | ཐབས་ | *thap.* |
| Oppose, to (dispute) | རྩོད་པ་རྒྱབ་པ་ | *tsö-pa gyap-pa.* |
| Do. *hon.* | རྩོད་པ་སྐྱོན་པ་ | *tsö-pa kyöm-pa.* |
| Oppose, to (thwart) | བཀག་པ་ (འགེགས་པ་) | *kak-pa.* |
| Do. *hon.* | བཀག་ག་ (འགེགས་པ་) གནང་བ་ | *kak-ka nang-wa.* |
| Opposite (different) | མི་...གཅིག་པ་ | *mi . chik-pa.* |
| Do. (facing) | ཁ་ཐུག་ལ་ | *kha-thu-la.* |
| Opposite side | ཕར་ཕྱོགས་ | *pha-chho.* |
| Oppress, to (press against) | གནན་པ་ (ནོན་པ་) | *nem-pa.* |
| Do. *hon.* | གནན་ (ནོན་) པ་གནང་བ་ | *nem-pa nang-wa.* |
| Oppress, to (use severely) | སྡུག་པོ་བཏང་ (གཏོང་) བ། བཟོ་བལྟ་བཟོ་བ་ | *duk-po tang-wa ; śop-ta śo-wa.* |
| Do. *hon.* | སྡུག་པོ་བཏོང་ང་ (བ་) གནང་བ་ | *duk-po tong-nga nang wa.* |
| Opthalmia | མིག་ནད་ | *mik-ne.* |
| Do. *hon.* | སྤྱན་སྙུང་བ་ | *chen nyung-wa.* |
| Optical deception | མིག་འཁྲུལ་ | *mik-thrü.* |
| Option | ཐང་ | *thang.* |
| Opulent | ཕྱུག་པོ། ཅ་ (ཆ་) ལག་ཆེན་པོ་ | *chhuk-po; cha-la chhem-po.* |

| | | |
|---|---|---|
| Opulent, *hon.* | སྐུ་ཅས་ (ཆས་) ཆེན་པོ་ | *ku-che chhem-po.* |
| Or | ཡང་མེན་ན། ཡང་ན་ | *yang-men-na; yang-na.* |
| Oracle (prophecy) | ལུང་བསྟན་ | *lung-ten.* |
| Do. *hon.* | བཀའ་ལུང་ | *ka-lung.* |
| Oracle, to deliver (by beads or dice) | མོ་རྒྱབ་པ་ | *mo gyap̄-pa.* |
| Do. *hon.* | ཕྱག་མོ་སྐྱོན་པ་ | *chha-mo kyöm-pa.* |
| Oral | ཁའི་ | *khe.* |
| Orally | ཁ་ནས་ | *kha-ne.* |
| Orange | ཚ་ལུམ་མ་ (པ་) | *tsha-lum-ma.* |
| Orchard | ལྡུམ་ར་ | *dum-ra.* |
| Order, *s.* (command) | བཀའ་ | *ka.* |
| Order (rank) | གོ་ས། གོ་གནས། རིམ་པ་ | *k̄o-sa; k̄o-ne; rim-pa.* |
| Order, written (of Government) | བཀའ་རྒྱ་ | *ka-gya.* |
| Do. (of official) | བསྐུལ་གཏམ་ | *kü-tam.* |
| Do. verbal (of official) | བཀའ་ཁྱབ། བཀའ་བཀོད་ | *ka-khyap̄; ka-kö.* |
| Do. (written judgment in a judicial case). | བཅད་མཚམས། ཁྲ་མ་ | *che-tsham; thra-ma.* |
| Do. (series) | རིམ་པ་ | *rim-pa.* |
| Do. (rank) | གྲལ་ | *t̄re.* |

| | | |
|---|---|---|
| Order, to | བཀའ་གནང་བ་ | *ka-nang-wa.* |
| Order, to (things from shop, etc.) | མངག་པ་ | *ngaḱ-pa.* |
| Do. *hon.* | བཀའ་མངག་གནང་བ་ | *ka-nga nang-wa.* |
| Order to, in | དོན་ལ་ | *ťön-la.* |
| Ordinarily | ཕལ་ཆེར་ | *phe-chher.* |
| Ordinary language, *opp.* to *hon.* | ཞེ་ས་མེད་པ་ | *sḱe-sa me-pa.* |
| Ordinary (in quality) | དཀྱུས་མ་ | *kyü-ma.* |
| Orifice | ཨི་ཁུང་ | *i-khung.* |
| Origin | བྱུང་སྟངས་ (འབྱུང་ཁུང་) | *cḱung-tang.* |
| Ornament | རྒྱན་ཆ་ | *gyen-chha.* |
| Do. *hon.* | སྐུ་རྒྱན་ | *ku-gyen.* |
| Orphan | ད་ཕྲུག་ | *ťa-thru.* |
| Orthography | དག་ཡིག་ | *ťaḱ-yi.* |
| Ostentatious | ཉམས་དོད་པོ་ | *nyam-ťö-po.* |
| Do. *hon.* | སྐུ་ཉམས་དོད་པོ་ | *ku-nyam ťö-po.* |
| Other | གཞན་པ། ཡན་པ་ | *sḱem-pa ; yem-pa.* |
| Otter | སྲམ་ | *hram.* |
| Ought | དགོས་པ་ | *gö-pa.* |
| Our | ང་ཚོའི་ | *nga-tshö.* |

| | | |
|---|---|---|
| **Out (outside)** | ཕྱི་ལོགས་ལ་ | *chhi-lo-la.* |
| **Out of** | ནས་ | *ne.* |
| **Outcry** | ཨུར་སྒྲ་ | *u-dra.* |
| **Outlet** | སྒོ་ | *go.* |
| **Outside,** *adv.* | ཕྱི་ལོགས་ལ་ | *chhi-lo-la.* |
| **Outward** | ཕྱིའི་ | *chhi-i.* |
| **Oven** | ཐབ་ | *thap.* |
| Do. *hon.* | གསོལ་ཐབ་ | *sö-thap.* |
| **Over (above)** | ཡ་གེའི་ | *ya-ke.* |
| Do. (more) | ལྷག་ | *hla.* |
| **Overbear, to** | རྒྱལ་བ། ཀླག་འཁས་པ་ | *gye-wa ; la khe-pa.* |
| Do. *hon.* | རྒྱལ་ར་ (བ་) གནང་བ། ཀླག་འཁས་ར་ (པ་) གནང་བ་ | *gye-ra nang-wa ; la khe-ra nang-wa.* |
| **Overbearing** | ཉམས་ཆེན་པོ། ཛ་ཁོག་ཆེན་པོ་ | *nyam-chhem-po ; dza-kho chhem-po.* |
| **Overcome, to** | རྒྱལ་བ། ཀླག་འཁས་པ་ | *gye-wa ; la khe-pa.* |
| Do. *hon.* | རྒྱལ་ར་ (བ་) གནང་བ། ཀླག་འཁས་ར་ (པ་) གནང་བ་ | *gye-ra nang-wa ; la khe-ra nang-wa* |

| | | |
|---|---|---|
| Overflow, to | ལྷུད་པ་ | *lü-pa.* |
| Overpower, to | རྒྱལ་བ། ལྷག་འཁས་པ་ | *gye-wa ; la khe-pa.* |
| Do *hon.* | རྒྱལ་ར་ (བ་) གནང་བ། ལྷག་འཁས་ར་ (པ་) གནང་བ་ | *gye-ra nang-wa ; la khe-ra nang-wa.* |
| Overtake, to | རྗེས་ཟིན་པ་ | *je-śim-pa.* |
| Do. *hon.* | རྗེས་ཟིན་པ་གནང་བ་ | *je-śim-pa nang-wa.* |
| Do. *inf.* to *sup.* | ཕེབ་རྗེས་ཟིན་པ་ | *phep-je śim-pa.* |
| Overthrow, to | རྒྱལ་བ་ | *gye-wa.* |
| Do. *hon.* | རྒྱལ་ར་ (བ་) གནང་བ་ | *gye-ra nang-wa.* |
| Overturn, to | མགོ་གཞུག་ལོག་པ། ཨ་ལོག་རྒྱབ་པ་ | *go-sku lok-pa ; a-lo gyap-pa.* |
| Do. *hon.* | མགོ་གཞུག་ལོག་ག་ (པ་) གནང་བ། ཨ་ལོག་སྐྱོན་པ་ | *go-sku lok-ka nang-wa ; a-lo kyöm-pa.* |
| Owe, to | བུ་ལོན་གཟུག་པ་ | *pu-lön śuk-pa.* |
| Do. *hon.* | ཕྱག་བུན་གཟུག་པ་ | *chha pün śuk-pa.* |
| Owl | འུག་པ་ | *uk-pa.* |
| Own, *adj.* | རང་གི་ | *rang-ki.* |
| Owner | བདག་པོ་ | *dak-po.* |
| Ox | གླང་། གླང་གོག་ | *lang ; lang-ko.* |

# P

| | | |
|---|---|---|
| Pace (stride) | གོམ་པ་ | *kom-pa.* |
| Do. *hon.* | ཞབས་གོམ་ | *shap-kom.* |
| Paces (of a horse) | འགྲོས་ | *drö.* |
| Do. *hon.* | ཆིབས་འགྲོས་ | *chhip-drö.* |
| Pack (load) | ཁལ་ | *khe.* |
| Pack on, to (load) | བཀལ་བ་ (འགེལ་བ་) | *kel-wa.* |
| Do. *hon.* | བཀལ་ར་ (འགེལ་བ་) གནང་བ་ | *ke ra nang-wa* |
| Pack-horse | ཁལ་རྟ་ | *khe-ta.* |
| Pack-mule | ཁལ་དྲེ་ | *khe-tre.* |
| Pack-pony | ཁལ་རྟ་ | *khe-ta.* |
| Pack-saddle | སྒ་ | *ga.* |
| Packet of paper, large | ཤོག་སྒྲིལ་ | *shok-dri.* |
| Do. small | ཤོག་གུའི་ (ཤོག་བུའི་) ཆག་པ་ | *shok-kü chhak-pa.* |
| Padlock | སྒོ་ལྕགས་ | *gö-cha* |
| Do. *hon.* | གཟིམ་ལྕགས། ཕྱག་ལྕགས་ | *sim-cha: chhu-cha* |
| Pagan | ཕྱི་པ་ | *chhi-pa.* |
| Page of book | ཤོག་ལེབ་ | *shok-le.* |
| Do. number of, in a book | ཤོག་གྲངས་ | *shok-trang.* |
| Do. (attendant) | གཡོག་པོ་ | *yok-po.* |

| | | |
|---|---|---|
| Page (attendant), *hon.* | ཞབས་ཕྱི་ | *sḱaṕ-chhi.* |
| Pail (of wood) | ཟོ་ལག་ | *śo-la.* |
| Do. (of iron) | ལྕགས་ཀྱི་ཟོ་ལག་ | *cha-kyi śo-la.* |
| Pain, bodily | གཟུག་ | *śu.* |
| Do. *hon.* | སྙུང་གཟུག་ | *nyung-śu.* |
| Pain, mental | སྡུག་བསྔལ་ | *dung-nge.* |
| Do. *hon.* | ཐུགས་འཁྲལ་ | *thuḱ-thre.* |
| Pain (punishment by beating) | ཁྲིམས་ | *thrim.* |
| Do. *hon.* | བཀའ་ཁྲིམས་ | *ka-thrim.* |
| Pain (punishment by fine) | ཉེས་པ། ཆད་པ་ | *nye-pa ; chhe-pa.* |
| Do. *hon.* | བཀའ་ཉེས། བཀའ་ཆད | *ka-nye ; ka-chhe.* |
| Painful | གཟུག་ཆེན་པོ་ | *śuḱ-chhem-po.* |
| Painstaking | སྙིང་རུས་ཆེན་པོ་ | *nying-rü chhem-po.* |
| Paint, *s.* | ཚོན་ | *tshön.* |
| Paint, to (cover with colour) | ཚོན་བཏང་ (གཏོང་) བ་ | *tshön tang-wa.* |
| Do. *hon.* | ཚོན་གཏོང་ང་ (བ་) གནང་བ་ | *tshön tong-nga nang-wa.* |
| Paint, to (picture) | བྲིས་པ་ (འབྲི་བ་) | *ťri-pa.* |
| Do. *hon.* | བྲིས་པ་ (འབྲི་བ་) གནང་བ་ | *ťri-pa nang-wa.* |
| Painter | ལྷ་བྲི་ (འབྲི་) པ་ | *hlaṕ-ri-pa.* |

| | | |
|---|---|---|
| Painting | རི་མོ་ | *ri-mo.* |
| Pair | ཆ་ | *chha.* |
| Palace | ཕོ་བྲང་ | *pho-ťrang.* |
| Palanquin | མགྱོགས་དཔྱང་ (འཁྱོགས་དཔྱང་) | *gyo-chang.* |
| Do. *hon.* | ཕེབ་དཔྱང་ | *phep̌-chang.* |
| Palate | དཀན་ | *ken.* |
| Pale | དཀར་པོ་དཀར་ཀྱང་ | *kar-po kar-kyang.* |
| Pallid | དཀར་པོ་དཀར་ཀྱང་ | *kar-po kar-kyang.* |
| Palm (of hand) | ལག་མཐིལ་ | *lak̆-thi.* |
| Do. *hon.* | ཕྱག་མཐིལ་ | *chha-thi.* |
| Palsy | གྲུམ་བུ་ཆུ་སེལ་ | *ťrum-p̌u chhu-se.* |
| Paltry | དོན་དག་ཆུང་ཆུང་ | *ťön-ťa chhung-chhung.* |
| Do. *hon.* | སྐུ་དོན་ཆུང་ཆུང་ | *ku ťön chhung-chhung.* |
| Pan | སླ་ང་ | *la-nga.* |
| Pang, mental | སྡུག་བསྔལ་ | *du-nge.* |
| Do. *hon.* | ཐུགས་འཁྲལ་ | *thu-thre.* |
| Pang, physical | གཟུག་ | *śu.* |
| Do. *hon.* | སྙུང་གཟུག་ | *nyung-śu.* |
| Pankah | རླུང་ཡབ་ | *lung-yap̌.* |

| | | |
|---|---|---|
| Pang (of grief) | སྡུག་བསྔལ་ | *dung-nge.* |
| Pant, to (for breath) | དབུགས་བསགས་ (གསོག་) པ་ | *u sak-pa.* |
| Do. *hon.* | ལྗགས་དབུགས་བསགས་ག་ (གསོག་པ་) གནང་བ་ | *ja-u sak-ka nang-wa.* |
| Pant, to (when the breath is taken away by cold water) | ཧམ་པ་ | *ngam-pa.* |
| Do. *hon.* | ཧམ་པ་གནང་བ་ | *ngam-pa nang-wa.* |
| Pantaloons | གོས་ཐུང་། དོར་མ་ | *ko-thung ; tor-ma.* |
| Do. *hon.* | ཞབས་དོར་ | *sKap-to.* |
| Panther | གཟིག་ | *sik.* |
| Pantry | གཉེར་ཚང་ | *nyer-tshang.* |
| Paper | ཤུ་གུ་ (ཤོག་བུ་) | *shu-gu.* |
| Do. *hon.* | ཕྱག་ཤོག་ | *chha-sho.* |
| Parable | དཔེ། འདྲ་དཔེ་ | *pe ; dra-pe.* |
| Paradise | བདེ་བ་ཅན་གྱི་ཞིང་ཁམས་ | *de-wa-chen-kyi sKing-kham.* |
| Parasol | ཉི་གདུགས་ | *nyi-du.* |
| Do. *hon.* | དབུ་གདུགས་ | *u-du.* |
| Parcel (round) | ཐུམ་རི་ | *thum-ti.* |
| Parcel out, to | བགོད་པ། བགོ་བཤའ་རྒྱབ་པ་ | *gö-pa ; gop-sha gyap-pa.* |

| | | |
|---|---|---|
| **Parcel out, to,** ***hon.*** | བགོད་པ་གནང་བ། བགོ་བཤའ་སྐྱོན་པ་ | *gö-pa nang-wa ; goṕ-sha kyöm-pa.* |
| **Parched (dry)** | སྐམ་པོ་ | *kam-po.* |
| **Pardon** | དགོངས་པ་ | *gong-pa.* |
| **Pardon, to** | དགོངས་པ་བཏང་ (གཏོང་) བ་ | *gong-pa tang-wa.* |
| **Do.** ***hon.*** | དགོངས་པ་གཏོང་ང་ (བ་) གནང་བ་ | *gong-pa tong nga nang-wa.* |
| **Pardon, to ask** | ཐུགས་དགོངས་དག་ཞུ་བ་ | *thu-gong-ťa sḱu-wa.* |
| **Pare, to** | པགས་པ་ཤུ་བ་ | *paḱ-pa shu-wa.* |
| **Do.** ***hon.*** | པགས་པ་ཤུ་བ་གནང་བ་ | *paḱ-pa shu-wa nang-wa.* |
| **Parents** | ཕ་མ་ | *pha-ma.* |
| **Do.** ***hon.*** | ཡབ་ཡུམ་ | *yaṕ-yum.* |
| **Park** | གླིང་ཀ་ | *ling-ka.* |
| **Parrot** | ཨའུ་ནེ་ཙོ། ནེ་ཙོ་ | *a-u-nen tso ; nen-tso.* |
| **Parsimonious** | ལག་པ་དམ་པོ་ | *laḱ-pa ťam-po.* |
| **Do.** ***hon.*** | ཕྱག་དམ་པོ་ | *chha-ťam-po.* |
| **Part** | དུམ་བུ་ | *ťum-ṕu.* |
| **Do. (share)** | སྐལ་ལ་ (སྐལ་བ་ | *ke-la.* |
| **Do.** ***hon.*** | སྐུ་སྐལ་ | *ku-ke.* |
| **Part, to** | ཁ་གྱེས་པ་ (འགྱེ་བ་) | *kha-ḱye-pa.* |

| | | |
|---|---|---|
| Part, to, *hon.* | ཞལ་བྲེས་ར་ (འབྲེ་བ་) གནང་བ་ | *ske-kye-ra nang-wa.* |
| Partial, to be (biassed) | ཉེ་རིང་བྱེད་པ་ | *nye-ring-che-pa.* |
| Do. *hon.* | ཉེ་རིང་གནང་བ་ | *nye-ring nang-wa.* |
| Particular (exact) | ཁྲིག་ཁྲིག། ཏེན་ཏེན་ | *thrik-thrik; ten-ten.* |
| Particularly | ཁྱད་པར་དུ་ | *khye-par-tu.* |
| Partly | དོག་ཙ་ | *tok-tsa.* |
| Partner (in business) | ཚོང་རོགས་ | *tshong-ro.* |
| Party (faction) | ཕྱོགས་ | *chho.* |
| Do. (in law-suit) | གྱོད་ཡ་ | *kyo-ya.* |
| Pass, *s.* (over mountains) | ལ་ | *la.* |
| Pass, to (go), *v.i.* | འགྲོ་བ་ | *dro-wa.* |
| Do. *hon.* | ཕེབ་པ་ | *phe-pa.* |
| Pass, to, *h. hon.* | འཆིབ་ཀྱུ་གནང་བ་ | *chhip-gyu nang-wa.* |
| Pass the time, to | མགོ་འཁོར་བ་ | *go-khor-wa.* |
| Do. *hon.* | དབུ་འཁོར་བ་ | *u-khor-wa.* |
| Passenger (traveller) | འགྲུལ་པ་ | *drü-pa.* |
| Passion (rage) | ཚིག་པ། ཁོང་ཁྲོ་ | *tshik-pa; khong-thro.* |
| Do. *hon.* | དགོངས་པ། རྣམ་མཁྱེན་ | *gong-pa; nam-khyen.* |
| Passion (lust) | འདོད་ཆགས་ | *dö-chha.* |

| | | |
|---|---|---|
| Passionate | རུ་ངར་པོ་ | *ru-ngar-po.* |
| Passport | ལམ་ཡིག་ | *lam-yi.* |
| Pastime (game) | རྩེད་མོ་ | *tse-mo.* |
| Do. *hon.* | སྐུ་རྩེད་ | *ku-tse.* |
| Pastry-puff | མོག་མོག་ | *mo mo.* |
| Do. *hon.* | བཞེས་མོག་ | *sKe-mo.* |
| Patch, *s.* | ལྷན་པ་ | *hlem-pa* |
| Patch, to | ལྷན་པ་རྒྱབ་པ་ | *hlem-pa gyap pa.* |
| Do. *hon.* | ལྷན་པ་སྐྱོན་པ་ | *hlem-pa kyöm-pa.* |
| Path | ལམ་ཀ་ | *lang-ka.* |
| Do. *hon.* | ཕེབ་ལམ་ | *phep-lam.* |
| Path (by cliff) | ཕྲང་ | *thrang.* |
| Patience (forbearance) | བཟོད་པ་ | *śö-pa.* |
| Patient, to be (to endure) | བཟོད་པ་སྒོམ་པ་ | *śö-pa gom pa.* |
| Do. *hon.* | བཟོད་པ་སྒོམ་པ་གནང་བ་ | *śö-pa gom-pa nang-wa.* |
| Patiently, to wait | བསྒུགས་བསྡད་ (སྡོད་) པ་ | *gu de-pa.* |
| Do. *hon.* | བསྒུགས་བཞུགས་པ་ | *gu sKuk-pa.* |
| Patron | མགོ་འདྲེན་གནང་མཁན་ | *gön-dren nang-khen.* |
| Patronage | མགོ་འདྲེན་ | *gön-dren.* |
| Patronize, to | མགོ་འདྲེན་གནང་བ་ | *gön-dren nang-wa.* |

| | | |
|---|---|---|
| Pattern | དཔེ་ | *pe.* |
| Do. (sample) | ཕྱུས་ཚད་ | *pü-tshe.* |
| Pauper | ཉམས་ཆུང་། སྐྱོ་པོ་ | *nyem chhung; kyo-po.* |
| Paw | སྡེར་མོ་ | *der-mo.* |
| Pawn, to | གཏའ་མ་བཞག་ (འཇོག) པ་ | *ta-ma sḱaḱ-pa.* |
| Do. *hon.* | གཏའ་མ་གཞོག་ག་ (འཇོག་པ་) གནང་བ་ | *ta-ma sḱoḱ-ḱa nang-wa.* |
| Pay | གླ། ཕོགས་ | *la; pho.* |
| Do. *hon.* | གསོལ་ཕྱོགས་ | *sö-pho.* |
| Pay, to | གླ་སྤྲད་པ། ཕོགས་སྤྲད་པ་ | *la-tre-pa; pho-tre-pa.* |
| Do. *hon.* | གླ་གནང་བ། ཕོགས་གནང་བ་ | *la nang-wa; pho nang-wa.* |
| Pay back, to | སྐྱིན་ཚབ་སྤྲད་པ་ | *kyin tshaṕ tre-pa.* |
| Do. *hon.* | སྐྱིན་ཚབ་གནང་བ་ | *kyin-tshaṕ nang-wa.* |
| Do. *inf.* to *sup.* | སྐྱིན་ཚབ་ཕུལ་ (འབུལ་) བ་ | *kyin-tshaṕ phü-wa.* |
| Pay taxes, to | ཁྲལ་འཇལ་བ་ | *thre je-wa.* |
| Paymaster | ཕོགས་དཔོན་ | *pho-pön.* |
| Pea | སྲན་མ་ | *trem-ma.* |
| Peace | སྐྱིད་པོ། དུས་བདེ་པོ་ | *kyi-po; tü de-po.* |
| Peaceable (condition of country) | ལྷིངས་ཆག་པོ། འཇམ་ཐིང་ཐིང་ | *hling-chhaḱ-po; jam-thing-thing.* |

| | | |
|---|---|---|
| Peaceful (condition of country) | ལྷིངས་ཆག་པོ། འཇམ་ཐིང་ཐིང་ | *hling-chhaḱ-po ; jam-thing-thing.* |
| Peach | ཁམ་བུ་ | *kham-ṕu.* |
| Peacock | རྨ་བྱ་ | *maṕ-cḱe.* |
| Peak (of mountain) | རྩེ་ | *tse.* |
| Pear | སླི་ | *li.* |
| Do. *hon.* | བཞེས་སླི་ | *sḱe-li* |
| Pearl | མུ་ཏིག་ | *mu-ti.* |
| Do. *hon.* | དབུ་ཏིག་ | *u-ti.* |
| Peasant | སོ་ནམས་བྱེད་མཁན་ | *so-nam cḱe-khen.* |
| Pebble | རྡོ་ཧྲུག་ | *do-hru.* |
| Peculiar | ཁྱད་མཚར་པོ། ཡ་མཚན་པོ་ | *khye-tsha po ; yam-tshem-po.* |
| Pedestrian | རྐང་ཐང་ང་ (པ་) | *kang-thang-nga.* |
| Peel, *s.* | པགས་པ་ | *paḱ-pa.* |
| Peel, to | པགས་པ་ཤུ་བ་ | *paḱ pa shu-wa.* |
| Do. *hon.* | པགས་པ་ཤུ་བ་གནང་བ་ | *paḱ-pa shu wa nang-wa.* |
| Peg, iron | ལྕགས་ཕུར་ | *cha-phu.* |
| Do. wooden | ཕུར་པ་ | *phu pa.* |
| Pelt, to (stone) | གཞུ་བ་ | *sḱu wa.* |
| Do. *hon.* | གཞུ་བ་གནང་བ་ | *sḱu-wa nang-wa.* |

| | | |
|---|---|---|
| Pen | སྙུ་གུ་ | *nyu-ḱu.* |
| Do. *hon.* | ཕྱག་སྙུ་ | *chha-nyu.* |
| Penalty | ཆད་པ། ཉེས་པ་ | *chhe-pa ; nye-pa.* |
| Do. *hon.* | བཀའ་ཆད། བཀའ་ཉེས་ | *ka chhe ; ka-nye.* |
| Pencil | སྙུ་གུ་ | *nyu-ḱu.* |
| Do. *hon.* | ཕྱག་སྙུ་ | *chha-nyu.* |
| Pending | མ་ཚར་བ་ | *ma-tshar-wa.* |
| Penetrate, to (enter) | འཛུལ་བ་ | *dzü-wa.* |
| Do. (pierce) | ཕིགས་པ་ (འབིགས་པ་) | *phi-pa.* |
| Do. *hon.* | འབིགས་ག་ (པ་) གནང་བ་ | *bi-ḱa nang-wa.* |
| Penis | མཇེ། ཕོ་རྟགས་ | *je ; pho-ta.* |
| Do. *hon.* | སོ་མཇེ་ | *so je.* |
| Penurious | སྐྱོ་པོ། སྙེམས་ཆུང་ (ཉམས་ཆུང་) | *kyo-po ; nyem-chhung.* |
| People | མི་ | *mi.* |
| Do. (nation) | མི་བརྒྱུད། རིགས་བརྒྱུད་ | *mi-gyü ; ri-gyü* |
| Pepper | ཕོ་བ་རིལ་བུ་ | *pho-wa ri-ṕu.* |
| Peradventure | གཅིག་བྱེད་ན་ | *chiḱ-cḱe-na.* |
| Perceive, to (with the eye) | མཐོང་བ་ | *thong-wa.* |
| Do. *hon.* | གཟིགས་པ་ | *śi-pa.* |

| | | |
|---|---|---|
| Perceive, to (understand) | ཤེས་པ། ཧ་གོ་བ་ | *she-pa ; ha-ḱo-wa.* |
| Do. *hon.* | མཁྱེན་པ་ | *khyem-pa.* |
| Do. *h. hon.* | དགོངས་པ་རྟོགས་པ་ | *gong-pa toḱ-pa.* |
| Perfect (possessed of grace, glory, and wealth) | ཕུན་སུམ་ཚོགས་པ་ | *phün-sum tshoḱ-pa.* |
| Perform, to | བྱེད་པ་ | *cḱe-pa.* |
| Do. *hon.* | གནང་བ་ | *nang-wa.* |
| Perfume | དྲི་མ་ | *ťri-ma.* |
| Perhaps | གཅིག་བྱེད་ན་ | *chiḱ-cḱe-na.* |
| Peril | ཉེན་ཁ་ | *nyen-kha.* |
| Perilous | ཉེན་ཁ་ཆེན་པོ་ | *nyen-kha chhem-po.* |
| Period | དུས། བསྐལ་པ་ | *ťü, kel-pa.* |
| Perish, to | ཞི་བ་ | *shi-wa.* |
| Do. *hon.* | གྲོངས་པ་ (འགྲོང་བ་) | *ťrong-pa.* |
| Do. *h. hon.* | བཞགས་པ་ | *shaḱ-pa.* |
| Permission | དགོངས་པ་ | *gong-pa.* |
| Permit, to | བཅུག་པ་ (འཇུག་པ་) | *chuḱ-pa.* |
| Do. *hon.* | བཅུག་ག་ (འཇུག་པ་) གནང་བ་ | *chuḱ-ḱa nang-wa.* |
| Permitted, to be | ཆོག་པ་ | *chhoḱ-pa.* |
| Perpetual | རྒྱུན་ཆད་རྒྱུ་མེད་པ་ | *gyün-chhe-gyu me-pa.* |

| | | |
|---|---|---|
| Perpetually | ནམ་རྒྱུན། དུས་རྒྱུན་ | *nam-gyün ; tü-gyün.* |
| Perplexed, to be | མགོ་འཐོམས་པ་ | *go-thom-pa.* |
| Do. *hon.* | དབུ་འཐོམས་པ་གནང་བ་ | *u thom-pa nang-wa.* |
| Perplexing | མགོ་ཉོག་ཚ་པོ་ | *go-nyo tsha-po.* |
| Perplexity | མགོ་ཉོག་ | *go-nyo.* |
| Persecute, to | གནོད་པ་བྱེད་པ་ | *nö-pa cḱe-pa.* |
| Do. *hou.* | གནོད་པ་གནང་བ་ | *nö-pa nang wa.* |
| Persecution | གནོད་པ་ | *nö-pa.* |
| Perseverance | སྙིང་རུས་ | *nying-rü.* |
| Do. *hon.* | ཐུགས་རུས་ | *thu-rü.* |
| Persevere, to | སྙིང་རུས་བྱེད་པ་ | *nying-rü cḱe-pa.* |
| Do. *hon.* | ཐུགས་རུས་གནང་བ་ | *thuḱ-rü nang-wa.* |
| Persia | ད་ཟིག་ | *ta-śi.* |
| Persian | ད་ཟིག་པ་ | *ta śiḱ-pa.* |
| Persist, to | ཨུ་ཚུགས་བྱེད་པ་ | *u tshu cḱe-pa.* |
| Do. *hon.* | ཨུ་ཚུགས་གནང་བ་ | *u-tshu nang-wa.* |
| Persistence | ཨུ་ཚུགས་ | *u·tshu.* |
| Person | མི་ | *mi.* |
| Personally | རང་ | *rang.* |
| Perspiration | རྔུ་ལ་ནག་ | *ngü-na.* |

| | | |
|---|---|---|
| Perspire, to | རྔུལ་ནག་འཐོན་པ་ | *ngü-na thöm-pa.* |
| Do. *hon.* | རྔུལ་ནག་འཐོན་པ་གནང་བ་ | *ngü-na thöm-pa nang-wa.* |
| Persuade, to | བསླབ་བྱ་བྱེད་པ་ | *lap-cKa cKe-pa.* |
| Do. *hon.* | བཀའ་སློབ་གནང་བ་ | *ka-lop nang-wa.* |
| Peruse, to | ཀློག་པ་ | *loK-pa.* |
| Do. *hon.* | ལྗགས་ཀློག་གནང་བ་ | *ja-lo nang-wa.* |
| Perverse | གྱོང་པོ་ | *Kyong-po.* |
| Pessimistic, to be (hopeless) | རེ་བ་མེད་པ་ | *re-wa me-pa.* |
| Do. *hon.* | ཐུགས་རེ་མེད་པ་ | *thu-re me-pa.* |
| Pestle | ཡ་ཀྱུག། གཏུན་རིལ་ | *ya-gya ; ting-ri.* |
| Pet, to | གཅེས་པོ་བྱེད་པ་ | *che-po cKe-pa.* |
| Do. *hon.* | གཅེས་པོ་གནང་བ་ | *che-po nang-wa.* |
| Petition | སྙན་ཞུ་ | *nye-sKu.* |
| Petition, to | སྙན་ཞུ་ཞུ་བ་ | *nye-sKu sKu-wa.* |
| Petroleum | ས་སྣུམ་ | *sa-num.* |
| Petticoat | སྨད་གཡོགས་ | *me-yo.* |
| Do. *hon.* | ཞབས་ཁྱེན་ | *sKap-khyen.* |
| Petty (matter) | དོན་གནད་ཆུང་ཆུང་ | *tön-ne chhung-chhung.* |
| Do. *hon.* | ཐུགས་དོན་ཆུང་ཆུང་ | *thuK-tön chhung-chhung.* |

| | | |
|---|---|---|
| Pewter | དིག་ཚ་ | *tiḱ-tsha.* |
| Phantom | གདོང་འདྲེ། འདྲེ་ | *dong-dre ; dre.* |
| Pheasant, Blood | ཟེ་མོ་ | *śe-mo.* |
| Do. Monal | ཁྲ་མདངས་ | *cḱam-dang.* |
| Phlegm | ལུད་པ་ | *lü-pa.* |
| Do. *hon.* | ལྗགས་ལུད་ | *ja-lü.* |
| Photographic mount | པར་གྱི་རྒྱབ་ཤ་ཤོག་གུ་ (བུ་) | *par-ḱyi gyaṕ-sha shoḱ-ḱu.* |
| Phthisis | གཅོང་ནད་ | *chong-ne.* |
| Physic | སྨན་ | *men.* |
| Do. *hon.* | གསོལ་སྨན་ | *sö-men.* |
| Physician | ཨེམ་ཆི་ | *am-chhi.* |
| Do. *hon.* | ཨེམ་ཆི་ལགས་ | *am-chhi-la.* |
| Pick, to (flowers, etc.) | གཏོག་པ་ | *toḱ-pa.* |
| Do. *hon.* | གཏོག་ག་ (པ་) གནང་བ་ | *toḱ-ḱa nang-wa.* |
| Pick, to (a quarrel) | སྙད་སྐོ་བ་ | *nye-ko-wa.* |
| Do. (choose) | འདམ་པ་ | *dam-pa.* |
| Do. *hon.* | འདམ་པ་གནང་བ་ | *dam-pa nang-wa.* |
| Pick up, to | ཡར་སྒྲུག་པ། ཡར་ཁྱག (འཁྱགས་) པ་ | *ya-druḱ-pa ; ya-khyaḱ-pa.* |

| | | |
|---|---|---|
| Pick up, to, *hon.* | ཡར་སྒྲུག་ག་ (པ་) གནང་བ། ཡར་ཁྱག་ག་ (འཁྱོགས་པ་) གནང་བ་ | *ya-druk̄-k̄a nang-wa ; ya-khyak̄-k̄a nang-wa.* |
| Pictorial representation | རི་མོ་ | *ri-mo.* |
| Picture | ཐང་ཀ་ | *thang-ka.* |
| Do. *hon.* | ཞལ་ཐང་ | *sk̄e-thang.* |
| Piebald (horse) | ཏ་ཁྲ་ | *tap̄-thra.* |
| Piece | ཏུམ་བུ་ | *tum-p̄u.* |
| Do. (round in shape) | རྡོག་རྡོག་ | *dok̄-do.* |
| Do. (roll of cotton cloth) | ཐ་ན་ *Hind.* | *tha-na.* |
| Do. (roll of silk) | ཡུག་ | *yuk̄.* |
| Do. (roll of woollen cloth) | བུབས་ | *p̄up̄.* |
| Pierce, to | ཕིགས་པ (འབིགས་པ་) | *phi-pa.* |
| Do. *hon.* | འབིགས་ག་ (པ་) གནང་བ་ | *bi-k̄a nang-wa.* |
| Piety | ཆོས་སེམས། དགེ་སེམས་ | *chhö-sem ; ge-sem.* |
| Pig | ཕག་པ་ | *phak̄-pa.* |
| Pig-sty | ཕག་ཚང་ | *phak̄-tshang.* |
| Pig-tail | ལྕང་ལོ་ | *chang-lo.* |
| Do. *hon.* | དབུ་ལྕང་ | *u-chang.* |
| Pigeon | ཨང་གུ། (ཕུག་རོན་) | *ang-k̄u.* |

| | | |
|---|---|---|
| Pike (spear) | མདུང་ | *dung.* |
| Do. *hon.* | ཕྱག་མདུང་ | *chhan-dung.* |
| Pile, *s.* | སྤུང་ | *pung.* |
| Pile, to | སྤུང་ནས་བཞག་ (འཇོག་) པ་ | *pung-ne sḱak-pa.* |
| Do. *hon.* | སྤུང་ནས་གཞོག་ག་ (པ་) གནང་བ་ | *ṗung-ne sḱok-ka nang-wa.* |
| Piles | གྲང་ཐོར་ | *ṫrang-thor.* |
| Pilgrim | གནས་སྐོར་ར་ (པ་) | *ne-kor-ra.* |
| Pilgrimage | གནས་སྐོར་ | *ne-kor.* |
| Do. to go on | གནས་སྐོར་ལ་འགྲོ་བ་ | *ne-kor-la dro-wa.* |
| Do. *hon.* | གནས་སྐོར་ལ་ཕེབ་པ་ | *ne-kor-la phe-ṗa.* |
| Do. *h. hon.* | གནས་སྐོར་ལ་འཆིབ་རྒྱུ་ གནང་བ་ | *ne-kor-la chhiṕ-gyu nang-wa.* |
| Pill | རིལ་བུ་ | *ri-ṕu.* |
| Pillage, to (rob) | ཇག་པ་རྒྱབ་པ་ | *cḱak-pa gyaṕ-pa.* |
| Pillar | ཀ་བ་ | *ka-a.* |
| Pillow | སྔས། སྔས་འབོལ་ | *nge ; ngem böl.* |
| Do. *hon.* | དབུ་སྔས་ | *u-nge.* |
| Pimple | ཐོར་པ་ | *thor-pa.* |
| Do. *hon.* | མགུལ་ཐོར་ | *gü-thor.* |

| | | |
|---|---|---|
| **Pin** | གཟེར་ | *śer.* |
| **Pincers** | སྐམ་པ་ | *kam-pa.* |
| **Pinch, to** | སེན་འཐོག་རྒྱབ་པ་ | *sem-tho gyap-pa.* |
| **Do.** ***hon.*** | སེན་འཐོག་སྐྱོན་པ་ | *sem-tho kyöm-pa.* |
| **Pinch, to (twisting the skin)** | ཤ་བཙུས་ (འཛུས་) རྒྱབ་པ་ | *shap-chü gyap-pa.* |
| **Do.** ***hon.*** | ཤ་བཙུས་ (འཛུས་) སྐྱོན་པ་ | *shap-chü kyöm-pa.* |
| **Pine-tree (Pinus Excelsa)** | ཐང་ཤིང་ | *thang-shing.* |
| **Pinnacle** | ལྷ་བཙུགས། ལྕོག་ | *hla-tsuk ; cho.* |
| **Pions** | ཆོས་སེམས་ཆེན་པོ་ | *chhö-sem chhem-po.* |
| **Pipe (musical) instrument)** | གླིང་བུ་ | *ling pu.* |
| **Do.** ***hon.*** | ཞལ་གླིང་ | *she-ling.* |
| **Pipe (tobacco)** | གང་ཟག་ | *kang-śa.* |
| **Do.** ***hon.*** | བཞེས་ཟག་ | *ske-śa.* |
| **Pistol** | གྲོ་མདའ་ | *trom-da.* |
| **Pit** | ས་དོང་། དོང་ | *sa-tong ; tong.* |
| **Pitch (of the voice)** | གདངས་ | *dang.* |
| **Pitcher** | ཆུ་སྣོད། ཆུ་བན་ | *chhu-nö ; chhu-pen.* |
| **Pitiless, to be** | སྙིང་རྗེ་...མེད་པ་ | *nying-je...me-pa.* |
| | ཁྲམས་སྙིང་རྗེ་...མེད་པ་ | *ckam-nying-je ...me pa.* |
| **Do.** ***hon.*** | ཐུགས་རྗེ་...མེད་པ་ | *thuk-je...me-pa.* |

| | | |
|---|---|---|
| Pity | སྙིང་རྗེ། བྱམས་སྙིང་རྗེ་ | *nying-je ; cKam-nying-je.* |
| Do. *hon.* | ཐུགས་རྗེ་ | *thuk-je.* |
| Place, *s.* | ས་ཆ་ | *sa-chha.* |
| Place, to | བཞག་པ་ (འཇོག་པ་) | *sKak-pa.* |
| Do. *hon.* | གཞོག་ག་ (འཇོག་པ་) གནང་བ་ | *sKok-ka nang-wa.* |
| Place in, to | བཙུག་པ་ (འཛུག་པ་) | *chuk-pa.* |
| Do. *hon.* | བཙུག་ག་ (འཛུག་པ་) གནང་བ་ | *chuk-ka nang-wa.* |
| Placenta | ཤ་མ་ | *sha-ma* |
| Plague | གཉན་ནད་ | *nyen-ne.* |
| Plain | ཐང་ | *thang.* |
| Plain, *adj.* (clear) | གསལ་པོ་ | *se-po.* |
| Do. (level) | སྙོམས་པོ་ | *nyom-po.* |
| Plaintiff | ཞུ་གདུག་བྱེད་པོ་ | *sKu-tuk cKe-po.* |
| Do. *hon.* | ཞུ་གདུག་གནང་མཁན་ | *sKu-tuk nang-khen.* |
| Plait (of hair) | ལྕང་ལོ་ | *chang-lo.* |
| Do. *hon.* | དབུ་ལྕང་ | *u-chang.* |
| Plan (pattern) | རི་མོ་ | *ri-mo.* |
| Do. (map) | ས་ཁྲ་ | *sap-thra.* |
| Do. (contrivance) | ཐབས་ | *thap.* |
| Plane | སྦྱུ་ལྷན | *bu-hlen.* |

| | | |
|---|---|---|
| Plane, to | སྦུ་ལྷན་རྒྱབ་པ་ | *bu-hlen gyaṕ-pa.* |
| Do. *hon.* | སྦུ་ལྷེན་སྐྱོན་པ་ | *bu hlen kyöm-pa.* |
| Planet | གཟའ་ | *śa.* |
| Plank | སྤང་ལེབ་ | *pang-le.* |
| Plant, to | བཙུགས་པ་ (འཛུགས་པ་) | *tsuḱ-pa.* |
| Do. *hon.* | བཙུགས་ག་ (འཛུགས་པ་) གནང་བ་ | *tsuḱ-ḱa nang-wa.* |
| Plantain | སྐྱེ་སྡོང་ *Sik.* | *kye-dong.* |
| Plat, to (weave) | འཐག་འཐག་པ་ | *tha thaḱ-pa.* |
| Do. *hon.* | འཐག་ཐག་ག་གནང་བ་ | *tha thaḱ-ḱa nang-wa.* |
| Plate | སྡེར་མ། ཐར་དཔག་ | *der-ma ; tha-pa.* |
| Do. *hon.* | གསོལ་སྡེར་ | *sö-der.* |
| Play | རྩེད་མོ་ | *tse-mo.* |
| Do. *hon.* | སྐུ་རྩེད་ | *ku-tse.* |
| Play, to | རྩེད་མོ་རྩེ་བ་ | *tse mo tse-wa.* |
| Do. *hon.* | སྐུ་རྩེད་གནང་བ་ | *ku-tse nang-wa.* |
| Play-fellow | རྩེད་རོགས་ | *tse-ro.* |
| Do. *hon.* | སྐུ་རྩེད་གནང་རོགས་ | *ku-tse nang-ro.* |
| Plea (controversy) | ལབ་གཞི། རྩོད་པ་ | *laṕ-sḱi ; tsö-pa.* |
| Plead, to | ཞུ་བ་ | *sḱu-wa.* |

| | | |
|---|---|---|
| Plead, to, *hon.* | ཞུ་བ་གནང་བ་ | *sKu-wa nang-wa.* |
| Pleader | བར་མི་བྱེད་མཁན་ | *par-mi cKe-khen.* |
| Do. *hon.* | བར་མི་གནང་མཁན་ | *par-mi nang-khen.* |
| Pleasant | སྐྱིད་པོ་ | *kyi-po.* |
| Do. *hon.* | སྤྲོ་པོ་ | *tro-po.* |
| Please, if you | རོགས་གནང་། རོགས་བྱེད་ | *ro nang ; ro-cKe.* |
| Pleased, to be | དགའ་བ་ | *ga-wa.* |
| Do. *hon.* | ཐུགས་མཉེས་པ་ | *thu nye-pa.* |
| Do. *h. hon.* | ཐུགས་དགྱེས་པ་ | *thu-gye-pa.* |
| Pleasure | དགའ་ཚོར་ | *ga-tshor.* |
| Do. *hon.* | མཉེས་ཚོར་ | *nye-tshor.* |
| Pledge | གཏའ་མ་ | *ta-ma.* |
| Plenteous | འབེལ་པོ། རྫག་ཏོ་ | *be-po ; dzak-to.* |
| Plentiful | འབེལ་པོ། རྫག་ཏོ་ | *be-po ; dzak-to.* |
| Pliable | མཉེན་པོ་ | *nyem-po.* |
| Pliant (flexible) | མཉེན་པོ་ | *nyem-po.* |
| Plough, *s.* | གཤོལ་ | *shö.* |
| Plough, to | རྨོན་པ་རྒྱབ་པ་ | *möm-pa gyap-pa.* |
| Ploughman | རྨོན་པ་རྒྱབ་མཁན། ཐོན་མཁན་ (ཐོང་པ་) | *möm-pa gyang-khen ; thön-khen.* |

| | | |
|---|---|---|
| Pluck, to (*e.g.* from tree) | གཏོག་པ་ | *toḱ-pa.* |
| Do. *hon.* | གཏོག་ག་ (པ་) གནང་བ་ | *toḱ-ḱa nang-wa.* |
| Plump | ཤ་རྒྱགས་པ་ | *sha-gyaḱ-pa.* |
| Do. *hon.* | སྐུ་ཤ་འབྱོར་པོ་ | *ku-sha jor-po.* |
| Plunder, to (by stealth) | རྐུ་བ་ | *ku-wa.* |
| Do. (by highway robbery) | ཇག་པ་རྒྱབ་པ་ | *cḱaḱ-pa gyaṕ pa.* |
| Pneumonia | བད་ཁྲག་ | *ṕe-thra.* |
| Pocket | ཨམ་ཕྲག་ | *am-ṕa.* |
| Do. *hon.* | སྐུ་ཕྲག་ | *kum-ṕa.* |
| Pock-mark | འབར་ཙག་ | *bar-tsa.* |
| Pod | གང་བུ་ | *ḱam-ṕu.* |
| Do. *hon.* | བཞེས་གང་ | *sḱe-ḱam.* |
| Poem | སྙན་ངག་ | *nye-nga.* |
| Poet | སྙན་ངག་བྲིས་མཁན་ | *nye-nga t́ri-khen.* |
| Point (*e.g.*, of nail) | རྩེ་ | *tse.* |
| Do. (of argument) | དོན་དག་ | *t́ön-t́a.* |
| Do. *hon.* | སྐུ་དོན་ | *ku-t́ön.* |
| Point out, to (indicate) | མིག་སྟོན་པ་ | *mi-töm-pa.* |
| Do. *hon.* | མིག་སྟོན་པ་གནང་བ་ | *mi-töm-pa nang-wa.* |

| | | |
|---|---|---|
| Point out, to (indicate) *inf.* to *sup.* | སྤྱན་ཕེབ་ཞུ་བ། སྤྱན་དར་ཞུ་བ་ | *chem-phe sḱu-wa ; chen-ťar sḱu-wa.* |
| Poised evenly, to be | ཡང་ལྗི་མེད་པ་ | *yang-ji me-pa.* |
| Poison | དུག་ | *ťu.* |
| Do. *hon.* | གསོལ་དུག་ | *sö-ťu.* |
| Policeman | སྐོར་ལྕག་པ་ | *ko-chaḱ-pa.* |
| Policy | ལུགས་སྲོལ་ | *luḱ-sö.* |
| Polite language | ཞེ་ས་ | *sḱe-sa.* |
| Pollute, to | བཙོག་པ་བཟོ་བ་ | *tsoḱ-pa śo-wa.* |
| Do. *hon.* | བཙོག་པ་བཟོ་བ་གནང་བ་ | *tsoḱ-pa śo-wa nang-wa.* |
| Pollution | གྲིབ་ | *ťriṕ.* |
| Do. *hon.* | སྐུ་གྲིབ་ | *ku-ťriṕ.* |
| Pond | ཆུ་འཁྱིལ་ | *chhu-khyil.* |
| Ponder, to | བསམ་བློ་བཏང་ (གཏོང་) བ་ | *sam-lo tang-wa.* |
| Do *hon.* | ཐུགས་བསམ་བཞེས་པ་ | *thu-sam sḱe-pa.* |
| Ponderous (heavy) | ལྗི་པོ་ | *ji-po.* |
| Pony | རྟ་ | *ta.* |
| Do. *hon.* | ཆིབས་པ་ | *chhiḱ-pa.* |
| Pony, riding | ཞོན་རྟ་ | *sḱön-ta.* |
| Do. *hon.* | ཆིབས་པ་ | *chhiḱ-pa.* |

| | | |
|---|---|---|
| Pony, riding (of very high official or lama) | ཆིབས་ཆེན་ | *chhiṕ-chhen.* |
| Pony, pack | ཁལ་རྟ་ | *khe-ta.* |
| Pool (small) | ཆུ་འཁྱིལ་ | *chhu-khyil.* |
| Poor | སྐྱོ་པོ། སྙེམས་ཆུང་ (ཉམས་ཆུང་) | *kyo-po ; nyem-chhung.* |
| Poplar | སྤྱར་པ་ | *ja-pa.* |
| Poppy | སྟོབས་ལྡན་མེ་ཏོག་ | *tom-den me to.* |
| Population | མི་གྲངས་ | *mi-t́rang.* |
| Porch | ཕྱི་སྒོ་ | *chhi-go.* |
| Porcupine | གཟིག་མོ་ | *śiḱ-mo.* |
| Pork | ཕག་ཤ་ | *phaḱ-sha.* |
| Porridge | བག་ཐུག་ | *ṕa-thu.* |
| Do. *hon.* | བཞེས་བག་བག་ཐུག་ | *sḱe-ṕa ṕa-thu.* |
| Portent | རྟེན་འབྲེལ་ | *tem-dre.* |
| Portion | སྐལ་ལ་ (སྐལ་བ་) | *ke-la.* |
| Do. *hon.* | སྐུ་སྐལ་ | *ku-ke.* |
| Position (in society) | རྒྱུད་ | *gyü.* |
| Positive | རྟེན་རྟེན་ | *ten-ten.* |
| Possessor | བདག་པོ་ | *daḱ-po.* |

| | | |
|---|---|---|
| Possible, to be | ཐུབ་པ་ | *thup-pa.* |
| Post (pillar) | ཀ་བ་ | *ka-a.* |
| Post-office | ཡིག་ཁང་ | *yik-khang.* |
| Posterior (anus) | ཀུབ་ | *kup.* |
| Do. *hon.* | ཞབས་ཕོང་ | *sKam-phong.* |
| Postpone, to (adjourn) | བཞག་པ་ (འཇོག་པ་) | *sKak-pa.* |
| Do. *hon.* | གཞོག་ག་ (འཇོག་པ་) གནང་བ་ | *sKok-ka nang-wa.* |
| Posture | བརྡབ་ (བརྡ་) | *dap.* |
| Pot | ཁོག་མ་ | *kho-ma.* |
| Do. earthen | རྫ་ཁོག་ | *dza-kho.* |
| Do. flower | མེ་ཏོག་ཁོག་མ་ | *me-to kho-ma.* |
| Potato | ཞོ་གོག་ | *sKo-ko.* |
| Do. (a sweet variety) | གྲོ་མ་ | *tro-ma.* |
| Do. *hon.* | བཞེས་གྲོ་ | *ske-tro.* |
| Potency | དབང་ | *wang.* |
| Do. *hon.* | སྐུ་དབང་ | *ku-wang.* |
| Potter | རྫ་མཁན་ | *dza-khen.* |
| Pouch (for tobacco) | ཐ་ཁུག་ | *tha-khu.* |
| Do. *hon.* | བཞེས་ཁུག་ | *ske-khu.* |

| | | |
|---|---|---|
| Pound, to (crush) | རྫོག་པ་ | *dzok̄-pa.* |
| Do. *hon.* | རྫོག་ག་ (པ་) གནང་བ་ | *dzok̄-k̄a nang-wa.* |
| Pour, to | ལྡུག་པ་ | *luk̄-pa.* |
| Do. *hon.* | ལྡུག་ག་ (པ་) གནང་བ་ | *luk̄-k̄a nang-wa.* |
| Powder | ཕྱེ་མ་ | *chhe-ma.* |
| Do. gun | རྫས་ | *dze.* |
| Power (official) | དབང་ | *wang.* |
| Do. *hon.* | སྐུ་དབང་ | *ku-wang.* |
| Power (physical) | ཤེད་ | *she.* |
| Do. *hon.* | སྐུ་ཤེད་ | *ku-she.* |
| Powerful (officially) | དབང་ཆེན་པོ་ | *wang chhem-po.* |
| Do. *hon.* | སྐུ་དབང་ཆེན་པོ་ | *ku-wang chhem-po.* |
| Powerful (physically) | ཤེད་ཆེན་པོ་ | *she chhem-po.* |
| Do. *hon.* | སྐུ་ཤེད་ཆེན་པོ་ | *ku-she chhem-po.* |
| Practicable, to be | ཐུབ་པ་ | *thup̄-pa.* |
| Practice (custom) | ལུགས་སྲོལ་ | *luk̄-sö.* |
| Practise, to | སྦྱང་བ་ | *jang-wa.* |
| Do. *hon.* | སྦྱང་ང་ (བ་) གནང་བ་ | *jang-nga nang-wa.* |
| Praise, *s.* | སྟོད་ར་ | *tö-ra.* |
| Praise, to | སྟོད་ར་བཏང་ (གཏོང་) བ་ | *tö-ra tang-wa.* |

| | | |
|---|---|---|
| Praise, to, *hon.* | སྟོད་ར་གཏོང་ང་ (བ་) གནང་བ་ | *tö-ra tong-nga nang-wa.* |
| Do. *inf.* to *sup.* | སྟོད་ར་ཞུ་བ་ | *tö-ra sKu-wa.* |
| Pray, to (request) | ཞུ་བ་ | *sKu-wa.* |
| Do. *hon.* | ཞུ་བ་གནང་བ་ | *sKu-wa nang-wa.* |
| Pray to deity, to (extempore prayer) | སྨོན་ལམ་བཏབ་ (འདེབས་) པ་ | *mö-lam tap-pa.* |
| Do. *hon.* | ཐུགས་སྨོན་གནང་བ་ | *thu-mön nang wa.* |
| Do. (written prayers) | ཁ་འདོན་བྱེད་པ་ | *khan-dön cKe-pa.* |
| Do. *hon.* | ཞལ་འདོན་གནང་བ་ | *sKen-dön nana-wa.* |
| Prayer (extempore) | སྨོན་ལམ་ | *mö-lam.* |
| Do. *hon.* | ཐུགས་སྨོན་ | *thu-mön.* |
| Prayer (written) | ཁ་འདོན་ | *khan-dön.* |
| Do. *hon.* | ཞལ་འདོན་ | *sKen-dön.* |
| Prayer-wheel | མ་ཎི། ལག་སྐོར་ | *ma-ni ; la-kor.* |
| Do. *hon.* | ཕྱག་སྐོར་ | *chha-kor.* |
| Preach, to | ཆོས་བཤད་པ་ | *chhö she-pa.* |
| Do. *hon.* | བཀའ་ཆོས་གསུང་བ་ | *ka-chhö sung-wa.* |
| Precede, to | སྔན་ (སྔོན་) ལ་འགྲོ་བ་ | *ngen-la dro-wa.* |
| Do. *hon.* | སྔན་ (སྔོན་) ལ་ཕེབ་པ་ | *ngen-la phe-pa.* |

| | | |
|---|---|---|
| Precede, to, *h. hon.* | སྔན་ (སྔོན་) ལ་འཆིབ་རྒྱུ་ གནང་བ་ | *ngen-la chhip-gyu nang-wa.* |
| Preceding | སྔོན་གྱི། དང་པོ་ | *ngön-kyi ; tang-po.* |
| Precept (maxim) | གཏམ་དཔེ་ | *tam-pe.* |
| Precious | རྩ་ཆེན་པོ་ | *tsa-chhem-po.* |
| Precipice | གཡང་ | *yang.* |
| Precipitate (rash) | ཁ་མེད་མིག་མེད་ | *kha-me mik-me.* |
| Precise | ཁྲིག་ཁྲིག། ཏེན་ཏེན་ | *thrik-thrik ; ten-ten.* |
| Precisely | རང་ | *rang.* |
| Preclude, to | བཀག་པ་ (འགེགས་པ་) | *kak-pa.* |
| Do. *hon.* | བཀག་ག་ (འགེགས་པ་) གནང་བ་ | *kak-ka nang-wa.* |
| Predict, to | མངོན་ཤེས་བཤད་པ་ | *ngön-she she-pa.* |
| Do. *hon.* | མངོན་མཁྱེན་གསུང་བ་ | *ngön-khyen sung-wa.* |
| Prediction | ལུང་བསྟན་ | *lung-ten.* |
| Do. *hon.* | བཀའ་ལུང་ | *ka-lung.* |
| Prefix, *s.* | སྔོན་འཇུག་ | *ngön-ju.* |
| Pregnant, to be | བུ་གུ་སྐྱེད་རྒྱུ་ཡོད་པ་ | *pu-gu kye-gyu yö-pa.* |
| Do. *hon.* | ཨ་ཝ་འཁྲུང་རྒྱུ་ཡོད་པ་ | *a-wa thrung-gyu yö-pa.* |
| Prejudice | རྣམ་རྟོག་ | *nam-to.* |

| | | |
|---|---|---|
| Prepare, to | གྲལ་སྒྲིག་བྱེད་པ་ | *ṫra-dri cḱe-pa.* |
| Do. *hon.* | གྲལ་སྒྲིག་གནང་བ་ | *ṫra-dri nang-wa.* |
| Prerogative | ཐོབ་ཐང་ | *thop̄-thang.* |
| Presage, *s.* | རྟེན་འབྲེལ་ | *tem dre.* |
| Presence of, in the | མདུན་ལ་ | *dün-la.* |
| Do. *hon.* | སྐུ་མདུན་ལ་ | *kun-dün-la.* |
| Present, *s.* (alms to poor) | སྦྱིན་པ་ | *jim-pa.* |
| Do. (to lama) | འབུལ་བ་ | *bül-wa.* |
| Do. (tip) | ཆང་རིན་ | *chhang-rin.* |
| Do. *hon.* | གསོལ་རས། ཕྲུང་རིན་ | *sö-re; thrung-rin.* |
| Present, to | སྟེར་བ་ | *ter-wa.* |
| Do. *hon.* | གནང་བ་ | *nang-wa.* |
| Do. *inf.* to *sup.* | ཕུལ་བ་ | *phü-wa.* |
| Do. *hon.* | འབུལ་ར་ (བ་) གནང་བ་ | *bü-ra nang wa.* |
| Present, to be | བསྡད་ (སྡོད་) ཡོད་པ་ | *de yö-pa.* |
| Do. *hon.* | བཞུགས་ཡོད་པ་ | *sḱu yö-pa.* |
| Do. *h. hon.* | བཞུགས་གདན་འཛག་ཡོད་པ་ | *sḱu-den-ja yö-pa.* |
| Present, at | ད་ལྟ་ | *ṫan-da.* |
| Presently (in a few minutes) | ཧྲིབ་ཙ་ (ཙམ་) གཅིག། མགྱོགས་པོ་ | *hrip-tsa-chi; gyoḱ-po.* |

| | | |
|---|---|---|
| Preserve, to (keep care of) | ཉར་བ་ | *nyar-wa.* |
| Do. *hon.* | ཉར་ར་ (བ་) གནང་བ་ | *nyar-ra nang-wa.* |
| Do. *h. hon.* | ཐུགས་ཅག་གནང་བ་ | *thuḱ-cha nang-wa.* |
| Press, to (physically) | གནན་པ་ (གནོན་པ་) | *nem-pa.* |
| Do. *hon.* | གནན་ (གནོན་) པ་གནང་བ་ | *nem-pa nang-wa.* |
| Press, to (insist) | ཨུ་ཚུགས་བྱེད་པ་ | *u-tshu cḱe-pa.* |
| Do. *hon.* | ཨུ་ཚུགས་གནང་བ་ | *u-tshu nang-wa.* |
| Pressing (work) | ཐྲལ་ཐྲལ་བྱེད་དགོས་ཡ་ | *thre-thre cḱe gö-ya.* |
| Pretend, to | གྱོད་བཞད་པ་ | *ḱyö she-pa.* |
| Do. *hon.* | གྱོད་གསུང་བ་ | *ḱyö sung-wa.* |
| Pretty (of woman) | ཚར་པོ། མཛེས་པོ་ | *tshar-po ; dze-po.* |
| Do. *hon.* | ཐུགས་ཚར་པོ་ | *thu tshar-po.* |
| Pretty (of things) | སྙིང་རྗེ་པོ་ | *nying-je-po.* |
| Prevail over, to (overcome) | རྒྱལ་བ། ཀླག་འཁས་པ་ | *gye-wa ; la khe-pa.* |
| Do. *hon.* | རྒྱལ་ར་ (བ་) གནང་བ། ཀླག་འཁས་ར་ (པ་) གནང་བ་ | *gye-ra nang-wa ; la khe-ra nang-wa.* |
| Prevent, to | བཀག་པ་ (འགེགས་པ་) | *kaḱ-pa.* |
| Do. *hon.* | བཀག་ག་ (འགེགས་པ་) གནང་བ་ | *kaḱ-ḱa nang-wa.* |

| | | |
|---|---|---|
| Previous | སྔོན་ཀྱི། དང་པོ་ | *ngön-k̔yi; t̔ang-po.* |
| Previously | སྔན་མ། སྔོན་ལ་ | *ngen-ma; ngen-la.* |
| Price | གོང་། རིན་ | *k̔ong; ring.* |
| Do. *hon.* | ལྗགས་གོང་ | *ja-k̔ong.* |
| Prick, to | བཙུགས་པ་ (འཛུགས་པ་) | *tsuk̔-pa.* |
| Do. *hon.* | བཙུགས་ཀ་ (འཛུགས་པ་) གནང་བ་ | *tsuk̔-k̔a nang-wa.* |
| Pride | ཉམས། རྫག་ཁོག་ | *nyam; dza-kho.* |
| Priest | བླ་མ་ | *la-ma.* |
| Prince | རྒྱལ་སྲས་ | *gye-se.* |
| Princess | རྒྱལ་པོའི་སྲས་མོ་ | *gye-pö sé-mo.* |
| Principal | ཆེ་ཤོས་ | *chhe-shö.* |
| Do. (of a loan) | མ་རྩ་ | *ma-tsa.* |
| Principally | ཕལ་ཆེར་ | *phe-chher.* |
| Principle (origin) | བྱུང་སྟངས་ (འབྱུང་ཁུང་) | *ch̔ung-tang.* |
| Do. (cause) | རྐྱེན། རྒྱུ་རྐྱེན་ | *kyen; gyu-kyen.* |
| Do. (motive) | དོན་དག་ | *t̔ön-t̔a.* |
| Do. *hon.* | སྐུ་དོན་ | *ku-t̔ön.* |
| Print, to | པར་རྒྱབ་པ་ | *par-gyap̔-pa.* |
| Do. *hon.* | སྐུ་པར་སྐྱོན་པ་ | *ku-par kyöm-pa.* |

| | | |
|---|---|---|
| Printed matter | པར་མ་ | *par-ma.* |
| Printer | པར་པ་ | *par-pa.* |
| Printer (cutter of types) | པར་རྐོད་ (རྐོ་) པ་ | *par-kö-pa.* |
| Do. *hon.* | པར་དཔོན་ | *par-pön.* |
| Printing-office | པར་ཁང་ | *par-khang.* |
| Prior, *adj.* | སྔོན་གྱི། དང་པོ་ | *ngön-k̔yi ; t̔ang-po.* |
| Prison | བཙོན་ཁང་ | *tsön-khang.* |
| Prisoner | བཙོན་པ་ | *tsöm-pa.* |
| Private | གསང་བ་ | *sang-wa.* |
| Private property, *hon.* | སྐུ་སྒེར་གྱི་སྐུ་ཆས་ | *ku-ger-k̔yi ku-chhe.* |
| Privately | གསང་བ་བྱས་ནས་ | *sang-wa c̔he-ne.* |
| Do. *hon.* | གསང་བ་གནང་ནས་ | *sang-wa nang-ne.* |
| Privilege (right) | ཐོབ་ཐང་ | *thop̔-thang.* |
| Prize | གསོལ་རས་ | *sö-re.* |
| Probably | གཅིག་བྱེད་ན་ | *chik̔-c̔he-na.* |
| Probationer (in monastery) | ཨེན་ཆུང་ | *en-chhung.* |
| Proceed, to | འགྲོ་བ། ཕྱིན་པ་ | *dro-wa ; chhim-pa.* |
| Do. *hon.* | ཕེབ་བ། ཐས་པ་ | *phe-pa ; the-pa.* |
| Do. *h. hon.* | འཆིབ་སྒྱུ་གནང་བ་ | *chhip̔-gyu nang-wa.* |
| Proclaim, to | སྒྲོག་པ་ | *drok̔-pa.* |

| | | |
|---|---|---|
| Proclaim, to, *hon.* | སྒྲོག་ག་ (པ་) གནང་བ་ | *drok-ka nang wa.* |
| Proclamation (of Government) | བཀའ་རྒྱ་ | *ka-gya.* |
| Do. (of official) | བསྐུལ་གཏམ་ | *kü-tam.* |
| Procrastinating | ཉ་སི་དགུ་སི་ | *nya-si-gu-si.* |
| Procreate, to | སྐྱེད་པ་ | *kye-pa.* |
| Procure, to | འབྱོར་བ། ཐོབ་པ་ | *jor-wa ; thop-pa.* |
| Do. *hon.* | ཕྱག་འབྱོར་ཡོང་བ་ | *chhan-jor yong-wa.* |
| Prodigal (profuse) | འཕེལ་པོ། ཛག་ཏོ་ | *be-po ; dzak-to.* |
| Prodigious | ཆེ་ཐག་ཆོད་ | *chhe-thak-chhö.* |
| Prodigy | ཡ་མཚན་ | *yam-tshen.* |
| Produce, to (bring) | འཁྱེར་ཡོང་བ་ | *khyer-yong-wa.* |
| Do. *hon.* | བསྣམས་ (སྣོམས་) ཕེབ་པ་ | *nam-phe-pa.* |
| Productive (of soil) | ལུད་ཆུ་འཛོམ་པོ་ | *lü-chhu dzom-po.* |
| Profane | ཆོས་སེམས་མེད་པ་ | *chhö-sem me-pa.* |
| Profession | ལས་ཀ་ | *le-ka.* |
| Do. *hon.* | ཕྱག་ལས་ | *chha-le.* |
| Professor | མཁན་པོ་ | *khem-po.* |
| Profit | ཁེ་བཟང་ | *khep-śang.* |
| Do. *hon.* | སྐུ་ཁེ་ | *ku-khe.* |
| Profit, to make a | ཁེ་བཟང་ཟབ་ | *khep-śang śa wa.* |

| | | |
|---|---|---|
| Profit, to make a, *hon.* | སྐུ་ཁེ་བཞེས་པ་ | *ku-khe sḱe-pa.* |
| Profitable, to be | ཕན་ཐོགས་པ་ | *phen-thoḱ-pa.* |
| Do. *hon.* | ཐུགས་ཕན་གསོལ་བ་ | *thu-phen söl-wa.* |
| Profound (deep) | གཏིང་རིང་པོ་ | *ting-ring-po.* |
| Profuse | འབེལ་པོ། ཛག་དོ་ | *be-po ; dzaḱ-ťo.* |
| Progeny | ཕྲུ་གུ་ | *pu-gu.* |
| Prognostication | ལུང་བསྟན་ | *lung-ten.* |
| Do. *hon.* | བཀའ་ལུང་ | *ka-lung.* |
| Prohibit, to | བཀག་པ་ (འགེགས་པ་) | *kaḱ-pa.* |
| Do. *hon.* | བཀག་ག་ (འགེགས་པ་) གནང་བ་ | *kaḱ-ka nang-ẇa.* |
| Prolific (of soil) | ལུད་ཆུ་འཛོམ་པོ་ | *lü-chhu dzom-po.* |
| Prominent (eminent) | སྐད་གྲགས་ཆེན་པོ་ | *ke-ťra chhem-po.* |
| Do. *hon.* | སྙན་གྲགས་ཆེན་པོ་ | *nyen-ťra chhem-po.* |
| Promise, to | ཁས་བླང་བ་ | *khe-lang-wa.* |
| Do. *hon.* | ཞལ་བཞེས་པ་ | *sḱe-sḱe-pa.* |
| Promoted, to be | གོ་གནས་འཕར་བ་ | *ḱo-ne phar-wa.* |
| Do. *hon.* | གོ་གནས་འཕར་ར་ (བ་) གནང་བ་ | *ḱo-ne phar-ra nang-wa.* |
| Promptly | མགྱོགས་པོར་ | *gyoḱ-po.* |

| | | |
|---|---|---|
| **Promptly,** ***hon.*** | ཚོལ་པོར་ | *tsö-po.* |
| Promulgate, to | སྒྲོག་པ་ | *drok̄-pa.* |
| Do. *hon.* | སྒྲོག་ག་ (པ་) གནང་བ་ | *drok̄-k̄a nang-wa.* |
| Pronunciation | ལབ་སྟངས། ཤོད་སྟངས་ | *lap̄-tang ; shö-tang.* |
| Do. *hon.* | གསུང་སྟངས་ | *sung-tang.* |
| Proof | རྟགས་ | *ta.* |
| Prop, *s.* | ཀ་སྐྱོར་ | *ka-kyor.* |
| Prop, to | སྐྱོར་བ་ | *kyor-wa.* |
| Do. *hon.* | སྐྱོར་ར་ (བ་) གནང་བ་ | *kyor-ra nang-wa.* |
| Proper (befitting) | འོས་པོ་ | *ö po.* |
| Property (in land) | ས་ཆ་ | *sa-chha.* |
| Do. (in goods) | ཆ་ལག་ | *cha-la.* |
| Do. *hon.* | སྐུ་ཆས་ | *ku-che.* |
| Prophecy | ལུང་བསྟན་ | *lung-ten.* |
| Do. *hon.* | བཀའ་ལུང་ | *ka-lung.* |
| Prophesy, to | མངོན་ཤེས་ཤེས་པ་ | *ngön-she she-pa.* |
| Do. *hon.* | མངོན་མཁྱེན་མཁྱེན་པ་ | *ngön-khyen khyem-pa.* |
| Propitious | རྟེན་འབྲེལ་ཡག་པོ་ | *tem-dre yak̄-po.* |
| Proportion | ཚོད་ | *tshö.* |
| Proprietor | བདག་པོ་ | *dak̄-po.* |

| | | |
|---|---|---|
| Prose | ལྷུག་མ་ | *lhuk-ma.* |
| Prosperity (good fortune) | བསོ་བདེ་ (བསོད་བདེ།) བསོད་ནམས་ | *so-de ; sö-nam.* |
| Do. *hon.* | སྐུ་བསོད་ | *ku-sö.* |
| Prosperous | གཡང་ཆེན་པོ་ | *yang-chhem-po.* |
| Prostrate oneself, to | ཕྱག་འཚལ་བ་ | *chha-tshe-wa.* |
| Do. *hon.* | སྐུ་ཕྱག་འཚལ་ར་ (བ་) གནང་བ་ | *ku-chha tshe-ra nang-wa.* |
| Prostitute | ཆལ་མོ། ཞང་ཚོང་མ་ | *chhe-mo ; sḱang-tshong-ma.* |
| Protect, to | སྲུང་བ་ | *sung-wa.* |
| Do *hon.* | སྲུང་ང་ (བ་) གནང་བ་ | *sung-nga nang-wa.* |
| Protector | སྐྱབས་མགོན་ | *kyam-gön.* |
| Protectorate (over a country) | སྐྱབས་ཁོངས་ | *kyaṕ-khong.* |
| Proud | ཉམས་ཆེན་པོ། ཛག་ཁོག་ཆེན་པོ་ | *nyam-chhem-po ; dza-kho chhem-po.* |
| Prove, to (a case) | ར་འཕྲོད་པ་ | *ra-thrö-pa.* |
| Do. *hon.* | ར་འཕྲོད་པ་གནང་བ་ | *ra-thrö-pa nang-wa.* |
| Prove, to (test) | ཚོད་ལྟ་བ་ | *tshö ta-wa.* |
| Do. *hon.* | ཚོད་གཟིགས་པ་ | *tsho śi-pa.* |

| | | |
|---|---|---|
| Proverb | གཏམ་དཔེ་ | *tam-pe.* |
| Provide, to | སྒྲུབ་པ་ | *druṕ-pa.* |
| Do. *hon.* | སྒྲུབ་པ་གནང་བ་ | *druṕ-pa nang-wa.* |
| Province | ཞིང་ཆེན། ཁུལ་ | *sḱing-chhen ; khü.* |
| Provisions | ཁ་ལག། ལྟོ་ | *kha-la ; to.* |
| Do. *hon.* | ཞལ་ལག་ | *sḱe-la.* |
| Provisions for journey | ལམ་ཆས་ | *lam-chhe.* |
| Provoke, to (annoy) | ཁོང་ཁྲོ་སློང་བ་ | *khong-thro lang-wa.* |
| Do. *hon.* | དགོངས་པ་དཀྲུག་པ་ | *gong-pa truḱ-pa.* |
| Proximity | ཉེ་འཁོར་ | *nye-khor.* |
| Proxy | ཚབ་ | *tshaṕ.* |
| Do. *hon.* | སྐུ་ཚབ་ | *ku-tshaṕ.* |
| Prudence (wisdom) | བློ་གྲོས་ | *lo-t́rö.* |
| Prudent | མཁས་པོ་ | *khe-po.* |
| Puddle (small pool) | ཆུ་འཁྱིལ་ | *chhu-khyil.* |
| Puff (pastry) | མོག་མོག་ | *mo-mo.* |
| Do. *hon.* | བཞེས་མོག་ | *sḱe-mo.* |
| Pull, to | འཐེན་པ་ | *them-pa.* |
| Do. *hon.* | འཐེན་པ་གནང་བ་ | *them-pa nang-wa.* |
| Pull, to (of horses) | ངར་པོ་བྱེད་པ་ | *ngar-po cḱe-pa.* |

| | | |
|---|---|---|
| **Pulling**, *adj.* (of horses) | ངར་པོ་ | *ngar-po.* |
| **Pulse** (of the body) | རྩ་ | *tsa.* |
| Do. *hon.* | ཕྱག་རྩ་ | *chha-tsa* |
| **Punctually** | ཏེན་ཏེན་བྱས་ནས། མ་འཕྱུག་པ་བྱས་ནས་ | *ten-ten cḱe-ne; ma-chhuḱ-pa cḱe-ne.* |
| Do. *hon.* | ཏེན་ཏེན་གནང་ནས། མ་འཕྱུག་པ་གནང་ནས་ | *ten-ten nang-ne; ma-chhuḱ-pa nang-ne.* |
| **Pungent** | ཁ་ཚ་པོ་ | *kha-tsha-po.* |
| Do. *hon.* | ཞལ་ཚ་པོ་ | *sḱe-tsha-po.* |
| **Punish, to** (by fine) | ཉེས་པ་བཏང་ (གཏོང་) བ་ | *nye-pa tang-wa.* |
| Do. *hon.* | བཀའ་ཉེས་གནང་བ་ | *ka-nye nang-wa.* |
| **Punish, to** (by beating) | ཁྲིམས་བཏང་ (གཏོང་) བ་ | *thrim tang-wa.* |
| Do. *hon.* | བཀའ་ཁྲིམས་གནང་བ་ | *ka-thrim nang-wa.* |
| **Punishment** (by fine) | ཉེས་པ། ཆད་པ་ | *nye-pa; chhe-pa.* |
| Do. *hon.* | བཀའ་ཉེས། བཀའ་ཆད་ | *ka-nye; ka-chhe.* |
| **Punishment** (by beating) | ཁྲིམས་ | *thrim.* |
| Do. *hon.* | བཀའ་ཁྲིམས་ | *ka-thrim.* |
| **Pupil** | བསླབ་ཕྲུག་ | *laṕ-thru.* |
| Do. (monk) | དགེ་ཕྲུག་ | *ge-thru.* |
| **Puppy** | ཨ་ཡོ་ (ཁྱི་ཕྲུག་) | *a-yo.* |

| | | |
|---|---|---|
| Purchase, to | ཉོ་བ་ | *nyo-wa.* |
| Do. *hon.* | གཟིགས་པ་ | *śi-pa.* |
| Pure | གཙང་མ་ | *tsang-ma.* |
| Purgative | འཁྲིན་སྨན། བཤམ་སྨན་ | *dri-men ; she-men.* |
| Purge, to | འཁྲིན་པ། བཤལ་བ་ | *drim-pa ; she-wa* |
| Do. *hon.* | འཁྲིན་པ་གནང་བ། བཤལ་ར་ (བ་) གནང་བ་ | *drim-pa nang-wa ; she-ra nang-wa.* |
| Purified | དག་པོ་ | *ťak-po.* |
| Purple | ཀུན་འབྲུམ་མདོག་ | *gün-drum-do.* |
| Purport | དོན་དག་ | *ťön-ťa.* |
| Do. *hon.* | སྐུ་དོན་ | *ku-ťön.* |
| Purpose, *s.* | དོན་དག་ | *ťön-ťa.* |
| Do. *hon.* | སྐུ་དོན་ | *ku-ťön.* |
| Purpose, to | སེམས་ལ་བསམ་པ་ | *sem-la sam-pa.* |
| Do. *hon.* | ཐུགས་ལ་དགོངས་པ་ | *thuǩ-la gong-pa.* |
| Purr, to | ངུག་པ་རྒྱབ་པ་ | *nguǩ-pa gyaṗ-pa.* |
| Purse | སྦ་ཁུག་ (སྣོད་ཁུག་) | *ba-khu.* |
| Do. *hon.* | ཕྱག་ཁུག་ | *chha-khu.* |
| Pursue, to | གཞུག་དེད་ཕྱིན་པ་ | *sǩuǩ-de chhim pa.* |
| Do. *hon.* | གཞུག་དེད་ཕེབ་པ་ | *sǩuǩ-de phe-pa.* |

| | | |
|---|---|---|
| Pus | རྣག་ | *na.* |
| Do. *hon.* | སྐུ་རྣག་ | *ku-na.* |
| Push, to | འབེད་ཀྱག་བཏང་ ( གཏོང་ ) བ་ | *be-kya tang-wa.* |
| Do. *hon.* | འབེད་ཀྱག་གཏོང་ང་ ( བ་ ) གནང་བ་ | *be-kya tong-nga nang-wa.* |
| Pustule | ཐོར་པ་ | *thor-pa.* |
| Do. *hon.* | མགུལ་ཐོར་ | *gü-thor.* |
| Put, to (place) | བཞག་པ་ ( འཇོག་པ་ ) | *sKak-pa.* |
| Do. *hon.* | བཞོག་ག་ ( འཇོག་པ་ ) གནང་བ་ | *sKok-ka nang-wa.* |
| Put in, to | ཆུག་པ་ ( འཇུག་པ་ ) | *chuk-pa.* |
| Do. *hon.* | འཇུག་ག་ ( པ་ ) གནང་བ་ | *juk-ka nang-wa.* |
| Put in order, to | སྒྲིག་པ་ | *drik-pa.* |
| Do. *hon.* | སྒྲིག་ག་ ( པ་ ) གནང་བ་ | *drik-ka nang-wa.* |
| Put on, to (clothes) | གོན་པ་ | *köm-pa.* |
| Do. *hon.* | བཞེས་པ་ | *sKe-pa.* |
| Put off, to (defer) | པ་རུ་བཞག་ ( འཇོག་ ) པ་ | *pa-ru sKak-pa.* |
| Do. *hon.* | པ་རུ་གཞོག་ག་ ( འཇོག་པ་ ) གནང་བ་ | *pa-ru sKok-ka nang-wa.* |
| Put off, to (divest) | ཕིས་པ་ ( འབུད་པ་ ) | *pi-pa.* |
| Do. *hon.* | ཕིས་ ( འབུད་ ) པ་གནང་བ་ | *pi-pa nang-wa.* |

| | | |
|---|---|---|
| Putrefy, to | རུལ་འགྲོ་བ་ | *rü-dro-wa.* |
| Putrid, to be | རུལ་བ་ | *rü-wa.* |
| Puzzled, to be | མགོ་འཐོམས་པ་ | *go-thom-pa.* |
| Do. *hon.* | དབུ་འཐོམས་པ་གནང་བ་ | *u-thom-pa nang-wa.* |

# Q

| | | |
|---|---|---|
| Quaint | ཡ་མཚན་པོ། ཁྱད་མཚར་པོ་ | *yam-tshen-po ; khye-tsha-po.* |
| Quake, to (shudder) | འདར་བ་ | *dar-wa.* |
| Do. *hon.* | སྐུ་འདར་སྐྱོན་པ་ | *kün-dar kyöm-pa.* |
| Qualified | འོས་པོ་ | *ö-po.* |
| Quality | ཡག་ཉེས། ཕུལ་ཁ་ | *ya-nye ; pü-kha.* |
| Quarrel | རྒྱབ་འདྲེ་ | *gyam-dre.* |
| Do. *hon.* | གསུང་འཁྲུག་ | *sung-thru.* |
| Quarrel, to | རྒྱབ་འདྲེ་རྒྱབ་པ་ | *gyam-dre gyaṕ-pa.* |
| Do. *hon.* | གསུང་འཁྲུག་སྐྱོན་པ་ | *sung-thru kyöm-pa.* |
| Quarrel, to pick a | སྙད་སྐོ་བ་ | *nye-ko-wa.* |
| Quarrelsome | རུ་ངར་པོ་ | *ru-ngar-po.* |
| Queen | རྒྱལ་མོ་ | *gye-mo.* |
| Queen-consort | རྒྱལ་པོའི་བཙུན་མོ་ | *gye-pö tsö-mo.* |
| Queer | ཁྱད་མཚར་པོ་ | *khye-tsha-po.* |
| Query, to (question) | དྲི་བ་ (འདྲི་བ་) | *t́ri-wa.* |
| Do. *hon.* | བཀའ་འདྲི་གནང་བ་ | *kan-dri nang-wa.* |
| Do. *inf.* to *sup.* | ཞུ་བ་ | *sḱu-wa.* |
| Question, to | དྲི་བ་ (འདྲི་བ་) | *t́ri-wa.* |
| Do. *hon.* | བཀའ་འདྲི་གནང་བ་ | *kan-dri nang-wa.* |

| | | |
|---|---|---|
| Queue (pig-tail) | ལྕང་ལོ་ | *chang-lo.* |
| Do. *hon.* | དབུ་ལྕང་ | *u-chang.* |
| Quick (rapid) | མགྱོགས་པོ་ | *gyoḱ-po.* |
| Do. *hon.* | རྩོལ་པོ་ | *tsö-po.* |
| Quick (active) | ཧུར་པོ་ | *hur-po.* |
| Do. (clever) | རིག་པ་ཆེན་པོ་ | *riḱ-pa chhem-po.* |
| Do. *hon.* | ཐུགས་རིག་ཆེན་པོ་ | *thu-riḱ chhem-po.* |
| Quick (irritable) | རུ་ངར་པོ་ | *ru-ngar-po.* |
| Do. *hon.* | ཐུགས་རུ་ངར་པོ་ | *thu-ru ngar-po.* |
| Quick (living) | གསོན་པོ་ | *söm-po.* |
| Quickly (rapidly) | མགྱོགས་པོར་ | *gyoḱ-po.* |
| Do. *hon.* | རྩོལ་པོར་ | *tsö-po.* |
| Quick-silver | དངུལ་ཆུ་ | *ngü-chhu.* |
| Quiet (of persons) | ཁ་ཉུང་ཉུང་ | *kha nyung-nyung.* |
| Do. *hon.* | ཞལ་ཉུང་ཉུང་ | *sḱe nyung-nyung.* |
| Quiet (of places) | ཁ་གུ་སིམ་པོ་ | *kha-ḱu sim-po.* |
| Do. (calm condition of country) | གླིང་ཆགས་པོ། འཇམ་ཐིང་ཐིང་ | *hling-chhaḱ-po; jam-thing-thing.* |
| Do. (of horses) | གླིང་བུ་ | *hling-ṕu.* |
| Quilt | ཉལ་གཟན་ | *nye-śen.* |

| | | |
|---|---|---|
| Quilt, *hon.* | གཟིམ་གཟན་ | *śim-śen.* |
| Quill-pen | སྒྲོ་སྨྱུག་ | *dro-nyu.* |
| Quit, to (depart) | འཐོན་པ། ཕྱིན་པ་ | *thöm-pa ; chhim-pa.* |
| Do. *hon.* | ཕེབ་པ་ | *phe-pa.* |
| Do. *h. hon.* | འཆིབ་སྒྱུ་གནང་བ་ | *chhiṕ-gyu nang-wa.* |
| Quit, to (a country, etc.) | བཞག་ནས་ཡོང་བ་ | *sḱa-ne yong-wa.* |
| Do. *hon.* | བཞག་ནས་ཕེབ་པ་ | *sḱa-ne phe-pa.* |
| Do. *h. hon.* | བཞག་ནས་འཆིབ་སྒྱུ་གནང་བ་ | *sḱa-ne chhiṕ-gyu nang-wa.* |
| Quite (used negatively) | བད་དེ། ཁྱོན་ནས་ | *be-t́e ; khyön-ne.* |
| Quite so ! | ད་ག་རང་རེད་ | *t́a-ḱa-rang-re.* |
| Do. *hon.* | ལགས་ད་ག་རང་རེད་ | *la t́a-ḱa-rang-re.* |
| Do. *h. hon.* | བཀའ་གནང་རང་རེད་ | *ka-na-rang-re.* |
| Quiver, *s.* | མདའ་དོང་ | *da-t́ong.* |
| Quiver, to (of animate things) | འདར་བ་ | *dar-wa.* |
| Do. *hon.* | སྐུ་འདར་སྐྱོན་པ་ | *kün-dar kyöm-pa.* |
| Quiver, to (of inanimate things) | འཁྲུག་པ་ | *thruḱ-pa.* |
| Quota | སྐལ་ལ་ ( སྐལ་བ་ ) | *ke-la.* |
| Do. *hon.* | སྐུ་སྐལ་ | *ku-ke.* |

# R

| | | |
|---|---|---|
| Rabbit | རི་གོང་ (རི་བོང་) | *ri-kong.* |
| Rabid | སྨྱོན་པ་ | *nyöm-pa.* |
| Rabid, to be | སྨྱོ་བ་ | *nyo-wa.* |
| Race, foot | མི་རྒྱུག་ | *mi-gyu.* |
| Do. horse | རྟ་རྒྱུག་ | *ta-gyu.* |
| Race (tribe) | མི་བརྒྱུད། རིགས་བརྒྱུད་ | *mi-gyü ; ri-gyü.* |
| Radiance | གཟི་བརྗིད། འོད་ | *śi-ji ; ö.* |
| Radiant | གཟི་བརྗིད་ཆེན་པོ། འོད་ཆེན་པོ་ | *śi-ji chhem-po ; ö chhem-po.* |
| Radish | ལ་ཕུག་ | *la-phu.* |
| Do. *hon.* | བཞེས་ལབ་ | *ske-lap.* |
| Rafter | ལྕམ་ | *cham.* |
| Rag | ཨ་ཚོར་ | *a-chho.* |
| Do. *hon.* | ཞལ་ཚོར་ | *ske-chho.* |
| Rage | ཚིག་པ། ཁོང་ཁྲོ་ | *tshik-pa ; khong-thro.* |
| Do. *hon.* | དགོངས་ཚུང་། རྣམ་མཁྱེན་ | *gong-tshung ; nam-khyen.* |
| Ragged | བཙབ་རལ་ (རྡུལ་པོ་) | *tsap-re.* |
| Railing (fence) | ར་བ་ | *ra-wa.* |
| Do. iron | ལྕགས་ཀྱི་ར་བ་ | *cha-kyi ra-wa.* |
| Raiment | དུག་ལོ་ | *tu-lo.* |

| | | |
|---|---|---|
| Raiment, *hon.* | ན་བཟའ་ | *nam-śa.* |
| Rain | ཆར་པ་ | *chhar-pa.* |
| Do. *hon.* | སྐུ་ཆར་ | *sKu-chhar.* |
| Rain, light shower of | སྤྲིན་ཆར་ | *tring-chhar.* |
| Do. mixed with hail | དྲག་ཆར་ | *t́rak-chhar.* |
| Rain, to | ཆར་པ་བཏང་ (གཏོང་) བ་ | *chhar-pa tang-wa.* |
| Do. *hon.* | སྐུ་ཆར་བཏང་ (གཏོང་) བ་ | *sKu-chhar tang-wa.* |
| Rain heavily, to | ཆར་པ་ཞེ་སྐྲག་རྒྱབ་པ་ | *chhar-pa sKe-tra gyap-pa.* |
| Rainbow | འཇའ་ | *ja.* |
| Raise up, to | ཡར་ཀྱག་ (འཁྱོག་) པ། ཡར་ལེན་པ་ | *yar-kyaK-pa; yar-lem-pa.* |
| Do. *hon.* | ཡར་ཀྱག་ག་ (འཁྱོག་པ་) གནང་བ་ | *yar-kyaK-Ka nang-wa.* |
| Raisin | རྒུན་འབྲུམ་དཀར་པོ་ | *gün-drum ka-po* |
| Rake | རྒྱ་གཟེབ་ | *gya-śep.* |
| Ram | ལུག་ཕོ་ | *luK-pho.* |
| Ramble, to | ཆམ་ཆམ་ (འཁྲམས་ འཁྲམས་) བྱེད་པ་ | *chham-chham cKe-pa.* |
| Do. *hon.* | སྐུ་ཆམ་ (འཁྲམས་) གནང་བ་ | *Kün-chham nang-wa.* |
| Ramrod of gun | སིན་འབིད་ | *sim-bi.* |

| | | |
|---|---|---|
| Rancid | ཁ་རྩུབ་པོ་ | *kha-tsup-po.* |
| Rancour | གནོད་སེམས་ | *nö-sem.* |
| Range, to (rove over) | ཆམ་ཆམ་ (འཁྱམས་འཁྱམས་) ལ་འགྲོ་བ་ | *chham-chham la dro-wa.* |
| Do. *hon.* | སྐུ་ཆམ་ (འཁྱམས་) ལ་ཕེབ་པ་ | *kün-chham la phe-pa.* |
| Do. *h. hon.* | སྐུ་ཆམ་ (འཁྱམས་) ལ་འཆིབ་རྒྱུ་གནང་བ་ | *kün-chham la chhip-gyu nang-wa.* |
| Rank (degree) | གོ་ས། གོ་གནས། རིམ་པ་ | *ko-sa ; ko-ne ; rim-pa.* |
| Do. (row) | གྲལ་ | *tre.* |
| Ransack, to | ཇག་པ་རྒྱབ་པ་ | *chak-pa gyap-pa* |
| Ransom (for killing a man) | སྟོང་ | *tong.* |
| Ransom, to | བླུ་བ་ | *lu-wa.* |
| Do. *hon.* | བླུ་བ་གནང་བ་ | *lu-wa nang-wa.* |
| Rap, *s.* (on door, etc.) | དག་དག་ | *tak-tak.* |
| Rap, to | དག་དག་བཏང་ (གཏོང་) བ་ | *tak-tak tang-wa.* |
| Do. *hon.* | དག་དག་གཏོང་ང་(བ་) གནང་བ་ | *tak-tak tong-nga nang-wa.* |
| Rapacious | འདོད་པ་ཆེན་པོ། ཧམ་པ་ཚ་པོ་ | *dö-pa chhem-po ; ham-pa tsha-po.* |
| Rapacity | ཧམ་པ་ | *ham-pa.* |
| Rapid | མགྱོགས་པོ་ | *gyok-po.* |

| | | |
|---|---|---|
| Rapid, *hon.* | རྩོལ་པོ་ | *tsö-po.* |
| Rare | དཀོན་པོ་ | *köm-po.* |
| Rascal | བསྟན་བཞིག། འཛབ་ཆེན་ | *ten-ski ; dzap-chhen.* |
| Rase, to | བཤིག་པ་ (འཇིག་པ་) | *shik-pa* |
| Do. *hon.* | བཤིག་ག་ (འཇིག་པ་) གནང་བ་ | *shik-ka nang-wa* |
| Rash, *adj.* | ཁ་མེད་མིག་མེད་ | *kha-me mik-me.* |
| Rat | ཙི་ཙི་ (ཙིག་གེ་) | *tsi-tsi.* |
| Rate (price) | གོང་ | *kong.* |
| Do. *hon.* | ཕྱགས་གོང་ | *ja-kong.* |
| Rate (tax) | ཁྲལ། འབབ་ | *thre ; bap.* |
| Do. on land | ས་ཁྲལ་ | *sa-thre.* |
| Ratify, to (confirm) | གཏན་ལྡན་བྱེད་པ་ | *ten-den cke-pa.* |
| Do. *hon.* | གཏན་ལྡན་གནང་བ་ | *ten-den nang-wa.* |
| Rattle, to, *v.t.* | དཀྲོག་དཀྲོག་བཏང་ (གཏོང་) བ་ | *trok-tro tang-wa.* |
| Do. *hon.* | དཀྲོག་དཀྲོག་གཏོང་ང་ (བ་) གནང་བ་ | *trok-tro tong-nga nang-wa.* |
| Ravage, to (rob) | ཇག་པ་རྒྱབ་པ་ | *chak-pa gyap-pa.* |
| Raven | ཕོ་རོག་ | *pho-ro.* |

| | | |
|---|---|---|
| Ravine | རོང་ | *rong.* |
| Raw (uncooked) | རྗེན་པ་ | *jem-pa.* |
| Do. (of weather) | གྲང་མོ། བསིལ་པོ་ | *t́rang-mo ; si-po.* |
| Do. *hon.* | སྐུ་བསིལ་པོ་ | *ku-si-po.* |
| Ray | འོད་གཟེར་ | *ö-śer.* |
| Raze, to | བཤིག་པ་ (འཇིག་པ་) | *shiḱ-pa.* |
| Do. *hon.* | བཤིག་ག་ (འཇིག་པ་) གནང་བ་ | *shiḱ-ḱa nang-wa.* |
| Razor | སྐྲ་གྲི་ | *tra-t́ri.* |
| Reach, to (by stretching hand, etc.) | སྙོབ་པ་ | *nyoṕ-pa.* |
| Do. *hon.* | སྙོབ་པ་གནང་བ་ | *nyoṕ-pa nang-wa.* |
| Reach, to (arrive at) | སླེབ་པ་ | *leṕ-pa* |
| Do. *hon.* | ཕེབ་པ་ | *ṕhe-pa.* |
| Do. *h. hon.* | འཆིབ་སྒྱུ་གནང་བ་ | *chhiṕ-gyu nang-wa.* |
| Read, to | ཀློག་པ་ | *loḱ-pa.* |
| Do. *hon.* | ཀློག་ག་ (པ་) གནང་བ་ | *loḱ-ḱa nang-wa.* |
| Do. *h. hon.* | ལྗགས་ཀློག་གནང་བ་ | *ja-lo nang-wa.* |
| Ready | གྲལ་སྒྲིག་ | *t́ra-dri.* |
| Ready, to make | གྲལ་སྒྲིག་བྱེད་པ་ | *t́ra-dri cḱe-pa.* |

| | | |
|---|---|---|
| **Ready, to make,** *hon.* | གྲལ་སྒྲིག་གནང་བ་ | *ťra-dri nang-wa.* |
| **Real** | ངོ་ཐོག། དངོས་ནས་ | *ngo-tho ; ngö-ne.* |
| Do. (of price, etc.) | ཡང་ཏིག་ | *yang-tiǩ.* |
| **Realise, to** (obtain) | འབྱོར་བ། ཐོབ་པ་ | *jor-wa ; thoṕ-pa.* |
| Do. *hon.* | ཕྱག་འབྱོར་ཡོང་བ་ | *chhan-jor yong-wa.* |
| **Realise, to** (understand) | ཤེས་པ། ཧ་གོ་བ་ | *she-pa; ha-ǩo-wa.* |
| Do. *hon.* | མཁྱེན་པ་ | *khyem-pa.* |
| Do. *h. hon.* | དགོངས་པ་རྟོགས་པ་ | *gong-pa toǩ-pa.* |
| **Really** | ངེས་པར། དངོས་ནས་དྲང་ནས་ | *nge-par; ngö-ne ťrang-ne.* |
| **Realm** (kingdom) | རྒྱལ་སྲིད་ | *gye-si.* |
| **Reap, to** | རྔ་བ་ | *nga-wa.* |
| Do. *hon.* | རྔས་པ་གནང་བ་ | *nge-pa nang-wa.* |
| **Reaper** | རྔ་མཁན་ | *nga-khen.* |
| Do. *hon.* | རྔ་བ་གནང་མཁན་ | *nga-a nang-khen.* |
| **Rear, in the** | རྒྱབ་ལ་ | *gyaṕ-la.* |
| **Reason** (mind) | བློ། སེམས་ | *lo ; sem.* |
| Do. *hon.* | ཐུགས་ | *thu.* |
| **Reason** (purpose) | དོན་དག་ | *ťon-ťa.* |
| Do. *hon.* | སྐུ་དོན་ | *ku-ťön.* |
| **Reason, to** (argue) | རྩེ་རྒྱབ་པ་ | *tse gyaṕ-pa.* |

| | | |
|---|---|---|
| Reason, to (argue), *hon.* | ཞལ་རྩེ་སྐྱོན་པ་ | *sḱe-tse kyöm-pa.* |
| Reasoning | རྩོད་པ་ | *tsö-pa.* |
| Rebel, to | སྡེ་འཁྲུག་པ་ | *de-thruḱ-pa.* |
| Rebellion | སྡེ་འཁྲུག་ | *de-thru.* |
| Rebuke, *s.* | གཤེ་གཤེ་ | *she-she.* |
| Do. *hon.* | བཀའ་བཀྱོན་ | *kaṕ-kyön.* |
| Rebuke, to | གཤེ་གཤེ་བཏང་ (གཏོང་) བ་ | *she-she tang-wa.* |
| Do. *hon.* | བཀའ་བཀྱོན་གནང་བ་ | *kaṕ-kyön nang-wa.* |
| Recede, to (retreat) | ཕྱིར་ལོག་རྒྱབ་པ་ | *chhi-lo gyaṕ-pa.* |
| Do. *hon.* | ཕྱིར་ལོག་སྐྱོན་པ་ | *chhi-lo kyöm-pa.* |
| Receipt | འཛིན་ | *dzin.* |
| Do. *hon.* | ཕྱག་འཛིན་ | *chhan-dzin.* |
| Receive, to | འབྱོར་བ། ཐོབ་པ་ | *jor-wa; thoṕ-pa.* |
| Do. *hon.* | ཕྱག་འབྱོར་ཡོང་བ་ | *chhan-jor yong-wa.* |
| Recent | གསར་པ་ | *sa-pa.* |
| Recently | ཁ་སང་ནས་ | *kha-sang-ne.* |
| Recite, to | ཆོས་ཀློག་པ་ | *chhö loḱ-pa.* |
| Do. *hon.* | ཆོས་ཀློག་ག་ (པ་) གནང་བ་ | *chhö loḱ-ḱa nang-wa.* |
| Reckless | ཁ་མེད་མིག་མེད་ | *kha-me miḱ-me.* |
| Reckon, to | རྩིས་རྒྱབ་པ་ | *tsi-gyaṕ-pa.* |

| | | |
|---|---|---|
| Reckon, to, *hon.* | ཕྱགས་རྩིས་སྐྱོན་པ་ | *ja-tsi kyöm-pa.* |
| Reckoning | རྩིས་ | *tsi.* |
| Do. *hon.* | ཕྱགས་རྩིས་ | *ja-tsi.* |
| Recline, to | ཉལ་ནས་བསྡད་ (སྡོད་) པ་ | *nye-ne de-pa.* |
| Do. *hon.* | གཟིམ་ནས་བཞུགས་པ་ | *śim-ne sǩu-pa.* |
| Recluse | སྒོམ་ཆེན་ | *gom-chhen.* |
| Recognise, to (a person) | ངོ་ཤེས་པ་ | *ngo-shem-pa.* |
| Do. *hon.* | ཐུགས་ངོ་མཁྱེན་པ།ཞལ་ཚོར་བ་ | *thu-ngo khyem-pa; she-tsho-wa.* |
| Recollect, to | དྲན་གསོ་བ་ | *t́ren-so-wa.* |
| Do. *hon.* | ཐུགས་དྲན་གསོ་བ་གནང་བ་ | *thu-tren so-wa nang-wa.* |
| Recollection | དྲན་པ་ | *t́rem-pa.* |
| Do. *hon.* | ཐུགས་དྲན་ | *thu-t́ren.* |
| Reconcile, to | ནང་སྒྲིག་བྱེད་པ་ | *nang-dri cǩe-pa.* |
| Do. *hon.* | ནང་སྒྲིག་གནང་བ་ | *nang-dri nang-wa.* |
| Reconciliation | ནང་སྒྲིག་ | *nang-dri.* |
| Record | ཐོ་ | *tho.* |
| Do. *hon.* | ཕྱག་ཐོ་ | *chha-tho.* |
| Recover, to (health) | དྲག་པ་ | *t́raḱ-pa.* |
| Do. *hon.* | སྐུ་དྭངས་པ་ | *ku-t́ang-pa.* |

| | | |
|---|---|---|
| Recover, to (find) | རྙེད་པ་ | *nye-pa.* |
| Do. *hon.* | རྙེད་པ་གནང་བ་ | *nye-pa nang-wa.* |
| Recreation (game) | རྩེད་མོ་ | *tse-mo.* |
| Do. *hon.* | སྐུ་རྩེད་ | *ku-tse.* |
| Recreation, to have | ཐུགས་སྤྲོ་བཏང་ (གཏོང་) བ་ | *thu-tro tang-wa.* |
| Do. *hon.* | ཐུགས་སྤྲོ་གཏོང་ང་ (བ་) གནང་བ་ | *thu-tro tong-nga nang-wa.* |
| Rectify, to (correct) | ཞུ་དག་བྱེད་པ་ | *sḱu-ťa cḱe-pa.* |
| Do. *hon.* | ཞུ་དག་གནང་བ་ | *sḱu-ťa nang-wa.* |
| Red | དམར་པོ་ | *ma-po.* |
| Redeem, to | བླུ་བ་ | *lu-wa.* |
| Do. *hon.* | བླུ་བ་གནང་བ་ | *lu-wa nang-wa.* |
| Redeemer | སྐྱབས་མགོན་ | *kyam-gön.* |
| Redemption | ཐར་པ་ | *thar-pa.* |
| Reduce in number, to | ཉུང་རུ་ (དུ་) བཟོ་བ་ | *nyung-ru śo-wa.* |
| Do. *hon.* | ཉུང་རུ་ (དུ་) བཟོ་བ་གནང་བ་ | *nyung-ru śo-wa nang-wa.* |
| Reduce in price, to | གོང་བཅག་ (གཅོག་) པ་ | *ḱong chaḱ-pa.* |
| Do. *hon.* | ལྗགས་གོང་གཅོག་ག་ (པ་) གནང་བ་ | *ja-ḱong choḱ-ḱa nang-wa.* |
| Reduce, to (conquer) | རྒྱལ་བ། ཀླག་འཁས་པ་ | *gye-wa ; la khe-pa.* |

| | | |
|---|---|---|
| Reduce, to (conquer), *hon.* | རྒྱལ་ར་ (བ་) གནང་བ། གླག་འཁབས་ར་ (པ་) གནང་བ་ | *gye-ra nang-wa ; la khe-ra nang-wa.* |
| Reduce, to (degrade) | ཀོ་གནས་བབ་པ་ | *ko-ne pap-pa.* |
| Reed | སྨྱུག་མ་ | *nyung-ma.* |
| Reel, to (stagger) | འཁྱོར་ནས་འགྲོ་བ་ | *khyor-ne dro-wa.* |
| Do. *hon.* | སྐུ་འཁྱོར་ནས་ཕེབ་པ་ | *ku-khyor-ne phe-pa.* |
| Do. *h. hon.* | སྐུ་འཁྱོར་ནས་འཆིབ་རྒྱུ་ གནང་བ་ | *ku-khyor-ne chhip-gyu nang-wa.* |
| Reflect, to | བསམ་བློ་བཏང་ (གཏོང་) བ་ | *sam-lo tang-wa.* |
| Do. *hon.* | ཐུགས་བསམ་བཞེས་པ་ | *thu-sam sKe-pa.* |
| Reform, to (amend) | བཅོ་སྐྱོར་བྱེད་པ་ | *ś o-kyor cKe-pa.* |
| Do. *hon.* | བཅོ་སྐྱོར་གནང་བ་ | *ś o-kyor nang-wa.* |
| Refrain, to (forbear) | ཁོག་པ་བྱེད་པ་ | *khok-pa cKe-pa.* |
| Do. *hon.* | ཐུགས་ཁོག་གནང་བ་ | *thu-kho nang-wa* |
| Refuge (shelter) | སྐྱབས་གནས་ | *kyam-ne.* |
| Refuse, to (withhold) | མི་····སྟེར་བ་ | *mi...ter-wa.* |
| Do. *hon.* | མི་····གནང་བ་ | *mi...nang-wa.* |
| Refuse, to (a request) | མི་····ཉན་པ་ | *mi...nyem-pa.* |
| Do. *hon.* | མི་····གསན་པ་ | *mi...śem-pa.* |
| Regard, to (look at) | ལྟ་བ་ | *ta-wa.* |

| | | |
|---|---|---|
| Regard, to (look at), ***hon.*** | གཟིགས་པ་ | *śi-pa.* |
| Regarding (concerning) | དོན་ལ། སྐོར་ལ་ | *tön-la ; kor-la.* |
| Regent | རྒྱལ་ཚབ་ | *gye-tshap.* |
| Regent of Tibet | བོད་རྒྱལ་པོ་ | *pö-gye-po.* |
| Regiment | དམག་དཔུང་ | *ma-pung.* |
| Region | ལུང་པ་ | *lung-pa.* |
| Register, *s.* | ཐོ་ | *tho.* |
| Do. *hon.* | ཕྱག་ཐོ་ | *chha-tho.* |
| Register, to | ཐོ་བྲིས་པ་ (འབྲི་པ་) | *tho-tri-pa.* |
| Do. *hon.* | ཕྱག་ཐོ་སྐྱོན་པ་ | *chha-tho kyöm-pa.* |
| Regret, *s.* (heavy sorrow) | སྡུག་བསྔལ། སེམས་འཁྲལ་ | *du-nge ; sem-thre.* |
| Do. *hon.* | ཐུགས་འཁྲལ་ | *thuk-thre.* |
| Regret, *s.* (repentance) | འགྱོད་པ་ | *gyö-pa.* |
| Do. *hon.* | ཐུགས་འགྱོད་ | *thung-gyö.* |
| Regret, to, *v.i.* (heavy sorrow) | སྡུག་བསྔལ་བྱེད་པ། མྱ་ངན་བྱེད་པ་ | *du-nge che-pa ; nya-ngen che-pa.* |
| Do. *hon.* | ཐུགས་ངན་གནང་བ་ | *thu-ngen nang-wa.* |
| Regret, to, *v.i.* (in lesser matters) | སེམས་སྐྱོ་བ། སེམས་སྡུག་པ་ | *sem-kyo-wa ; sem-duk-pa.* |
| Do. *hon.* | ཐུགས་སེམས་སྐྱོ་བ་གནང་བ་ | *thu-sem kyo-wa nang-wa.* |
| Regulate, to (arrange) | སྒྲིག་པ་ | *drik-pa.* |

| | | |
|---|---|---|
| Regulate, to (arrange), *hon.* | སྒྲིག་ག་ (པ་) གནང་བ་ | *drik-ka nang-wa.* |
| Regulation (law) | ཁྲིམས་ | *thrim.* |
| Do. *hon.* | བཀའ་ཁྲིམས་ | *ka-thrim.* |
| Regulation (religious) | ཆོས་ཁྲིམས་ | *chhö-thrim.* |
| Reign, *s.* | རྒྱལ་སྲིད་ | *gye-si.* |
| Reign, to | རྒྱལ་སྲིད་གནང་བ་ | *gye-si nang-wa.* |
| Reinforcement | རྒྱབ་སྣོན་ | *gyam-nön.* |
| Reins | སྲབ་ཐག་ | *trap-tha.* |
| Reject, to | སྤང་བ་ | *pang-wa.* |
| Do. *hon.* | སྤོང་ང་ (བ་) གནང་བ་ | *pong-nga nang-wa.* |
| Rejoice, to | དགའ་བ་ | *ga-wa.* |
| Do. *hon.* | མཉེས་པོ་གནང་བ་ | *nye-po nang-wa.* |
| Do. *h. hon.* | ཐུགས་དགྱེས་པོ་གནང་བ་ | *thu-gye-po nang-wa.* |
| Rejoicing, *s.* | དགའ་ཚོར་ | *ga-tshor.* |
| Relate, to | བཤད་པ་ | *she-pa.* |
| Do. *hon.* | གསུང་བ་ | *sung-wa.* |
| Relation | ཉེ་བ་ | *nye-wa.* |
| Do. *hon.* | སྐུ་གཉེན་ | *ku-nyen.* |
| Relative, *s.* | ཉེ་བ་ | *nye-wa.* |
| Do. *hon.* | སྐུ་གཉེན་ | *ku-nyen.* |

| | | |
|---|---|---|
| Relative to (concerning) | དོན་ལ། སྐོར་ལ་ | *t́ön-la; kor-la.* |
| Release, to | ཐར་ར་ (བར་) བྱེད་པ། བཏང་བ་ (གཏོང་བ་) | *thar-ra cḱe-pa; tang-wa.* |
| Do. *hon.* | ཐར་ར་ (བར་) གནང་བ། གཏོང་ང་ (བ་) གནང་བ་ | *thar-ra nang-wa; tong-nga nang-wa.* |
| Release, to (by ransom) | བླུ་བ་ | *lu-wa.* |
| Do. *hon.* | བླུ་བ་གནང་བ་ | *lu-wa nang-wa.* |
| Released, to be | ཐར་བ་ | *thar-wa.* |
| Relentless, to be | སྙིང་རྗེ་མེད་པ་ | *nying-je me-pa.* |
| Do. *hon.* | ཐུགས་རྗེ་མེད་པ་ | *thuḱ-je me-pa.* |
| Reliable | བློས་ (བློ་) ཁེལ་བ་ | *lö khe-wa.* |
| Do. *hon.* | ཐུགས་བློས་ཁེལ་བ་ | *thu-lö khe-wa.* |
| Reliance | བློ་གཏད་ | *lo-te.* |
| Relief (help) | རོགས་ | *ro.* |
| Do. *hon.* | མགོ་འདྲེན་ | *gön-dren.* |
| Relief (in coming troops) | རྗེས་ཚབ་ | *je-tshaṕ.* |
| Relieve, to (help) | རོགས་བྱེད་པ་ | *ro cḱe-pa.* |
| Do. *hon.* | མགོ་འདྲེན་གནང་བ་ | *gön-dren nang-wa.* |
| Religion | ཆོས་ | *chhö.* |
| Religion, to practise | ཆོས་བྱེད་པ་ | *chhö cḱe-pa.* |

| | | |
|---|---|---|
| Religion, to practise, *hon.* | སྐུ་ཆོས་གནང་བ་ | *ku-chhö nang-wa.* |
| Religious | ཆོས་སེམས་ཆེན་པོ་ | *chhö-sem chhem-po.* |
| Relinquish, to (abandon) | སྤང་བ་ | *pang-wa.* |
| Do. *hon.* | སྤོང་ང་ (བ་) གནང་བ་ | *pong-nga nang-wa.* |
| Relish, *s.* (taste) | བྲོ་བ་ | *t́ro-a.* |
| Do. *hon.* | ལྗགས་བྲོ་ | *ja-t́ro.* |
| Rely on, to | བློས་ (བློ་) བཀལ་བ་ | *lö kel-wa.* |
| Do. *hon.* | ཐུགས་བློ་བཀལ་ར་ (བ་) གནང་བ་ | *thu-lo ke-ra nang-wa.* |
| Remain, to | བསྡད་པ་ (སྡོད་པ་) | *de-pa.* |
| Do. *hon.* | བཞུགས་པ་ | *sḱu-pa.* |
| Do. *h. hon.* | བཞུགས་གདན་འཛག་པ་ | *sḱu-den jaḱ-pa.* |
| Remainder | ལྷག་མ་ | *hla-ma.* |
| Remains (corpse) | རོ་ | *ro.* |
| Do *hon.* | སྐུ་སྤུར། སྐུ་ཕུང་ | *ku-pur ; ku-phung.* |
| Do. *hon.* (of lamas) | སྐུ་གདུང་ | *ku-dung.* |
| Remarkable | ཁྱད་མཚར་པོ་ | *khye-tsha-po.* |
| Remedy, to | བཅོས་ཐབས་བྱེད་པ་ | *chö-thaṕ cḱe-pa.* |
| Do. *hon.* | བཅོས་ཐབས་གནང་བ་ | *chö-thaṕ nang-wa.* |
| Remember, to | དྲན་གསོ་བ་ | *t́ren-so-wa.* |

| | | |
|---|---|---|
| Remember, to, *hon.* | ཐུགས་དྲན་གསོ་བ་གནང་བ་ | *thu-t́ren so-wa nang-wa.* |
| Remembrance | དྲན་པ་ | *t́rem-pa.* |
| Do. *hon.* | ཐུགས་དྲན་ | *thu-t́ren.* |
| Remind, to | དྲན་གསོས་བཏང་ (གཏོང་) བ་ | *t́ren-sö tang-wa.* |
| Do. *hon.* | དྲན་གསོས་གནང་བ་ | *t́ren-sö nang-wa.* |
| Do. *inf.* to *sup.* | བསྙེལ་གསོལ་ཞུ་བ་ | *nye-sö sḱu-wa.* |
| Reminder | དྲན་གསོ་ | *t́ren-so.* |
| Do. *hon.* | བསྙེལ་གསོ་ | *nye-so.* |
| Remorse (regret) | འགྱོད་པ་ | *gyö-pa.* |
| Do. *hon.* | ཐུགས་འགྱོད་ | *thung-gyö.* |
| Remorseless, to be (merciless) | སྙིང་རྗེ་མེད་པ་ | *nying-je me-pa.* |
| Do. *hon.* | ཐུགས་རྗེ་མེད་པ་ | *thuḱ-je me-pa.* |
| Remote | ཐག་རིང་པོ་ | *tha-ring-po.* |
| Do. *hon.* | ཕེབ་ཐག་རིང་པོ་ | *phep̍-tha-ring-po.* |
| Remove, to | ཕར་ཤིད་པ་ | *pha shi-pa.* |
| Do. *hon.* | ཕར་ཤིད་པ་གནང་བ་ | *pha shi-pa nang-wa.* |
| Remove, to (take off) | ཕྱིས་པ་ (འབུད་པ་) | *pi-pa.* |
| Do. *hon.* | བསིལ་ར་ (བ་) གནང་བ་ | *si-ra nang-wa.* |
| Remuneration | རྔན་པ་ | *ngem-pa.* |
| Rend, to | གཤག་པ་ | *shaḱ-pa.* |

| | | |
|---|---|---|
| **Rend, to,** *hon.* | གཤག་ག་ (པ་) གནང་བ་ | *śhak-ḱa nang-wa.* |
| **Renounce, to (sins, certain kinds of foods, etc.)** | སྤང་བ་ | *pang-wa.* |
| **Do.** *hon.* | སྤོང་ང་ (བ་) གནང་བ་ | *pong-nga nang-wa.* |
| **Renown** | སྐད་གྲགས་ | *ke-ťra.* |
| **Do.** *hon.* | སྙན་གྲགས་ | *nyen-ťra.* |
| **Renowned** | མིང་ཆེན་པོ་ | *ming chhem-po.* |
| **Do.** *hon.* | མཚན་ཆེན་པོ་ | *tshen chhem-po.* |
| **Rent** | སེར་ཀ་ | *se-ka.* |
| **Rent of a house** | ཁང་གླ་ | *khang-la.* |
| **Do.** *hon.* | གཟིམ་ཁང་གི་གླ་ | *śim-khang ḱi-la.* |
| **Rent, to (house)** | ཁང་གླ་བྱས་ནས་བསྡད་ (སྡོད་) པ་ | *khang-la cḱe-ne de-pa.* |
| **Do.** *hon.* | ཁང་གླ་གནང་ནས་བཞུགས་པ་ | *khang-la nang-ne sḱu-pa.* |
| **Repair, to** | གསོས་སྐྱོར་བྱེད་པ་ | *sö-kyor cḱe-pa.* |
| **Do.** *hon.* | གསོས་སྐྱོར་གནང་བ་ | *sö-kyor nang-wa.* |
| **Repair, to (a house)** | ཞིག་གསོས་བྱེད་པ་ | *sḱik-sö cḱe-pa.* |
| **Do.** *hon.* | ཞིག་གསོས་གནང་བ་ | *sḱik-sö nang-wa.* |
| **Repast** | ཁ་ལག། ལྟོ་ | *kha-la; to.* |
| **Do.** *hon.* | ཞལ་ལག་ | *sḱe-la.* |

| | | |
|---|---|---|
| Repay, to | སྐྱིན་ཚབ་སྤྲད་པ་ | *khin-tshaṗ tre-pa.* |
| Do. *hon.* | སྐྱིན་ཚབ་གནང་བ་ | *kyin-tshaṗ ṅang-wa.* |
| Do. *inf.* to *sup.* | སྐྱིན་ཚབ་ཕུལ་བ་ | *kyin-tshaṗ phü-wa.* |
| Repeat, to (recite) | ཆོས་ཀློག་པ་ | *chhö-loḱ-pa.* |
| Do. *hon.* | ཆོས་ཀློག་ག་ (པ་) གནང་བ་ | *chhö-loḱ-ḱa nang-wa.* |
| Repent, to | འགྱོད་པ་སྐྱེད་པ་ | *gyö-pa kye-pa.* |
| Do. *hon.* | ཐུགས་འགྱོད་གནང་བ་ | *thung-gyö nang-wa.* |
| Repentance | འགྱོད་པ་ | *gyö-pa.* |
| Do. *hon.* | ཐུགས་འགྱོད་ | *thung-gyö.* |
| Reply, *s.* | ལན་ | *len.* |
| Do. *hon.* | བཀའ་ལན་ | *ka-len.* |
| Reply to a letter, *s.* | ཡིག་ལན་ | *yiḱ-len.* |
| Do. *hon.* | ཕྱག་བྲིས་བཀའ་ལན་ | *chha-ri ka-len.* |
| Reply, to | ལན་རྒྱབ་པ་ | *len gyaṗ-pa.* |
| Do. *hon.* | ལྗགས་ལན་སྐྱོན་པ་ | *ja-len kyöm-pa.* |
| Reply, to (letter) | ཡིག་ལན་བཏང་ (གཏོང་) བ་ | *yiḱ-len tang-wa.* |
| Do. *hon.* | ཕྱག་བྲིས་བཀའ་ལན་གནང་བ་ | *chha-ri ka-len nang-wa.* |
| Report (rumour) | སྐད་ཆ། གཏམ་ | *ke-chha ; tam.* |
| Report, to | སྙན་ཞུ་བཏང་ (གཏོང་) བ་ | *nyen-sḱu tang-wa.* |
| Do. *inf.* to *sup.* | སྙན་ཞུ་ཕུལ་ (འབུལ་) བ་ | *nyen-sḱu phü-wa.* |

| | | |
|---|---|---|
| Report, to (after investigation), *inf.* to *sup.* | ཁྲ་མ་ཕུལ་ (འབུལ་) བ་ | *thra-ma phü-wa.* |
| Do. *hon.* | ཁྲ་མ་འབུལ་ར་ (བ་) གནང་བ་ | *thra-ma bü-ra nang-wa.* |
| Repository | བང་མཛོད་ | *ṕang-dzö.* |
| Representative, *s.* | ཚབ། འཐུས་མི་ | *tsh́aṕ; thü-mi.* |
| Do. *hon.* | སྐུ་ཚབ་ | *ku tshaṕ.* |
| Reprimand, *s.* | གཤེ་གཤེ་ | *she-she.* |
| Do. *hon.* | བཀའ་བཀྱོན་ | *kaṕ-kyön.* |
| Reprimand, to | གཤེ་གཤེ་བཏང་ (གཏོང་) བ་ | *she-she tang-wa.* |
| Do. *hon.* | བཀའ་བཀྱོན་གནང་བ་ | *kaṕ-kyön nang-wa.* |
| Reproduce, to (copy) | དཔེ་ཤུ་བ་ | *pe-shu-wa.* |
| Do. *hon.* | དཔེ་ཤུ་བ་གནང་བ་ | *pe-shu-wa nang-wa.* |
| Reproduce, to (imitate) | མིག་འདྲེན་བྱེད་པ་ | *miḱ-dren cḱe-pa.* |
| Repulsive | སྐྱུག་བྲོ་པོ་ | *kyuḱ-ťro-po.* |
| Reprove, to | གཤེ་གཤེ་བཏང་ (གཏོང་) བ་ | *she-she tang-wa.* |
| Do. *hon.* | བཀའ་བཀྱོན་གནང་བ་ | *kaṕ-kyön nang-wa.* |
| Reputable | ཡ་རབས་ | *ya-raṕ.* |
| Reputation (fame) | སྐད་གྲགས་ | *ke-ťra.* |
| Do. *hon.* | སྙན་གྲགས་ | *nyen-ťra.* |
| Repute, *s.* | སྐད་གྲགས་ | *ke-ťra.* |

| | | |
|---|---|---|
| Repute, *s. hon.* | སྙན་གྲགས་ | *nyen-ťra.* |
| Request, *s.* | ཞུ་བ་ | *sǩu-wa.* |
| Request, to | ཞུ་བ་ | *sǩu-wa.* |
| Do. *hon.* | ཞུ་བ་གནང་བ་ | *sǩu-wa nang-wa.* |
| Require, to | དགོས་པ་ | *gö-pa.* |
| Do. *hon.* | ཐུགས་དགོས་པ་ | *thu-gö-pa.* |
| Requisite | དགོས་པ་ | *gö-pa.* |
| Do. *hon.* | ཐུགས་ཁོ་ | *thung-kho.* |
| Requite, to (revenge) | དགྲ་ལན་ལོག་པ་ | *dra-len loǩ-pa.* |
| Do. *hon.* | དགྲ་ལན་ལོག་ག་ (པ་) གནང་བ་ | *dra-len loǩ-ǩa nang-wa.* |
| Rescue, to | བསྐྱབས་པ་ (སྐྱོབ་པ།) སྐྱོང་བ་ | *kyap̌-pa; kyong-wa.* |
| Do. *hon.* | སྐྱབས་འཇུག་གནང་བ་ | *kyam-ǰuǩ nang-wa.* |
| Resent, to | འཚེར་བ་ | *tsher-wa.* |
| Do. *hon.* | ཐུགས་འཚེར་གནང་བ་ | *thu-tsher nang-wa.* |
| Resentment | ཚིག་པ།, ཁོང་ཁྲོ་ | *tshiǩ-pa; khong-thro.* |
| Do. *hon.* | དགོངས་ཚུང་། རྣམ་མཁྱེན་ | *gong-tshung; nam-khyen.* |
| Resentment, to cause | ཁོང་ཁྲོ་སློང་བ་ | *khong-thro lang-wa.* |
| Do. *hon.* | དགོངས་པ་དཀྲུག་པ་ | *gong-pa truǩ pa.* |

| | | |
|---|---|---|
| Reside, to | བསྡད་པ་ (སྡོད་པ་) | *de-pa.* |
| Do. *hon.* | བཞུགས་པ་ | *sḱu-pa.* |
| Do. *h. hon.* | བཞུགས་གདན་འཇག་པ་ | *sḱu-den jaḱ-pa.* |
| Residence (house) | ཁང་པ། ནང་། སྡོད་ས་ | *khang-pa ; nang ; dö-sa.* |
| Do. *hon.* | གཟིམ་ཁང་། བཞུགས་ས་ | *śim-khang ; sḱuḱ-sa.* |
| Do. *h. hon.* | གཟིམ་ཤག། བཞུགས་གདན་འཇག་ས་ | *śim-sha ; sḱu-den ja-sa.* |
| Resident | སྡོད་མཁན་ | *dö-khen.* |
| Do. *hon.* | བཞུགས་མཁན་ | *sḱu-khen.* |
| Do. *h. hon.* | བཞུགས་གདན་འཇག་མཁན་ | *sḱu-den ja-khen.* |
| Residue | ལྷག་མ་ | *hla-ma.* |
| Resistless, to be | བཀག་…མི་ཐུབ་པ་ | *kaḱ…mi-thuṕ-pa.* |
| Resolute | བརྟན་པོ་ | *tem-po.* |
| Resolve, to (decide) | ཐག་བཅད་ (གཅོད་) པ་ | *tha-che-pa.* |
| Do. *hon.* | ཐག་གཅོད་པ་གནང་བ་ | *tha-chö-pa nang-wa.* |
| Do. *h. hon.* | ཐུགས་ཐག་གཅོད་པ་གནང་བ་ | *thu-tha chö-pa nang-wa.* |
| Respect to, with | དོན་ལ། སྐོར་ལ་ | *ťön-la ; kor-la.* |
| Respect (reverence) | བསྙེན་བཀུར་ | *nyen-kur.* |
| Respect, to | བསྙེན་བཀུར་བྱེད་པ་ | *nyen-kur cḱe-pa.* |
| Do. *inf.* to *sup.* | བསྙེན་བཀུར་ཞུ་བ་ | *nyen-kur sḱu-wa.* |

| | | |
|---|---|---|
| Respectable (socially) | ཡ་རབས་ | *ya-rap̌.* |
| Respectful language | ཞེ་ས་ | *sk̃e-sa.* |
| Respecting (concerning) | དོན་ལ། སྐོར་ལ་ | *tön-la; kor-la.* |
| Respiration | དབུགས་ | *u.* |
| Do. *hon.* | ལྗགས་དབུགས་ | *ja-u.* |
| Resplendence | གཟི་བརྗིད་ | *śi-ji.* |
| Resplendent | གཟི་བརྗིད་ཆེན་པོ། འོད་ཆེན་པོ་ | *śi-ji chhem-po; ö chhem-po.* |
| Respond, to | ལན་རྒྱབ་པ་ | *len gyap̌-pa.* |
| Do. *hon.* | ལྗགས་ལན་སྐྱོན་པ་ | *ja-len kyöm-pa.* |
| Responsibility | ཁག། འགན་ | *kha; gen.* |
| Do. *hon.* | ཐུགས་ཁག་ | *thu-kha.* |
| Responsible, to become | ཁས་ཁྱག་ (ཁག་ཐེག་) པ་ | *khe-khyak̃-pa.* |
| Do. *hon.* | ཞལ་ཁྱག་ (ཐེག་) གནང་བ་ | *sk̃e-khya nang-wa.* |
| Rest (for Tibetan gun) | མེ་མདའི་རུ་ | *men-de ru.* |
| Do. *hon.* | ཕྱག་མདའི་རུ་ | *chhan-de ru.* |
| Rest, to | ངལ་གསོ་བ་ | *nge-so-wa.* |
| Do. *hon.* | སྐུ་ངལ་གསོ་བ་གནང་བ་ | *ku-nge so-wa nang-wa.* |
| Rest, to (elbows on table, etc.) | སྦོ་སྙེ་རྒྱབ་པ་ | *bo-nye gyap̌-pa.* |
| Do. *hon.* | སྐུ་སྙེ་སྐྱོན་པ་ | *ku-nye kyöm-pa.* |
| Rest, to (lean back) | རྒྱབ་སྙེ་རྒྱབ་པ་ | *gyam-nye gyap̌-pa.* |

| | | |
|---|---|---|
| Rest, to (lean back), *hon.* | སྐུ་སྙེ་སྐྱོན་པ་ | *ku-nye kyöm-pa.* |
| Rest, to (lie down) | ཉལ་བསྡད་ (སྡོད་) པ་ | *nye-de-pa.* |
| Do. *hon.* | གཟིམ་བཞུགས་པ་ | *śim-sḱu-pa.* |
| Restaurant | ཟ་ཁང་ | *śa-khang.* |
| Restrain, to | བཀག་པ་ (འགེགས་པ་) | *kaḱ-pa.* |
| Do. *hon.* | བཀག་ག་ (འགེགས་པ་) གནང་བ་ | *kaḱ-ḱa nang-wa.* |
| Result | སྙིང་པོ་ | *nying-po.* |
| Retain, to | བཞག་པ་ (འཇོག་པ་) | *sḱaḱ-pa.* |
| Do. *hon.* | གཞོག་ག་ (འཇོག་པ་) གནང་བ་ | *sḱoḱ-ḱa nang-wa.* |
| Retaliate, to | དགྲ་ལན་ལོག་པ་ | *dra-len loḱ-pa.* |
| Do. *hon.* | དགྲ་ལན་ལོག་ག་ (པ་) གནང་བ་ | *dra-len loḱ-ḱa nang-wa.* |
| Retaliation | དགྲ་ལན་ | *dra-len.* |
| Retard to (obstruct) | བཀག་པ་ (འགེགས་པ་) | *kaḱ-pa.* |
| Do. *hon.* | བཀག་ག་ (འགེགས་པ་) གནང་བ་ | *kaḱ-ḱa nang-wa.* |
| Retinue | འཁོར་གཡོག་ | *khor-yo.* |
| Do. *hon.* | ཞབས་ཕྱི་ | *sḱaṕ-chhi.* |

| | | |
|---|---|---|
| Retire, to (retreat) | ཕྱིར་ལོག་རྒྱབ་པ་ | *chhi-lo gyaṕ-pa.* |
| Do. *hon.* | ཕྱིར་ལོག་སྐྱོན་པ་ | *chhi-lo kyöm-pa.* |
| Retreat, *s.* (shelter) | སྐྱབས་གནས་ | *kyam-ne.* |
| Retreat, to | ཕྱིར་ལོག་རྒྱབ་པ་ | *chhi-lo gyaṕ-pa.* |
| Do. *hon.* | ཕྱིར་ལོག་སྐྱོན་པ་ | *chhi-lo kyöm-pa.* |
| Return, to | ལོག་པ་ | *loḱ-pa.* |
| Do. *hon.* | ཚུར་ཕེབ་པ་ | *tshur-phe-pa.* |
| Do. *h. hon.* | ཚུར་འཆིབ་རྒྱུ་གནང་བ་ | *tshur-chhiṕ-gyu nang-wa.* |
| Return, to, *v.t.* (property committed to one's charge) | རྩིས་སྤྲོད་པ་ | *tsi tre-pa.* |
| Do. *hon.* | ཕྱགས་རྩིས་གནང་བ་ | *ja-tsi nang-wa.* |
| Revenge, *s.* | དགྲ་ལན་ | *dra-len.* |
| Revenge, to | དགྲ་ལན་ལོག་པ་ | *dra-len loḱ-pa.* |
| Do. *hon.* | དགྲ་ལན་ལོག་ག་ (པ་) གནང་བ་ | *dra-len loḱ-ḱa nang-wa.* |
| Revenue | ཁྲལ་དངུལ་ | *thre-ngü.* |
| Revenue, government | གཞུང་གི་འབབ་ | *sḱung-gi baṕ.* |
| Revere, to | བསྙེན་བཀུར་བྱེད་པ་ | *nyen-kur cḱe-pa.* |
| Do. *inf.* to *sup.* | བསྙེན་བཀུར་ཞུ་བ་ | *nyen-kur sḱu-wa.* |
| Reverence, *s.* | བསྙེན་བཀུར་ | *nyen-kur.* |

| | | |
|---|---|---|
| Reverence, to | བསྙེན་བཀུར་བྱེད་པ་ | *nyen-kur cḱe-pa.* |
| Do. *inf.* to *sup.* | བསྙེན་བཀུར་ཞུ་བ་ | *nyen-kur sḱu-wa.* |
| Reverend (title) | རྗེ་བཙུན་ | *je-tsün.* |
| Reverse, to (turn up-side down) | མགོ་གཞུག་ལོག་པ། ཨ་ལོག་རྒྱབ་པ་ | *go-sḱu loḱ-pa; a-lo gyaṕ-pa.* |
| Do. *hon.* | མགོ་གཞུག་ལོག་ག་ (པ་) གནང་བ། ཨ་ལོག་སྐྱོན་པ་ | *go-sḱu loḱ-ḱa nang-wa; a-lo kyöm-pa.* |
| Reverse, to (turn back to front) | ཁ་ཕྱོགས་ལོག་པ་ | *kha-chho loḱ-pa.* |
| Do. *hon.* | ཞལ་ཕྱོགས་ལོག་ག་ (པ་) གནང་བ་ | *sḱe-chho loḱ-ḱa nang-wa.* |
| Revile, to | སྨད་ར་བཏང་ (གཏོང་) བ་ | *me-ra tang-wa.* |
| Do. *hon.* | སྨད་ར་གཏོང་ང་ (བ་) གནང་བ་ | *me-ra tong-nga nang-wa.* |
| Do. *inf.* to *sup* | སྨད་ར་ཞུ་བ་ | *me-ra sḱu-wa.* |
| Revise, to | ཞུ་དག་བཏང་ (གཏོང་) བ་ | *sḱu-t́a tang-wa.* |
| Do. *hon.* | ཞུ་དག་གཏོང་ང་ (བ་) གནང་བ་ | *sḱu-t́a tong-nga nang-wa.* |
| Revision | ཞུ་དག་ | *sḱu-t́a.* |
| Revolt, *s.* | སྡེ་འཁྲུགས་ | *de-thru.* |
| Revolt, to | སྡེ་འཁྲུག་པ་ | *de-thruḱ-pa.* |
| Revolting (disgusting) | སྐྱུག་བྲོ་པོ་ | *kyuḱ-t́ro-po.* |
| Revolve, to | འཁོར་བ་ | *khor-wa.* |

| | | |
|---|---|---|
| Reward | རྔན་པ་ | *ngem-pa.* |
| Do. *hon.* | གསོལ་རས་ | *sö-re.* |
| Reward, to | རྔན་པ་སྟེར་བ་ | *ngem-pa ter-wa.* |
| Do. *hon.* | གསོལ་རས་གནང་བ་ | *sö-re nang-wa.* |
| Rheumatism | འབམ་ | *bam.* |
| Do. *hon.* | ཞབས་འབམ་ | *sKam-bam.* |
| Rhinoceros | བསེ་རུ་ | *se-ru.* |
| Rhododendron | སྟག་མ་ཤིང་ | *ta-ma-shing.* |
| Rhubarb | ཆུ་ཆུ་ | *chhu-chhu.* |
| Rib | རྩིབ་མ་ | *tsi-ma.* |
| Ribbon | ལྷས་མ་ | *hle-ma.* |
| Rice | འབྲས་ | *dre.* |
| Do. *hon.* | བཞེས་འབྲས་ | *sKen-dre.* |
| Rich (wealthy) | ཕྱུག་པོ། ཅ་ (ཆ་) ལག་ཆེན་པོ་ | *chhuK-po; cha-la chhem-po.* |
| Do. *hon.* | སྐུ་ཅས་ (ཆས་) ཆེན་པོ་ | *ku-che chhem-po.* |
| Rich (fertile) | ལུད་ཆུ་འཛོམ་པོ་ | *lü-chhu dzom-po* |
| Ride, to | ཞོན་པ་ | *sKöm-pa.* |
| Do. *hon.* | འཆིབ་པ་ | *chhip-pa.* |
| Ridge | སྒང་ | *gang.* |

| | | |
|---|---|---|
| **Ridiculous** | དོན་མེད་ | ***ťön-me.*** |
| **Riding horse** | ཞོན་རྟ་ | ***sǩön-ta.*** |
| **Do.** ***hon.*** | ཆིབས་པ་ | ***chhiǩ-pa.*** |
| **Riding horse (of very high official or lama)** | ཆིབས་ཆེན་ | ***chhip̌-chhen.*** |
| **Riding mule** | ཞོན་དྲེ་ | ***sǩön-ťre.*** |
| **Do.** ***hon.*** | ཆིབས་དྲེ་ | ***chhip̌-ťre.*** |
| **Riding pony** | ཞོན་རྟ་ | ***sǩön-ta.*** |
| **Do.** ***hon.*** | ཆིབས་པ་ | ***chhiǩ-pa.*** |
| **Riding pony (of very high official or lama)** | ཆིབས་ཆེན་ | ***chhip̌-chhen.*** |
| **Rifle** | མེ་མདའ་ | ***men-da.*** |
| **Do.** ***hon.*** | ཕྱག་མདའ་ | ***chhan-da.*** |
| **Rift** | སེར་ཀ་ | ***se-ka.*** |
| **Right (privilege)** | ཐོབ་ཐང་ | ***thop̌-thang.*** |
| **Right (not left)** | གཡས་ | ***ye.*** |
| **Right (not wrong)** | དག་པོ་ | ***ťaǩ-po.*** |
| **Right, to be** | འགྲིག་པ་ | ***driǩ-pa.*** |
| **Right! (very well)** | ལགས་སི། ལགས་ལགས་སི་ | ***la-si; la-la-si.*** |
| **Righteous** | དྲང་པོ་ | ***ťrang-po.*** |
| **Rigid** | མཁྲགས་པོ་ (མཁྲིགས་པ་) | ***thraǩ-po.*** |

| | | |
|---|---|---|
| Rind | པགས་པ་ | *pak-pa.* |
| Rinderpest | ཡོར་ | *yor.* |
| Ring (for finger) | ཚིགས་ཁོག་ | *tshi-kho.* |
| Do. *hon.* | ཕྱག་རྒྱུས་ | *chha-gyü.* |
| Ring (for thumb) | སྤྲས་ཁོག་ | *tre-kho.* |
| Do. *hon.* | ཕྱག་སྤྲས་ | *chha-tre.* |
| Ring (circle) | ཨ་ལོང་ | *a-long.* |
| Ring, to (bell) | དཀྲོལ་བ་ (འཁྲོལ་བ་) | *tröl-wa.* |
| Ringleader | གདེ་པོ། མི་བྱེད་མགོ་བྱེད་བྱེད་མཁན་ | *te-po; mi-cKe go-cKe cKe-khen.* |
| Rinse, to | བཤལ་བཤལ་བཏང་ (གཏོང་) བ་ | *she-she tang-wa.* |
| Do. *hon.* | བཤལ་བཤལ་གནང་བ་ | *she-she nang-wa.* |
| Ripen, to | སྨིན་པ་ | *mim-pa.* |
| Rise, to (get up) | ལང་བ་ | *lang-wa.* |
| Do. *hon.* | བཞང་བ་ (བཞེང་བ་) | *sKang-wa.* |
| Do. *h. hon.* | སྐུ་བཞང་ (བཞེང་) གནང་བ་ | *ku-sKang nang-wa.* |
| Rise, to (of sun) | ཤར་བ་ | *shar-wa.* |
| Do. (of water) | རྒྱས་པ་ | *gye-pa.* |
| Risk | ཉེན་ཁ་ | *nyen-kha.* |
| Risky | ཉེན་ཁ་ཆེན་པོ་ | *nyen-kha chhem-po.* |

| | | |
|---|---|---|
| Rite, religious | ཆོས་ལུགས་ | *chhö-lu.* |
| Rival | ཁ་ཐེག་ | *khap-the.* |
| River, large | གཙང་པོ་ | *tsang-po.* |
| Do. small | ཆུ་ | *chhu.* |
| Road | ལམ་ཀ་ | *lang-ka.* |
| Do. *hon.* | ཕེབ་ལམ་ | *phep-lam.* |
| Road, main | རྒྱ་ལམ་ | *gya-lam.* |
| Roam, to | ཆམ་ཆམ་ (འཁྱམ་འཁྱམ་) བྱེད་པ་ | *chham-chham che-pa.* |
| Do. *hon.* | སྐུ་ཆམ་ (འཁྱམ་) གནང་བ་ | *kün-chham nang-wa.* |
| Roar, to (wild beasts) | ངར་སྐད་རྒྱབ་པ་ | *ngar-ke gyap-pa.* |
| Roast, to | རྔོད་པ་ | *ngö-pa.* |
| Do. *hon.* | རྔོད་པ་གནང་བ་ | *ngö-pa nang-wa.* |
| Rob, to (by stealth) | རྐུ་ (རྐུན་) མ་རྐུ་བ་ | *ku-ma ku-wa.* |
| Do. (openly) | ཇག་པ་རྒྱབ་པ་ | *chak-pa gyap-pa.* |
| Robber (by stealth) | རྐུ་མ་ (རྐུན་མ་) | *ku-ma.* |
| Do. (openly) | ཇག་པ་ | *chak-pa.* |
| Robe | དུག་ལོག་ | *tu-lo.* |
| Do *hon.* | ན་བཟའ་ | *nam-sa.* |
| Robust | ཤེད་ཆེན་པོ་ | *she chhem-po.* |

| | | |
|---|---|---|
| Robust, *hon.* | སྐུ་ཤེད་ཆེན་པོ་ | *ku-she chhem-po.* |
| Rock | བྲག་ | *t́ra.* |
| Rod | འཁར་རྒྱུག་ | *khar-gyu.* |
| Roe (of fish) | ཉའི་སྒོ་ང་ | *nye-go-nga.* |
| Do. *hon.* | བཞེས་ཉའི་བཞེས་སྒོང་ | *sḱe-nye sḱe-gong.* |
| Rogue | བསྟན་བཞིག། འཛབ་ཆེན་ | *ten-sḱi; dzaṕ-chhen.* |
| Roll (of woollen cloth) | ཕྲུབས་ | *ṕuṕ.* |
| Do. (of cotton cloth) | ཐ་ན། *Hin.* ཡུག་ | *tha-na; yuḱ.* |
| Do. (of silk) | དབ་རིལ་ | *taṕ-ri.* |
| Roll, to | སྒྲིལ་བ་ | *dril-wa.* |
| Do. *hon.* | སྒྲིལ་ར་ (བ་) གནང་བ་ | *dri-ra nang-wa.* |
| Roof | ཐོག་ཁ་ | *tho-kha.* |
| Rook | ཁྭ་ཏ་ | *kha-ta.* |
| Room (in house) | ཁང་མིག་ | *khang-mi.* |
| Do. *hon.* | གཟིམས་ཆུང་ | *śim-chhung.* |
| Room (space) | ས་ཆ་ | *sa-chha.* |
| Root | རྩ་བ་ | *tsa-wa.* |
| Rope | ཐག་པ་ | *thaḱ-pa* |
| Rosary | འཕྲང་ང་ (འཕྲེང་བ་) | *thrang-nga.* |
| Do. *hon.* | ཕྱག་འཕྲང་ (ཕྱག་འཕྲེང་) | *chhan-thrang.* |

| | | |
|---|---|---|
| se | སེ་བའི་མེ་ཏོག་ | *se-we me-to.* |
| osin | ཐང་ཆུ་ | *thang-chhu.* |
| t, to | རུལ་བ་ | *rül-wa.* |
| otten | རུལ་པ་ | *rü-pa.* |
| ough | རྩུབ་པོ། རྩིང་པོ་ | *tsup-po; tsing-po.* |
| ound (like a disc) | སྒོར་སྒོར་ | *go-gor.* |
| Do. (like a sphere) | རྡོག་རྡོག་ | *dok-do.* |
| ouse, to (from sleep) | གཉིད་བསད་ (གསོད་) པ་ | *nyi se-pa.* |
| Do. *hon.* | གཉིད་གསོད་པ་གནང་བ་ | *nyi sö-pa nang-wa.* |
| Do. *inf.* to *sup.* | མཉེན་ (མཉལ་) སད་པ་ | *nyen se-pa.* |
| oute | ལམ་ཀ་ | *lang-ka.* |
| Do. *hon.* | ཕེབ་ལམ་ | *phep-lam.* |
| oute (highway) | རྒྱ་ལམ་ | *gya-lam.* |
| ove, to | ཆམ་ཆམ་ (འཁྱམ་འཁྱམ་) བྱེད་པ་ | *chham-chham che-pa.* |
| Do. *hon.* | སྐུ་ཆམ་ (འཁྱམ་) གནང་བ་ | *kün-chham nang wa.* |
| ow (noise) | ཨུར་སྒྲ་ | *u-dra.* |
| Do. (quarrel) | རྒྱབ་འདྲེ་ | *gyam-dre.* |
| Do. *hon.* | གསུང་འཁྲུག | *sung-thru.* |
| ow (line) | གྲལ་ | *tre.* |

| | | |
|---|---|---|
| Row, to (boat) | སྐྱ་རྒྱབ་པ་ | *kya-gyap-pa.* |
| Royal | རྒྱལ་པོའི་ | *gye-pö.* |
| Rub, to | འཕུར་འཕུར་བྱེད་པ་ | *phu-phu cKe-pa* |
| Do. *hon.* | འཕུར་འཕུར་གནང་བ་ | *phu-phu nang-wa.* |
| Rub out, to (erase) | སུབ་པ་ | *sup-pa.* |
| Do. *hon.* | སུབ་པ་གནང་བ་ | *sup-pa nang-w* |
| Rubber | སྐྱིགས་ | *gyi.* |
| Rubbish (refuse) | གད་སྙིགས། ཕྱག་སྙིགས་ | *ke-nyi ; chha-ny* |
| Ruby | པདྨ་རཱ་ག་ | *pe-ma ra-ga.* |
| Rudder | སྐྱ་མཇུག་ | *kyam-ju.* |
| Rude (impolite) | འཇིང་པ་སྦོམ་པོ། གྱོང་པོ་ | *jing-pa bom-po kyong-po.* |
| Do. (ignorant) | ཡོན་ཏན་མེད་པ་ | *yön-ten me-pa.* |
| Do. (rough) | རྩུབ་པོ་ | *tsup-po.* |
| Do. (robust) | ཤེད་ཆེན་པོ་ | *she chhem-po.* |
| Do. *hon.* | སྐུ་ཤེད་ཆེན་པོ་ | *ku-she chhem-p* |
| Ruffian | འཛབ་ཆེན་ | *dzap-chhen.* |
| Rug (bedding) | ཉལ་གཟན་ | *nye-śen.* |
| Do. *hon.* | གཟིམ་གཟན་ | *śim-śen.* |
| Rugged | རྩུབ་པོ་ | *tsup-po.* |
| Ruin, to | མེད་པར་བཟོ་བ་ | *me-pa śo-wa.* |

| | | |
|---|---|---|
| Ruin, to, *hon.* | མེད་པར་བཟོ་བ་གནང་བ་ | *me-pa śo-wa nang-wa.* |
| Rule (government) | གཞུང་། གཞུང་ཐོག་ | *sḱung ; sḱung-tho.* |
| Rule (law) | ཁྲིམས་ | *thrim.* |
| Do. *hon.* | བཀའ་ཁྲིམས་ | *ka-thrim.* |
| Do. (religious) | ཆོས་ཁྲིམས་ | *chhö-thrim.* |
| Rule (maxim) | གཏམ་དཔེ་ | *tam-pe.* |
| Rule (power) | དབང་ | *wang.* |
| Do. *hon.* | སྐུ་དབང་ | *ku-wang.* |
| Rule, as a (usually) | ནམ་རྒྱུན་ | *nam-gyün.* |
| Rule, to (govern) | དབང་བྱེད་པ་ | *wang cḱe-pa.* |
| Do. *hon.* | སྐུ་དབང་གནང་བ་ | *ku-wang nang-wa.* |
| Rule, to (decide) | ཐག་བཅད་ (གཅོད་) པ་ | *tha-che-pa.* |
| Do. *hon.* | ཐག་གཅོད་པ་གནང་བ་ | *tha-chö-pa nang-wa.* |
| Do. *h. hon.* | ཐུགས་ཐག་གཅོད་པ་གནང་བ་ | *thu-tha chö-pa nang-wa.* |
| Rule a country, to (secular rule) | རྒྱལ་སྲིད་གནང་བ་ | *gye-si nang-wa.* |
| Do. (spiritual rule) | ཆོས་སྲིད་གནང་བ་ | *chhö-si nang-wa.* |
| Ruler (king) | རྒྱལ་པོ་ | *gye-po.* |
| Do. (for drawing lines) | ཐིག་ཤིང་ | *thiḱ-shing.* |
| Rumour | སྐད་ཆ། གཏམ་ | *ke-chha ; tam.* |

| | | |
|---|---|---|
| **Rump** (anus) | རྐུབ་ | *kup.* |
| Do. *hon.* | ཞབས་ཕོངས་ | *sKam-phong.* |
| **Run, to** | རྒྱུག་པ་ | *gyuk-pa.* |
| Do. *hon.* | རྒྱུག་ཕེབ་པ་ | *gyuk phe-pa.* |
| Do. *h. hon.* | རྒྱུག་འཆིབ་རྒྱུ་གནང་བ་ | *gyuk chhip-gyu nang-wa.* |
| **Run away, to** (flee) | བྲོས་ཕྱིན་པ་ | *pö-chhim-pa.* |
| Do. *hon.* | བྲོས་ཕེབ་པ་ | *pö-phep-pa.* |
| Do. *h. hon.* | བྲོས་འཆིབ་རྒྱུ་གནང་བ་ | *pö-chhip-gyu nang-wa.* |
| **Rupee** | སྒོར་མོ་ | *gor-mo.* |
| **Rush, to** (run) | རྒྱུག་པ་ | *gyuk-pa.* |
| Do. *hon.* | རྒྱུག་ཕེབ་པ་ | *gyuk phe-pa.* |
| Do. *h. hon.* | རྒྱུག་འཆིབ་རྒྱུ་གནང་བ་ | *gyuk chhip-gyu nang-wa.* |
| **Russia** | ཨུ་རུ་སུ་ | *u-ru-su.* |
| **Russian** | ཨུ་རུ་སུ་གི་ | *u-ru-su-ki.* |
| **Rust** | བཙའ་ | *tsa.* |
| **Rut** (furrow) | རོལ་ | *röl.* |
| **Ruthless, to be** | སྙིང་རྗེ་མེད་པ་ | *nying-je me-pa.* |
| Do. *hon.* | ཐུགས་རྗེ་མེད་པ་ | *thuk-je me-pa.* |

## S

| | | |
|---|---|---|
| Sabbath | ངལ་གསོ་བའི་ཉི་མ་ | *nge-so-we nyi-ma.* |
| Sabre | ཞོག་ལང་ | *sho-lang.* |
| Sack (small) | ཕད་གོག་ | *phe-k̔o.* |
| Do. (large) | སྒྱེ་མོ་ | *gye-mo.* |
| Do. (small, of cotton) | རས་ཁུག་ | *re-khu.* |
| Do. (large, of cotton) | རས་ཕད་ | *re-phe.* |
| Do. leather | རྐྱལ་པ་ | *kye-pa.* |
| Sacred | དམ་པ། ཆོས་ལྡན་ | *t̔am-pa; chhön-den.* |
| Sacrifice (religious offering) | མཆོད་པ་ | *chhö-pa.* |
| Sacrifice, to | མཆོད་པ་ཕུལ་ (འབུལ་) བ་ | *chhö-pa phü-wa.* |
| Do. *hon.* | མཆོད་པ་འབུལ་ར་ (བ་) གནང་བ་ | *chhö-pa bü-ra nang-wa.* |
| Sad, to be | སེམས་སྐྱོ་བ། སེམས་སྡུག་པ་ | *sem-kyo-wa; sem-duk̔-pa.* |
| Do. *hon.* | ཐུགས་སེམས་སྐྱོ་བ་གནང་བ། ཐུགས་སེམས་སྡུག་ག་ (པ་) གནང་བ་ | *thu-sem kyo-wa nang-wa; thu-sem duk̔-k̔a nang-wa.* |
| Saddle | སྒ། རྟའི་སྒ་ | *ga; te-ga.* |
| Do. *hon.* | ཆིབས་སྒ་ | *chhip̔-ga.* |
| Saddle, pack | ཁལ་སྒ་ | *khe-ga.* |

| | | |
|---|---|---|
| Saddle, to | རྟའི་སྒ་རྒྱབ་པ་ | *te-ga gyap̓-pa.* |
| Do. *hon.* | ཆིབས་སྒ་སྐྱོན་པ་ | *chhip̓-ga kyöm-pa.* |
| Saddle-bag | རྟ་སྒྲོག་ | *ta-dro.* |
| Do. *hon.* | ཆིབས་སྒྲོག་ | *chhip̓-dro.* |
| Saddle-cloth | སྨ་སྦྲན་ *Ch.* | *ma-tren.* |
| Do. *hon.* | ཆིབས་སྨ་སྨ་སྦྲན་ | *chhip̓-ma ma-tren.* |
| Saddle-girth | གློ་ | *lo.* |
| Do. *hon.* | ཆིབས་གློ་ | *chhip̓-lo.* |
| Safe (steadfast) | བརྟན་པོ་ | *tem-po.* |
| Safflower (Saffron) | གུར་གུམ་ | *k̓ur-k̓um.* |
| Saffron | ཁ་ཆེ་ཤ་ཀ་མ་ | *kha-chhe sha-ka-ma.* |
| Sagacious | རིག་པ་ཆེན་པོ་ | *rik̓-pa chhem-po.* |
| Do. *hon.* | ཐུགས་རིག་ཆེན་པོ་ | *thu-ri chhem-po.* |
| Sagacity | རིག་པ་ | *rik̓-pa.* |
| Do. *hon.* | ཐུགས་རིག་ | *thu-ri.* |
| Sailor | མཉན་པ་ | *nyem-pa.* |
| Do. *hon.* | མཉན་དཔོན་ལགས་ | *nyem-pön-la.* |
| Saint, Buddhist | བྱང་ཆུབ་སེམས་དཔའ་ | *c̓hang-chhup̓ sem-pa.* |
| Saintly | དམ་པ། ཆོས་ལྡན་ | *t̓am-pa ; chhön-den.* |
| Sake of, for the | དོན་ལ་ | *t̓ön-la.* |

| | | |
|---|---|---|
| ake of, for the *hon.* | སྐུ་དོན་ལ་ | *ku-ťön-la.* |
| al ammoniac | རྒྱ་ཚྭ་ | *gya-tsha.* |
| alary | ཕོགས་ | *pho.* |
| Do. *hon.* | གསོལ་ཕོགས་ | *sö-pho.* |
| alesman | ཚོང་པ་ | *tshong-pa.* |
| Do. *hon.* | ཚོང་དཔོན་ | *tshong-pön.* |
| aliva | ཁ་ཆུ་ | *kha-chhu.* |
| Do. *hon.* | ཞལ་ཆུ་ | *sḱe-chhu.* |
| alt | ཚྭ་ | *tsha.* |
| Do. *hon.* | ལྗགས་ཚྭ་ | *ja-tsha.* |
| altpetre | ཟེ་ཚྭ་ | *śe-tsha.* |
| alute, to | ཕྱག་འབུལ་ཞུ་བ་ | *chham-bü sḱu-wa.* |
| Do. *hon.* | ཕྱག་འབུལ་ཞུ་བ་གནང་བ་ | *chham-bü sḱu-wa nang-wa.* |
| alvation | ཐར་པ་ | *thar-pa.* |
| ame | གཅིག་པ་ | *chiḱ-pa.* |
| ample | དཔེ། སྤུས་ཚད་ | *pe; pü-tshe.* |
| anctify, to (consecrate) | རབ་གནས་བྱེད་པ་ | *raṕ-ne cḱe-pa.* |
| Do. *hon.* | རབ་གནས་གནང་བ་ | *raṕ-ne nang-wa.* |
| anction | དོན་སྨིན་ | *ťön-min.* |
| and | ཕྱེ་མ་ | *chhe-ma.* |

| | | |
|---|---|---|
| Sand-grouse | གང་ག་ལིང་ | *kang-ka-ling.* |
| Sandal | ཀྲད་པ་ | *tre-pa.* |
| Sandal-wood | ཙན་དན་ | *tsen-ten.* |
| Sanskrit | སྔགས་སྐད་ | *nga-ke.* |
| Sap | ཆུ་ | *chhu.* |
| Sapient | ཡོན་ཏན་ཆེན་པོ་ | *yön-ten chhem-po.* |
| Do. *hon.* | སྐུ་ཡོན་ཆེན་པོ་ | *ku-yön chhem-po* |
| Sapphire | ཨིནྡྲ་ནཱི་ལ་ | *in-tra-ni-la.* |
| Sash | སྐེ་རགས་ | *ke-ra.* |
| Do. *hon.* | སྐུ་རགས་ | *ku-ra.* |
| Satan | བདུད་ | *dü.* |
| Satin (cloth) | ཟླུབ་ | *sup.* |
| Satisfied, to be | འདོད་པ་གང་བ་ | *dö-pa kang-wa.* |
| Do. *hon.* | ཐུགས་འདོད་གང་བ་ | *thung-dö kang-wa.* |
| Satisfied, to be (with food) | འགྲང་བ་ | *drang-wa.* |
| Do. (with water) | ཁ་ངོམས་པ་ | *kha ngom-pa.* |
| Do. *hon.* | ཞལ་ངོམས་པ་གནང་བ་ | *she ngom-pa nang-wa.* |
| Saturday | གཟའ་སྤེན་པ་ | *sa-pem-pa.* |
| Sauce | ཤ་ཁུ་ | *sha-khu.* |
| Do. *hon.* | སྲུམ་ཁུ་ | *trung-khu.* |

| | | |
|---|---|---|
| **Saucepan** | ཚལ་སླང་ | *tshe-lang.* |
| **Saucer** | དྲ་ཀྱ་ | *t́ra-kya.* |
| **Do.** *hon.* | ཞལ་ཀྱ་ | *sḱe-kya.* |
| **Saucy** (rude) | འཛིང་པ་སྦོམ་པོ། ཀྱོང་པོ་ | *jing-pa bom-po; ḱyong-po.* |
| **Saunter, to** (linger) | འགོར་བ་ | *gor-wa.* |
| **Do.** *hon.* | ཕེབ་འགོར་གནང་བ་ | *phe-gor nang-wa.* |
| **Sausage** | རྒྱུ་མ་ | *gyu-ma.* |
| **Do.** *hon.* | བཞེས་རྒྱོང་ (བཞེས་རྒྱུ་) | *sḱe-gyong.* |
| **Savage,** *s.* (barbarian) | ཀླ་ཀློ་ | *la-lo.* |
| **Do.** *adj.* (ferocious) | ངན་པ་ | *ngem-pa.* |
| **Save, to** (rescue) | བསྐྱབས་པ་ (སྐྱོབ་པ་) | *kyaṕ-pa.* |
| **Do.** *hon.* | སྐྱབས་འཇུག་གནང་བ་ | *kyam-juḱ nang-wa.* |
| **Save, to** (money) | བསག་པ་ (གསོག་པ་) | *saḱ-pa.* |
| **Do.** *hon.* | གསོག་ག་ (པ་) གནང་བ་ | *soḱ-ḱa nang-wa.* |
| **Saviour** | སྐྱབས་མགོན་ | *kyam-gön.* |
| **Savour** | བྲོ་ | *t́ro.* |
| **Do.** *hon.* | ལྗགས་བྲོ་ | *ja-t́ro.* |
| **Savoury** | ཞིམ་པོ་ | *sḱim-po.* |
| **Do.** *hon.* | སྦྲོ་པོ་ | *tro-po.* |
| **Saw** (cutting instrument) | སོག་ལེ་ | *so-le.* |

| | | |
|---|---|---|
| Saw (proverb) | གཏམ་དཔེ་ | *tam-pe.* |
| Saw, to | སོག་ལེ་རྒྱབ་པ་ | *so-le gyaṕ-pa.* |
| Say, to | ལབ་པ། ཟེར་བ་ | *laṕ-pa ; śe-wa.* |
| Do. *hon.* | གསུང་བ་ | *sung-wa.* |
| Saying | སྐད་ཆ་ | *ke-chha.* |
| Scab | རྨ་ཁོག་ | *ma-kho.* |
| Scabbard | ཤུབས་ | *shuṕ.* |
| Scalded, to be | ཆུ་འཁོལ་མས་འཚིག་པ་ | *chhu-khö-me tshiḱ-pa.* |
| Do. *hon.* | ཆབ་ཆུ་འཁོལ་མས་འཚིག་པ་ | *chhaṕ-chhu khö-me tshiḱ-pa.* |
| Scales, a pair of | ཉ་ག་ | *nya-ga.* |
| Scamp | བསྟན་བཞིག། འཛབ་ཆེན་ | *ten-sḱi ; dzaṕ-chhen.* |
| Scan, to (look at) | ལྟ་བ་ | *ta-wa.* |
| Do. *hon.* | གཟིགས་པ་ | *śi-pa.* |
| Scanty | ཉུང་ཉུང་ | *nyung-nyung.* |
| Scar | རྨ་རྗེས་ | *ma-ǰe.* |
| Do. *hon.* | སྐུ་རྨའི་རྗེས་ | *ku-me-ǰe.* |
| Scarce | དཀོན་པོ་ | *köm-po.* |
| Scare, to | ཞེད་སྐྲག་སླང་བ་ | *sḱe-tra lang-wa.* |
| Do. *hon.* | ཞེད་སྐྲག་སློང་ང་(བ་) གནང་བ་ | *sḱe-tra long-nga nang-wa.* |
| Scared, to be | ཞེད་པ་ | *sḱe-pa.* |

| | | |
|---|---|---|
| Scared, to be, *hon.* | ཞེད་པ་གནང་བ་ | *sḱe-pa nang-wa.* |
| Scarf, complimentary | ཁ་བཏགས་ | *kha-ta.* |
| Do. *hon.* | མཇལ་དར་ | *je-t́ar.* |
| Scarf, complimentary, best | ནང་མཛོད་ | *nang-dzö.* |
| Do. second best | ཨ་ཤེ་ | *a-she.* |
| Do. third best | ཕྱི་སྤྲག་ | *chhi-pa.* |
| Do. fourth best | ཟུར་ཨ་ཤེ་ | *su a-she.* |
| Do. fifth best | ཕྱི་མཛོད་ | *chhi-dzö.* |
| Do. sixth best | ཁ་སྔོན་ | *kha-ngön.* |
| Do. seventh best | གསོལ་བཏགས་ | *sö-ta.* |
| Do. cheapest | རྒྱས་སྤྲག་ | *gye-pa.* |
| Scarlet | དམར་པོ་ | *ma-po.* |
| Scatter, to (strew) | གཏོར་བ་ | *tor-wa.* |
| Do *hon.* | གཏོར་ར་ (བ་) གནང་བ་ | *tor-ra nang-wa.* |
| Schedule | ཟུར་ཐོ་ | *śur-tho.* |
| Scent, *s.* | དྲི་མ་ | *t́ri-ma.* |
| Sceptre (thunder bolt) | རྡོ་རྗེ་ | *dor-je.* |
| Scholar (pupil) | བསླབ་ཕྲུག་ | *lap̓-thru.* |
| Scholarly (learned) | ཡོན་ཏན་ཆེན་པོ་ | *yön-ten chhem-po.* |
| Do. *hon.* | སྐུ་ཡོན་ཆེན་པོ་ | *ku-yön chhem-po.* |

| | | |
|---|---|---|
| School | བསླབ་གྲྭ་ | *laṕ-ťra.* |
| School-master | དགེ་རྒན་ | *ge-gen.* |
| Science (skill) | རིག་པ | *riḱ-pa.* |
| Do. *hon.* | ཐུགས་རིག་ | *thu-ri.* |
| Science (knowledge) | ཤེས་བྱ་ | *she-cḱa.* |
| Scissors | ཇེམ་ཙེ་ (ཅེམ་ཙེ་) | *cḱem-tse.* |
| Do. *hon.* | ཕྱག་ཇེམ་ (ཕྱག་ཅེམ་) | *chha-cḱem.* |
| Scoff, to | ཀྱག་ཀྱག་བྱས་ནས་ལབ་པ་ | *kya-kya cḱe-ne laṕ-pa.* |
| Do. *hon.* | ཀྱག་ཀྱག་གནང་ནས་གསུང་བ་ | *kya-kya nang-ne sung-wa.* |
| Scold, to | གཤེ་གཤེ་བཏང་ (གཏོང་) བ་ | *she-she tang-wa.* |
| Do. *hon.* | བཀའ་བཀྱོན་གནང་བ་ | *kaṕ-kyön nang-wa.* |
| Scoop, *s.* | སྐྱོགས་ | *kyo.* |
| Scoop, to | སྐྱོགས་ཀྱིས་བཏོན་ (འདོན་) པ་ | *kyo-kyi töm-pa.* |
| Do. *hon.* | སྐྱོགས་ཀྱིས་འདོན་པ་གནང་བ་ | *kyo-kyi dom-pa nang-wa.* |
| Scope (intention) | དོན་དག་ | *ťön-ťa.* |
| Do. *hon.* | སྐུ་དོན་ | *ku-ťön.* |
| Scorch, to | འཚིག་པ་ | *tshiḱ-pa.* |
| Score (twenty) | ཉི་ཤུ | *nyi-shu.* |
| Scorn, to | ཀྱག་ཀྱག་བྱས་ནས་ལབ་པ་ | *kya-kya cḱe-ne laṕ-pa.* |
| Do. *hon.* | ཀྱག་ཀྱག་གནང་ནས་གསུང་བ་ | *kya-kya nang-ne sung-wa.* |

| | | |
|---|---|---|
| Scorpion | སྡིག་པ་ར་ཛ་ | *dik-pa ra-dza.* |
| Scoundrel | བསྟན་བཤིག། འཛབ་ཆེན་ | *ten-sKi; dzap-chhen.* |
| Scourge, to | རྟའི་ལྕག་གཞུ་བ་ | *te-cha sKu-wa.* |
| Scraggy (of persons and animals) | ཤ་སྐམ་པོ་ | *sha kam-po.* |
| Do. *hon.* (of persons) | སྐུ་ཤ་སྐམ་པོ་ | *ku-sha kam-po.* |
| Do. *hon.* (of animals) | བཞེས་ཤ་སྐམ་པོ་ | *she-sha kam-po.* |
| Scrap | དུམ་བུ་ | *tum-pu.* |
| Scrape, to | བྲད་བྲད་ (འབྲད་འབྲད་) བཏང་ (གཏོང་) བ་ | *tre-tre tang-wa.* |
| Do. *hon.* | བྲད་བྲད་ (འབྲད་འབྲད་) གཏོང་ང་ (བ་) གནང་བ་ | *tre-tre tong-nga nang-wa* |
| Scrape off, to | ཤུད་ཤུད་བྱེད་པ་ | *shü-shü cKe-pa.* |
| Do. *hon.* | ཤུད་ཤུད་གནང་བ་ | *shü-shü nang-wa.* |
| Scratch, to | སྦར་ཤད་རྒྱབ་པ་ | *bar-she gyap-pa.* |
| Do. *hon.* | ཕྱག་ཤད་སྐྱོན་པ་ | *chha-she kyöm-pa.* |
| Scream, to | སྐད་རྒྱབ་པ་ | *ke-gyap-pa.* |
| Do. *hon.* | གསུང་སྐད་སྐྱོན་པ་ | *sung-ke kyöm-pa.* |
| Screen | ཡོལ་ལ་ (ཡོལ་བ་) | *yö-la.* |
| Scriptures | གསུང་རབ་ | *sung-rap.* |

| | | |
|---|---|---|
| Scroll | ཤུག་གུའི་ཆག་པ་ | *shuḱ-ḱü chhaḱ-pa.* |
| Scruple | ཐེ་ཚོམ་ | *the-tshom.* |
| Sea | རྒྱ་མཚོ་ | *gyam-tsho.* |
| Seal | དམ་ཕྲུག། ཐེ་ཙེ་ | *t́am-thru ; the-tse.* |
| Do. *hon.* | ཕྱག་དམ་ | *chha-t́am.* |
| Seal, to | དམ་ཕྲུག་རྒྱབ་པ། ཐེ་ཙེ་རྒྱབ་པ་ | *t́am-thru gyaṕ-pa ; the-tse gyaṕ-pa.* |
| Do. *hon.* | ཕྱག་དམ་སྐྱོན་པ་ | *chha-t́am-kyöm-pa.* |
| Sealing-wax | ལ་ཆ་ | *la-chha.* |
| Seam | ཚེམ་བུ་ | *tshem-ṕu.* |
| Do. *hon.* | ཕྱག་ཚེམ་ | *chha-tshem.* |
| Search, to | འཚལ་བ་ (འཚོལ་བ་) | *tshel-wa.* |
| Do. *hon.* | འཚལ་ར་ (འཚོལ་བ་) གནང་བ་ | *tshe-ra nang-wa* |
| Season | ནམ་དུས་ | *nam-t́ü.* |
| Seat | ཀུབ་ཀྱག། ཁྲིའུ་ཤིང་ | *kuṕ-kya ; thri-u shing.* |
| Do. *hon.* | ཞབས་ཀྱག་ | *sḱaṕ-kya.* |
| Secluded place | དབེན་གནས་ | *en-ne.* |
| Second | གཉིས་པ་ | *nyi-pa.* |
| Secondly | གཉིས་པར་ | *nyi-pa.* |
| Secret | གསང་བ་ | *sang-wa.* |

| | | |
|---|---|---|
| Secretary | དྲུང་ཡིག་བགྲེས་པ་ | *ťrung-yi dre-pa.* |
| Secretary, Chief | དྲུང་ཡིག་ཆེན་མོ་བ་ | *ťrung-yi chhem-mo-wa.* |
| Secrete, to | སྦེད་པ་ | *be-pa.* |
| Do. *hon.* | སྦེད་པ་གནང་བ་ | *be-va nang-wa.* |
| Sect (religious) | ཆོས་ལུགས་ | *chhö-lu.* |
| Secular | འཇིག་རྟེན་པ་ | *jiǩ-tem-pa.* |
| Secure (steadfast) | བརྟན་པོ་ | *tem-po.* |
| Security (bail) | ཁས་ཁྱགས་ | *khe-khya.* |
| Do. *hon.* | ཞལ་ཁྱགས་ | *sǩe-khya.* |
| Security, to give | ཁས་ཁྱགས་བྱེད་པ་ | *khe-khya cǩe-pa.* |
| Do. *hon.* | ཞལ་ཁྱགས་གནང་བ་ | *sǩe-khya nang-wa.* |
| Sedan-chair | མགྱོགས་དབྱུང་ (འཁྱོགས་དབྱུང་) | *gyo-chang.* |
| Do. *hon.* | ཕེབ་དབྱུང་ | *phep̌-chang.* |
| Sediment | སྙིགས་ | *nyi.* |
| Seduce, to | སླུ་བ་ | *lu-wa.* |
| Do. *hon.* | སླུ་བ་གནང་བ་ | *lu-wa nang-wa.* |
| See, to | མཐོང་བ་ | *thong-wa.* |
| Do. *hon.* | གཟིགས་པ་ | *śi-pa.* |
| Seed | སོན། ས་བོན་ | *sön ; sa-p̌ön.* |

| | | |
|---|---|---|
| Seek, to | འཚལ་བ་ (འཚོལ་བ་) | *tshel-wa.* |
| Do. *hon.* | འཚལ་ར་ (འཚོལ་བ་) གནང་བ་ | *tshe-ra nang-wa.* |
| Seemingly (probably) | ཡིན་པ་འདྲ་ | *yim-pa-dra.* |
| Seemly (becoming) | འོས་པོ་ | *ö-po.* |
| Seize, to | ཟིན་པ་ (འཛིན་པ་) | *śim-pa.* |
| Do *hon.* | ཟིན་ (འཛིན་) པ་གནང་བ་ | *śim-pa nang-wa.* |
| Select, to | འདམ་པ་ | *dam-pa.* |
| Do. *hon.* | འདམ་པ་གནང་བ་ | *dam-pa nang-wa.* |
| Self | རང་ | *rang.* |
| Selfish | རང་འདོད་ཚ་པོ་ | *rang-dö tsha-po.* |
| Selfishness | རང་འདོད་ | *rang-dö.* |
| Sell, to | འཚོང་བ་ | *tshong-wa.* |
| Do. *hon.* | འཚོང་ང་ (བ་) གནང་བ་ | *tshong-nga nang-wa.* |
| Send, to | བཏང་བ་ (གཏོང་བ་) | *tang-wa.* |
| Do. *hon.* | གཏོང་ང་ (བ་) གནང་བ་ | *tong-nga nang-wa.* |
| Senior | རྒན་པ་ | *gem-pa.* |
| Sense (opinion) | བསམ་པ་ | *sam-pa.* |
| Do. *hon.* | ཐུགས་སེམས་ | *thu-sem.* |
| Sense (purport) | དོན་དག་ | *ťön-ťa.* |
| Do. *hon.* | སྐུ་དོན་ | *ku-ťön.* |

| | | |
|---|---|---|
| Sense (understanding) | བློ་གྲོས་ | *lo-t́rö.* |
| Senseless (nonsensical) | དོན་མེད་ | *t́ön-me.* |
| Do. (unconscious) | དྲན་མེད་ | *trem-me.* |
| Sensible (intelligent) | རིག་པ་ཡག་པོ་ | *riḱ-pa yaḱ-po.* |
| Do. *hon.* | ཐུགས་རིག་ཡག་པོ་ | *thu-ri yaḱ-po.* |
| Sentence *s.* (in a book) | ཤོག་ལོ་ | *shoḱ-lo.* |
| Do. a single | ཤོག་ལོ་ཁ་གཅིག་ | *shoḱ-lo kha-chi.* |
| Sentence, to (punish) | ཁྲིམས་བཏང་ (གཏོང་) བ་ | *thrim tang-wa.* |
| Do. *hon.* | ཁྲིམས་གཏོང་ང་ (བ་) གནང་བ་ | *thrim tong-nga nang-wa.* |
| Do. *h. hon.* | བཀའ་ཁྲིམས་གནང་བ་ | *ka-thrim nang-wa.* |
| Sentence, to (fine) | ཉེས་པ་བཏང་ (གཏོང་) བ་ | *nye-pa tang-wa.* |
| Do. *hon.* | ཉེས་པ་གནང་བ་ | *nye-pa nang-wa.* |
| Do. *h. hon.* | བཀའ་ཉེས་གནང་བ་ | *ka-nye nang-wa.* |
| Sentiment (opinion) | བསམ་པ་ | *sam-pa.* |
| Do. *hon.* | ཐུགས་སེམས་ | *thu-sem.* |
| Sentinel | སོ་པ་ | *so-pa.* |
| Separate, to | དབྱེན་ (དབྱེ་བ་) ཕྱེ་བ་ | *yen chhe-wa.* |
| Do. *hon.* | དབྱེན་ (དབྱེ་བ་) ཕྱེ་བ་གནང་བ་ | *yen chhe-wa nang-wa.* |
| Separately | ཁ་ཁ་བྱས་ནས་ | *kha-kha ćhe-ne.* |
| Sepoy | དམག་མི་ | *ma-mi.* |

| | | |
|---|---|---|
| Sepulchre | རོ་སྦེད་ས་ | *ro be-sa.* |
| Series | རིམ་པ་ | *rim-pa.* |
| Serpent | སྦྲུལ་ | *drü.* |
| Serpent-demon | ཀླུ་ | *lu.* |
| Servant | གཡོག་པོ་ | *yoḱ-po.* |
| Do. *hon.* | ཞབས་ཕྱི་ | *sḱaṕ-chhi.* |
| Servant, female | ཞལ་ལྟ་མ་ | *sḱe-ta-ma.* |
| Serve, to | གཡོག་བྱེད་པ་ | *yo ḱe-pa.* |
| Do. *hon.* | ཞབས་ཕྱི་ཞུ་བ་ | *sḱaṕ-chhi sḱu-wa.* |
| Service, religious | ཆོ་ག། སྐུ་རིམ་ | *chho-ga ; ku-rim.* |
| Serviceable, to be | ཕན་ཐོགས་པ་ | *phen-thoḱ-pa.* |
| Do. *hon.* | ཐུགས་ཕན་གསོ་བ་ | *thu-phen so-wa.* |
| Sesamum | ཏིལ་ *Hind.* | *til.* |
| Set, to (place) | བཞག་པ་ (འཇོག་པ་) | *sḱaḱ-pa.* |
| Do. *hon.* | གཞོག་ག་ (འཇོག་པ་) གནང་བ་ | *sḱoḱ-ka nang-wa.* |
| Set, to (of the sun) | རྒས་པ་ | *ge-pa.* |
| Set out, to (depart) | འཐོན་པ་ | *thöm-pa.* |
| Do. *hon.* | ཕེབ་པ་ | *phe-pa.* |
| Set right, to (adjust) | སྒྲིག་པ་ | *driḱ-pa.* |

| | | |
|---|---|---|
| Set right, to (adjust), *hon.* | སྒྲིག་ག་ (པ་) གནང་བ་ | *drik-ka nang-wa.* |
| Settle, to (decide) | ཐག་བཅད་ (གཅོད་) པ་ | *tha che-pa.* |
| Do. *hon.* | ཐག་གཅོད་པ་གནང་བ་ | *tha chö-pa nang-wa.* |
| Do. *h. hon.* | ཐུགས་ཐག་གཅོད་པ་གནང་བ་ | *thu-tha chö-pa nang-wa.* |
| Settle, to (a lawsuit out of court) | འདུམ་བཏང་ (གཏོང་) བ་ | *dum tang-wa.* |
| Do. *hon.* | བཀའ་འདུམ་གནང་བ་ | *kan-dum nang-wa.* |
| Settle, to (arrange) | སྒྲིག་པ་ | *drik-pa.* |
| Do. *hon.* | སྒྲིག་ག་ (པ་) གནང་བ་ | *drik-ka nang-wa.* |
| Seven | བདུན་ | *dün.* |
| Seventh | བདུན་པ་ | *dün-pa.* |
| Seventeen | བཅུ་བདུན་ | *chup-dün.* |
| Seventeenth | བཅུ་བདུན་པ་ | *chup-dün-pa.* |
| Seventieth | བདུན་ཅུ་པ་ | *dün-chu-pa.* |
| Seventy | བདུན་ཅུ་ | *dün-chu.* |
| Sever, to (cut) | བཅད་པ་ (གཅོད་པ་) | *che-pa.* |
| Do. *hon.* | བཅད་ (གཅོད་) པ་གནང་བ་ | *che-pa nang-wa.* |
| Several | འགའ་ཆེན་ | *ga-chhen.* |
| Severally | སོ་སོ་བྱས་ནས་ | *so-so ke-ne.* |
| Severe (harsh, of human beings) | གྱོང་པོ་ | *kyong-po.* |

| | | |
|---|---|---|
| Severe (of gods) | དྲག་པོ་ | *ťrak-po.* |
| Severe (strict) | དམ་པོ། བཙན་པོ་ | *ťam-po; tsem-po.* |
| Sew, to | འཚེམ་པ། འཚེམ་བུ་རྒྱབ་པ་ | *tshem-pa; tshem-p̒u gyap̒-pa.* |
| Do. *hon.* | ཕྱག་འཚེམ་གནང་བ། ཕྱག་འཚེམ་སྐྱོན་པ་ | *chha-tshem nang-wa; chha-tshem kyöm-pa.* |
| Sew, to (together) | སྒྲིལ་བ་ | *drel-wa.* |
| Do. *hon.* | སྒྲིལ་ར་ (བ་) གནང་བ་ | *dre-ra nang-wa.* |
| Shackles (for hands) | ལག་ལྕགས་ | *lak̒-cha.* |
| Do. (for feet) | རྐང་ལྕགས་ | *kang-cha.* |
| Shade | བསིལ་གྲིབ་ | *sil-ťrip̒.* |
| Shadow | གྲིབ་མ་ | *ťri-ma.* |
| Shaggy | རྩུབ་པོ་ | *tsup̒-po.* |
| Shake, to *v.t.* | འགུལ་འགུལ་བཏང་ (གཏོང་) བ། དཀྲུག་དཀྲུག་བྱེད་པ་ | *gü-gü tang-wa; truk̒-truk̒ ck̒e-pa.* |
| Do. *hon.* | འགུལ་འགུལ་གཏོང་ང་ (བ་) གནང་བ། དཀྲུག་དཀྲུག་གནང་བ་ | *gü-gü tong-nga nang-wa; truk̒-truk̒ nang-wa.* |
| Shake, to *v.i.* | འཁྲུག་པ་ | *thruk̒-pa.* |
| Do. (of human being) | འདར་བ་ | *dar-wa.* |

| | | |
|---|---|---|
| Shake, to (of human being), *hon.* | སྐུ་འདར་སྐྱོན་པ་ | *kün-dar kyöm-pa.* |
| Shake, to (of bridge, etc.) | ལྡེམ་ལྡེམ་བྱེད་པ་ | *dem-dem cḱe-pa.* |
| Shallow, to be | གཏིང་རིང་པོ་མེད་པ་ | *ting-ring-po me-pa.* |
| Sham (false) | རྫུས་མ་ | *dzü-ma.* |
| Sham, to | ཁྱོད་བཤད་པ་ | *ḱyö she-pa.* |
| Do. *hon.* | ཁྱོད་གསུང་བ་ | *ḱyö sung-wa.* |
| Sham illness, to | ན་རྫུ་བཏབ་ (འདེབས་) པ་ | *na-dzu taṕ-pa.* |
| Do. *hon.* | སྙུང་རྫུ་བཏབ་ (འདེབས་) པ་ | *nyung-dzu taṕ-pa.* |
| Shame | ངོ་ཚ་ | *ngo-tsha.* |
| Shame, to feel | ངོ་ཚ་བ་ | *ngo-tsha-wa.* |
| Do. *hon.* | ཐུགས་ངོ་ཚ་བ་ | *thu-ngo-tsha-wa.* |
| Shamefaced | ངོ་ཚ་པོ་ | *ngo-tsha-po.* |
| Shameful | ངོ་ཚ་པོ་ | *ngo-tsha-po.* |
| Shameless, to be | ངོ་ཚ་མེད་པ་ | *ngo-tsha me-pa.* |
| Shape, *n.* | བཟོ་བལྟ་ | *śoṕ-ta.* |
| Do. *hon.* | སྐུ་བཟོ་ | *ku-śo.* |
| Share | སྐལ་ལ་ (སྐལ་བ་) | *ke-la.* |
| Do. *hon.* | སྐུ་སྐལ་ | *ku-ke.* |
| Share, to | བགོད་པ། བགོ་བཤའ་རྒྱབ་པ་ | *gö-pa ; goṕ-sha gyaṕ-pa.* |

| | | |
|---|---|---|
| Share, to, *hon.* | བགོད་པ་གནང་བ། བགོ་བཤའ་སྐྱོན་པ་ | *gö-pa nang-wa ; gop-sha kyöm-pa.* |
| Sharp (not blunt) | རྣོ་པོ་ | *no-po.* |
| Do. (shrewd) | གཙང་པོ་ | *chang-po.* |
| Do. *hon.* | ཐུགས་གཙང་པོ་ | *thu-chang-po.* |
| Sharpen, to | བདར་བ་ | *dar-wa.* |
| Do. *hon.* | བདར་ར་ (བ་) གནང་བ་ | *dar-ra nang-wa.* |
| Sharpen, to (by blacksmith) | ཁ་འདོན་བྱེད་པ་ | *khan-dön cKe-pa.* |
| Shatter, to | ཧྲུག་ཧྲུག་བཏང་ (གཏོང་) བ་ | *hru-hru tang-wa.* |
| Shave, to | སྐྲ་བཞར་བ་ | *tra sKar-wa.* |
| Do. *hon.* | དབུ་སྐྲ་བཞར་བ་ | *u-tra sKar-wa.* |
| Shaved head, having a (as a monk) | མགོ་རིལ་རིལ་ | *go-ri-ri.* |
| Do. *hon.* | དབུ་རིལ་རིལ་ | *u-ri-ri.* |
| Shawl (of lamas) | གཟན་ | *śen.* |
| Do. *hon.* | སྐུ་གཟན་ | *ku-śen.* |
| She | མོ་ | *mo.* |
| Sheaf | ཆག་པ་ | *chhak-pa.* |
| Shear, to | བལ་བག་ (འབྲེག་) པ་ | *pe pak-pa.* |

| | | |
|---|---|---|
| Shear, to, *hon.* | བལ་བག་ (འབྲེག་) ག་ (པ་) གནང་བ་ | *ṕe ṕak-ḱa nang-wa.* |
| Sheath | ཤུབས་ | *shuṕ.* |
| Sheep | ལུག་ | *lu.* |
| Sheep, flock of | ལུག་ཁྱུ་ | *luk-khyu.* |
| Sheep-skin | ལུག་པགས་ | *luk-pa.* |
| Sheet of paper | ཤོག་གུ་ (ཤོག་བུ་) | *shu-ḱu.* |
| Do. *hon.* | ཕྱག་ཤོག་ | *chha-sho.* |
| Shelf | བང་ཁྲི། བང་ག་ | *ṕang-thri; ṕang-ḱa.* |
| Shell | འགྲོན་བུ་ | *dröm-ṕu.* |
| Shell, conch | དུང་ | *ṫung.* |
| Shelter (refuge) | སྐྱབས་གནས་ | *ḱyam-ne.* |
| Shepherd | ལུག་རྫི་ | *luk-dzi.* |
| Shield | ཕུབ་ | *phuṕ.* |
| Shift, to (move) | སྤོ་བ་ | *po-wa.* |
| Do. *hon.* | སྤོ་བ་གནང་བ་ | *po-wa nang-wa.* |
| Shin, shin-bone | ངར་དུང་ | *ngar-ṫung.* |
| Do. *hon.* | ཞབས་པིས་ངར་དུང་ | *sḱaṕ-pi ngar-ṫung.* |
| Shine (brightness) | འོད་ | *ö.* |
| Shine, to | འོད་རྒྱབ་པ་ | *ö gyaṕ-pa.* |

| | | |
|---|---|---|
| Shine, to (of the sun) | ཤར་བ་ | *shar-wa.* |
| Do. (of the moon) | ཟླ་དཀར་ཤར་བ་ | *da-ka shar-wa.* |
| Ship | གྲུ་ | *ťru.* |
| Shirt | འོག་འཇུག་ | *ön-ju.* |
| Do. *hon.* | སྐུ་འཇུག་ | *kün-ju.* |
| Shiver, to (with fear, cold, etc.) | འདར་བ་ | *dar-wa.* |
| Do. *hon.* | སྐུ་འདར་སྐྱོན་པ་ | *kun-dar kyöm-pa.* |
| Shock | ཧམས་སྐྲག་ | *ngam-tra.* |
| Shoe | ལྷམ། ལྷམ་ཁོག་ | *hlam ; hlam-kho.* |
| Do. *hon.* | ཞབས་ཆགས་ | *sǩaṕ-chha.* |
| Shoe (European style) | འཇུ་ཏ་ *Hin.* | *ju-ta.* |
| Shoe-maker | ལྷམ་བཟོ་ | *hlam-śo.* |
| Shoot, to (with gun, etc.) | རྒྱབ་པ་ | *gyaṕ-pa.* |
| Do. *hon.* | སྐྱོན་པ་ | *kyöm-pa.* |
| Shop | ཚོང་ཁང་ | *tshong-khang.* |
| Shore | འགྲམ་ | *dram.* |
| Short | ཐུང་ཐུང་ | *thung-thung.* |
| Short man | དེ་པོ་ | *te-po.* |
| Do. *hon.* | སྐུ་གཟུགས་ཆུང་ཆུང་ | *ku-śu chhung chhung.* |

| | | |
|---|---|---|
| Short-cut (road) | མགྱོགས་ལམ་ | *gyo-lam.* |
| Shorten, to (abbreviate) | སྡུད་པ། དུམ་དུམ་བྱེད་པ་ | *dü-pa ; dum-dum cḱe-pa.* |
| Shortly (soon) | ཧྲིབ་ཙ་ (ཙམ་) གཅིག་ལ་ | *hrip-tsa-chi-la.* |
| Shoulder | དཔུང་པ་ | *pung-pa.* |
| Do. *hon.* | ཕྱག་དཔུང་ | *chha-pung.* |
| Shout, to | སྐད་རྒྱབ་པ་ | *ke-gyaṕ-pa.* |
| Do. *hon.* | གསུང་སྐད་སྐྱོན་པ་ | *sung-ke kyöm-pa.* |
| Shovel | འཇག་མ་ | *ja-ma.* |
| Show | བལྟས་མོ་ | *te-mo.* |
| Do. *hon.* | གཟིགས་མོ་ | *śi-mo.* |
| Show, to | བསྟན་པ་ (སྟོན་པ་) | *tem-pa.* |
| Do. *hon.* | བསྟན་ (སྟོན་) པ་གནང་བ་ | *tem-pa nang-wa.* |
| Do. *inf.* to *sup.* | སྤྱན་ཕེབ་ཞུ་བ། སྤྱན་དར་ཞུ་བ་ | *chen-phe sḱu-wa; chen-ťar sḱu-wa.* |
| Show off, to (in dress) | དང་འདོད་བྱེད་པ་ | *ťang-dö cḱe-pa.* |
| Do. *hon.* | ཐུགས་དང་འདོད་གནང་བ་ | *thu ťang-dö nang-wa.* |
| Shower of rain, light | སྦྲིན་ཆར་ | *tring-chhar.* |
| Do. mixed with hail | དྲག་ཆར་ | *ťrak-chhar.* |
| Shrewd | གཅང་པོ་ | *chang-po.* |
| Do. *hon.* | ཐུགས་གཅང་པོ་ | *thu-chang-po.* |
| Shrine | ལྷ་ཁང་ | *hla-khang.* |

| | | |
|---|---|---|
| Shrink, to (of cloth, etc.) | འཁུམ་པ་ | *khum-pa.* |
| Shrivel, to | འཁུམ་པ་ | *khum-pa.* |
| Shrub | ཤིང་སྡོང་ཆུང་ཆུང་ | *shing-dong-chung-chung.* |
| Shudder, to | འདར་བ་ | *dar-wa.* |
| Do. *hon.* | སྐུ་འདར་སྐྱོན་པ་ | *kün-dar kyöm-pa.* |
| Shun, to (persons) | དབྱོལ་བ། ཟུར་ནས་འགྲོ་བ་ | *yö-wa ; śur-ne dro-wa.* |
| Do. *hon.* | ཟུར་ནས་ཕེབ་པ་ | *śur-ne phe-pa.* |
| Shun, to (things) | དབྱུག་བཞག་ (འཇོག་) པ། སྤང་བ་ | *yuk-skak-pa ; pang-wa.* |
| Do. *hon.* | དབྱུག་གཞོག་ག་ (འཇོག་པ་) གནང་བ། སྤོང་ང་ (ཀ་) གནང་བ་ | *yuk-sko-ka nang-wa ; pong-nga nang-wa.* |
| Shut, to (door) | རྒྱབ་པ་ | *gyap-pa.* |
| Do. *hon.* | སྐྱོན་པ་ | *kyöm-pa.* |
| Shut the mouth, to | ཁ་བཙུམ་ (འཛུམ་) པ་ | *kha tsum-pa.* |
| Shut up! (keep quiet) | ཁ་ཁ་སྡོད། ཁ་བཙུམ་ (ཁ་ཚུམ་) | *kha-kha-dö ; kha-tsum.* |
| Do. *hon.* | ཞལ་བཙུམ་ (ཞལ་ཚུམ་) | *ske-tsum.* |
| Shutter | སྒོ་སྤང་ | *go-pang.* |
| Shuttle-cock | ཐེ་བེ་ | *the-be.* |
| Shy, to (of horses) | འདྲོག་པ་ | *drok-pa.* |

| | | |
|---|---|---|
| Shy, to be (bashful) | ངོ་ཚ་བ་ | *ngo-tsha-wa.* |
| Do. *hon.* | ཞལ་རས་ཚ་བ་གནང་བ་ | *sḱe-re tsha-wa nang-wa.* |
| Sick, to be | ན་བ་ | *na-wa.* |
| Do. *hon.* | སྙུང་བ་ | *nyung-wa.* |
| Sickle | ཟོར་ར་ ( ཟོར་བ་ ) | *śor-ra.* |
| Sickness | ན་ཚ་ | *na-tsha.* |
| Do. *hon.* | སྙུང་གཞི་ | *nyung-sḱi.* |
| Side (of the body) | ཟུར་ | *śur.* |
| Do. (direction) | ཕྱོགས། ངོས་ | *chho; ngö.* |
| Side of, at the | རྩ་ལ་ ( རྩར་ལ་ ) | *tsa-la.* |
| Side of, the far | ཕར་ཕྱོགས་ | *phar-chho.* |
| Side of, the near | ཚུར་ཕྱོགས་ | *tshur-chho.* |
| Sides, on all | ཕན་ཚུན་ | *phen-tshün.* |
| Sift, to | བཙག་པ་ ( འཚག་པ་ ) | *tsaḱ-pa.* |
| Do. *hon.* | བཙག་ག་ (འཚག་པ་) གནང་བ་ | *tsaḱ-ḱa nang-wa.* |
| Sigh | དབུགས་རིང་ | *u-ring.* |
| Sigh, to | དབུགས་རིང་བཏང་ (གཏོང་) བ་ | *u-ring tang-wa.* |
| Do. *hon.* | དབུགས་རིང་གཏོང་ང་ ( བ་ ) གནང་བ་ | *u-ring tong-nga nang-wa.* |
| Sight (of a gun) | སོ་ཁུང་ | *so-khung.* |

| | | |
|---|---|---|
| Sightless | ལོང་ང་ (ལོང་བ་) | *long-nga.* |
| Do. *hon.* | སྤྱན་ལོང་ང་ (བ་) | *chen-long-nga.* |
| Sign (mark) | རྟགས་ | *ta.* |
| Signal | ལག་བརྡ་ | *laḱ-da.* |
| Signature | ལག་རྟགས་ | *laḱ-ta.* |
| Do *hon.* | ཕྱག་རྟགས་ | *chha-ta.* |
| Significant (important) | གནད་ཁག་ཆེན་པོ། གལ་ཆེན་པོ་ | *nen-kha chhem-po ; ḱe chhem-po.* |
| Signification | དོན་དག་ | *t́ön-t́a.* |
| Do. *hon.* | སྐུ་དོན་ | *ku-t́ön.* |
| Sikkim | འབྲས་ལྗོངས་ | *dren-jong.* |
| Silent, to be | ཁ་ཁ་བསྡད་ (སྡོད་) པ་ | *kha-kha de-pa.* |
| Do. *hon.* | ཞལ་རགས་བཞུགས་པ་ | *sḱe-ra sḱu-pa.* |
| Silk | གོས་ཆེན་ | *ḱö-chhen.* |
| Do. (tussore silk) | འབུ་རས་ | *bu-re.* |
| Silly (weak in intellect) | སྐུགས་པ། གླེན་པ་ | *kuḱ-pa ; lem-pa.* |
| Do. (nonsensical) | དོན་མེད་ | *t́ön-me.* |
| Silver, *s.* | དངུལ་ | *ngü.* |
| Do. *adj.* | དངུལ་གྱི་ | *ngü-ḱyi.* |
| Silversmith | དངུལ་བཟོ་བ་ | *ngü śo-wa.* |

| | | |
|---|---|---|
| Similar | ནང་བཞིན། འདྲ་པོ། གཅིག་པ། འདྲ་འདྲ་ | *nang-sḱin ; dra-po ; chik-pa ; dran-dra.* |
| Simple (easy) | ལས་སླ་པོ་ | *le-la-po.* |
| Do. (foolish) | ལྐུགས་པ། གླེན་པ་ | *kuḱ-pa ; lem-pa.* |
| Simpleton | ལྐུགས་པ། གླེན་པ་ | *kuḱ-pa ; lem-pa.* |
| Simply (merely) | གཅིག་གོ་ (གཅིག་པོ་) | *chiḱ-ḱo.* |
| Simulate, to | ཁྱོད་བཞད་པ་ | *ḱyö she-pa.* |
| Do. *hon.* | ཁྱོད་གསུང་བ་ | *ḱyö sung-wa.* |
| Sin | སྡིག་པ་ | *diḱ-pa.* |
| Do. *hon.* | སྐུ་སྡིག་ | *ku-di.* |
| Sin, to | སྡིག་པ་བསགས་ (སོག་) པ་ | *diḱ-pa saḱ-pa.* |
| Do. *hon.* | སྐུ་སྡིག་བསགས་ག་ (སོག་པ་) གནང་བ་ | *ku-dı saḱ-ka nang-wa.* |
| Since (afterwards) | གཞུག་ལ། རྗེས་ལ་ | *sḱu-la ; je-la.* |
| Sincere | དྲང་པོ་ | *ťrang-po.* |
| Do. *hon.* | ཐུགས་དྲང་པོ་ | *thuḱ-ťrang-po.* |
| Sincerely | དངོས་ནས་དྲང་ནས་ | *ngö-ne ťrang-ne.* |
| Sinew | རྒྱུས་པ་ | *gyü-pa.* |
| Sinful | ངན་པོ་ | *ngem-po.* |
| Do. *hon.* | ཐུགས་ངན་པོ་ | *thu ngem-po.* |

| | | |
|---|---|---|
| Sing, to | གཞེས་བཏང་ ( གཏོང་ ) བ་ | *sKe tang-wa.* |
| Do. *hon.* | མགུལ་གླུ་བཞེས་པ་ | *gü-lu sKe-pa.* |
| Sing, to (hymns) | མགུར་མ་ལེན་པ་ | *gur-ma lem-pa.* |
| Do. *hon.* | གསུང་མགུར་བཞེས་པ་ | *sung-gur sKe-pa.* |
| Single (separate) | གཅིག་པོ་ | *chiK-po.* |
| Do. *hon.* | སྐུ་རྐྱང་ | *ku-kyang.* |
| Single (individual) | རེ་རེ་ | *re-re.* |
| Singly | རེ་རེ་བྱས་ནས་ | *re-re cKe-ne.* |
| Sink, to (of persons) | ཐིམ་པ་ | *thim-pa.* |
| Do. *hon.* | ཐིམ་པ་གནང་བ་ | *thim-pa nang-wa.* |
| Sink, to (of things) | གཟགས་པ་ ( འཛོག་པ་ ) | *śaK-pa.* |
| Do. *hon.* | གཟགས་ག་ ( འཛོག་པ་ ) གནང་བ་ | *śaK-ka nang-wa* |
| Sinner | སྡིག་ཅན་ | *diK-chen.* |
| Sinuous | ཀྱོག་ཀྱོག་ | *kyo-kyo.* |
| Sip, to | ཏོག་ཙོ་ཏོག་ཙོ་འཐུང་བ་ | *toK-tso toK-tso thung-wa.* |
| Do. *hon.* | ཏོག་ཙོ་ཏོག་ཙོ་བཞེས་པ་ | *toK-tso toK-tso sKe-pa.* |
| Sir | སྐུ་གཞོགས་ ( སྐུ་ཞབས་ ) | *ku-sKo.* |
| Sister (general term) | སྤུན་ཀྱག་ | *pün-kya.* |
| Do. *hon.* | སྐུ་མཆེད་ | *kum-chhe.* |

| | | |
|---|---|---|
| Sister, elder | ཨ་ཆེ་ | *a-chhe.* |
| Sister, young | སྤུན་ཀྱག་ཆུང་ང་ (བ་) | *pün-kya chhung-nga.* |
| Do. *hon.* | སྐུ་མཆེད་ཆུང་ང་ (བ་) | *kum-chhe chung-nga.* |
| Sister-in-law (husband's sister) | ཁྱོ་གའི་སྤུན་ཀྱག་ | *khyo-ge pün-kya.* |
| Do. *hon.* | སྐུ་ཟླའི་སྐུ་མཆེད་ | *kum-de kum-chhe.* |
| Sister-in-law (wife's sister) | སྐྱེ་དམན་གྱི་སྤུན་ཀྱག་ | *kyi-men-K̄yi pün-kya.* |
| Do. *hon.* | སྐུ་ཟླའི་སྐུ་མཆེད་ | *kum-de kum-chhe.* |
| Sister-in-law (brother's wife) | སྤུན་ཀྱག་གི་སྐྱེ་དམན་ | *pün-kya K̄i kyi-men.* |
| Do. *hon.* | སྐུ་མཆེད་ཀྱི་སྐུ་ཟླ་ | *kum-chhe kyi kum-da.* |
| Sit, to | བསྡད་པ་ (སྡོད་པ་) | *de-pa.* |
| Do. *hon.* | བཞུགས་པ་ | *sK̄u-pa.* |
| Do. *h. hon.* | བཞུགས་གདན་འཇགས་པ་ | *sK̄u-den jaK̄-pa.* |
| Sit cross-legged, to | སྐྱིལ་ཀྲུང་བྱས་ནས་བསྡད་ (སྡོད་) པ་ | *kyi-trung cK̄e-ne de-pa.* |
| Site | ས་ཆ་ | *sa-chha.* |
| Situation (locality) | ས་ཆ་ | *sa-chha.* |
| Do. (state of affairs, etc.) | གནས་ཚུལ་ | *ne-tshü* |
| Six | དྲུག་ | *t́ruK̄.* |
| Sixteen | བཅུ་དྲུག་ | *chu-t́ruK̄.* |

| | | |
|---|---|---|
| Sixteenth | བཅུ་དྲུག་པ་ | *chu-t́ruḱ-pa.* |
| Sixth | དྲུག་པ་ | *truḱ-pa.* |
| Sixtieth | དྲུག་ཅུ་པ་ | *t́ruḱ-chu-pa.* |
| Sixty | དྲུག་ཅུ་ | *t́ruḱ-chu.* |
| Size | ཆེ་ཆུང་ | *chhe-chhung.* |
| Skeleton | རུས་ཀྲང་ | *rü-trang.* |
| Sketch | རི་མོ་ | *ri-mo.* |
| Sketch, to | རིས་མོ་བྲིས་པ་ (འབྲི་བ་) | *ri-mo t́ri-pa.* |
| Do. *hon.* | རིས་མོ་བྲིས་པ་ (འབྲི་བ་) གནང་བ་ | *ri-mo t́ri-pa nang-wa.* |
| Skilful | མཁས་པོ་ | *khe-po.* |
| Skill | རིག་པ་ | *riḱ-pa.* |
| Do. *hon.* | ཐུགས་རིག་ | *thu-ri.* |
| Skin | པགས་པ་ | *paḱ-pa.* |
| Skin, to | པགས་པ་ཤུ་བ་ | *paḱ-pa shu-wa.* |
| Do. *hon* | པགས་པ་ཤུ་བ་གནང་བ་ | *paḱ-pa shu-wa nang-wa.* |
| Skinny (of persons and animals) | ཤ་སྐམ་པོ་ | *sha kam-po.* |
| Do. *hon.* (of persons) | སྐུ་ཤ་སྐམ་པོ་ | *ku-sha kam-po.* |
| Do. *hon.* (of animals) | བཞེས་ཤ་སྐམ་པོ་ | *sḱe-sha kam-po.* |

| | | |
|---|---|---|
| **Skull** | ཐོད་པ། ཀ་པཱ་ལི་ *Hind.* | *thö-pa; kap-li.* |
| **Skull-drum** | ཐོད་རྔམ་ | *thön-tam.* |
| **Sky** | གནམ། ནམ་མཁའ་ | *nam; nam-kha.* |
| **Slack** (languid) | ཉ་རེ་ (ར་) ཉོ་རེ་ | *nya-re nyo-re.* |
| Do. (slow) | འགོར་པོ་ | *gor-po.* |
| **Slacken, to** | ལྷོད་ལྷོད་བཏང་ (གཏོང་) བ་ | *hlö-hlö tang-wa.* |
| Do. *hon.* | ལྷོད་ལྷོད་གཏོང་ང་ (བ་) གནང་བ་ | *hlö-hlö tong-nga nang-wa.* |
| **Slander, *s.*** | སྨད་ར་ | *me-ra.* |
| **Slander, to** | སྨད་ར་བཏང་ (གཏོང་) བ་ | *me-ra tang-wa.* |
| Do. *hon.* | སྨད་ར་གཏོང་ང་ (བ་) གནང་བ་ | *me-ra tong-nga nang-wa.* |
| Do. *inf.* to *sup.* | སྨད་ར་ཞུ་བ་ | *me-ra sǩu-wa.* |
| **Slap, to** | གཞུ་བ་ | *sǩu-wa.* |
| Do. *hon.* | གཞུ་བ་གནང་བ་ | *sǩu-wa nang-wa.* |
| **Slate** (for writing) | ཡང་བག་ | *yam-p̌a.* |
| Do. wooden | སྦྱང་ཤིང་ | *jang-shing.* |
| **Slaughter, to** | བསད་པ་ (གསོད་པ་) | *se-pa.* |
| Do. *hon.* | བསད་ (གསོད་) པ་གནང་བ་ | *se-pa nang-wa.* |
| **Slave** | ཚེ་གཡོག་ | *tshe-yo.* |
| **Slay, to** | བསད་པ་ (གསོད་པ་) | *se-pa.* |

| | | |
|---|---|---|
| Slay, to *hon.* | བསད་ (གསོད་) པ་གནང་བ་ | *se-pa nang-wa.* |
| Slay, to (a person of good position) | བཀྲོངས་པ་ (འགྲོང་བ་) | *trong-pa.* |
| Sleep, *s.* | གཉིད་ | *nyi.* |
| Do. *hon.* | མཉལ་ (མནལ་) | *nye.* |
| Sleep, to | ཉལ་བསྡད་ (སྡོད་) པ་ | *nye de-pa.* |
| Do. *hon.* | གཟིམ་བཞུགས་པ་ | *śim sḱu-pa.* |
| Sleep, to go to | གཉིད་ཁུག་པ་ | *nyi khuḱ-pa.* |
| Do. *hon.* | མཉལ་ (མནལ་) གཟིམ་པ་ | *nye śim-pa.* |
| Sleeping draught | ཞི་སྨན་ | *sḱi-men.* |
| Sleepy, to be | གཉིད་ཚོག་རྒྱབ་པ་ | *nyi-tso gyaṕ-pa.* |
| Do. *hon.* | མཉལ་ (མནལ་) ཚོག་སྐྱོན་པ་ | *nye-tso* **kyöm-pa.** |
| Sleeve | ཕུ་དུང་ | *phu-t́ung.* |
| Do. *hon.* | ཕྱག་ཕུང་ | *chha-phung.* |
| Slender | ཕྲ་པོ་ | *thra-po.* |
| Slice, to | གཏུབ་པ་ | *tuṕ-pa.* |
| Do. *hon.* | གཏུབ་པ་གནང་བ་ | *tuṕ-pa nang-wa.* |
| Slice | ཁྲ་པོ་ | *tra-po.* |
| Slight, *adj.* (thin) | ཤ་སྐམ་པོ་ | *sha kam-po.* |
| Do. *hon.* | སྐུ་ཤ་སྐམ་པོ་ | *ku-sha* **kam-po.** |

| | | |
|---|---|---|
| Sling (for stone) | སྒུ་རྡོ་ | *gu-do.* |
| Slip, to, *v.i.* | འདྲེད་དག་ཤོར་བ་ | *dre-ťa shor-wa.* |
| Do. *hon.* | ཞབས་འདྲེད་ཤོར་བ་ | *sȟam-dre shor-wa.* |
| Slit (fissure) | སེར་ཀ་ | *ser-ka.* |
| Slit, to be (cloth) | རལ་བ་ | *re-wa.* |
| Slope (upward) | གྱེན་ | *ǩyen.* |
| Do. (downward) | ཐུར་ | *thur.* |
| Slothful | སྙོབས་པོ། ལེ་ལོ་ཆེན་པོ་ | *nyop̌-po ; le-lo chhem-po.* |
| Slow | འགོར་པོ་ | *gor-po.* |
| Slowly | ག་ལེ་ག་ལེ་ | *ǩa-le ǩa-le.* |
| Sluggard | སྙོབས་པོ་ | *nyop̌-po.* |
| Sluggish (languid) | ཉ་རེ་ (ར་) ཉོ་རེ་ | *nya-re nyo-re.* |
| Slumber, to | གཉིད་ཚོག་རྒྱབ་པ་ | *nyi-tso gyap̌-pa.* |
| Do. *hon.* | མཉལ་ (མནལ་) ཚོག་སྐྱོན་པ་ | *nye-tso kyöm-pa.* |
| Sly (artful) | གཅང་པོ་ | *chang-po.* |
| Do. *hon.* | ཐུགས་གཅང་པོ་ | *thu-chang-po.* |
| Small | ཆུང་ཆུང་ | *chhung-chhung.* |
| Small-pox | ལྷན་འབྲུམ་ | *hlan-drum.* |
| Smash, to | བཅག་པ་ (གཅོག་པ་) | *chaǩ-pa.* |
| Do. *hon.* | བཅག་ཀ་ (པ་) གནང་བ་ | *chaǩ-ǩa nang-wa.* |

| | | |
|---|---|---|
| Smear, to | བྱུག་པ་ (འབྱུག་པ།) སྐུ་བ་ | *chuk-pa ; ḱu-wa.* |
| Do. *hon.* | བྱུགས་ཀ་ (འབྱུག་པ་) གནང་བ། སྐུ་བ་གནང་བ་ | *chuḱ-ḱa nang-wa ; ku-wa nang-wa.* |
| Smell | དྲི་མ་ | *t́ri-ma.* |
| Smell, to (use the sense of smell) | སྣོམ་པ་ | *nom-pa.* |
| Do. *hon.* | སྣོམ་པ་གནང་བ་ | *nom-pa nang-wa.* |
| Smell, to (have odour) | དྲི་མ་ཁ་བ་ | *t́ri-ma kha-wa.* |
| Smile, to | ཁ་ཚེ་ཚེ་བྱེད་པ་ | *kha tshe-tshe cḱe-pa.* |
| Do. *hon.* | ཞལ་ཚེ་ཚེ་གནང་བ་ | *sḱe tshe-tshe nang-wa.* |
| Smite, to | གཞུ་བ། རྡུང་བ་ | *sḱu-wa ; dung-wa.* |
| Do. *hon.* | གཞུ་བ་གནང་བ། ཕྱག་འཇུག (འཇུས་) གནང་བ་ | *sḱu-wa nang-wa ; chhan-ju nang-wa.* |
| Smith | མགར་ར་ (མགར་བ་) | *gar-ra.* |
| Smoke, *s.* | དུ་བ་ (དུད་པ་) | *t́u-wa.* |
| Smoke, to (tobacco) | འཐུང་བ། འཐེན་པ་ | *thung-wa ; them-pa.* |
| Do. *hon.* | བཞེས་པ་ | *sḱe-pa.* |
| Smooth | སྙོམ་པོ་ | *nyom-po.* |
| Smother, to | གློ་སུབ་རྒྱབ་པ་ | *lo-suṕ gyaṕ-pa.* |
| Do. *hon.* | གློ་སུབ་སྐྱོན་པ་ | *lo-suṕ kyöm-pa.* |
| Snake | སྦྲུལ་ | *drü.* |

| | | |
|---|---|---|
| Snap the finger, to | སིར་གོར་ (སེ་གོལ་) རྡབ་པ་ | *sir-ḱor daṕ-pa.* |
| Do. *hon.* | སིར་གོར་ (སེ་གོལ་) རྡབ་པ་ གནང་བ་ | *sir-ḱor daṕ-pa nang-wa.* |
| Snare | རྙི་ | *nyi.* |
| Snatch, to | འཕྲོག་པ་ | *throḱ-pa.* |
| Do. *hon.* | འཕྲོག་ག་ (པ་) གནང་བ་ | *throḱ-ḱa nang-wa.* |
| Sneeze, to | ཧབ་ཕྲིད་ (སྦྲིད་) རྒྱབ་པ་ | *haṕ-ťri gyaṕ-pa.* |
| Do. *hon.* | ཧབ་ཕྲིད་ (སྦྲིད་) སྐྱོན་པ་ | *haṕ-ťri kyöm-pa.* |
| Sneer, to | ཀྱག་ཀྱག་བྱས་ནས་ལབ་པ་ | *kya-kya cḱe-ne laṕ-pa.* |
| Do. *hon.* | ཀྱག་ཀྱག་གནང་ནས་གསུང་བ་ | *kya-kya nang-ne sung-wa.* |
| Snore, to | སྔུར་པོ་རྒྱབ་པ་ | *ngur-po gyaṕ-pa.* |
| Do. *hon.* | སྔུར་པོ་སྐྱོན་པ་ | *ngur-po kyöm-pa.* |
| Snow | གངས་ | *ḱang.* |
| Snow, to | གངས་རྒྱབ་པ་ | *ḱang gyaṕ-pa.* |
| Snow, eye-shade for | མིག་ར་ | *miḱ-ra.* |
| Do. *hon.* | སྤྱན་ར་ | *chen-ra.* |
| Snow-avalanche | གངས་རུད་ | *ḱang-rü.* |
| Snow-blindness | གངས་ཁྲིད་ | *ḱang-chhi.* |
| Snow-cock, | ལྷ་བྱ་གོང་མོ་ | *lhaṕ-cḱa ḱong-mo.* |
| Snow-leopard | གསའ་ | *sa.* |

| | | |
|---|---|---|
| **Snow-storm** | གངས་ཚུབ་ | *k̇ang-tshup̣.* |
| **Snuff** | སྣ་ཐག་ | *na-tha.* |
| Do. *hon.* | ཞངས་ཐག་ | *shang-tha.* |
| **Snuff-box** | སྣ་རུ་ | *na-ru.* |
| Do. *hon.* | ཞངས་རུ་ | *shang-ru.* |
| So and so | དེ་འདྲས་ | *den-dre.* |
| **Soak, to** | སྦང་བ་ | *bang-wa.* |
| Do. *hon.* | སྦང་ང་ (བ་) གནང་བ་ | *bang-nga nang-wa.* |
| **Soap** | ཡི་རྩེ་ *Ch.* | *yi-tse.* |
| Do. globular (for washing clothes) | གླང་གླད་ | *lang-le.* |
| **Do.** powdered (of Tibetan manufacture) | སུག་པ་ | *suk̇-pa.* |
| Do. *hon.* | ཕྱག་སུག་ | *chha-su.* |
| Soar, to | ལྡིང་བ་ | *ding-wa.* |
| **Sob, to** | ངུ་བ་ | *ngu-wa.* |
| Do. *hon.* | ཤུམ་པ་ | *shum-pa.* |
| **Sober** (not **drunk**), to be | ར་མ་ཟི་པ་ | *ra ma śi-pa.* |
| Do. *hon.* | སྐུ་ར་མ་བེད་པ་ | *ku-ra ma be-pa.* |
| **Sock** | ཨོ་མོ་སུ་ *Mon.* | *o-mo-su.* |
| Do. *hon.* | ཞབས་སུ་ | *sk̇ap̣-su.* |

| | | |
|---|---|---|
| **Socket** of the eye | མིག་ཁུང་ | *mik-khung.* |
| Do. *hon.* | སྤྱན་ཁུང་ | *chen-khung.* |
| **Sod** | སྤང་ | *pang.* |
| **Soda** | བུལ་ཏོག་ | *ṕü-to.* |
| **Soft** | འཇམ་པོ་ | *jam-po.* |
| **Softly** | ཀ་ལེ་ཀ་ལེ་ | *ḱa-le ḱa-le.* |
| **Soil** (earth) | ས་ | *sa.* |
| **Soil, to** | བཙོག་པ་བཟོ་བ་ | *tsoḱ-pa śo-wa.* |
| Do. *hon.* | བཙོག་པ་བཟོ་བ་གནང་བ་ | *tsoḱ-pa śo-wa nang-wa.* |
| **Sojourn, to** | བསྡད་པ་ (སྡོད་པ་) | *de-pa.* |
| Do. *hon.* | བཞུགས་པ་ | *sḱu-pa.* |
| Do. *h. hon.* | བཞུགས་གདན་འཇག་པ་ | *sḱu-den jaḱ-pa.* |
| **Solace, to** | སེམས་གསོ་བཏང་ (གཏོང་) བ་ | *sem-so tang-wa.* |
| Do. *hon.* | སེམས་གསོ་གཏོང་ང་ (བ་) གནང་བ་ | *sem-so tong-nga nang-wa.* |
| Do. *inf.* to *sup.* | ཐུགས་གསོ་ཕུལ་ (འབུལ་) བ་ | *thu-so phü-wa.* |
| **Solder,** *s.* | དཀར་ཡ་ | *ka-ya.* |
| **Soldier** | དམག་མི་ | *ma-mi.* |
| **Sole** (of foot) | རྐང་མཐིལ་ | *kang-thi.* |
| Do. *hon.* | ཞབས་མཐིལ་ | *sḱaṕ-thi.* |

| | | |
|---|---|---|
| Sole, *adj.* | གཅིག་པོ་ | *chiḱ-pa.* |
| Do. *hon.* | སྐུ་རྐྱང་ | *ku-kyang.* |
| Solely | ཤ་སྟག་ | *sha-ta.* |
| Solicit, to | ཞུ་བ་ | *sḱu-wa.* |
| Do. *hon.* | ཞུ་བ་གནང་བ་ | *sḱu-wa nang-wa.* |
| Solitary | གཅིག་པོ་ | *chiḱ-po.* |
| Do. *hon.* | སྐུ་རྐྱང་ | *ku-kyang* |
| Solitary place | དབེན་གནས་ | *en-ne.* |
| Solid (firm) | བརྟན་པོ་ | *tem-po.* |
| Sombre, to be, (melancholy) | སེམས་སྐྱོ་སྣང་བྱེད་པ་ | *sem kyo-nang ḱe-pa.* |
| Do. *hon.* | ཐུགས་སེམས་སྐྱོ་སྣང་གནང་པ་ | *thu-sem kyo-nang nang-wa.* |
| Some (a little, *e.g.* salt) | ཏོག་ཙཾ་ | *toḱ-tsa.* |
| Some (a few, *e.g.* men) | ཁ་ཤས་ | *kha-she.* |
| Something | ག་རེ་ཡིན་ནས་གཅིག་ | *ḱa-re yin-ne chi.* |
| Sometimes | མཚམས་མཚམས་ | *tsham-tsham.* |
| Do. *hon.* | ཐུགས་སངས་ཐུགས་སངས་ལ་ | *thuḱ-sang thuḱ-sang la.* |
| Somnolent, to be | གཉིད་ཚོག་རྒྱབ་པ་ | *nyi-tso gyaṕ-pa.* |
| Do. *hon.* | མཉལ་ (མནལ་) ཚོག་སྐྱོན་པ་ | *nye-tso kyöm-pa.* |
| Son | བུ་ | *ṕu.* |
| Do. *hon.* | སྲས་ | *se.* |

| | | |
|---|---|---|
| Son-in-law | མག་པ་ | *mak-pa.* |
| Do. *hon.* | སྐུ་བག་ | *ku-pa.* |
| Song | གཞས་ | *she.* |
| Do. *hon.* | གསུང་གཞས་ | *sung-she.* |
| Song, religious | མགུར་མ་ | *gur-ma.* |
| Do. *hon.* | གསུང་མགུར་ | *sung-gur.* |
| Soon | མགྱོགས་པོར་ | *gyok-po.* |
| Soothsay, to | མངོན་ཤེས་ཤེས་པ་ | *ngön-she she-pa.* |
| Do. *hon.* | མངོན་མཁྱེན་མཁྱེན་པ་ | *ngön-khyen khyem-pa.* |
| Soothsay, to (in a trance) | ལུང་བསྟན་ (སྟོན་) པ་ | *lung tem-pa.* |
| Do. *hon.* | བཀའ་ལུང་བསྟན་ (སྟོན་) པ་གནང་བ་ | *ka-lung tem-pa nang-wa.* |
| Soothsayer | རྩིས་པ་ | *tsi-pa.* |
| Soothsaying | མངོན་ཤེས་ | *ngon-she.* |
| Do. *hon.* | མངོན་མཁྱེན་ | *ngön-khyen.* |
| Soothsaying (in a trance) | ལུང་བསྟན་ | *lung-ten.* |
| Do. *hon.* | བཀའ་ལུང་ | *ka-lung.* |
| Sorcerer | མཐུ་རྒྱབ་མཁན་ | *thu-gyap-khen.* |
| Do. *hon.* | མཐུ་སྐྱོན་མཁན་ | *thu kyön-khen.* |
| Sorcery | མཐུ་ | *thu.* |

| | | |
|---|---|---|
| Sordid (niggardly) | ལག་པ་དམ་པོ་ | *laḱ-pa t́am-po.* |
| Do. *hon.* | ཕྱག་དམ་པོ་ | *chha t́am-po.* |
| Sore, *s.* | རྨ་ | *ma.* |
| Sore throat, to have a | སྐེ་ན་བ་ | *ke-na-wa.* |
| Sorrow | སྡུག་བསྔལ་ | *du-nge.* |
| Do. *hon.* | ཐུགས་འཁྲུལ། ཐུགས་བསྔལ་ | *thu-thre ; thu-nge.* |
| Sorrowful, to be | སེམས་སྐྱོ་བ། སེམས་སྡུག་པ་ | *sem-kyo-wa ; sem-duḱ-pa.* |
| Do. *hon.* | ཐུགས་སེམས་སྐྱོ་བ་གནང་བ། ཐུགས་སེམས་སྡུག་ག་ (པ་) གནང་བ་ | *thu-sem kyo-wa nang-wa ; thu-sem duḱ-ḱa nang-wa.* |
| Sorry, to be | སེམས་སྐྱོ་བ་ | *sem-kyo-wa.* |
| Do. *hon.* | ཐུགས་སེམས་སྐྱོ་བ་གནང་བ་ | *thu-sem kyo-wa nang-wa.* |
| Sort, *s.* (class of man) | རྒྱུ། རིགས་ | *gyu ; ri.* |
| Do. *hon.* | སྐུ་རྒྱུ། སྐུ་རིགས་ | *ku-gyu ; ku-ri.* |
| Sort, *s.* (of things) | རྒྱུ་དག་ | *gyu-t́a.* |
| Sorts, different | སྣ་ཚོགས་ | *na-tsho.* |
| Soul | སེམས་ | *sem.* |
| Do. *hon.* | ཐུགས་སེམས་ | *thu-sem.* |
| Sound (noise) | སྐད་ | *ke.* |
| Sound (healthy) | གཟུགས་པོ་བདེ་པོ་ | *śuḱ-po de-po.* |

| | | |
|---|---|---|
| Sound (healthy), *hon.* | སྐུ་གཟུགས་བཟང་པོ་ | *ku-śuk śang-po.* |
| Soup | ཁུ་བ་ | *khu-a.* |
| Do. *hon.* | སྐྲུམ་ཁུ་ | *trung-khu.* |
| Soup (made from meat) | ཤ་ཁུ་ | *sha-khu.* |
| Do. *hon.* | སྐྲུམ་ཁུ་ | *trung-khu.* |
| Sour (acid) | སྐྱུར་པོ་ | *kyur-po.* |
| Source (of river, etc.) | བྱུང་སྟངས་ (འབྱུང་ཁུངས་) | *cKung-tang.* |
| Do. (cause) | རྐྱེན་ | *kyen.* |
| South | ལྷོ་ | *hlo.* |
| Sovereign (king) | རྒྱལ་པོ་ | *gye-po.* |
| Sow, *s.* | ཕག་མོ་ | *pha-mo.* |
| Sow, to (seed) | བཏབ་པ་ (འདེབས་པ་) | *tap̍-pa.* |
| Do. (broad-cast) | སོན་རྒྱབ་པ་ | *sön gyap̍-pa.* |
| Sower | སོན་རྒྱབ་མཁན་ | *sön gyam-khen.* |
| Space for, sufficient | ཤོང་ས་ | *shong-sa.* |
| Spacious | གུ་ཡངས་པོ་ | *ku-yang-po.* |
| Spade | འཇག་མ་ | *ja-ma.* |
| Span | མཐོ་ | *tho.* |
| Spare (thin) | ཤ་སྐམ་པོ་ | *sha kam-po.* |
| Do. *hon.* | སྐུ་ཤ་སྐམ་པོ་ | *ku-sha kam-po.* |

| | | |
|---|---|---|
| Spare time (leisure) | ལོངས་ | *long.* |
| Spark | མེ་ཚག་ | *me-tsha.* |
| Sparkle, to, *v.i.* | འོད་རྒྱབ་པ་ | *ö gyap̍-pa.* |
| Speak, to | ལབ་པ་ | *lap̍-pa.* |
| Do. *hon.* | གསུང་བ་ | *sung-wa.* |
| Spear | མདུང་ | *dung.* |
| Do. *hon* | ཕྱག་མདུང་ | *chhan-dung.* |
| Specially | ཁྱད་པར་དུ་ | *khye-par-t́u.* |
| Species (of human beings) | རྒྱུ། རིགས་ | *gyu ; ri.* |
| Do. *hon.* | སྐུ་རྒྱུ། སྐུ་རིགས་ | *ku-gyu ; ku-ri.* |
| Species (of things) | རྒྱུ་དག་ | *gyu-t́a.* |
| Do. (different) | སྣ་ཚོགས་ | *na-tsho.* |
| Specimen | དཔེ་ | *pe.* |
| Spectacle | བལྟད་མོ་ | *te-mo.* |
| Do. *hon.* | གཟིགས་མོ་ | *śi-mo.* |
| Spectacles | མིག་ཤེར་ (མིག་ཤེལ་) | *mik̍-sher.* |
| Do. *hon.* | སྤྱན་ཤེར་ (སྤྱན་ཤེལ་) | *chen-sher.* |
| Spectre (ghost) | གདོང་འདྲེ། འདྲེ་ | *dong-dre ; dre.* |
| Speech | སྐད་ | *ke.* |
| Do. *hon.* | གསུང་སྐད་ | *sung-ke.* |

| | | |
|---|---|---|
| Speechless, to be | ཁ་ཁ་བསྡད་ (སྡོད་) པ་ | *kha-kha de-pa.* |
| Do. *hon.* | ཞལ་རགས་བཞུགས་པ་ | *sḱe-ra sḱu-pa.* |
| Speed | ཚ་དྲག་ | *tsha-t́ra.* |
| Speed, to | མགྱོགས་པོ་བྱེད་པ་ | *gyoḱ-po cḱe-pa.* |
| Do. *hon.* | རྩོལ་པོ་གནང་བ་ | *tsö-po nang-wa.* |
| Do. *h. hon.* | ཐུགས་རྩོལ་པོ་གནང་བ་ | *thu-tsö-po nang-wa.* |
| Speedy | མགྱོགས་པོ་ | *gyoḱ-po.* |
| Do. *hon.* | རྩོལ་པོ་ | *tsö-po.* |
| Spell, to | སྦྱོང་ཀློག་རྒྱབ་པ་ | *jong-lo gyaṕ-pa.* |
| Spelling | སྦྱོང་ཀློག་ | *jong-lo.* |
| Spend waste-fully, to (money) | གཏོར་བ་ | *tor-wa.* |
| Do. *hon.* | གཏོར་ར་ (བ་) གནང་བ་ | *tor-ra nang-wa.* |
| Spice | ཤ་སྨན་ | *sha-men.* |
| Spider | འདོམ་ | *dom.* |
| Spider's web | འདོམ་ཐག་ | *dom-tha.* |
| Spike, iron | ལྕགས་ཕུར་ | *chaḱ-phur.* |
| Do. wooden | ཕུར་པ་ | *phu-pa.* |
| Spill, to | ཕོ་བ་ (འཕོ་བ་) | *pho-wa.* |
| Do. *hon.* | ཕོ་ (འཕོ་) བ་གནང་བ་ | *pho-wa nang-wa.* |

| | | |
|---|---|---|
| Spin, to | འཁེལ་བ་ | *khe-wa.* |
| Do. *hon.* | འཁེལ་ར་ (བ་) གནང་བ་ | *khe-ra nang-wa.* |
| Spindle | ཡོ་ག་ | *yo-ga.* |
| Do. (another kind) | འཕང་ | *phang.* |
| Spine | སྒལ་ཚིགས་ | *ge-tshi.* |
| Spirit (soul) | སེམས་ | *sem.* |
| Do. (wine) | ཨ་རག་ | *a-ra.* |
| Do. *hon.* | བསྐྱེས་རག་ | *sKe-ra.* |
| Spirit, evil | གདོང་འདྲེ། བདུད་ | *dong-dre ; dü.* |
| Spirited | ཧུར་པོ་ | *hur-po.* |
| Spiritual | དགེ་སེམས་ཆེན་པོ་ | *ge-sem chhem-po* |
| Spit, to | མཆིལ་མ་གཏོར་བ་ | *chhi-ma tor-wa.* |
| Do. *hon.* | ལྗགས་ཆུ་གཏོར་ར་ (བ་) གནང་བ་ | *ja-chhu tor-ra nang-wa.* |
| Spite | གནོད་སེམས་ | *nö-sem.* |
| Spittle | མཆིལ་མ་ | *chhi-ma.* |
| Do. *hon.* | ལྗགས་ཆུ་ | *ja-chhu.* |
| Splendid | གཟི་བརྗིད་ཆེན་པོ། གཡང་མཛེས་ | *śi-ji chhem-po ; yang-dze.* |
| Splendour | གཟི་བརྗིད་ | *śi-ji.* |

| | | |
|---|---|---|
| Splice, to | འཐུད་རྒྱབ་པ་ | *thü gyap-pa.* |
| Do. *hon.* | འཐུད་སྐྱོན་པ་ | *thü kyöm-pa.* |
| Split, to | གཤགས་པ་ | *shak-pa.* |
| Do. *hon.* | གཤག་ག་ (པ་) གནང་བ་ | *shak-ka nang-wa.* |
| Spoil, to | མེད་པར་བཟོ་བ་ | *me-pa so-wa.* |
| Do. *hon.* | མེད་པར་བཟོ་བ་གནང་བ་ | *me-pa so-wa nang-wa.* |
| Spoon | ཐུར་མ་ | *thur-ma.* |
| Do. *hon.* | བཞེས་ཐུར་ | *sKip-thu.* |
| Sport, *s.* | རྩེད་མོ་ | *tse-mo.* |
| Do. *hon.* | སྐུ་རྩེད་ | *ku-tse.* |
| Sport, to | རྩེད་མོ་རྩེ་བ་ | *tse-mo tse-wa.* |
| Do. *hon.* | སྐུ་རྩེད་གནང་བ་ | *ku-tse nang-wa* |
| Spot (stain) | ཐིག་པ་ | *thik-pa.* |
| Do. (place) | ས་ཆ་ | *sa-chha.* |
| Spouse (wife) | སྐྱེས་དམན་ | *kyi-men.* |
| Do. *hon.* (of well-to-do villager) | སྙི་སྙིང་ལགས་ | *nyi-nying-la.* |
| Do. (of ordinary official) | ལྕམ་སྐུ་གཞོགས་ | *cham ku-sKo.* |
| Do. (of third grade and upwards) | ལྷ་ལྕམ་སྐུ་གཞོགས་ | *hla-cham ku-sKo,* |
| Sprain, to | ཚིགས་འཁྲོག་ (འབུད་) པ་ | *tshi throk-pa.* |

| | | |
|---|---|---|
| Sprain, to, *hon.* | ཞབས་ཚིགས་འཁྲོག་ག་ (འབུད་པ་) གནང་བ་ | *sKaṕ-tshi throk-ka nang-wa.* |
| Spread, to (mat, etc.) | བཏིང་བ་ (འདིང་བ་) | *ting-wa.* |
| Do. *hon.* | བཏིང་ང་ (འདིང་བ་) གནང་བ་ | *ting-nga nang-wa.* |
| Spring (season) | དཔྱིད་ཀ་ | *chi-ka.* |
| Spring (of water) | ཆུ་མིག་ | *chhu-mi.* |
| Spring, to (jump) | མཆོངས་པ། མཆོངས་རྒྱག་རྒྱབ་པ་ | *chhọng-pa ; chhong-gya gyaṕ-pa.* |
| Do. *hon.* | མཆོངས་རྒྱག་སྐྱོན་པ་ | *chhong-gya kyöm-pa.* |
| Sprinkle, to (*e.g.* water on ground) | གཏོར་བ་ | *tor-wa.* |
| Do. *hon.* | གཏོར་ར་ (བ་) གནང་བ་ | *tor-ra nang-wa.* |
| Sprite | གདོང་འདྲེ། འདྲེ་ | *dong-dre ; dre.* |
| Sprout, to | སྐྱེ་བ་ | *kye-wa.* |
| Spruce (tree) | སད་ཤིང་ | *se-shing.* |
| Spur (of mountain) | སྒང་ | *gang.* |
| Spy, *s.* | སོ་པ་ | *so-pa.* |
| Spy, to | སོ་ལྟ་བ་ | *so ta-wa.* |
| Squabble (row) | རྒྱབ་འདྲེ་ | *gyam-dre.* |
| Do. *hon.* | གསུང་འཁྲུག་ | *sung-thru.* |

| | | |
|---|---|---|
| Squabble, to | རྒྱབ་འདྲེ་རྒྱབ་པ་ | *gyam-dre gyaṕ-pa.* |
| Do. *hon.* | གསུང་འཁྲུག་སྐྱོན་པ་ | *sung-thru kyöm-pa.* |
| Squander, to | གཏོར་བ་ | *tor-wa.* |
| Do. *hon.* | གཏོར་ར་ (བ་) གནང་བ་ | *tor-ra nang-wa.* |
| Square | གྲུ་བཞི་ | *t́ruṕ-sḱi.* |
| Squeeze, to | བཙིར་བ་ (འཚིར་བ) | *tsir-wa.* |
| Do. *hon.* | བཙིར་ར་ (བ་) གནང་བ་ | *tsir-ra nang-wa.* |
| Squirrel | སྲེ་མོང་ | *tre-mong.* |
| Stab, to | བཙུགས་པ་ (འཛུགས་པ་) | *tsuḱ-pa.* |
| Do. *hon.* | བཙུགས་ཀ་ (འཛུགས་པ་) གནང་བ་ | *tsuḱ-ḱa nang-wa.* |
| Stable, *adj.* (firm) | བརྟན་པོ་ | *tem-po.* |
| Stable, *s.* | རྟ་ར་ | *ta-ra.* |
| Do. *hon.* | ཆིབས་ར་ | *chhiṕ-ra.* |
| Stable gear | རྟ་ཆས་ | *taṕ-chhe.* |
| Stack, to | རྩིག་བཞག་ (འཇོག་) པ་ | *tsiḱ sḱaḱ-pa.* |
| Do. *hon.* | རྩིག་གཞོག་ཀ་ (འཇོག་པ་) གནང་བ་ | *tsiḱ sḱoḱ-ḱa nang-wa.* |
| Staff | འཁར་རྒྱུག། རྒྱུག་པ་ (དབྱུག་པ་) | *khar-gyu ; gyuk-pa.* |

| | | |
|---|---|---|
| Stag | ཤ་ཕོ་ | *sha-pho.* |
| Do. young | ཤ་ཕྲུག་ | *sha-thru.* |
| Stage of a journey | ཞག་ས། རྒྱ་ཚུག་ | *sḱaḱ-sa ; gya-tshu.* |
| Do. *hon.* | བཞུགས་ཞག་ | *sḱu-sḱa.* |
| Stagger, to, *v.i.* | འཁྱོར་ནས་འགྲོ་བ་ | *khyor-ne dro-wa.* |
| Do. *hon.* | སྐུ་འཁྱོར་ནས་ཕེབ་པ་ | *ku-kyyor-ne phe-pa.* |
| Do. *h. hon.* | སྐུ་འཁྱོར་ནས་འཆིབ་རྒྱུ་གནང་བ་ | *ku-khyor-ne chhiṕ-gyu nang-wa.* |
| Stagger, to (astonish) | ཡ་མཚན་བྱེད་པ་ | *yam-tshen cḱe-pa.* |
| Do. *hon.* | ཡ་མཚན་གནང་བ་ | *yam-tshen nang-wa.* |
| Stain, *s.* | ཐིག་པ་ | *thiḱ-pa.* |
| Stain, to | བཙོག་པ་བཟོ་བ་ | *tsoḱ-pa śo-wa.* |
| Do. *hon.* | བཙོག་པ་བཟོ་བ་གནང་བ་ | *tsoḱ-pa śo-wa nang-wa.* |
| Stair-case | ཀན་ཙ་ (སྐས་འཛེག་) | *ken-tsa.* |
| Do. *hon.* | ཕེབ་སྐས་ | *pheṕ-ke.* |
| Staircase (of stone) | རྡོ་ཀྱག་ | *doṕ-kya.* |
| Stake (wager) | རྒྱན་ | *gyen.* |
| Do. *hon.* | སྐུ་རྒྱན་ | *ku-gyen.* |
| Stake, to | རྒྱན་བཞག་ (འཛོག་) པ་ | *gyen sḱaḱ-pa.* |

| | | |
|---|---|---|
| Stake, to, *hon.* | སྐུ་རྒྱན་གཞོག་ག་ (འཛོག་པ་) གནང་བ་ | *ku-gyen sḱok-ḱa nang-wa.* |
| Stake | སྙིང་པ་ | *nying-pa.* |
| Stalk | ཀང་ | *kang.* |
| Stallion | གསེབ་ | *sep̍.* |
| Do. *hon.* | ཆིབས་གསེབ་ | *chhip̍-sep̍.* |
| Stalwart | ཤེད་ཆེན་པོ་ | *she chhem-po.* |
| Do. *hon.* | སྐུ་ཤེད་ཆེན་པོ་ | *ku-she chhem-po.* |
| Stammering | ཁ་ལྡིག་ | *kha-di.* |
| Stamp, *s.* (seal) | ཐེ་ཙེ། དམ་ཕྲུག་ | *the-tse ; t́am-thru.* |
| Do. *hon.* | ཕྱག་དམ་ | *chha-t́am.* |
| Stampede, to | འདྲོག་ནས་འབོས་ (འབྲོས་) པ་ | *drok̍-ne p̍ö-pa.* |
| Stand, to | ལངས་ནས་བསྡད་ (སྡོད་) པ་ | *lang-ne de-pa.* |
| Do. *hon.* | བཞང་ (བཞེངས་) ནས་བཞུགས་པ་ | *sḱang-ne sḱu-pa* |
| Standard (flag) | དར་ལྕོག་ | *t́ar-cho.* |
| Star | སྐར་མ་ | *kar-ma.* |
| Stare, to | མིག་འདིར་ (བསྒྲིམས་) ནས་ལྟ་བ་ | *mik̍-dir-ne ta-wa.* |

| | | |
|---|---|---|
| Stare, to, *hon.* | སྤྱན་འདིར་ (བསྒྲིམས་) ནས་ གཟིགས་པ་ | *chen-dir-ne śi-pa.* |
| Start, to (on a journey) | འགྲོ་བ། ཕྱིན་པ་ | *dro-wa ; chhim-pa.* |
| Do. *hon.* | ཕེབ་པ་ | *phe-pa.* |
| State (condition) | གནས་ཚུལ་ | *ne-tshü.* |
| Do. (kingdom) | རྒྱལ་སྲིད་ | *gye-si.* |
| Station (rank) | གོ་ས་ | *ḱo-sa.* |
| Statue | སྐུ་འདྲ་ | *kun-dra.* |
| Status quo | ཆབ་སྲིད་སྔོན་ཡོད་ | *chhaṕ-si ngön-yö* |
| Status quo, maintenance of | ཆབ་སྲིད་སྔོན་ཡོད་རང་འཇགས་བཞག་རྒྱུ་ | *chhaṕ-si ngön-yö rang-ja sḱaḱ-gyu.* |
| Stay, to | བསྡད་པ་ (སྡོད་པ་) | *de-pa.* |
| Do. *hon.* | བཞུགས་པ་ | *sḱu-pa.* |
| Do. *h. hon.* | བཞུགས་གདན་འཇག་པ་ | *sḱu-den jaḱ-pa.* |
| Stay, to (wait) | སྒུག་བསྡད་ (སྡོད་) པ་ | *gu de-pa.* |
| Do. *hon.* | སྒུག་བཞུགས་པ་ | *gu sḱu-pa.* |
| Steadfast | བརྟན་པོ་ | *tem-po.* |
| Steadily | ཏེན་ཏེན་བྱས་ནས་ | *ten-ten cḱe-ne.* |
| Steady (resolute) | བརྟན་པོ་ | *tem-po.* |
| Steal, to | ཀུན་མ་ཀུ་བ། ཀུ་བ་ | *kü-ma ku-wa ; ku-wa.* |

| | | |
|---|---|---|
| Steam | རླངས་པ་ | *lang-pa.* |
| Steed | རྟ་ | *ta.* |
| Do. *hon.* | ཆིབས་པ་ | *chhi-pa.* |
| Steel | ཁ་ལྕགས་ | *kha-cha.* |
| Steep | གཟར་པོ་ | *śar-po.* |
| Steep, to | སྦང་བ་ | *bang-wa.* |
| Do. *hon.* | སྦང་ང་ (བ་) གནང་བ་ | *bang-nga nang-wa.* |
| Stem | སྡོང་པོ་ | *dong-po.* |
| Stench, to | དྲི་མ་ཁ་བ་ | *ťri-ma kha-wa.* |
| Step (pace) | གོམ་པ་ | *ǩom-pa.* |
| Do. *hon.* | ཞབས་གོམ་ | *sǩaṕ-ǩom.* |
| Step, to (move by paces) | གོམ་པ་རྒྱབ་པ་ | *ǩom-pa gyaṕ-pa.* |
| Do. *hon.* | ཞབས་གོམ་སྐྱོན་པ་ | *sǩaṕ-ǩom kyöm-pa.* |
| Step-father | ཕ་གཡར་ | *p̱ha-ya.* |
| Step-mother | མ་གཡར་ | *ma-ya.* |
| Steps, flight of wooden | ཀན་རྩ་ (སྐས་འཛེག་) | *ken-tsa.* |
| Do. *hon.* | ཕེབ་སྐས་ | *pheṕ-ke.* |
| Steps, stone | རྡོ་ཀྱག་ | *doṕ-kya.* |
| Sterile (of women) | རབས་ཆད་ | *raṕ-chhe.* |
| Do. (of land) | རྩ་ཆུ་འཛོམ་པོ་...མེད་པ་ | *tsa-chhu dzom-po...me-pa.* |

| | | |
|---|---|---|
| Stern, *adj.* | གྱོང་པོ་ | *ḱyong-po.* |
| Steward | ཕྱག་མཛོད་ | *chhang-dzö.* |
| Stick, *s.* | འཁར་རྒྱུག། རྒྱུག་པ་ (དབྱུག་པ་) | *khar-gyu ; gyuḱ-pa.* |
| Stick, to (paste) *v.t.* | སྦྱར་བ་ | *jar-wa.* |
| Do. *hon.* | སྦྱར་ར་ (བ་) གནང་བ་ | *jar-ra nang-wa.* |
| Stiff | གྱོང་པོ་ | *ḱyong-po.* |
| Stifle to | གློ་སུབ་རྒྱབ་པ་ | *lo-suṕ gyaṕ-pa.* |
| Do. *hon.* | གློ་སུབ་སྐྱོན་པ་ | *lo-suṕ kyöm-pa.* |
| Still, *adv.* | ད་རུང་། ད་འདོ་ | *t́a-rung ; t́an-do.* |
| Still, to sit | ཁ་ཁ་བསྡད་ (སྡོད་) པ་ | *kha-kha de-pa.* |
| Do. *hon.* | ཁ་ཁ་བཞུགས་པ་ | *kha-kha sḱu-pa.* |
| Still-birth | ཤི་རོ་སྐྱེས་པ་ | *shi-ro kye-pa.* |
| Sting, to | སོ་རྒྱབ་པ་ | *so gyaṕ-pa.* |
| Stingy | ལག་པ་དམ་པོ་ | *laḱ-pa t́am-po.* |
| Do. *hon.* | ཕྱག་དམ་པོ་ | *chha-t́am-po.* |
| Stink, to | དྲི་མ་ཁ་བ་ | *t́ri-ma kha-wa.* |
| Stipend | གླ། ཕོགས་ | *la ; pho.* |
| Do. *hon.* | གསོལ་ཕོགས་ | *sö-pho.* |
| Stir, to (move), *v.t.* | དཀྲུག་པ་ | *truḱ-pa.* |

| | | |
|---|---|---|
| Stir, to (move), *v.t.*, *hon.* | དཀྲུག་ག་ (པ་) གནང་བ་ | *truk-ka nang-wa.* |
| Stir, to, *v.i.* | འཁྲུག་པ་ | *thruk-pa.* |
| Do. *hon.* | འཁྲུག་ག་ (པ་) གནང་བ་ | *thruk-ka-nang-wa.* |
| Stirrup | ཡོབ་ | *yop.* |
| Do. *hon.* | ཆིབས་ཡོབ་ | *chhip-yop.* |
| Stirrup-leather | ཡོབ་ཐག་ | *yop-tha.* |
| Do. *hon.* | ཆིབས་ཡོབ་ཀྱི་ཐག་པ་ | *chhip-yop kyi thak-pa.* |
| Stitch, to (clothes) | འཚེམ་པ་ | *tshem-pa.* |
| Do. *hon.* | ཕྱག་འཚེམ་སྐྱོན་པ་ | *chha-tshem kyöm-pa.* |
| Stitch, to (together) | སྒྲེལ་བ་ | *drel-wa.* |
| Do. *hon.* | སྒྲེའ་ར་ (བ་) གནང་བ་ | *dre-ra nang-wa.* |
| Stock (of gun) | སྒུམ་ཤིང་ | *gum-shing.* |
| Stocking | ཨོ་མོ་སུ་ *Mon.* | *o-mo-su.* |
| Stocks (for criminals) | ཨན་གདས་ | *an-de.* |
| Stomach | གྲོ་ཁོག་ (གྲོད་ཁོག་) | *tro-kho.* |
| Do. *hon.* | གསོལ་གྲོད་ | *sö-trö.* |
| Stone | རྡོ་ | *do.* |
| Do. *hon.* | ཕྱག་རྡོ་ | *chha-do.* |
| Stool (foot-stool) | རྐང་སྟེགས་ | *kang-tek.* |
| Do. *hon.* | ཞབས་སྟེགས་ | *skap-tek.* |

| | | |
|---|---|---|
| Stoop, to | གུག་གུག་ (སྒུར་སྒུར་) བྱེད་པ་ | *kuḱ-ḱu cḱe-pa.* |
| Do. *hon.* | གུག་གུག་ (སྒུར་སྒུར་) གནང་བ་ | *kuḱ-ḱu nang-wa* |
| Stop, to, *v.t.* | བཀག་པ་ (འགེགས་པ་) | *kaḱ-pa.* |
| Do. *hon.* | བཀག་ཀ་ (འགེགས་པ་) གནང་བ་ | *kaḱ-ḱa nang-wa.* |
| Stop, to, *v.i.* | བསྡད་པ་ (སྡོད་པ་) | *de-pa.* |
| Do. *hon.* | བཞུགས་པ་ | *sḱu-pa.* |
| Do. *h. hon.* | བཞུགས་གདན་འཇག་པ་ | *sḱu-den jaḱ-pa.* |
| Stop raining, to | ཆར་པ་འཆད་པ་ | *chhar-pa chhe-pa.* |
| Store-house | མཛོད། མཛོད་ཁང་ | *dzö ; dzö-khang.* |
| Stork | ཀྲུང་ཀྲུང་དཀར་མོ་ | *trung-trung ka-mo.* |
| Storm | རླུང་ཚུབ་ | *lung-tshuṕ.* |
| Do. snow | གངས་ཚུབ་ | *ḱang-tshuṕ.* |
| Story (of house) | ཐོག་ | *tho.* |
| Do. second | བར་ཐོག | *ṕar-tho.* |
| Do. third | གསུམ་ཐོག་ | *sum-tho.* |
| Do. top | རྩེ་ཐོག་ | *tse-tho.* |
| Story (legend) | སྒྲུང་། རྣམ་ཐར་ | *drum ; nam-thar.* |
| Do. *hon.* | ཞལ་སྒྲུང་ | *sḱe-drum.* |

| | | |
|---|---|---|
| Stout (of men and animals) | ཤ་རྒྱགས་པ་ | *sha gyaḱ-pa.* |
| Do. *hon.* | སྐུ་ཤ་འབྱོར་པོ་ | *ku-sha jor-po.* |
| Stout (of things) | སྦོམ་པོ་ | *bom-po.* |
| Stove, iron | ལྕག་ཐབ་ | *chaḱ-thaṕ.* |
| Straight | འདྲོང་པོ་ (དྲང་པོ་) | *drong-po.* |
| Do. (of road) | ཁ་ཐུག་ | *kha-thu.* |
| Do. (honourable) | དྲང་པོ་ | *t́rang-po.* |
| Straighten, to | འདྲོང་ (དྲང་) པོ་བཟོ་བ་ | *drong-po śo-wa.* |
| Do. *hon.* | འདྲོང་ (དྲང་) པོ་བཟོ་བ་ གནང་བ་ | *drong-po śo-wa nang-wa.* |
| Straightforward (just) | ཁྲིམས་དྲང་པོ་ | *thrim-t́rang-po.* |
| Do. *hon.* | བཀའ་ཁྲིམས་དྲང་པོ་ | *ka-thrim t́rang-po.* |
| Straightway | ལམ་སང་ | *lam-sang.* |
| Strain, to | བཙག་པ་ (འཚག་པ་) | *tsaḱ-pa.* |
| Do. *hon.* | བཙག་ག་ (འཚག་པ་) གནང་བ་ | *tsaḱ-ḱa nang-wa.* |
| Strainer, tea | ཇ་འཚག་ | *cḱa-tsha.* |
| Strait (narrow) | དོག་པོ། སྦུགས་སྦུབ་དོག་པོ་ | *t́oḱ-po; bu-su t́oḱ-po.* |
| Strange | ཁྱད་མཚར་པོ་ | *khye-tsha-po.* |
| Stranger | ཕྱི་མི་ | *chhi-mi.* |

| | | |
|---|---|---|
| Strangle, to | སྐེ་བཀག་བཏང་ནས་བསད་ (གསོད་) པ་ | *ke-kak tang-ne se-pa.* |
| Strategy | དམག་ཇུས་ | *mak-chü.* |
| Do. *hon.* | སྐུ་ཇུས་ | *ku-chü.* |
| Straw | ཟན་པ་ | *śem-pa.* |
| Strawberry (Chumbi Valley dialect) | དམར་ལུམ་ | *ma-lum.* |
| Stray, to | ལམ་ཀ་ནོར་བ་ | *lang-ka nor-wa.* |
| Do. *hon.* | ཕེབ་ལམ་ནོར་ར་ (བ་) གནང་བ་ | *phep-lam nor-ra nang-wa.* |
| Stream | རྒྱུག་ཆུ་ | *gyuk-chhu.* |
| Street | ལམ་ཀ་ | *lang-ka.* |
| Do. narrow | སྲང་འགག་ | *hrang-ga.* |
| Strength | ཤེད་ | *she.* |
| Do. *hon.* | སྐུ་ཤེད་ | *ku-she.* |
| Stretch, to | བརྐྱང་བ་ (རྐྱོང་བ་) | *kyang-wa.* |
| Do. *hon.* | རྐྱོང་ང་ (བ་) གནང་བ་ | *kyong-nga nang-wa.* |
| Strew, to (grass, etc.) | གཏོར་བ་ | *tor-wa.* |
| Do. *hon.* | གཏོར་ར་ (བ་) གནང་བ་ | *tor-ra nang-wa.* |
| Strewing oblation | གཏོར་མ་ | *tor-ma.* |

| | | |
|---|---|---|
| Strict | དམ་པོ། བཙན་པོ་ | *ťam-po; ťsem-po.* |
| Strife | རྒྱབ་འདྲེ་ | *gyam-dre.* |
| Do. *hon.* | གསུང་འཁྲུག་ | *sung-thru.* |
| Strike, to (hit) | འཕོག་པ་ | *phoḱ-pa.* |
| Strike, to (a blow) | རྡུང་བ་ | *dung-wa.* |
| Do. *hon.* | ཕྱག་འཇུག་ (འཇུས་) གནང་བ་ | *chhan-ju nang-wa.* |
| String | སྐུད་པ་ | *kü-pa.* |
| Do. *hon.* | ཕྱག་སྐུད་ | *chha-kü.* |
| Strive, to | སྙིང་རུས་བྱེད་པ་ | *nying-rü cḱe-pa.* |
| Do. *hon.* | ཐུགས་རུས་གནང་བ་ | *thuḱ-rü nang-wa.* |
| Strip, to | ཤུ་བ་ | *shu-wa.* |
| Stroke | ལྕག་ | *cha.* |
| Stroll, to | ཆམ་ཆམ་ (འཁྱམ་འཁྱམ་) ལ་འགྲོ་བ་ | *chham-chham-la dro-wa.* |
| Do. *hon.* | ཆམ་ཆམ་ (འཁྱམ་འཁྱམ་) ལ་ཕེབ་པ་ | *chham-chham la phe-pa.* |
| Do. *h. hon.* | ཆམ་ཆམ་ (འཁྱམ་འཁྱམ་) ལ་འཆིབ་རྒྱུ་གནང་བ་ | *chham-chham la chhiṕ-gyu nang-wa.* |

| | | |
|---|---|---|
| Strong (of human beings, animals, etc.) | ཤེད་ཆེན་པོ་ | *she chhem-po.* |
| Do. *hon.* | སྐུ་ཤེད་ཆེན་པོ་ | *ku-she chhem-po.* |
| Strong (of forts, houses, etc.) | བཙན་པོ་ | *tsem-po.* |
| Struggle, to (wrestle) | འཛིང་བ། འཛིང་རེ་བཏང་ (གཏོང་) བ་ | *dzing-wa ; dzing-re tang-wa.* |
| Do. *hon.* | འཛིང་ང་ (བ་) གནང་བ་ | *dzing-nga nang-wa.* |
| Stubble | སོག་མ་ | *so-ma.* |
| Stubborn | གྱོང་པོ་ | *ḱyong-po.* |
| Student | བསླབ་གྲྭ་ | *laṕ-tra.* |
| Do. religious | གྲྭ་པ་ | *t́ra-pa.* |
| Stumble, to (of persons) | ཁ་རྡབ་པ་ | *kha daṕ-pa.* |
| Do. *hon.* | ཞལ་རྡབ་པ་གནང་བ་ | *sḱe daṕ-pa nang-wa.* |
| Stumble, to (of animals) | ཚིགས་བུར་རྒྱབ་པ་ | *tshiḱ-ṕu gyaṕ-pa.* |
| Stupid (weak in intellect) | ལྐུགས་པ། གླེན་པ་ | *kuḱ-pa ; lem-pa.* |
| Do. (senseless, of things) | དོན་མེད་ | *t́ön-me.* |
| Sturdy | ཤེད་ཆེན་པོ་ | *she chhem-po.* |
| Do. *hon.* | སྐུ་ཤེད་ཆེན་པོ་ | *ku-she chhem-po.* |
| Stuttering | ཁ་ལྡིག་ | *kha-di.* |
| Sty | ཕག་ཚང་ | *phaḱ-tshang.* |

| | | |
|---|---|---|
| Style (of persons) | རྒྱུ། རིགས་ | *gyu; ri.* |
| Do. *hon.* | སྐུ་རྒྱུ། སྐུ་རིགས་ | *ku-gyu; ku-ri.* |
| Style (of things) | རྒྱུ་དག་ | *gyu-t́a.* |
| Styles, different | སྣ་ཚོགས་ | *na-tsho.* |
| Subdue, to | རྒྱལ་བ། ཀླག་འཁས་པ་ | *gye-wa; la khe-pa.* |
| Do. *hon.* | རྒྱལ་ར་ (བ་) གནང་བ། ཀླག་འཁས་ར་ (པ་) གནང་བ་ | *gye-ra nang-wa; la khe-ra nang-wa.* |
| Subject (of a government), *s.* | མངའ་འབངས་ | *nga-bang.* |
| Do. *hon.* | མངའ་ཞབས་ | *nga-sḱaṕ.* |
| Subjoin, to | འཐུད་རྒྱབ་པ་ | *thü gyaṕ-pa.* |
| Do. *hon.* | འཐུད་སྐྱོན་པ་ | *thü kyöm-pa.* |
| Subjugate, to | རྒྱལ་བ། ཀླག་འཁས་པ་ | *gye-wa; la khe-pa.* |
| Do. *hon.* | རྒྱལ་ར་ (བ་) གནང་བ། ཀླག་འཁས་ར་ (པ་) གནང་བ་ | *gye-ra nang-wa; la khe-ra nang-wa.* |
| Sublime | གཡང་མཛེས་ | *yang-dze.* |
| Submissive (humble) | སེམས་ཆུང་ཆུང་ | *sem-chhung-chhung.* |
| Do. *hon.* | ཐུགས་སེམས་ཆུང་ཆུང་ | *thuḱ-sem chhung-chhung.* |
| Submit, to | མགོ་དགུར་བ་ | *go gur-wa.* |
| Do. *hon.* | དབུ་དགུར་ར་ (བ་) གནང་བ་ | *u gur-ra nang-wa.* |

| | | |
|---|---|---|
| Submit, to (a petition or report) | འབུལ་བ། འབུལ་ལམ་ཞུས་པ་ (ཞུ་བ་) | *bül-wa ; bü-lam sḱü-pa.* |
| Do. *hon.* | འབུལ་ར་ (བ་) གནང་བ། འབུལ་ལམ་ཞུ་བ་གནང་བ་ | *bü-ra nang-wa ; bü-lam sḱu-wa nang-wa.* |
| Subside, to (of water, flood, etc.) | ཆག་པ་ | *chhaḱ-pa.* |
| Substance | དངོས་པོ། རྒྱུ་ | *ngö-po ; gyu.* |
| Do. (of document, etc.) | དོན་སྙིང་ | *ťön-nying.* |
| Substantiate, to (statement) | གཏན་ལྡན་བྱེད་པ་ | *ten-den cḱe-pa.* |
| Do. *hon.* | གཏན་ལྡན་གནང་བ་ | *ten-den nang-wa.* |
| Substitute | ཚབ་ | *tshaṕ.* |
| Do. *hon.* | སྐུ་ཚབ་ | *ku-tshaṕ.* |
| Subtility | གཡོ་སྒྱུ་ | *yo-gyu.* |
| Subtle | གཡོ་ཆེན་པོ་ | *yo chhem-po.* |
| Subtract, to | འཐེན་པ་ | *them-pa.* |
| Do. *hon.* | འཐེན་པ་གནང་བ་ | *them-pa nang-wa.* |
| Succeed, to (be successful) | ཐུབ་པ་ | *thuṕ-pa.* |
| Do. (follow) | གཞུག་ལ་ཕྱིན་པ་ | *sḱu-la chhim-pa.* |
| Do. *hon.* | གཞུག་ལ་ཕེབ་པ་ | *sḱu-la phe-pa.* |
| Do. *h. hon.* | གཞུག་ལ་འཆིབ་རྒྱུ་གནང་བ་ | *sḱu-la chhiṕ-gyu nang-wa* |

| | | |
|---|---|---|
| Successful, to be | མགོ་འཐོན་པ་ | *go thöm-pa.* |
| Succession, (descendants) | རིགས་བརྒྱུད། མི་བརྒྱུད་ | *ri-gyü ; mi-gyü.* |
| Do. *hon.* (of laity) | སྐུ་བརྒྱུད་ | *ku-gyü.* |
| Do. *hon.* (of lamas) | གདུང་བརྒྱུད་ | *dung-gyü.* |
| Succour, *s.* | རོགས་ | *ro.* |
| Do. *hon.* | མགོ་འདྲེན་ | *gön-dren.* |
| Succour, to | རོགས་བྱེད་པ་ | *ro ch'e-pa.* |
| Do. *hon.* | དབུ་འདྲེན་གནང་བ་ | *u-dren nang-wa.* |
| Such | འདི་འདྲ་ | *din-dra.* |
| Suck, to | འཇིབ་པ་ | *jiṕ-pa.* |
| Do. *hon.* | འཇིབ་པ་གནང་བ་ | *jiṕ-pa nang-wa.* |
| Suckle, to | འོ་མ་སྟེར་བ་ | *o-ma ter-wa.* |
| Do. *hon.* | འོ་མ་གནང་བ་ | *o-ma nang-wa.* |
| Suddenly | ལམ་སང་ | *lam-sang.* |
| Suffer, to (endure) | བཟོད་པ་སྒོམ་པ་ | *śö-pa gom-pa.* |
| Do. *hon.* | བཟོད་པ་བཞེས་པ་ | *śö-pa sh'e-pa.* |
| Suffer, to (pain) | གཟུག་རྒྱབ་པ་ | *śu-gyaṕ-pa.* |
| Do. *hon.* | སྙུང་གཟུག་སྐྱོན་པ་ | *nyung-śu kyöm-pa.* |
| Suffer, to (permit) | བཅུག་པ་ (འཇུག་པ་) | *chuḱ-pa.* |
| Do. *hon.* | བཅུག་ག་ (འཇུག་པ་) གནང་བ་ | *chuḱ-ḱa nang-wa.* |

| | | |
|---|---|---|
| Suffering (mental) | སྡུག་བསྔལ་ | *du-nge.* |
| Do. *hon.* | ཐུགས་འཁྲལ་ | *thu-thre.* |
| Suffering (physical) | གཟུག་ | *śu.* |
| Do. *hon.* | སྙུང་གཟུག་ | *nyung-śu.* |
| Sufficient, to be | ལྡང་བ། འགྲིག་པ་ | *dang-wa ; driḱ-pa.* |
| Suffocate, to | གློ་སུབ་རྒྱབ་པ་ | *lo-suṕ gyaṕ-pa.* |
| Do. *hon.* | གློ་སུབ་སྐྱོན་པ་ | *lo-suṕ ḱyöm-pa.* |
| Suffocated, to be | དབུགས་འགག་པ་ | *u gaḱ-pa.* |
| Sugar | བྱེ་མ་ཀ་ར་ | *cḱe-ma ḱa-ra.* |
| Sugar-candy | ཤེལ་ཀ་ར་ | *she ḱa-ra.* |
| Suicide, to commit | རང་སྲོག་བཅད་ (གཅོད་) པ་ | *rang-so che-pa.* |
| Do. *hon.* | རང་སྲོག་གཅོད་པ་གནང་བ་ | *rang-so chö-pa nang-wa.* |
| Suit, to (befit) | འོས་པ་ | *ö-pa.* |
| Do. (agree) | འགྲིག་པ། འཆམ་པ་ | *driḱ-pa ; chham-pa.* |
| Suitable | འོས་པོ། འོས་བབས་ | *ö-po ; ö-ṕaṕ.* |
| Suite | འཁོར་གཡོག་ | *ḱhor-yo.* |
| Sulk, to | གདོང་ནག་པོ་བསྟན་ (སྟོན་) པ་ | *dong naḱ-po tem-pa.* |
| Do. *hon.* | ཞལ་རས་ནག་པོ་སྟོན་པ་གནང་བ་ | *sḱe-re naḱ-po töm-pa nang-wa.* |
| Sullen | རྒྱོང་པོ་ | *ḱyong-po.* |

| | | |
|---|---|---|
| Sully, to | བཙོག་པ་བཟོ་བ་ | *sok-pa śo-wa.* |
| Do. *hon.* | བཙོག་པ་བཟོ་བ་གནང་བ་ | *tsok-pa śo-wa nang-wa.* |
| Sulphur | མུ་ཟི་ | *mu-śi.* |
| Sum up, to | སྡོམ་པ་ | *dom-pa.* |
| Do. *hon.* | སྡོམ་པ་གནང་བ་ | *dom-pa nang-wa.* |
| Summer | དབྱར་ཀ་ | *yar-ka.* |
| Summit | རྩེ་ | *tse.* |
| Summon, to | སྐད་བཏང་ (གཏོང་) བ་ | *ke tang-wa.* |
| Do. *hon.* | ཤོག་བཀའ་གནང་བ་ | *sho ka-nang-wa.* |
| Sun | ཉི་མ་ | *nyi-ma.* |
| Do. *hon.* | ཞོ་ཉི་ (ཞུ་ཉི་) | *sko-nyi.* |
| Sunbeam | ཉི་མའི་གཟེར་ | *nyi-me śer.* |
| Sunrise | ཉི་མ་ཤར་ར་ (བ་) | *nyi-ma shar-ra.* |
| Sunset | ཉི་མ་རྒས་པ་ | *nyi-ma ge-pa.* |
| Sunstroke, to get | ཉི་གཟེར་འཕོག་པ་ | *nyi-śer phok-pa.* |
| Sunday | གཟའ་ཉི་མ་ | *śa-nyi-ma.* |
| Sundry (various) | མི་གཅིག་པ་ | *mi-chik-pa.* |
| Superabundant | ཧ་ཅང་མང་པོ། གཡོ་མ་སུ་ | *ha-chang mang-po; yo-ma-su.* |
| Superb | གཡང་མཛེས་ | *yang-dze.* |
| Supercilious (haughty) | ཉམས་ཆེན་པོ། ཛ་ཁོག་ཆེན་པོ་ | *nyam-chhem-po; dza-kho chhem-po.* |

| | | |
|---|---|---|
| Superfluous | ལྷག་པོ་ | *hlaḱ-po.* |
| Superintend | དོ་དམ་བྱེད་པ་ | *t́o-t́am cḱe-pa.* |
| Do. *hon.* | དོ་དམ་གནང་བ་ | *t́o-t́am nang-wa.* |
| Superintendent | དོ་དམ་པ་ | *t́o-t́am-pa.* |
| Superstition | རྣམ་རྟོག་ | *nam-to.* |
| Superior (rank of persons) | མཐོ་པོ་ | *tho-po.* |
| Do. (of things) | ཡག་པོ་ | *yaḱ-po.* |
| Supervise, to | དོ་དམ་བྱེད་པ་ | *t́o-t́am cḱe-pa.* |
| Do. *hon.* | དོ་དམ་གནང་བ་ | *t́o-t́am nang-wa.* |
| Supper | དགོངས་མོའི་ཁ་ལག་ | *gong-mö kha-la.* |
| Do. *hon.* | དགོངས་མོའི་ཞལ་ལག་ | *gong-mö sḱe-la.* |
| Supple | མཉན་པོ་ | *nyem-po.* |
| Supplicate, to | ཞུ་བ་ | *sḱu-wa.* |
| Do. *hon.* | ཞུ་བ་གནང་བ་ | *sḱu-wa nang-wa.* |
| Supplication | ཞུ་བ་ | *sḱu-wa.* |
| Supply, to | སྒྲུབ་པ་ | *druṕ-pa.* |
| Do. *hon.* | སྒྲུབ་པ་གནང་བ་ | *druṕ-pa nang-wa.* |
| Support, to (prop up) | སྐྱོར་བ་ | *kyor-wa.* |
| Do. *hon.* | སྐྱོར་ར་ (བ་) གནང་བ་ | *kyor-ra nang-wa.* |
| Support to (endure) | བཟོད་པ་སྒོམ་པ་ | *śö-pa gom-pa.* |

| | | |
|---|---|---|
| Support, to (endure), *hon.* | བཟོད་པ་སྒོམ་པ་གནང་བ་ | *śö-pa gom-pa nang-wa.* |
| Support, to (nourish) | གསོ་བ་ | *so-wa.* |
| Do. *hon.* | གསོ་བ་གནང་བ་ | *so-wa nang-wa.* |
| Suppose, to | བསམ་པ་ | *sam-pa.* |
| Do. *hon.* | དགོངས་པ་ | *gong-pa.* |
| Supposition (opinion) | བསམ་པ་ | *sam-pa.* |
| Do. *hon.* | ཐུགས་སེམས་ | *thu-sem.* |
| Suppress, to (restrain) | བཀག་པ་ (འགོགས་པ་) | *kaḱ-pa.* |
| Do. *hon.* | བཀག་ག་ (འགོགས་པ་) གནང་བ་ | *kaḱ-ḱa nang-wa.* |
| Suppression of urine, to suffer from | གཅིན་པ་འགག་པ་ | *chim-pa gaḱ-pa.* |
| Suppurate, to | རྣག་བསག་ (གསོག་) པ་ | *na saḱ-pa.* |
| Do. *hon.* | རྣག་བསག་ག་ (གསོག་པ་) གནང་བ་ | *na saḱ-ḱa nang-wa.* |
| Sure | ཏེན་ཏེན། ཁྲིག་ཁྲིག་ | *ten-ten ; thriḱ-thri.* |
| Surely | ངེས་པར་ | *nge-par.* |
| Surety | ཁས་ཁྱགས་ | *khe-khya.* |
| Do. *hon.* | ཞལ་ཁྱགས་ | *sḱe-khya.* |
| Surety, to stand | ཁས་ཁྱགས་བྱེད་པ་ | *khe-kya cḱe-pa.* |

| | | |
|---|---|---|
| Surety, to stand, *hon.* | ཞལ་ཁྱགས་གནང་བ་ | *sḱe-khya nang-wa.* |
| Surgeon | ཨེམ་ཆི་ | *am-chhi.* |
| Surly | གྱོང་པོ་ | *ḱyong-po.* |
| Surmise, to (suspect) | རྟོགས་པ་ཟ་བ་ | *t́ok-pa śa-wa.* |
| Do. *hon.* | ཐུགས་རྟོགས་གནང་བ་ | *thu-t́o nang-wa.* |
| Surmise, to (conjecture) | བསམ་པ་ | *sam-pa.* |
| Do. *hon.* | དགོངས་པ་ | *gong-pa.* |
| Surplus | ལྷག་མ་ | *hla-ma.* |
| Surprise, *s.* | ཡ་མཚན་ | *yam-tshen.* |
| Surprise, to | ཡ་མཚན་བྱེད་པ་ | *yam-tshen ch́e-pa.* |
| Do. *hon.* | ཡ་མཚན་གནང་བ་ | *yam-tshen nang-wa.* |
| Surprising | ཡ་མཚན་པོ། ཁྱད་མཚར་པོ་ | *yam-tshem-po; khye-tsha-po.* |
| Surrender, to (abandon) | སྤང་བ་ | *pang-wa.* |
| Do. *hon.* | སྤོང་ང་ (བ་) གནང་བ་ | *pong-nga nang-wa.* |
| Surrender, to (submit) | མགོ་བཏགས་ཞུ་བ་ | *goṕ-te sḱu-wa.* |
| Surround, to | སྐོར་ར་རྒྱབ་པ་ | *kor-ra gyaṕ-pa.* |
| Do. *hon.* | ཞབས་སྐོར་སྐྱོན་པ་ | *sḱaṕ-kor kyöm-pa.* |
| Survey, to (look at) | ལྟ་བ་ | *ta-wa.* |
| Do. *hon.* | གཟིགས་པ་ | *śi-pa.* |
| Suspect, to | རྟོགས་པ་ཟ་བ་ | *t́ok-pa śa-wa.* |

| | | |
|---|---|---|
| Suspect, to, *hon.* | ཐུགས་དོགས་གནང་བ་ | *thu-ťo nang-wa.* |
| Suspense (doubt) | ཐེ་ཚོམ་ | *the-tshom.* |
| Suspense, to be in (doubt) | ཐེ་ཚོམ་ཟ་བ་ | *the-tshom śa-wa.* |
| Do. *hon.* | ཐེ་ཚོམ་གནང་བ་ | *the-tshom nang-wa.* |
| Suspend, to | བཀལ་བ་ (འགེལ་བ་) | *kel-wa.* |
| Do. *hon.* | བཀལ་ར་ (འགེལ་བ་) གནང་བ་ | *ke-ra nang-wa.* |
| Suspend, to (from office) | བདོན་པ་ (འདོན་པ་) | *töm-pa.* |
| Do. *hon.* | བདོན་ (འདོན་) པ་གནང་བ་ | *töm-pa nang-wa.* |
| Suspicion | དོགས་པ་ | *ťok-pa.* |
| Do. *hon.* | ཐུགས་དོགས་ | *thu-ťo.* |
| Suspicious and angry, to be | བལྟ་ཕྱོགས་བྱེད་པ་ | *ta-chhok cȟe-pa.* |
| Do. *hon.* | གཟིགས་ཕྱོགས་གནང་བ་ | *śi-chhok nang-wa.* |
| Sustain, to (endure) | བཟོད་པ་སྒོམ་པ་ | *śö-pa gom-pa.* |
| Do. *hon.* | བཟོད་པ་སྒོམ་པ་གནང་བ་ | *śö-pa gom-pa nang-wa.* |
| Sustain, to (nourish) | གསོ་བ་ | *so-wa.* |
| Do. *hon.* | གསོ་བ་གནང་བ་ | *so-wa nang-wa.* |
| Sustain, to (prop) | སྐྱོར་བ་ | *kyor-wa.* |
| Do. *hon.* | སྐྱོར་ར་ (བ་) གནང་བ་ | *kyor-ra nang-wa.* |
| Swallow, to | མིད་པ་ | *mi-pa.* |

| | | |
|---|---|---|
| Swarm (crowd) | ཚོགས་ | *tsho.* |
| Sway | དབང་ | *wang.* |
| Do. *hon.* | སྐུ་དབང་ | *ku-wang.* |
| Sway, to (govern) | དབང་བྱེད་པ་ | *wang-cḱe-pa.* |
| Do. *hon.* | སྐུ་དབང་གནང་བ་ | *ku-wang nang-wa.* |
| Swear, to | མནའ་སྐྱེལ་བ་ | *na kyel-wa.* |
| Do. *hon.* | དབུ་མནའ་བཞེས་པ་ | *u-na sḱe-pa.* |
| Sweat, *s.* | རྔུལ་ནག་ | *ngü-na.* |
| Sweat, to | རྔུལ་ནག་འཐྲོན་པ་ | *ngü-na thöm-pa.* |
| Do. *hon.* | རྔུལ་ནག་འཐྲོན་པ་གནང་བ་ | *ngü-na thöm-pa nang-wa.* |
| Sweep, to | གེ་རྒྱབ་པ་ | *ḱe gyaṕ-pa.* |
| Do. *hon.* | གེ་སྐྱོན་པ་ | *ḱe-kyöm-pa.* |
| Sweeper | གེ་པ། ར་རྒྱ་པ་ | *ḱe-pa; ra-gya-pa.* |
| Do. chief | ར་རྒྱ་དཔོན་པོ་ | *ra-gya pöm-po.* |
| Sweet, *adj.* | མངར་མོ། ཞིམ་པོ་ | *ngar-mo; sḱim-po.* |
| Sweetheart | སྙིང་སྡུག་ | *nying-du.* |
| Sweetmeat | ཁྲི་རིལ་ | *cḱi-ri.* |
| Sweet-scented | དྲི་མ་ཞིམ་པོ་ | *ťri-ma sḱim-po.* |
| Swell, to | སྦྲང་བ་ | *trang-wa.* |
| Do. *hon.* | སྦྲང་ང་ (བ་) གནང་བ་ | *trang-nga nang-wa.* |

| | | |
|---|---|---|
| Swift | མགྱོགས་པོ་ | *gyoḱ-po.* |
| Do. *hon.* | རྩོལ་པོ་ | *tsö-po.* |
| Swim, to | རྐྱལ་རྒྱབ་པ་ | *kye gyaṕ-pa.* |
| Do. *hon.* | རྐྱལ་སྐྱོན་པ་ | *kye kyöm-pa.* |
| Swine | ཕག་པ་ | *phaḱ-pa.* |
| Swineherd | ཕག་རྫི་ | *phaḱ-dzi.* |
| Swing, (*e.g.* branch in wind) | ལིང་ལིང་བྱེད་པ་ | *ling-ling cḱe-pa.* |
| Do. (brandish) | དབྱུག་དབྱུག་བྱེད་པ་ | *yuḱ-yuḱ cḱe-pa.* |
| Do. *hon.* | དབྱུག་དབྱུག་གནང་བ་ | *yuḱ-yuḱ nang-wa.* |
| Switch | རྟའི་ལྕག། ལྕང་སྨྱུག་ | *te-cha ; chang-nyu.* |
| Do. *hon.* | ཆིབས་ལྕག་ | *chhiṕ-cha.* |
| Swoon, to | དྲན་མེད་བརྒྱལ་བ་ | *t́ren-me gyel-wa.* |
| Do. *hon.* | ཐུགས་དྲན་མེད་བརྒྱལ་ར་ (བ་) གནང་བ་ | *thu-t́ren-me gye-ra nang-wa.* |
| Sword | དཔའ་དམ། ཤོག་ལང་ | *pa-dam ; sho-lang.* |
| Do. (two-edged) | རལ་གྲི་ | *re-t́ri.* |
| Do. short | རྩེབ་སག་ | *tseṕ-sa.* |
| Symbol | རྟགས་ | *ta.* |
| Symmetry (proportion) | ཚོད་ | *tshö.* |

| | | |
|---|---|---|
| Sympathy | སྙིང་རྗེ། ཁམས་སྙིང་རྗེ་ | *nying-je; ckam-nying-je.* |
| Do. *hon.* | ཐུགས་རྗེ་ | *thuk-je.* |
| Symptom (of disease) | ན་སྟངས་ | *na-tang.* |
| Do. *hon.* | སྙུང་སྟངས་ | *nyung-tang.* |
| Syphilis | སྲི་མོག་ | *se-mo.* |
| System (method) | ཐབས་ | *thap.* |

# T

| | | |
|---|---|---|
| Table, small | ལྕོག་ཙེ་ | *choḱ-tse.* |
| Do. *hon.* | གསོལ་ལྕོག་ | *sö-cho.* |
| Table, European | རྒྱ་ལྕོག་ | *gya-cho.* |
| Table-cloth | ལྕོག་ཁེབས་ | *cho-kheṕ.* |
| Taciturn, to be | ཁ་ཁ་བསྡད་ (སྡོད་) པ་ | *kha-kha de-pa.* |
| Do. *hon.* | ཞལ་ཁ་བཞུགས་པ་ | *sḱe-kha sḱu-pa.* |
| Tact | ཐབས་མཁས་ | *thaṕ-khe.* |
| Tail | གཞུག་གུ་ | *sḱu-gu.* |
| Tailor | ཚེམ་བུ་ | *tshem-ṕu.* |
| Do. *hon.* | དབུ་མཛད་ | *um-dze.* |
| Taint (contamination) | གྲིབ་ | *ťriṕ.* |
| Do. *hon.* | སྐུ་གྲིབ་ | *ku-ťriṕ.* |
| Take, to | ལེན་པ་ | *lem-pa.* |
| Do. *hon.* | བཞེས་པ་ | *sḱe-pa* |
| Take, to (carry) | འཁྱེར་འགྲོ་བ་ | *khe dro-wa.* |
| Do. *hon.* | སྣོམ་ཕེབ་པ་ | *nom phe-pa.* |
| Do. *h. hon.* | སྣོམ་འཆིབ་རྒྱུ་གནང་བ་ | *nom chhiṕ-gyu nang-wa.* |
| Take, to (conduct) | འཁྲིད་འགྲོ་བ་ | *thri dro-wa.* |
| Do. *hon.* | འཁྲིད་ཕེབ་པ་ | *thri phe-pa.* |

| | | |
|---|---|---|
| Take, to (conduct), *h. hon.* | འཁྲིད་འཆིབ་རྒྱུ་གནང་བ་ | *thri chhiṕ-gyu nang-wa.* |
| Take, to (forcibly | འཕྲོག་པ་ | *phoḱ-pa.* |
| Do. *hon.* | འཕྲོག་ག་ (པ་) གནང་བ་ | *phoḱ-ḱa nang-wa.* |
| Take hold of, to | ཟིན་པ་ | *śim-pa.* |
| Do. *hon.* | ཟིན་པ་གནང་བ་ | *śim-pa nang-wa.* |
| Take off, to (clothes, etc.) | ཕིས་པ་ (འབུད་པ་) | *pi-pa.* |
| Do. *hon.* | བསིལ་ར་ (བ་) གནང་བ་ | *si-ra nang-wa.* |
| Take out, to | བཏོན་པ་ (འདོན་པ་) | *töm-pa.* |
| Do. *hon.* | འདོན་པ་གནང་བ་ | *döm-pa nang-wa.* |
| Tale | སྒྲུང་། རྣམ་ཐར་ | *drum; nam-thar.* |
| Do. *hon.* | ཞལ་སྒྲུང་ | *sḱe-drum.* |
| Talent (natural gift) | ཡོན་ཏན་ | *yön-ten.* |
| Talented (person) | རིག་པ་ཆེན་པོ་ | *riḱ-pa chhem-po.* |
| Do. *hon.* | ཐུགས་རིག་ཆེན་པོ་ | *thu-ri chhem-po.* |
| Talisman | སྲུང་བ་ | *hrung-nga.* |
| Do. (used by high lamas) | སྲིད་པ་ཧོ་ | *si-pa-ho.* |
| Talk, *s.* (conversation) | སྐད་ཆ་ | *ke-chha.* |
| Do. *hon.* | གསུང་གྲོས་ | *sung-t́rö.* |
| Talk (rumour) | སྐད་ཆ། གཏམ་ | *ke-chha; tam.* |
| Talk, to | ལབ་པ་ | *laṕ-pa.* |

| | | |
|---|---|---|
| **Talk, to,** *hon.* | གསུང་བ་ | *sung-wa.* |
| Do. *h. hon.* | བཀའ་གནང་བ་ | *ka nang-wa.* |
| **Tall** | གཟུགས་པོ་རིང་པོ་ | *śuḱ-po ring-po.* |
| Do. *hon.* | སྐུ་གཟུགས་རིང་པོ་ | *ku-śu ring-po.* |
| **Tallow** | ཚིལ་ལུ་ (ཚིལ་བུ་) | *tshi-lu.* |
| **Talon** | སྡེར་མོ་ | *der-mo.* |
| **Tame, to** | ལྷིང་པོ་བཟོ་བ་ | *hling-po śo-wa.* |
| Do. *hon.* | ལྷིང་པོ་བཟོ་བ་གནང་བ་ | *hling-po śo-wa nang-wa.* |
| **Tan, to** | མཉེད་པ་ | *nye-pa.* |
| **Tanner** | ཀོ་བ་མཉེད་མཁན་ | *ko-wa nye-khen.* |
| **Tap, to** | དག་དག་བཏང་ (གཏོང་) བ་ | *taḱ-ta tang-wa.* |
| Do. *hon.* | དག་དག་གཏོང་ང་ (བ་) གནང་བ་ | *taḱ-ta tong-nga nang-wa.* |
| **Tape, measuring** | ཐག་ཚད་ | *thaḱ-tshe.* |
| **Tape-worm** | ཀྲུབ་འབུ་ | *kuṕ-bu.* |
| **Tardy** | ཕྱི་པོ་ | *chhi-po.* |
| **Target** | རྒྱབ་འབེན་ | *gyam-be.* |
| **Tarnish, to** | བཙོག་པ་བཟོ་བ་ | *tsoḱ-pa śo-wa.* |
| Do. *hon.* | བཙོག་པ་བཟོ་བ་གནང་བ་ | *tsoḱ-pa śo-wa nang-wa.* |
| **Tarry, to** | འགོར་པོ་བྱེད་པ་ | *gor-po cḱe-pa.* |

| | | |
|---|---|---|
| Tarry, to, *hon.* | འགོར་པོ་གནང་བ་ | *gor-po nang-wa.* |
| Tartar (on the teeth) | སོ་དྲེག་ | *so-ťre.* |
| Do. *hon.* | ཚེམས་དྲེག་ | *tshem-ťre.* |
| Task | ལས་ཀ་ | *le-ka.* |
| Do. *hon.* | ཕྱག་ལས་ | *chha-le.* |
| Task, school | ཡིག་ཚད་ | *yiǩ-tshe.* |
| Tassel (for hat) | དོང་སྐུད་ | *tong-kü.* |
| Taste, *s.* | བྲོ་བ་ | *ťro-a.* |
| Do. *hon.* | ལྗགས་བྲོ་ | *ja-ťro.* |
| Taste, to | བྲོ་བ་ལྟ་བ་ | *ťro-a ta-wa.* |
| Do. *hon.* | ལྗགས་བྲོ་གཟིགས་པ་ | *ja-ťro śi-pa.* |
| Taunt, to | ཀྱག་ཀྱག་བྱས་ནས་ལབ་པ་ | *kya-kya cǩe-ne laṕ-pa.* |
| Do. *hon.* | ཀྱག་ཀྱག་གནང་ནས་གསུང་བ་ | *kya-kya nang-ne sung-wa.* |
| Tavern | ཆང་ཁང་ | *chhang-khang.* |
| Tax (general) | ཁྲལ། འབབ་ | *thre ; baṕ.* |
| Do. (customs-duty) | ཤོ་ཁྲལ་ | *sho-thre.* |
| Do. on land | ས་ཁྲལ་ | *sa-thre.* |
| Tax, to pay | ཁྲལ་འཇལ་བ་ | *thre-je-wa.* |
| Tea | ཇ་ | *cǩa.* |
| Do. *hon.* | གསོལ་ཇ་ | *sö-cǩa.* |

| | | |
|---|---|---|
| Tea, best quality | འབྲུ་ཐང་ | *dru-thang.* |
| Do. 2nd quality | འབྲུ་གཉིས་ | *dru-nyi.* |
| Do. 3rd quality | བཅུ་པ་ | *chu-pa.* |
| Do. 4th quality | བརྒྱད་པ་ | *gye-pa.* |
| Tea, brick of | ཇ་པག་ | *cḱa-ṕa-ka.* |
| Do. *hon.* | གསོལ་ཇ་པག་ | *sö-cḱa ṕa-ka.* |
| Tea-pot | ཁོག་ཏི་ | *k̇ho-ti.* |
| Do. *hon.* | གསོལ་ཏི་ | *sö-ti.* |
| Tea-strainer | ཇ་ཚགས་ | *cḱa-tsha.* |
| Teach, to | བསླབ་པ་ (སློབ་པ་) | *laṕ-pa.* |
| Do. *hon.* | བསླབས་ (སློབ་) པ་གནང་བ་ | *laṕ-pa nang-wa.* |
| Teacher | དགེ་རྒན། སློབ་དཔོན་ | *ge-gen; lo-pön.* |
| Tear, *s.* | མིག་ཆུ་ | *miḱ-chhu.* |
| Do. *hon.* | སྤྱན་ཆབ་ | *chen-chhaṕ.* |
| Tear, to (cloth, etc.) | རལ་བ་ | *re-wa.* |
| Do. *hon.* | རལ་ར་ (བ་) གནང་བ་ | *re-ra nang-wa.* |
| Tear, to (flesh) | བཀོག་པ་ (འགོག་པ་) | *koḱ-pa.* |
| Do. *hon.* | བཀོག་ག་ (འགོག་པ་) གནང་བ་ | *koḱ-ḱa nang-pa.* |
| Tears, to shed | མིག་ཆུ་ཤོར་བ་ | *miḱ-chhu shor-wa.* |

| | | |
|---|---|---|
| Tears, to shed, *hon.* | སྤྱན་ཆབ་ཤོར་བ་ | *chen-chhaṕ shor-wa.* |
| Tedious | དཀའ་ལས་ཁག་པོ་ | *ka-le khaḱ-po.* |
| Do. *hon.* | སྐུ་མཉེལ་པོ་ | *ku-nye-po.* |
| Telegram | གློག་སྐད་ཡི་གེ་ | *lo-kü yi-ge.* |
| Telegraph | ལྕགས་སྐད། གློག་སྐད་ | *cha-kü; lo-kü.* |
| Telephone | ཁ་པར་ | *kha-ṕar.* |
| Do. *hon.* | ཞལ་པར་ | *sḱe-ṕar.* |
| Telescope | རྒྱང་ཤེལ་ | *gyang-she.* |
| Tell, to | ལབ་པ་ | *laṕ-pa.* |
| Do. *hon.* | གསུང་བ་ | *sung-wa.* |
| Do. *h. hon.* | བཀའ་གནང་བ་ | *ka nang-wa.* |
| Temper (passion) | ཚིག་པ། ཁོང་ཁྲོ་ | *tshiḱ-pa ; khong-thro.* |
| Tempered, good | བློ་རྒྱུ་རིང་པོ་ | *lo-gyu ring-po.* |
| Do. *hon.* | ཐུགས་རྒྱུ་རིང་པོ་ | *thu-gyu ring-po.* |
| Tempered, bad | རུ་ངར་པོ་ | *ru ngar-po.* |
| Do. *hon.* | ཐུགས་རུ་ངར་པོ་ | *thu-ru ngar-po.* |
| Temperate (climate) | བསིལ་དྲོས་སྙོམས་པོ་ | *si-t́rö nyom-po.* |
| Temperate, to be (moderate) | ཚོད་ཟིན་པ་ | *tshö-śim-pa.* |
| Temperature | གྲང་ལོས་ | *t́rang-lö.* |
| Tempest | རླུང་ཚུབ་ | *lung-tshuṕ.* |

| | | |
|---|---|---|
| Temple | མཆོད་ཁང་ | *chhö-khang.* |
| Tempt, to (cheat) | མགོ་སྐོར་བཏང་ (གཏོང་) བ་ | *go-kor tang-wa.* |
| Do. *hon.* | མགོ་སྐོར་གཏོང་ང་ (བ་) གནང་བ་ | *go-l or tong-nga nang-wa.* |
| Tempt, to (entice) | སེམས་བསླུས་པ་ | *sem lü-pa.* |
| Do. *hon.* | སེམས་བསླུས་པ་གནང་བ་ | *sem lü-pa nang-wa.* |
| Do. *inf.* to *sup.* | ཐུགས་སེམས་བསླུས་པ་ | *thuk-sem lü-pa.* |
| Tenacious (obstinate) | གྱོང་པོ་ | *ḱyong-po.* |
| Tenant | མི་སེར། འབངས་ | *mi-ser; bang.* |
| Do. poorer class of | མོ་ཡན་ | *mo-yen.* |
| Tender | འཇམ་པོ་ | *jam-po.* |
| Tendon | རྒྱུས་པ་ | *gyü-pa.* |
| Tenet | ཆོས་ལུགས་ | *chhö-lu.* |
| Ten | བཅུ་ | *chu.* |
| Tenth | བཅུ་པ་ | *chu-pa.* |
| Ten thousand | ཁྲི་ | *thri.* |
| Tent | གུར་ | *ḱur.* |
| Do. *hon.* | དབུ་གུར་ | *u-ḱur.* |
| Tent-pole | གུར་རྒྱུག་ | *ḱur-gyu.* |
| Tepid | དྲོན་འཇམ་ | *trön-jam.* |

| | | |
|---|---|---|
| Term (limit) | མཐའ་ | *tha.* |
| Do. (period) | དུས། བསྐལ་པ་ | *t́ü ; kel-pa.* |
| Do. (word) | ཚིག་ | *tshi.* |
| Terminate, to | འཚར་བ་ | *tshar-wa.* |
| Do. *hon.* | གྲུབ་པ་ | *t́ruṕ-pa.* |
| Terrible | ཞེད་སྐྲག་ཚ་པོ་ | *sḱe-tra tsha-po.* |
| Terribly | ཞེད་སྐྲག་ | *sḱe-tra.* |
| Terrified, to be | ཞེད་པ་ | *sḱe-pa.* |
| Do. *hon.* | ཞེད་པ་གནང་བ་ | *sḱe-pa nang-wa.* |
| Terrify, to | ཞེད་སྐྲག་སླང་བ་ | *sḱe-tra lang-wa.* |
| Do. *hon.* | ཞེད་སྐྲག་སློང་ང་ (བ་) གནང་བ་ | *sḱe-tra long-nga nang-wa.* |
| Terrifying | ཞེད་སྐྲག་ཚ་པོ་ | *sḱe-tra tsha-po.* |
| Territory | ས་ཆ་ | *sa-chha.* |
| Terror | ཞེད་སྐྲག་ | *sḱe-tra.* |
| Test, to | ཚོད་ལྟ་བ་ | *tshö ta-wa.* |
| Do. *hon.* | ཚོད་གཟིགས་པ་ | *tshö śi-pa.* |
| Testament (will) | ཁ་ཆེམས་ | *kha-chhem.* |
| Do. *hon.* | ཞལ་ཆེམས་ | *sḱe-chhem.* |
| Testicle | རླིག་པ་ | *lik-pa.* |

| | | |
|---|---|---|
| Testify, to | དཔང་པོ་བྱེད་པ་ | *pang-po cḱe-pa.* |
| Do. *hon.* | དཔང་པོ་གནང་བ་ | *pang-po nang-wa.* |
| Than | ལས་ | *le.* |
| Thankful, to be | དྲིན་དྲན་པ་ | *t́rin t́rem-pa.* |
| Do. *hon.* | དྲིན་དྲན་པ་གནང་བ་ | *t́rin t́rem-pa rang-wa.* |
| Do. *inf.* to *sup.* | བཀའ་དྲིན་དྲན་པ་ | *ka-t́rin t́rem-pa.* |
| Thank you! | འོ་ཡག་བྱུང་ | *o ya-cḱung.* |
| Do. *hon.* | ཐུགས་ཆེ་ | *thu-chhe.* |
| Do. *h. hon.* | ཐུགས་རྗེ་ཆེ་གནང་ | *thu-je chhe-nang.* |
| That | དེ་ | *t́e.* |
| That down there | མ་གི་ | *ma-ḱi.* |
| That, just like | ད་ག་རང་། དེ་འདྲ་ | *t́a-ḱa-rang; t́en-dra.* |
| That over there | ཕ་གི་ | *pha-ki.* |
| That up there | ཡ་གི་ | *ya-ḱi.* |
| That very | ཕ་གེ་རང་ | *pha-ḱe-rang.* |
| Thaw, to | ཞུ་བ་ | *sḱu-wa.* |
| The, *def. art.* | འདི། དེ་ | *di; t́e.* |
| Theft | རྐུན་མ་ | *ku-ma.* |
| Their | ཁོང་ཚོའི་ | *khon-tshö.* |
| Them | ཁོང་ཚོ་ | *khon-tsho.* |

| | | |
|---|---|---|
| Then (after that) | དེ་ནས་ | *t́e-ne.* |
| Do. (at that time) | དེའི་སྐང་ལ་ | *t́e-i gang-la.* |
| There | དད་ (དེ་ཙུ།) ཕ་གི་ | *t́e ; pha-gi.* |
| Therefore | བྱས་ཙང་། དེའི་རྐྱེན་བྱས་ནས། དེའི་རྐྱེན་གྱིས་ | *cḱe-tsang ; t́e-i kyen cḱe-ne ; t́e-i kyen-ḱyi* |
| Thermometer | ཚ་གྲང་ལྟ་ཡ་ | *tsha-t́rang ta-ya.* |
| These | འདི་ཚོ་ | *di-tsho.* |
| They | ཁོ་ཚོ་ | *khon-tsho.* |
| Thibet | བོད་ | *ṕo.* |
| Thibetan | བོད་པ་ | *ṕö-pa.* |
| Do. language | བོད་སྐད་ | *ṕö-ke.* |
| Do. manuscript characters | དབུ་མེད་ | *u-me.* |
| Do. printed characters | དབུ་ཅན་ | *u-chen.* |
| Thick (of flat objects) | འཐུག་པོ་ | *thuḱ-po.* |
| Do. (of round objects) | སྦོམ་པོ་ | *bom-po.* |
| Do. (turbid) | རྙོག་པོ་ | *nyoḱ-po.* |
| Thief | རྐུན་མ་ | *ku-ma.* |
| Thieve, to | རྐུན་མ་རྐུ་བ་ | *ku-ma ku-wa.* |
| Thigh | བརླ་ཤ་ | *le-sha.* |

| | | |
|---|---|---|
| Thigh-bone trumpet | རྐང་གླིང་ | *kang-ling.* |
| Thimble | ཙོ་མོ་ | *cho-mo.* |
| Thin (of flat objects) | སྲབ་པོ་ | *traṕ-po.* |
| Do. (of round objects) | ཕྲ་པོ་ | *thra-po.* |
| Do. (of persons and animals) | ཤ་སྐམ་པོ་ | *sha kam-po.* |
| Do. *hon.* (of persons) | སྐུ་ཤ་སྐམ་པོ་ | *ku-sha kam-po.* |
| Do. *hon.* (of animals) | བཞེས་ཤ་སྐམ་པོ་ | *sḱe-sha kam-po.* |
| Thine | ཁྱོད་རེའི་ (ཁྱོད་ཀྱི་) | *khyö-re.* |
| Do. *hon.* | ཁྱེད་ཀྱི་ | *khye-kyi.* |
| Do. *h. hon.* | སྐུ་གཞོགས་ཀྱི་ | *ku-sḱo kyi.* |
| Thing | ཅ་ལག་ (ཆ་ལག་) | *cha-la.* |
| Do. *hon.* | སྐུ་ཅས་ (སྐུ་ཆས་) | *ku-che.* |
| Think, to (suppose) | བསམ་པ་ | *sam-pa.* |
| Do. *hon.* | དགོངས་པ་ | *gong-pa.* |
| Think, to (reflect) | བསམ་བློ་བཏང་ (གཏོང་) བ་ | *sam-lo tang-wa.* |
| Do. *hon.* | ཐུགས་བསམ་བཞེས་པ་ | *thu-sam sḱe-pa.* |
| Third | གསུམ་པ་ | *sum-pa.* |
| Thirdly | གསུམ་པར་ | *sum-pa.* |
| Thirsty, to be | ཁ་སྐོམ་པ་ | *kha kom-pa.* |
| Do. *hon.* | ཞལ་སྐྱེམས་པ་ | *sḱe kyem-pa.* |

| | | |
|---|---|---|
| Thirteen | བཅུ་གསུམ་ | *chuk-sum.* |
| Thirteenth | བཅུ་གསུམ་པ་ | *chuk-sum-pa.* |
| Thirty | སུམ་ཅུ་ | *sum-chu.* |
| Thirtieth | སུམ་ཅུ་པ་ | *sum-chu-pa.* |
| This | འདི་ | *di.* |
| This very | ད་ག་རང་ | *ta-ka-rang* |
| Thither | དད་ (དེ་རུ་) | *te.* |
| Thorn | ཚེར་མ་ | *tsher-ma.* |
| Thorough, to be (complete) | ཕུགས་འཁྱོལ་བ་ | *phu khyö-wa.* |
| Thoroughly | ཐད་དེ་ | *be-te.* |
| Those | དེ་ཚོ་ | *te-tsho.* |
| Thou | ཁྱོད། ཁྱོད་རང་ | *khyö ; khyö-rang.* |
| Do. *hon.* | ཁྱེད་ | *khye.* |
| Do. *h. hon* | སྐུ་གཞོགས་ | *ku-sko.* |
| Though | ནས། ཀྱང་། རུང་། ན་ཡང་ | *ne ; kyang ; rung na-yang.* |
| Thought (intention) | དོན་དག་ | *tön-ta.* |
| Do. *hon.* | སྐུ་དོན་ | *ku-tön.* |
| Thought (opinion) | བསམ་པ་ | *sam-pa.* |
| Do. *hon* | ཐུགས་སེམས་ | *thu-sem.* |

| | | |
|---|---|---|
| Thousand | སྟོང་ཕྲག་ | *tong-thra.* |
| Thousand, hundred | འབུམ་ | *bum.* |
| Thousand, ten | ཁྲི་ | *thri.* |
| Thrash, to | གཡོ་མ་སྲུ་རྡུང་བ་ | *yo-ma-su dung-wa.* |
| Thread | སྐུད་པ་ | *kü-pa.* |
| Threaten, to | འཛོག་འཛོག་ (འཛིག་འཛིག་) བཏང་ (གཏོང་) བ་ | *dziḱ-dziḱ tang-wa.* |
| Three | གསུམ་ | *sum.* |
| Thresh, to (corn) | རྡུང་བ་ | *dung-wa.* |
| Threshhold | ཐེམ་པ་ | *them-pa.* |
| Thrice | ཚར་གསུམ་ | *tshar-sum.* |
| Thriving | གཡང་ཆེན་པོ་ | *yang-chhem-po.* |
| Throat | མིག་པ་ | *miḱ-pa.* |
| Do. *hon.* | མགུལ་མིག་ | *gü-mi.* |
| Throne | བཞུགས་ཁྲི་ | *sḱuḱ-thri.* |
| Throng (of men) | མི་ཚོགས་ | *mi-tsho.* |
| Through (by the agency of) | བརྒྱུད་ནས | *gyü-ne.* |
| Throw, to | རྒྱབ་པ། དབྱུག་པ་ | *gyaṕ-pa; yuḱ-pa.* |
| Do. *hon.* | དབྱུག་ཀ་ (པ་) གནང་བ | *yuḱ-ka nang-wa.* |
| Throw at, to | གཞུ་བ་ | *sḱu-wa.* |

| | | |
|---|---|---|
| Throw at, to, *hon.* | སྐྱོན་པ་གནང་བ་ | *kyöm-pa nang-wa.* |
| Thumb | མཐེ་བོ་ | *the-po.* |
| Do. *hon.* | ཕྱག་མཐེ་ | *chha-the.* |
| Thunder | འབྲུག་སྐད་ | *druḱ-ke.* |
| Thunder, to | འབྲུག་སྐད་སྐྱོན་པ་ | *druḱ-ke kyöm-pa.* |
| Thunderbolt | ཐོག་ | *tho.* |
| Do. sacred | རྡོ་རྗེ་ | *dor-je.* |
| Thursday | གཟའ་ཕུར་བུ་ | *śa-phur-ṕu.* |
| Thus | འདི་འདྲས། དག་ག་ཟེ་ | *din-dre ; t́a-ḱa-śe.* |
| Thwart, to | བཀག་པ་ (འགེགས་པ་) | *kaḱ-pa.* |
| Do. *hon.* | བཀག་ག་ (འགེགས་པ་) གནང་བ་ | *kaḱ-ḱa nang-wa.* |
| Tibet | བོད་ | *ṕö.* |
| Tibetan | བོད་པ་ | *ṕö-pa.* |
| Do. language | བོད་སྐད་ | *ṕö-ke.* |
| Do. printed characters | དབུ་ཅན་ | *u-chen.* |
| Do. manuscript characters | དབུ་མེད་ | *u-me.* |
| Tickle, to | ཨི་ཀུ་ལུ་ཀུ་སག་པ་ | *i-ḱu lu-ḱu saḱ-pa.* |
| Tidings | གནས་ཚུལ། གསར་འགྱུར་ | *ne-tshü ; sang-gyu.* |

| | | |
|---|---|---|
| Tiffin | ཉིན་གུང་ཁ་ལག་ | nyin-kung kha-la. |
| Do. *hon.* | ཉིན་གུང་ཞལ་ལག་ | nyin-kung ske-la. |
| Tie, to | བསྡམས་པ་ (སྡོམ་པ་) | dam-pa. |
| Do. *hon.* | བསྡམས་ (སྡོམ་)་་གནང་བ་ | dam-pa nang-wa. |
| Tiger | སྟག་ | ta. |
| Tight | དམ་པོ་ | tam-po. |
| Till | ཐུག་ལ། བར་དུ་ | thuk-la; par-tu. |
| Till, to | རྨོན་པ་རྒྱབ་པ་ | möm-pa gyap-pa. |
| Tillage | སོ་ནམས་ | so-nam. |
| Tiller, *s.* (one who tills) | རྨོན་པ་རྒྱབ་མཁན། ཐོན་ཁས་ (ཐོན་པ་) | möm-pa gyang-khen; thön-khe. |
| Timber | ཤིང་ཆ་ | shing-chha. |
| Time | དུས། དུས་ཚོད་ | tü; tü-tshö. |
| Do. (o'clock) | ཆུ་ཚོད་ | chhu-tshö. |
| Do. (proper time for doing something) | རན་ | ren. |
| Do. (three times, etc.) | ཚར། ཐེངས་ | tshar; theng. |
| Do. (life) | ཚེ་ | tshe. |
| Time, at the present (now-a-days) | དེ་རིང་སང་། དེང་སང་ | te-ring sang; teng-sang. |
| Time, to pass the | དགོ་འཁོར་བ་ | go-khor-wa. |

| | | |
|---|---|---|
| Time, to pass the, *hon.* | དབུ་འཁོར་བ་ | *u-khor-wa.* |
| Tin | ཤ་དཀར་ | *sha-ka.* |
| Tinder | སྤྲ་བ་ | *pa-a.* |
| Tip (point) | རྩེ་ | *tse.* |
| Tip (gratuity) | ཆང་རིན་ | *chhang-ring.* |
| Do. *hon.* | གསོལ་རས་ | *sö-re.* |
| Tipsy | ར་བཟི་ | *raṕ-śi.* |
| Do. to be | ར་བཟི་བ་ | *ra-śi-wa.* |
| Do. *hon.* | སྐུ་ར་བྲེད་པ་ | *ku-ra be-pa.* |
| Tired | བཀའ་ལས་ཁག་པོ་ | *ka-le khaḱ-po* |
| Do. *hon.* | སྐུ་མཉེལ་པོ་ | *ku-nye-po.* |
| Tired, to be | ཐང་ཆད་པ་ | *thang-chhe-pa.* |
| Do. *hon.* | སྐུ་ཐང་ཆད་པ་གནང་བ་ | *ku-thang chhe-pa nang-wa.* |
| Tiresome (tedious) | དཀའ་ལས་ཁག་པོ་ | *ka-le khaḱ-po.* |
| Do. *hon.* | སྐུ་མཉེལ་པོ་ | *ku-nye-po.* |
| Titan (demi-god) | ལྷ་མ་ཡིན་ | *hla-ma-yin.* |
| Title | གོ་ས། གོ་གནས་ | *ḱo-sa; ḱo-ne.* |
| To (in presence of a person) | རྩ་ལ་ | *tsa-la.* |
| Do. *inf.* to *sup.* | སྐུ་མདུན་ལ་ | *kun-dün-la.* |
| To (as far as) | བར་ལ་ | *ṕar-la.* |

| | | |
|---|---|---|
| Tobacco | ཐ་མག་ | *tha-ma.* |
| Do. *hon.* | བཞེས་ཐ་ | *sk̓e-tha.* |
| Tobacco pipe | གང་ཟག་ | *k̓ang-śa.* |
| Do. *hon.* | བཞེས་ཟག་ | *sk̓e-śa.* |
| Tobacco pouch | ཐ་ཁུག་ | *tha-khu.* |
| Do. *hon.* | བཞེས་ཁུག་ | *sh̓e-khu.* |
| To-day | དེ་རིང་ | *t̓e-ring.* |
| Toe | རྐང་པའི་མཛུག་གུ་ | *kang-pe dzuk̓-k̓u.* |
| Do. *hon.* | ཞབས་ཀྱི་ཕྱག་མཛུག་ | *sk̓ap̓-kyi chhan-dzu.* |
| Toe, the big | རྐང་པའི་མཐེ་བོ་ | *kang-pe the-p̓o.* |
| Do. *hon.* | ཞབས་ཀྱི་མཐེ་བོ་ | *sk̓ap̓-kyi the-p̓o.* |
| Together with, *prep.* | དང་མཉམ་དུ་ | *t̓ang-nyam-t̓u.* |
| Together, *adv.* (jointly) | མཉམ་སྦྲེལ་ | *nyam-drel.* |
| Do. *hon.* | ཕྱག་སྦྲེལ་ | *chha-drel.* |
| Toilsome | དཀའ་ལས་ཁག་པོ་ | *ka-le khak̓-po.* |
| Do. *hon.* | སྐུ་མཉེལ་པོ་ | *ku-nye-po.* |
| Token | རྟགས་ | *ta.* |
| Tolerate, to (endure) | བཟོད་པ་སྒོམ་པ་ | *śö-pa gom-pa.* |
| Do. *hon.* | བཟོད་པ་སྒོམ་པ་གནང་བ་ | *śö-pa gom-pa nang-wa.* |
| Tolerate to (permit) | བཅུག་པ་ (འཇུག་པ་) | *chuk̓-pa.* |

| | | |
|---|---|---|
| Tolerate, to (permit), *hon.* | བཅུག་ག་ (འཇུག་པ་) གནང་བ་ | *chuḱ-ḱa nang-wa.* |
| Tomb | དུར་ཁུང་ | *t́ur-khung.* |
| Tom-cat | ཕོ་ཞིམ་ | *pho-sḱim.* |
| To-morrow | སང་ཉིན་ | *sang-nyi.* |
| To-morrow morning | སང་ཞོགས་སྔ་པོ་ | *sang-sḱo nga-po.* |
| Tone | གདངས་ | *dang.* |
| Tongue | ལྕེ་ | *che.* |
| Do. *hon.* | ལྗགས་ | *ja.* |
| Tongue (dialect) | སྐད་ལུགས་ | *ke-lu.* |
| To-night | དོ་དགོངས་དགོངས་མོ་ | *t́o-gong gong-mo.* |
| Too, *conj.* | ཡང་ | *yang.* |
| Too (very) | ཧ་ཅང་ | *ha-chang.* |
| Too few, to be | ཉུང་དྲག་པ་ | *nyung t́raḱ-pa.* |
| Too little, to be | ཆུང་དྲག་པ་ | *chhung t́raḱ-pa.* |
| Too many, to be | མང་དྲག་པ་ | *mang t́raḱ-pa.* |
| Too much, to be | ལྷག་པ་ | *hlaḱ-pa.* |
| Tool | ལག་ཆ་ | *laḱ-chha.* |
| Tooth | སོ་ | *so.* |
| Do. *hon.* | ཚེམས་ | *tshem.* |

| | | |
|---|---|---|
| Toothless | སོ་མེད་ | *so-me.* |
| Do. *hon.* | ཚེམས་མེད་ | *tshem-me.* |
| Tooth, front | མདུན་སོ་ | *dün-so.* |
| Do. *hon.* | མདུན་གྱི་ཚེམས་ | *dün-kyi tshem.* |
| Tooth, lower | སྨད་སོ་ | *me-so.* |
| Do. *hon.* | སྨད་ཀྱི་ཚེམས་ | *me-kyi tshem.* |
| Tooth, molar | འགྲམ་སོ་ | *dram-so.* |
| Do. *hon.* | ཞལ་འགྲམ་གྱི་ཚེམས་ | *ske-dram kyi-tshem* |
| Tooth, upper | ཡ་སོ་ | *ya-so.* |
| Do. *hon.* | ཡས་ཀྱི་ཚེམས་ | *ye-kyi tshem.* |
| Top (summit) | རྩེ | *tse.* |
| Do. (lid) | ཁ་གཅོད་ | *khap-chö.* |
| Do. *hon.* | ཞལ་གཅོད་ | *ske-chö.* |
| Torch | སྦྱད་འབར་ (སྦྱ་འབར་) | *pem-bar.* |
| Torment, to (annoy) | ཁོང་ཁྲོ་སློང་བ་ | *khong-thro lang-wa.* |
| Do. *hon.* | དགོངས་པ་དཀྲུག་པ་ | *gong-pa truk-pa.* |
| Torn, to be | རལ་བ་ | *re-wa.* |
| Tortoise | རུས་སྦལ་ | *rü-be.* |
| Tortuous (crooked) | ཀྱོག་ཀྱོག་ | *kyo-kyo.* |
| Do. (deceitful) | གཡོ་ཅན། བློ་སྐྱོགས་སྐྱོགས་ | *yo-chen ; lo kyok-kyok.* |

| | | |
|---|---|---|
| Tortuous (deceitful), *hon.* | ཐུགས་གཡོ་ཅན། ཐུགས་སྐྱོགས་སྐྱོགས་ | *thu yo-chen ; thu kyoḱ-kyoḱ.* |
| Torture (agony of mind) | སྡུག་བསྔལ་ | *du-nge.* |
| Do. *hon.* | ཐུགས་འཁྲལ་ | *thu-thre.* |
| Total, in the | བསྡོམས་ནས་ | *dom-ne* |
| Totter, to | འཁྱོར་ནས་འགྲོ་བ་ | *khyor-ne dro-wa.* |
| Do. *hon.* | སྐུ་འཁྱོར་ནས་ཕེབ་པ་ | *ku-khyor-ne phe-pa.* |
| Do. *h. hon.* | སྐུ་འཁྱོར་ནས་འཆིབ་རྒྱུ་གནང་བ་ | *ku-khyor-ne chhiṕ-gyu nang-wa.* |
| Touch, to | ཐུག་པ། འཆང་བ་ | *thuḱ-pa ; chhang-wa.* |
| Do. *hon.* | ཐུག་ག་ (པ་) གནང་བ་ | *thuḱ-ḱa nang-wa.* |
| Touch, to (by stretching out hand, etc.) | སྙོབ་པ་ | *nyoṕ-pa.* |
| Do. *hon.* | སྙོབ་པ་གནང་བ་ | *nyoṕ-pa nang-wa.* |
| Towards | ཕྱོགས་ལ། ངོས་ལ་ | *chhoḱ-la ; ngö-la.* |
| Towel | ཨ་ཆོར་ | *a-chor.* |
| Do. *hon.* | ཞལ་ཆོར་ | *sḱe-chor.* |
| Town | གྲོང་ཁྱེར་ | *t́rong-khyer.* |
| Toy | རྩེད་མོ་རྩེ་ཡ་ | *tse-mo tse-ya.* |
| Do. *hon.* | སྐུ་རྩེ་གནང་ཡ་ | *ku-tse nang-ya.* |

| | | |
|---|---|---|
| Track (path) | ལམ་ཀ་ | *lang-ka.* |
| Do. *hon.* | ཕེབ་ལམ་ | *pheṕ-lam.* |
| Track (on face of cliff) | ཕྲང་ | *thrang.* |
| Track (foot-print) | རྐང་རྗེས་ | *kang-je.* |
| Do. *hon.* | ཞབས་རྗེས་ | *sḱaṕ-je.* |
| Tract (of country) | ལུང་པ་ | *lung-pa.* |
| Trade, *s.* | ཚོང་ | *tshong.* |
| Do. *hon.* | རྒྱ་ཚོང་ | *gya-tshong.* |
| Trade, to | ཚོང་རྒྱབ་པ་ | *tshong-gyaṕ-pa.* |
| Do. *hon.* | རྒྱ་ཚོང་སྐྱོན་པ་ | *gya-tshong kyöm-pa.* |
| Trader, tradesman | ཚོང་པ་ | *tshong-pa.* |
| Do. *hon.* | ཚོང་དཔོན་ | *tshong-pön.* |
| Traduce, to | སྨད་ར་བཏང་ (གཏོང་) བ་ | *me-ra tang-wa.* |
| Do. *hon.* | སྨད་ར་གཏོང་ང་ (བ་) གནང་བ་ | *me-ra tong-nga nang-wa.* |
| Do. *inf.* to *sup.* | སྨད་ར་ཞུ་བ་ | *me-ra sḱu-wa.* |
| Traffic | ཚོང་ | *tshong.* |
| Do. *hon.* | རྒྱ་ཚོང་ | *gya-tshong.* |
| Train, to (teach) | བསླབས་པ་ (སློབ་པ་) | *laṕ-pa.* |
| Do. *hon.* | བསླབས་ (སློབ་) པ་གནང་བ་ | *laṕ-pa nang-wa.* |
| Trammel *s.* (hindrance) | བཀག་ཆ་ | *kaḱ-chha.* |

| | | |
|---|---|---|
| Trammel, to | བཀག་པ་ (འགེགས་པ་) | *kak̄-pa.* |
| Do. *hon.* | བཀག་ག་ (འགེགས་པ་) གནང་བ་ | *kak̄-k̄a nang-wa.* |
| Tramp, *s.* (loafer) | རྒྱལ་ཁམས་ལ་སྐོར་མཁན་ | *gyeng-kham kor-khen.* |
| Trample, to | རྐང་པས་རྫི་བ་ | *kang-pe dzi-wa.* |
| Do. *hon.* | ཞབས་ཀྱིས་རྫི་བ་གནང་བ་ | *sk̄ap̄-kyi dzi-wa nang-wa.* |
| Tranquil (of places) | ཁ་གུ་སིམ་བུ་ | *kha-k̄u sim-p̄u.* |
| Do. *hon.* | ཞལ་གུ་སིམ་བུ་ | *sk̄e-k̄u sim-p̄u.* |
| Transfer, to | རྗེ་བ་ | *je-wa.* |
| Do. (soldiers, etc.) | རྗེ་པོ་རྒྱབ་པ་ | *je-po gyap̄-pa.* |
| Do. *hon.* | རྗེ་པོ་སྐྱོན་པ་ | *je-po kyöm-pa.* |
| Transgress, to | སྡིག་པ་བསགས་ (སོག་) པ་ | *dik̄-pa sak̄-pa.* |
| Do. *hon.* | སྐུ་སྡིག་བསགས་ག་ (སོག་པ་) གནང་བ་ | *ku-di sak̄-k̄a nang-wa.* |
| Transgression | སྡིག་པ་ | *dik̄-pa.* |
| Do. *hon.* | སྐུ་སྡིག་ | *ku-di.* |
| Translate, to | སྒྱུར་བ་ | *gyur-wa.* |
| Do. *hon.* | སྒྱུར་ར་ (བ་) གནང་བ་ | *gyur-ra nang-wa.* |
| Transmigrate, to | སྐྱེ་བ་འཕོས་པ་ | *kye-wa phö-pa.* |
| Do. *hon.* | སྐུ་སྐྱེ་འཕོས་པ་ | *ku-kye phö-pa.* |

| | | |
|---|---|---|
| Transmigration, cycle of | སྲིད་པ་འཁོར་ལོ་ | *si-pa khor-lo.* |
| Transport | ཁལ་མ་ | *khe-ma.* |
| Do. *hon.* | ཆིབས་ཁལ་ | *chhiṕ-khe.* |
| Transport (compulsory service) | རྟའུ་ | *ta-u.* |
| Do. *hon.* | ཆིབས་རྟའུ་ | *chhiṕ-ta-u.* |
| Transport, to | རྟའུ་སྐྱེལ་བ་ | *ta-u kyel-wa.* |
| Do. *hon.* | ཆིའུ་སྐྱེལ་ར་ (བ་) གནང་བ་ | *chhi-u kye-ra nang-wa.* |
| Trap | རྙི་ | *nyi.* |
| Travail (child-birth) | སྐྱེ་གཟུག་ | *kye-śu.* |
| Traveller | འགྲུལ་པ་ | *drü-pa.* |
| Tray | ཤིང་ཁྲོལ་ | *shing-thrö.* |
| Do. *hon.* | གསོལ་ཁྲོལ་ | *sö-thrö.* |
| Tread, to | རྐང་ལེབ་འཐེབ་པ་ | *kang-le theṕ-pa.* |
| Do. *hon.* | ཞབས་ལེབ་འཐེབ་པ་ | *sḱaṕ-le theṕ-pa.* |
| Treasure, *s.* | བཀང་འཛུག་ | *kang-juḱ.* |
| Treasurer | ཕྱག་མཛོད་ | *chhan-dzö.* |
| Treasury | དངུལ་ཁང་ | *ngü-khang.* |
| Treat, *s.* (feast) | མགྲོན་པོ་ | *dröm-po.* |
| Do. *hon.* | ཐུགས་སྤྲོ་ | *thu-tro.* |

| | | |
|---|---|---|
| Treat, to (entertain) | མགྲོན་པོ་བཏང་ (གཏོང་) བ་ | *dröm-po tang-wa.* |
| Do. *hon.* | ཐུགས་སྤྲོ་གཏོང་ང་ (བ་) གནང་བ་ | *thu-tro tong-nga nang-wa.* |
| Treaty | འཆིང་ཡིག་ | *chhing-yi.* |
| Tree | ཤིང་སྡོང་ | *shing-dong.* |
| Tremble, to (of animate beings) | འདར་བ་ | *dar-wa.* |
| Do. *hon* | སྐུ་འདར་སྐྱོན་པ་ | *kun-dar kyöm-pa.* |
| Tremble, to (of inanimate things) | འཁྲུག་པ་ | *thruk-pa.* |
| Trench | དོང་ | *t́ong.* |
| Trial (experiment) | ཞིབ་ཆ་ | *sḱiṕ-chha.* |
| Do. (by judge) | ཞིབ་དཔྱོད་ | *sḱiṕ-chö.* |
| Do. *hon.* | བཀའ་ཞིབ་ | *ka-sḱiṕ.* |
| Trial, to make a | ཞིབ་ཆ་ལྟ་བ་ | *sḱiṕ-chha ta-wa.* |
| Do. *hon.* | ཞིབ་ཆ་གཟིགས་པ་ | *sḱiṕ-chha śi-pa* |
| Triangle | ཟུར་གསུམ་ | *śur-sum.* |
| Tribe | མི་བརྒྱུད། རིགས་བརྒྱུད་ | *mi-gyü ; ri-gyü.* |
| Tribunal | ཁྲིམས་ཁང་ | *thrim-khang.* |
| Tribute | ཁྲལ། འབབ་ | *thre ; bap.* |
| Trick (deceit) | མགོ་སྐོར་ | *go-kor.* |

| | | |
|---|---|---|
| Trick (deceit), *hon.* | དབུ་སྐོར་ | *u-kor.* |
| Trickle, to | ཐིགས་པ་རྒྱབ་པ་ | *thiḱ-pa gyaṕ-pa.* |
| Tricky (artful) | གཅང་པོ་ | *chang-po.* |
| Do. *hon.* | ཐུགས་གཅང་པོ་ | *thu-chang-po.* |
| Trident | ཁ་ཊཾ་ | *kha-tam.* |
| Trifling, (matter), *adj.* | དོན་གནད་ཆུང་ཆུང་ | *t́ön-ne chhung-chhung.* |
| Do. *hon.* | ཐུགས་དོན་ཆུང་ཆུང་ | *thuḱ-t́ön chhung-chhung.* |
| Trigger | སྐམ་པ་ | *kam-pa.* |
| Tripod | རྐང་གསུམ་ | *kang-sum.* |
| Do. iron (for fire) | ལྕགས་སྒྲིད་ | *cha-gyi.* |
| Trivial | དོན་གནད་ཆུང་ཆུང་ | *t́ön-ne chhung-chhung.* |
| Do. *hon.* | ཐུགས་དོན་ཆུང་ཆུང་ | *thuḱ-t́ön chhung-chhung.* |
| Tromowa (inhabitant of Chumbi Valley) | གྲོ་མོ་བ་ | *t́ro-mo-wa.* |
| Troop | དམག་དཔུང་ | *maḱ-pung.* |
| Trot, to | གོམ་ས་རྒྱབ་པ་ | *ḱom-sa gyaṕ-pa.* |
| Do. *hon.* | གོམ་ས་སྐྱོན་པ་ | *ḱom-sa kyöm-pa.* |
| Trouble | དཀའ་ལས་ | *ka-le.* |
| Do. to be in | དཀའ་ལས་ཕྱུང་བ་ | *ka-le ḱung-wa.* |

| | | |
|---|---|---|
| Troublesome (of persons) | ཅ་སྙུན་པོ་ | *cha-sing-po.* |
| Do. *hon.* | ཐུགས་ཅ་སྙུན་པོ་ | *thuk-cha sing-po.* |
| Troublesome (of things) | དཀའ་ལས་ཁག་པོ་ | *ka-le khak-po.* |
| Do. *hon.* | སྐུ་མཉེལ་པོ་ | *ku-nye-po.* |
| Trousers | གོ་ཐུང་ (གོས་ཐུང་།) དོར་མ | *ko-thung ; tor-ma.* |
| Do. *hon.* | ཞབས་དོར་ | *skap-to.* |
| True | ངོ་ཐོག། དངོས་ནས་ | *ngo-tho : ngö-ne.* |
| Truly | དངོས་ནས་ | *ngö-ne.* |
| Trumpet | དུང་ | *tung.* |
| Trumpet, thigh bone | རྐང་གླིང་ | *kang-ling.* |
| Trunk (box) | སྒམ་ | *gam.* |
| Do. *hon.* | ཕྱག་སྒམ་ | *chha-gam.* |
| Trunk (of elephant) | མཆུ་རྡོ་ | *chhu-do.* |
| Trunk, iron (box) | ལྕགས་སྒམ་ | *cha-gam.* |
| Do. leather (box) | ཀོ་སྒམ་ | *ko-gam.* |
| Trunk (of tree) | སྡོང་པོ་ | *dong-po.* |
| Trust (confidence) | བློ་གཏད་ | *lo-te.* |
| Trust, to | བློས་བཀལ་བ་ | *lö ke-wa.* |
| Do. *hon* | ཐུགས་བློ་བཀལ་ར་ (བ་) གནང་བ་ | *thu-lo ke-ra nang-wa.* |

| | | |
|---|---|---|
| Trustworthy | བློས་ (བློ་) ཁེལ་ར་ (བ་) | *lö khe-ra.* |
| Do. *hon.* | ཐུགས་བློ་ཁེལ་ར་ (བ་) | *thu-lo khe-ra.* |
| Truth | ངོ་ཐོག། དངོས་ནས་ | *ngo-tho; ngö-ne.* |
| Try, to (make effort) | སྙིང་རུས་བྱེད་པ་ | *nying-rü cḱe-pa.* |
| Do. *hon.* | ཐུགས་རུས་གནང་བ་ | *thuḱ-rü nang-wa.* |
| Try, to (test) | ཚོད་ལྟ་བ། ཁོག་པ་ལེན་པ་ | *tshö ta-wa; khoḱ-pa lem-pa.* |
| Do. *hon.* | ཚོད་གཟིགས་པ་ | *tshö śi-pa.* |
| Tuesday | གཟའ་མིག་དམར་ | *śa miḱ-mar.* |
| Tumble, to (on ground which one is already touching) | འགྱེལ་བ་ | *gye-wa.* |
| Do. *hon.* | འགྱེལ་ར་ (བ་) གནང་བ་ | *gye-ra nang-wa.* |
| Tumble, to (from a height) | གཟགས་པ་ (འཛག་པ་) | *śaḱ-pa.* |
| Do. *hon.* | གཟགས་ག་ (འཛག་པ་) གནང་བ་ | *śaḱ-ḱa nang-wa.* |
| Tumour | གཉེན་འབུར་ | *nyem-bur.* |
| Tumult | རྒྱབ་འདྲེ། འཁྲུག་པ་ | *gyam-dre; thruḱ-pa.* |
| Tune | གདངས་ | *dang.* |
| Turban | ལེ་དོས་ | *le-tö.* |
| Turbid | ཉོག་པོ་ | *nyoḱ-po.* |

| | | |
|---|---|---|
| Turf | སྤང་ | *pang.* |
| Turkistan | ཧོར་ལུང་པ། ཧོར་ཡུལ་ | *hor lung-pa; hor-yü.* |
| Do. man of | ཧོར་པ་ | *hor-pa.* |
| Turn round, to, *v.i.* | འཁོར་བ་ | *khor-wa.* |
| Do. *hon.* | ཞབས་འཁོར་གནང་བ་ | *sKap-khor nang-wa.* |
| Turn round, to, *v.t.* | སྐོར་ར་ (བ་) རྒྱབ་པ་ | *kor-ra gyap-pa.* |
| Do. *hon.* | སྐོར་ར་ (བ་) སྐྱོན་པ་ | *kor-ra kyöm-pa.* |
| Turn back to front, to | ཁ་ཕྱོགས་ལོག་པ་ | *kha-chho lok-pa.* |
| Do. *hon.* | ཁ་ཕྱོགས་ལོག་ག་ (པ་) གནང་བ་ | *kha-chho lok-ka nang-wa.* |
| Turn upside down, to | མགོ་གཞུག་ལོག་པ། ཨ་ལོག་རྒྱབ་པ་ | *ao-sKu lok-pa; a-lo gyap-pa.* |
| Do. *hon.* | མགོ་གཞུག་ལོག་ག་ (པ་) གནང་བ། ཨ་ལོག་སྐྱོན་པ་ | *go-sKu lok-ka nang-wa; a-lo kyöm-pa.* |
| Turnip | ཉུང་མ་ | *nyung-ma.* |
| Do. *hon.* | བཞེས་ཉུང་ | *sKe-nyung.* |
| Turquoise | གཡུ་ | *yu.* |
| Do. *hon.* | ཕྱག་གཡུ་ | *chha-yu.* |
| Turquoise ear-ring | ཟི་གཡུ་ | *ši-yu.* |
| Turquoise (worn in head-dress) | གཡུ་ | *yu.* |

| | | |
|---|---|---|
| Turquoise (worn in head-dress) *hon.* | དབུ་གཡུ་ | *u-yu.* |
| Tusk | མཆེ་བ་ | *chhe-wa.* |
| Tutelary deity | ཡི་དམ་ | *yi-dam.* |
| Tutor | དགེ་རྒན་ | *ge-gen.* |
| Do. *hon.* | དགེ་རྒན་ལགས་ | *ge-gen-la.* |
| Twelfth | བཅུ་གཉིས་པ་ | *chu-nyi-pa.* |
| Twelve | བཅུ་གཉིས་ | *chu-nyi.* |
| Twentieth | ཉི་ཤུ་པ་ | *nyi-shu-pa.* |
| Twenty | ཉི་ཤུ་ | *nyi-shu.* |
| Twice | ཚར་གཉིས་ | *tshar-nyi.* |
| Twilight, at | ས་རིབ་ (སྲིབ་) ནས་ | *sa rip-ne.* |
| Twin | མཚེ་མ་ | *tshe-ma.* |
| Do. *hon.* | ཨ་ཝ་མཚེ་མ་ | *a-wa tshe-ma.* |
| Twine | སྐུད་པ་ | *kü-pa.* |
| Do. *hon.* | ཕྱག་སྐུད་ | *chha-kü.* |
| Twist, to | སྒྲིམ་པ་ | *drim-pa.* |
| Do. *hon.* | སྒྲིམ་པ་གནང་བ་ | *drim-pa nang-wa.* |
| Two | གཉིས་ | *nyi.* |
| Do. (in weighing, measuring, etc.) | དོ་ | *to.* |

## U

| | | |
|---|---|---|
| Udder | གཞོས་ | *sKö.* |
| Ugly | ཁ་མདོག་ཉེས་པོ་ | *kha-do nye-po.* |
| Do. *hon.* | ཞལ་མདོག་ཉེས་པོ་ | *sKe-do nye-po.* |
| Ulcer | ཤུ་བ་ | *shu-wa.* |
| Do. *hon.* | སྐུ་ཤུ་ | *ku-shu.* |
| Ultimate | གཞུག་ཤོས་ | *sKuk-shö.* |
| Umbrage, to take | འཚེར་བ་ | *tsher-wa.* |
| Do. *hon.* | ཐུགས་འཚེར་གནང་བ་ | *thu-tsher nang-wa.* |
| Umbrella | ཉི་གདུགས་ | *nyi-du.* |
| Do *hon.* | དབུ་གདུགས་ | *u-du.* |
| Unable, to be | མི་ཐུབ་པ་ | *mi thup-pa.* |
| Unavailing, to be (useless) | ཕན་མི་ཐོགས་པ་ | *phen mi thok-pa.* |
| Do. *hon.* | ཐུགས་ཕན་མི་གསོ་བ | *thu-phen mi so-wa.* |
| Unbearable (pain) | སྒྲོང་མི་ཐུབ་པ་ | *gong mi thup-pa.* |
| Do. *hon.* | སྒྲོང་ང་ (སྒྲོམ་པ་) གནང་མི་ཐུབ་པ་ | *gong-nga nang mi thup-pa.* |
| Unbiassed | ཁྲིམས་དྲང་པོ་ | *thrim trang-po.* |
| Do. *hon.* | བཀའ་ཁྲིམས་དྲང་པོ་ | *ka-thrim trang-po.* |
| Unbreakable, to be | ཆག་རྒྱུ་མེད་པ་ | *chhak-gyu me-pa.* |

| | | |
|---|---|---|
| Unbridled (licentious) | འདོད་ཆགས་ཆེན་པོ་ | *dö-chha chhem-po.* |
| Unceasing | རྒྱུན་ཆད་རྒྱུ་མེད་པ་ | *gyün-chhe-gyu me-pa.* |
| Unceasingly | རྣམ་རྒྱུན། དུས་རྒྱུན་ | *nam-gyün ; t́ü-gyün.* |
| Uncertain, to be | ཐེ་ཚོམ་ཟ་བ་ | *the-tshom śa-wa.* |
| Do. *hon.* | ཐེ་ཚོམ་གནང་བ་ | *the-tshom nang-wa.* |
| Uncertainty | ཐེ་ཚོམ་ | *the-tshom.* |
| Unchaste | འདོད་ཆགས་ཆེན་པོ་ | *dö-chha chhem-po.* |
| Uncivil | སྒྲིག་མེད་ | *driḱ-me.* |
| Uncle, maternal | ཞང་ཞང་ (ཨ་ཞང་) | *sḱang·sḱang.* |
| Do. paternal | ཨ་ཀུ་ | *a-ḱu.* |
| Unclean | བཙོག་པ་ | *tsoḱ-pa.* |
| Unclothed | དམར་ཧྲང་ང་ | *mar-hrang-nga.* |
| Uncommon (rare) | དཀོན་པོ་ | *köm-po.* |
| Unconquerable | གླགས་···མི་ཁ་བ་ | *la...mi kha-wa.* |
| Undaunted | བློ་ཁོག་ཆེན་པོ་ | *lo-kho chhem-po.* |
| Do. *hon.* | ཐུགས་ཁོག་ཆེན་པོ་ | *thu-kho chhem-po.* |
| Undefined | བརྟན་པོ་མེད་པ་ | *tem-po me-pa.* |
| Under | འོག་ལ་ | *o-la.* |
| Understand, to | ཤེས་པ། ཧ་གོ་བ་ | *she-pa ; ha-ḱo-wa.* |
| Do. *hon.* | མཁྱེན་པ་ | *khyem-pa.* |

| | | |
|---|---|---|
| Understand, to, *h. hon.* | དགོངས་པ་རྟོགས་པ་ | *gong-pa toḱ-pa.* |
| Understanding | རིག་པ་ | *riḱ-pa.* |
| Do. *hon.* | ཐུགས་རིག | *thu-ri.* |
| Undo, to (nullify) | མེད་པར་བཟོ་བ་ | *me-pa so-wa.* |
| Do. *hon.* | མེད་པར་བཟོ་བ་གནང་བ་ | *me-pa śo-wa nang-wa.* |
| Undo, to (untie) | བཀྲོལ་བ་ (འགྲོལ་བ།) བཤིག་པ་ | *tröl-wa ; sḰiḱ-pa.* |
| Do. *hon.* | བཀྲོལ་ར་ (འགྲོལ་བ་) གནང་བ། བཤིག་ག་ (པ་) གནང་བ་ | *trö-ra nang-wa ; sḰiḱ-ḱa nang-wa.* |
| Undress, to | ཕྱིས་པ་ (འབུད་པ་) | *pi-pa.* |
| Do. *hon.* | ཕྱིས་ (འབུད་) པ་གནང་བ་ | *pi-pa nang-wa.* |
| Unendurable (pain) | སྐོང་ (སྐོམ་) མི་ཐུབ་པ་ | *gong mi thuṕ-pa.* |
| Do. *hon.* | སྐོང་ང་ (སྐོམ་པ་) གནང་མི་ཐུབ་པ་ | *gong-nga nang mi thuṕ-pa.* |
| Uneven, to be | སྙོམས་པོ་མེད་པ་ | *nyom-po me-pa.* |
| Unfasten, to (button, etc.) | ཕྱིད་པ་ | *pi-pa.* |
| Do. *hon.* | ཕྱིད་པ་གནང་བ་ | *pi-pa nang-wa.* |
| Untasten, to (knot, etc.) | བཤིག་པ་ | *sḰiḱ-pa.* |
| Do. *hon.* | བཤིག་ག་ (པ་) གནང་བ་ | *sḰiḱ-ḱa nang-wa.* |

| | | |
|---|---|---|
| Unfit | འོས་པོ་མེད་པ་ | *ö-po me-pa.* |
| Do. *hon.* | ཐུགས་འོས་པོ་མེད་པ་ | *thu-ö-po me-pa.* |
| Unfortunate | བསོད་བདེ་མེད་པ། བསོད་བདེ་ཆུང་ཆུང་ | *so-de me-pa ; so-de chhung-chhung.* |
| Do. *hon.* | སྐུ་བསོད་མེད་པ། སྐུ་བསོད་ཆུང་ཆུང་ | *ku-sö me-pa ; ku-sö chhung-chhung.* |
| Unfortunate, to be | བསོད་བདེ་མེད་པ་ | *so-de me-pa.* |
| Do. *hon.* | སྐུ་བསོད་མེད་པ་ | *ku-sö me-pa.* |
| Unintelligible | མི་གོ་བ་ | *mi ko-wa.* |
| Do. *hon.* | མི་གསན་པ་ | *mi sem-pa.* |
| Unhappy, to be | སྐྱིད་པོ་མེད་པ་ | *kyi-po me-pa.* |
| Do. *hon.* | ཐུགས་སྤྲོ་པོ་མེད་པ་ | *thu-tro-po me-pa.* |
| Uniform (dress) | དམག་ཆས་ | *mak-chhe.* |
| Uniform (alike) | གཅིག་པ། འདྲ་འདྲ་ | *chik-pa ; dran-dra.* |
| Unimportant | དོན་དག་ཆུང་ཆུང་ | *tön-ta chhung-chhung.* |
| Do. *hon.* | ཐུགས་དོན་ཆུང་ཆུང་ | *thuk-tön chhung-chhung.* |
| Uninterrupted | རྒྱུན་ཆད་རྒྱུ་མེད་པ་ | *gyün-chhe-gyu me-pa.* |
| Uninterruptedly | ནམ་རྒྱུན། དུས་རྒྱུན་ | *nam-gyün ; tü-gyün.* |
| Unite, to | འཐུད་རྒྱབ་པ་ | *thü-gyap-pa.* |
| Do. *hon.* | འཐུད་སྐྱོན་པ་ | *thü-kyöm-pa.* |

| | | |
|---|---|---|
| Unitedly (jointly) | མཉམ་སྦྲེལ་ | *nyam-drel.* |
| Do. *hon.* | ཕྱག་སྦྲེལ་ | *chha-drel.* |
| Universal (all) | ཚང་མ། ཐམས་ཅད། སྒང་ཁ། རུ་ | *tshang-ma ; tham-che ; gang-kha ; ru.* |
| Unlawful | ཁྲིམས་མེད་ | *thrim-me.* |
| Unlearned | ཡོན་ཏན་མེད་པ་ | *yön-ten me-pa.* |
| Do. *hon.* | སྐུ་ཡོན་མེད་པ་ | *ku-yön me-pa.* |
| Unless, with *verb* "to do" | མ་བྱེད་ན་ | *ma cKe-na.* |
| Unlimited | ཚོད་མེད་པ་ | *tshö me-pa.* |
| Unloose, to (dress, etc.) | སྤྲིད་པ་ | *pi-pa.* |
| Do. *hon.* | སྤྲིད་པ་གནང་བ་ | *pi-pa nang-wa.* |
| Unlucky | བསོད་བདེ་མེད་པ། བསོ་ (བསོད་) བདེ་ཆུང་ཆུང་ | *so-de me-pa ; so-de chhung-chhung* |
| Do. *hon.* | སྐུ་བསོད་མེད་པ། སྐུ་བསོད་ཆུང་ཆུང་ | *ku-sö me-pa ; ku-sö chhung-chhung.* |
| Unlucky, to be | བསོད་བདེ་མེད་པ་ | *so-de me-pa.* |
| Do. *hon.* | སྐུ་བསོད་མེད་པ་ | *ku-sö me-pa.* |
| Unmarried man | ཕོ་ཧྲང་ང་ | *pho-hrang-nga.* |
| Do. woman | མོ་ཧྲང་ང་ | *mo-hrang-nga.* |
| Unmerciful, to be | སྙིང་རྗེ་མེད་པ་ | *nying-je me-pa.* |

| | | |
|---|---|---|
| Unmerciful, to be, *hon.* | ཐུགས་རྗེ་མེད་པ་ | *thuǩ-je me-pa.* |
| Unprejudiced (of judge) | ཁྲིམས་དྲང་པོ་ | *thrim ťrang-po.* |
| Do. *hon.* | བཀའ་ཁྲིམས་དྲང་པོ་ | *ka-thrim ťrang-po.* |
| Unprofitable, to be | ཕན་མི་ཐོགས་པ་ | *phen mi thoǩ-pa.* |
| Do. *hon.* | ཐུགས་ཕན་མི་གསོ་བ་ | *thu-phen mi so-wa.* |
| Unreasonable | དོན་མེད་ | *ťon-me.* |
| Unrelenting, to be | སྙིང་རྗེ་མེད་པ་ | *nying-je me-pa.* |
| Do. *hon.* | ཐུགས་རྗེ་མེད་པ་ | *thuǩ-je me-pa.* |
| Unserviceable, to be | ཕན་མི་ཐོགས་པ་ | *phen mi thoǩ-pa.* |
| Do. *hon.* | ཐུགས་ཕན་མི་གསོ་བ་ | *thu-phen mi so-wa.* |
| Unsettled (indefinite) | བརྟན་པོ་མེད་པ་ | *tem-po me-pa.* |
| Untie, to | བཀྲོལ་བ་ (འགྲོལ་བ།) བཤིག་པ་ | *tröl-wa ; sǩik-pa.* |
| Do. *hon.* | བཀྲོལ་ར་ (འགྲོལ་བ་) གནང་བ། བཤིག་ག་ (པ་) གནང་བ་ | *trö-ra nang-wa ; sǩik-ǩa nang-wa.* |
| Until | ཐུག་ལ་ | *thuǩ-la.* |
| Untruth | ཧམ་པ། ཀྱག་རྫུན་ | *ham-pa ; kyaǩ-dzün.* |
| Do. *hon.* | ཞལ་རྫུན་ | *sǩe-dzün.* |
| Unusual (rare) | དཀོན་པོ་ | *köm-po.* |

| | | |
|---|---|---|
| Unusual (extraordinary) | ཡ་མཚན་པོ། ཁྱད་མཚར་པོ་ | *yam-tshem-po ; khye-tsha-po.* |
| Unwell, to be | བདེ་པོ་མེད་པ། གཟུགས་པོ་ ཐང་པོ་མེད་པ་ | *de-po me-pa ; śuḱ-po thang-po me-pa.* |
| Do. *hon.* | སྐུ་གཟུགས་བདེ་པོ་མེད་པ། སྐུ་གཟུགས་ཐང་པོ་མེད་པ་ | *ku-śu de-po me-pa ; ku-śu thang-po me-pa.* |
| Up | ཡར་ | *ya.* |
| Up to | ཐུག་ལ་ | *thuḱ-la.* |
| Up-hill | གྱེན་ | *ḱyen.* |
| Do. steep | གྱེན་དམ་པོ་ | *ḱyen-ťam-po.* |
| Upon | སྟེང་ལ། སྒང་ལ་ | *teng-la ; gang-la.* |
| Upper | ཡ་གི་ | *ya-ḱi.* |
| Upper arm | ལག་ཉ་ | *laḱ-nya.* |
| Do. *hon.* | ཕྱག་ཉ་ | *chha-nya.* |
| Upper tooth | ཡ་སོ་ | *ya-so.* |
| Do. *hon.* | ཡས་ཀྱི་ཚེམས་ | *ye-kyi tshem.* |
| Upraid, to | གཤེ་གཤེ་བཏང་ (གཏོང་) བ་ | *she-she tang-wa.* |
| Do. *hon.* | བཀའ་བཀྱོན་གནང་བ་ | *kaṕ-kyön nang-wa.* |
| Upright (erect) | ཀྱེ་རེ་ | *kye-re.* |
| Do. (just) | ཁྲིམས་དྲང་པོ་ | *thrim ťrang-po.* |
| Do. *hon.* | བཀའ་ཁྲིམས་དྲང་པོ་ | *ka-thrim ťrang-po.* |

| | | |
|---|---|---|
| Upright (moral, virtuous) | ཚུལ་ལྡན་ | *tshün-den.* |
| Upshot | སྙིང་པོ་ | *nying-po.* |
| Upstairs | ཡ་ཐོག་ | *yap-tho.* |
| Urge, to (insist) | ཨུ་ཚུགས་བྱེད་པ་ | *u-tshu cKe-pa.* |
| Do. *hon.* | ཨུ་ཚུགས་གནང་བ་ | *u-tshu nang-wa.* |
| Urgent (work) | འཕྲལ་འཕྲལ་བྱེད་དགོས་ཡ་ | *thre-thre cKe gö-ya.* |
| Urine | གཅིན་པ་ | *chim-pa.* |
| Do. *hon.* | ཆབ་གསང་ | *chhap-sang.* |
| Do. *h. hon.* | སྐུ་གསང་ | *ku-sang.* |
| Urine, to discharge | གཅིན་པ་བཏང་ (གཏོང་) བ་ | *chim-pa tang-wa.* |
| Do. *hon.* | ཆབ་གསང་བཏང་ (གཏོང་) བ་ | *chhap-sang tang-wa.* |
| Do. *h. hon.* | སྐུ་གསང་གནང་བ་ | *ku-sang nang-wa.* |
| Urn (containing ashes of dead lama) | སྐུ་གདུང་ | *ku-dung.* |
| Us | ང་ཚོ་ | *nga-tsho.* |
| Usage | ལུགས་སྲོལ་ | *luk-sö.* |
| Use (custom) | ལུགས་སྲོལ་ | *luk-sö.* |
| Use, to (employ) | སྐོ་བ་ | *ko-wa.* |
| Do. *hon.* | སྐོ་བ་གནང་བ་ | *ko-wa nang-wa.* |
| Use, to be of | ཕན་ཐོགས་པ་ | *phen thok-pa.* |

| | | |
|---|---|---|
| Use, to be of *hon.* | ཐུགས་ཕན་གསོ་བ་ | *thu-phen so-wa.* |
| Used to, to be | གོམས་པ་ | *ḱom-pa.* |
| Used to, to become | གོམས་སོང་བ་ | *ḱom-song-wa.* |
| Used up, to be | རྫོགས་པ་ | *dzoḱ-pa.* |
| Do. *hon.* | རྫོགས་ག་ (པ་) གནང་བ་ | *dzoḱ-ḱa nang-wa.* |
| Useful, to be | ཕན་ཐོགས་པ་ | *phen thoḱ-pa.* |
| Do. *hon.* | ཐུགས་ཕན་གསོ་བ་ | *thu-phen so-wa.* |
| Useless, to be | ཕན་མི་ཐོགས་པ་ | *phen mi thoḱ-pa* |
| Do. *hon.* | ཐུགས་ཕན་མི་གསོ་བ་ | *thu-phen mi so-wa.* |
| Usually | ཕལ་ཆེར་ | *phe-chhe.* |
| Usurp, to | འཕྲོག་པ་ | *throḱ-pa.* |
| Do. *hon.* | འཕྲོག་ག་ (པ་) གནང་བ་ | *throḱ-ḱa nang-wa.* |
| Utensils | ལག་ཆ་ | *laḱ-chha.* |
| Do. cooking | ཐབ་ཆས་ | *thaṕ-chhe.* |
| Utter (entire) | ཚང་མ། ཐམས་ཅད། སྒང་ཁ. | *tshang-ma; thum-che; gang-kha.* |
| Utter, to (speak) | ལབ་པ་ | *laṕ-pa.* |
| Do. *hon.* | གསུང་བ་ | *sung-wa.* |
| Utterance | སྐད་ | *ke.* |
| Do. *hon.* | གསུང་སྐད་ | *sung-ke.* |
| Utterly (used negatively) | བད་དེ། ཁྱོན་ནས་ | *be-t́e; khyön-ne.* |

# V

| | | |
|---|---|---|
| Vacant | སྟོང་པ་ | *tong-pa.* |
| Vagrant | རྒྱལ་ཁམས་སྐོར་མཁན་ | *gyeng-kham kor-khen.* |
| Vaccine lymph | ཐོར་པའི་སྨན་ | *thor-pe-men.* |
| Vacillate, to | ཐེ་ཚོམ་ཟ་བ་ | *the-tshom za-wa.* |
| Do. *hon.* | ཐེ་ཚོམ་གནང་བ་ | *the-tshom nang-wa.* |
| Vacillation | ཐེ་ཚོམ་ | *the-tshom.* |
| Vague | ཏན་པོ་མེད་པ་ | *tem-po me-pa.* |
| Vain | རང་སྟོད་ཚ་པོ་ | *rang-tö tsha-po.* |
| Do. in personal appearance | དང་འདོད་ཚ་པོ་ | *tang-dö tsha-po.* |
| Valiant | སྙིང་ཆེན་པོ་ | *nying-chhem-po.* |
| Do. *hon.* | ཐུགས་སྙིང་ཆེན་པོ་ | *thu-nying chhem-po.* |
| Valley | རོང་། ལུང་པ་ | *rong ; lung-pa.* |
| Do. upper part of | ལུང་པའི་ཕུ་ | *lung-pe phu.* |
| Do. lower part of | ལུང་པའི་མདོ་ | *lung-pe do.* |
| Valorous | སྙིང་ཆེན་པོ་ | *nying-chhem-po.* |
| Do. *hon.* | ཐུགས་སྙིང་ཆེན་པོ་ | *thu-nying chhem-po.* |
| Valuable | རྩ་ཆེན་པོ་ | *tsa chhem-po.* |
| Value. *s.* | གོང་ | *kong.* |

| | | |
|---|---|---|
| **Value**, *hon.* | ལྗགས་གོང་ | *ja-kong.* |
| Valueless | གོང་མེད་ | *kong-me.* |
| Vanish, to | ཡལ་བ་ | *ye-wa.* |
| Vanity | རང་སྟོད་ | *rang-tö.* |
| Do. in personal appearance | དང་འདོད་ | *tang-dö.* |
| Vanquish, to | རྒྱལ་བ། གླག་འཁས་པ་ | *gye-wa ; la khe-pa.* |
| Do. *hon.* | རྒྱལ་ར་ (བ་) གནང་བ། གླག་འཁས་ར་ (པ་) གནང་བ་ | *gye-ra nang-wa ; la khe-ra nang-wa.* |
| Vanquished, to be | འཕམ་པ་ | *pham-pa.* |
| Do. *hon.* | འཕམ་པ་གནང་བ་ | *pham-pa nang-wa.* |
| Vapour | རླངས་པ་ | *lang-pa.* |
| Variable, to be | བརྟན་པོ་……མེད་པ་ | *tem-po...me-pa.* |
| Variation (difference) | ཁྱད། ཧེ་བག་ | *khye ; he-pa.* |
| Do. *hon.* | ཐུགས་ཁྱད་ | *thu-khye.* |
| Variety | ཁྱད། ཧེ་བག་ | *khye ; he-pa.* |
| Do. *hon.* | ཐུགས་ཁྱད་ | *thu-khye.* |
| Various | མི་གཅིག་པ། མི་འདྲ་བ་ | *mi chik-pa ; min dra-wa.* |
| Various kinds of | སྣ་ཚོགས་ | *na-tsho.* |
| Vase | བུམ་པ་ | *pum-pa.* |

| | | |
|---|---|---|
| Vase, *hon.* | ཕྱག་བུམ་ | *chha-pum.* |
| Vast | རྒྱ་ཆེན་པོ་ | *gya-chhem-po.* |
| Vaunt, to | རང་སྟོད་བྱེད་པ་ | *rang-tö cḱe-pa.* |
| Veal | བེ་བེའི་ཤ་ | *ṕe-ṕe sha.* |
| Vegetable | ཚས་ *Ch.* | *tshe.* |
| Vegetable drug | སྔོ་སྨན་ | *ngo-men.* |
| Vegetable garden | ཚས་གཡང་ཙེ་ *Ch.* | *tshe yang-tse.* |
| Vein | རྩ་ | *tsa.* |
| Do. *hon.* | སྐུ་རྩ་ | *ku-tsa.* |
| Velveteen | སྤུ་མ་ | *pu-ma.* |
| Venerable (title) | རྗེ་བཙུན་ | *je-tsün.* |
| Venerate, to | བསྙེན་བཀུར་བྱེད་པ་ | *nyen-kur cḱe-pa.* |
| Do. *inf.* to *sup.* | བསྙེན་བཀུར་ཞུ་བ་ | *nyen-kur sḱu-wa.* |
| Veneration | བསྙེན་བཀུར་ | *nyen-kur.* |
| Vengeance | དགྲ་ལན་ | *dra-len.* |
| Vengeance, to take | དགྲ་ལན་ལེན་པ་ | *dra-len lem-pa.* |
| Do. *hon.* | དགྲ་ལན་བཞེས་པ་ | *dra-len sḱe-pa.* |
| Venial (trivial) | དོན་གནད་ཆུང་ཆུང་ | *ṫön-ne chhung-chhung.* |
| Do. *hon.* | ཐུགས་དོན་ཆུང་ཆུང་ | *thuk-ṫon chhung-chhung.* |
| Venison | ཤྭ་གི་ཤ་ (ཤྭ་བའི་ཤ་) | *sha-ki sha.* |

| | | |
|---|---|---|
| Venom (poison) | དུག་ | *t́u.* |
| Do. *hon.* | གསོལ་དུག་ | *sö-t́u.* |
| Venom (spite) | གནོད་སེམས་ | *nö-sem.* |
| Venture, to | ནུས་པ་ | *nü-pa.* |
| Do. *hon.* | ནུས་པ་གནང་བ་ | *nü-pa nang-wa.* |
| Venturesome | ཁ་མེད་མིག་མེད་ | *kha-me miḱ-me.* |
| Verandah (roofed in) | ཐོག་གཡང་ | *tho-yang.* |
| Do. (in upper story) | གཡབ་སྟེང་ | *yaṕ-teng.* |
| Do. (upper, running round a house) | གཡབ་འཁོར་ | *yaṕ-khor.* |
| Verbal | ཁའི་ | *khe.* |
| Verbally | ཁ་ནས་ | *kha-ne.* |
| Verdict (judgment) | བཅད་མཚམས་། ཁྲ་མ་ | *che-tsham; thra-ma.* |
| Vermilion | མཚལ། རྒྱ་མཚལ་ | *tshe; gyam-tshe.* |
| Vermin | འབུ་ | *bu.* |
| Verse | ཚིགས་བཅད་ | *tshiḱ-che.* |
| Vertebræ | སྒལ་ཚིགས་ | *ge-tshi.* |
| Do. *hon.* | སྐུ་སྟོད་ཚིགས་ | *ku-tö tshi.* |
| Vertigo | བད་རླུང་མགོ་འཁོར་ | *ṕe-lung go-khor.* |
| Very | ཧ་ཅང་ | *ha-chang.* |

| | | |
|---|---|---|
| Vessel (for water) | ཆུ་སྣོད་ | *chhu-nö.* |
| Do. *hon.* | ཆབ་སྣོད་ | *chhaṕ-nö.* |
| Vessel (ship) | གྲུ་ | *t́ru.* |
| Do. *hon.* | ཕེབ་གྲུ་ | *pheṕ-t́ru.* |
| Vex, to | ཁོང་ཁྲོ་སློང་བ་ | *khong-thro lang-wa.* |
| Do. *hon.* | དགོངས་པ་དཀྲུག་པ་ | *gong-pa truḱ-pa.* |
| Vexed, to be | ཚིག་པ་ཟ་བ་ | *tshiḱ-pa śa-wa.* |
| Do. *hon.* | དགོངས་པ་ཚུང་བ་ | *gong-pa tshung-pa.* |
| Viands | ཁ་ལག། ལྟོ་ | *kha-la ; to.* |
| Do. *hon.* | ཞལ་ལག་ | *sḱe-la.* |
| Vibrate, to | འཁྲུག་པ་ | *thruḱ-pa.* |
| Vice | སྡིག་པ་ | *diḱ-pa.* |
| Do. *hon.* | སྐུ་སྡིག་ | *ku-di.* |
| Vicinity | ཉེ་འཁོར་ | *nye-khor.* |
| Vicious | ངན་པོ་ | *ngem-po.* |
| Do. *hon.* | ཐུགས་ངན་པོ་ | *thu ngem-po.* |
| Victorious, to be | རྒྱལ་བ་ | *gye-wa.* |
| Do. *hon.* | རྒྱལ་ར་ (བ་) གནང་བ་ | *gye-ra nang-wa.* |
| Victuals | ཁ་ལག། ལྟོ་ | *kha-la ; to.* |
| Do. *hon.* | ཞལ་ལག་ | *sḱe-la.* |

| | | |
|---|---|---|
| View (opinion) | བསམ་པ་ | *sam-pa.* |
| Do. *hon.* | ཐུགས་སེམས་ | *thu-sem.* |
| View (purpose) | དོན་དག་ | *ťön-ťa.* |
| Do. *hon.* | སྐུ་དོན་ | *ku-ťön.* |
| View, to | མཐོང་བ། ལྟ་བ་ | *thong-wa ; ta-wa.* |
| Do. *hon.* | གཟིགས་པ་ | *śi-pa.* |
| Vigorous | ཤེད་ཆེན་པོ་ | *she chhem-po.* |
| Do. *hon.* | སྐུ་ཤེད་ཆེན་པོ་ | *ku-she chhem-po.* |
| Vigour | ཤེད་ | *she.* |
| Do. *hon.* | སྐུ་ཤེད་ | *ku-she.* |
| Vile (dirty) | བཙོག་པ་ | *tsoǩ-pa.* |
| Do. (odious) | སྐྱུག་བྲོ་པོ་ | *kyuǩ-ťro-po.* |
| Vilification | སྨད་ར་ | *me-ra.* |
| Vilify, to | སྨད་ར་བཏང་ (གཏོང་) བ་ | *me-ra tang-wa.* |
| Do. *hon.* | སྨད་ར་གཏོང་ང་ (བ་) གནང་བ་ | *me-ra tong-nya nang-wa.* |
| Do. *inf.* to *sup.* | སྨད་ར་ཞུ་བ་ | *me-ra sǩu-wa.* |
| Village | གྲོང་པ་ | *ťrong-pa.* |
| Villager | གྲོང་པ་ | *ťrong-pa.* |
| Villain | འཛབ་ཆེན་ | *dzap̌-chhen.* |
| Vine | རྒྱུན་འབྲུམ་ཤིང་ | *gün-drum-shing.* |

| | | |
|---|---|---|
| Vinegar | ཚུའུ་ *Ch.* | *tshu-u.* |
| Violence (force) | དབང་ཡོད་ | *wang-yö.* |
| Violence, to show | དབང་ཡོད་བྱེད་པ་ | *wang-yö cḱe-pa.* |
| Violet (colour) | རྒུན་འབྲུམ་མདོག་ | *gün-drum do.* |
| Virgin | བུ་མོ་ | *ṕu-mo.* |
| Virtue | དགེ་བ་ | *ge-wa.* |
| Virtuous | ཚུལ་ལྡན་ | *tshün-den.* |
| Virus (poison) | དུག་ | *t́u.* |
| Do. *hon.* | གསོལ་དུག་ | *sö-tu.* |
| Visible, to be | མཐོང་བ་ | *thong-wa.* |
| Do. *hon.* | གཟིགས་པ་ | *śi-pa.* |
| Vision (spectre) | གདོང་འདྲེ། འདྲེ་ | *dong-dre ; dre.* |
| Visit, to (a person) | བཅར་བ་ | *char-wa.* |
| Do. *inf.* to *sup.* | སྐུ་མདུན་ལ་བཅར་བ་ | *kun-dün-la char-wa.* |
| Vituperate, to | སྨད་ར་བཏང་ (གཏོང་) བ་ | *me-ra tang-wa.* |
| Do. *hon.* | སྨད་ར་གཏོང་ང་ (བ་) གནང་བ་ | *me-ra tong-nga nang-wa.* |
| Do. *inf.* to *sup.* | སྨད་ར་ཞུ་བ་ | *me-ra sḱu-wa.* |
| Vituperation | སྨད་ར་ | *me-ra.* |
| Vocabulary | མིང་མཛོད་ | *ming-dzö.* |
| Vocation | ལས་ཀ་ | *le-ka.* |

| | | |
|---|---|---|
| Vocation, *hon.* | ཕྱག་ལས་ | *chha-le.* |
| Voice | སྐད། སྒྲ་ | *ke ; dra.* |
| Do. *hon.* | གསུང་ | *sung.* |
| Void (empty) | སྟོང་པ་ | *tong-pa.* |
| Volume (of book) | པོ་ཏི་ | *po-ti.* |
| Vomit, to | སྐྱུག་པ་ | *kyuK-pa.* |
| Do. *hon.* | ཞལ་སྐྱུག་གནང་བ་ | *sKe-kyu nang-wa.* |
| Voracious (gluttonous) | གྲོད་ཆེན་པོ་ | *ťrö-chhem-po.* |
| Vouch, to | ཁས་ཁྱགས་བྱེད་པ་ | *khe-khya cKe-pa.* |
| Do. *hon.* | ཞལ་ཁྱགས་གནང་བ་ | *sKe-khya nang-wa.* |
| Voucher (guarantor) | ཁས་ཁྱགས་བྱེད་མཁན་ | *khe-khya cKe-khen.* |
| Do. *hon.* | ཞལ་ཁྱགས་གནང་མཁན་ | *sKe-khya nang-khen.* |
| Vow (religious) | དམ་བཅའ་ | *ťam-cha.* |
| Do. to make) | དམ་བཅའ་ཕུལ་ (འབུལ་) བ་ | *ťam-cha phü-wa.* |
| Do. *hon.* | དམ་བཅའ་འབུལ་ར་ (བ་) གནང་བ་ | *ťam-cha bü-ra nang-wa.* |
| Vowels | དབྱངས་ | *yang.* |
| Vulgar (of language, *opp.* to *hon.*) | ཞེ་ས་མེད་པ་ | *sKe-sa me-pa.* |
| Do. (of persons, *opp.* to high-born) | དཀྱུས་མ་ | *kyü-ma.* |

## W

| | | |
|---|---|---|
| Wag (jester) | དབུ་འཁོར་ཞུ་མཁན་ | *u-khor sKu-khen.* |
| Wag, to (shake) | དབྱུག་དབྱུག་བྱེད་པ་ | *yuk-yu cKe-pa.* |
| Do. *hon.* | དབྱུག་དབྱུག་གནང་བ་ | *yuk-yu nang-wa.* |
| Wag, to (dog's tail) | རིལ་རིལ་བྱེད་པ་ | *ri-ri cKe-pa.* |
| Wager | རྒྱན་ | *gyen.* |
| Do. *hon.* | སྐུ་རྒྱན་ | *ku-gyen.* |
| Wager, to | རྒྱན་བཞག་ (འཛོག་) པ་ | *gyen sKak-pa.* |
| Do. *hon.* | སྐུ་རྒྱན་གཞོག་ག་ (འཛོག་པ་) གནང་བ་ | *ku-gyen sKok-ka nang-wa.* |
| Wages | གླ། ཕོགས་ | *la ; pho.* |
| Waggish | བགད་མོ་བྲོ་པོ་ | *ge-mo tro-po.* |
| Do. *hon.* | ཞལ་མོ་བྲོ་པོ་ | *sKe-mo tro-po.* |
| Waggon | ཤིང་རྟ་འཁོར་ལོ་ | *shing-ta khor-lo.* |
| Wail, to | ངུ་བ་ | *ngu-wa.* |
| Do. *hon.* | ཤུམ་པ་ | *shum-pa.* |
| Waist | སྐེད་པ་ | *ke-pa.* |
| Do. *hon.* | སྐུ་སྐེད་ | *ku-ke.* |
| Waist band | སྐེད་རགས་ | *ke-ra.* |
| Do. *hon.* | སྐུ་རགས་ | *ku-ra.* |

| | | |
|---|---|---|
| Waistcoat | ཁན་སྦྱར་ | *khen-jar.* |
| Wait, to, *v.t.* | སྒུག་བསྡད་ (སྡོད་) པ་ | *gu de-pa.* |
| Do. *hon.* | སྒུག་བཞུགས་པ་ | *gu-sku-pa.* |
| Wait on, to | སྐུ་མདུན་ལ་བཅར་བ་ | *kun-dün-la char-wa.* |
| Wake, to | གཉིད་སད་པ་ | *nyi se-pa.* |
| Do. *hon.* | མཉན་ (མནལ་) སད་པ་ | *nyen se-pa.* |
| Walk, to | ཀང་ཐང་ལ་འགྲོ་བ་ | *kang-thang la dro-wa.* |
| Do. *hon.* | ཞབས་ཐང་ལ་ཕེབ་པ་ | *skap-thang la phe-pa.* |
| Do. *h. hon.* | ཞབས་ཐང་ལ་འཆིབ་རྒྱུ་གནང་བ་ | *skap-thang la chhip-gyu nang-wa.* |
| Walk, to (of horses) | གོམ་པ་འགྲོ་བ་ | *kom-pa dro-wa.* |
| Walk, to take a | ཆམ་ཆམ་ (འཁྲམ་འཁྲམ་) ལ་འགྲོ་བ་ | *chham-chham la dro-wa.* |
| Do. *hon.* | སྐུ་ཆམ་ (འཁྲམ་) ལ་ཕེབ་པ་ | *kün-chham la phe-pa.* |
| Do. *h. hon.* | སྐུ་ཆམ་ (འཁྲམ་) ལ་འཆིབ་རྒྱུ་གནང་བ་ | *kün-chham la chhip-gyu nang-wa.* |
| Wall | རྩིག་པ་ | *tsik-pa.* |
| Do. city | ལྕགས་རི་ | *cha-ri.* |
| Do. fortified | འཛིང་ར་ | *dzing-ra.* |
| Walnut | སྟར་ཀ་ | *tar-ka.* |

| | | |
|---|---|---|
| Wan | དཀར་པོ་དཀར་ཀྱང་ | *kar-po kar-kyang.* |
| Wander, to (stroll) | ཆམ་ཆམ་ (འཁྱམ་འཁྱམ་) ལ་འགྲོ་བ་ | *chham-chham la dro-wa.* |
| Do. *hon.* | སྐུ་ཆམ་ (འཁྱམ་, ལ་ཕེབ་པ་ | *kün-chham la phe-pa.* |
| Do. *h. hon.* | སྐུ་ཆམ་ (འཁྱམ) ལ་འཆིབ་རྒྱུ་གནང་བ་ | *kün-chham la chhiṕ-gyu nang-wa.* |
| Wander, to (go astray) | ལམ་ཀ་ནོར་བ་ | *lam-ka nor-wa.* |
| Do. *hon.* | ཕེབ་ལམ་ནོར་ར་ (བ་) གནང་བ་ | *pheṕ-lam nor-ra nang-wa.* |
| Want, to (need) | དགོ་བ་ (དགོས་པ་) | *go-wa.* |
| Do. *hon.* | དགོ་བ་གནང་བ་ | *go-wa nang-wa.* |
| Want, to (wish) | འདོད་པ་བྱེད་པ་ | *dö-pa cḱe-pa.* |
| Do. *hon.* | ཐུགས་འདོད་གནང་བ་ | *thung-dö nang-wa.* |
| Wanton | འདོད་ཆགས་ཆེན་པོ་ | *dö-chha chhem-po.* |
| War | དམག་ | *ma.* |
| Wardrobe | དུག་ལོག་བླུག་སའི་སྒམ་ | *ťu-lo luḱ-se gam.* |
| Do. *hon.* | ན་བཟའ་བླུག་སའི་ཕྱག་སྒམ་ | *nam-śa luḱ-se chha-gam.* |
| Wares | ཚོང་ཡ་ | *tshong-ya.* |
| Do. *hon.* | རྒྱ་ཚོང་གནང་ཡ་ | *gya-tshong nang-ya.* |
| Warm | དྲོ་པོ་ | *ťro-po.* |
| Warn, to | བསླབ་བྱ་བྱེད་པ་ | *laṕ-cḱa cḱe-pa.* |

| | | |
|---|---|---|
| **Warn, to,** ***hon.*** | བསླབ་བྱ་གནང་བ་ | *lap̓-cḱa nang-wa.* |
| **Warp,** *s.* **(of loom)** | རྒྱུ་ | *gyu.* |
| **Do.** ***hon.*** | ཕྱག་རྒྱུ་ | *chha-gyu.* |
| **Warrant, to (authorize)** | དབང་སྤྲད་པ་ | *wang tre-pa.* |
| **Do.** ***hon.*** | དབང་གནང་བ་ | *wang nang-wa.* |
| **Warrant, to (guarantee)** | ཁས་ཁྱགས་བྱེད་པ་ | *ḱhe-khya cḱe-pa.* |
| **Do.** ***hon.*** | ཞལ་ཁྱགས་གནང་བ་ | *sḱe-khya nang-wa.* |
| **Warranty** | ཁས་ཁྱགས་ | *ḱhe-khya.* |
| **Do.** ***hon.*** | ཞལ་ཁྱགས་ | *sḱe-khya.* |
| **Warrior** | དམག་མི་ | *ma-mi.* |
| **Wart,** *s.* | སྨན་ (སྨེ་བ་) | *men.* |
| **Do** ***hon.*** | སྐུ་སྨན་ (སྐུ་སྨེ་) | *ḱu-men.* |
| **Wash, to** | འཁྲུད་པ་ | *thrü-pa.* |
| **Do.** ***hon.*** | བསིལ་ར་ (བ་) གནང་བ་ | *si-ra nang-wa.* |
| **Wasp** | དུག་སྦྲང་ | *ťuḱ-drang.* |
| **Waste, to** | གཏོར་བ་ | *tor-wa.* |
| **Do.** ***hon.*** | གཏོར་ར་ (བ་) གནང་བ་ | *tor-ra nang-wa.* |
| **Watch,** *s.* | ཆུ་ཚོད་འཁོར་ལོ་ | *chhu-tshö khor-lo.* |
| **Watch, to** | མིག་ལྟ་བ་ | *miḱ ta-wa.* |
| **Do.** ***hon.*** | སྤྱན་གཟིགས་པ་ | *chen śi-pa.* |

| | | |
|---|---|---|
| Watch, to (guard) | སྲུང་བ་ | *sung-wa.* |
| Do. *hon.* | སྲུང་ང་ (བ་) གནང་བ་ | *sung-nga nang-wa.* |
| Watchman | མིག་ལྟ་མཁན། སྲུང་མཁན་ | *miḱ-ta-khen ; sung-khen.* |
| Water | ཆུ་ | *chhu.* |
| Do. *hon.* | ཆབ་ | *chhaṕ.* |
| Water (for drinking) | འཐུང་ཡ་གི་ཆུ་ | *thung-ya-ḱi chhu.* |
| Do. *hon.* | བཞེས་ཡ་གི་ཆབ་ | *sḱe-ya-ḱi chhaṕ.* |
| Waterfall | བབ་ཆུ་ (འབབ་ཆུ་) | *ṕaṕ-chhu.* |
| Do. over rocks | བྲག་ཆུ་ | *t́raḱ-chhu.* |
| Water-mill | ཆུ་འཁོར་ | *chhu-kho.* |
| Water-vessel | ཆུ་སྣོད་ | *chhu-nö.* |
| Do. *hon.* | ཆབ་སྣོད་ | *chhaṕ-nö.* |
| Wave, *s.* | དབའ་རླབས་ | *ba-laṕ.* |
| Wave, to | དབྱུག་དབྱུག་བྱེད་པ་ | *yuḱ-yu cḱe-pa.* |
| Waver, to | ཐེ་ཚོམ་ཟ་བ་ | *the-tshom śa-wa.* |
| Do. *hon.* | ཐེ་ཚོམ་གནང་བ་ | *the-tshom nang-wa.* |
| Wavering | ཐེ་ཚོམ་ | *the-tshom.* |
| Wax, sealing | ལ་ཆ་ | *la-chha.* |
| Way (road) | ལམ་ཀ་ | *lang-ka.* |
| Do. *hon.* | ཕེབ་ལམ་ | *pheṕ-lam.* |

| | | |
|---|---|---|
| Way (highway) | རྒྱ་ལམ་ | *gya-lam.* |
| Way (manner) | ཐབས་ | *thaṕ.* |
| We | ང་ཚོ། ང་རང་ཚོ་ | *nga-tsho ; nga-rang-tsho.* |
| Weak (in muscle) | ཤེད་ཆུང་ཆུང་ | *she chhung-chhung.* |
| Do. *hon.* | སྐུ་ཤེད་ཆུང་ཆུང་ | *ku-she chhung-chhung.* |
| Weak (prone to illness) | གཟུགས་པོ་གཅོང་པོ་ | *śuḱ-po chong-po.* |
| Do. *hon.* | སྐུ་གཟུགས་གཅོང་པོ་ | *ku-śuḱ chong-po.* |
| Weakminded | ཀླུགས་པ། གླེན་པ་ | *kuḱ-pa ; lem-pa.* |
| Wealthy | ཕྱུག་པོ། ཅ་ (ཆ་) ལག་ཆེན་པོ་ | *chhuḱ-po ; cha-la chhem-po.* |
| Do. *hon.* | སྐུ་ཅས་ (ཆས་) ཆེན་པོ་ | *ku-che chhem-po.* |
| Weapon | མཚོན་ཆ་ | *tshön-chha.* |
| Wear, to | གོན་པ་ | *ḱöm-pa.* |
| Do. *hon.* | བཞེས་པ་ | *sḱe-pa.* |
| Wearisome | དཀའ་ལས་ཁག་པོ་ | *ka-le ḱhaḱ-po.* |
| Do. *hon.* | སྐུ་མཉེལ་པོ་ | *ḱu-nye-po.* |
| Weariness | ངལ་ | *ngel.* |
| Do. *hon.* | སྐུ་ངལ་ | *ḱu-ngel.* |
| Weary, to be | ཐང་ཆད་པ་ | *thang chhe-pa.* |
| Do. *hon.* | སྐུ་ཐང་ཆད་པ་གནང་བ་ | *ku-thang chhe-pa nang-wa.* |

| | | |
|---|---|---|
| Weasel | སྲེ་མོང་ | *tre-mong.* |
| Weather | གནམ་ | *nam.* |
| Do. clear | གནམ་དྭངས་པོ་ | *nam ťang-po.* |
| Weave, to | འཐག་འཐག་པ་ | *tha thaǩ-pa.* |
| Do. *hon:* | འཐག་འཐག་ག་ (པ་) གནང་བ་ | *ťha thaǩ-ǩa nang-wa.* |
| Weaver | འཐག་མཁན་ | *thang-khen.* |
| Web | ཐགས་ | *tha.* |
| Do. *hon.* | ཕྱག་ཐགས་ | *chha-tha.* |
| Wed, to (take husband) | མག་པ་བསླང་ (སློང་) བ་ | *maǩ-pa lang-wa* |
| Do. *hon.* | སྐུ་བག་བཞེས་པ་ | *ku-ṕa sǩe-pa.* |
| Wed, to (take wife) | མནའ་མ་ལེན་པ་ | *na-ma lem-pa.* |
| Do. *hon.* | མནའ་མ་བཞེས་པ་ | *na-ma sǩe-pa.* |
| Wedding | ཆང་ས་ | *chhang-sa.* |
| Do. *hon.* | འཁྲུང་ས་ | *thrung-sa.* |
| Wedge | ཀེའུ་ | *ke-u.* |
| Wednesday | གཟའ་ལྷག་པ་ | *śa-hlaǩ-pa.* |
| Weed | རྩ་ངན་ | *tsa-ngen.* |
| Weed, to | ཡུར་མ་རྒྱབ་པ་ | *yur-ma gyaṕ-pa.* |
| Do. *hon.* | ཡུར་མ་སྐྱོན་པ་ | *yur-ma kyöm-pa* |
| Week | བདུན་ཕྲག་ | *dün-thra.* |

| | | |
|---|---|---|
| Weep, to | ངུ་བ་ | *ngu-wa.* |
| Do. *hon.* | ཤུམ་པ་ | *shum-pa.* |
| Weft | སྤུན་ | *pün.* |
| Do. *hon.* | ཕྱག་སྤུན་ | *chha-pün.* |
| Weigh, to | ཀྱག་ (འགྱོགས་) པ་ | *kyak-pa.* |
| Do. *hon.* | ཀྱག་ག་ (འགྱོགས་པ་) གནང་བ་ | *kyak-ka nang-wa.* |
| Weigh, to (consider) | བསམ་བློ་བཏང་ (གཏོང་) བ་ | *sam-lo tang-wa.* |
| Do. *hon.* | ཐུགས་བསམ་བཞེས་པ་ | *thu-sam she-pa.* |
| Weight | ཡང་ལྗི་ | *yang-chi.* |
| Weighty (heavy) | ལྗི་པོ་ | *ji-po.* |
| Do. (important) | གནད་ཁག་ཆེན་པོ། གལ་ཆེན་པོ་ | *nen-kha chhem-po ; ke chhem-po.* |
| Welcome! | ཕྱག་ཕེབ་གནང་བྱུང་ | *chha-phe nang-chung.* |
| Well, *s.* | ཁྲོམ་པ་ (ཁྲོན་པ་) | *throm-pa.* |
| Do. *adj.* | ཡག་པོ་ | *yak-po.* |
| Well, to be (in health) | གཟུགས་པོ་བདེ་པོ་ཡོད་པ་ | *suk-po de-po yö-pa.* |
| Do. *hon.* | སྐུ་གཟུགས་བཟང་པོ་ཡོད་པ་ | *ku-suk sang-po yö-pa.* |
| Well! *interj.* | འོ་ན་ | *o-na.* |
| Well-behaved | ཡ་རབས་ | *ya-rap.* |
| Well-known (celebrated) | སྐད་གྲགས་ཆེན་པོ་ | *ke-tra chhem-po.* |

| | | |
|---|---|---|
| Well-known (celebrated), *hon.* | མཚན་སྙན་གྲགས་ཆེན་པོ་ | *tshen-nyen-t́ra chhem-po.* |
| Well-modelled (of metal-work, wood-work, etc.) | བཀོད་པ་དོད་པོ་ | *kö-pa t́ö-po.* |
| West | ནུབ་ | *nuṕ.* |
| Westward | ནུབ་ངོས། ནུབ་ཕྱོགས་ | *nuṕ-ngö ; nuṕ-chho.* |
| Wet | རློན་པ་ | *löm-pa.* |
| Wet, to | སྦང་བ་ | *bang-wa.* |
| Do. *hon.* | སྦང་ང་ (བ་) གནང་བ་ | *bang-nga nang-wa.* |
| Wether | ལུག་ཕོ་ | *luk-pho.* |
| What, *interr.* and *rel.* | ག་རེ་ | *ḱa-re.* |
| Whatever it is | ག་རེ་ཡིན་ནས་ | *ḱa-re yin-ne.* |
| Wheat | གྲོ་ | *t́ro.* |
| Wheat-flour | གྲོ་ཞིབ་ | *t́ro-sḱiṕ.* |
| Wheedle, to (for good object) | བསླབ་བྱ་རྒྱབ་པ་ | *laṕ-cḱa gyaṕ-pa.* |
| Do. *hon.* | བཀའ་སློབ་གནང་བ་ | *ka-loṕ nang-wa.* |
| Wheedle, to (for bad object) | སླུ་བ་ | *lu-wa.* |
| Do. *hon.* | སླུ་བ་གནང་བ་ | *lu-wa nang-wa.* |
| Wheel | འཁོར་ལོ་ | *khor-lo.* |
| When, *rel.* | དུས་ (w. root of verb) | *t́ü.* |

| | | |
|---|---|---|
| When, *interr.* | ག་དུས་ | *ḱa-ťü.* |
| Whenever | ག་དུས་……ཡང་ | *ḱa-ťü...yang.* |
| Whence | ག་ནས་ | *ḱa-ne.* |
| Where, *interr.* and *rel.* | ག་པ་ | *ḱa-pa.* |
| Wherever | ག་པ་……ཡང་ | *ḱa-pa...yang* |
| Whet, to | རྡར་བ་ | *dar-wa.* |
| Do. *hon.* | རྡར་ར་ (བ་) གནང་བ་ | *dar-ra nang-wa.* |
| Whether | ནས་ (ནོ་) | *ne.* |
| Whetstone | བདར་རྡོ་ | *dar-do.* |
| Which, *interr.* and *rel.* | ག་རེ་ | *ḱa-re.* |
| Which of them | ག་གི་ | *ḱa-ḱi.* |
| While, *adv.* | དུས་ (w. root of verb) | *ťü.* |
| Whip | རྟའི་ལྕག་ | *te-cha.* |
| Do. *hon.* | ཆིབས་ལྕག་ | *chhiṕ-cha.* |
| Whirlwind | རླུང་ཚུབ་ | *lung-tshuṕ.* |
| Whiskers | རྒྱཨུ་ | *gya-u.* |
| Whisper, *s.* | ཤབ་ཤོབ་ (ཤབ་ཤུབ་) | *shaṕ-shoṕ.* |
| Whisper, to | ཤབ་ཤོབ་ (ཤབ་ཤུབ་) ལབ་པ་ | *shaṕ-shoṕ laṕ-pa.* |
| Do. *hon.* | ཤབ་ཤོབ་ (ཤབ་ཤུབ་) གསུང་བ་ | *shaṕ-shoṕ sung-wa.* |

| | | |
|---|---|---|
| Whistle, to | སི་རྒྱབ་པ་ | *si gyaṕ-pa.* |
| Do. *hon.* | སི་སྐྱོན་པ་ | *si kyöm-pa.* |
| Whistle a tune, to | སི་གླུ་བཏང་ (གཏོང་) བ་ | *si-lu tang-wa.* |
| Do. *hon.* | སི་གླུ་བཞེས་པ་ | *si-lu sḱe-pa.* |
| White | དཀར་པོ་ | *ḱar-po.* |
| Whitewash | ས་དཀར། དཀར་རྩི་ | *sa-kar; kar-tsi.* |
| Whisher | ག་པ་ | *ḱa-pa.* |
| Who | སུ་ | *su.* |
| Whoever (you, he, tc.) be | སུ་ཡིན་ནས་ | *su yin-ne.* |
| Whole | ཚང་མ། ཐམས་ཅད། སྒང་ཁ་ | *tshang-ma, tham-che; gang-kha.* |
| Do. (healthy) | གཟུགས་པོ་བདེ་པོ་ | *śuḱ-po de-po.* |
| Do. *hon.* | སྐུ་གཟུགས་བཟང་པོ་ | *ku-śuḱ śang-po.* |
| Wholly (used negatively) | བད་དེ། ཁྱོན་ནས་ | *be-ťe; khyön-ne* |
| Whore | གཞང་ཚོང་མ་ | *sḱang-tshong-ma.* |
| Why, *interr.* | ག་རེ་དོན་ལ་ | *ḱa-re ťön-la.* |
| Do. *interj.* | འོ་ན་ | *o-na.* |
| Wick | སྡོང་རས་ | *dong-re.* |
| Wicked | ངན་པོ་ | *ngem-po.* |
| Do. *hon.* | ཐུགས་ངན་པོ་ | *thu ngem-po.* |

| | | |
|---|---|---|
| Wickedness | སྡིག་པ་ | *diḱ-pa.* |
| Do. *hon.* | སྐུ་སྡིག | *ku-di.* |
| Wide | ཞང་ (ཞེང་) ཆེན་པོ་ | *sḰang-chhem-po.* |
| Do. (of valley, etc.) | རྒྱ་ཆེན་པོ་ | *gya chhem-po.* |
| Widow (term of reproach) | ཡུགས་ཟ་མ་ | *yuḱ-śa-ma.* |
| Width | ཞང་ (ཞེང་) | *sḰang.* |
| Wife | སྐྱེ་དམན་ | *kyi-men.* |
| Do. (of well-to-do villager) | སྙི་སྙིང་ལགས་ | *nyi-nying-la.* |
| Do. (of ordinary official) | ལྕམ་སྐུ་གཞོགས་ | *cham ku-sḰo.* |
| Do. (of third grade and upwards) | ལྷ་ལྕམ་སྐུ་གཞོགས་ | *hla-cham ku-sḰo.* |
| Wild (fierce, of human beings) | ངན་པ་ | *ngem-pa.* |
| Do. (of animals) | ཚུབ་པོ་ | *tshuṕ-po.* |
| Wild animal | རི་དྭགས་ | *ri-t́a.* |
| Wilderness | བྱེ་ཐང་ | *cḰe-thang.* |
| Wile, *s.* | མགོ་སྐོར་ | *go-kor.* |
| Do. *hon.* | དབུ་སྐོར་ | *u-kor.* |
| Will, *s.* (wish) | འདོད་པ་ | *dö-pa.* |
| Do. *hon.* | ཐུགས་འདོད་ | *thung-dö.* |
| Will, *s.* (testament) | ཁ་ཆེམས་ | *kha-chhem.* |

| | | |
|---|---|---|
| **Will,** *s.* (testament), *hon.* | ཞལ་ཆེམས་ | *sKe-chhem.* |
| **Willing, to be** | འདོད་པ་ཡོད་པ་ | *dö-pa yö-pa.* |
| Do. *hon.* | ཐུགས་འདོད་ཡོད་པ་ | *thung-dö yö-pa* |
| **Willow** | ལྕང་མ་ | *chang-ma.* |
| **Wily** | གཅང་པོ་ | *chang-po.* |
| Do. *hon.* | ཐུགས་གཅང་པོ་ | *thu chang-po.* |
| **Win, to** (conquer) | རྒྱལ་བ་ | *gyel-wa.* |
| Do. *hon.* | རྒྱལ་ར་ (བ་) གནང་བ་ | *gye-ra nang-wa.* |
| **Win, to** (obtain) | འབྱོར་བ། ཐོབ་པ་ | *jor-wa ; thop-pa.* |
| Do. *hon.* | ཕྱག་འབྱོར་ཡོང་བ་ | *chhan-jor yong-wa.* |
| **Wind** | ལྷགས་པ། རླུང་ | *hlak-pa ; lung.* |
| **Wind, to** | སྒྲིལ་བ་ | *dril-wa.* |
| Do. *hon.* | སྒྲིལ་ར་ (བ་) གནང་བ་ | *dri-ra nang-wa.* |
| **Winding** | ཀྱོག་ཀྱོག་ | *kyo-kyo.* |
| **Window** | སྒི་ཁུང་ (རྒྱལ་ཁུང་) | *gi-khung.* |
| **Window-grating** | ཁྲ་མ་ (དྲ་མ་) | *thra-ma.* |
| Do. *hon.* | ཞལ་ཁྲ་ | *sKe-thra.* |
| **Wine** (beer) | ཆང་ | *chhang.* |
| Do. *hon.* | མཆོད་ཆང་ | *chhö-chhang.* |
| **Wing** | གཤོག་པ་ | *shok-pa.* |

| | | |
|---|---|---|
| Wink, to | མིག་ཁྲབ་ཁྲབ་བྱེད་པ་ | *miḱ thraṕ-thraṕ ćhe-pa.* |
| Do. *hon.* | སྤྱན་ཁྲབ་ཁྲབ་གནང་བ་ | *chen thraṕ-thraṕ nang-wa.* |
| Winter | དགུན་ཀ་ | *gün-ka.* |
| Wintry (cold) | གྲང་མོ། བསིལ་པོ་ | *t́rang-mo ; si-po.* |
| Do. *hon.* | སྐུ་བསིལ་པོ་ | *ku-si-po.* |
| Wipe, to | འཕྱིད་པ་ | *chhi-pa.* |
| Do. *hon.* | འཕྱིད་པ་གནང་བ་ | *chhi-pa nang-wa.* |
| Wipe out, to (efface) | སུབ་པ་ | *suṕ-pa.* |
| Do. *hon.* | སུབ་པ་གནང་བ་ | *suṕ-pa nang-wa.* |
| Wire | ལྕགས་སྐུད་ | *cha-kü.* |
| Wireless telegraphy | ལྕགས་སྐུད་མེད་པའི་དར་ | *cha-kü me-pe tar.* |
| Wisdom | བློ་གྲོས་ | *lo-t́rö.* |
| Wise (skilful) | མཁས་པོ་ | *khe-po.* |
| Do. (learned) | ཡོན་དན་ཆེན་པོ་ | *yön-ten chhem-po.* |
| Do. *hon.* | སྐུ་ཡོན་ཆེན་པོ་ | *ku-yön chhem-po.* |
| Wish | འདོད་པ་ | *dö-pa.* |
| Do. *hon.* | ཐུགས་འདོད་ | *thung-dö.* |
| Wish, to | འདོད་པ་བྱེད་པ་ | *dö-pa ćhe-pa.* |
| Do. *hon.* | ཐུགས་འདོད་གནང་བ་ | *thung-dö nang-wa.* |
| Wit (intellect) | བློ་གྲོས་ | *lo-t́rö.* |

| | | |
|---|---|---|
| Witchcraft | མཐུ་ | *thu.* |
| With (together with) | དང་མཉམ་དུ་ | *ťang-nyam-tu.* |
| Do. *hon.* | ལྷན་རྒྱས་ | *hlen-gye.* |
| With regard to | དོན་ལ། སྐོར་ལ་ | *ťön-la ; kor-la.* |
| Withdraw, to, *v.i.* (retreat) | ཕྱིར་ལོག་རྒྱབ་པ་ | *chhi-lo gyap̓-pa.* |
| Do. *hon.* | ཕྱིར་ལོག་སྐྱོན་པ་ | *chhi-lo kyöm-pa.* |
| Wither, to | སྙིད་པ་ | *nyi-pa.* |
| Within | ནང་ལ་ | *nang-la.* |
| Withhold, to (restrain) | བཀག་པ་ (འགེགས་པ་) | *kaǩ-pa.* |
| Do. *hon.* | བཀག་ག་ (འགེགས་པ་) གནང་བ་ | *kaǩ-ǩa nang-wa.* |
| Without (*opp.* to "with") | མེད་པར་ | *me-pa.* |
| Without (*opp.* to "within") | ཕྱི་ལོགས་ལ་ | *chhi-lo-la.* |
| Withstand, to (restrain) | བཀག་པ་ (འགེགས་པ་) | *kaǩ-pa.* |
| Do. *hon.* | བཀག་ག་ (འགེགས་པ་) གནང་བ་ | *kaǩ-ǩa nang-wa.* |
| Witless | སྐུགས་པ། གླེན་པ་ | *kuǩ-pa ; lem-pa.* |
| Witness | དཔང་པོ་ | *pang-po.* |
| Witness, to | དཔང་པོ་བྱེད་པ་ | *pang-po cǩe-pa.* |
| Do *hon.* | དཔང་པོ་གནང་བ་ | *pang-po nang-wa.* |

| | | |
|---|---|---|
| Woe | སྡུག་བསྔལ། སེམས་འཁྲལ་ | *du-nge; sem-thre.* |
| Do. *hon.* | ཐུགས་འཁྲལ་ | *thuk-thre.* |
| Wolf | སྤྱང་ཀུ་ | *chang-ku.* |
| Woman | སྐྱེས་དམན་ | *kyi-men.* |
| Do. (wife of well-to-do villager) | སྙི་སྙིང་ལགས་ | *nyi-nying-la.* |
| Do. (wife of ordinary official) | ལྕམ་སྐུ་གཞོགས་ | *cham ku-sKo.* |
| Do. (third grade and upwards) | ལྷ་ལྕམ་སྐུ་གཞོགས་ | *hla-cham ku-sKo.* |
| Womb | ཕུ་སྣོད་ | *pu-nö.* |
| Wonder | ཡ་མཚན་ | *yam-tshen.* |
| Wonder, to | ཁྱད་མཚར་བ་ | *khye tshar-wa.* |
| Do. *hon.* | ཐུགས་ཁྱད་མཚར་ར་ (བ་) གནང་བ་ | *thu-khye tshar-ra nang-wa.* |
| Wonderful | ཡ་མཚན་པོ། ཁྱད་མཚར་པོ་ | *yam-tshem-po; khye-tsha-po.* |
| Wondrous | ཡ་མཚན་པོ། ཁྱད་མཚར་པོ་ | *yam-tshem-po; khye-tsha-po.* |
| Wood | ཤིང་ | *shing.* |
| Do. (forest) | ཤིང་ནགས། ནགས་གསེབ་ | *shing-na; nak-sep.* |
| Wooden | ཤིང་གི་ | *shing-ki.* |
| Woof, *s.* (of loom) | སྤུན་ | *pün.* |

| | | |
|---|---|---|
| Woof, *s.* (of loom), *hon.* | ཕྱག་སྤུན་ | *chha-pün.* |
| Wool | བལ་ | *ṕe.* |
| Woollen | བལ་གྱི་ | *ṕe-ḱyi.* |
| Woollen cloth | སྣམ་བུ་ | *nam-ṕu.* |
| Do. *hon.* | ཕྱག་སྣམ་ | *chha-nam.* |
| Word | ཚིག་ | *tshi.* |
| Do. (tidings) | གནས་ཚུལ། གསར་འགྱུར་ | *ne-tshü ; sang-gyu.* |
| Do. (command) | བཀའ་ | *ka.* |
| Word, to give one's (promise) | ཁས་བླང་བ་ | *khe-lang-wa.* |
| Do. *hon.* | ཞལ་བཞེས་པ་ | *sḱe-sḱe-pa.* |
| Work | ལས་ཀ་ | *le-ka.* |
| Do. *hon.* | ཕྱག་ལས་ | *chha-le.* |
| Work, to | ལས་ཀ་བྱེད་པ | *le-ka cḱe-pa.* |
| Do. *hon.* | ཕྱག་ལས་གནང་བ་ | *chha-le nang-wa.* |
| Work, to be, occupied with | བྲེལ་བ་ཡོད་པ་ | *t́re-wa yö-pa.* |
| Do. *hon.* | ཐུགས་བྲེལ་ཡོད་པ་ | *thu-t́re yö-pa.* |
| World | འཛམ་བུ་གླིང་། འཇིག་རྟེན་ | *dzam-ṕu-ling ; jiḱ-ten.* |
| Worm | འབུ་ | *bu.* |
| Worry, to, *v.t.* (vex) | ཁོང་ཁྲོ་སློང་བ་ | *khong-thro lang-wa.* |
| Do. *hon.* | དགོངས་པ་དཀྲུག་པ་ | *gong-pa truḱ-pa* |

| | | |
|---|---|---|
| Worry, to, *v.i.* | སེམས་འཕྲལ་བྱེད་པ་ | *sem-thre cḱe-pa.* |
| Do. *hon.* | ཐུགས་འཕྲལ་གནང་བ་ | *thuḱ-thre nang-wa.* |
| Worship, to (extempore prayers) | སྨོན་ལམ་བཏབ་ (འདེབས་) པ་ | *mö-lam tap-pa.* |
| Do. *hon.* | ཐུགས་སྨོན་གནང་བ་ | *thu-mön nang-wa.* |
| Worship, to (written prayers) | ཁ་འདོན་བྱེད་པ་ | *khan-dön cḱe-pa.* |
| Do. *hon.* | ཞལ་འདོན་གནང་བ་ | *sḱen-dön nang-wa.* |
| Worst | སྡུག་ཤོས་ | *duḱ-shö.* |
| Worst of, to get the | འཕམ་པ་ | *pham-pa.* |
| Do. *hon.* | འཕམ་པ་གནང་བ་ | *pham-pa nang-wa.* |
| Worth | གོང་ | *ḱong.* |
| Do. *hon.* | ལྗགས་གོང་ | *ja-ḱong.* |
| Worth, to be | གོང་བྱེད་པ་ | *ḱong-cḱe-pa.* |
| Worthless (valueless) | གོང་མེད་ | *ḱong-me.* |
| Do. (useless) | དོན་མེད་ | *ṫön-me.* |
| Do. (wicked) | ངན་པོ་ | *ngem-po.* |
| Do. *hon.* | ཐུགས་ངན་པོ་ | *thu ngem-po.* |
| Worthy | འོས་པོ་ | *ö-po.* |
| Wound, *s.* | རྨ་ | *ma.* |
| Wound, to | རྨ་བཟོ་བ་ | *ma ṡo-wa.* |

| | | |
|---|---|---|
| Wound, to, *hon.* | རྨ་བཟོ་བ་གནང་བ་ | *ma śo-wa nang-wa.* |
| Wrangle, to | རྒྱབ་འདྲེ་རྒྱབ་པ་ | *gyam-dre gyap-pa.* |
| Do. *hon.* | གསུང་འཁྲུག་སྐྱོན་པ་ | *sung-thru kyöm-pa.* |
| Wrap, to | སྒྲིལ་བ་ | *dril-wa.* |
| Do. *hon.* | སྒྲིལ་ར་ (བ་) གནང་བ་ | *dri-ra nang-wa.* |
| Wrath | ཚིག་པ། ཁོང་ཁྲོ་ | *tshik-pa ; khong-thro.* |
| Do. *hon.* | དགོངས་ཚུང་། རྣམ་མཁྱེན་ | *gong-tshung ; nam-khyen.* |
| Wrathful, to be | ཚིག་པ་ཟ་བ། ཁོང་ཁྲོ་ཟ་བ་ | *tshik-pa śa-wa ; khong-thro śa-wa.* |
| Do. *hon.* | དགོངས་པ་ཚུང་པ། རྣམ་མཁྱེན་འགལ་བ་ | *gong-pa tshung-pa ; nam-khyen gel-wa.* |
| Wrest, to | འཕྲོག་པ་ | *throk-pa.* |
| Do *hon.* | འཕྲོག་ག་ (པ་) གནང་བ་ | *throk-ka nang-wa.* |
| Wrestle, to | འཛིང་རེ་བཏང་ (གཏོང་) བ་ | *dzing-re tang-wa.* |
| Wretched (bad) | སྡུག་རྩུལ་ | *duk-rü.* |
| Do. (unhappy) | སྡུག་བསྔལ་ཆེན་པོ་ | *dung-nge chhem-po.* |
| Do. *hon.* | ཐུགས་བསྔལ་ཆེན་པོ་ | *thuk-nge chhem-po.* |
| Wretchedness | སྡུག་བསྔལ། སེམས་འཁྲལ་ | *dung-nge ; sem-thre.* |
| Do. *hon.* | ཐུགས་འཁྲལ་ | *thuk-thre.* |
| Wring, to (twist) | སྒྲིམ་པ་ | *drim-pa.* |

| | | |
|---|---|---|
| Wring, to. (twist), *hon.* | སྒྲིམ་པ་གནང་བ་ | *drim-pa nang-wa* |
| Wrinkle (on face) | གཉེར་མ་ | *nye-ma.* |
| Wrist | ལག་ཚིགས་ | *laḱ-tshi.* |
| Do. *hon.* | ཕྱག་ཚིགས་ | *chhaḱ-tshi.* |
| Write, to | བྲིས་པ་ (འབྲི་བ་) | *t́ri-pa.* |
| Do. *hon.* | ཕྱག་བྲིས་གནང་བ་ | *chha-t́ri nang-wa.* |
| Writer (author) | རྩོམ་མཁན་ | *tsom-khen.* |
| Do. *hon.* | རྩོམ་པ་གནང་མཁན་ | *tsom-pa nang-khen.* |
| Writer (clerk) | དྲུང་ཡིག་ | *t́rung-yi.* |
| Do. *hon.* | དྲུང་ཡིག་ལགས་ | *t́rung-yi-la.* |
| Wrong, *adj.* (incorrect) | མ་དག་པ་ | *ma...t́aḱ-pa.* |
| Do. (unjust) | ཁྲིམས་མེད་ | *thrim-me.* |
| Do. (wicked) | ངན་པ་ | *ngem-pa.* |
| Wrong, *s.* (error) | ནོར་ | *nor.* |
| Do. (guilt) | སྐྱོན། ཉེས་པ་ | *kyön; nye-pa.* |
| Do. (sin) | སྡིག་པ་ | *diḱ-pa.* |
| Do. *hon.* | སྐུ་སྡིག་ | *ku-di.* |
| Wrong (crime), to commit | ཁྲིམས་འགལ་བ་ | *thrim gel-wa.* |
| Do. *hon.* | བཀའ་ཁྲིམས་འགལ་ར་ (བ་) གནང་བ་ | *ka-thrim ge-ra nang-wa.* |

## X

| | | |
|---|---|---|
| Xylograph, to make a | ཤིང་བསྐོས་རྒྱབ་པ་ | *shing-kö gyap-pa.* |
| Do. *hon.* | ཤིང་བསྐོས་སྐྱོན་པ་ | *shing-kö kyöm-pa.* |

# Y

| | | |
|---|---|---|
| Yak, *m.* | གཡག་ | *ya.* |
| Do. *f.* | འབྲི་ | *dri.* |
| Yak, wild | འབྲོང་ | *drong.* |
| Yak, half-breed with ordinary cattle | མཛོ་ | *dzo.* |
| Yak-dung | ལྕོ་ (ལྕི་བ་) | *cho.* |
| Yak's meat | ཚག་ཤ་ | *tshak̄-sha.* |
| Yama | གཤིན་རྗེ་ཆོས་རྒྱལ་ | *shin-je chhö-gye.* |
| Yap, to | འཆང་བ་ | *chhang-wa.* |
| Yard, court | སྒོ་ར་ | *go-ra.* |
| Yarn | སྲིང་སྐུད་ | *hring-kü.* |
| Do. black | སྲིང་ནག་ | *hring-na.* |
| Do. blue | སྲིང་སྔོན་ | *hring-ngön.* |
| Do. green | སྲིང་ལྗང་ | *hring-jang.* |
| Do. red | སྲིང་དམར་ | *hring-mar.* |
| Do. white | སྲིང་དཀར་ | *hring-kar.* |
| Do. yellow | སྲིང་སེར་ | *hring-ser.* |
| Yawn, to | ཨ་སྟོང་རྒྱབ་པ་ | *a-tong gyap̄-pa.* |
| Do. *hon.* | ཨ་སྟོང་སྐྱོན་པ་ | *a-tong kyöm-pa.* |

| | | |
|---|---|---|
| Year | ལོ་ | *lo.* |
| Year, this | ད་ལོ་ | *t́a-lo.* |
| Year, last | ཟླ་སྙིང་ (ན་ནིང་) | *da-nyi.* |
| Year before last | ཞི་སྙིང་ (ཞི་ནིང་) | *sḱi-nyi.* |
| Year, next | ཕྱི་ལོ། སང་སྤོད་ | *chhi-lo ; sang-pö.* |
| Year, first four months of a | ཟླ་སྟོད་ | *da-tö.* |
| Year, middle four months of a | ཟླ་དཀྱིལ་ | *da-kyi.* |
| Year, last four months of a | ཟླ་སྨད་ | *da-me.* |
| Yearn for, to | དྲན་པ་ | *t́rem-pa.* |
| Do. *hon.* | ཐུགས་དྲན་པ་གནང་བ་ | *thu-t́rem-pa nang-wa.* |
| Yeast (for bread) | ཕྱི་སྨན་ | *chhi-men.* |
| Do. (for fermenting liquor) | ཕབ་ | *phaṕ.* |
| Yell, to (of children crying) | ངུ་བ་ | *ngu-wa.* |
| Do. *hon.* | ཤུམ་པ་ | *shum-pa.* |
| Yell, to (of dogs) | སྡུག་སྐད་རྒྱབ་པ་ | *duḱ-ḱe gyaṕ-pa.* |
| Yellow | སེར་པོ་ | *se-po.* |
| Yellow, dark | སྙུག་སེ་ | *nyuḱ-se.* |
| Yelp, to (of dogs) | འཆང་བ་ | *chhang-wa.* |
| Yes | ལགས་སི། ལགས་ w. auxiliary verb | *la-si ; la.* |

| | | |
|---|---|---|
| Yes, *hon.* | ལགས་ལགས་སི། ལ་འོང་ | *la-la-si; la-ong.* |
| Do. *h. hon.* | ལགས་བཀའ་གནང་རང་ | *la ḱa-nang-rang.* |
| Yesterday | ཁས་ས་ (ཁ་སང་) | *khe-sa.* |
| Yesterday evening | མདང་དགོང་ | *dang-gong.* |
| Yet, *adv.* (in addition) | ད་འདོ། ད་རུང་ | *ťan-do; ťa-rung.* |
| Yet, *conj.* (nevertheless) | ཡིན་ནས། ཡིན་ཀྱང་། ཡིན་ན་ཡང་ | *yin-ne; yin-kyang; yin-na-yang.* |
| Yield, to (admit) | ཁས་ལེན་པ་ | *khe-lem-pa.* |
| Do. *hon.* | ཞལ་བཞེས་གནང་བ། ཞལ་གྱིས་བཞེས་པ་ | *sḱe-sḱe nang-wa; sḱe-ḱyi sḱe-pa.* |
| Yield, to (forego) | སྤང་བ་ | *pang-wa.* |
| Do. *hon.* | སྤོང་ང་ (བ་) གནང་བ་ | *pong-nga nang-wa.* |
| Yield, to (give) | སྟེར་བ་ | *ter-wa.* |
| Do. *hon.* | གནང་བ་ | *nang-wa.* |
| Yield, to (surrender) | མགོ་དགུར་བ་ | *go gur-wa.* |
| Do. *hon.* | དབུ་དགུར་ར་ (བ་) གནང་བ་ | *u gur-ra nang-wa.* |
| Yielding (flexible) | མཉེན་པོ་ | *nyem-po.* |
| Yoke (for oxen) | གཉའ་ཤིང་ | *nya-shing.* |
| Yolk | སེར་སྒོང་། སེར་སྤྲིན་ | *ser-gong; ser-trin.* |
| Yonder | ཕ་གི་ | *pha-gi.* |

| | | |
|---|---|---|
| You | ཁྱོད། ཁྱོད་རང་ | *khyö ; khyö-rang.* |
| Do. *hon.* | ཁྱེན་ (ཁྱེད་) | *khyen.* |
| Do. *h. hon.* | སྐུ་གཞོགས་ | *ku-sKo.* |
| Young | གཞོན་པ། ལོ་གཞོན་གཞོན་ | *sKöm-pa ; lo sKön-sKön.* |
| Your | ཁྱོད་རེའི་ (ཁྱོད་ཀྱི་) | *khyö-re.* |
| Do. *hon.* | ཁྱེན་གྱི་ (ཁྱེད་ཀྱི་) | *khyen-kyi.* |
| Do. *h. hon.* | སྐུ་གཞོགས་ཀྱི་ | *ku-sKo kyi.* |
| Youthful | གཞོན་པ། ལོ་གཞོན་གཞོན་ | *sKöm-pa ; lo sKön-sKön.* |

## Z

| | | |
|---|---|---|
| Zeal | སྙིང་རུས་ | *nying-rü.* |
| Do. *hon.* | ཐུགས་རུས་ | *thu-rü.* |
| Zealous | སྙིང་རུས་ཆེན་པོ་ | *nying-rü chhem-po.* |
| Do. *hon.* | ཐུགས་རུས་ཆེན་པོ་ | *thu-rü. chhem-po.* |
| Zealous, to be | སྙིང་རུས་བྱེད་པ་ | *nying-rü cKe-pa.* |
| Do. *hon.* | ཐུགས་རུས་གནང་བ་ | *thu-rü nang-wa.* |
| Zealously | སྙིང་རུས་བྱས་ནས་ | *nying-rü cKe-ne.* |
| Do. *hon.* | ཐུགས་རུས་གནང་ནས་ | *thu-rü nang-ne.* |
| Zero | ཀླད་སྐོར་ | *le-kor.* |
| Zigzag | ལམ་སྐྱོགས་ | *lam-kyo.* |

THE END.